CHURCH, IDENTITY, *and* CHANGE

CHURCH, IDENTITY, *and* CHANGE

Theology and Denominational Structures in Unsettled Times

Edited by

David A. Roozen & James R. Nieman

WILLIAM B. EERDMANS PUBLISHING COMPANY
GRAND RAPIDS, MICHIGAN / CAMBRIDGE, U.K.

Wm. B. Eerdmans Publishing Co.
255 Jefferson Ave. S.E., Grand Rapids, Michigan 49503 /
P.O. Box 163, Cambridge CB3 9PU U.K.

Printed in the United States of America

10 09 08 07 06 05   7 6 5 4 3 2 1

Library of Congress Cataloging-in-Publication Data

Church, identity, and change: theology and denominational structures in unsettled times /
    edited by David A. Roozen & James Nieman.
        p.   cm.
    Includes bibliographical references.
    ISBN 0-8028-2819-1 (pbk.: alk. paper)
        1. Protestant churches — United States — History. 2. Protestant churches —
    Doctrines — History. 3. United States — Church history.
    I. Roozen, David A.   II. Nieman, James R., 1956–

BR515.C526   2005
280′.4′0973 — dc22

                                        2004060785

www.eerdmans.com

Contents

Contents

Contents

Introduction

David A. Roozen and James R. Nieman

Eighty years after Nietzsche's madman shouted "God is dead,"[1] that same cry was used to label the supposed religious climate of the late 1960s. The report, however, was exaggerated. In fact, that decade was an extremely energetic period of theological exploration, finding conflict mixed with creativity, bewilderment with innovation, and anxiety with renewal in a way that is typical during major, unsettling transitions. A closer examination of the period reveals that God's viability was less the issue than how we think about God and structure that into practice. Today, another rumor of death is often heard: the demise of denominationalism. Could it again be that life and death are less the issue than how denominations think about God and structure such reflection into organizational identity and practice? We believe that the historical introductions, sociological case studies, and theological essays in this collection support such a conclusion.

This conclusion should not be misunderstood. We neither deny nor minimize the fact that all denominations today are feeling unique sources of stress. For many, this strain has edged into crisis and seeking strategies to cope. The search for strategies has been especially marked by contentiousness, disorientation, apprehension, fear of loss, and sense of hurt. Even so, several transitions suggest a story more complex and compelling than any simple prediction of doom.

- Many people are investing considerable energy in the future of their denominations. It is probably true that there is a growing layer of privatistic

1. Friedrich Nietzsche, *The Gay Science: With a Prelude in Rhymes and an Appendix in Songs,* trans. Walter Kaufmann (New York: Vintage Books, 1974), sec. 125, 343.

and localistic indifference to denominations across our society. This is not the dominant story, however. Instead, by actually looking closely at denominations, as did the contributors to this collection, what emerges is a commitment to affirm and engage these groups, even to the point of sometimes fighting with friends and colleagues.

- Many denominations, particularly within oldline Protestantism, face serious problems and may never regain the numerical, missiological, or cultural prominence they once enjoyed. Yet in this study, neither social analysts nor denominational leaders actually believed that even the most challenged denominations were in imminent danger of collapse. Even groups facing great struggle show indications of adaptive resources and pockets of vitality. In denominations beyond the oldline, images of steadfast purpose and high energy predominate.

- While the major sources of stress and strain, transition and change that challenge denominations are clear and well known, so are the organizational and theological resources for coping with these challenges. Equally in abundance are the strategies that can be applied to or enhance these resources.

- Historians have noted that during the roughly 350 years of Protestantism in North America, there have been several distinct transitions in the nature of denominations. Just as important, the organizational embodiments of all the major colonial religious bodies from America's founding period, as well as the major indigenous movements that joined them along the way (such as Methodism, Assemblies of God, and the historic black denominations), have survived these transitions in recognizable form. As Russell Richey succinctly remarked in his sketch of the five historical stages of American denominationalism, "Radical change is not a new experience."[2]

- Scholars have reminded us that denominations, in addition to being organizations, are also traditions and cultures. As such, they typically have a more foundational and adaptable permanence than their organizational carriers, enabling a greater durability than appearances might first suggest.[3]

- As will be noted later in this introduction, transition is the pervasive real-

---

2. Russell E. Richey, "Denominations and Denominationalism: An American Morphology," in *Reimagining Denominationalism: Interpretive Essays,* ed. Robert Bruce Mullin and Russell E. Richey (New York: Oxford University Press, 1994), p. 74.

3. Nancy T. Ammerman, "Denominations: Who and What Are We Studying?" in *Reimagining Denominationalism,* pp. 111-33; Jackson Carroll and Wade Clark Roof, eds., *Beyond Establishment: Protestant Identity in a Post-Protestant Age* (Louisville: Westminster John Knox, 1993).

ity affecting the way secular America in general and corporate America in particular organize their work. This reality is no less true for religious groups in America, obviously including the denominations in and beyond this study.

Others may wish to speculate on what motivates the rumor that denominationalism is dying. Our interest is the reality of denominations, not the rumors. *The issue facing American denominations as they enter the new millennium is not death but instead how they can and do bear their particular legacies faithfully and effectively into a changing future.*

Since colonial days, religious work in America has happened through denominations. At least since the start of the twentieth century, these religious bodies consisted of a fairly tight, intradenominationally connected system of congregations, regional judicatories, and national offices. This system was the product of more than two centuries of consolidation among America's historic immigrant and indigenous churches.[4] The vast majority of these structures are still in place, retain some semblance of internal coherence, have considerable social and religious significance, and will be with us for the foreseeable future. Nevertheless, the stresses upon them today clearly indicate that they are entering an unsettled period of transition.[5] A constellation of technological, economic, demographic, and cultural changes is transforming all of American society, as well as the world. Many organizational analysts argue that these changes are so fundamental as to signal a major paradigm shift from modern to postmodern forms of organization, a shift affecting all institutional segments of American life, including the religious.[6] *The purpose of this collection is to examine part of that shift, using the national structures of eight diverse Protestant denominations as a window into the nature of this transition.*

---

4. On the history of denominationalism, see Richey, "Denominations and Denominationalism"; Craig Dykstra and James Hudnut-Beumler, "The National Organizational Structures of Protestant Denominations: An Invitation to a Conversation," in *The Organizational Revolution: Presbyterians and American Denominationalism,* ed. Milton J. Coalter, John M. Mulder, and Louis B. Weeks (Louisville: Westminster John Knox, 1992), pp. 307-31; and Ben Primer, *Protestants and American Business Methods* (Ann Arbor, Mich.: UMI Research Press, 1978).

5. For a provocative perspective on organizational change in such an unsettled period, see Ann Swidler, "Culture in Action: Symbols and Strategies," *American Sociological Review* 51 (1986): 273-86.

6. Stewart Clegg, *Modern Organizations: Organizational Studies in the Postmodern World* (Newbury Park, Calif.: Sage, 1990); Nancy T. Ammerman, "SBC Moderates and the Making of a Postmodern Denomination: Locating a Niche," *Christian Century* 110, no. 26 (September 22, 1993): 896-99.

Because denominations are both religious and institutional in nature, the broad frame of our inquiry is the relationship between the *theological and the organizational nature* of national denominational structures as they *adapt to the changing situation* of the twenty-first century. The method of our inquiry is to draw the reader into the actual situation of the national structures of eight denominations, using a distinctive collection of articles:

> **Historical introductions** to each denomination, giving background to its national structure and the theological legacy that undergirds this;
> **Sociological case studies** of how each denomination defines and attempts to redefine the purposes and organization of its national structure;
> **Theological essays** that treat the work, organization, and rethinking of each denomination as instances of embodied, practical theology; and
> **Concluding reflections**, one focused from an organizational perspective and the other highlighting the theological dimension.

In a demanding time for organizations attempting to do God's work, we seek to help those who are committed to their denominations turn the challenges they face into opportunities. We also seek to help students of American religion and postmodern organizations who are attempting to deepen their understanding of the adaptive capacities inherent in the broader social and cultural transitions within which denominations are embedded.

Features of the Study

The two most recent examinations of denominationalism in the United States share a common orientation.[7] On the one hand, they acknowledge that denominations are a distinctive mark if not the historically fundamental organizational unit of American religious experience. On the other hand, they express the pervasive sense that, "Born in an earlier era to give expression to free and voluntary religion in a country without an established church, the denomination often appears out of kilter, if not hopelessly obsolete, in an America where religion has become more pluralistic and privatized."[8] Particularly among commentators on and practitioners within oldline Protestantism, assessments of denominationalism are often cast in the gloomy tones of demise.

---

7. Carroll and Roof, *Beyond Establishment;* Mullin and Richey, *Reimagining Denominationalism.*
   8. Carroll and Roof, *Beyond Establishment,* p. 11.

Even for oldline Protestantism with its downsizing, such assessments seem overdramatic. Beyond the oldline, however, the claims are flatly erroneous, especially when considering that many such groups are bursting with growth and optimism. The Holiness/Pentecostal segment and the independent megachurch movement are perhaps the most noticeable examples of this, and they share three characteristics worth noting.[9] First, their national connectional systems are less hierarchical and bureaucratic when compared to oldline Protestantism. Second, prompted by the combination of organizational growth and bureaucratic skepticism, they are searching for nonhierarchical ways to strengthen their national connectional systems for the sake of mission. Third, there are noticeable tensions in these national connectional systems between fellowship-resource functions and regulatory-accountability functions. Two of the denominations in this collection derive from this stream of American religious expression, and their inclusion alone sets this study apart from others, causing a reconsideration of earlier assessments about the fate of denominations. Indeed, the very breadth and diversity represented by all eight denominations in this study is also a distinctive feature. The vast majority of recent literature on American denominations, including the rumored demise of denominationalism, has focused on oldline Protestantism. Four of the denominations contained herein clearly belong to this family. We have intentionally balanced these, however, with four other groups from beyond that family. Among other things, this means that we were able to compare the experience of several denominations that confront the current period of unsettled transition in a weakened state with several more that engage these changes from a position of vitality and growth.

Another unique aspect of this study is its attention to how the national level relates to the overall structures of a denomination. Simply put, *a denomination is a group of congregations united under a common and distinct faith, name, and organization.* Even such a basic definition immediately indicates that a denomination is a layered organizational system. In the United States these layers typically have a geographical quality, connecting local congregations with national offices and agencies through one or two layers of regional divisions generically called "judicatories" (classes, associations, or districts for relatively circumscribed clusters of congregations, and dioceses, conferences, or

9. Kimon Howland Sargeant, "The Post-Modern Denomination: An Organizational Analysis of the Willow Creek Association" (paper presented at the Religious Research Association Annual Meeting, Nashville, 1996); Scott L. Thumma, "Megachurches Today: A Summary of Data from the 'Faith Communities Today' Project," found at http://hirr.hartsem.edu/org/faith_megachurches_FACTsummary .html; Scott L. Thumma, "Exploring the Megachurch Phenomena: Their Characteristics and Cultural Context," found at http://hirr.hartsem.edu/bookshelf/thumma_article2.html.

synods for larger regional groupings). The important point is that a denomination is more than its national structure. While the intentional focus of this study is on national structures, the sociological cases and the theological essays will to a great extent use those structures as a vehicle for examining aspects of the entire denominational system, especially the relationship between a denomination's internal diversity and its identity.

The traditional geographic layering of organizational connections within denominations is also germane to how this study was uniquely related to two parallel projects, one on congregations and the other on judicatories. All three projects were part of a comprehensive study entitled "Organizing Religious Work for the Twenty-First Century: Exploring Denominationalism." Located within and staffed by faculty of Hartford Seminary's Institute for Religion Research, the entire project received major funding from the Lilly Endowment, Inc., beginning in the fall of 1997. In the language of the original funding proposal, the study would consist of "three distinct, but closely coordinated, subprojects. One sub-project will take the national 'denomination' as its focus; a second will focus on regional judicatories; and a third will take the local congregation as the starting point, moving outward to ask how congregations form the functional networks through which they accomplish their work in the world and by which they themselves are shaped." The congregation subproject was directed by Nancy T. Ammerman, assisted by Scott Thumma. It included surveys, interviews, and ethnographic examination of congregations and the local organizations with which they were connected in seven representative areas of the United States. The sampling of congregations in the seven locales included all faith traditions, but oversampled congregations from the eight denominations of the national subproject.[10] The judicatory subproject was directed by Adair Lummis. It included in-depth interviews with judicatory staff from the eight denominations of the national subproject and in the seven locales used by the congregation subproject. In addition, mailed surveys and telephone interviews were used with a broader sample of judicatory leaders in the eight denominations.[11]

10. Nancy Tatom Ammerman, *Pillars of Faith: American Congregations and Their Partners* (Berkeley: University of California Press, 2005); Nancy T. Ammerman, "Doing Good in American Communities: Congregations and Service Organizations Working Together," found at http://hirr.hartsem.edu/about/about_orw_cong-report.html.

11. Adair T. Lummis, "Brand Name Identity in a Post-Denominational Age: Regional Leaders' Perspectives on Its Importance for Churches" (paper presented at the Society for the Scientific Study of Religion Annual Meeting, Columbus, Ohio, 2001); Adair T. Lummis, "The Art and Science of Subtle Proactivity: Regional Leaders and Their Congregations" (paper presented at the Religious Research Association Annual Meeting, Columbus, Ohio, 2001); Adair T.

Although each subproject of the Organizing Religious Work (ORW) project had its own integrity, the subprojects were also designed and implemented in close coordination. Emerging insights were a continuing point of conversation among the project coprincipals. In addition, several consultations involving an interdisciplinary mix of scholars and an ecumenical mix of church leaders were convened to discuss the implications of and relations between the joint findings of the three subprojects. Therefore, the national level perspective of this collection was uniquely expanded by an ongoing dialogue with careful studies conducted at congregation and judicatory levels. Together they treated the denomination as an inclusive connectional system.

By attending to the layered organizational system of denominations, another unusual (though not utterly unique) aspect of this study comes to the fore: the seriousness it gives to organizational perspectives, including secular literature on organizations. It may seem strange, if not dangerous and misguided, for a study of religious organizations to take cues from the study of secular organizations. While we examined the embodiment of denominational theology and tradition in organizational structures, the vast majority of organizational theory, including extensions to emerging forms of postmodern organization, is secular in derivation and tone.[12] There are good reasons why such insights are important, however. For example, there is clear evidence that the twentieth-century development and refinement of Protestant national structures was heavily affected by the importing of cutting edge organizational structures and processes from corporate America.[13] There are also striking parallels between the calls for reorganization in denominations and those heard in secular organizations, such as the need for decentralization, greater local autonomy, network connections instead of hierarchy, and resourcing functions rather than regulation. Indeed,

---

Lummis, "The Role of Judicatories in Interpreting Denominational Identity" (paper presented at the Religious Research Association Annual Meeting, Boston, 1999); Adair T. Lummis, "Judicatory Niches and Negotiations" (paper presented at the Association for the Sociology of Religion Annual Meeting, San Francisco, 1998). These papers can be found at http://hirr.hartsem.edu/about/lummis_articles.htm.

12. An interest in the organizational embodiment of traditions is particularly salient in two streams of sociological theory: (1) the merging of cultural and structural perspectives in neo-institutionalism, and (2) the merging of cultural and resource mobilization perspectives in constructivist approaches to social movement theory. Walter W. Powell and Paul DiMaggio, *The New Institutionalism in Organizational Analysis* (Chicago: University of Chicago Press, 1991), is perhaps the most comprehensive summary of the former. Ulf Hjelmar, "Constructivist Analysis and Movement Organizations: Conceptual Clarifications," *Acta Sociologica* 39, no. 2 (1996): 169-86, is the most recent systemization of the latter.

13. Richard W. Reifsnyder, "Managing the Mission: Church Restructuring in the Twentieth Century," in *The Organizational Revolution*, pp. 55-95.

Ammerman's characterization of the postmodern denomination draws its framework directly from sociologist Stewart Clegg's recent work.[14]

The basic definition mentioned earlier indicated that denominations have an explicitly religious dimension, organizing around a common faith. As Richey put it, a denomination "is *ecclesial,* a movement or body understanding itself to be legitimate and self-sufficient, a proper 'church' (or religious movement)."[15] Ammerman was still more direct:

> Set out to write about denominations, and one can hardly avoid writing about beliefs and practices. That, after all, is what denominations are supposed to be. The great reformers of the sixteenth, seventeenth, and eighteenth centuries argued over how best to honor God and reach heaven. They argued that what one believed, how one worshiped, the religious devotions of one's life mattered. . . . As Christians began to transform the Church Universal into the Church Denominational, they did so with differences over beliefs and practices at the forefront of their fights. . . . The person on the street, like the theologian in the seminary, knows that denominations are supposed to be identifiable by their beliefs and practices. Defining denominations by the ideas and rituals that distinguish them from others is the commonsense thing to do.[16]

The national structures of denominations are not simply organizations, but religious ones as well. Any adequate understanding of denominations therefore must include the question of the relationship between (in our case) their *Christian* nature and their *organizational* nature. Highlighting this very relationship, especially the religious aspect of how these organizations face massive transition, is one of the unique aspects of this study. By contrast, much recent literature on denominations has been segregated into academic disciplines. There are books and articles written by historians for historians, by sociologists for sociologists, by theologians for theologians, and by practitioners for practitioners. Our alternative was to create an explicit dialogue among a church historian, a sociologist, a theologian, and a national level executive within each denomination. The resulting sets of histories, case studies, and essays emerged from each denominational team's own internal dialogue. Our goal was to generate critical but appreciative reflection that provides grounded, comparative, and multidisciplinary insights for both scholars and practitioners who care about how denominations seek to embody God's work.

14. Ammerman, "SBC Moderates"; Clegg, *Modern Organizations.*
15. Richey, "Denominations and Denominationalism," pp. 75-76.
16. Ammerman, "Denominations," p. 113.

Traditional ecclesiological treatments of polity provide one perspective on the relationship between organization and theology,[17] as do the limited number of more ideal-type taxonomies[18] and the few (mostly polemical) accounts of specific denominational structures.[19] In most respects, however, it was a new challenge to develop what we envisioned, an empathetic examination of denominational structures as embodied theology, one that does justice to both the organizational and the religious nature of those structures.[20] Our theological point of departure in accepting this challenge was, to borrow appreciatively from Thomas Jeavons's recent study of Christian service organizations: "What makes this organization, what it does, and the way it does it, Christian?"[21]

Another aspect of denominations mentioned earlier in our basic definition seems so obvious that its broader significance may easily be overlooked: a denomination has a name. Each is "denominated." Among other things, this means that it exists alongside other groups similarly named, that is, other denominations. As Richey noted, "The denomination exists in a situation of religious pluralism, typically a pluralism of denominations." Such denominationalism "is voluntary and therefore presupposes a condition of legal or *de facto* toleration and religious freedom — an environment within which it is possible, in fact, willingly to join or not join."[22] Ever the historian, Richey was also quick to add that such voluntaristic denominationalism is a relatively recent phenomenon. Many American denominations, including all colonial imports (Lutheran, Presbyterian, Mennonite, Anglican, Baptist, and Congrega-

17. Robert S. Paul, *The Church in Search of Its Self* (Grand Rapids: Eerdmans, 1972).

18. For the most comprehensive sociological treatment, see Gary P. Burkart, "Patterns of Protestant Organization," in *American Denominational Organization: A Sociological View,* ed. Ross P. Scherer (Pasadena, Calif.: William Carey Library, 1980), pp. 36-83. For a more theologically informed approach, see Avery Robert Dulles, *Models of the Church,* expanded ed. (Garden City, N.Y.: Image Books, 1987).

19. Andy Langford and William H. Willimon, *A New Connection: Reforming the United Methodist Church* (Nashville: Abingdon, 1995), provides a recent example of the polemical literature; Reifsnyder, "Managing the Mission," is a recent example of a more descriptively neutral treatment.

20. The most direct methodological models for what we envision come from the merging of congregational studies and practical and local theology in the recent work of Don S. Browning, *A Fundamental Practical Theology: Descriptive and Strategic Proposals* (Minneapolis: Fortress, 1991), and Robert J. Schreiter, "Theology in the Congregation: Discovering and Doing," in *Studying Congregations: A New Handbook,* ed. Nancy T. Ammerman, Jackson W. Carroll, Carl S. Dudley, and William McKinney (Nashville: Abingdon, 1998), pp. 23-39.

21. Thomas Jeavons, *When the Bottom Line Is Faithfulness: Management of Christian Service Organizations* (Bloomington: Indiana University Press, 1994), p. 139.

22. Richey, "Denominations and Denominationalism," p. 75.

tional), had a predenominational ecclesial existence, such that even a radical change today should not necessarily be interpreted as a signal of demise. It may instead be simply another metamorphosis.[23]

Being denominated also connotes that something is distinct, having recognizable boundaries. Most denominational analysts have long recognized that the distinctness of a denomination is not solely or in some cases even primarily carried by its beliefs. As will become apparent in what follows, distinctness can also arise from social class, race or ethnicity, polity or governance, and worship or other practices. How all these elements and others besides merge to form a recognizably distinct entity is what Ammerman referred to as a denomination's "cultural identity."[24] In a related way, we invite the reader to pay special attention to the notion of *denominational identity*. To be clear, denominational identity is a characteristic of the entire denominational system, not solely or even primarily the privileged domain of the national level. Nevertheless, as a central part of the overall system, a denomination's national structures are intimately linked to overall identity issues, sometimes as cause, sometimes as beneficiary (or victim). The material in this collection is distinctive in showing that, to the extent that the current state of transition and adaptation in national structures is problematic, *it is most immediately a problem of identity*. The place of national structures in this broader identity work, particularly what they are presently doing or might yet do to strengthen denominational identity, therefore becomes a central topic in the concluding reflections of this volume, as well as something worth noticing in the descriptive material throughout the collection.

The eight denominations in this study, like the vast majority of American denominations, have a set of interrelated national structures, including both a national assembly that meets periodically and various ongoing administrative or program offices and agencies. To the extent that a denomination has a primary national governance structure, it typically takes the shape of a national assembly operating with some form of representative, participatory democratic process. Theoretically, the role of denominational assemblies is analogous to

23. Richey, "Denominations and Denominationalism," p. 76.

24. Ammerman, "Denominations," pp. 119-22. For a similar perspective as applied to congregations, see Jackson W. Carroll and James F. Hopewell, "Identity," in *Handbook for Congregational Studies,* ed. Jackson W. Carroll, Carl S. Dudley, and William McKinley (Nashville: Abingdon, 1986), pp. 21-47. For a perspective applied to organizations more generically, see Joanne Martin, *Cultures in Organizations: Three Perspectives* (New York: Oxford University Press, 1992); Edgar H. Schein, *Organizational Culture and Leadership,* 2nd ed. (San Francisco: Jossey-Bass, 1997); Terrence E. Deal and Allan A. Kennedy, *Corporate Cultures: The Rites and Rituals of Corporate Life* (Cambridge, Mass.: Perseus Books, 2000); Mats Alvesson, *Understanding Organizational Culture* (Thousand Oaks, Calif.: Sage, 2002).

that of federal and state legislatures. Of course, such governmental legislatures are nearly full-time operations. By contrast, a denominational assembly typically meets only one or two weeks annually, biennially, or even, as with the United Methodist Church, quadrennially. It is therefore not hard to imagine that a denomination's ongoing national offices and agencies have considerably more power and importance than its periodic national assembly, especially when compared to similar structures in federal and state governments.

A denomination's ongoing national offices and agencies typically include some that are largely independent from the national assembly (such as pension boards and publishing houses) and some that are directly mandated by and accountable to that assembly. A key and enduring structural issue in all denominations, and a distinctive concern in this collection, is the relationship of national offices and agencies to the national assembly and to each other. A related and persistent structural issue is the degree to which a denomination's national structures are representative of or responsive to congregations and persons in the pew. There are at least two dimensions to notice. One is that the accountability of the staff of ongoing national offices and agencies to the grass roots typically runs through the national assembly. Given the relative power of national staff in comparison to the national assembly, the ability of the grass roots to hold national staff accountable is episodic and arduous at best. The other dimension to notice is the extent to which delegates to the national assembly, typically unpaid volunteers elected at the congregation or regional level, represent the grass roots. When such questions about the accountability and representativeness of the national level are combined with concerns about the fundamental identity, direction, beliefs, and practices of a denomination, it is little wonder that denominational politics occasionally make the front pages of the secular press. If this much is publicly on the surface, there can be little doubt that more resides beneath.

The fundamental, rational-legal process of representative democracies, a process that most denominations have used since the days of their American founding, is clearly political. The political nature of national level decision making in denominations has therefore been a reality for our country's dominant national religious structures during more than 250 years of good times and bad. Nevertheless, this political quality appears to become more visible, complex, and heated during the unsettledness of change and transition. Such periods also make the interaction between theology and cultural context more challenging. Indeed, the negotiation among diverse constituencies and theological perspectives is a prominent theme throughout this book, as is the tension between more singular and more multistranded theological perspectives.

Our examination of the national level of denominational organization focuses primarily on the national assembly and particularly its derivative agencies, the latter typically directed by the denominational office of the president or the CEO equivalent, such as a presiding bishop or executive secretary. Especially in the organizationally descriptive portions of this collection, attention is paid to the potentially changing nature of the national level's work, both what that work is and how it is being done. Since the national level includes not only the roles, rules, and relationships that arrange how the organization does its work but also the goals and purposes to which that work is oriented, we are consequently interested in both form and function. Many might argue that form should follow function. When both form and function carry theological value as well as the weight of tradition, however, the commonsense or utilitarian sequence of the two (form follows function) becomes questionable. To complicate matters further, the negotiated balance between form, function, and theological warrant is not always consistently systematic. William Warren Sweet remarked in the 1930s that Presbyterians had developed "a more democratic government but a 'monarchial gospel,' while Methodists developed a 'monarchial' government but preached a more 'democratic gospel.'"[25] The attempt to document the relationship between form, function, and theological warrant, let alone how this connects with a changing social and cultural context, is a unique feature of this book.

The governmental structure of Protestant denominations, frequently referred to as polity, is typically described as episcopal (Episcopalian, United Methodist), presbyterian (Presbyterian Church [U.S.A.], Reformed Church in America), congregational (various Baptist denominations, United Church of Christ), or some combination of these (how the Assemblies of God mixes presbyterian and congregational). All three use national structures, but in congregational polities the local congregation has final authority over all aspects of its life, so that compliance with national and regional directives is, with few exceptions, voluntary (or to use the religiously preferred term, covenantal). The congregation owns its property and hires or fires its clergy. Theologically, each congregation is fully the church. In both episcopal and presbyterian polities, the national assembly sets general policy and standards to which congregations must conform, but the regional structures mediate and elaborate this to and for congregations. Regional structures are where congregations and clergy hold standing in the denomination, have a voice in clergy placement, and typically hold claim to local church property. This connectional arrangement is theologically the dominant ecclesial structure. In episcopal polities the primary regional structures are

25. William Warren Sweet, *The Story of Religion in America* (New York: Harper and Brothers, 1939), p. 319.

headed by bishops, while in presbyterian systems they are representative democracies. To use nonreligious descriptors of organizational structure, both episcopal and presbyterian systems are fundamentally federative, with congregations having some of the characteristics of franchises. By contrast, the national structures in congregational systems are best understood as associative or coalitional in light of the autonomy of their congregations.

In practice, the role and prominence of national structures within their overall denominational systems varies more than these three traditional and generalized types of polity would suggest. There is also a considerably greater range in how a denomination's national assembly actually relates to its agencies and offices, and vice versa. In perhaps surprising contrast, the general kind of work done by national structures differs less than one might expect, although the priority and resources given to various tasks can diverge greatly. In any case, this collection gives ample opportunity to consider the disparities between theory (formal polity) and practice in several different national level models.

We have noted that the national structures of denominations have certain parallels with state and federal governments. Accordingly, one can find legislative, executive, and judicial functions within all national denominational structures. Legislatively, each denomination's national assembly establishes the rules of governance for all levels of the system. In episcopal and presbyterian systems, the national assembly also establishes general policy on matters of faith, ordination, and religious practice. National assemblies within congregational polities also regularly deal with such matters, but their resolutions are more guidelines than binding rules for other levels of the denomination. Additionally, the legislative function of national assemblies in virtually every established denomination sets broad policy directives for a range of programs, implementation of which is usually delegated to the various programmatic offices and agencies within a denomination's "executive branch."

National program initiatives are of four general kinds. At the most abstract level, national directives can set the theological principles and goals that should undergird program initiatives and their implementation by judicatories and congregations. This is a regulatory function. At a more concrete level, all national structures help to provide program resource materials, especially educational curricula and worship materials for congregations. Third, all national structures run at least some domestic and international mission programs. Finally, all national structures provide a measure of training and information, opportunities for celebration and fellowship, systems of denomination-wide communication, and support for the denomination's judicial system (if not actually convening it). Even if through fully or quasi-independent agencies, most national structures provide pension funds and insurance programs, and many have publishing houses. Some national structures are also directly responsible for a system of seminaries, colleges, and/or parochial schools, as well as providing placement assistance for clergy.

While much of a national structure's work is internal to the larger denominational system, in all instances there is also an external dimension. This moves in two different directions. The first is providing a public voice for a denomination's religious values and commitments. The second is providing mechanisms for relating to other denominations and faith groups, both nationally and internationally.

With such a diverse complex of functions, it is not surprising that national structures can evolve into sizable bureaucracies, complete with specialized professional staff. Related to this, the historical record of accomplishment of these corporate earthen vessels of the Christian gospel is immense. Among other things, they helped to create and sustain the highest level of individual religious participation in the Western world, the largest sector both of nonprofit organizations (namely, congregations) and of charitable giving in the United States, and a wide array of domestic and international networks of humanitarian aid, social welfare agencies, colleges, hospitals, and specialized housing. When considering the corporate power and productivity of the United States, few people immediately connect such organizational virtuosity and innovation with the religious system. Our focus on denominations through their national structures makes a distinctive and compelling case for this claim, fascinating if for no other reason than their special blend of collective, corporate, and governmental functions. At the same time, few people view corporate America as an unmixed blessing or believe that state and federal governments operate at peak efficiency. The same concerns might well be voiced about the national structures of denominations, especially during a period of broad social and cultural change. For this reason, we will also find denominational structures rife with tensions between inertia and change, theology and efficiency, tradition and adaptation, and local interests and national priorities, all amidst increasingly diverse constituencies.

Description of the Collection

Selected Denominations

Our selection of denominations assumed that the organization of religious work in the United States is in a transitional period, with no broadly shared consensus about how God's work should be done. In order to see how different groups are trying to adapt, it was therefore essential to involve as broad a spectrum of denominations as possible. Within a Protestant frame, we tried to maximize the diversity of these denominations in light of five considerations:

Theology: Whether sacramental, confessional, progressive, reformed, pietistic, or Pentecostal, traditions differ in what they think the church should say and do in the world.

Polity: Episcopal, presbyterian, congregational, and mixed polities vary by how authority and responsibility are allocated and exercised at different levels of organization.

Scale: Larger groups obviously have more resources than smaller ones, but at the same time face greater contingencies.

Ethnicity: Immigrant and African American groups, for example, bear quite distinct traditions of organizing in the larger social milieu today.

History: Older groups have had longer to compromise with society and constituencies, as well as formally institutionalize. A denomination's original structure also reflects the currents of that period and is carried onward as a resource or liability of that tradition.

Trying to maximize diversity on the basis of these factors led to the selection of the eight denominations that are the immediate focus of this collection. They are listed in alphabetical order below, which is the same order in which they appear in the book. Following the name of each is its common abbreviation and a brief sketch of its theology, polity, size (approximate number of congregations), historical ethnicity (if still significant), and period of founding. Later in this introduction we will describe the content of the chapters related to each denomination and suggest several paths through the entire collection.

Assemblies of God (AG): Pentecostal theology, presbyterian-congregational polity, 12,000 congregations, founded 1914.

Association of Vineyard Churches (Vineyard): Postmodern Pentecostal theology, presbyterian-congregational polity, 500 congregations, founded 1982.

Episcopal Church (Episcopal): Sacramental theology, episcopal polity, 7,500 congregations, the dominant church of the southern British colonies.

Lutheran Church–Missouri Synod (LC-MS): Conservative theology, episcopal-congregational polity, 6,000 congregations, historically German, founded 1840s.

National Baptist Convention, USA (NBC): Restorationist theology, congregational polity, 20,000 congregations, historically African American, founded 1895.

Reformed Church in America (RCA): Reformed theology, presbyterian polity, 900 congregations, historically Dutch, founded 1628 in New Amsterdam (New York City).

United Church of Christ (UCC): Liberal Reformed theology, congregational polity, 5,800 congregations, product of several mergers including descendants of the *Mayflower* Puritans.

United Methodist Church (UMC): Wesleyan theology, episcopal polity, 35,000 congregations, founded 1784.

Research Teams

The examination of the adaptive tactics and resources at the national level of these eight denominations was conducted by a four-person research team for each denomination. As noted earlier, each team consisted of a church historian, a sociologist, a theologian, and a national level executive. In collaboration with others on the team, the historian wrote an introduction that provided historical context for the denomination and the other writers, the sociologist wrote a sociological case study, and the theologian wrote a theological essay. The national level executive was both a consultant to the writers and an entrée to the national structures. Teams met both separately and collectively, starting with an orientation meeting for the entire project in the spring of 1998. The sociological case studies were researched and drafted between the fall of 1998 and the fall of 2000. Some writing on the historical introductions and the theological essays happened during this same period, with first drafts of most chapters completed a year later and the final versions finished by the spring of 2002.

The specific assignment for each sociologist was to select at least one theme or issue that was central to understanding the then current (1998-2000) adaptive challenges faced by the national structure of her or his denomination, especially as it sought to determine, articulate, and act on its identity and mission. These were then to serve as a window into:

- How the national structure defined its work (mission, functions, tasks), and what historical continuities and discontinuities this definition represented;
- How the national structure organized its resources to accomplish this work, and what historical continuities or discontinuities this organization revealed; and

• Why the national structure had arrived at defining and organizing its work in the aforementioned ways.

The core of the case study was to be descriptive. Nevertheless, the writers were also invited to conclude with an empathetic evaluation, reflecting on the case's implications for denominational leaders, the emerging nature of organized religion, and organizational adaptiveness.

The sociologists used a variety of methods for obtaining the information upon which their studies were based. In all instances this included interviews with national leaders and staff, as well as a review of published and unpublished documents, memos, and reports. One of the responsibilities of the national level executive on each team was to help in gaining access to these people and documents. All sociologists also had access to reports from the interviews conducted by the ORW judicatory subproject and congregational surveys conducted by the ORW congregation subproject. In a few instances this information was supplemented with clergy surveys conducted by the sociologists themselves and/or participant observation at national meetings. Every team member for a denomination had access to all this information, and on several teams many or all team members participated in the interview and observation processes. With only a few exceptions, team members had some history of personal involvement with the denominations they studied.

The case studies were developed in close cooperation with the theological essays, in some cases providing essential background to them. The task of integrating organizational perspectives with theological reflection is formidable, with scant literature concerning the national structures of denominations upon which to draw. Recent attention to practical, contextual, and local theology has emphasized that the development of action strategies within religious organizations can be a fundamentally theological activity, but literature in this is focused almost exclusively on congregations. Don Browning, for example, has argued that congregations can be communities of memory, tradition, and practical theological reason,[26] while Robert Schreiter has illumined the rich theological practices that relate particular religious gatherings to their broader traditions.[27] Without any models for applying such insights to denominations, however, we were essentially asking the theologians on each team to pioneer a new kind of research. By embracing this challenge, they not only expanded the present scope of practical theology but also reaffirmed that the work of denominations is deeply theological.

26. Browning, *A Fundamental Practical Theology*.
27. Robert J. Schreiter, *Constructing Local Theologies* (Maryknoll, N.Y.: Orbis, 1985).

17

The specific assignment for each theologian was to offer a theological portrayal of the denomination based on information assembled by the team, including but not limited to the case study. Each essay was to convey the actual, operative theologies used at the national level and, if possible, how these intersected with theological expressions throughout the denomination. In other words, this required venturing beyond official theological statements into the wider claims and commitments embodied in daily practices and organizational arrangements. Although there was no set pattern for the research or reflection that resulted in these essays, the theologians were advised to bring careful observation and description of a presenting situation and its implicit faith commitments into conversation with the larger historical and systematic theological memory of the denomination. A more detailed discussion of this task and a summary of the results can be found in the concluding reflection on theology at the end of this volume.

From the outset two premises served as points of departure for this entire study. First, the national structures of denominations are organizationally embodied traditions whose religious character includes an intrinsic commitment to being a community of memory. Second, these same structures are presently facing a period of transition in the United States. Taken together, these premises obviously foreground questions of continuity and change. To highlight the importance of such questions and to provide resources for their consideration, we therefore included a historian on each denominational team. The perspective these historians brought to their respective denominations and fellow team members is reflected in the introductions that begin each denominational set within this collection. These introductions, besides giving the historical background for the case studies and essays that follow in each set, will be especially valuable for those without a working knowledge of a particular denomination.

A biographical note about the writers whose work is presented here can be found in the List of Contributors (pp. 654-56). We also wish to recognize the national level executives who contributed their time, insight, and patience as members of the denominational teams:

LeRoy Bartel, Secretary for Education — AG
Kenneth R. Bradsell, Director of Policy, Planning, and Administrative Services — RCA
Lorin Cope, Assistant to the President — UCC
Todd Hunter, National Director — Vineyard
C. David Lundquist, General Secretary, General Council on Ministries — UMC
Kenneth Schurb, Assistant to the President — LC-MS
Bruce Woodcock, Church Pension Board — Episcopal

(The NBC used several national and state leaders as key informants rather than a single national executive.) In addition, we wish to acknowledge several team members who began the journey with us but needed to withdraw for various reasons along the way: Marilyn Dubasak, Samuel Solivan, Richard Valantasis, and George O. Wood. Finally, we wish especially to remember the lives and contributions of Peter Becker (sociologist, LC-MS) and John Wimber (national level executive, Vineyard), both of whom died during this project.

Chapter Précis

Given the focus of this study, each writer had a broad mandate: to provide a strategic and practical glimpse into the purposes, organizational arrangements, and adaptability of a denomination's national structures, as well as into its theological and historical resources. Each chapter, therefore, contains a virtual feast of topics, situations, questions, and conclusions, so that any one of them could profitably be read alone. Nevertheless, since each religious tradition represents an organizationally and theologically integrated reality, we recommend at the very least that the chapters be read as they were produced, in denominational sets. Such a strategy naturally means moving beyond one's typical disciplinary expertise. Since denominations are messy wholes and not neat abstractions, an appreciative understanding therefore requires an interdisciplinary approach. While we have no illusions about completeness or accuracy in portraying denominational complexity and wholeness (for example, perhaps one coauthored, integrated article on each denomination would have been stronger), we still believe the assembled sets for each denomination offer a step in the right direction.

Because of the richness of topics that dance in varying ways across the chapters of this collection, there was simply no one best way to order them. For the sake of simplicity in locating material, we therefore settled on a conventional alphabetic arrangement by denominational name. Before suggesting several ways to read through the entire collection, we first offer a brief précis of each of the twenty-four chapters.

ASSEMBLIES OF GOD

Historical Introduction (Gary B. McGee)

Through a hundred years of robust growth, the AG has managed to maintain a healthy balance in regard to two enduring tensions. The one tension is between its restoration Pentecostal heritage and evangelical respectability. The other is between charisma and institutional structure. Both tensions have faced an increasing amount of pressure in the transition to the twenty-first century.

Sociological Case Study (Margaret M. Poloma)

Thomas O'Dea's five dilemmas of institutionalization are a well-known statement of the trade-offs between the positive and negative aspects of religious organization. These are used for a close analysis of the tensions evident in the AG today, especially the pressure from both new Pentecostal and new evangelical developments. The ambiguity produced by such pressures appears to function as a safety valve protecting the AG's historical balance between charisma and institution building.

Theological Essay (William W. Menzies)

The growing role of the national level of the AG reflects a growing complexity of challenges that has required much intervention and leadership. Eight specific theological challenges are studied to show how these were addressed with a deepened attention to doctrine, prayer, and Scripture. Ongoing tensions and relationships with evangelicals and other Pentecostals raise new questions about how the AG will retain its distinctive place.

ASSOCIATION OF VINEYARD CHURCHES

Historical Introduction (Bill Jackson)

The primary way of expressing the Vineyard's history is through the biography of its founder, John Wimber. Wimber embarked upon a quest for a radical middle between a doctrinal evangelicalism and Pentecostal power that covered at least seven distinct periods until his death in 1997. Todd Hunter became national director in the spring of 1998 and challenged the Vineyard to honor Wimber by looking forward and defining itself not in ecclesiastical but in biblical terms.

Sociological Case Study (Donald E. Miller)

John Wimber's successor, Todd Hunter, inherited a remarkably successful, innovative, and yet tumultuous organization that was only twenty years old. Rather than routinizing and consolidating the movement, he tried to remove its layers of emerging bureaucracy by radically decentering its authority, hoping to create a "charismatic moment" within the movement and ignite a new level of spiritual entrepreneurship. The reasons for Hunter's hopes and the implications of his resignation in May of 2000 are explored.

Theological Essay (Don Williams)

The biography and commitments of founder John Wimber reveal many parallels between his theology and that of the Vineyard itself. In addition, the Vineyard *Statement of Faith* is examined to show how it draws from doctrinal insights of earlier periods of church history. The highly flexible and relationship-oriented polity of the Vineyard, woven from these several theological strands, positions it for effective witness in the postmodern period.

EPISCOPAL CHURCH

Historical Introduction (Ian T. Douglas)

The denomination's political, economic, and social ascendancy led Episcopalians to believe they were the established church in the United States. Over the last three decades a dramatically pluralistic America and the global Anglican Communion have challenged the presumed cohesion of the national church ideal. In partial response, Episcopal bishops recently dedicated themselves to becoming agents of reconciliation in a church divided over issues of human sexuality and in a world torn apart by violence, poverty, and disease.

Sociological Case Study (William H. Swatos, Jr.)

The changing role of the presiding bishop and a 1995 embezzlement scandal in the national offices are used as ways for exploring what Episcopalians consider the national church to be. The former shows a movement from an authority-orientated hierarchical church to an autonomy-oriented network of discernment rather than decision making. The latter shows that diffuse organizational structures and competing strategic visions in the denomination allowed for creative, healthy resolution of the scandal's breach of trust.

Theological Essay (Jennifer M. Phillips)

The 1995 embezzlement scandal in the national offices raised basic questions about the way church structures reflect the theological leadership and commitments of the presiding bishop. Even more strikingly, the aftermath of that scandal continues to pose a theological challenge to this highly liturgical denomination on matters of forgiveness and reconciliation, and whether its ritual practices in these areas have suffered a lack of imagination and courage.

David A. Roozen and James R. Nieman

LUTHERAN CHURCH–MISSOURI SYNOD

Historical Introduction (Paul Marschke)

For nearly a century, the primary adaptive challenge of the LC-MS was distinguishing German from Lutheran identity in its witness and work. These tensions were at least partly responsible for the duality of structure that emerged, with centralization in matters of doctrine and decentralization elsewhere. More recently, the tension between doctrinal purity and effective mission outreach has become the new LC-MS identity issue, reinvigorating historic tensions around centralization and decentralization.

Sociological Case Study (David L. Carlson)

A crisis over communion threatens a second major schism in the LC-MS in a little over a quarter-century. This crisis is driven by differing views of what constitutes fellowship (who ought to be invited to share the sacrament) and complicated by the postmodern drift from hierarchical to persuasive authority. While the congregational dimension of LC-MS governance gives space for inventive governance, a lack of trust in this political model has pushed the denomination into an earlier European exercise of hierarchy amidst crisis.

Theological Essay (Eugene W. Bunkowske)

Communion, particularly as seen through the Lord's Supper, is the theological focus for this essay. Recent national level discussions about the Supper are examined on the basis of evidence from formal resolutions and informal conversations. Especially important are the perceived qualities, possibilities, and limits for communion, as well as how this theological conversation within the denomination reveals broader religious challenges facing society at large.

NATIONAL BAPTIST CONVENTION

Historical Introduction (Quinton Hosford Dixie)

Despite all the NBC's growth and significance, it has since its origins possessed contradictory impulses that keep the organization at odds with itself. These impulses include the denomination's birth during the period of "separate but equal," the tension between efficiency and harmony in Baptist polity, the pulls of congregational autonomy versus centralized authority, and the role of women within the denomination. These typically become increasingly troublesome in unsettled times.

Sociological Case Study (Aldon D. Morris and Shayne Lee)

The office of the NBC president and a scandal related to it reveal both resilience and rigidity in the practices and culture of the denomination as it struggles to remain relevant and vital. What unfolds is an illuminating account of how loose formal structures can have strong cohesiveness, how loose coalitions can have multiple points for adaptation, and how the lack of explicit policies can contribute to the maintenance of marginalizing informal practices.

Theological Essay (David Emmanuel Goatley)

Tracing the many historic sources and struggles of the NBC, this essay explores the denomination's relation to other parts of the black church tradition and to the dominant white American culture. These subtle theological contours help explain why the NBC responded as it did to the fiscal misappropriation crisis that engulfed its presidency in 1998. Honesty about sin and deep commitment to forgiveness are seen as foundational theological resources for the members.

REFORMED CHURCH IN AMERICA

Historical Introduction (John Coakley)

Its presbyterian polity notwithstanding, the RCA's historic definition of the church as the locus of preaching and sacraments construes the church as something essentially local. At the same time, there is the conviction that the church must be "purposive," activist about its mission. However, it appears that mission in the purposive sense is increasingly being considered as the very essence of the church. In addition, there is a growing challenge to the assumption that the national level most properly has the job of mission.

Sociological Case Study (Donald A. Luidens)

The implications of the 1997 Mission Statement for rethinking the purpose and organization of the RCA's national structure are analyzed. In an unprecedented fashion, congregations are coming to see themselves as autonomous actors within the historically connectional RCA. The corporate model of the denomination has not died, however. Instead, it seems to be in transition from an agency acting on *behalf of* congregations to one acting *on* congregations, a national structure fully engaged with local matters.

Theological Essay (Steve Mathonnet-VanderWell)

The 1997 Mission Statement is used as a window into the RCA's theology. Both the process of its adoption and its overall content reflect key changes in the functional theological commitments of the denomination. At issue is whether the statement's strong emphasis upon the congregation shifts the theological basis for classic Reformed ecclesiology, obscures the value of denominational heritage, and risks impairing the very mission it seeks to promote.

UNITED CHURCH OF CHRIST

Historical Introduction (Barbara Brown Zikmund)

The growing nineteenth-century concern about Christian unity generated an ecumenical movement that encouraged mergers and reunions early in the twentieth century. The UCC is rooted in this history, in which unity through shared life and work took precedence over issues of faith and order. The 1999 UCC restructuring seems to suggest a different vision of Christian unity rooted in who makes up the church rather than what it confesses or what it does.

Sociological Case Study (Emily Barman and Mark Chaves)

The nature, rationale, and implications of the 1999 UCC restructuring at its national level are the focus of this case study. The restructure had the goals of creating new relationships among the various units of the denomination and pushing the UCC to emphasize and value diversity of various sorts. Emerging issues concern the reasons congregations become alienated from national structures, the national wariness about covenant, and a possible shift from an ecumenical to a multicultural view of the meaning of diversity.

Theological Essay (Roger L. Shinn)

Formed over forty years ago as an intentionally ecumenical denomination, the UCC today faces a reorganization that reveals theological concerns unresolved since the time of its origins. Most noticeable is the growing theological distance between national boards and local congregations, particularly in areas of cultural diversity. Pressured by declining membership and finances, the denomination seeks to be true to its heritage while creatively engaging new social challenges.

UNITED METHODIST CHURCH

Historical Introduction (Russell E. Richey)

From its outset, American Methodism has agonized over its highly stylized, disciplined, and centralized apparatus for decision making and resourcing. This agony and the calls for reform have grown in intensity as the inadequacies of established bureaucratic patterns grow increasingly stark. Although restructure remains elusive, there has also been an emerging awareness that such habitual Methodist practices as itinerancy, superintending, and conferencing actually enact important theological principles.

Sociological Case Study (James Rutland Wood)

The UMC faces vast changes driven both by broader social forces and internal struggles precipitated by those forces. In response, eleven transformational directions were reported by a Connectional Process Team to the UMC General Conference in 2000. Potential changes are analyzed in three areas: greater structural flexibility that allows local mission response to the call of the Spirit, the meaning and priority of biblical authority, and the reduced structural centrality of the UMC in global Methodism.

Theological Essay (Pamela D. Couture)

Practical theology in the Wesleyan tradition is deeply committed to mutual bonds of relationship (restructuring), public implications of the spiritual life (reshaping), and connections between the theological heritage and contemporary concerns (reclaiming). These commitments are explored in relation to three recent national level projects of the UMC and how these exemplify a distinctively Wesleyan manner of doing theology in practice.

Reading Strategies

Armed with some sense of the range of insights in each chapter and denominational set, you may consider planning a route through this material a daunting task. We have already recommended that an entire set be read as a unity, rather than selectively reading, say, only the sociological case studies or the theological essays. While such a selective reading at first sounds beneficial for those with more limited disciplinary interests, the complexity of the denomination could easily be lost by dropping out the other disciplinary perspectives. Beyond these initial cautions, however, we want to suggest several reading strategies that seek to connect particular reader interests with the specific features of each denominational set.

As a starting point, it is fruitful to recall the list from earlier in this introduction about the considerations that led to the selection of the eight denominations in the first place: theology, polity, scale, ethnicity, and history. We then briefly sketched each selected denomination in light of these five considerations. Therefore, one simple strategy would be to select whichever consideration holds greatest interest and read through the collection by emerging clusters or natural sequences. For example, a *cluster* strategy would look for common qualitative or quantitative features, such as representatives of the same theological family (Pentecostal or Reformed) or similar forms of polity (congregational or episcopal). By contrast, a *sequential* strategy would identify a typical scale of comparison and move through that scale in some predetermined order, such as smaller to larger in scale or older to younger based on the period of founding.

A *blending* of cluster and sequential strategies is another possibility especially germane to those interested in history and the continuing influence of the period of founding. Looking at all eight denominations in the order of their founding also reveals three broad clusters in that sequence. First are the colonial establishment denominations of the UCC, Episcopal, and RCA, although all three also include later waves of immigration. Next, the UMC is largely an indigenous movement emerging in the late eighteenth century and affected by frontier expansion well into the nineteenth century. By contrast, the LC-MS represents a mid-nineteenth-century European immigration, while the NBC develops out of the freedom of slaves following the Civil War. Finally, the twentieth century is bracketed at its start by the formation of the AG (reflecting the dislocations due to American industrialization and urbanization) and near its end by the establishment of the Vineyard (with roots in the California Jesus movements of the late 1960s). A more abbreviated approach might begin with the establishment-oriented, colonially grounded Episcopal, move to the LC-MS as it continues to struggle with its nineteenth-century and ethnic immigrant roots, proceed to the AG at the turn of century, and then close with the quite contemporary Vineyard. Of course, this in no way implies that the four denominations not mentioned have uninteresting or unimportant histories. It is worth noting, however, that those histories are somewhat more complex, so that the impact of each group's respective period of founding on its contemporary efforts and commitments is not as easy to isolate.

Beyond clusters, sequences, or blends of the two, one other reading strategy would be to identify *themes* mentioned in the chapter précis. For example, a reader with special interest in the relation of *structure and purpose* might focus on the four denominations whose sets particularly emphasize that theme: the RCA, AG, Vineyard, and UCC. The RCA set uses a new mission statement as a way of exploring the denomination, especially how that statement departs from both the denomination's polity and the role of its national structure. The AG set examines the classic tension between a movement's foundational religious experience and the need to institutionalize that experience so it can be extended to future generations. The Vineyard set looks at a denomination on a journey from being a loose coalition to a more formalized organization and facing the daunting transition brought by the death of its founder and leader. Finally, the UCC set draws our attention back to the ongoing struggle for renewal and adaptability by America's colonial denominations. The theme in all four sets is how foundational theological values are evolving in new circumstances, both redefining the priorities of the national structure and provoking significant changes within denominational polity.

A different thematic strategy might look at *dominant tensions,* especially those between unity and diversity or fragmentation and reconciliation. Four sets attend to this particular theme. The LC-MS set focuses on the dynamics and struggles of a denomination trying to reassert traditional, exclusivist boundaries. The UMC set presents a denomination almost paralyzed by conflict generated by diverse constituencies, with one of the most contested issues being the very breadth of diversity that can be tolerated. Both the NBC and Episcopal sets look at how the crisis of scandal can accentuate existing organizational tensions and fissures while at the same time bring out a denomination's resources for solidarity and reconciliation.

One last example of a thematic strategy for reading through this collection would be to look at the *adaptive strategies* different denominations use. All eight denominations face some measure of division or discord, but their means for responding to such threats are quite distinct. The LC-MS attempts to increase national command and control in order to preserve the purity of the tradition. The AG has a strong core identity that allows for some tolerance of and patience with threats from margins. In the tension between spirit and structure, the Vineyard has resolved to err on the side of spirit. The NBC has learned to close ranks around ethnic solidarity. The Episcopal set notes an intentional connection between the pastoral style of the presiding bishop and the denomination's historic theological resources for reconciliation. The UCC attempts to respond by readjusting national purpose and structure, while the RCA tries to respond by redefining these. Finally, the UMC is working to articulate a renewed theological core by which it can restore a sense of direction amidst transition.

Literature on Denominations and Organizations

Eleven months a *New York Times* best-seller, *Thriving on Chaos* resonated with the experience of the reading public in the late 1980s. It called for a revolution that "challenges everything we thought we knew about managing, and often challenges over a hundred years of American tradition. Most fundamentally, the times demand that flexibility and love of change replace our longstanding penchant for mass production and mass markets, based as it is upon a relatively predictable environment now vanished."[28] It proposed turning uncertainty into opportunity through becoming obsessed with listening, flattened networked structures, and fostering "fast failures" (that is, creating an ethos that encourages both the risk of innovation and the accountability to discontinue those experiments that fail). Many similar books quickly followed during the 1990s, including *The Boundaryless Organization* and *The New Management*.[29] The former claimed to provide the practical strategies necessary to sweep away the artificial obstacles of hierarchy and turf that stand in the way of creating the organizational forms required in the new millennium: virtual organizations, horizontal organizations, team-based structures, and so forth. The mantra of the latter book was to lead from the bottom up and the outside in. Among other things, it called for creating competition within an organization and then balancing the tension so generated by establishing communal, democratic decision-making processes. Finally, the turn of the century was marked by a readable explication of the new electronic global economy, *The Lexus and the Olive Tree*. It warned of the inevitable tension between retribalization and consumerism as globalization replaces the Cold War economic system with an integration of capital, technology, and information across national borders.[30] All four of these books exemplify how technological, economic, demographic, and cultural changes during the past quarter- to half-century have prompted a paradigm shift from modern to postmodern forms of corporate organization.

There are striking parallels to these insights in the organization of American religion. A good place to begin tracing these changes in the religious sector is with a little-noticed but symbolically profound fact from 1966. In that year the Southern Baptist Convention surpassed the United Methodist Church in membership to become the largest Protestant denomination in the United States. Something was happening within American religion, but typical for most major transitions, it was not immediately clear what. The emergence of a new market leader among Protestant denominations that year was caused by a

28. Tom Peters, *Thriving on Chaos: Handbook for a Management Revolution* (New York: Knopf, 1987), p. xiii.

29. Ron Ashkenas, *The Boundaryless Organization: Breaking the Chains of Organizational Structure* (San Francisco: Jossey-Bass, 1995); William E. Halal, *The New Management: Democracy and Enterprise Are Transforming Organizations* (San Francisco: Berrett-Koehler, 1998).

30. Thomas L. Friedman, *The Lexus and the Olive Tree: Understanding Globalization* (New York: Harper Collins, 1999).

nearly equal mix of Methodist decline and Southern Baptist ascent. Most initial reflection, however, focused on the decline, locating Methodism within the broader, ebbing mainline. Writing about the 1960s, Sydney Ahlstrom was one of the first to locate the changed fortunes of the mainline in a wider perspective. "[I]t may even have ended a distinct quadricentennium — a unified four-hundred-year period — in the Anglo-American experience. A Great Puritan Epoch can be seen as beginning in 1558 with the death of Mary Tudor . . . and the terms 'post-Puritan' and 'post-Protestant' are first popularly applied to America in the 1960s."[31] Ahlstrom was speaking in particular of the demise of the white Anglo-Saxon Protestant establishment. The 1960s may well have marked the end of WASP cultural hegemony, but to expand this into a "post-Protestant" assessment fails to account for several details. Perhaps most important, it ignores the ascendancy of Southern Baptists as well as the growth of many other noncolonial groups, including the Assemblies of God and several of the historic black denominations. Indeed, even Methodism was not part of the colonial, religious establishment, and Sweet noted as early as 1948 that this establishment had already lost numerical dominance in the early years of the nineteenth century. Unsurprisingly, this dominance was lost to Baptists, Methodists, and other left-wing sectarian bodies, denominations better adapted to the conditions of the movement westward.[32] Their dominance was further eroded by the immigration of large numbers of non-Protestant groups beginning just before the start of the twentieth century.[33]

Why Conservative Churches Are Growing was the first book to bring a more integrated perspective on the changes symbolized by the denominational shifts of 1966.[34] In simple outline, it argued that the stricter a denomination was in enforcing doctrinal and behavioral norms, the more serious and committed its members were. Conservative groups were strict, and therefore their beliefs and practices remained plausible, even against the onslaught of an increasingly secular popular culture. The mainline (rapidly becoming "oldline") denominations had become less strict, and therefore their brand of religion

31. Sydney E. Ahlstrom, *A Religious History of the American People* (New Haven: Yale University Press, 1972), p. 1079.

32. The link between vitality and the adaptive innovation of newly emergent religious movements has recently been popularized in economic, entrepreneurial terms as the major thesis of Roger Finke and Rodney Stark, *The Churching of America, 1776-1990: Winners and Losers in Our Religious Economy* (New Brunswick, N.J.: Rutgers University Press, 1992).

33. William W. Sweet, "The Protestant Churches," *Annals of the American Academy of Political and Social Science* 256 (1948): 43-52.

34. Dean M. Kelley, *Why Conservative Churches Are Growing: A Study in Sociology of Religion* (New York: Harper and Row, 1972).

provided little if any plausible difference from secular culture, especially for newer generations of young adults.

The 1979 *Understanding Church Growth and Decline* added three nuances to Dean Kelley's theory.[35] First, it empirically confirmed that the most significant portion of the oldline decline involved young adult dropouts. Second, it confirmed that the baby boomers raised in oldline churches but now leaving them as young adults were not, for the most part, entering more conservative churches. Instead, they were moving into the ranks of the unchurched because they found that even oldline churches, especially at the congregational level, were out of step with the progressive values of 1960s countercultural revolution. Third, as historian James Smiley persuasively argued, oldline Protestantism's historical roots in evangelical strictness, its dominant ethos of comforting and culture-affirming devotionalism, and its prophetic predisposition toward the strange countercultural mix of emergent personal and social liberation were producing a major identity crisis.[36] Equally important, this weakening of identity was both cause and consequence of what Hoge argued were the increasing divisions in the oldline Protestant house.[37]

A decade later, *The Restructuring of American Religion* provided the most comprehensive and integrated treatment to date of the dramatic changes occurring since the Second World War.[38] A primary theme and conclusion was the declining significance of denominationalism. Robert Wuthnow meant by this both the weakening of denominational attachments among members and potential members and the erosion of the symbolic barriers that distinguished one denomination from another. Among the major factors contributing to this were increased intradenominational diversity (which contests and blurs a denomination's distinctive identity), growing consumerist individualism (which emphasizes subjective interpretation that erodes the tacit acceptance of official denominational creeds and changes the nature of theology), and hundreds of new, small, special-purpose religious groups (which deliver more attention to the varied self-interests of niche constituencies than can inclusive denominations). The combination of indistinct denominational identity and increased

35. Dean R. Hoge and David A. Roozen, eds., *Understanding Church Growth and Decline, 1950-1978* (New York: Pilgrim Press, 1979).

36. James H. Smiley, "Church Growth and Decline in Historical Perspective: Protestant Quest for Identity, Leadership, and Meaning," in *Understanding Church Growth and Decline, 1950-1978*, pp. 69-93.

37. Dean R. Hoge, *Division in the Protestant House: The Basic Reasons behind Intra-Church Conflicts* (Philadelphia: Westminster, 1976).

38. Robert Wuthnow, *The Restructuring of American Religion: Society and Faith Since World War II* (Princeton: Princeton University Press, 1988).

expressive individualism echoes the "new voluntarism" mentioned in *American Mainline Religion*.[39] The two have also come to be major themes in subsequent literature on the changing fortunes of American denominations, along with subjective individualism's organizational equivalent, congregational localism. By the mid-1990s, each theme was being consistently presented as a manifestation of the transition from modernity to postmodernity.

The Greening of America was the first best-selling articulation of the countercultural values that captured so much of the baby boom generation during the 1960s. A decade later, *New Rules: Searching for Self-Fulfillment in a World Turned Upside Down* provided a succinct, popularly written account of the inward turn this generation made during the early 1970s.[40] It was, however, the "Sheilaism" presented in *Habits of the Heart* that most forcefully captured the nature and potential implications of the expressive individualism of baby boomers for the religious community.[41] As noted above, the religious impact of this emerging new form of American individualism was further popularized by William McKinney and Wade Clark Roof as "new voluntarism." This was considerably nuanced in an article by Penny Marler and David Roozen as a fundamental social-psychological shift in American culture from an objective to a subjective locus of authority that gave rise to the "the dual edges of church as choice."[42] Prior treatments of privatized "church as choice" focused exclusively on the baby boomers' decision to drop out of religion. The authors pointed out that a choice could also be made for religious participation, and their national survey analysis provided evidence of both choices being made. Their article is important because it provided the basis for merging the expressive individualism, spirituality, and seeker orientation of baby boomers in *A Generation of Seekers*.[43] This widely influential book argued that many baby boomers were not opting out of religion altogether, but showed a predisposition toward more subjective and spiritual forms of religious expression instead of doctrinal and institutional forms. *The Post-War Generation and Establishment Religion* was

39. Wade Clark Roof and William McKinney, *American Mainline Religion: Its Changing Shape and Future* (New Brunswick, N.J.: Rutgers University Press, 1987).

40. Charles A. Reich, *The Greening of America: How the Youth Revolution Is Trying to Make America Livable* (New York: Random House, 1970); Daniel Yankelovich, *New Rules: Searching for Self-Fulfillment in a World Turned Upside Down* (New York: Random House, 1981).

41. Robert N. Bellah and others, *Habits of the Heart: Individualism and Commitment in American Life* (Berkeley: University of California Press, 1985).

42. Penny Long Marler and David A. Roozen, "From Church Tradition to Consumer Choice: Two Gallup Surveys of Unchurched Americans," in *Church and Denominational Growth*, ed. David A. Roozen and C. Kirk Hadaway (Nashville: Abingdon, 1993), pp. 253-77.

43. Wade Clark Roof, *A Generation of Seekers: The Spiritual Journeys of the Baby Boom Generation* (San Francisco: Harper San Francisco, 1993).

among the first religious treatments that tied this emergent, expressive individualistic spirituality to postmodernism.[44] More importantly, several contributions from Europe drove home the point that the spiritual preference of the postwar generation was not, in the majority of cases, a solitary experience.[45] Rather it tended to be embedded in small group experiences that gave priority to the expressive and communal.

There is a significant body of literature arguing that one of the divides between a denomination's national staff and its local congregations is that the former gives priority to mission and the latter gives priority to the communal. In light of the communal and anti-institutional views of baby boomers, let alone the increased fragmentation within denominations that further erodes the national-level sense of common identity and purpose, the relatively recent rediscovery of local congregations is unsurprising. Perhaps the only unusual aspect about this rediscovery was its almost simultaneous mention by both a sociologist writing in a prestigious, academic journal and a folksy church consultant writing for church practitioners, each referring to "a new paradigm." A difference between the two versions of this paradigm, however, was that the former emphasized the communal nature of congregations while the latter emphasized mission. Stephen Warner went to the theoretical crux of the matter when he asserted, "We shall see below that religion in the United States has typically expressed not the culture of the society as a whole but the subcultures of its many constituents; therefore it should not be thought of as either the Parsonian conscience of the whole or the Bergian refuge of the periphery, but as the vital expression of groups."[46] As evidence of this, he cited a variety of recent studies showing the development of "assertive particularism, resurgent traditionalism, creative innovation, and all-round vitality in American religion."[47] Among the organizational implications of this new innovative group vitality were the fading of national denominational structures and the rise of "*de facto* congregationalism*," the latter grounded in the growing prominence of

44. Wade Clark Roof, Jackson W. Carroll, and David A. Roozen, eds., *The Post-War Generation and Establishment Religion: Cross-Cultural Perspectives* (Boulder, Colo.: Westview Press, 1995).

45. See, for example, Danièle Hervieu-Léger, "The Case of French Catholicism," and Liliane Voyé, "From Institutional Catholicism to 'Christian Inspiration': Another Look at Belgium," in *The Post-War Generation and Establishment Religion*, pp. 151-70 and 191-206 respectively.

46. R. Stephen Warner, "Work in Progress toward a New Paradigm for the Sociological Study of Religion in the United States," *American Journal of Sociology* 98, no. 5 (March 1993): 1047.

47. Warner, "Work in Progress," p. 1048.

"affectively significant associations under local and lay control."[48] This same paradigm shift from national denominational prominence to local congregation was also at the heart of Loren Mead's *The Once and Future Church*.[49] His normative agenda for the congregation was clearer in the book's subtitle, however: *Reinventing the Congregation for a New Mission Frontier*.

It is too early to tell whether these differing communal and missional interpretations show that church professionals, especially in oldline Protestantism, still do not understand the changing nature of baby boomer religious expression. It is worth noting, however, that the priority of the congregation was also soon adopted as a core tenet of faith within several emergent theological streams, most with an emphasis on mission.[50] The major exception to this missional thrust in recent theological writing giving priority to the congregation is found in works that emphasize the Holy Spirit and the experience of the Spirit in worship.[51] *Reinventing American Protestantism* is one of the first sociological studies that appreciatively examines the new wave of Pentecostal denominations and their megachurch, seeker orientation, asking what their innovative and apparently successful style suggests for oldline Protestant groups.[52] This book is also one of the first to connect the experiential priority on the local with postmodernism.

Finally, back on the denominational level, the twin and interrelated threats of increased diversity and eroded denominational identity have received major attention within oldline Protestantism. Indeed, the subtitle of *Beyond Establishment* (mentioned much earlier in this introduction) is *Protestant Identity in a Post-Protestant Age*. This book is a collection of essays addressing recent changes across a broad spectrum of programs and institutions that used traditional carriers of denomination identity: Sunday schools, women's organizations, church-related colleges, campus ministries, seminaries, hymnals, and so forth. The editors concluded:

> Protestantism has moved 'beyond establishment' in the sense of an unofficial hegemony that mainline Protestants exercised culturally and socially in

48. Warner, "Work in Progress," p. 1066.

49. Loren B. Mead, *The Once and Future Church: Reinventing the Congregation for a New Mission Frontier* (Washington, D.C.: Alban Institute, 1991).

50. Darrell L. Guder, ed., *Missional Church: A Vision for the Sending of the Church in North America* (Grand Rapids: Eerdmans, 1998).

51. For a mainline Protestant example, see Peter Crafts Hodgson, *Winds of the Spirit: A Constructive Christian Theology* (Louisville: Westminster John Knox, 1994). Examples from a Pentecostal perspective can be found in the theological essays by Don Williams and William W. Menzies within this collection.

52. Donald E. Miller, *Reinventing American Protestantism: Christianity in the New Millennium* (Berkeley: University of California Press, 1997).

nineteenth and early twentieth century America. The combined impact of pluralism and privatization in matters of religion and culture has eroded much of this hegemony. This erosion, together with the serious hemorrhaging at the level of membership, has left mainline Protestants with a severe crisis of identity and purpose.[53]

Writing a year later and again focusing on oldline Protestantism, Richey outlined five stages through which he perceives denominations moved during more than three hundred years of American history.[54] Each stage represents a distinctive style of being a denomination based on adhesive and dynamic principles. These include the commitments, ideals, and purposes that hold a denomination together and direct its energy. In historical order, these five stages are: ethnic voluntarism, purposive missionary association, churchly denominationalism, corporate organization, and postdenominational confessionalism. The last stage represents the current state of oldline denominations, and Richey chose the name to suggest "that denominations have lost or are losing longfamiliar adhesive and dynamic principles and are groping, often desperately, for tactics that work and unite."[55] After a familiar litany of challenges faced today, including the frequent contentiousness among a denomination's diverse constituencies, Richey asked, "Might the problem, the cause, lie in the collapse of denominational purpose and in the loss of a real reason for hanging together?"[56]

Expressive individualism, congregational localism, and pluralism's potential for fragmentation are among the pervasive and significant challenges that the postmodern situation of American society places before denominations. While some denominations seem up to the challenge, others are struggling to cope — but none are left unaffected. It is to the stories of eight of these diverse and resourceful religious groups that we now turn.

53. Roof and Carroll, *Beyond Establishment*, pp. 343-44.
54. Richey, "Denominations and Denominationalism."
55. Richey, "Denominations and Denominationalism," p. 87.
56. Richey, "Denominations and Denominationalism," p. 88.

"More Than Evangelical":
The Challenge of the Evolving Identity
of the Assemblies of God

Gary B. McGee

I n the cauldron of doctrinal controversy at the sixth national gathering of the
General Council of the Assemblies of God in Springfield, Missouri, in 1918,
the delegates announced as their "distinctive testimony" that speaking in
tongues represents the uniform "initial physical sign" of the postconversion experience of baptism in the Holy Spirit. In so doing, they voiced the sentiments
of the large majority of Pentecostals who had insisted since the inception of the
Pentecostal movement at the turn of the twentieth century, that glossolalic utterance marked the inauguration of the Spirit-filled Christian life. Eventually
this became known as the doctrine of "initial physical evidence," or simply "initial evidence."

Pentecostals saw themselves as an end-times movement raised up by God
to evangelize the world before the imminent return of Jesus Christ. Forming
new denominations, like the ones they had left or been forced out of, was the
last thing on their minds. Cold ritual, the "Social Gospel," and arid discussions
on theological issues had no place on their agenda. A common goal to proclaim
the good news in the power of the Spirit knit them together. But despite the idealized sense of unity that prevailed, quarrels over correct doctrine quickly divided them, revealing how seriously they considered scriptural teaching and
authority. As early as 1906, they parted ways over the absolute requirement of
tongues for Spirit baptism. Four years later, in 1910, the house again divided
over the nature of sanctification. Then, in 1913, a major dispute arose over the
biblical understanding of the Godhead. An excessive use of biblical literalism
mixed with the Jesus-centered piety of the Holiness Movement prompted a
march of events that climaxed in a division between trinitarian and "Jesus'
Name" or "Oneness" Pentecostals. Hardest hit by the controversy was the Assemblies of God.

In order to affix the stamp of historic Christian belief (especially that of the Trinity) on the public perception of its name, the General Council approved the Statement of Fundamental Truths in 1916, just two years after its incorporation. The statement pledges allegiance to orthodox teachings to preserve the doctrinal integrity of the organization and avoid the charge of heresy from the wider Christian community. It maps out common ground shared with other conservative Christians, while the teachings on Spirit baptism, the availability of the charismatic gifts in the contemporary life and mission of the church (1 Cor. 12:7-11), and divine healing (usually referred to by outside observers as "faith healing") explain the distance between them.[1] Even though the council adopted the creedal declaration with reluctance, the times demanded a forthright exposition of doctrine.[2] Hopefully, the trinitarian statement would also limit the further antagonizing of evangelical Christians whose opinions about Pentecostals had been stridently negative.[3]

Like the larger Pentecostal movement, the Assemblies of God finds its heritage in the family photo album of evangelical revivalism and the nineteenth-century Holiness Movement. The frames include the Trinity, the inspiration and infallibility of the Bible, the lostness of humankind, redemption through the substitutionary atonement of Jesus Christ, justification by faith, the resurrection of Christ, Spirit baptism as an event in the believer's life subsequent to conversion, and the premillennial version of the "Blessed Hope." With other Pentecostals, Assemblies of God believers summed up their unique be-

---

1. Largely drafted by Daniel W. Kerr, a former pastor with the Christian and Missionary Alliance who joined the Assemblies of God, it reveals an almost wholesale borrowing of Alliance teachings and reflects the influence of the latter on first-generation Assemblies of God leaders. Charles W. Nienkirchen analyzes this legacy in *A. B. Simpson and the Pentecostal Movement* (Peabody, Mass.: Hendrickson, 1992). See also Russell P. Spittler, "Are Pentecostals and Charismatics Fundamentalists? A Review of American Uses of These Categories," in *Charismatic Christianity as a Global Culture*, ed. Karla Poewe (Columbia: University of South Carolina Press, 1994), pp. 103-16.

2. The disclaimer in the original preface to the Statement of Fundamental Truths contradicts its actual creedal function and immediate application at the time for the credentialing of ministers: "This . . . is not intended as a creed for the Church, nor as a basis of fellowship among Christians, but only as a basis of unity for the ministry alone (i.e., that we all speak the same thing 1 Cor. 1:10; Acts 2:42). The human phraseology employed in such statement is not inspired nor contended for, but the truth set forth in such phraseology is held to be essential to a full Gospel ministry. No claim is made that it contains all truth in the Bible, only that it covers our present needs as to these fundamental matters"; Combined Minutes of the General Council of the Assemblies of God, 1914-1917, p. 12.

3. Grant A. Wacker, "Travail of a Broken Family: Radical Evangelical Responses to the Emergence of Pentecostalism in America, 1906-1916," in *Pentecostal Currents in American Protestantism*, ed. Edith L. Blumhofer et al. (Urbana: University of Illinois Press, 1999), pp. 23-49.

liefs with the term "full gospel" (Jesus Christ as Savior, Healer, Baptizer [in the Holy Spirit], and Coming King), which highlighted salvation by grace, divine healing, Spirit baptism (with tongues), and the soon return of Jesus Christ.[4]

This christocentric orientation had characterized teachings in various wings of the Holiness and healing movements. Well before the close of the century, the popularity of Wesleyan Holiness and the Reformed revivalist "Higher Life" teachings had generated interest in the baptism and gifts of the Spirit. Wesleyan Holiness preachers told their hearers that a crisis experience of sanctification, the "second blessing," would instantaneously eradicate their sinful dispositions and elevate them to a new plateau of Christian living. Higher Life advocates, sharing the notion of a second work of grace but avoiding the "sinless perfection" of the Wesleyans, preferred to look at it as "full consecration" that empowered them for evangelism.[5] By the end of the century, both camps chose to use Pentecostal imagery from the New Testament to describe the event. Thus the experience of "sinless perfection" and "full consecration" constituted the baptism in the Holy Spirit, believed to be identical to that received by the disciples on the Day of Pentecost (Acts 2). In this way Holiness and Higher Life believers — "radical evangelicals" — regarded themselves as "Pentecostal" in spirituality.[6]

Another formative influence came in the latter part of the century as radical evangelicals in the Protestant missions movement, whose worldview resounded with actions of the Spirit, longed for the restoration of apostolic power in "signs and wonders" (Acts 5:12) to expedite gospel proclamation. Given the slow pace of conversions overseas and the nearness of Christ's return, they wondered how the Great Commission could be achieved in such a short time. Desirous of preaching upon arrival at their respective mission fields, they became frustrated when several years of language study were required before sufficient fluency could be attained. Beginning at least by the 1880s, some speculated that with mustering enough faith, God might enable them to "speak with new tongues" (Mark 16:17 AV) in order to avoid the nuisance of language school.[7]

Building on his Wesleyan Holiness theology, eschatological speculation, and passion for world evangelization, Kansas preacher Charles F. Parham con-

---

4. For the historical and theological background of the term "full gospel," see Donald W. Dayton, *Theological Roots of Pentecostalism* (Peabody, Mass.: Hendrickson, 1987), pp. 19-23.

5. Dayton, *Theological Roots of Pentecostalism*, pp. 87-113.

6. "Radical evangelicals" refers to Wesleyan Holiness and Higher Life (Reformed revivalist) believers; for a discussion of the term, see Wacker, "Travail," pp. 25-26.

7. Gary B. McGee, "Short-Cut to Language Preparation? Radical Evangelicals, Missions, and the Gift of Tongues," *International Bulletin of Missionary Research* 25 (July 2001): 118-20, 122-23.

ceived the doctrine of initial evidence in the fall of 1900 and deserves credit for making it the chief distinctive of classical Pentecostal faith.[8] His aspirations began to be realized with a revival at his Bethel Bible School in Topeka, Kansas, in January 1901 that marked the beginning of the Pentecostal movement. Along with the students, he testified to speaking in unlearned human languages through the agency of the Holy Spirit. To Parham and his sometime student William J. Seymour, the best-known leader of the Azusa Street Revival in Los Angeles, California (1906-9), and other pioneers, glossolalia signaled the predicted "outpouring" of the Spirit at the close of human history (Joel 2:28-29), verified the reception of Spirit baptism, and provided linguistic expertise for God's elite band of end-times missionaries. Such supernatural enablement would make formal language study an anachronism. Parham contended that "if Balaam's mule could stop in the middle of the road and give the first preacher that went out for money a *bawling out* in Arabic [then] anybody today ought to be able to preach in any language of the world if they had horse sense enough to let God use their tongue and throat."[9] As a writer in the *Apostolic Faith* (Los Angeles), the voice of the Apostolic Faith Mission on Azusa Street, put it, "God is solving the missionary problem, sending out new-tongued missionaries on the apostolic faith line."[10]

Pentecostals lamented that tongues had virtually disappeared after the apostolic age, including the doctrine of initial evidence. Not until the turn of the century did believers rediscover and reinstate the doctrine. From their perspective this paralleled Martin Luther's recovery of justification by faith, John Wesley's teaching on Christian perfection, and the divine provision for physical healing as taught by such faith healers as Charles C. Cullis, John Alexander Dowie, A. J. Gordon, and A. B. Simpson.[11]

Nevertheless, as early as 1906 some began to have reservations about the function of tongues for missions. Reports from missionaries proved to be disappointing in this respect. A period of theological reflection then began in which Pentecostals sought for a better biblical understanding of the role of tongues. Most came to recognize that speaking in tongues, though still consid-

8. James R. Goff, Jr., *Fields White unto Harvest: Charles F. Parham and the Missionary Origins of Pentecostalism* (Fayetteville: University of Arkansas Press, 1988), pp. 74-75.

9. Charles F. Parham, quoted in Sarah E. Parham, *The Life of Charles F. Parham* (Baxter Springs, Kans.: Apostolic Faith Bible College, 1930), pp. 51-52.

10. *Apostolic Faith* (Los Angeles), November 1906, p. 2, col. 4.

11. D. W. Kerr, "The Basis of Our Distinctive Testimony," *Pentecostal Evangel*, September 2, 1922, p. 4; cf. Charles Nienkirchen, "Conflicting Visions of the Past: The Prophetic Use of History in the Early American Pentecostal-Charismatic Movements," in *Charismatic Christianity as a Global Culture*, pp. 120-25.

ered recognizable languages and intrinsic to Spirit baptism, represented worship and prayerful intercession in the Spirit (Rom. 8:26; 1 Cor. 14:2). For the most part they seemed to accept the transition in the meaning of tongues from preaching to prayer since on either reading — glossolalia for functioning effectively in a foreign language, or for spiritual worship — the notion of receiving languages denoted zeal and empowerment for evangelism.[12] Hence, Pentecostalism cannot be accurately interpreted apart from its mission ethos.

Accordingly, tongues speech, now principally comprehended as a mystical operation of the Holy Spirit, would reveal and exalt Christ in the heart of the seeker, and inspire a deeper Christ-centered life and witness. It would also make the believer receptive to the exercise of the charismatic gifts in worship and evangelism.[13] According to Simon Chan, it serves as "an essential part of a coherent schema of spiritual development in which one experiences growing intimacy with God and holiness of life."[14] Some considered the possibility that tongues might not follow in every instance of Spirit baptism and allowed for the possibility of exceptions.[15] However, all attested to its importance for the Spirit-filled life.

More than anything else, therefore, the uniqueness of Pentecostal identity among radical evangelicals rested primarily on tongues.[16] When the issue of the indispensability of tongues resurfaced in the Assemblies of God in 1918, the council had to clarify yet another doctrinal stance. But to whom was the resolu-

12. Gary B. McGee, "Early Pentecostal Hermeneutics: Tongues as Evidence in the Book of Acts," in *Initial Evidence: Biblical and Historical Perspectives on the Pentecostal Doctrine of Spirit Baptism*, ed. Gary B. McGee (Peabody, Mass.: Hendrickson, 1991), pp. 96-118.

13. For contemporary expositions on baptism in the Holy Spirit by Assemblies of God scholars, see William W. Menzies and Robert P. Menzies, *Spirit and Power: Foundations of Pentecostal Experience* (Grand Rapids: Zondervan, 2000); Frank D. Macchia, "Tongues as a Sign: Towards a Sacramental Understanding of Pentecostal Experience," *Pneuma: The Journal of the Society for Pentecostal Studies* 15 (spring 1993): 61-76; Macchia, "The Struggle for Global Witness: Shifting Paradigms in Pentecostal Theology," in *The Globalization of Pentecostalism: A Religion Made to Travel,* ed. Murray W. Dempster, Byron D. Klaus, and Douglas Petersen (Irvine, Calif.: Regnum Books International, 1999), pp. 8-29. For a recent study by a Pentecostal Assemblies of Canada scholar whose books have been highly influential in the American Assemblies of God, see Roger Stronstad, *The Prophethood of All Believers: A Study in Luke's Charismatic Theology* (Sheffield, U.K.: Sheffield Academic Press, 1999).

14. Simon Chan, *Pentecostal Theology and the Christian Spiritual Tradition* (Sheffield, U.K.: Sheffield Academic Press, 2000), p. 64.

15. For example, F. F. Bosworth, *Do All Speak with Tongues?* (New York: Christian Alliance Publishing Co., n.d.).

16. A theme stated clearly on the cover page of the first issue of the *Apostolic Faith* (Los Angeles), "Pentecost Has Come," September 1906, p. 1, col. 1; also R. E. Massey, "Tongues, the Bible Evidence; the Great Issue," *Cloud of Witnesses to Pentecost in India*, August 1909, pp. 5-6.

tion about "our distinctive testimony" largely aimed? The membership of the General Council was the first audience. The resolution also spoke implicitly to other Pentecostals who questioned or hesitated about the connection of tongues with Spirit baptism. If the Statement of Fundamental Truths had certified general theological integrity to outsiders, the "distinctive testimony," though carrying less weight in the hierarchy of truths than the pronouncement on the Trinity, protected the foundation of Pentecostal spirituality for insiders.

Through the years the Assemblies of God has postured itself between the poles of evangelical respectability and its restorationist Pentecostal heritage.[17] The current general superintendent, Thomas E. Trask, has accurately expressed the long-standing tension: "The Assemblies of God was raised up to be a Pentecostal voice. I have great respect and love for evangelical churches, but we are more than evangelical; we are Pentecostal!"[18] It is this ideal of being "more than evangelical" that presents the greatest challenge to the denomination as it enters the twenty-first century.

Within three decades of its founding in 1914, the Assemblies of God began to align itself with conservative evangelicals by joining the National Association of Evangelicals and its affiliate agencies, leading to what Russell P. Spittler has called "the evangelicalization of the Assemblies of God."[19] "More than evangelical" also suggests that the process has in part diminished the "testimony" and other restorationist teachings, particularly through the widespread attraction of Reformed evangelical scholarship with its objections to distinctive Pentecostal beliefs. Nowhere has the impact been greater than on the doctrine of initial evidence.[20] While earlier Pentecostals could appeal to the hermeneutical under-

17. On the restorationist impulse in Assemblies of God history, see Edith L. Blumhofer, *Restoring the Faith: The Assemblies of God, Pentecostalism, and American Culture* (Urbana: University of Illinois Press, 1993); Lewis Wilson explores the limitations of this hypothesis in his review of *Restoring the Faith*, by Edith L. Blumhofer, *Pneuma: The Journal of the Society for Pentecostal Studies* 17 (spring 1995): 119-22. For a perceptive essay on the evolution of Assemblies of God theology during its middle period, consult Douglas Jacobsen, "Knowing the Doctrines of Pentecostals: The Scholastic Theology of the Assemblies of God, 1930-55," in *Pentecostal Currents in American Protestantism*, pp. 90-107.

18. Thomas E. Trask and David A. Womack, *Back to the Altar: A Call to Spiritual Awakening* (Springfield, Mo.: Gospel Publishing House, 1994), p. 25.

19. Russell P. Spittler, "A Celebration of Sovereignty," *Agora* 5 (summer 1981): 13-14; see also his "Maintaining Distinctives: The Future of Pentecostalism," in *Pentecostals from the Inside Out*, ed. Harold B. Smith (Wheaton, Ill.: Victor, 1990), pp. 121-34.

20. Menzies and Menzies, *Spirit and Power*, pp. 33-34. Del Tarr speaks of the "curse of Reformed theology" in "Transcendence, Immanence, and the Emerging Pentecostal Academy," in *Pentecostalism in Context: Essays in Honor of William W. Menzies*, ed. Wonsuk Ma and Robert P. Menzies (Sheffield, U.K.: Sheffield Academic Press, 1997), pp. 209-17.

pinning of Wesleyan Holiness and Higher Life teachings that upheld Spirit baptism as an experience of grace subsequent to conversion, the popularity of this school of thought gradually declined. Most evangelical theologians today, revealing the influence of classical Reformed theology, hold that the gift of salvation and Spirit baptism are one and the same, and without the necessity of glossolalic utterance.

In another crucial development in the last half-century, the tenet of divine healing, the second most distinguishing belief of early Pentecostalism and the Assemblies of God in particular, underwent a transformation. With unprecedented advances in medical science, church members began to consult doctors and take medicines for their ailments. As a result, the original antimedical tone of the doctrine gave way to a holistic view of healing in many quarters, one that balanced prayer for the sick with the care of physicians and seemed to better answer lingering theological questions.[21] A pivotal change also came when Pentecostals and evangelicals alike experienced social and economic lift after World War II. Accompanied by the inculturation of middle-class values, it led to steady erosion of eschatological expectancy.[22]

Just as the last sixty years have seen the "evangelicalization" of the denomination, so a parallel "Pentecostalization" of evangelicals has occurred with many now praying for the sick, reporting the restoration of the "charismatic gifts" in their churches (1 Cor. 12:7-11), and adopting charismatic modes of worship.[23] At the beginning of the twenty-first century, with the previous boundaries between evangelicals and Pentecostals now blurred, innovative "evangelical/Pentecostal" models of worship and mission have emerged in the United States and many parts of the world, ones that affirm the charismatic dimension of spirituality in various ways but do not require tongues.[24] Notwithstanding, the insistence on glossolalia with baptism in the Holy Spirit remains the hallmark of Assemblies of God belief and practice, even though some pastors and congregations have moved in the direction of these new patterns.

21. "Divine Healing: An Integral Part of the Gospel," in *Where We Stand* (Springfield, Mo.: Gospel Publishing House, 1990), p. 53.

22. Margaret M. Poloma, *The Assemblies of God at the Crossroads: Charisma and Institutional Dilemmas* (Knoxville: University of Tennessee Press, 1989), pp. 140-55; also Blumhofer, *Restoring the Faith*, pp. 242-60.

23. Tim Stafford, "Testing the Wine from John Wimber's Vineyard," *Christianity Today*, August 8, 1986, pp. 17-22; Vinson Synan, *The Century of the Holy Spirit: 100 Years of Pentecostal and Charismatic Renewal* (Nashville: Nelson, 2001), pp. 349-80.

24. Corwin E. Smidt et al., "The Spirit-Filled Movements in Contemporary America: A Survey Perspective," and Helen Lee Turner, "Pentecostal Currents in the SBC: Divine Intervention, Prophetic Preachers, and Charismatic Worship," both in *Pentecostal Currents in American Protestantism*, pp. 111-30 and 209-25 respectively.

For General Council leaders the resurgence of Pentecostal revival in the ranks, enhanced by promoting the "distinctive testimony" as the desirable norm for believers, holds the key to jump-starting church planting and evangelism on a large scale. In turn, it is hoped that this will restore and surpass the level of momentum in growth that the Assemblies of God once enjoyed on the American scene, especially in the sector of its dominant white constituency.[25] Not surprisingly the expression "revival is our survival" has become a top priority.[26] Indeed, as Margaret M. Poloma noted: "The Assemblies of God cannot be understood apart from the stress it has placed on religious experience available through the baptism with the Holy Spirit. Spirit baptism, the tangible sign of which is a recipient's ability to speak in tongues, brings with it a host of other paranormally accepted phenomena." Such happenings ("miracles, divine healing, and prophetical abilities") constitute "the best indicator of evangelistic activities that would facilitate church growth."[27]

Officials, pastors, and missionaries in the AG have traditionally centered their energies on "doing" rather than "theorizing." This activism stems from a strong commitment to missions, inspired by an eschatology that views the approaching end of the age with a sense of great urgency. This combination has sown a strong pragmatism, at times even risking the peril of an unreflective activism.[28] Along with the experiential nature of Pentecostal spirituality, these seeds have also inadvertently yielded a lingering anti-intellectualism and occasional fears of the academic study of the denomination's history and theology.[29] Still, substantial funding for the Assemblies of God Theological Seminary and other institutions of higher education, as well as the preservation of historical materials at the Flower Pentecostal Heritage Center, both located in Springfield, Missouri, with the latter now the foremost repository for such resources in North America, exhibit important and enduring commitments to Pentecostal scholarship. Certainly at no time in its pilgrimage has the Assemblies of God

---

25. George O. Wood, "From the General Secretary," in "Assemblies of God Minister" (Exclusive Release to Assemblies of God Ministers), July 1, 2000, pp. 7-8.

26. Trask and Womack, *Back to the Altar*, p. 102.

27. Poloma, *Assemblies of God*, p. 232.

28. Grant Wacker analyzes the primitive and pragmatic impulses of Pentecostalism in *Heaven Below: Early Pentecostals and American Culture* (Cambridge: Harvard University Press, 2001), pp. 10-14.

29. James K. Bridges, "Assemblies of God Schools and Scholars for the Twenty-First Century," *Enrichment*, fall 1999, pp. 94-97; Bridges, "The Full Consummation of the Baptism in the Holy Spirit," *Enrichment*, fall 2000, pp. 92-95; cf. Cecil M. Robeck, Jr., "An Emerging Magisterium? The Case of the Assemblies of God," in *The Spirit and Spirituality: Essays in Honor of Russell P. Spittler*, ed. Wonsuk Ma and Robert P. Menzies (Sheffield, U.K.: Sheffield Academic Press, forthcoming).

had greater need of its theologians, historians, missiologists, and educational specialists to interpret the spiritual legacy to the next generation. Yet, perhaps due to its activist focus and reluctance to relate to the larger church world, it is ironic that the Assemblies of God with its considerable size and multifarious programs remains an enigma to many outsiders.

The two chapters that follow offer discerning sociological, historical, and theological insights into the complex mosaic of the Assemblies of God. Poloma bases her organizational case study on an extensive survey of ministers since they, more than any other personnel, communicate the spiritual vision to the faithful and connect the congregations to the judicatories that hold the organization together. Her work analyzes changes currently under way that have resulted from the tension between charisma (Pentecostal spirituality) and increasing institutionalization. It explores social, political, and spiritual forces that have molded the denomination as it presently exists.

The evidence indicates that the core identity, the supernatural worldview that has undergirded Pentecostalism and differentiated it most from evangelicalism, now stands in jeopardy. In spite of the determined efforts of leaders to encourage believers to seek for Spirit baptism and for ministers to reinforce its value from their pulpits, an inconsistency exists in the grass roots between what is verbally espoused and practiced. A variety of opinions over the validity of certain revival movements, both within and without the AG, expose reservations about phenomena that have historically characterized Pentecostal spirituality. Likewise, the declining frequency of glossolalic tongues and interpretations, as well as prophetic utterances in church services, coupled with the failure to see spectacular demonstrations of divine power (e.g., physical healings), depicts a shifting landscape.

In his theological essay, William W. Menzies investigates the dynamics behind the spiritual locomotion of the Assemblies of God. He looks at the typical worship pattern — especially its participatory nature, highlighted by experiential encounter with the Holy Spirit in praise and singing, preaching, prayer for the hurting, and manifestations of the charismatic gifts.[30] In this regard, the spiritual effectiveness of the local congregation thrives as believers secure the "fullness" of empowerment that comes with Spirit baptism. This orientation explains how individual callings to begin particular ministries, prompted by the "leading of the Holy Spirit," have pragmatically shaped the development of denominational programs and structure.

---

30. For the nature of Pentecostal worship, see Daniel E. Albrecht, *Rites in the Spirit: A Ritual Approach to Pentecostal/Charismatic Spirituality* (Sheffield, U.K.: Sheffield Academic Press, 1999).

Menzies also traces how doctrinal exposition has progressed from the Statement of Fundamental Truths to the more recent preparation of "position papers." Through the years the council has had to address many challenging issues, including pacifism, divorce and remarriage, sanctification, divine healing, and the initial physical evidence of Spirit baptism. And of no less importance are the meaning of revival and the impact of "evangelicalization."

It is significant that both authors detect an ongoing healthy balance between charisma and institutional structure, suggesting that the future may see additional growth. Even with the changing complexion of congregations and rising diversity of thought on specific core features of doctrine and practice, the organization still enjoys a strong base of support, loyalty to the Statement of Fundamental Truths, and appreciation of its agencies. Indeed, the robust energy currently displayed in financial giving and the extensive involvement of laypersons and professional clergy in home and foreign mission endeavors engender optimism about continuing expansion.

In the estimation of Peter Hocken, "Pentecostalism represents a protest for Spirit against a powerless and largely cerebral Protestantism, in which attachment to the Word was not evidently accompanied by the vitality of the Spirit."[31] Consequently, observers propose that the last century witnessed a seismic shift toward recapturing the ministry of the Holy Spirit in the life and mission of the churches, and much of the credit for this goes to the stimulus of the Pentecostal movement.[32] Given its conservative point of reference, it is clear that the AG will not settle for being "less than evangelical." The greatest hurdle, therefore, in its path into the twenty-first century stands in how successfully it recaptures what it means to be "more than evangelical."

31. Peter Hocken, *The Glory and the Shame: Reflections on the Twentieth-Century Outpouring of the Holy Spirit* (Guildford, Surrey, U.K.: Eagle, 1994), p. 156.

32. See Harvey Cox, *Fire from Heaven: The Rise of Pentecostal Spirituality and the Reshaping of Religion in the Twenty-First Century* (Reading, Mass.: Addison-Wesley, 1995); Edward L. Cleary, "Introduction: Pentecostals, Prominence, and Politics," in *Power, Politics, and Pentecostals in Latin America,* ed. Edward L. Cleary and Hannah W. Stewart-Gambino (Boulder, Colo.: Westview Press, 1997), pp. 1-24.

Charisma and Structure in the Assemblies of God: Revisiting O'Dea's Five Dilemmas

Margaret M. Poloma

Prologue

> Charisma, in final analysis, is a gift — a breath that is illusive and fragile. She can launch a new institution and breathe life into existing ones. The Assemblies of God, birthed by her spirit, has been renewed by her grace. Whether she will continue to seek and to find a home within the Assemblies of God remains a critical question that only the future can answer.[1]

Nearly twenty-five years have passed since I first launched a sociological study of the Assemblies of God (AG) — a research adventure published as *The Assemblies of God at the Crossroads* in 1989. My conclusion about the fate of charisma in this rapidly growing Pentecostal denomination was cautious and tentative. Its destiny, despite the gloomy Weberian prognosis on the inevitable routinization of charisma, was then colored by the revitalization of the Assemblies of God brought about by the rise of the charismatic movement during the 1960s and 1970s, bringing Pentecostal experiences to the mainline Christian churches. The charismatic movement soon waxed and waned, as had the earlier revival on Azusa Street in Los Angeles (1906-9) that birthed Pentecostalism during the first decade of the twentieth century. It was not long, however, before another move of the Spirit, the so-called Third Wave, crossed the American continent during the 1980s — a move which marked the rise of more contemporary and youth-oriented charismatic groups, many of which developed out of the Jesus movement of the 1970s.[2] Rumors of a fresh renewal in the early

---

1. Margaret M. Poloma, *The Assemblies of God at the Crossroads: Charisma and Institutional Dilemmas* (Knoxville: University of Tennessee Press, 1989), p. 243.

2. Although most Pentecostals were wary of both the charismatic movement and the

1990s attracted international attention with the outbreak of the so-called Toronto Blessing. It developed in the Third Wave sector but soon spilled over into the Pentecostal and charismatic streams of the larger movement. With its nightly revival meetings beginning in January 1994 attracting pilgrims from around the world, the Toronto Airport Christian Fellowship became the epicenter of a fresh revival fire that torched similar gatherings at numerous other North American sites. One such site emerged on Father's Day 1995, at Brownsville Assembly of God in Pensacola, Florida, where the new revival found an inroad into the increasingly routinized and bureaucratized Pentecostal stream of the Spirit-filled movement.[3]

The "Pensacola Outpouring" caused some degree of tension within the AG, blurring the boundaries and raising questions about denominational identity. But tension has always found a home within the AG; and, as I have discussed at length elsewhere,[4] a degree of tension between charisma and structure has been an important factor in accounting for the vitality enjoyed by the AG.[5] Indeed, William Menzies' following theological essay effectively presents a case for the AG's ability to live with theological tension by demonstrating "continued evidence of a reasonable balance between charisma and organization." Maintaining a free flow of charisma, however, requires skill not unlike that of a unicycle rider: despite great skill, there is always the risk of a fall.

The fear of falling into the abyss of "carnal," unregulated religious experi-

---

Third Wave (just as they were of the New Order of the Latter Rain movement of the 1940s), the AG was revitalized by an influx of new converts from more recent revivals. The rapid growth of the AG during the 1970s and 1980s, which reached a plateau by the mid-1980s when the renewal crested, can be linked to revitalization movements which originated outside the AG. See Donald E. Miller, *Reinventing American Protestantism* (Berkeley: University of California Press, 1997), and David Di Sabatino, *The Jesus People Movement: An Annotated Bibliography and General Resource* (Westport, Conn.: Greenwood Press, 1999).

3. Margaret M. Poloma, "The 'Toronto Blessing': Charisma, Institutionalization and Revival," *Journal for the Scientific Study of Religion* 37, no. 2 (1997): 257-71, and Margaret M. Poloma, "Inspecting the Fruit of the 'Toronto Blessing': A Sociological Assessment," *Pneuma: The Journal for the Society for Pentecostal Studies* 20, no. 1 (1998): 43-70.

4. Poloma, *The Assemblies of God at the Crossroads*; Margaret M. Poloma and Brian F. Pendleton, "Religious Experiences and Institutional Growth within the Assemblies of God," *Journal for the Scientific Study of Religion* 24 (winter 1989): 415-31.

5. As Lewis Coser (*Continuities in the Study of Social Conflict* [Glencoe, Ill.: Free Press, 1967]) convincingly argued almost forty years ago, tension and conflict can have positive institutional consequences. Tension with an out-group (external conflict), for example, can serve to establish a strong group identity, and Pentecostalism's status as a "third force" within Christianity owes much to the hostility Pentecostalism experienced as a newly emerging sect during the first half of the twentieth century. Tension within the group (internal conflict) can also have positive repercussions, especially for loosely knit structures such as the Assemblies of God.

ence has often caused established Pentecostalism to quench charisma as it sought to protect its emergent structure. Fresh charismatic outbursts seem to find more fertile ground outside organized denominations in the growing numbers of parachurch networks and independent churches. Sociologist Peter Berger was correct in his passing assessment that "religious experiences are institutionally dangerous."[6] Newly formed networks and emerging congregations appear to have less to risk in embracing fresh experiences than do established sects and denominations.[7]

A tolerance for a moderate amount of tension between charisma and institution, however, is seemingly built into the DNA of Pentecostalism where religious distinctiveness centers on paranormal experiences believed to be generated by Spirit baptism. The inherent tension between what Grant Wacker has called primitivism and pragmatism — the paranormal working of the Holy Spirit and the organizational matrix that promotes the Pentecostal mission — is rooted in its earliest history. As Wacker succinctly summarizes his thesis: "My main argument can be stated in a single sentence. *The genius of the Pentecostal movement lay in its ability to hold two seemingly incompatible impulses in productive tension. I call the two impulses the primitive and the pragmatic.*"[8] This tension between charisma (the "primitive") and organization (a facet of the "pragmatic") continues to be central for understanding the AG today, just as it is for understanding its past.

As I have done in my earlier work on the AG, I will use the framework of dilemmas of institutionalization developed by Thomas O'Dea to explore the tension between charisma and organizing religious work by the AG.[9] For each of O'Dea's five dilemmas, I will identify an issue in Pentecostalism and explore its "core" and "peripheral" dimensions. A *core* value, according to Lewis Coser, is a central component of the relationship (in contrast to a pe-

6. Peter L. Berger, *The Heretical Imperative* (Garden City, N.Y.: Anchor Press/Doubleday, 1979).

7. The birth of the AG itself provides an excellent example of embracing risk and institutional resistance to seemingly unregulated religious experience by established sects and denominations. Those who reported being Spirit-baptized during the first decade of the twentieth century, complete with paranormal experiences (especially glossolalia, but also healing, prophecy, deliverance, and miracles), usually (voluntarily or involuntarily) withdrew from what they regarded as "dead denominations." History was to repeat itself throughout the twentieth century with the development of fresh charismatic experiences and the splits and schisms resulting from failed attempts to agree on the essence and meaning of such experiences.

8. Grant Wacker, *Heaven Below: Early Pentecostals and American Culture* (Cambridge: Harvard University Press, 2001), p. 10.

9. Thomas O'Dea, "Sociological Dilemmas in the Institutionalization of Religion," *Journal for the Scientific Study of Religion* 1, no. 1 (1961): 30-41.

ripheral issue), an attack upon which threatens the social group.[10] If a core
value is attacked, a single line of cleavage that may have seriously negative
consequences threatens the organization. Loosely knit organizations, such as
the AG, may actually be strengthened by the tension that develops around
multiple peripheral issues, conflict which tends to diffuse an attack on a core
issue. Coser contends that when stress mounts within a group, making allowance for tension may serve a positive force in "sewing" diverse factions together.[11] Different alliances often made on different peripheral but potentially divisive issues paradoxically can further group integration. The
problematic face of conflict arises when a single core issue is made focal and
threatens to bifurcate the group.

In addressing key core and peripheral issues currently facing the AG,
Coser's and O'Dea's theoretical framework will be grounded in data collected
from a random sample of 447 AG pastors who were mailed surveys in early
1999.[12] The major conclusion from the survey analysis: *The AG has a solid core
around which there are varying levels of ambiguity.* The ambiguity that exists on
peripheral issues appears to function as a safety-valve mechanism feeding the
ongoing dialectical interrelationship between charisma and institution building.[13] In sum, the AG continues to successfully balance charisma with institutionalization, as it has for much of its history. Institutionalization has not
sounded the death knell for charisma, nor has revitalization of charisma
brought about organizational anarchy.

O'Dea's Five Dilemmas in the Institutionalization of Religion: Ambiguities and Creative Tension

Thomas O'Dea's well-known "five institutional dilemmas" point to the inherent tension found to some degree in all religious organizations. Each dilemma
reflects the "basic antinomy" or "fundamental tension" that exists between charisma (that is, the immediacy of direct religious experience) and institutional
forces. The ongoing tension between spontaneity and stability that permeates
all five dilemmas can be described as "transforming the religious experience to
render it continuously available to the mass of men [*sic*] and to provide for it a

10. Lewis A. Coser, *Functions of Social Conflict* (Glencoe, Ill.: Free Press, 1956), p. 73.

11. Coser, *Functions of Social Conflict*, p. 72.

12. A copy of the questionnaire and summary of responses is available at: http://
www.hirr.hartsem.edu/sociology/sociology_online_articles.html#P.

13. S. N. Eisenstadt, introduction to *Max Weber on Charisma and Institution Building*
(Chicago: University of Chicago Press, 1969).

stable institutional context."[14] Once free-flowing, nonnormative, and seemingly chaotic, charisma must (at least to some extent) be transformed into something stable, normal, and ordered. Although an important catalyst in the development of all world religions, charisma is usually quenched in favor of the patterned and predictable institutional features of social life. Each of the dilemmas — mixed motivation, symbolic, delimitation, power, and administrative order — provides a unique vantage point to explore the working of the AG as seen by its pastors as evidenced in their survey responses.

The Dilemma of Mixed Motivation: Assessing Identity

According to O'Dea's theory, the emergence of a stable structure brings with it the capability of eliciting a wide range of individual motives that follow the ideal-typical state where a charismatic leader is able to generate "single-mindedness."[15] It should be noted that the Pentecostal/charismatic movement (PCM) has never had a single charismatic leader similar to Methodism's John Wesley, Quakerism's George Fox, Mormonism's Joseph Smith, or Christian Science's Mary Baker Eddy. In a movement that has democratized charisma, the relationship between a charismatic leader and his disciples described by O'Dea has not been the prime motivating factor. Rather, the single-mindedness of the movement has been energized by a common experience of the Holy Spirit out of which a diffused leadership and organizations have emerged. Countless churches, networks, and small sects came out of the particular experiences of the Holy Spirit which were reported in the nineteenth century, became better labeled and identified in the early twentieth century, and spread globally through the Azusa Street Revival in Los Angeles from 1906 to 1909.[16] It was in 1914 that the leaders and pastors of some of these groups came together in Hot Springs, Arkansas, giving birth to the AG, the largest and most influential white Pentecostal denomination in the United States.

Although the dilemma of mixed motivation can be illustrated through the rise of an ordained clergy and the correspondent development of leadership roles (as suggested by O'Dea and described in *Assemblies of God at the Crossroads*), it can also be assessed through a discussion of religious identity issues

14. O'Dea, "Sociological Dilemmas," p. 38.
15. O'Dea, "Sociological Dilemmas," p. 33.
16. Wacker identifies Pentecostals as part of a genre of believers he calls "radical evangelicals" who emphasized a fourfold gospel of "personal salvation, Holy Ghost baptism, divine healing, and the Lord's soon return." The emphasis of the streams differs somewhat, with Pentecostals putting their focus on "Holy Ghost baptism." Wacker, *Heaven Below*.

Margaret M. Poloma

found in its distinctive worldview. A passage from Zechariah 4:6 that serves as a motto for the AG provides a succinct statement about Pentecostal identity: "'Not by might, nor by power, but by my Spirit,' says the Lord Almighty." This simple profession reflects what AG theologian Frank Macchia describes as a "paradigm shift from an exclusive focus on holiness to an outward thrust that invoked a dynamic filling and an empowerment for global witness."[17]

As routinization extracts its due, however, this emphasis on "dynamic filling" and "empowerment" increasingly shifts from personal experience and testimony to profession and expansion of doctrinal decree. Testimonies of lived experience that empowered early believers take a backseat to a selective reconstruction of AG history and doctrine that often fails to capture the diversity that found expression in the larger PCM. As Robeck effectively argues in his discussion of Pentecostal identity, Pentecostalism has demonstrated a host of "indigenous entries," including "Oneness Pentecostalism," "World Faith Pentecostalism," "Feminist Pentecostalism," and even "Gay Pentecostalism," all of which have been rejected by the AG.[18] The AG has increasingly defined itself primarily as "evangelical Pentecostalism," or perhaps more accurately, as Menzies argues in the following essay, as "evangelicalism plus tongues." Robeck goes on to state:

> Pentecostals have historically disagreed with one another on what constitutes a real Pentecostal, and as a result, on what constitutes genuine Pentecostalism. The fact may not be easy for some Pentecostals to accept, but it is true nonetheless. Each group seems to want to identify its own specific character as providing the best, if not *the only legitimate identity* for all real Pentecostals. Insofar as their distinctives become all that define Pentecostalism, the real character, contribution, and impact of the whole Movement may be lost.[19]

What appears to happen, particularly in more established classical Pentecostal denominations like the AG, is that the breadth and depth of the PCM is eclipsed as each segment identifies with a single appendage much like the blind men in their respective attempts to describe the proverbial elephant. The es-

17. Frank D. Macchia, "The Struggle for Global Witness: Shifting Paradigms in Pentecostal Theology," in *The Globalization of Pentecostalism: A Religion Made to Travel*, ed. M. W. Dempster, B. D. Klaus, and D. Petersen (Carlisle, U.K.: Regnum Books International, Paternoster Publishing, 1999), p. 16.

18. Cecil M. Robeck, Jr., "Toward Healing Our Divisions: Reflecting on Pentecostal Diversity and Common Witness" (paper presented at the 28th Annual Meeting of the Society of Pentecostal Studies, March 11-13, 1999).

19. Robeck, "Toward Healing Our Divisions."

sence of Pentecostalism as a "new paradigm" — with the natural and supernatural engaged in a dialectical dance — is compromised by accommodative forces that threaten to dilute Pentecostal identity. As evangelicals find a prominent place in the American religious mosaic, some would put aside the "new paradigm" to embrace a modernist religious identity that downplays controversial issues that come with "dynamic filling" and "empowerment."

It should be noted that Spirit-filled Christianity, unlike Christian fundamentalism and evangelicalism, is not primarily a reaction to modernity. It has proactively developed certain characteristics which taken together make its worldview distinct from other forms of Christianity, both of the liberal and conservative stripes. The Pentecostal worldview is experientially centered with followers in a dynamic and personal relationship with a deity who is both immanent and transcendent. According to Johns, "The Spirit-filled believer has a predisposition to see a transcendent God at work in, with, through, above and beyond all events. Therefore, all space is sacred space and all time is sacred time." God is seen as active in all events past, present, and future which work together in a kind of master plan. It is a worldview that tends to be "transrational," professing that knowledge is "not limited to realms of reason and sensory experience."[20] Consistent with this transrational characteristic, Pentecostal Christians also tend to be anticreedal, believing that "knowing" comes from a right relationship with God rather than through reason or even through the five senses. Theirs is a God who can and often does defy the laws of nature with the miraculous and unexplainable. Without doubt the Bible holds an important place in their worldview, but for many it is a kind of catalyst and litmus test for the authenticity of personal and corporate experience rather than a manual of rigid doctrine and practices. As Johns succinctly states: "In summary, a Pentecostal paradigm for knowledge and truth springs from an experiential knowledge of God which alters the believer's approach to reading and interpreting reality."[21]

This paradigm is shared by both classical Pentecostalism and more recent PCM streams. The newer groups together with some classical Pentecostals, however, tend to self-identify as "charismatic" or as "Spirit-filled" Christians and, as products of more recent renewals or revivals, tend to be stronger in primitivism and weaker on pragmatism. Although the distinction Menzies makes in his following essay between Pentecostals and charismatics as being one over the "enduement of power for evangelism and missions" has some

---

20. Jackie David Johns, "Yielding to the Spirit: The Dynamics of a Pentecostal Model of Praxis," in *The Globalization of Pentecostalism,* p. 75.

21. Johns, "Yielding to the Spirit," p. 75.

merit, I would contend that "involvement in ministry" is a by-product of Spirit baptism for both groups.[22] The primary distinction I have observed between the two major streams of the PCM in North America is their somewhat different expressions of its common core Pentecostal spirituality. At the risk of some oversimplification, those who self-identify as "charismatic" are more likely to be open to a range of paranormal experiences (including prophecy, miracles, healing, and physical manifestations of an altered state of consciousness) as signs of Spirit baptism, while most Pentecostals tend to place a doctrinal emphasis on the gift of tongues (as does the AG). Furthermore, established classical Pentecostal denominations (like the AG) tend to have well-developed bureaucratic structures while thriving neo-Pentecostal organizations tend to be nondenominational with members focusing on relational ties expressed in loosely knit networks.[23]

What can be said about the PCM, regardless of the stream, is that it is more about a distinct spirituality than about religion.[24] Members share a common transcendent worldview rather than particular doctrines, defined ritual practices, or denominational involvement. This worldview is a curious blend of premodern miracles, modern technology, and postmodern mysticism in which the natural blends with the supernatural. Signs and wonders analogous to those described in premodern biblical accounts are expected as normal occurrences in the lives of believers.[25] Johns asserts that what underlies Pentecostal identity is a Pentecostal epistemology "congruous with the ancient Jewish approach to knowledge" — one that represents an alternative to modern ways of knowing: "Pentecostals have an alternative epistemology because they have an alternative world-view. At the heart of the Pentecostal world-view is transforming experience with God. God is known through relational encounter which finds its penultimate expression in being filled with the Holy Spirit. This experience becomes the normative epistemological framework and thus

---

22. Poloma, "Inspecting the Fruit of the 'Toronto Blessing.'"

23. The heightened primitivism of neo-Pentecostal spirituality and eschewing of traditional organizational structures have led one British sociologist to make the following wager: "I would put my money on the old Pentecostal denominations still to be with us, and thriving at the end of the next century. I'm not prepared to put my shirt on the new churches, and don't relish the long-odds on the Renewal." Andrew Walker, foreword to *Pentecostals in Britain*, by William K. Kay (Carlisle, U.K.: Paternoster Press, 2000), pp. vii-ix.

24. See Daniel E. Albrecht, *Ties in the Spirit: A Ritual Approach to Pentecostal/Charismatic Spirituality* (Sheffield, U.K.: Sheffield Academic Press, 1999), and Steven Land, *Pentecostal Spirituality: A Passion for the Kingdom* (Sheffield, U.K.: Sheffield Academic Press, 1993).

25. Margaret M. Poloma, "Mysticism as a Social Construct: Religious Experience in Pentecostal/Charismatic Context" (paper presented at the annual meetings of the Association for the Sociology of Religion, Anaheim, Calif., 2001).

shifts the structures by which the individual interprets the world."[26] The general issue of Pentecostal identity is the core of this analysis — an issue that impacts each of the other dilemmas.

A report of the survey findings on the Pentecostal identity of AG pastors will add details to this brief description of Pentecostal identity and the importance of its worldview in maintaining the dialectical tension between charisma and organization that has been at the heart of Pentecostalism's success. Through data provided by the survey questions, identity issues can be empirically explored to reveal core tenets as well as attendant ambiguities. What does it mean to be Pentecostal (specifically AG) at the turn of this new century? Is there congruence between the reported identity self-perceptions of pastors and the congregations they represent? Is there a goodness of fit between these perceptions of identity and the denominational work performed by national and regional administrative offices? These and other related questions are used to tap the core identity and the ambiguities that exist around it, including the importance of being a member of the AG and a Pentecostal, and social distance between AG and adherents of other religious worldviews.

Pentecostal Core Identity

AG scholar Everett Wilson[27] put the question to pen: "What makes a Pentecostal?" Difficulties of providing a simple description are deeply embedded in Pentecostal history. Wilson concludes that the social identity of a Pentecostal is rooted in a worldview based on the "mystical, the 'supernatural' and the allegedly miraculous," which tended to stigmatize and marginalize early Pentecostals. For Wilson, being labeled a Pentecostal was the result of more than a confessional act — it signaled a worldview that separated these believers from other Christians. As Wilson comments:

> Like the proverbial duck, if the person looked like one, walked like one and talked like one — especially if one were supportive of the beliefs and practices that Pentecostals advanced — friends and neighbours could assume that he or she in fact belonged. At least the often-sung refrain, "I'm so glad I can say I am one of them" apparently gained favour not just to establish identity or to convince believers that they were with the right crowd, but because adherents gave assent to the Pentecostal way of looking at reality,

---

26. Johns, "Yielding to the Spirit," pp. 74-75.

27. Everett A. Wilson, "They Crossed the Red Sea, Didn't They? Critical History and Pentecostal Beginnings," in *The Globalization of Pentecostalism*, pp. 85-115.

something about which they may have felt deeply even when their convictions were not overtly displayed.[28]

Although professing to be a Pentecostal certainly does not tell the whole story of AG identity, it is a good place to begin a discussion of single-mindedness. Are pastors still singing "I am one of them," as the denomination has taken a more accepted place in the religious mosaic? For the vast majority of pastors the answer appears to be "yes." Self-identity can be gleaned from a question which instructed respondents to "indicate how important it is to identify with each of these groups" — Assemblies of God, Pentecostalism, revival/renewal, charismatic movement/Third Wave, and evangelicalism. Pastors were most likely to report their primary self-identity as Pentecostal (55 percent claimed it was "extremely important," with another 33 percent saying it was "very important"). Nearly identical figures are reported for a personal identification with "revival/renewal," implying a conscious decision to support a revitalization of Pentecostal identity through fresh religious experiences. Reporting self-identification with the AG was only slightly less than being Pentecostal and in revival/renewal.[29] Forty-nine percent reported self-identification with the AG as "extremely important," and another 36 percent said it was "very important."[30] The vast majority of the pastors report a religious identity that can be described as Pentecostal and being a member of the AG. These same pastors also identify very strongly with the need to be involved in revival/renewal, suggesting that Pentecostalism is largely regarded as a dynamic process rather than a staid structure. These labels of self-identity, however, need to be further explored. Probing into the nature of Pentecostal identity will reveal some of the ambiguities that beset the denomination.

Ambiguity around the Core Identity

Despite the strong approval of retaining and reviving Pentecostal identity, an old dilemma lurks beneath the "single-mindedness" reflected in the pastors' responses. The AG historically has found itself in the paradoxical position of pro-

28. Wilson, "They Crossed," pp. 88-89.

29. The mean scores for Pentecostal identification and for identifying with revival/renewal was 3.4 (on a 4-point scale). The mean score for identification with being Assemblies of God was 3.3.

30. Although the solid majority figures are being highlighted, the strength of the minority position should not be overlooked. For 16 percent of the pastors, identity with the AG is only "somewhat important" or "not important"; for 14 percent, being in revival is relatively unimportant; and for 13 percent, Pentecostal identity is not particularly relevant.

moting a distinct Pentecostal perspective while seeking a rapport with fundamentalism and later with a more moderate evangelicalism, sectors of which have been very critical of the PCM. Within two years of its founding in 1914, the AG's message and mission, as Edith Blumhofer noted, "would be held within the boundaries drawn by traditional evangelical doctrines."[31] Its attempt to become "fundamentalism with a difference" (fundamentalism plus Spirit baptism) was not always well received, and Pentecostals, including the AG, became the target in 1928 of the World's Christian Fundamentals Association, which went on record as "unreservedly opposed to Modern Pentecostalism." It was not until the development of the more moderate National Association of Evangelicals (NAE) in the early 1940s that the AG found acceptance in this newly formed transdenominational conservative network. However, support for the NAE by AG constituents was far from universal. Blumhofer reports the critical response of one influential AG pastor to AG membership in the NAE: "This association is not Pentecostal and many of their speakers who are listed for a convention . . . not only do not favor Pentecost, but speak against it. This [cooperating with the NAE] is what I call putting the grave clothes again on Lazarus, while the Scripture says: 'Come out from among them, and be ye separate, saith the Lord, and touch not the unclean thing; and I will receive you and will be a Father unto you, and ye shall be my sons and daughters, saith the Lord Almighty.'"[32]

The old controversy appears to be far from resolved, and it is here that ambiguity surfaces. Clergy remain divided about the threat that evangelicalism presents to the Pentecostal worldview that provides the AG with its distinct identity. A clear majority (60 percent) of pastors agreed or strongly agreed with the statement, "Too many AG churches have stressed a general evangelical identity at the expense of their Pentecostal heritage." Those AG congregations that clearly downplay their ties to the denomination often select a name for their congregation that gives the impression of its being an independent evangelical church. Ritual in such congregations (as will be discussed in a later section) often follows an evangelical format in which Pentecostal practices are discouraged — or at least their public display is not encouraged.

Over two-thirds of the pastors responding to the survey self-identified as evangelical, a nomenclature that is somewhat less important for most respondents than Pentecostal, AG, and revival/renewal identities. The evangelical label is clearly more important, however, than is self-identity with cousins in the

31. Edith Blumhofer, *Restoring the Faith: The Assemblies of God, Pentecostalism, and American Culture* (Urbana and Chicago: University of Illinois Press, 1993), p. 135.

32. Blumhofer, *Restoring the Faith*, p. 187.

charismatic/Third Wave sector of the PCM.[33] Despite the Pentecostal-like worldview of charismatic/Third Wave churches, only 28 percent of AG pastors reported that self-identification with these newer streams of the PCM was "extremely important" or "very important."[34] While self-identifying as Pentecostal and evangelical is central to the identity of a clear majority of AG pastors, only a minority self-identify with newer streams of the PCM where revitalization and renewal are often accompanied by a range of "signs and wonders" strikingly similar to those reported in the history of Pentecostalism.[35]

Further ambiguity may be observed in the response to the question about belief in a dispensationalist interpretation of the Scriptures — a fundamentalist "fundamental" of long-standing tension within the AG. The dispensationalist perspective, popularized in the notes of the Scofield Bible and permeating sectors of evangelical Christianity, has been used to disparage Pentecostalism as at best delusional and at worst heretical. As Blumhofer has noted: "Dispensationalists generally held that miracles had ceased with the Apostles; Pentecostalism thus could not be authentic, for its premise that New Testament gifts would mark the end-times church was false. Rejecting the latter-rain views by which Pentecostals legitimated their place in church history, dispensationalists effectively eliminated the biblical basis for Pentecostal theology."[36] Reflecting the fact that many Pentecostals did embrace the Scofield Bible (while rejecting its teachings on spiritual gifts in the contemporary church), 58 percent of the pastors strongly agreed or agreed with the statement, "I believe in a dispensationalist interpretation of Scripture."

The interface with the fundamentalists goes back to the earliest days of

33. Evangelical identity had a mean score of 3 (on a 4-point scale) while charismatic/Third Wave identity scores had a mean of 2.

34. In North America the term "Pentecostal" usually refers to persons in denominations born out of or having some connection with the Azusa Street Revival in Los Angeles (1906-9). "Charismatic" applies to those in mainline and newer (often independent) churches which embraced a Pentecostal worldview in the mid–twentieth century or later. In the United States some 23 percent of all evangelical Protestants, 9 percent of mainline Protestants, 13 percent of Roman Catholics, and 36 percent of black Protestants claim to be "Spirit-filled," another appellation for those persons embracing the PCM (John C. Green, James L. Guth, Corwin E. Smidt, and Lyman A. Kellstedt, *Religion and the Culture Wars* [Lanham, Md.: Rowman and Littlefield, 1997], p. 228). Americans who claim to be Spirit-filled tend to self-identify as Pentecostal (4.7 percent) or charismatic (6.6 percent), but much less frequently as both charismatic and Pentecostal (0.8 percent). It is thus not surprising that these clearly Pentecostal pastors would express some social distance from charismatics. Despite a worldview and theology that are more similar than dissimilar, most persons involved in the PCM are likely to identify with a particular stream of the movement.

35. Wacker, *Heaven Below*.

36. Blumhofer, *Restoring the Faith*, p. 107.

the AG. As Blumhofer has observed, "The causes espoused by fundamentalists seemed to coincide in meaningful ways with AG denominational interests and to offer as well an opportunity for declaring Pentecostal sympathies with doctrinal 'fundamentals.' It was not long before 'right belief replaced right experience,' causing even further erosion of AG distinctiveness."[37] The danger that fundamentalism (and its softer evangelical expression) poses for Pentecostal identity has been noted by, for example, Cox, Hollenweger, and Spittler.[38] Although the AG can be placed securely within the walls of larger evangelicalism, there is evidence that such positioning fragments its identity and, as O'Dea's dilemma of mixed motivation suggests, leaves the denomination with possibly dissonant agendas that may not be easy to resolve.

As reflected in our "collective fellowship" survey questions, dissonance between what AG ministers say and what they do to live out the common PCM paradigm can be seen in the groups with which they and their congregations are willing to cooperate in promoting issues of common concern. When pastors were asked to indicate the "extent you would like to see the AG cooperate with different religious groups," they were most likely to choose full cooperation with other Pentecostals. Sixty-five percent indicated a desire for full support with other Pentecostal churches. Despite paradigmatic differences, over half the pastors (57 percent) advocated full cooperation with evangelical churches on issues of common concern. Pastors were much less likely to support full cooperation with associations of charismatics in mainline Protestantism (26 percent) or with independent charismatic organizations (27 percent).[39]

Clearly there is widespread support for a Pentecostal identity among AG pastors, but the essence of this distinct identity, especially when considered in light of fundamentalist opposition and evangelical indifference to Pentecostalism's worldview, is much less evident. Part of the explanation may come from Pentecostalism's success in spreading their once-distinct worldview to the larger Christian church. A popular cessationist position teaching that the su-

---

37. Blumhofer, *Restoring the Faith,* p. 159.

38. Harvey Cox, *Fire from Heaven: The Rise of Pentecostal Spirituality and the Reshaping of Religion in the Twenty-First Century* (Reading, Mass.: Addison-Wesley, 1995); Walter J. Hollenweger, *Pentecostalism: Origins and Developments Worldwide* (Peabody, Mass.: Hendrickson, 1997); and Russell P. Spittler, "Are Pentecostals and Charismatics Fundamentalists? A Review of American Uses of These Categories," in *Charismatic Christianity as a Global Culture,* ed. Karla Poewe (Columbia: University of South Carolina Press, 1994).

39. The mean scores for cooperating with various religious groups "on issues of common concern" (on a 3-point scale marking none, limited, and full) are as follows: with evangelicals = 2.6; with Pentecostals = 2.6; with independent/nondenominational churches = 2.3; with charismatic organizations = 2.2; with mainline Protestant churches = 2.1; with the Roman Catholic Church = 1.7; and with non-Christian religious groups = 1.4.

pernatural gifts were meant only to jump-start early Christianity (and then ceased) may have lost ground in many evangelical circles. This perspective seems to have been found wanting in a postmodern culture that is hungry for spiritual means to counter the inadequacies of materialism and rationalism. Much of the argument about the availability of "signs and wonders" for contemporary Christianity appears to be about semantics and doctrinal statements rather than popular belief. As Jon Ruthven has noted in his review of *Are Miraculous Gifts for Today?*, the work edited by Wayne Grudem: "One is left with the feeling that the whole debate could be resolved by a simple change in labels (not 'prophecy,' or 'a word of knowledge,' but 'leadings'; not '*gifts* of healing,' but 'healings'). Here the issue is not so much what God actually *does* today, so long as one avoids identifying these events as 'miracles' accrediting new doctrine."[40] The real issue underlying the controversy that comes to the surface in Grudem's collection is *how frequently and how intensely* these events should be expected. It may be that a version of the early Pentecostal worldview is widely accepted by both Pentecostals and non-Pentecostal Christians, but it is a domesticated version that has diluted the original paradigm. As we shall see in the next section, the twin issue of frequency and intensity is not only relevant for dialogue between Pentecostals and non-Pentecostals, but also points to an ambiguity within Pentecostalism.

In summary, there appears to be single-mindedness about key aspects of AG identity: the overwhelming majority of pastors claim that being AG and Pentecostal is "important" or "very important" to them, with a significant majority claiming evangelical identity and only a minority self-identifying with the charismatic/Third Wave streams of the PCM. A convergence of Pentecostal and evangelical identities is reflected in the pastors' acceptance of a more refined Pentecostal worldview at a time when some evangelicals are abandoning a dispensationalist hermeneutic that preached against "signs and wonders" for contemporary Christianity. An analysis of how a converging of seemingly dissonant identities translates into theology and religious cooperation reveals some AG fragmentation. Pentecostal support for fundamentalist theology and for evangelical alliances (after the founding of the NAE in 1943) seems to have sowed seeds of ambiguity that continue to this day that prevent established Pentecostal denominations like the AG from being on the cutting edge of the PCM.

---

40. Jon Ruthven, review of Wayne Grudem, ed., *Are Miraculous Gifts for Today? Four Views* (Grand Rapids: Zondervan, 1996), in *Pneuma* 21:1 (Spring 1999); also in *Journal of the Evangelical Theological Society* 42:3 (Sept. 1999): 531-32.

The Symbolic Dilemma: Assessing the
Prevalence of Pentecostal Experience

The worldview of the early Pentecostals not only accorded ideological legitimacy to the paranormal experiences reported in biblical times but restored them to a normative position in the twentieth-century Western world. Although glossolalia, or speaking in tongues, became the pivotal experiential doctrine in the AG, accounts of divine healing, prophetic words, miracles, and demonic exorcisms were also part and parcel of the Pentecostal package. More controversial were the strange physical manifestations that generated the pejorative label "Holy Rollers" ascribed by outsiders to Pentecostal believers who sometimes fell in a faint to the floor, jumped pews, violently jerked and shook, laughed, barked or rolled in the aisles under the alleged influence of the Spirit. Despite the denials of many contemporary cultural Pentecostals about their occurrence in early Pentecostalism, these same controversial manifestations erupted again during the New Order of the Latter Rain movement, spread to the "second wave" as Pentecost came to mainline denominations, and intensified during the contemporary "third wave" revivals.[41]

A dilemma facing Pentecostal believers from the earliest days of Azusa Street was how to allow the Spirit free movement while controlling excesses judged to be fanatic. This challenge was met by sorting out the more controversial physical responses (often difficult to justify from biblical texts) from less controversial experiences (more readily defined as "biblical") that frequently have accompanied the perceived presence of the Holy Spirit. In the AG glossolalia and healing became doctrines while many other alleged expressions of the Spirit's presence were relegated to the realms of fanaticism and heresy. Despite the solid ideological support for revival expressed in pastoral responses to the Pentecostal identity issues already discussed, much ambiguity continues around the incarnation of this ideology. What is perceived to be "extreme" and "fanatical" has fluctuated in AG history, thus contributing to a mixed message about the current streams of revival. This ambivalence about once commonly experienced revival phenomena can be gleaned in reviewing survey data through the lenses of the symbolic dilemma.

At the heart of the symbolic dilemma is ritual — "the cultic re-presentation of the religious experience [that] is central to the life of the religious group."[42] In

---

41. See Wacker, *Heaven Below*, and Ann Taves, *Fits, Trances, and Visions* (Princeton: Princeton University Press, 1999).

42. Thomas O'Dea and Janet O'Dea Aviad, *The Sociology of Religion*, 2nd ed. (Englewood Cliffs, N.J.: Prentice-Hall, 1983), p. 58.

Pentecostalism, however, the goal was never to simply remember the past but rather to provide a forum for ongoing religious experiences. As described at some length in *The Assemblies of God at the Crossroads,* the report card on this dilemma is mixed, as noted in this concluding paragraph of the chapter titled "Maintaining a Pentecostal Worldview through Ritual":

> The symbolic dilemma is deemed one of the most important in maintaining charisma, yet it is, paradoxically, perhaps the most difficult to keep alive. In an attempt to minimize the dangers of both disorder and inauthenticity, some pastors are placing less emphasis on experiences in their services. Opting for set programs, well-timed services, and a high level of professionalism, these pastors are often openly critical of "emotionalism" in services. The dilemma is further jeopardized by the fact that some very successful Assemblies of God congregations have exchanged charisma for institutional techniques to promote church growth.[43]

Core Ritual Expressions within the AG

The debates within the AG about choirs and choir robes, printed bulletins, and ritualized services have over the years been increasingly resolved in favor of order and predictability. As noted in Menzies' following essay, pragmatic decisions to accommodate multiple services, to make services more inviting for non-Pentecostals, and to deal with time-conscious Americans have produced a ritual in many churches that is indistinguishable from non-Pentecostal evangelical services. Mechanisms used to maintain order are the same ones that stifle the free flow of Pentecostal experiences. Earlier years of distinctive Pentecostal ritual when congregants commonly "tarried," waiting for the Holy Spirit to move in the gathering, sometimes with unpredictable results, are the makings of AG history.[44] Some recall this history with fondness and longing; others are more cautious about feared abuses found in unregulated meetings. The result is for the Pentecostal spirit to be unevenly distributed, a story that can be developed from statistics on the personal religious experiences of pastors as well as from pastoral reports about congregational services.

The most frequently practiced Pentecostal expression reported by pastors is speaking in tongues, or glossolalia. All ministers must sign a document annually when their credentials are renewed certifying that they accept the doctrine of tongues as the "initial physical evidence" of Spirit baptism. Although the

---

43. Poloma, *Crossroads*, p. 206.
44. See Wacker, *Heaven Below.*

doctrine has repeatedly been challenged by those outside the denomination, as well as some within, it appears to have strong support among pastors. Eighty-five percent of the pastors agreed with this statement: "A person who has never spoken in tongues cannot claim to be Spirit baptized." However, there appears to be a significant increase over the last quarter-century in the number of pastors who do not agree with the AG position on tongues as initial evidence of Spirit baptism. The 16 percent figure indicating disagreement is up from 2 percent in the 1980s survey. Although increasing numbers of AG congregants do not speak in tongues and a significant percentage of pastors disagree with the doctrinal statement, the experience of glossolalia and professing the creed of "initial evidence" continue to be a prerequisite for receiving and retaining AG ordination papers.[45]

The overwhelming majority of pastors in our survey (82 percent) did report praying in tongues weekly or more, with no pastor reporting not having prayed in tongues this past year. Tongues (at least on occasion) is a nearly universal part of the prayer lives of AG pastors. Pastors are somewhat less likely, however, to use this gift in a church service. Eighteen percent reported that they never gave an utterance in tongues or an interpretation of a glossolalic word during the past year, with another 36 percent indicating they did so only a few times. Forty-seven percent gave expression to glossolalia in a congregational setting more regularly, reportedly giving an "utterance" or an "interpretation" once a month or more. The fact that pastors *pray* in tongues in private ritual but are less likely to use the *gift of tongues* in a corporate setting suggests a dissonance in this expression of Pentecostal identity. Despite a more vocal yet clear minority who have reservations about the *doctrine* of tongues, it appears that the *use* of glossolalia is nearly universal for pastors in private prayer. Its corporate form of expression as "tongues and interpretation," however, is practiced regularly by fewer than half the pastors surveyed.

Glossolalia is central to AG doctrinal identity, as reflected in its inclusion as one of the sixteen items found in the AG Statement of Fundamental Truths. It is, however, only one of many paranormal expressions found in early Pentecostalism or in the larger Spirit movement within Christianity. Experiences of other gifts and manifestations common at Azusa Street, during the early history of the AG, and during subsequent renewals and revivals are now seemingly few and far between. This narrowing range of Pentecostal experi-

---

45. Data from the CCSP (Cooperative Congregational Studies Project) found that "40% of churches estimated that half or less of their members have been baptized in the Holy Spirit with evidence of speaking in other tongues." Sherri Doty and Efraim Espinoza, "FACT Survey Analysis: A 2000 Survey of Assemblies of God Churches," General Council of the Assemblies of God, 2000.

ences was true for the pastors' accounts of their personal experiences as well as for their reports of corporate experiences within their congregational services.

Only a minority of pastors regularly experienced prophecy, healing, deliverance, or other phenomena believed by many to be signs of the activity and presence of the Holy Spirit. For example, 34 percent claimed to have given a prophecy once a month or more. Forty-six percent reported being a prayer facilitator for a physical healing, and 41 percent for a mental and emotional healing. Only 13 percent, however, claimed regular involvement in deliverance from demonic oppression as a result of prayer. Put another way, 66 percent never or rarely gave a prophecy, 55 percent never or rarely witnessed a physical healing through their prayer, 60 percent were never or rarely a witness to emotional or mental healing, and 88 percent never witnessed deliverance. Other physical manifestations common to contemporary revival meetings outside the AG were similarly less likely to be part of experiences reported by pastors: 94 percent were never or rarely slain in the Spirit, 83 percent had never or rarely experienced holy laughter, and 76 percent had never or rarely experienced the bodily manifestation of shaking or jerking, all of which were commonly experienced during the recent revivals.

A similar pattern was found for corporate ritual experiences. Tongues and interpretations were reported as a regular experience for only 43 percent of the congregations. While only 2 percent of the pastors said tongues and interpretation (as dictated by Pentecostal protocol) were never a part of their public ritual, they still occurred infrequently for the remaining majority. Only 33 percent reported regular experiences of prophecy, a gift that serves a function similar to that of tongues and interpretations. Both are regarded as inspired words or messages from God delivered to the congregation, with prophecy being a simple message without the glossolalic prelude.

Although prayer for healing was a regular feature of 90 percent of congregational services, fewer than half the congregations (41 percent) provided regular opportunity for sharing healing testimonies. It appears that healing prayer has become a nearly universal ritual in AG churches, but that fewer churches include opportunities for testimonials commonly used to encourage and build faith for miraculous healing.[46] The fact that testimonies about healings received were far less likely to be reported than regular prayer for healing may point to underlying ambiguity about healing ritual as well as glossolalia. The

46. In reviewing these statistics, I was reminded of a comment made by an AG graduate student in one of my courses during which I was discussing my research on divine healing. The young man commented, "I have heard stories like you are reporting all of my life, but I have never seen one case of such healing in my church. Healing is professed but I have seen little evidence of its being practiced or experienced."

survey responses regarding pastoral involvement in the expression of charisma during worship services and the pastoral reports of congregational use of gifts during worship demonstrate how ongoing charismatic practices vary widely within the AG.

Ambiguity and the Ritual Dilemma

The history of the AG, as we have already seen, is one of a revitalization movement that emphasizes an experiential baptism distinct from baptism with water. In the words of David du Plessis, a central Pentecostal actor in the charismatic movement of the 1960s and 1970s, "God has no grandchildren." Because the identity of Pentecostals is rooted in paranormal religious experiences, their children cannot rely on their parents' experiences to claim Spirit baptism. Many adherents, however, appear to be lapsing into a cultural Pentecostalism that increasingly assumes an evangelical identity at the expense of Pentecostal experience. This may be demonstrated by the changes in Pentecostal ritual over the decades, particularly the decrease in revival meetings where signs and wonders drew both the faithful and potential converts to be refreshed by Pentecostal experiences. In a recent discussion of the history of Pentecostalism, Everett Wilson emphasized the important role revival plays in the spread of this global movement:

> Whatever success the historian has in identifying the succession of Pentecostal outpourings in the early century, the issue is not "who begat whom," but who or what brought to life and enthusiasm those many different specimens of Pentecostalism in diverse settings and sequences. A pedigree can show the relationship of each ascending generation to its predecessor, but each new generation still has to be born in reproductive passion. Revivals last not because the movement had an impressive beginning, but rather because periodic renewal keeps the enthusiasm vibrant despite energy-sapping generational, organizational and circumstantial changes.[47]

Revivals, once common in the AG, have gradually taken a backseat in many sectors of the denomination to "seeker-sensitive" churches and well-promoted programs. They were first banished from Sunday morning time slots and relegated to Sunday evening church gatherings and summer camps. They increasingly have been replaced by other rituals in many AG churches, lingering only as rumors from a seemingly distant historical past, as fewer pastors and their congregants experience the range of charisma found in early Pentecostal-

47. Wilson, "They Crossed," p. 92.

ism. When new outpourings of charisma come along that revive the larger PCM, the AG has been reluctant to accept them as authentic moves of God. That isolationist and protectionist mentality has cost them opportunity to participate in charismatic outpourings in other sectors of Christianity.

Blumhofer's observations about the consonant notes found in the New Order (Latter Rain) revival of the 1940s and early Pentecostalism provide some insight for understanding the ambivalence of the AG toward the fresh outpouring of charisma:

> Some first-generation Pentecostals had begun within a decade to bemoan their movement's waning power and had pointed to a future, more copious shower of the latter rain. Consequently, there was even precedent for the eschatological innovation by the New Order advocates. Daniel Kerr, for example, noting a declining focus on healing as early as 1914, had heralded a coming dispensation in which healing would have the prominence accorded to tongues at the turn of the century. As Pentecostal groups had organized and charismatic fervor had waned in some places — or was largely confined to revival campaigns and campmeetings — voices had been raised asserting that the turn-of-the-century Apostolic Faith Movement had seen only the beginning of a revival whose more copious latter rains were yet to come.[48]

While Blumhofer goes on to describe the AG rationale for rejecting the Latter Rain or New Order movement (particularly its rejection of religious organizations and its indictment of "old Pentecost"), the fact remains that the AG has been at times ambivalent and at times hostile to Pentecostal experiences in other streams of the PCM. The Latter Rain, the subsequent healing revival of the 1950s, and the charismatic movement of the 1960s and 1970s all, for the most part, occurred outside the AG. It had a positive effect on AG growth during this period largely through pastors who risked the criticism of their peers and sometimes censure from leadership for their support of this newer movement.

Most pastors in our survey do seem to be aware that the Pentecostal worldview is in continual need of revitalization. A vast majority (84 percent) either agreed or strongly agreed with the statement, "The AG must actively seek to revitalize its early Pentecostal roots." Very few (5 percent) agreed that to reach the unchurched "the AG must downplay the public use of the gifts of the Spirit" which are believed to accompany baptism with the Holy Spirit. The overwhelming majority of pastors verbally support AG identity as a Pentecostal

48. Edith Blumhofer, *The Assemblies of God: A Chapter in the Story of American Pentecostalism,* vol. 2 (since 1941) (Springfield, Mo.: Gospel Publishing House, 1989), p. 58.

denomination in which paranormal gifts are openly displayed, even if these manifestations should cause some discomfort for first-time visitors. Moreover, 85 percent of the respondents reported that their congregations are of "one mind" regarding "expressive worship practices" which have at times caused divisions and disagreements in the past.

Despite the verbal acquiescence, there appears to be an unresolved paradox between the widely acclaimed support for revival with an openness to paranormal gifts and the absence or near absence of Pentecostal vitality in at least half the AG churches. With the possible exception of tongues and interpretations (experienced regularly in 43 percent of the congregations included in this study), other gifts and manifestations commonly witnessed in the larger PCM do not appear to be a regular part of AG ritual. The discrepancy between sentiments and behavior — between what people say and what they do — has been long observed by social psychologists,[49] and can be once again seen in the responses to questions about the Brownsville Outpouring and other renewal tributaries.

The revival/renewal of the 1990s in North America can be traced to a revival begun with the AG in Argentina — a revival that continues into the twenty-first century. Although it first took form in North America in 1994 (at the then Toronto Airport Vineyard, a Third Wave congregation) and quickly spread to the United Kingdom (largely in independent "new" or "restoration churches" and Anglican charismatic churches), in 1995 similar revival phenomena found expression in an AG congregation in Pensacola, Florida. Brownsville Assembly of God (BAOG) quickly became a pilgrimage site for Spirit-thirsty Pentecostals and charismatics alike. Its leaders soon offered a traveling version of the revival as Awake America Crusades and began monthly treks to local communities. In June 1997 the *Pentecostal Evangel* ("The Official Magazine of the Assemblies of God") devoted a special issue to the question, "Is America on the verge of spiritual awakening?" It presented revival updates on twenty-four AG congregations throughout the United States. Full-length articles appeared on churches in the Golden State (AG churches in Sacramento, Modesto, and Bakersfield, California); First Assemblies of God in Fort Wayne, Indiana; the Tabernacle in Orchard Park, New York; Bethel Temple in Hampton, Virginia; and Bettendorf, Iowa, Assembly of God. Editor Hal Donaldson acknowledged that this issue is "by no means a comprehensive report . . . [but the churches] featured here are merely representative of congregations across America —

---

49. See Irwin Deutscher, *What We Say/What We Do: Sentiments and Acts* (New York: Aldine de Gruyter, 1973), and Irwin Deutscher, Fred P. Pestello, and Frances G. Pestello, *Sentiments and Acts* (New York: Aldine de Gruyter, 1993).

large and small, urban and rural — that are recognizing fresh spiritual life." The tone of the issue was affirming of renewal sprinkled with only a bit of caution. Donaldson offered this editorial comment: "Historians will judge whether the burgeoning revival in America deserves to be dubbed the next great awakening. But signs suggest this is more than a spiritual tremor."[50]

The response paper adopted by the General Presbytery in August 2000, "Endtime Revival — Spirit-Led and Spirit Controlled," appeared to be more cautionary about the excesses of renewal than it was affirming. While stating that the "last thing any sincere Pentecostal believer wants to do is to quench or grieve the Holy Spirit," much of the paper was devoted to cautioning against "revival extremes." These two publications — the special issue of the *Pentecostal Evangel* and the "Response Paper to Resolution 16" dealing with "Endtime Revival" — demonstrate the ambiguity that readily can be found in the AG about revival/renewal.

The survey data collected from AG pastors about the 1990s revivals reflect the same dissonance. As reported earlier, 86 percent of pastors identify with Pentecostal *renewal* or *revival* (R/R), reporting that being involved in R/R is extremely important or very important to them. Nearly all (98 percent) were aware of the R/R movement found at BAOG and other congregations in North America through reading articles in AG literature (100 percent) or in other Christian magazines (86 percent) and by talking with AG leaders/pastors (72 percent), with church members (70 percent), or with other persons who have visited popular R/R sites (86 percent). The overwhelming majority of the pastors appear to be aware of the current Pentecostal revival and seem to have a single mind about the importance of reviving authentic Pentecostal spirituality. This does not necessarily mean, however, that AG pastors are of one mind about BAOG and the revival of the 1990s. Pastors were evenly divided on whether "America is in the midst of a revival similar to the one that gave birth to Pentecostalism." This suggests that even AG national leaders' cautious approval and support of the revival at BAOG may have been ahead of the ambivalence among pastors.[51]

Nearly all the pastors surveyed support revival in principle and nearly all had heard about BAOG and the R/R movement, but far fewer had experienced

50. Hal Donaldson, "Labeling Churches," *Pentecostal Evangel* 8 (June 1997): 4.

51. It was interesting to review the selection of readings found in the eighty-fifth anniversary edition, 1913-98, of the *Pentecostal Evangel,* the weekly publication of the AG. An article on Pentecostal revival was reprinted from the July 12, 1924, issue that lamented how "many folks are blind" to the Pentecostal revival that was still in process. The anniversary issue, although published three years after the revival began at BAOG, failed to mention the Pensacola Outpouring (as it is often called) as one of the significant events of AG history.

this latest outpouring of charisma for themselves. It is noteworthy that despite the verbal assent to the importance of revival, approximately two-thirds *have not* personally checked out the nightly meetings at the BAOG in Pensacola or any of the other AG and non-AG renewal sites that dot the nation. The vast majority have not invited R/R speakers to their churches (67 percent), nor have they attended an Awake America Crusade sponsored by BAOG in various cities throughout the United States (80 percent). Given this lack of firsthand contact, it is not surprising that only 30 percent of the pastors report their churches "to be actively engaged in the Renewal/Revival."

In sum, it is clear that most pastors perceive a decline in Pentecostal practices within the denomination. It is noteworthy that 70 percent either strongly agree or agree that "the gifts of the Holy Spirit are losing their prominence in AG churches as a whole." They report concern about the loss of Pentecostal power, embrace a renewal/revival identity, and are informed about the various renewal sites, but surprisingly most have made little effort to check out for themselves the rumors of revival.[52] Being of one mind around the core value of revival has apparently not translated into an acceptance of revival in contemporary dress. Present-day pastors, much like their predecessors, have been reluctant to accept charisma as it has taken flesh in periodic revivals of the latter half of the twentieth century. At least among some pastors, revitalization in Pentecostalism is being relegated to doctrine rather than personal experience. Revivals are often acknowledged to be "messy" — even by their supporters. Established Pentecostal denominations like the AG may well prefer the safety of doctrine to the unpredictability of religious experience.

The Dilemma of Delimitation: Doctrine and Pentecostal Experience

The dilemma of delimitation addresses the threat to charisma posed by the relativizing of the original religious message in relation to new conditions. One horn of the dilemma is the danger of watering down the message to fit the times, often rendering commonplace what was originally a call to the extraordinary. The AG (as may be gleaned from earlier discussion) runs a risk of grabbing on to this horn with its long history of courting noncharismatic evangelicals who are

---

52. Ambiguity and ambivalence appear to be heightened by the fact that only 6 percent of the respondents did not believe that the denomination is responsible for promoting revival. Sixty percent of the pastors surveyed believed it was the task of the national office, and another 34 percent reported that it was the task of the district offices.

indifferent and often hostile to the distinct Pentecostal worldview. Primitive charismatic tendencies are tamed as favor is bestowed on more pragmatic ritual and organizations. The other horn of the dilemma is the creation of rigid doctrines and religious legalisms set up in an attempt to capture and reproduce the charisma of the original movement. The early founders of the AG were initially resistant to forming any kind of doctrinal statement, but they soon found it necessary to produce a statement of faith, consisting largely of a reiteration of the "fundamentals" drawn up earlier by Protestant fundamentalists. The stage was set for the replacing of right experience with right belief — a move that tends to water down the distinct Pentecostal worldview where the Spirit of God moves freely, openly, and creatively in the lives of ordinary believers.

During the 1914 founding meeting of the AG in Hot Springs, Arkansas, there was strong resistance to the development of a creedal statement, but the Oneness "heresy" that developed between 1914 and 1916 forced leaders to quickly adopt one. As elaborated in Menzies' following essay, most of the tenets were derived from the Fundamentalist Statement of Truths, with two important additions: tongues as "initial evidence" of Spirit baptism and "healing by the atonement." The belief in divine healing is not distinctively Pentecostal, being promoted by other sectlike non-Pentecostal groups even at the time the AG creed was formulated. The doctrine of "initial evidence," however, is distinctively Pentecostal and has been embraced to varying degrees by most Pentecostal groups in North America.[53] Accounts of Pentecostal-like revivals that did not promote a doctrine of initial evidence have usually been lost in unexamined historical archives.[54] At its core, however, the AG Statement of Fundamental Truths is basically a fundamentalist-dispensationalist creedal statement, with "initial evidence" added to the other largely eschatological concerns. Its adoption from fundamentalism set the stage for the unfolding of the dilemma of delimitation. O'Dea and Aviad describe the dangers of delimitation as follows: "While the dangers of distortion of the faith require these definitions of dogma and morals, once established, the definitions themselves pose the possibility of another kind of distortion. They become a vast intellectual structure which serves not to guide the faith of untrained specialists but rather to burden it."[55]

53. See Gary B. McGee, "Initial Evidence," in *New International Dictionary of the Pentecostal and Charismatic Movements*, ed. Stanley M. Burgess (Grand Rapids: Zondervan, 2000), and Wacker, *Heaven Below*.

54. See Gary B. McGee, "'Latter Rain' Falling in the East: Early-Twentieth-Century Pentecostalism in India and the Debate over Speaking in Tongues," *American Society of Church History* 68 (fall 1999): 648-65, for one such account of the rise of Pentecostalism in India.

55. O'Dea and Aviad, *The Sociology of Religion*, p. 61.

In theory, it is the task of the Holy Spirit to ensure that Pentecostalism does not sink into the abyss of contentless mysticism or become caged in a cavern of rigid doctrine. Pentecostalism in its various faces has continuously needed to balance experience with biblical teachings, describing itself as both people of the Spirit and people of the Word. At the heart of Pentecostalism is a conviction that the Bible is the inspired word of God. Pentecostals do differ, however, in their hermeneutics, with scholarship tending toward an evangelical rational/propositional theology with some pastors uncritically adding an undefined narrative to the fundamentalist core. Some Pentecostals, as already noted, have "aligned themselves with Evangelicals in their move toward adopting the methods of higher criticism."[56] The text is easily reduced to the meaning intended by the author of the Scripture without sufficient exploration of the insight that can be gleaned from integrating this hermeneutic with narrative theology. Traditional Pentecostalism, despite its official fundamentalist creed, notes Cagel, often placed greater "emphases on the immediacy of the text and multiple dimensions of meaning."[57] It allowed for subjective experiences and subjective interpretations to exist alongside the more objective critical-historical-literary methods. Even the doctrine of tongues as "initial evidence" emerged not from the pens of theologians versed in higher criticism but from the accounts told by those who experienced glossolalia and sought to align this experience with their reading of the Bible.

Today's Pentecostalism is more likely to appear dressed in the rationalism of contemporary American society, devoid of the colorful and emotional accounts that found expression through the anointed preaching and testimonies of its earlier days. As already noted, the seeds for this condition can be found in the early history of the AG as its leaders sought to find acceptance and legitimation from the dispensationalist fundamentalists. As Gerald Shepherd noted in his discussion of the "uneasy relationship between Pentecostalism and dispensationalism," embraced evangelical views "have raised new problems for the identity of Pentecostals — hermeneutically, sociologically, and politically."[58] Other scholars have also cautioned against the danger of an uncritical wedding of Pentecostalism with evangelical/fundamentalist theology. Harvey Cox, for example, noted the paradoxical relationship between fundamentalist Christianity and modernity, cautioning that fundamentalism is but a crude

---

56. Timothy B. Cagel, "Beyond the Fundamentalist-Modernist Controversy: Pentecostals and Hermeneutics in a Postmodern Age," *Pneuma: The Journal for Pentecostal Studies* 15 (fall 1993): 163.

57. Cagel, "Fundamentalist-Modernist Controversy," p. 163.

58. Gerald T. Shepherd, "Pentecostals and the Hermeneutics of Dispensationalism: The Anatomy of an Uneasy Relationship," *Pneuma: The Journal for Pentecostal Studies* 6 (fall 1984): 6.

Margaret M. Poloma

form of nineteenth-century rationalism that is not compatible with a Pentecostal worldview.[59]

Evangelical rational thought with its propositional truth tends to undermine the importance of religious experiences, the stuff out of which Pentecostalism is made and through which it maintains its vitality. At the same time, it has provided a useful form for professing the faith, one that gains common and uncritical acceptance by most AG pastors. The present study of AG pastors, as well as an earlier one by Guth, Green, Smidt, Kellstedt, and Poloma,[60] suggests that AG pastors are of a near single mind on most common theological issues. Of the eight Protestant denominations included in the study by Guth et al., the AG clearly is the group in most accord on basic doctrine. This theological core and some attendant ambiguities provide the contents for discussing the delimitation dilemma.

The Bible, Fundamentals, and Orthodoxy

On matters of biblical orthodoxy, AG pastors score higher in the Guth et al. study than clergy in the Southern Baptist Convention, Evangelical Covenant Church, Christian Reformed Church, Reformed Church in America, United Methodist Church, Presbyterian Church (U.S.A.), or the Disciples of Christ. On basic biblical beliefs coupled with premillennial eschatology, AG pastors responding to our survey demonstrated almost unanimous agreement. One hundred percent of the pastors agreed or strongly agreed that "there is no other way to salvation but through belief in Jesus Christ," 99 percent believe "the devil actually exists," and 98 percent agreed or strongly agreed that "Scriptures are the inerrant, literally accurate word of God not only in matters of faith, but in all matters." Ninety-four percent agreed or strongly agreed that the "Bible clearly teaches a 'premillennial' view of history and the future," and 98 percent reported believing "in the imminent 'rapture' of the church."

Widespread agreement on basic Christian tenets, which appears to be stronger in the AG than in other denominations, may be due in part to its tendency to downplay the refinement of doctrine. As AG historian William Menzies observed nearly thirty years ago, the AG "has been surprisingly free of theological controversy, possibly owing to the relative unconcern of the fellowship with the niceties of doctrinal distinctions." Menzies goes on to state: "The

59. Cox, *Fire from Heaven*.
60. James L. Guth, John C. Green, Corwin E. Smidt, Lyman A. Kellstedt, and Margaret M. Poloma, *The Bully Pulpit: The Politics of Protestant Clergy* (Lawrence: University of Kansas Press, 1997).

traditional emphasis has been experiential and practical, not ideological. Absolute trust in the Bible and general agreement on fundamentals of the faith have served to furnish a fairly tolerant basis of fellowship."[61]

However, some ambiguities can be seen lurking beneath the surface of the seemingly placid doctrinal waters. As shown before, the survey suggests an ambiguity about a dispensationalist hermeneutic that hints at a major potential cleavage. While 58 percent reported accepting a dispensationalist interpretation of Scripture, 42 percent rejected this approach. The uncritical wedding of dispensationalism and Pentecostalism by a majority of pastors points to the downside of not wrestling with theological "niceties" within the denomination. A de facto theology has emerged, but one that often suffers from a lack of coherence and relevance in its failure to mirror a clear Pentecostal worldview. Of particular concern in exploring the dilemma of delimitation is the degree to which the "definitions of dogma and morals" within the AG contribute toward maintaining or quenching a distinct Pentecostal identity.

Ambiguity and Dissent on Select Doctrinal Issues

Traditional Pentecostalism has birthed a movement that it has been unable to monitor. The Spirit blows how and where it will, and much of the activity within the past fifty years has been outside of classical Pentecostalism within the so-called Latter Rain, charismatic, and Third Wave sectors of the Spirit movement. Robeck describes the dilemma faced in the wake of an expanded PCM as follows:

> While it is indisputable that the needs of some people are being met in these newer congregations, sometimes the very categories with which they choose to identify suggests a new form of elitism. Older Pentecostals are now being portrayed as *passé*, while these groups promise that God is on the move in their midst. They are the latest "wave" of what God is doing. Older "waves" have been passed by. As members of the first "wave" of what

---

61. William W. Menzies, *Anointed to Serve: The Story of the Assemblies of God* (Springfield, Mo.: Gospel Publishing House, 1971), p. 376. Unpublished interviews conducted with AG pastors by a team of Organizing Religious Work (ORW) researchers under the direction of Nancy Ammerman at Hartford Seminary seem to confirm Menzies' observation about the focus being on the sixteen fundamentals, with little concern for "niceties of doctrinal distinctions." It is significant that while some respondents talked about being "big on sound doctrine," it was largely with regard to issues decided at the 1916 Council. Interestingly, none of the twenty-eight pastors interviewed talked about their disagreement with any of the fundamentals of the denomination, not even the somewhat controversial "initial evidence" tenet on glossolalia which insists that speaking in tongues is *the* evidential sign of Spirit baptism.

God is said to be doing in the Church today, Pentecostals must now deal with the same feelings that members of the historic churches had when they were first faced with the claims that Pentecostals were proclaiming the "Full Gospel." For some older Pentecostal groups, this has introduced questions of self-doubt or very human desires to discredit the "new" as not sufficiently up to God's standards.[62]

Of significance for this discussion is that many of these newer streams have tended to de-emphasize the importance of glossolalia for Spirit baptism, much to the chagrin of classical Pentecostals.[63] This diminished emphasis on tongues while emphasizing the presence and power of the Holy Spirit has appealed to others outside the larger PCM. Popular American Baptist sociologist/theologian Tony Campolo raises the issue of how to be Pentecostal without speaking in tongues in a book written for a larger evangelical audience.[64] Campolo joined others outside the Pentecostal camp in rediscovering the power of the Holy Spirit. They adopt and adapt the Pentecostal worldview of Spirit baptism, suggesting that there is more to being a Christian than believing the accepted doctrines and practicing the right rituals. As is evident in Menzies' following essay, glossolalia as a symbol of distinct Pentecostal identity is being eroded by the influence of the larger Spirit movement that refuses to accept the centrality of tongues as "initial evidence," causing AG leaders to cling even more to the one plank of doctrine that makes them different.

There has been a growing awareness that the Pentecostal perspective is no longer marginalized but has gone mainstream. As AG scholar Glen Menzies commented:

> [Most Christians once] regarded glossolalia in particular as a token of fanaticism and emotional excess. But due to the eruption of the charismatic movement in the 1960s and its widespread success in popularizing this Pen-

---

62. Cecil M. Robeck, Jr., "The Holy Spirit and Ecumenism" (paper presented at a symposium on the Holy Spirit and ecumenism sponsored by the Cardinal Suenens Foundation, Leuven, Belgium, December 1999).

63. It is interesting to note the estimate that only 35 percent of Pentecostals speak in tongues. In other words, only one in three members of churches who teach that glossolalia is the "initial evidence" of Spirit baptism is actually glossolalic. Walter J. Hollenweger, "Roman Catholics and Pentecostals in Dialogue," *Pneuma: The Journal of the Society for Pentecostal Studies* 21 (spring 1999): 147, comments on this statistic: "If we add to this number those Pentecostal denominations who refuse to subscribe to the doctrine of 'initial sign' (for instance, the very strong Chilean movement), the percentage is even higher."

64. Tony Campolo, *How to Be Pentecostal without Speaking in Tongues* (Waco: Word, 1994).

tecostal understanding of spiritual gifts outside Pentecostal circles, the notion that all of the gifts of the Spirit are available to the contemporary church no longer constitutes a "distinctive" of Pentecostalism. And while Pentecostals rejoice that in this regard the rest of the church has moved in their direction, this "success" has only intensified the need for Spirit baptism and evidential tongues to provide distinctive identity and internal cohesion to Pentecostalism.[65]

The logic of the leaders, some of whom are currently proposing tightening up the doctrinal wording to minimize the mental gymnastics some pastors engage in annually as they check the form to renew their ordination credentials, runs something like this: the key to Spirit baptism is tongues, the key to revival is Spirit baptism, the key to church growth is revival. Without tongues there can be no Spirit baptism, no revival, no church growth. To back down on what is increasingly becoming a controversial doctrine in some sectors of the AG, according to this logic, would insure the AG traveling down a slippery slope of losing its Pentecostal identity and jeopardizing the institutional well-being of this thriving denomination. At the same time that this particular symbol is being sharpened, the use of glossolalia and other experiences that birthed Pentecostalism seems to be waning within the AG.

As discussed earlier, glossolalia remains a litmus test for "true" Pentecostalism for many AG leaders and pastors (at least in North America), but increasingly it is a doctrine held up for scrutiny. While the vast majority (85 percent) of pastors affirmed the doctrine in their survey responses, a significant minority (15 percent) expressed disagreement with it.[66] If glossolalia is in fact the "initial physical evidence" attesting to Spirit baptism, how is it that others

65. Glen Menzies, "Tongues as 'The Initial Physical Sign' of Spirit Baptism in the Thought of D. W. Kerr," *Pneuma: The Journal of the Society for Pentecostal Studies* 20 (fall 1998): 175.

66. The figure for those disagreeing with the tongues doctrine represents a significant increase over the 2 percent figure reported from a 1985 data set on pastors for the same question (Poloma, *Crossroads,* p. 40). Also of interest from the results of the study of congregations and pastors in the mid-1980s is the gap between the pastoral and congregational responses to the issue of tongues as initial evidence. At that time, 39 percent of the congregants did not agree with this fundamental doctrine (as compared with 2 percent of the pastors). Anecdotal evidence further supports the concern about an erosion of consensus regarding the tongues doctrine. Specifically, at least some pastors have quietly been neglecting to check the box asking about a belief in tongues as "initial physical evidence" of Spirit baptism, noting that the constitution and by-laws do not authorize the collection of such information. Those seeking ordination papers for the first time are the ones caught in the most precarious position. Reportedly the Executive Presbytery has added the term "immediate," reading "tongues as the immediate initial physical evidence," to close in on those who have been acquiescing to the words but not the spirit of increasing doctrinal rigidity.

are experiencing a range of Pentecostal-like phenomena without emphasizing tongues? Some answered the question by saying that eventually the Spirit-baptized person will speak in tongues, leading to the attempt to insert the word "immediate" before "initial physical evidence." Even more disconcerting to those who would make tongues a litmus test for Spirit baptism is the fact that in many AG congregations the majority of adherents do not report speaking in tongues. Such observations plus an evangelical hermeneutic have caused a small but growing number of pastors to question the biblical base for the doctrine. Although a majority of pastors appear to support the official position (we have no way of determining how many are engaged in personal mental revisions as they acquiesce to this plank of AG doctrine), there is a significant minority opposition movement present in the AG. Those who tackle the issue, however, do so at the risk of their own status as ordained AG ministers.[67]

The doctrine surrounding glossolalia is one of two major issues that have generated controversy over the years that I have been a systematic observer of the AG. The other is divorce and remarriage among AG laity, and especially among church pastors. In the congregational survey that provided data for *The Assemblies of God at the Crossroads,* approximately half the adherents of AG churches reported beliefs that were not in compliance with the stance of the denomination on divorce. The 1973 Statement on Divorce and Remarriage clearly proscribed divorce, but left the question of remarriage for adherents to "be resolved by the believer as he walks in the light of God's Word."[68] While adherents were given permission to discern the issue of divorce for themselves, until very recently divorced ministers were granted no such freedom of conscience about remarriage after divorce. Even if the divorce and remarriage occurred before the person's conversion, a divorced and remarried person could not be ordained. (Rumblings could be heard, however, about annulments being granted which have enabled some high-ranking ministers to avoid the censure of losing credentials after divorce and remarriage or after marrying a divorced person.)

---

67. One interesting caveat may be found in a testimony by J. Roswell Flower, the first general superintendent of the AG, on his Spirit baptism. In the original article appearing in the *Pentecostal Evangel* in 1933, it is clear that Flower, while clearly believing in the fundamental about glossolalia, regarded himself as having received the baptism some months before he actually spoke in tongues and *after* leading evangelistic crusades deemed to be Spirit empowered. When the article was reprinted in the *Pentecostal Evangel* in 1993, it was abridged in such a way as to make it appear that Flower actually spoke in tongues on the occasion of his Spirit baptism that he reports empowered him for the crusades. For an AG defense against critiques of the existing doctrine on tongues, see James K. Bridges, "The Full Consummation of the Baptism in the Holy Spirit," *Theological Enrichment,* fall 2000, pp. 92-95.

68. Poloma, *Crossroads,* pp. 148-49.

After defeating a similar measure in 1991 and 1997, the AG General Council passed a resolution in August 2001 that allows divorced persons to become pastors *as long as the divorce occurred before their conversion.*

This action has partially resolved the divorce and remarriage issue. Significant numbers of pastors appear to be in favor of even more flexibility in dealing with the divorce and remarriage of pastors, just as there has been for laity. Pastors responding to the survey reported considerably less support for the official AG position on ministers divorcing and remarrying than at the time of my first pastoral survey in 1985, when only 10 percent disagreed with the AG policy of defrocking divorced and remarried pastors. The present survey found that 43 percent agreed or strongly agreed with the statement, "Persons who have been divorced and remarried should be permitted to serve as AG pastors." Only 19 percent reported a *strong disagreement* with the statement that would ban divorced and remarried pastors from the ministry, suggesting that most desire increased flexibility in dealing with the thorny issue of divorce and remarriage. Further, only a minority of pastors (23 percent) would prohibit divorced and remarried persons from assuming leadership in local congregations — a position which further illustrates the denomination's inability to withstand accommodative forces stemming from a widespread acceptance of divorce and remarriage in the larger culture.

Other moral proscriptions remain as vestiges from a past in which all worldly amusements were shunned by Pentecostals who set themselves apart from the larger world to live "holy" and "separate" lives. Questions were asked on the survey about four such practices: drinking alcohol, gambling, dancing, and movies. Proscriptive attitudes toward such behavior remain fairly strong among pastors (although sermons are rarely preached on these issues in most urban AG churches). A clear majority disapproved of "gambling, including lotteries" (98 percent), even "the occasional use of alcoholic beverages" (82 percent), social dancing (80 percent), and Christians patronizing "movie theaters" (51 percent).

In a more striking way than in other well-established Protestant denominations, there is an intact seamless robe around Christian orthodoxy in the AG extending even to its particular eschatology and most moral and behavioral taboos. The garment wrapping distinct Pentecostal theology, however, does show some signs of wear. Pastors are seemingly divided on some remnant moral issues that once seemed central to Pentecostal identity — behavior and practices that set Pentecostals aside as a "peculiar people." Attempts to select any doctrinal items, as the leadership has done with glossolalia and divorced ministers, to prevent the further slide down what is commonly referred to as the slippery slope, appear more likely to cause division than to reinforce Pentecostal identity. What seems needed to deal with the slippery slope is not a tightening of doctrinal reins but rather continued flexibility that allows controversy around peripheral issues not central to the larger Pentecostal worldview. Perhaps the best way to deal with controversial issues is to frame them theologically within the "new" Pentecostal paradigm discussed earlier — one that reflects an openness to personal experience and narrative that aligns with Pentecostal identity as a Spirit-led people.[69]

Spirit baptism remains a core feature of PCM identity, but increasingly it is not regarded as synonymous with the gift of tongues. Spirit baptism (or "infilling") is often treated as an ongoing process in which Pentecostals of all streams experience the power of God not only for personal pleasure and edification but also for empowerment for service. Power and empowerment cannot be legislated or mandated by doctrinal decrees or denominational edicts, but rather depend on hospitable terrain that allows the wind, rain, and fire of the Holy Spirit to fall as it will. A fertile environment can be created, but the desired work of the Spirit is in every sense *charisma* or gift — which takes us to the fourth dilemma, that of power. The accommodative forces at work in O'Dea's dilemma of power are important for understanding the interrelationship between attempts to enforce doctrinal decrees on pastors and the empowerment sought by early Pentecostals.

The Dilemma of Power: From Pilgrims to Citizens

The theme of accommodation to the larger culture runs through all the institutional dilemmas, but perhaps no dilemma focuses on a more important facet of accommodation than does the dilemma of power. O'Dea and Aviad succinctly describe the dilemma of power as follows: "Religion cannot but relate itself to the other institutions of society and to the cultural values. Yet such accommodation tends toward a coalescing of religion and power. The alliance of religion and secular power creates a situation in which apparent religiosity often conceals a deeper cynicism and a growing unbelief."[70]

Although the early Pentecostals were not trained in sociology, they seemed to have a natural instinct for the importance of separation from the larger world if their distinct worldview were to be retained. As Blumhofer noted, "[E]arly Assemblies of God members professed little interest in contem-

---

69. See Wonsuk Ma, "Biblical Studies in the Pentecostal Tradition: Yesterday, Today and Tomorrow," in *The Globalization of Pentecostalism*, pp. 52-69.

70. O'Dea and Aviad, *The Sociology of Religion*, p. 63.

porary society; they had either not yet glimpsed a broader social world or had consciously turned from it."[71] They began their sojourn as pilgrims, but slowly and steadily moved toward becoming citizens. Nowhere is this better illustrated than in the move from an apolitical (once pacifist) stance with a strong sense of Spirit-led destiny to embracing the political agenda of fundamentalism/evangelicalism. An eschatology proclaiming a soon-coming end times, the imminent rapture of the church, and premillennialism that once kept Pentecostals at bay from politics, now seems to undergird a staunchly conservative political agenda.[72] Spiritual power (empowerment) has, at least for some, been converted to political power.

The Core and the Periphery: Consonance and Dissonance in Political Thought

As the Religious Right began to flex its political muscles during the 1980s and 1990s, the AG struggled with its role in the political scene. Few AG pastors plunged into partisan politics (although a significant majority are self-reported Republicans), but rather they began to speak out on select issues. On the basis of both congregational and pastoral data as well as other research on conservative religions and politics, Poloma noted a distinction between private morality and public political issues that continues among AG pastors:

> Although the dividing lines are somewhat blurred, it appears that the Assemblies of God is quite concerned about private moral issues, such as divorce, pornography, drug and alcohol abuse, and abortion, that touch on "personal purity." Its leaders, however, are much more reluctant to step into the area of "public issues," including economic problems, social welfare legislation, and international affairs. Most appear not only to oppose political involvements that focus on the public sphere but also carefully to eschew partisan politics.[73]

The increased visibility of and attention paid to the Religious Right have prompted many AG pastors to take a place alongside other evangelicals in politics as well as theology, a stance Blumhofer has linked with the AG's one-sided involvement with the National Association of Evangelicals.[74] Not only are pastors now more likely to express concern over select political/moral issues, but

71. Blumhofer, *Restoring the Faith*, p. 142.
72. Guth et al., *The Bully Pulpit.*
73. Poloma, *Crossroads*, p. 157.
74. Blumhofer, *The Assemblies of God.*

many reportedly expect national and regional denominational representatives to lead the way in conservative political action. For example, 86 percent of the pastors in the present survey believed the national office should "serve as a political voice to combat homosexuality and abortion," with another 3 percent relegating this task to the district offices, and only 11 percent indicating such activity should be performed by neither office. Fewer pastors, although still a clear majority, support denominational action to promote select political candidates. Fifty-nine percent assigned this task to the national office and 8 percent to the districts, with 33 percent replying that such political activity is not appropriate for either denominational administrative office.

Eschatology has always played a role in AG political stances (or lack of them), and the overwhelming majority of pastors continue to support this plank of traditional AG theology. As we have seen, AG pastors are nearly unanimously committed to the premillennial eschatology held by their forebears. They still profess premillennial beliefs that once led their ancestors to resist political activities, but the impact and meaning of AG eschatology on pastoral politics has become somewhat fuzzy. Thirty-five percent of the pastoral respondents, for example, concurred with a statement that is more in accord with postmillennialism than with a traditional understanding of premillennial doctrine: "The Kingdom of God can be built in every institution and sphere of life before the Second Coming of Jesus Christ." For many the coming kingdom should be facilitated through the Christian Coalition, as "a proper channel to use to accomplish political goals" (59 percent in agreement). While there has been great resistance to ecumenism in the AG (especially dialogue with Roman Catholics and mainline Protestant organizations), paradoxically the vast majority (91 percent) would favor interfaith cooperation in politics "even if they can't agree on theology." Finally, underlying a more activist stance by many pastors is a more traditional majority opinion (70 percent) that "if enough people were brought to Christ, social ills would take care of themselves," a seeming holdover of a once dominant apolitical posture.

AG pastors are being increasingly drawn into an evangelical political agenda that fails to mirror an earlier Pentecostal understanding of power. As there has been a subtle transition of the AG from being pilgrims to citizens,[75] there has been a corresponding shift from reliance on Pentecostal power to that of political power. The passage from the book of Zechariah quoted earlier still can be found on the front cover of each issue of the *Pentecostal Evangel:* "Not by might, nor by power, but by My Spirit, saith the Lord." The classic Pentecostal understanding of that passage and the issue of Pentecostal empowerment war-

---

75. See Blumhofer, *The Assemblies of God.*

rant closer inspection for unpacking the relevance of the dilemma of power for the AG.

Power, Politics, and Empowerment: A Minority Report

The AG serves as a good illustration of the strong correlation that exists between theological conservatism and political conservatism in American politics. The history of Pentecostalism suggests, however, that this relationship is due more to social class concerns than to Pentecostal spirituality. When the PCM is in its charismatic moment, political agendas seem to lose significance as actual behavior may become (at least for the moment) somewhat radical. In the words of a popular renewal song that became a theme of the so-called Toronto Blessing, Spirit-filled people will "break dividing walls" — walls that can be found between men and women, blacks and whites, Pentecostals and non-Pentecostals, old and young (fill in other categories).[76] According to some Pentecostal historians, dividing walls fell at the Azusa Street Revival that birthed Pentecostalism but were quickly reconstructed during the years that followed. Gender, social class, race, ethnicity, and denomination all become less relevant (at least temporarily) when the power of the Spirit is sweeping over a gathering of people, leaving ecstasy in its wake.[77]

Despite their apolitical stance, many of the early Pentecostals seemed to understand that the Pentecostal experience was meant for service. As elaborated in Menzies' following essay, tongues, for example, was initially conceived as an infused knowledge of a foreign language for missionary activity. Those who tried to exercise their new language in foreign countries were usually disappointed, but their disappointment did not cause them to abandon glossolalia. Tongues was reconceptualized as a door that opened for the believer a storehouse of spiritual power, with missionaries coming to expect Pentecostal signs and wonders to provide for their necessities and to bring others to the Christian

76. See the video *Go Inside the Toronto Blessing,* an account of the outbreak of revival at the Toronto Airport Christian Fellowship in 1994 and its effects as reported in 1997. Distributed by Fresh Start Marketing, Canton, Ohio.

77. Perhaps the story of an egalitarian Pentecostalism is but a myth (as some historians have suggested); religious myth can be a powerful propellant for change. What is significant here is that the myth of early equality has been eroded with the aging of Pentecostalism. The vision of God's pouring out his Spirit on all people, as foretold in the book of Joel and reiterated by Peter on Pentecost, often fails to find modern expression. See Augustus Cerillo, "Interpretive Approaches to the History of American Pentecostal Origins," *Pneuma: The Journal of the Society for Pentecostal Studies* 19 (spring 1997): 29-52, for an excellent review of different historical approaches to reporting Pentecostal origins.

faith. Reports by missionaries then — and now — affirm this link between Pentecostal power and service. As AG scholar and veteran missionary Douglas Petersen describes the situation in a commentary on Macchia's excellent article calling for a paradigm shift in Pentecostal thinking: "From its inception, emphasis upon supernatural empowerment for ministry, observes Macchia, rather than academic formation was the motivational force behind the ever-expanding pastoral and missionary activity of the movement. Characterized by the active participation of its members as 'doers' of the word, assessment of Pentecostalism by themselves or others, according to Macchia, usually focused on their enthusiasm, emotional expressions, or exponential growth."[78] Macchia (and seemingly Petersen) would encourage a shift in emphasis to include the spiritual power underlying Pentecostal missionary activity, particularly the Pentecostal experiences of Spirit baptism and divine healing. "These spiritual encounter moments serve as a corrective antidote for these distinctive theological beliefs which are traditionally embodied within the uncritical constructs and limits of doctrinal guides. When supernatural experiences are integrally linked together with the person of Christ, Macchia argues, they offer potential for Pentecostals to move beyond a personal experience of self-gratification toward becoming part of a prophetic movement for both spiritual and social liberation."[79]

The AG's uncritical acceptance of a conservative political stance, at least in the United States, is not consistent with the nature of the potentially radical Pentecostal experience. The Azusa Street Revival, the event that catapulted the Pentecostal gospel on to the scene, according to some historical accounts empowered blacks and women long before the Civil Rights movement of the 1960s. However, this breaking down of dividing walls was short-lived, as organized Pentecostalism mirrored the same problems of racism and sexism that could be found in the dominant culture.

Sexism, social class inequities, racism, ecumenism, and other issues that captured the attention of liberal Protestantism more than a generation ago are slowly finding their way into AG awareness, causing more ambiguity around the core. Some have heard the challenge offered by scholars like Ronald Bueno, a Salvadorean Pentecostal anthropologist, to begin "listening to the margins"[80] — to reflect on Pentecostalism as it has been constructed by

78. Douglas Petersen, "Changing Paradigms: An Introductory Overview," in *The Globalization of Pentecostalism*, p. 175. Commentary on Macchia, "The Struggle for Global Witness," in the same book.

79. Petersen, "Changing Paradigms," p. 175.

80. Ronald N. Bueno, "Listening to the Margins: Re-historicizing Pentecostal Experiences and Identities," in *The Globalization of Pentecostalism*, pp. 268-88.

different ethnic groups.[81] Others are calling for greater openness to women's issues within Pentecostalism, noting how Pentecostalism's success has limited opportunities for women.[82] Still others have begun working on the challenge of interfaith dialogue as pioneered by the late David du Plessis (an AG minister, who was once defrocked for his ecumenical activity, known as "Mr. Pentecost" for the work he did to present the Pentecostal worldview to mainline churches) and continued by Cecil M. Robeck (an AG minister and professor at Fuller Theological Seminary who continues to serve as a Pentecostal representative to international ecumenical gatherings). The isolationist mentality that has made the AG so wary of "ecumenism" has inadvertently cut off the denomination not only from traditions that could provide much-needed insight for developing a truly Pentecostal theology, but also from fresh revival experiences. As we have discussed, the AG has tended to distance itself from those most likely to share its worldview, namely, neo-Pentecostals in mainstream Protestantism, Roman Catholics, and members of the independent charismatic movement.

There is evidence that the work done by Pentecostal scholars is slowly filtering through some pastors and into the pews, increasing an awareness of the importance of tackling issues beyond the narrow focus of so-called family values. This awareness is not shared by all, thus creating some additional ambiguity around the core of near universally accepted positions. Seventy percent of the pastors, for example, agreed that "issues of social concern really get to the heart of the Gospel." After years of encouraging black Americans to join the largely black "sister" organization, the Church of God in Christ, 93 percent of the pastors agreed or strongly agreed that the "AG should actively work to attract persons of color." Support for women's issues appears to be more divisive. Although the AG has ordained women throughout its history, only 72 percent of pastors support women serving as senior pastors. A smaller percentage (57

---

81. See David D. Daniels, "'Everybody Bids You Welcome': A Multicultural Approach to North American Pentecostalism," in *The Globalization of Pentecostalism*, pp. 222-52.

82. See Sherilyn Benvenutti, "Anointed, Gifted and Called: Pentecostal Women in Ministry," *Pneuma: The Journal of the Society for Pentecostal Studies* 17 (fall 1995): 229-36; Edith Blumhofer, "Reflections on the Source of Aimee Semple McPherson's Voice," *Pneuma: The Journal of the Society for Pentecostal Studies* 17 (spring 1995): 19-24; Janet Meyer Everts, "Brokenness as the Center of a Woman's Ministry," *Pneuma: The Journal of the Society for Pentecostal Studies* 17 (fall 1995): 237-44; Janet Meyer Everts, "'Your Daughters Shall Prophesy': Pentecostal Hermeneutics and the Empowerment of Women," in *The Globalization of Pentecostalism*, pp. 313-37; Deborah M. Gill, "The Contemporary State of Women in Ministry in the Assemblies of God," *Pneuma: The Journal of the Society for Pentecostal Studies* 17 (spring 1995): 33-36; and Margaret M. Poloma, "Charisma, Institutionalization and Social Change," *Pneuma: The Journal of the Society for Pentecostal Studies* 17 (fall 1995): 245-52.

percent) would support women in leadership positions within the national or district AG government or on local church boards (53 percent).

Although the AG has done an admirable job of establishing a loosely knit, cooperative worldwide network that is sensitive to regional and cultural differences, the American church has been relatively homogeneous. The sample of pastors responding to the survey reflects this homogeneity. Only 5 percent of the respondents were female; 97 percent self-identified as "white." Only one respondent was African American, two were Hispanic, two were Asian American, and two were "other." The congregations pastored by these respondents, not surprisingly, tended to be Caucasian, native-born American. Significantly, 6 percent of the congregations were either mostly (3 percent) or entirely (3 percent) comprised of Hispanic Americans. Less than 1 percent were primarily African American congregations, and 1 percent, Asian. The survey fails to capture a change seemingly under way in the ethnic composition of the American AG.

Figures on ten-year church growth of the AG reveal a slight decline in white AG churches during the decade from 1990 to 2000 and a noteworthy increase in the number of ethnic churches (which is responsible for the overall increase in the number of churches and adherents claimed by the AG for the past decade).[83] A document from the newly formed Commission of Ethnic Relations notes:

> Change doesn't happen overnight. It occurs in small stages. It is usually so subtle that it goes undetected until we are overwhelmed by it. Because of this we don't always understand the affect [sic] of change and we don't always know how to respond to change. We don't see it happening and when we look back we wonder how we could have missed it and what we should have done.
>
> I say this because I believe the Assemblies of God is now in the midst of what could be the most dramatic change since the founding of our Fellowship in 1914. I also believe we need to recognize and understand what this change means to us as a fellowship of Pentecostal believers. The change I speak of is not a doctrinal change and it is not a change that poses a threat, but rather an unparalleled opportunity. The change I

83. David J. Moore, director of the AG Center for Ethnic Relations, provided figures showing an increase of black (from 111 to 213), Hispanic (from 1,457 to 1,885), Native American (from 168 to 178), and "other" (from 53 to 125) congregations. "In 1990 ethnic minority congregations and those with no single majority represented 20.2% of all A/G churches. In ten years that has grown to 26.7%. If the current trend remains constant in 2010 they will account for one third of our churches."

speak of is a change in the composition of the church. **We are becoming more ethnic minority.**[84]

Pentecostals have been compelled by social forces to accept the increasingly pluralistic nature of American culture, with the AG being a beneficiary of the new waves of immigration that do promise to change the composition of the church. To date, however, the African Americans, Hispanics, Asians, and "others" are not found in the mainstream of the American AG polity but are often relegated to "special language districts."[85] The change in composition currently under way in the AG will undoubtedly have repercussions for the power dilemma considered in this section as well as the issue of delimitation discussed in the section that preceded.

It would appear, judging from historical accounts of religious isolationism and sometimes racist church policies, that the AG has already lost at least one opportunity to be a catalyst for social change that is consistent with the Pentecostal experience. The jury is still out as to whether it will continue to accept the political agenda of the evangelical subculture without reflecting on its own Pentecostal heritage or whether it will grant a greater voice to those on the margins of society.

The Dilemma of Administrative Order: Elaboration and Alienation

The final dilemma to be discussed brings us back to the brief history presented in the prologue of this article — back to the emergence of the AG and its transition from a "cooperative fellowship" to a denomination with its complex bureaucratic structure. It also returns us to the dilemma of mixed motivation, the first of the five dilemmas to be addressed, and in many ways the most significant one for understanding the AG. O'Dea and Aviad describe the relationship between concerns about the administrative order and mixed motivation as follows: "Since it is this structure of offices which becomes the mechanism for eliciting the mixed motivation . . . and mobilizing it behind organizational goals, the in-

---

84. Commission of Ethnic Relations, "The Church in Transition" (Assemblies of God, Springfield, Mo., 2000, photocopied; no page numbers; emphasis in original).

85. The overwhelming majority of respondents, reflecting their Anglo affiliation, either disagreed (61 percent) or strongly disagreed (28 percent) with the item stating that these special language districts have been detrimental to the AG. A significant minority of pastors, most of whom are themselves "on the margin," do seem to recognize the problems presented by the present structural arrangement.

dividuals involved come to have a vested interest in the structure as it is, and to resist change and reform, which they tend to see as threatening to themselves. Thus not only can the structure become overelaborated and alienated from contemporary problems, but it can contribute to the alienation of office holders from the rank-and-file members of the group."[86] As found in our study of the other four dilemmas, the dilemma of administrative order provides a portrait of the AG as reflecting some ambiguity around a solid core.

Charisma does not exist in pure form but requires some degree of organization to promote and protect her spirit. Despite an earlier resistance to organization, the AG is now a well-structured bureaucracy. At the top of the flowchart is the General Council of the Assemblies of God, clergy and congregational representatives from all member congregations, which gathers every two years. The overall administration of the AG is under the direction of the Executive Presbytery, four elected officers (general superintendent, assistant general superintendent, secretary, and treasurer) who together with various boards, directors, counselors, and committees govern the denomination and minister to its needs. Growth within the AG has led to a proliferation of programs to mobilize groups and resources. These programs embody an evangelistic emphasis, including missions, a drug program, university campus outreach, military and prison chaplaincies; there are also programs that focus on education, including a division of Christian education, Bible and liberal arts colleges, and a publishing house; and service programs adopted by most congregations to provide opportunities for fellowship and learning from cradle to grave. Buffered between the national office and the local congregations are the district offices with bureaus of their own, most of them based on geography but some based on ethnicity or special need (e.g., churches of the deaf). This is the complex organization which attempts to maintain the vision and carry out the mission of the AG — an organization which appears to have the respect and support of a vast majority of AG pastors.

Coherence around the Administrative Core

Whether based on the pastoral survey or an ancillary survey of 250 leaders of regional judicatories,[87] support appears to be solid for the work being carried out by the national and regional governing structures. In the ancillary survey, AG leaders tended to give high marks to the way the church has met ministry

86. O'Dea and Aviad, *Sociology of Religion*, p. 60.
87. Adair Lummis, "Summary of AG Results from the ORW Regional Judicatory Survey" (Hartford Seminary, 2000).

objectives, with only a small minority indicating that denominational effectiveness has decreased over the past five years. We list these objectives (and the percentage disapproving of task performance): providing resources for spiritual revitalization (2 percent), expanding overseas mission efforts and ministries (1 percent), attracting and keeping members in the denomination (14 percent), attracting ethnic minority members in particular (6 percent), maintaining high quality of clergy in local churches (7 percent), keeping unity of purpose within the denomination (10 percent), creating a financially stable national church (0 percent), developing an identity as a global church presence (2 percent), attracting ethnic minority clergy (8 percent), strengthening the health of local churches (9 percent), getting judicatories to share resources with one another (7 percent), and maintaining a denominational identity in local churches (20 percent). When this report card is reviewed internally or compared to those of other groups included in the ORW study, the AG administration appears to pass with high marks.

Similar expectations for and satisfaction with the governance of the denomination can be found in the pastors survey. A majority of pastors indicated the following tasks should be primarily the responsibility of the national office:[88] marshal available resources for world evangelism (91 percent), provide press information on the AG for the secular world (89 percent), serve as a political voice to combat homosexuality and abortion (86 percent), support seminary and Bible colleges (80 percent), safeguard doctrinal conformity (78 percent), support denominational liberal arts colleges (72 percent), develop congregational programs like Royal Rangers, Missionnettes (71 percent), coordinate missionary activities (66 percent), promote renewal/revival (60 percent), serve as a political voice to elect God-fearing candidates to public office (59 percent), and develop suitable educational resources for local congregations (58 percent).

The vast majority of the respondents were knowledgeable about the denominational work being done in the realm of missions and evangelism, and expressed strong approval of this work. Approval ratings between "good" and "excellent" were awarded to the Division of Foreign Missions, followed closely by three other evangelism programs: Teen Challenge, for drug and alcohol addiction; Speed the Light, for young people; and Light for the Lost, a more general evangelical support program. The vast majority of the pastors also re-

---

88. The survey question providing this information asked, "Which of the following tasks are best performed by the national office, which by the district office, and which are not appropriate for either denominational administrative office?" The three options were: National, District, and Not Appropriate.

ported being knowledgeable about and gave positive ratings to publications and Christian education programs developed by the national office. The weekly magazine *Pentecostal Evangel* and the work of Gospel Publishing House were both rated between good and excellent, with the Division of Christian Education receiving a slightly lower approval rating, midway between fair and good.

Two years after his election to the top church post in 1995, General Superintendent Thomas E. Trask noted that he wanted denomination programs to serve churches rather than have churches serve a denominational bureaucracy. Trask told *Charisma* magazine, the major publication for the PCM, "We want to address the needs of the local church and the pastor. We want to be known as servants of the local church."[89] For the most part, it appears that pastors and leaders give high marks for such effort. At the same time, as with each of the dilemmas, there are areas of ambiguity and potential alienation that merit some note.

Administrative Ambiguity and Potential Alienation

Given the history of the AG and its resolution not to become a denomination, perhaps it is not surprising that the report card provided by the pastoral survey on the administrative dilemma includes a few lower grades. There is a seeming and possibly increasing alienation among pastors from the national office, particularly if measured by decreased attendance at the biannual General Council meetings. Only 40 percent strongly agreed (4 percent) or agreed (36 percent) with the statement, "I always do whatever I possibly can do to attend General Council meetings." Another statement may provide a key for understanding the seeming apathy toward this once important gathering. Forty-six percent either agreed (10 percent) or strongly agreed (36 percent) that the General Council "does not provide an adequate forum for discussing differing opinions on key issues." In informal discussions, some AG pastors are quick to raise the Pensacola revival and "initial evidence" as examples of failures to hear differing opinions on these currently hot topics. These pastors also say they prefer to use their time and money going to conferences (very often outside the denomination) which are more relevant to their ministries than those of the AG. A concern about the AG becoming a denomination in a post-denominational society can also be heard in the pastoral survey. Over half (54 percent) the pastors agreed or strongly agreed with the statement that the AG needs to "focus more on being a religious network and less on being a denom-

89. Marcia Ford, "Trask Puts New Face on Assemblies," *Charisma*, July 1995, p. 62.

ination." My informal discussions with pastors suggest that many would like the denomination to do more to provide opportunities for fellowship and spiritual growth.

The AG has historically been ambivalent about higher education, and the survey responses may be reflecting current ambivalence — or possibly indifference — to the sponsorship of higher education by the denomination. Although a majority of pastors agreed that it was the responsibility of the national office to provide support for its colleges and seminary, over 40 percent of the respondents did not feel they knew enough about the denomination's colleges in Springfield, Missouri (where the AG national headquarters is located), to provide a rating, and 38 percent were unable to rate the seminary. The mean ratings for Evangel College, Central Bible College, and the Assemblies of God Theological Seminary were "fair" (with mean scores of 1.2, 1.8, and 2 respectively, on a 4-point scale). Pastors were most familiar with Berean University, the correspondence course designed to train AG ministers, giving it the highest ratings for the work done in the educational realm (mean = 2.3).

Silence, as suggested above in the discussion of AG institutions of higher education, may provide a porthole for discerning dissatisfaction. While fewer than 5 percent of respondents were unable to provide a scorecard for ministries like Gospel Publishing House, the Division of Foreign Missions, and the *Pentecostal Evangel,* this form of "no response" was fairly high for the Executive Presbytery and the General Presbytery. Twenty-two percent of the pastors were reluctant (reportedly unable because of a lack of knowledge) to rate the job being done by the Executive Presbytery or the General Presbytery. The mean scores for those who did rate them were somewhere between "good" and "fair," with means of 2.4 and 2.5 respectively.

Despite many comments I have heard over the years about the increased centralization of the AG, such hearsay appears to be the report of a minority (31 percent). Most pastors strongly disagreed (8 percent) or disagreed (61 percent) with the statement that "too much power is being centralized in the National Office." Respondents were nearly divided in whether their churches made "extensive use of the services provided by the National Office," with 56 percent either agreeing (51 percent) or strongly agreeing (5 percent).

Pastors seem to be somewhat more supportive of their respective district offices than of the national office. Given their dependence on and expectations of the district to provide networking opportunities (including nominations for church positions), they appear more likely to attend their district council meetings than the national General Assembly. Seventy-one percent strongly agreed or agreed that district councils "are a good investment of my time." Use of district office services appears to be strong, with 84 percent of the ministers strongly disagreeing (26 percent) or disagreeing (58 percent) with the statement, "I cannot find any service provided by the District Office that is of particular use to my congregation."

The services the majority of pastors expect from their district offices include the following: opportunities for pastoral fellowship (88 percent), workshops for ongoing pastoral training (73 percent), establishing appropriate networks for pastors (70 percent), providing resources for smaller churches (68 percent), providing pastoral/congregational "covering" (64 percent), developing programs to encourage pastoral spiritual growth (52 percent), and providing credentials for ministers (51 percent). The last item is of special interest given the fact that the national office provides the credentials, taking over even more authority after the disagreement between the Louisiana District and the National Headquarters over the Jimmy Swaggart censure in the 1980s. Only 48 percent of the pastors indicated support for the national credentialing of ministers, with 1 percent indicating that neither judicatory should be involved in this work.

Charisma and Administration

From its inception as a formal organization in 1914, adherents of the AG have had a love-hate relationship with institutionalization. Although the leaders of this new religious movement recognized the need for organizing to carry on its mission, they also recognized the perils structure would pose to their fragile newfound gift of charisma. The healthy tension that could be observed over the years in the AG continues today. Many are wary of the threat that administrative offices pose to charisma, but many also trust the Holy Spirit to lead both congregations and denominational administrative offices.

When pastors were asked, "To what extent does the manifest presence (e.g. prophetic leadings, tongues and interpretations, etc.) of the Spirit affect the decision making process of your local congregation?" only 19 percent reported "greatly" with another 54 percent replying "somewhat." Twenty-seven percent, a significant minority for a denomination whose identity is rooted in a worldview that has historically recognized the power of the Holy Spirit, responded "not at all." A clear majority of pastors report that the Holy Spirit guides the leaders and workers in various bureaus, agreeing (58 percent) or strongly agreeing (11 percent) that the "Holy Spirit directly affects the decision making process in most AG administrative agencies." Once again, however, a significant minority (31 percent) appear to regard the day-to-day operations of the denomination much like they might regard the workings of any modern secular organization.

Summary and Conclusion

> The Assemblies of God structure is sufficiently flexible and tolerant of am-
> biguity for the continued presence of charisma. The siren of accommoda-
> tive forces, however, can deafen believers to the whisper of charismatic
> voices, dreams, and visions. Waiting quietly and patiently for the leading of
> God is not readily compatible with the contemporary American culture,
> where instant lottery winners are heroes and fast-food chains a main ex-
> port. Worldly models of growth and success have subtly made inroads in
> this denomination that once sought to be separate from the world.[90]

The AG contains a solid core of beliefs and practices, with a healthy level of tension around peripheral issues. Its growing ethnic diversity positions it for an
even more visible place in the American religious mosaic of the twenty-first
century. The report cards provided by both the pastoral and judicatory surveys
demonstrate a solid core of pastoral support for the administrative functioning
of the denomination. Charisma and institutionalization, at least in the minds
of a majority of pastors, are still interwoven some eighty-five years after the
AG's founding.

The ambiguity found around the central core for each of O'Dea's five institutional dilemmas, however, provides some guidelines for charting the future. Perhaps the greatest challenge faced by the AG is what might be termed its
"identity crisis." There is a need for a paradigm shift — a move away from the
old modernist, doctrinal paradigm (embraced in word but not necessarily in
deed by earlier leaders) in favor of a new paradigm that could embody and empower the distinctive identity that is AG history and experience. Pentecostalism
is more than "evangelicalism plus tongues," and to limit it in this way robs the
AG of its rich identity. Globally the PCM has become a "third stream" within
Christianity as distinct from other streams as Catholicism is from Protestantism. (The uniqueness of the Pentecostal movement is particularly apparent
when it is removed from the American culture where it developed and from
where it spread and placed within the larger global culture where it is said to account for some one in four Christians.)

If the AG is going to be a major player in the American religious mosaic
in the twenty-first century, it will require a paradigm that can reflect its unique
qualities, qualities that fit better a postmodern paradigm than a modern one.
Among other things, Pentecostalism has made the common experience of the
divine available to a spiritually starved materialistic culture, taught the mean-

---

90. Poloma, *Crossroads*, p. 209.

ing of paradox to a Western world steeped in propositional logic, revived a sense of miracle and mystery among people trapped in the cage of rationality, and provided opportunities for catharsis in a civilization fearful of emotion. Increasingly AG identity, however, is expressed in terms of rational doctrine that masks the playful creative Spirit its believers have encountered during the last one hundred years of Pentecostalism's existence. The mixed motivation generated by the ambiguities in Pentecostal identity lies at the heart of the routinization of charisma.

While new paradigms reflecting a Pentecostal worldview are being embraced by more recent "waves" of the PCM, a significant number of AG pastors and their churches seem to be caught in a web of de facto dispensationalist-evangelical theology and its modern paradigm. These cultural Pentecostals are proclaiming a distinct identity but looking more and more like evangelicals in their beliefs and religious practices. Despite an overwhelming proclamation of the need to revitalize early Pentecostal roots, the revival at Brownsville Assembly of God and other AG and non-AG revival sites failed to interest two-thirds of the pastors enough to personally check out any of these events. With an identity shaped more by evangelical writings than by experiences of their black Pentecostal brothers or their charismatic cousins, it is perhaps not surprising that charismatic expressions and experiences are becoming less intense and less frequent at the average Assembly of God.

This failure to develop a consistent Pentecostal theology within an appropriate paradigm has made it difficult to affirm revivals within its own churches and renewal movements outside its boundaries. While some congregations have embraced fresh wind and fire, for the most part the reaction toward the new "waves" of charisma has been to critique and to tighten control on dissonant theologians and ministers who lacked a large congregational power base. The tendency to quench charisma can be most clearly seen in our discussion of the dilemma of delimitation. On one horn of the dilemma we find the watering down of Pentecostal identity due to inevitable accommodative forces; on the other, attempts to control ministers through doctrinal edicts in hopes of making them more "Pentecostal."

Also to be learned from assessing charismatic routinization through the lenses of O'Dea's dilemmas is how accommodative forces have eroded any distinct political voice that could have developed from a well-articulated Pentecostal theology and sense of Pentecostal history. The experiences of the early Pentecostals that challenged the sexist and racist culture of early-twentieth-century America could have paved the way for later disciples to make significant contributions to changes in women's roles and civil rights. Its early pacifist stance could have provided a plank for the peace movement. Its suspicion of rigid denominationalism in the face of a democratized baptism of the Spirit could have provided a platform for ecumenical activities. None of this happened, in part due to the isolation of Pentecostals during the first half of the twentieth century. Once they moved across the tracks to a more comfortable lifestyle, contemporary followers lost sight of Pentecostalism's unique identity as a marginalized people upon whom the Spirit released his power and presence in the earliest years of the twentieth century. As they made the journey from pilgrims to citizens, AG pastors seemed to take on the political voice of the fundamentalist-evangelical church expressed through the Republican Party.

The bureaucratic structure of the AG and its programs to serve churches and pastors have, for the most part, been rated well by pastors, especially in the area of missions and evangelism, including publications and church programs. As we have seen, pastors gave high marks to most of these services provided by the denomination. There is some indication, however, that some may feel that leaders have lost touch with the local churches (as reflected in increasingly fewer pastors making attendance at General Council meetings a priority). The reluctance of pastors to rate educational facilities and the performance of the Executive Presbytery is another indication of some estrangement between the national office and AG pastors.

In many respects the AG educational institutions are on the periphery of the organizational structure, a remnant of the ambivalence Pentecostals have traditionally had toward higher education. This is unfortunate. A long-range proactive approach toward appropriate self-definition could include harnessing some of the leading faculty in AG universities and the Assemblies of God Theological Seminary to help executives develop a distinct Pentecostal identity that goes beyond the doctrine of glossolalia as "initial evidence." The administrative offices could then be agents of disseminating the information and receiving feedback that would ensure that the articulation of Pentecostal identity would always be a dynamic process rather than perceived as a finished product.

The ambiguities reported in this study that exist around near universal attitudes and opinions can be regarded as indicators of vitality and catalysts for change within the AG. Tension and ambiguity are signs of life and are often positively functional for organizations. In allowing for the expression of differences and nurturing existing pluralism, the mechanisms of change are set in motion that can revitalize institutions. Since no institution can remain static and survive, some of the minority positions discussed in this paper may serve as catalysts of change that will assure that the AG remains true to its mission and identity.

The Assemblies of God is a religion where experience of the mystical is more than a memory, where the pragmatic and the supernatural can dance together in a worldview that transcends the premodern/modern dichotomy. Its structure and polity is permeable enough to ensure a medium for the charismatic play of the Spirit. Whether it can continue to surf the tension required to balance charisma with effective organization is the question that still begs an answer.

References

Albrecht, Daniel E. *Ties in the Spirit: A Ritual Approach to Pentecostal/Charismatic Spirituality.* Sheffield, U.K.: Sheffield Academic Press, 1999.
Benvenutti, Sherilyn. "Anointed, Gifted and Called: Pentecostal Women in Ministry." *Pneuma: The Journal of the Society for Pentecostal Studies* 17 (fall 1995): 229-36.
Berger, Peter L. *The Heretical Imperative.* Garden City, N.Y.: Anchor Press/ Doubleday, 1979.
Blumhofer, Edith. *The Assemblies of God: A Chapter in the Story of American Pentecostalism.* Vol. 2, *Since 1941.* Springfield, Mo.: Gospel Publishing House, 1989.
———. *Restoring the Faith: The Assemblies of God, Pentecostalism, and American Culture.* Urbana and Chicago: University of Illinois Press, 1993.
———. "Reflections on the Source of Aimee Semple McPherson's Voice." *Pneuma: The Journal of the Society for Pentecostal Studies* 17 (spring 1995): 19-24.
Bridges, James K. "The Full Consummation of the Baptism in the Holy Spirit." *Theological Enrichment,* 2000, pp. 92-95.
Bueno, Ronald N. "Listening to the Margins: Re-historicizing Pentecostal Experiences and Identities." In *The Globalization of Pentecostalism: A Religion Made to Travel,* edited by M. W. Dempster, B. D. Klaus, and D. Petersen, pp. 268-88. Carlisle, U.K.: Regnum Books International, Paternoster Publishing, 1999.
Cagel, Timothy B. "Beyond the Fundamentalist-Modernist Controversy: Pentecostals and Hermeneutics in a Postmodern Age." *Pneuma: The Journal for Pentecostal Studies* 15 (fall 1993): 163-87.
Campolo, Tony. *How to Be Pentecostal without Speaking in Tongues.* Waco: Word, 1994.
Cerillo, Augustus. "Interpretive Approaches to the History of American Pentecostal Origins." *Pneuma: The Journal for Pentecostal Studies* 19 (spring 1997): 29-52.
Coser, Lewis A. *Functions of Social Conflict.* Glencoe, Ill.: Free Press, 1956.

————. *Continuities in the Study of Social Conflict.* Glencoe, Ill.: Free Press, 1967.

Cox, Harvey. *Fire from Heaven: The Rise of Pentecostal Spirituality and the Reshaping of Religion in the Twenty-First Century.* Reading, Mass.: Addison-Wesley, 1995.

Daniels, David D. "'Everybody Bids You Welcome': A Multicultural Approach to North American Pentecostalism." In *The Globalization of Pentecostalism: A Religion Made to Travel,* edited by M. W. Dempster, B. D. Klaus, and D. Petersen, pp. 222-52. Carlisle, U.K.: Regnum Books International, Paternoster Publishing, 1999.

Deutscher, Irwin. *What We Say/What We Do: Sentiments and Acts.* New York: Aldine de Gruyter, 1973.

Deutscher, Irwin, Fred P. Pestello, and Frances G. Pestello. *Sentiments and Acts.* New York: Aldine de Gruyter, 1993.

Di Sabatino, David. *The Jesus People Movement: An Annotated Bibliography and General Resource.* Westport, Conn.: Greenwood Press, 1999.

Donaldson, Hal. "Labeling Churches." *Pentecostal Evangel* 8 (June 1997): 4.

Doty, Sherri, and Efraim Espinoza. "FACT Survey Analysis: A 2000 Survey of Assemblies of God Churches." General Council of the Assemblies of God, 2000.

Eisenstadt, S. N. Introduction to *Max Weber on Charisma and Institution Building.* Chicago: University of Chicago Press, 1969.

Everts, Janet Meyer. "Brokenness as the Center of a Woman's Ministry." *Pneuma: The Journal of the Society for Pentecostal Studies* 17 (fall 1995): 237-44.

————. "'Your Daughters Shall Prophesy': Pentecostal Hermeneutics and the Empowerment of Women." In *The Globalization of Pentecostalism: A Religion Made to Travel,* edited by M. W. Dempster, B. D. Klaus, and D. Petersen, pp. 313-37. Carlisle, U.K.: Regnum Books International, Paternoster Publishing, 1999.

Ford, Marcia. "Trask Puts New Face on Assemblies." *Charisma,* July 1995, pp. 62-63.

Gill, Deborah M. "The Contemporary State of Women in Ministry in the Assemblies of God." *Pneuma: The Journal of the Society for Pentecostal Studies* 17 (spring 1995): 33-36.

Green, John C., James L. Guth, Corwin E. Smidt, and Lyman A. Kellstedt. *Religion and the Culture Wars.* Lanham, Md.: Rowman and Littlefield, 1997.

Grudem, Wayne, ed. *Are Miraculous Gifts for Today? Four Views.* Grand Rapids: Zondervan, 1996.

Guth, James L., John C. Green, Corwin E. Smidt, Lyman A. Kellstedt, and Margaret M. Poloma. *The Bully Pulpit: The Politics of Protestant Clergy.* Lawrence: University of Kansas Press, 1997.

Hollenweger, Walter J. *Pentecostalism: Origins and Developments Worldwide.* Peabody, Mass.: Hendrickson, 1997.

————. "Roman Catholics and Pentecostals in Dialogue." *Pneuma: The Journal for Pentecostal Studies* 21 (spring 1999): 135-54.

Hyatt, Eddie L. *2000 Years of Charismatic Christianity.* Tulsa: Hyatt International Ministries, 1996.

Johns, Jackie David. "Yielding to the Spirit: The Dynamics of a Pentecostal Model of Praxis." In *The Globalization of Pentecostalism: A Religion Made to Travel,* edited by M. W. Dempster, B. D. Klaus, and D. Petersen, pp. 70-84. Carlisle, U.K.: Regnum Books International, Paternoster Publishing, 1999.

Land, Steven. *Pentecostal Spirituality: A Passion for the Kingdom.* Sheffield, U.K.: Sheffield Academic Press, 1993.

Ma, Wonsuk. "Biblical Studies in the Pentecostal Tradition: Yesterday, Today and Tomorrow." In *The Globalization of Pentecostalism: A Religion Made to Travel,* edited by M. W. Dempster, B. D. Klaus, and D. Petersen, pp. 52-69. Carlisle, U.K.: Regnum Books International, Paternoster Publishing, 1999.

Macchia, Frank D. "The Struggle for Global Witness: Shifting Paradigms in Pentecostal Theology." In *The Globalization of Pentecostalism: A Religion Made to Travel,* edited by M. W. Dempster, B. D. Klaus, and D. Petersen, pp. 8-29. Carlisle, U.K.: Regnum Books International, Paternoster Publishing, 1999.

McClung, L. Grant, Jr. "'Try to Get People Saved': Revisiting the Paradigm of an Urgent Pentecostal Missiology." In *The Globalization of Pentecostalism: A Religion Made to Travel,* edited by M. W. Dempster, B. D. Klaus, and D. Petersen, pp. 30-51. Carlisle, U.K.: Regnum Books International, Paternoster Publishing, 1999.

McGee, Gary B. "'Latter Rain' Falling in the East: Early-Twentieth-Century Pentecostalism in India and the Debate over Speaking in Tongues." *American Society of Church History* 68 (fall 1999): 648-65.

————. "Initial Evidence." In *New International Dictionary of the Pentecostal and Charismatic Movements,* edited by Stanley M. Burgess. Grand Rapids: Zondervan, 2000.

Menzies, Glen. "Tongues as 'The Initial Physical Sign' of Spirit Baptism in the Thought of D. W. Kerr." *Pneuma: The Journal of the Society for Pentecostal Studies* 20 (fall 1998): 174-89.

Menzies, William W. *Anointed to Serve: The Story of the Assemblies of God.* Springfield, Mo.: Gospel Publishing House, 1971.

Miller, Donald E. *Reinventing American Protestantism.* Berkeley: University of California Press, 1997.

O'Dea, Thomas. "Sociological Dilemmas in the Institutionalization of Religion." *Journal for the Scientific Study of Religion* 1 (1961): 30-41.

O'Dea, Thomas, and Janet O'Dea Aviad. *The Sociology of Religion.* 2nd ed. Englewood Cliffs, N.J.: Prentice-Hall, 1983.

Petersen, Douglas. "Changing Paradigms: An Introductory Overview." In *The Globalization of Pentecostalism: A Religion Made to Travel,* edited by M. W. Dempster, B. D. Klaus, and D. Petersen, pp. 3-8. Carlisle, U.K.: Regnum Books International, Paternoster Publishing, 1999.

Poloma, Margaret M. *The Charismatic Movement: Is There a New Pentecost?* Boston: Twayne Publishing Co., 1982.

————. *The Assemblies of God at the Crossroads: Charisma and Institutional Dilemmas.* Knoxville: University of Tennessee Press, 1989.

————. "Charisma, Institutionalization and Social Change." *Pneuma: The Journal of the Society for Pentecostal Studies* 17 (fall 1995): 245-52.

————. "The 'Toronto Blessing': Charisma, Institutionalization and Revival." *Journal for the Scientific Study of Religion* 37, no. 2 (1997): 257-71.

————. "Inspecting the Fruit of the 'Toronto Blessing': A Sociological Assessment." *Pneuma: The Journal for the Society for Pentecostal Studies* 20, no. 1 (1998): 43-70.

————. "The Spirit Movement in North America at the Millennium: From Azusa Street to Toronto, Pensacola and Beyond." *Journal of Pentecostal Theology* 37, no. 2 (1998): 253-73.

————. "Mysticism as a Social Construct: Religious Experience in Pentecostal/ Charismatic Context." Paper presented at the annual meetings of the Association for the Sociology of Religion, Anaheim, Calif., 2001.

Poloma, Margaret M., and Brian F. Pendleton. "Religious Experiences and Institutional Growth within the Assemblies of God." *Journal for the Scientific Study of Religion* 24 (winter 1989): 415-31.

Robeck, Cecil M., Jr. "The Holy Spirit and Ecumenism." Paper presented at a symposium on the Holy Spirit and ecumenism sponsored by the Cardinal Suenens Foundation, Leuven, Belgium, December 1999.

————. "Pentecostals and Ecumenism in a Pluralistic World." In *The Globalization of Pentecostalism: A Religion Made to Travel,* edited by M. W. Dempster, B. D. Klaus, and D. Petersen, pp. 338-62. Carlisle, U.K.: Regnum Books International, Paternoster Publishing, 1999.

————. "Toward Healing Our Divisions: Reflecting on Pentecostal Diversity and Common Witness." Paper presented at the 28th Annual Meeting of the Society of Pentecostal Studies, March 11-13, 1999.

Ruthven, Jon. "Book Review: Wayne Grudem, ed., *Are Miraculous Gifts for Today?*" *Pneuma: The Journal for the Society of Pentecostal Studies* 21, no. 1 (1999): 155-58.

Schmidt, David J., and Mike Messner. "Interview with J. David Schmidt and Mike Messner: Shaping the Vision." *Enrichment,* winter 2000, pp. 54-57.

Shepherd, Gerald T. "Pentecostals and the Hermeneutics of Dispensationalism: The Anatomy of an Uneasy Relationship." *Pneuma: The Journal for Pentecostal Studies* 6 (fall 1984).

Spittler, Russell P. "Are Pentecostals and Charismatics Fundamentalists? A Review of American Uses of These Categories." In *Charismatic Christianity as a Global Culture,* edited by Karla Poewe. Columbia: University of South Carolina Press, 1994.

Suurmond, Jean Jacques. *Word and Spirit at Play: Towards a Charismatic Theology.* London: SCM, 1994.

Taves, Ann. *Fits, Trances, and Visions.* Princeton: Princeton University Press, 1999.

Trask, Thomas E. "My Vision for the Twenty-First Century." *Enrichment: A Journal for Pentecostal Ministry,* winter 2000, pp. 8-9.

Wacker, Grant. *Heaven Below: Early Pentecostals and American Culture.* Cambridge: Harvard University Press, 2001.

Walker, Andrew. Foreword to *Pentecostals in Britain,* by William K. Kay, pp. vii-ix. Carlisle, U.K.: Paternoster Press, 2000.

Wilson, Everett A. "They Crossed the Red Sea, Didn't They? Critical History and Pentecostal Beginnings." In *The Globalization of Pentecostalism: A Religion Made to Travel,* edited by M. W. Dempster, B. D. Klaus, and D. Petersen, pp. 85-115. Carlisle, U.K.: Regnum Books International, Paternoster Publishing, 1999.

The Challenges of Organization and Spirit in the Implementation of Theology in the Assemblies of God

William W. Menzies

The modern Pentecostal movement began in 1901 in Charles F. Parham's informal Bible school in Topeka, Kansas (cf. the Gary B. McGee historical introduction, pp. 35-44). This is the point from which a connected historical narrative can be traced. It was here that the identifying characteristic of the movement was formed, a self-understanding that identified the phenomenon of speaking in other tongues as the accompanying biblical witness of Spirit baptism. This religious experience had been reported in a variety of settings over a period of some years, but it was not until the events in Topeka transpired that the meaning of these experiences was articulated, giving an ideological framework for the movement that soon developed.

The modern Pentecostal revival was propelled onto the stage of world events through the remarkable meetings that took place in Los Angeles from 1906 to 1909. This is generally known as the Azusa Street Revival. A black Holiness preacher, William J. Seymour, was the leader of the Azusa Street Meeting. Parham's attempt to control events in Los Angeles was rebuffed by Seymour and his followers, and with his repudiation in Los Angeles, his influence quickly waned. By 1910 Seymour had also been displaced by other charismatic figures, both in Los Angeles and elsewhere around the world. In effect, the revival had outgrown these early leaders. A worldwide network emerged almost at once. It should be noted that there was really no single "father" of the modern Pentecostal movement. What gave a sense of identity was the belief that believers should seek for and expect to receive a baptism in the Holy Spirit, and that they would know they had the full biblical experience when they spoke in other tongues. The common expectation was that God was pouring out his Spirit once again, just as he did in the book of Acts.

This revival, although so startling in some of its implications that it was often referred to as the "Latter Rain," was in reality an extension of common strands evident in American evangelicalism at the turn of the century. Some assert that the Pentecostal revival is a form of Restorationism.[1] To be sure, many of the earliest Pentecostals thought what they were experiencing was so remarkable that it was in truth a recovery of the purity of the apostolic church. Many of the early Pentecostal assemblies adopted the name "Apostolic Faith" as a witness to this conviction. In fact, however, virtually everything was already in place for the birth of the Pentecostal revival. Pentecostal groups that formed denominations, such as the Assemblies of God (AG), borrowed nearly everything from other Christian bodies, such as church polity and the full panoply of fundamentalist theology, including the Scofieldian dispensational system of hermeneutics. That fundamentalist dispensationalism was inherently anti-Pentecostal was no problem for AG scholars like Frank M. Boyd and Ralph M. Riggs. They gave Scofieldian premillennialism a "Pentecostal baptism." For them, the hiatus of the church age — the parenthesis between dispensations — instead of being shorn of the possibility of gifts of the Spirit (as the fundamentalists taught), became the age *of* the Spirit![2]

American evangelicalism had promoted the concept of a crisis experience of the Spirit subsequent to new birth as available to all believers. The concept "baptism in the Holy Spirit" had been popularized in American Christianity from the time of Phoebe Palmer in the 1830s. By 1875, revivalist Charles G. Finney was promoting this teaching. Wesleyan Holiness advocates were inclined to see baptism in the Spirit as a useful way of expressing the "second blessing" of entire sanctification. Many evangelicals from non-Wesleyan groups, however, employed this term to identify a crisis experience of empowerment for Christian witness, for evangelism and missions. Comparing the Baptist A. J. Gordon's *The Ministry of the Holy Spirit*,[3] published in 1895, with the Statement of Fundamental Truths adopted as the theological platform of the AG in 1916, one notices a striking parallel in virtually every respect but one. The only clearly different understanding lies in the attachment of speaking in other tongues to the baptism in the Holy Spirit. Gordon did not make this connection, but the early Pentecostals did. It is precisely here that the identity of the modern Pentecostal movement is to be distinguished.

The Pentecostal movement has grown at an astonishing rate. Although

1. Edith Blumhofer, *The Assemblies of God: A Chapter in the Story of American Pentecostalism* (Springfield, Mo.: Gospel Publishing House, 1989), 1:18-22.

2. William W. Menzies, *Anointed to Serve: The Story of the Assemblies of God* (Springfield, Mo.: Gospel Publishing House, 1971), pp. 328-29, which describes the Pentecostal revision of fundamentalist dispensationalism.

3. A. J. Gordon, *The Ministry of the Holy Spirit* (Philadelphia: Judson, 1894; reprint, 1950).

at the beginning of the second century of the Pentecostal revival there is no longer total agreement on the doctrine of the normative sign of tongues as the biblical criterion for Spirit baptism ("initial physical evidence"), nonetheless this is still the most widely held view among Pentecostals worldwide. Certainly this is true among the thirty million adherents to the many autonomous national AG bodies.

It is important to note a major difference between the modern charismatic movement and the Pentecostal movement. The Pentecostal movement highlights the experience of baptism in the Holy Spirit, understood to be an enduing of power for evangelism and missions. The charismatic movement, appearing on the scene from about 1955 onward, is best understood as openness to the charisms of the Spirit, specifically the manifestations enumerated in 1 Corinthians 12:8-10. Although Pentecostals make abundant room for the manifestations or gifts of the Spirit, a higher priority is given to the experience of baptism in the Spirit with the expectation that the participants will be deeply involved in ministry of one kind or another. Charismatics may or may not speak of a baptism in the Spirit, and not many of those who do make a necessary connection between that experience and speaking in tongues. Most charismatics would say that speaking in tongues is "normal" but not "normative."[4]

The Ethos of the Assemblies of God

Because the AG is strongly experientially oriented, its membership and leadership have not generally been overly concerned about the niceties of theological distinctions. Instead, the worldview of Pentecostals is best appreciated by examining its common practices. These practices reveal much about deeply felt values, values that do not readily translate into a set of doctrinal statements. An important means for capturing this worldview is to construct at least a brief description of typical worship patterns and other practices that are of central concern to this body of believers. Hopefully, such an introduction may promote an understanding of the belief structure of this denomination's adherents.

Over the years the AG has gone through considerable change. It is not worthwhile to stereotype a group as diverse as the AG particularly because of the high value placed on the autonomy of the local church. In a given city with

---

4. William W. Menzies, "A Taxonomy of Contemporary Pentecostal-Charismatic Theologies" (lecture delivered at the Society for Pentecostal Studies, Valley Forge, Pa., December 1978), which provides a chart identifying theological views of a variety of charismatic and evangelical scholars.

several AG churches, each will have its own identity marked by differing socio-economic profiles, ethnic origins, or tastes in music and worship style. Nonetheless, there are common values that are deeply shared and to some degree will be recognized in nearly all local AG churches. I have identified here some of the prominent characteristics that mark local churches. To a large degree, these characteristics are the practical implementation of the belief structure of these people. Later I will address those points that appear to be evidence of ambiguity and dissonance.

The local church is the primary arena for experiencing the manifestations of the Spirit. It is not surprising that the AG features a fairly strong sense of congregational church polity. Nevertheless, such localism is constrained by credentialing and disciplining of ordained ministers at the regional and national levels, reflecting a unique adaptation of presbyterial polity. In truth, then, the AG is really a hybrid of congregational and presbyterial structures. The focus, however, is clearly on the local church. The denomination is seen at its best in facilitating the work of the local church.

Pentecostals expect the Holy Spirit to break into any public gathering, be it an annual district council session, the biennial General Council, or a local assembly. It is the local church, however, that nurtures encounters with the Holy Spirit. It is here that parishioners are most likely to experience the activity of the Holy Spirit. In fact, a great attraction to AG churches is an environment conducive to the "flow of the Spirit." Few churches provide a printed order of service. This does not mean there is not a generally accepted pattern in the church service, but rather that the familiar routine is held tentatively, with the expectation that God might interrupt the meeting with an utterance in the Spirit, an interpretation of a "message in tongues," a prophecy, a word of wisdom, or a word of knowledge. Every service is expected to be marked by a degree of spontaneity. The generally recognized pattern that provides a sense of order is usually understood to be an opening prayer, group singing, special music, an offering and an offertory, a time of special intercessory prayer, and then a sermon. At the conclusion of the sermon, the pastor issues an altar call followed by a benediction. Following evening meetings, there is usually a time of prayer available for those seeking something from God, conducted around the altar at the front of the church or in an adjacent prayer room. This "after service" is usually confined to Sunday evening or Wednesday evening sessions since the Sunday morning service usually does not permit time for such protracted meetings in view of the impending dinner hour.

The style of worship varies considerably depending on geographical location and the level of sophistication of the congregation. The music and the form of worship, albeit attuned to the needs and tastes of the group, are designed to elevate individuals into an exalted state of praise and worship. This is often reflected by the raising of hands and, in some cases, individuals rising to sing while others sit quietly by. The content of the music in more recent years has moved away from the classic hymnal, with its mixture of traditional hymns and gospel songs, and toward the popular worship choruses generated by groups like Calvary Chapel or Hillsong from Australia. It is here that influences from the charismatic movement are clearly evident. Most churches have a means of projecting on a screen the music to be sung (choruses or hymns) for the convenience of the congregation. Conspicuous is the exuberant participation of the congregation in singing. One will observe some people singing (perhaps with eyes closed, as in prayer), some raising their hands, and most standing during at least part of the worship time. Intensity, enthusiasm, and participation characterize the worship.

In most AG churches prayer is a significant part of the church service. The services are punctuated by occasions when special prayer is offered, often with laypersons leading the prayer and the rest of the congregation audibly participating. During these times of "concert prayer," some may be praying in tongues. This time of corporate prayer is in reality a chorus of many private prayers being offered simultaneously. It is evident that the people are comfortable praying aloud and spontaneously. They are talking to God and they know it. Although it does not occur in all services, the pastor also fulfills the injunction to pray for the sick (James 5:14-15). The pastor will have a bottle of olive oil with which he anoints those who come forward at the designated time for such prayer, and elders of the church along with pastoral associates join him in laying hands on those seeking healing. The weekly periodical of the AG, the *Pentecostal Evangel,* regularly reports testimonies of divine intervention, often citing remarkable healings that have been authenticated by medical personnel. (Changing views on the theology of divine healing are addressed later in this paper.)

The content of AG preaching is clearly christocentric. It is widely understood that the work of the Holy Spirit is best seen as pointing to Christ (John 15:26). There is no prescribed liturgical calendar to govern the preaching in the local churches, but encouragement is provided for pastors to highlight the person and work of the Holy Spirit during the annual Pentecost season. That such encouragement is felt to be needed signifies that preaching on the Pentecostal experience of baptism in the Holy Spirit certainly is not the preoccupation of the ministers in the fellowship. AG ministers regularly subscribe in their annual credentials-renewal papers to the full list of doctrines cited in the *Statement of Fundamental Truths,* which is a thoroughly trinitarian document. The preaching of AG ministers is centered in Christ, followed by attention to the varied ministries of the Holy Spirit. It might be noted that although primary attention is given to preaching about Christ with substantial attention given to the person and work of the Holy Spirit, there does not seem to be commensurate attention devoted to the doctrine of God the Father.[5]

Church architecture is significant. The design of buildings, whether rural, small-church structures or urban, large-church facilities, expresses the theology of the immanence of God. The message is clear: God can be experienced in this place. The small-town church has bright lighting, large windows, simple platform layout with a pulpit in the center, and a bench across the front of the church below the platform. This is called the altar, understood as the place where people meet God in vital ways. These structural forms suggest that in this place God is accessible. Larger cities are likely to have grand structures, but the auditorium is arranged so that everyone seems to be near the pulpit. The balcony is likely to have steps descending to the main sanctuary near the platform area so that respondents to the altar calls can readily come forward. A generous area is provided below and in front of the platform so that many people can crowd forward for group prayer at the conclusion of a service. The platform area is usually quite large, giving space not only for a substantial choir but for musical instruments as well. Space for full drum sets, a piano, an organ, and various other instruments is typical. Many churches have a baptistry artfully placed at the rear of the platform. Such facilities enable the practice of baptism by immersion, a view universally held within AG churches.

Participation is a key word for understanding Pentecostal life and worship. The new birth brings converts into a spiritual fellowship. New believers are encouraged to seek God for the fullness of the Holy Spirit. Baptism in the Holy Spirit is understood to be an empowering experience available to all: young and old, male and female, clergy and laity. Participation is visible in the shared and meaningful congregational worship but goes far beyond this. Programs for mobilizing the energies of the people of God allow them to serve God in concrete ways. In earlier times the Sunday school proved to be an ideal mechanism for harnessing the energies of Spirit-filled laypersons. It was from such elementary leadership experiences that the pastor could observe emerging candidates for more conspicuous leadership. It was common practice for the pastor to select promising young leaders to join him in establishing a "home prayer meeting" in an area the local church wanted to evangelize. Eventually, one of the emerging leaders from the parent church might be asked to take over the responsibility for shepherding the fledgling home prayer meeting. Many of

---

5. C. M. Ward, *Sermon Classics,* ed. Gwen Jones (Springfield, Mo.: Revivaltime Media Ministries, 1991-93), contains typical examples of AG preaching.

these tiny beginnings eventually flowered into self-supporting churches. Observed leadership skills in the local environment were considered sufficient qualification for effective ministry, while attendance at one of the AG Bible schools remained a matter of debate. Some felt that academic endeavor at a Bible school might diminish the ardent spiritual vitality of the individual. In time, much of this anti-intellectual feeling dissipated (as noted in the McGee introduction), but the tension lingers for some. Historically, it was assumed that receiving the baptism in the Holy Spirit would lead to involvement in some form of ministry, with the individual selecting specifically what that calling might be. Although the patterns of church growth and lay ministry have changed over the years, it is significant that there remains a large pool of candidates for full-time Christian service both for ministry in domestic churches and for overseas missionary service. That AG churches still attract a large number of young people is an indicator of continuing vitality today and a hopeful sign for the church of tomorrow.[6]

A significant difference between groups like the AG and mainline denominations is that the people in AG churches have little interest in remote national entities passing resolutions on major issues such as poverty and injustice. AG people are more inclined to respond to concrete needs at the local level or to needs presented by the constant parade of missionaries who punctuate the church calendar, making vivid the specific needs at specific locations. Each year more than $100 million is given to missionary appeals, indicating a vigorous interest in reaching beyond the needs of one's own congregation. Most AG members and pastors are content to let the national office make official pronouncements on matters of national ethical concern. It would be a mistake, however, to confuse this relative indifference about national level resolutions with a lack of compassion for the needs of a hurting world.[7]

As previously noted, understanding an experience-oriented fellowship like the AG requires us to recognize how its group practices are particularly revealing, providing a useful means for getting at the real values held by participants. Experiencing God, participating in the "flow of the Spirit," is as impor-

---

6. Sherri Doty, Assemblies of God statistician, conversation with author, April 25, 2000. According to Doty, in 1978 there were 160,891 members of AG youth groups. By 1998 this figure had nearly doubled to 317,478.

7. David Martin, *Tongues of Fire: The Explosion of Protestantism in Latin America* (Cambridge: Basil Blackwell, 1990), an interesting study by a British sociologist who assessed which religious forces were most effective in bringing about social change among the poor of Latin America. He concluded that the Pentecostals were making a genuine difference in the lives of people, far beyond what other groups were doing. Although a similar study has not been undertaken for the American AG, it is possible that a comparable result would be observed.

tant as the theology that packages these experiences. Although the membership is strongly committed to the authority of the Bible, few seem to be greatly concerned about revamping the traditional doctrinal statements of the fellowship. Most seem content to study the Bible regularly within the framework of denominational teaching, whether in a Sunday school class or in the midweek Bible study, believing that the basic denominational truths are an adequate vehicle for experiencing God.

Many laypersons are content with traditional doctrinal statements. For a growing number of young pastors and many college and seminary students, however, there is a growing uneasiness about theological issues facing the Pentecostal movement. The tremendous current interest in the person and work of the Holy Spirit both within and beyond the Pentecostal movement has raised questions that were not considered in earlier days. In previous generations, one was either Pentecostal or anti-Pentecostal. There was little middle ground. There is, however, a great interest today in virtually all quarters of the Christian church in the Holy Spirit and how one may experience the Spirit. This fascination has produced a great volume of literature, much of it critical of the way Pentecostals have articulated their theology. Younger Pentecostals perceive a growing need for more persuasive responses to questions surfaced by astute theologians. Some of these theologians are genuinely interested in what is valid in the Pentecostal revival, yet they question the way these values have been supported by Pentecostal theologians. Sympathetic but unconvinced critics of Pentecostalism pose a continuing challenge for a new generation of Pentecostal scholars.

Analysis of surveys reported in Poloma's sociological case study (pp. 45-96) demonstrates a fairly high degree of satisfaction among AG pastors with the service provided to the local church by district judicatories and the national organization. As this dynamic and growing denomination has evolved over time, however, one would expect certain points of tension to arise. I will next examine some of the issues that have surfaced and attempt to trace how change has been addressed.

Structural Changes in the Assemblies of God

The AG did not begin with the intention of forming a denomination. Circumstances forced this. Rejection by fundamentalism, by virtually the entire Holiness cluster of churches, and by the mainline churches of American Protestantism forced Pentecostals to seek fellowship among their own. The AG came into being as a "cooperative fellowship" of autonomous Pentecostal local churches for the purposes of credentialing and disciplining ministers, regularizing acceptable teaching, providing for publications, arranging for the development of ministerial training schools, and facilitating the cause of missions. At the outset, strong sentiment prevailed against organizing as a denomination. There was an intuitive awareness of the tension between charisma and organization, as Margaret Poloma has elsewhere so eloquently articulated.[8]

Amorphous revival movements inevitably require some form of structure for survival, however. Within two years the infant AG found that it had to respond to theological issues that threatened to destroy the fellowship altogether. Occasioned by the "Jesus Only" crisis (as noted in the McGee introduction), a *Statement of Fundamental Truths* was adopted in 1916. This statement of faith was not intended to be a comprehensive creedal articulation. Nevertheless, it was only slightly edited over the years and has in truth become tantamount to a full-blown creed. How is one to evaluate this structuring of beliefs? Is this attempt to state core beliefs in propositional form simply a step toward routinization of charismata? I contend that the ability to articulate biblical boundaries for key concepts, including definitions of religious experience, has been an important means for preserving the integrity and continuity of the Pentecostal revival. A unique feature of the modern Pentecostal revival is its *survival*. Previous charismatic eruptions in history failed to survive, succumbing to fanaticism and/or heresy. Why did this transpire? Is it because they were not successful in expressing a coherent set of values having sufficient objectivity and biblical reference so that they had to be taken seriously? Certainly the history of charismatic movements is complex and each episode demands independent analysis, but I would argue that the modern Pentecostal revival survived long enough to gain a hearing in the larger church world precisely because it affirmed and enforced commitment to orthodox theology and to biblical foundations for all doctrine, experience, and practice. It is generally accepted that the AG has provided an important stabilizing influence on the modern Pentecostal movement.[9] Is it possible that a brief formulation of the understood and accepted basic doctrines actually set the people of the denomination free, within these parameters, to maintain the charismatic dimension of their religious experience?

By reorganizing the various resolutions that had been made in the General Council sessions since the founding of the AG in 1914, a constitution was adopted in 1927. In this move, this association of churches and ministers effec-

---

8. Margaret Poloma, *The Assemblies of God at the Crossroads: Charisma and Institutional Dilemmas* (Knoxville: University of Tennessee Press, 1989), pp. 90-92.

9. William W. Menzies, *Anointed to Serve*, p. 10.

tively passed from the category of an amorphous "movement" into the structured confines of a denomination. Leaders such as Thomas F. Zimmerman and Thomas Trask have been reluctant to surrender the term "movement," likely because it seems to convey the idea of vitality and growth more than does the term "denomination." The truth, however, is that the AG became a denomination within fifteen years of its birth.

Until the Second World War, the AG functioned at the national level with an extremely spare bureaucracy. A handful of people processed all the records and accounts of the denomination, in addition to operating a substantial printing plant at the Springfield, Missouri, headquarters. From 1941 to 1953, however, a dozen major service agencies were developed, creating a vastly increased bureaucracy at the national level. Gradually through the years, new programs have been called into being by action of the General Councils in session, necessitating a relentless upward thrust in the complexity of the national offices and a generally increasing number of personnel required to service them. Periodically there have been major attempts at restructuring the operations of the national headquarters with a view to effecting greater efficiency and, more importantly, insuring as much as possible that the energies expended there were indeed crucial for carrying out the primary objectives of the denomination. I have selected the Study Committee on Advance as a window into the process of such internal structural reform.

A long period of sustained, dramatic growth in the denomination came to an end in the middle 1950s. For the next decade, these growing patterns for opening new churches, credentialing new ministers, and adding new members essentially reached a plateau. Sociologists like David O. Moberg warned that the AG might mimic the rise and decline of Methodism, a concern that seemed to be a real and immediate possibility.[10] Driven by genuine anxiety, the Executive Presbytery of the AG called into being a Study Committee on Advance in 1967. The stated purpose of this special fifteen-member committee was to define the purpose of the church as gleaned from Scripture, and using this biblical model, to examine the present structures in the AG. The objective was to ascertain as accurately as possible which functions contributed directly to the denomination's central reasons for being, which supportive functions legitimately facilitated those primary functions, and which functions fit neither of these categories. Functions in this latter category were regarded as barnacles that should be scraped off. The importance of this committee lies primarily in being formed at a moment of truth for the AG, when the revival movement had reached a level

---

10. David O. Moberg, *The Church as a Social Institution: The Sociology of American Religion* (Englewood Cliffs, N.J.: Prentice-Hall, 1962), a study that features the AG.

of maturity and was called upon to reflect theologically on its reason for being. It was a time for self-conscious awareness, a pause in the midst of activity for reflecting on self-identity.

Based on the picture of the church at Antioch provided by Luke in Acts 13:1-3, the functions of the church were defined as threefold: to minister to believers inside the church (edification), to minister to the Lord (worship), and to minister to the world (missions). As an observer engaged in research at the time, I witnessed a singular event one Friday morning several months into the meetings of this committee. Bogged down for months in the initial definitional stage of the enterprise over such basic concerns as the meaning of "church," the members of the committee were clearly discouraged. These sessions were bathed in earnest prayer. On the Friday in question, there was a pause following a time of prayer and discussion during which one of the participants began to speak. He spoke for no more than three or four minutes. It was as if a dam had broken. Around the table, there was a great sense that the committee had heard from God! At the coffee break that followed, I asked this person how he had arrived at such a wise and fruitful proclamation, an utterance that was received so joyfully by those present. His response was simply that he had been impressed by the Holy Spirit to speak those words. In the months and years that followed, every subsequent decision flowed out of that single event. The results of this meeting were far-reaching. The bylaws of the denomination were overhauled to reflect this fresh rearticulation of the meaning of the church. Great national conferences were developed to focus attention on these three great, basic themes. Here, indeed, was a critical point where theology and praxis came together.

In writing the history of the AG, I was unsure what the next years would hold for the denomination. It was entirely uncertain whether the dire predictions of a downturn in the fortunes of this revival movement would be borne out or whether there would be a period of increased growth. At the time, in 1971, I looked at the AG as positioned for either decline or growth, considering the denomination to be at an optimum level of balance between charisma and organization. No one, however, could be certain what would transpire.[11]

The next twenty-five years were in fact marked by a surge of growth both at home and abroad. It appears that at least part of this growth in the 1970s and 1980s was a result of redefined identity and objectives, although the dramatic impact of the charismatic renewal certainly must be factored into the equation. Since the ministers surveyed in the Poloma case study seem relatively content with the services provided by regional and national judicatories, it may be rea-

11. William W. Menzies, *Anointed to Serve*, pp. 374-83.

sonable to claim that this optimal balance between charisma and structure still exists.

Additional reorganization followed during more recent years. There has been some fine-tuning of the highest echelons of the national bureaucracy, chiefly by enlarging the membership in the Executive Presbytery and the General Presbytery, the representative bodies that govern the affairs of the denomination in the intervals between the sessions of the General Council. More important have been changes effected around the "We Build People" program introduced in 1995. This program redefined the primary objectives of the denomination around four principles: fellowship (the principle of *inclusion*), discipleship (the principle of *instruction*), ministry (the principle of *involvement*), and evangelism/missions (the principle of *investment*). To these has recently been added a fifth: worship (the principle of *inspiration*). Of major significance is the decision to cut across traditional bureaucratic boundaries at AG headquarters to gather key people in various departments in order to network and achieve greater creativity for improving leadership in the discipleship process. This appears significantly to refine the previous three major biblical priorities gleaned by the Study Committee on Advance, which relied upon Acts 13:1-3 as a model for church life. Just as important was the decision to implement a process of networking among the various departments and divisions at the national headquarters.[12] Leroy Bartel was selected to head the new Commission on Discipleship in March 2000 by action of the Executive Presbytery. This new commission was charged with addressing a refined theological understanding of the functions of the local church.[13] At the same time, a parallel commission to accommodate networking with respect to evangelism issues was also instituted. Randy Hurst has been appointed to serve as chairman of this new Commission on Evangelism.[14]

The 1990s were to be a "Decade of Harvest," a time when concentrated effort at home and abroad was to be marshaled to open new churches and accelerate evangelism. This slogan was adopted by the newly formed World Assemblies of God Fellowship, a federation of autonomous national sister fellowships and largely the product of the American AG mission activity. Reported success proved to be uneven. Some nations such as the Philippines exceeded expectations in each of the years of the Decade of Harvest, reporting a doubling of the

12. Minutes of the General Council of the Assemblies of God (1999), pp. 146-48, which contain the articles detailing the function and composition of these two new commissions.

13. Sylvia Lee, "Assembly of God Leaders Meet to Discuss Discipleship," *Pentecostal Evangel,* April 30, 2000, p. 24.

14. Leroy Bartel, national director of the Division of Christian Education, interview with author, April 19, 2000.

number of churches.[15] In the United States, however, the American AG had little about which to cheer. Another plateau of growth had been reached, thus ending the dramatic growth of the 1970s and 1980s. Slogans and promotion were clearly inadequate. In fact, if the domestic growth among the Hispanic churches were discounted, the American AG in the Decade of Harvest experienced relatively little growth. In spite of a reduced rate of growth in recent years compared to previous ones, church membership had increased to more than 1.4 million by 1998 and the number of adherents passed the 2.5 million mark. The overseas constituency of sister national AG fellowships has grown to more than 30 million.[16]

The fairly steady pattern in Sunday school attendance nationwide over the past thirty years has been of considerable concern. Although actual attendance has held reasonably steady, the numbers are disappointing because they fail to keep pace with growing church attendance and membership. It appears that Sunday school attendance is no longer as useful a measure of actual Bible study activity as it once may have been. Bible study patterns in the AG are now much more diverse than participation in the traditional Sunday school program. Although statistics are not readily available to verify this, a burgeoning of new Bible study delivery systems providing services equivalent to the traditional Sunday school seems partly to compensate for the relative decline in Sunday school participation. Through the years the Sunday school was a key instrument for identifying emerging leadership in the local church, effectively mobilizing the energies of Spirit-baptized workers. With a multiplication of new, local church ministries presently available, however, lay leadership is now directed into a wide array of functions in addition to the traditional Sunday school.[17]

Bible institutes and Bible colleges have been the backbone of furnishing trained leadership for the AG. District-sponsored, regional-sponsored, and national colleges served the basic ministerial educational needs of the denomination for many years. Liberal arts programs and graduate education were eventually added to the academic services provided. There has been strong resistance to requiring a specific level of academic achievement as a criterion for credentials, but most of the districts stipulate that those considered for min-

15. Russell Turney, "A Decade of Harvest," *Pentecostal Evangel*, May 7, 2000, p. 15.

16. Doty, conversation with author, April 19, 2000. Based on information gleaned from the Annual Church Ministries Reports, statistics disclose that the number of net new churches from 1990 through 1998 averaged 83 per year, compared to 163 per year in the previous decade. Church membership between 1980 and 1990 grew at the rate of 22 percent, while in the first eight years of the Decade of Harvest growth had slowed to 12 percent. The number of ministers grew in the 1980s by 20 percent, but from 1990 to 1998 the number had grown only 5 percent.

17. Bartel, interview with author, April 19, 2000.

isterial credentials show evidence of fulfilling a slate of required readings or completing a required list of distance-education courses offered by Berean University. These nominal requirements are intended to insure theological harmony in the fellowship.

Historically, the three-year Bible institutes that served the earlier needs of the AG evolved upward into four-year degree-granting colleges. Several are now offering graduate programs and are classified as universities. A theological seminary has emerged. To meet a continuing need for entry-level Bible instruction, a whole new slate of schools is emerging. These are called "church-based Bible institutes." These local church Bible schools have tended to seek denominational endorsement as appropriate tracks for qualifying students for credentials. Application is made to the office of the General Secretary for such endorsement. It appears that courses offered through Berean University are important for certifying these local church Bible schools.[18] What is significant is that many laypeople, in addition to aspiring clergy, are enrolled in the multiplying range of serious Bible study opportunities now available, even though the traditional Sunday school seems to be in decline.[19]

The Assemblies of God Confronting Theological Challenges

To capture how the evolving structure of the national AG organization has related to the cascade of theological challenges over the years, I will review selected doctrinal issues with the intention of showing how a variety of organizational mechanisms have been employed to address perceived needs. Each of the following issues has a story of its own. From this tapestry, I will then draw several conclusions.

Pacifism

The AG in its beginnings featured a strong commitment to the imminent, premillennial return of Jesus Christ. Margaret Poloma has seen the pacifist pos-

---

18. Katy Attanasi, "New Global University Facility Nears Completion," *Pentecostal Evangel*, May 7, 2000, p. 28, reports that 400,000 students are participating in the distance-education delivery systems of Berean University and ICI University, combined. These two entities, one serving domestic United States needs and the other international needs, are being combined into a single enterprise called Global University.

19. Dayton Kingsriter, director of the Commission on Higher Education, interview with author, April 18, 2000.

ture of the emerging church as an authentic reflection of an otherworldly outlook. Preoccupied with reaching the lost before the cataclysmic end of the age, Pentecostals were little concerned with secular endeavors to reform a doomed world. Participation in war, even for a noble cause (as some portrayed the contours of the First World War), was not an option. Officially, the AG adopted a conscientious objection position.

When the United States was plunged into war in 1941, the situation was totally different. Pearl Harbor impacted the constituency of the AG very much like the rest of the nation. During the Second World War, fifty thousand AG young men served in the United States military. Only thirty-five served in camps for those asking for exemption as conscientious objectors.[20] This was a glaring cognitive dissonance for a denomination officially classified as pacifist!

During the Vietnam War, action was taken to address this problem. It was quite evident that the AG had acculturated to the point that its earlier pacifist position was no longer held by more than a handful of constituents. At the 1965 General Council held in Des Moines, Iowa, a decision was made to appoint a committee to study the matter with a view to making a recommendation for action at the next General Council convening two years later in Long Beach, California. What is significant about this issue is that never before had a major ideological issue been reexamined on the basis of a yearlong assessment by a theological committee. At the 1967 meeting of the General Council, the committee's recommendation was that the AG withdraw from its previous pacifist posture to the more realistic posture of honoring the right of individual members to adopt a position of conscientious objection to military service, of noncombatant military service, or of serving as a combatant. The committee's recommendation was adopted by the General Council, the first time such a decision was reached through the advice of a theological study commission.[21]

Divorce and Remarriage

No issue has resurfaced as frequently as the AG position on divorce and remarriage. From the beginning of the AG, the official position was essentially the same as that of the Roman Catholic Church: a virtual denial of the legitimacy of divorce. Under no circumstances other than by recognition of the annulment of a marriage could a married person with a living companion be remarried by an AG minister. An AG minister performing an unauthorized marriage

20. William W. Menzies, *Anointed to Serve*, pp. 327-28.
21. Minutes of the General Council (1967), p. 35.

did so at the risk of losing his credentials. In the years following World War II, more and more members of AG churches encountered the problem of divorce. In fact, the AG came increasingly to reflect the culture of which it was a part. By the 1960s, serious tension existed at this point, with larger urban churches more clearly reflecting the pressures of prevailing culture while rural and small-town churches appealed to sustaining traditional positions on the issue of divorce and remarriage. A standing committee of the General Council, "Doctrines and Practices Disapproved," was charged by the 1971 General Council with the responsibility of making a thorough study of this issue.

This committee, comprised of pastors, schoolmen, and church executives, spent more than a year studying the biblical foundations for marriage, divorce, and the conditions for possible remarriage. At the 1973 General Council in Miami, the recommendation of the committee was adopted with only slight revision. That decision effectively ratified the typical Protestant evangelical position on marriage and divorce, acknowledging that although divorce is not encouraged, it may be permitted for biblical reasons: adultery (Matt. 5:31-32 and 19:9) and abandonment (1 Cor. 7:15). Although affirming that divorce is therefore more than legal separation, the church recognized that when the conditions fell within biblical parameters, divorced persons could be allowed to remarry. Pastors of local churches were given the authority to perform such marriages, contingent on their being satisfied that the parties met the necessary qualifications. The committee recommended, however, that the denomination retain its previous standard for ministers and lay leaders in the local church. No minister could be ordained if he or she had been divorced and then remarried with the previous companion still living. One standard was therefore adopted for ordinary laypersons and another for clergy and local lay leadership. Not all have been satisfied with this position, even though it is a substantial change from the earlier position. The matter resurfaced in 1999 at the Orlando General Council, this time in the issue of same-sex marriages. A resolution was presented that added to the previous language on the divorce-remarriage issue by explicitly forbidding ministers to perform same-sex marriages. The motion was adopted.[22] At the General Council in 2001, a resolution was adopted permitting the credentialing of ministers if the divorce in question transpired prior to conversion.

Another means by which theological controversies have been addressed by the AG since 1970 has been the publication of occasional position papers. These documents do not have formal denominational sanction, being the product of a committee of scholars and churchmen. At the 1991 General Council meeting in Portland, the authority of such documents was clarified to insure

22. Minutes of the General Council (1999), p. 80.

that only those position papers recommended by the Executive Presbytery and approved by the General Council could be understood to have authority for credentialing purposes.[23] The publication of such documents tends to carry with it a kind of implicit influence, however, being perceived by the general public as the "official" position of the AG. In the years since the writing of the first position paper in 1970, only one has gained the approval of the General Council, thus becoming truly an official representation of AG belief. This was the "Divorce and Remarriage" paper, which was debated and adopted at the 1973 General Council.[24] From 1970 to 1997, twenty-two position papers have been promulgated.[25] All these have been approved by the General Presbytery, a broadly representative body. Most are the product of the standing General Council commission called Doctrines and Practices Disapproved, brought into being in 1971. As the title suggests, this commission reviews a variety of issues referred to it by the Executive Presbytery that are perceived to be of sufficient magnitude to warrant response. This commission was reconstituted in 1979 as the Doctrinal Purity Commission.[26]

Sanctification

From the beginning of the denomination, the doctrine of sanctification has been a matter of some ambiguity. The intention of the language employed on this point in the 1916 *Statement of Fundamental Truths* was purposely somewhat vague. This was done so that exponents of the Wesleyan Holiness crisis experience theology would not be overly offended, since the majority in the infant AG preferred the Keswickian, or Reformed, model of progressive sanctification. The terminology of "entire sanctification" was used, although it was generally defined to mean something less than the "second blessing" teaching of the Wesleyans. Over the years the term "entire sanctification" created sufficient ambiguity that a decision was made to drop it from the *Statement of Fundamental Truths*. Consequently, by action of the General Council in 1961, a clarification was supplied by amending the article in the *Statement of Fundamental Truths* accordingly.[27] It is a matter of curiosity that the annual ministerial ques-

---

23. Minutes of the General Council (1991), p. 60.

24. Minutes of the General Council (1973), p. 58.

25. Assemblies of God, General Council, *Where We Stand: The Official Position Papers of the Assemblies of God* (Springfield, Mo.: Gospel Publishing House, 2001).

26. Bylaws of the General Council of the Assemblies of God (revised August 7, 2001), art. IX, sec. A.

27. Minutes of the General Council (1961), p. 92.

tionnaire continues to ask the minister to verify that he or she conforms to the teaching of the denomination on entire sanctification, even though that terminology was abandoned nearly forty years ago.

Divine Healing

From the earliest days of the Pentecostal revival, it was a nearly universal belief that God's intervention occurred in concrete, physical ways. This included a belief in God's willingness to heal people. Borrowing from the slogan expressing core beliefs of evangelicals like A. J. Gordon and A. B. Simpson, AG people heralded confidence in the "fourfold gospel" (what Pentecostals tended to call the "full gospel"), which meant: "Jesus Christ the Savior, the Healer, the Baptizer in the Holy Spirit, and the Coming King." Of course, these themes were derived from their evangelical predecessors. Praying for the sick was a fairly common practice among a wide range of evangelicals in the late nineteenth century.[28] Implicit in the full gospel was the belief that Jesus, "the same yesterday, today, and forever" (Heb. 13:8), heals those who ask in faith. It was not uncommon for zealous advocates of this dimension of Pentecostalism to scorn those who employed the services of physicians. Over the years it became apparent that, although many did testify to remarkable healings, not all for whom prayer was offered were in fact healed. A strain appeared in the fabric of healing theology. How was one to report that healing is for all when common experience discloses that many are not healed?

The cognitive dissonance evident in the teaching on healing led to the promulgation of a position paper in 1974. This document is a clear retreat from the simplistic expectation of earlier years, with a clear acknowledgment that there remains a mystery in healing and that we must frankly report that all are not healed. In spite of this frank recognition of limitations, the reader is enjoined to "preach the Word and expect the signs to follow."[29] AG ministers cooperate fully with professional medical people today, accepting that healing is from God whether it comes in the form of special divine interventions or scientific medical skill.

Reaching a peak in the 1950s, the "Salvation-Healing" crusades often featured tent evangelism and citywide interdenominational support, but quickly waned in popularity when many of the traveling evangelists came under severe

---

28. Donald W. Dayton, *Theological Roots of Pentecostalism* (Grand Rapids: Francis Asbury Press, 1987), pp. 115-42.

29. Assemblies of God, *Where We Stand*, p. 54.

criticism for moral or financial shortcomings. The General Presbytery considered the problem of the lack of accountability of these marginal ministers, many of whom were independent. Eventually in 1965, the General Council adopted a resolution entitled "Criteria for Independent Corporations," which was aimed principally at AG ministers who had set up their own organizations in an effort to avoid the scrutiny of the denominational leadership.[30] The abuses of the Salvation-Healing evangelists quickly led to the virtual demise of this kind of ministry in the United States. The failure of these largely independent Pentecostal preachers, often making extravagant and unsubstantiated claims, led to considerable disillusionment among AG people regarding the ministry of divine healing, so that prayer for the sick diminished in local churches for a time. Gradually, however, a sustained level of local church healing practice was recovered and continues. A significant number of individuals report to have made commitments to Christ as a result of a physical healing of either themselves or a family member.

It does appear that remarkable healings are a significant factor in reaching people at the frontiers of Christianity. Evidently, supernatural interventions are more common in such situations. In the mission fields of Asia, Latin America, and Africa, as well as those of Europe, AG missionaries find a good response to the message that God delivers from sin, sickness, and the demonic. This seems to be particularly true among animist tribal peoples.[31]

Initial Physical Evidence

Close to the heart of Pentecostal ideology is the belief that there is, separable from the experience of new birth, the possibility for all believers to experience a baptism in the Holy Spirit. This belief was held by a significant array of evangelicals in the late nineteenth century, but for the first half of the twentieth century was largely shelved to avoid the possibility of being associated with Pentecostalism. Most Pentecostals adopted the evangelical "Higher Life" concept of Spirit baptism, identifying strongly with the view that this experience is to be understood principally as empowerment for Christian witness. To capture this intention, Pentecostals sometimes speak of the "expressive domain" of the Spirit. This language intends to include enrichment in private prayer and pub-

---

30. Minutes of the General Council (1965), pp. 54-58.

31. Julie C. Ma, *When the Spirit Meets the Spirits: Pentecostal Ministry among the Kankana-ey Tribe in the Philippines* (Frankfurt am Main: Peter Lang, 2000), which contains an excellent case study of healing among tribal animists in the mountains of Luzon, Philippines.

lic worship in addition to divine help in evangelism and missions. Sometimes the term "overflow of the Spirit" is employed as well. Nearly all Pentecostals, including AG people, claim that the biblical model for Spirit baptism includes speaking in other tongues (Acts 2:4) as the accompanying sign or "initial physical evidence" of Spirit baptism.[32]

This belief has not gone without challenge, however. In 1918 the first challenge to the commonly held "initial physical evidence" doctrine was mounted by F. F. Bosworth, a prominent leader in the AG. In a tract titled *Do All Speak with Tongues?* he minimized the role of tongues as evidence, placing the manifestation among other gifts of the Spirit. Bosworth felt that *any* of the gifts of the Spirit (1 Cor. 12:8-10) would suffice as evidence of Spirit baptism. He refused to make a distinction between evidential tongues associated with Spirit baptism and the gift of tongues employed in public worship, as did mainstream Pentecostals. He sought to distribute his tract at various conferences and camp meetings where AG ministers gathered, expecting to gain a following. Few of his colleagues joined his cause. It became apparent that Bosworth's view was not going to prevail and, if permitted to continue, would prove disruptive to the embryonic AG fellowship. Bosworth, a Christian gentleman, made a gracious, uncontentious exit, resigning from the AG at the General Council of 1918. He joined the Christian and Missionary Alliance, a denomination he served effectively for the rest of his life.[33] As a result of the issue raised by Bosworth, a resolution adopted at the 1918 General Council made the teaching of anything contrary to the initial physical evidence doctrine a matter of "serious disagreement."[34]

Only the matter of divorce and remarriage has surfaced more frequently at the national level than this question. In a 1959 quarterly letter sent to AG ministers, the general secretary noted that in one district, "a few of its preachers have confessed doubt in their attitude toward our doctrine of tongues as the initial physical evidence of the Baptism of the Holy Spirit."[35] Although the issue continued to recur, it did not seem to gain much momentum for many years.[36] In 1963 the general superintendent wrote a position paper that reported that "Time has brought changes, but no modification in the emphasis, teaching, and experi-

32. Minutes of the General Council (1999), p. 92.

33. Carl Brumback, *Suddenly . . . from Heaven: A History of the Assemblies of God* (Springfield, Mo.: Gospel Publishing House, 1961), pp. 217-19.

34. Minutes of the General Council (1918), p. 8.

35. Ralph Riggs, *Ministers Quarterly Letter* (Springfield, Mo.: General Council of the Assemblies of God), June 12, 1959, p. 3.

36. Bartlett Peterson, former general secretary of the Assemblies of God, interview with author, April 6, 1970.

ence of the baptism of the Spirit."[37] Later, the general secretary reaffirmed this understanding: "Our position is unchanged with regard to the Baptism of the Holy Spirit and speaking in other tongues."[38]

More recently, the Executive Presbytery in 1998 appointed a special committee to study the issue with a view to making recommendations for strengthening the teaching on the doctrine in local churches. That committee met over a period of many months, submitting a final report to the Executive Presbytery in January 2000. Concurrently the Doctrinal Purity Commission was at work on a revised position paper that was submitted to the General Presbytery in 1999 but was returned to the commission for further study. A revised report was adopted by the Executive Presbytery in March 2000 with the recommendation that this be submitted to the General Presbytery for its consideration at their August 2000 meeting.[39] This document is an updating of the previous position paper on the baptism in the Holy Spirit published in 1981, addressing important issues that have surfaced in the intervening years. The earlier position paper did not have the benefit of recent Pentecostal scholarship, so it was deemed necessary to update that publication. The newer document addresses hermeneutical questions, such as the availability of narrative materials in Acts for developing biblical theology. This is a new avenue of approach that Pentecostal scholars have pursued effectively in recent years.

Fifteen commonly asked questions are addressed in the document. Among these is, "What about the person who is convinced he or she was baptized in the Holy Spirit in a definite encounter with God, but did not speak in tongues until some time later?"

> Since the Bible teaches and demonstrates that tongues are the initial evidence of receiving the baptism in the Holy Spirit, the church cannot confirm the opinion of the individual until he or she actually speaks in tongues. But neither can we depreciate a special experience of the presence of the Holy Spirit of God. One might describe such an in-between time as involvement in a process that culminates when the person speaks in tongues. To take any other position on the question would open the door to individuals claiming to be baptized in the Holy Spirit, without having received the biblical evidence of speaking in tongues as the Spirit

37. T. F. Zimmerman, "The Pentecostal Position," *Pentecostal Evangel,* February 10, 1963, pp. 2-3, 7.

38. Bartlett Peterson, *Ministers Quarterly Letter* (Springfield, Mo.: General Council of the Assemblies of God), September 23, 1966, p. 4.

39. Minutes of the Executive Presbytery of the Assemblies of God (March 21-22, 2000), pp. 1-2.

gives utterance, and feeling content with what they already have experienced spiritually.[40]

Causing concern are data disclosing a significant number of church members claiming to believe the doctrine but also reporting never to have spoken in tongues. It is evident that there is enough uneasiness over the uncertainty with which some pastors hold this doctrine that the national leadership is struggling for better ways to support the traditional position.[41] Therefore, although in general the people of the AG are content with the basic doctrines described in the *Statement of Fundamental Truths,* the teaching about the initial physical evidence of baptism in the Spirit is a point of continuing uncertainty among some ministers.

Ecumenism

Prior to the Second World War, the AG participated on an unofficial basis in several agencies that in 1950 gathered into what became known as the National Council of Churches of Christ in America (NCC). As early as 1919, for example, Missionary Secretary J. Roswell Flower attended conventions of the Foreign Missions Conference of North America. Such interaction by the young and relatively unknown AG with such a missions organization proved helpful in getting visas and other necessary documents important for foreign missionaries. Through the years the AG participated constructively in such organizations as the Department of Church World Service, the Missionary Research Library, and the Associated Missions Medical Office. During the 1950s the AG also participated in the stewardship seminars offered by the NCC.[42]

In 1951 David du Plessis, a South African Pentecostal leader who had recently moved to the United States, became acquainted with John A. Mackay, president of Princeton Theological Seminary. Mackay had become interested in the Pentecostal movement from his travel in Latin America. Mackay introduced

40. Assemblies of God, General Council, "The Baptism in the Holy Spirit: The Initial Experience and the Continuing Evidences of the Spirit-Filled Life." Final revision to this position paper was made by the Commission on Doctrinal Purity, February 21, 2000, approved by the Executive Presbytery, March 21-22, 2000, and approved by the General Presbytery, August 11, 2000.

41. Statistics provided by Sherri Doty disclosed that in the latest year available, 94,721 people were reported having experienced baptism in the Holy Spirit, while 505,017 conversions were reported. Evidently fewer than 20 percent of the new converts moved on to the baptism in the Spirit, at least in that year.

42. William W. Menzies, *Anointed to Serve,* p. 220.

du Plessis to leaders of the World Council of Churches (WCC). Receiving a warm response, du Plessis was soon engaged in a wide range of activities within the WCC. He was responsible for leading dozens of World Council participants into the Pentecostal experience. All of this seemed to be a remarkable fulfillment of a prophecy given to him in 1936 by a British Pentecostal, Smith Wigglesworth. His well-publicized involvement with the WCC proved to be an embarrassment to the leadership of the AG, however. The AG had only recently been accepted as a collegial body within the National Association of Evangelicals (NAE) and was bent on proving that it was loyal to the core values of that group. Right-wing dissidents such as Carl McIntire had spurned membership in the NAE in 1943 at its founding. He chose instead to help form a separate fundamentalist coalition of churches, largely because the NAE had decided to include Pentecostal bodies such as the AG. Fundamentalists complained to the NAE that the AG was sojourning with the World Council. Stung by such accusations, the AG cut off all ties to World Council enterprises, including the very useful missions-oriented services, in order to appease critics. In 1962 the AG terminated the credentials of David du Plessis because of his World Council activities. Eighteen years later, his papers were restored.[43] The wry twist in this is that during these years many within the mainline National Council and World Council churches were experiencing the Pentecostal baptism, but very few were within evangelical churches.

By 1963 all of these associations had been terminated. On August 31, 1962, the General Presbytery unanimously adopted a resolution, subsequently ratified at the General Council of 1963, condemning the ecumenical movement. The reasons cited were:

1. We believe said movement to be a sign of the times and contrary to the real biblical doctrine of spiritual unity in the church of Jesus Christ, and
2. We are opposed to ecumenicity based on organic and organizational unity, and
3. We believe that the combination of many denominations into a World Super Church will probably culminate in the Scarlet Woman or Religious Babylon of Revelation. . . .[44]

The resolution did however seek to safeguard participation by ministers on a local level in such interdenominational activities as ministerial alliances. In the intervening years, many AG ministers participated in a variety of interdenominational activities, principally occasioned by the advent of the charismatic

---

43. Poloma, *Crossroads,* pp. 131-33, which has an excellent review of the du Plessis episode.
44. Minutes of the General Council (1963), p. 41.

movement. The current General Council bylaw article permits such activity provided it does not "promote the ecumenical movement."[45]

It has been difficult for Pentecostals to comprehend that the charismatic movement erupted within the more liberal mainline church bodies before it reached the evangelical cluster of churches. The problem of understanding the appropriate relation of the AG to various strands of the charismatic movement, especially those charismatics within the ecumenical movement and within the Roman Catholic Church, continues to be largely unresolved.[46] Most AG ministers are opposed to the ecumenical movement and feel that their loyalties lie with evangelical Christianity (see the Poloma case study). Yet many seek to find ways to nourish fellowship with charismatic Christians, particularly at the local level.[47] There is widespread recognition that true ecumenism is a spiritual fellowship across denominational boundaries generated by the Holy Spirit (John 17), but even stronger rejection of the kind of organizational union expressed by bodies such as the National Council and the World Council.

Revival

For some Christians the term "revival" evokes the image of unwelcome disturbance to the status quo, an intrusion into comfortable routines. The pejorative term "enthusiasm" has been used by some historians to cover this kind of religious phenomenon. In the context of the AG, however, this frequently employed term expresses the yearning of the people of God for "fresh wind and fresh fire." When the heightened sense of God's manifest presence diminishes in a church or a cluster of churches, prayer meetings may be organized to call upon God for a fresh outpouring of his Spirit. A significant proportion of AG preaching contains a sense of concern if not urgency to rekindle the fire of God among his people.

Revival, to be sure, does not mean the same thing to all. It appears that each major revival episode has unique characteristics. Historically, one can argue that some of the movements that have impacted the AG contained genuine elements of renewal but were not sustained because of abuses that threatened

45. Minutes of the General Council (1999), p. 134.

46. Cecil M. Robeck, "Pentecostals and the Apostolic Faith: Implications for Ecumenism," *Pneuma* 9 (spring 1987): 61-84. Robeck, professor of church history and ecumenics at Fuller Theological Seminary, Pasadena, is the leading authority in the AG on ecumenical relationships.

47. George Wood, general secretary of the Assemblies of God, interview with author, Springfield, Mo., April 17, 2000.

the stability of the denomination. The AG was particularly affected by some of these awakening movements.

In 1948 a movement that became known as "The New Order of the Latter Rain" first erupted in Saskatchewan and then moved into the United States, especially in Oregon, Michigan, and other Midwestern states. Features of this movement were the identification of latter-day apostles and prophets and the belief that spiritual gifts and ministries could be bestowed by the laying on of hands. Personal predictive prophecy was widespread, sometimes accompanied by disastrous consequences. Entire congregations were swept up in the enthusiasm, since the apparent fresh vitality being experienced suggested a higher level of spirituality than the traditional AG churches exhibited. At a 1949 annual district ministers' institute in Dearborn, Michigan, District Superintendent Charles Scott outlined the extravagances of the new movement and reported that these were not really new, but a reappearance of fringe phenomena from earlier times. This was for information only; no actions were taken. A year later, however, at the district council of May 1950, decisive action was taken. Out of two hundred ministers confronted with a decision regarding the Latter Rain movement, only two chose to leave. This effectively ended the flurry of events in that state.[48]

On the national level, the first evidence of concern came in February 1949 with the publication of the *Quarterly Letter* sent to all AG ministers. General Superintendent E. S. Williams provided a brief, general statement on the bestowal of spiritual gifts, pointing out acceptable biblical guidelines but not mentioning the Latter Rain phenomenon. The next *Quarterly Letter*, issued in April 1949, addressed the matter quite directly. At the General Council meeting later that year, a resolution was adopted denouncing Latter Rain practices deemed to be unbiblical extravagances. At the next General Council, the general secretary reported that very few churches had defected to the Latter Rain movement. Remnants of the Latter Rain movement persisted but had little further impact on the AG.[49]

How is one to assess the significance of this flurry of enthusiasm? Perhaps the Pentecostal movement had indeed slumped into a state of complacency. Phenomenal growth was being experienced. Perhaps some pastors had developed a routinized approach to ministry. They had learned how to "put it over." Was God shaking up a church, newly successful and grown complacent? Certainly the Latter Rain episode provoked many church leaders to a sober reassessment of spiritual priorities and to a healthy self-examination.

48. William W. Menzies, *Anointed to Serve*, pp. 323-24.
49. William W. Menzies, *Anointed to Serve*, p. 325.

More recently, what has become known as the "Brownsville Revival" has had a similar impact on the AG. At the Brownsville Assembly of God in Pensacola, Florida, in June 1995, a revival began that quickly reached international prominence. Ministers and laypersons from all over the world have flocked by the thousands to this revival center. Remarkable testimonies of physical healings, emotional healings, and transformed ministries have flowed from the Brownsville revival. Theologically, it is difficult to identify any particular teaching that is in conflict with standard AG belief and practice. As of this date, there appears to be good harmony between the Brownsville Assembly and the West Florida District in which it lies. It appears to serve as an instrument for deepening spiritual life and raising the horizons of expectation for local ministries without moving beyond acceptable AG understanding.

Some ministers and laypersons have returned to their local churches following a visit to Brownsville and have attempted to kindle a similar revival by instituting changes in schedule and practice they observed at Brownsville. Not all local churches have been ready to climb aboard the Brownsville bandwagon, however, sometimes resulting in church splits. Certainly the Brownsville revival and the widespread impact it has had, particularly within the AG, is an expression of a continued hungering for the presence of God. In spite of resistance to the threat it poses to some, it appears that a majority within the AG has looked favorably upon the revival.

As Poloma has so ably pointed out in her case study, revival movements are not readily contained and can introduce tension with existing structures. An appendage to the current wave of revival centered in northern California is known as "the River of God." This movement is clearly distinguishable from the Brownsville revival but has very likely drawn inspiration from it. The River of God has exhibited some of the same manifestations common to the New Order of the Latter Rain and has resulted in the splitting of churches. It has become such a serious issue that the 1999 General Council debated a strong resolution condemning what are deemed unbiblical practices in this new enthusiasm. A decision was reached that returned the matter to the Executive Presbytery for further consideration, with a recommendation that the Committee on Doctrinal Purity prepare a position paper for possible publication. The resolution reinforces the determination of the AG to circumscribe beliefs, experiences, and practices within the plain teaching of the Scriptures.[50] Traditional Pentecostal groups such as the AG draw theological lines somewhat differently from some charismatics. At the heart of the matter ultimately lies the issue of biblical hermeneutics.

50. Minutes of the General Council (1999), pp. 80-81.

Ethnic Diversity

The original Pentecost described in Acts 2 transcended significant sociological divisions occasioned by the fall. Pentecost seemed to be a statement about the divine intention to restore the harmony lost by the sinfulness of humanity. In an episode that seemed to reaffirm this Acts 2 principle, the Azusa Street Revival in Los Angeles (1906-9) was marked by ethnic diversity and bore a multicultural character. In fact, William Seymour, the first major leader in the revival, was an African American. This was especially remarkable during the Jim Crow era in the United States. It is sad to say, however, that the early Pentecostals acculturated to the segregation practiced in the larger society, so that by 1910 the Azusa Street Revival was reduced to a black congregation while the whites moved on to other venues.

By the time the AG was formed in 1914, a de facto segregation had already taken place. The largely black Church of God in Christ was looked upon as an appropriate counterpart to the white AG, so that black visitors coming to AG churches were routinely directed to the nearest Church of God in Christ congregation. The record of the AG in race relations up to the time of the Civil Rights era is unremarkable. The AG was neither better nor worse than other Pentecostal and evangelical bodies. Segregation, although not institutionalized and formalized, was the standard practice of all but a handful of congregations in the fellowship.

In more recent years, vigorous and proactive leadership has addressed the changing demography of the United States. By action of the General Council in 1997, the Executive Presbytery was enlarged to include representation from ethnic and linguistic minorities. At the same time, the General Presbytery was also enlarged to insure broader ethnic representation. Provision was made to establish a Commission on Ethnic Relations.[51] The report given to the General Presbytery by Ethnic Relations Commissioner Dr. David Moore discloses that during the "Decade of Harvest" (1990-2000), enormous changes took place in American society that deeply affected the AG. While there was a net growth in numbers of AG congregations and membership, there would be an actual loss were it not for the ethnic minority groups in the fellowship. White majority congregations declined by 205 while ethnic minority churches grew by 936![52]

Moore observes that much of the ethnic church growth must be attributed to immigrant leaders harvesting the Christians from their native lands

51. Minutes of the General Council (1997), pp. 22-24, 70-71.
52. David Moore, Report to the Annual Meeting of the General Presbytery of the Assemblies of God, Springfield, Mo., August 7, 2001, p. 62.

who had immigrated to the United States. The patterns of this immigration have been changing for the AG. No longer are Hispanics the fastest-growing component of the ethnic churches. The fastest-growing segments in the Decade of Harvest were from the Asia Pacific region, led by Koreans and Filipinos. Moore observes that the growth is not primarily because of proactive Anglo ministry but instead due to aggressive ministry undertaken by immigrants themselves.

Although Moore acknowledges that a few Anglo congregations have achieved a genuine multiracial character, he does not see this happening across socioeconomic lines. Those occasional churches that are multiethnic are inevitably monocultural in economic status. Moore does acknowledge that a variety of successful cooperative ventures have been undertaken by numerous AG congregations to reach out to ethnic groups. The most common expression of openness is the creative use of available space, so that several ethnic congregations share the same facilities on a scheduled basis. Some of these gather together periodically to celebrate their unity, but primarily these are separate congregations under a single roof. Not much blending is evident.

Moore sees a deeper problem in the AG. The denomination developed principally as a white organization, fitting well into the American pattern of western and northern European culture that characterized the broad development of the United States. In the 1990s, however, a dramatic cultural shift occurred. Until recently, immigrants were apparently well served by casting aside their ethnic and language identities and becoming absorbed in the great melting pot. This is no longer true. We have become an open society in which ethnic minorities are retaining their cultural identities but within the larger unity of American society. We are a cluster of many cultures, no longer a single culture.

The implications of this are significant for the AG. To encourage ethnic minority groups to give up their identity and meld into the dominant white culture of the congregation is no longer received well. The underlying assumption is that the dominant culture is superior. Moore sees that the challenge for the AG is to take seriously the need to respect immigrant populations for their diverse values. Proactive ethnic ministry must precede the attempt to gather minorities into the dominant white ethos. A sea change in attitude is required, not a structural change. Moore sees, for the well-being of the fellowship, an urgent need to face the monocultural ethos of the denomination.[53]

53. David Moore, Ethnic Relations Commissioner, interview with author, Springfield, Mo., August 14, 2001.

Evangelical Association: Theological Tensions

Born in isolation, the AG seems to have become fascinated by the approval and respect accorded the denomination by various evangelical parachurch organizations. Evangelicals have accepted groups like the AG as valid orthodox Christian bodies in spite of disagreement about the doctrine of the Holy Spirit. Herein lies a major point of ambiguity. The perplexity has been that believers belonging to liberal church bodies were more ready to seek Pentecostal-like experiences than the evangelicals with whom Pentecostals were more eager to identify. Some Pentecostals, recognizing the significance of this tension, have surfaced the notion that Pentecostals are better served by identifying themselves as a true "third force" in Christianity without being locked into either evangelicalism or liberal Christianity. Nevertheless, strong ties bind the AG to evangelicalism.

One way of demonstrating the dependence of the AG on evangelicalism is to consider the intellectual resources from which AG people draw. Without evangelical textbooks to line the shelves of AG college libraries, there would be little upon which students could draw. Apart from Sunday school materials and the reprinting of older books designed for lay readership, the Gospel Publishing House has over the years provided only limited help in support of Pentecostal theology. The books of E. S. Williams, Ralph M. Riggs, and Myer Pearlman — the old "classics" — are all nearly fifty years old or more. More recently, Stanley Horton has carried the theological freight for the AG. His popular book, *What the Bible Says about the Holy Spirit,* is widely read as an authentic representation of mainstream AG teaching.[54] The Gospel Publishing House has recently instituted a Pentecostal Textbooks Project with the objective of providing Pentecostal textbooks for use in AG colleges. These books are being published under the Logion banner. This enterprise was undertaken to fill a perceived need, since relatively little substantial Pentecostal theological material had been introduced for many years. Although AG leadership has not been conspicuous in encouraging theological scholarship, when scholars have produced useful materials these have been received with appreciation.

Until the advent of the charismatic movement in the late 1950s, simple

---

54. Stanley M. Horton, *What the Bible Says about the Holy Spirit* (Springfield, Mo.: Gospel Publishing House, 1976); and Myer Pearlman, *Knowing the Doctrines of the Bible* (Springfield, Mo.: Gospel Publishing House, 1937). E. S. Williams, *Systematic Theology,* 3 vols. (Springfield, Mo.: Gospel Publishing House, 1953), is an authentic representation of Pentecostal belief but is not really a systematic theology, being instead the collected notes from classes he taught at Central Bible Institute. See also Ralph M. Riggs, *We Believe: A Comprehensive Statement of Christian Faith* (Springfield, Mo.: Gospel Publishing House, 1954).

statements articulating basic Pentecostal beliefs seemed to serve the needs of the AG. With the sudden development of interest in the person and work of the Holy Spirit among Christians in virtually every sector of the church, new ways of expressing life in the Spirit appeared. Questions confronted Pentecostals from an avalanche of published materials. Most of the new charismatics had indeed invited the manifestation of the Holy Spirit, but generally expressed their new understanding in ways puzzling to Pentecostals. Many talked about Spirit baptism but few expressed belief in speaking in other tongues as the normative biblical evidence of it. When evangelicals entered the arena, advocates of dramatic interventions of the Holy Spirit for healing and deliverance from demonic power (such as Peter Wagner and John Wimber) distanced themselves conspicuously from Pentecostalism.[55] For many evangelicals, what some call baptism in the Spirit is not separable from new birth but is merely an actualization of that which is incipient from the moment of regeneration.[56] Perhaps the most difficult theological challenge confronting Pentecostals today comes from evangelicals who have eagerly entered into the domain that Pentecostals once held virtually alone but who understand these values in a significantly different way. Today the lines are considerably blurred, principally because of evangelical actualization theology.[57]

AG officialdom has responded to the theological challenges to Pentecostal doctrine by attempting to reinforce the statements of faith ministers are regularly required to sign. It is not a new practice in the AG to use annual questionnaires for maintaining credentials. These reach back at least to 1922. Questions respecting conformity to AG doctrine were instituted for the first time in 1960. Two basic questions were asked of each ordained minister, the one about subscription "without reservation" to the *Statement of Fundamental Truths* spelled out in the General Council constitution, and the other about publicly proclaiming these from the pulpit. The next year a third question was introduced, asking the minister to affirm his or her commitment to AG doctrine on six specific issues. If the minister differed in some respect on any of these six points, he

55. John Wimber and Kevin Springer, *Power Healing* (San Francisco: Harper and Row, 1987); and C. Peter Wagner, *Territorial Spirits: Insights on Strategic-Level Spiritual Warfare from Nineteen Christian Leaders* (Chichester, U.K.: Sovereign World Limited, 1991), both of which are examples of typical "Third Wave" theology.

56. Michael Green, *I Believe in the Holy Spirit* (Grand Rapids: Eerdmans, 1975), pp. 123-47.

57. James D. G. Dunn, *Baptism in the Holy Spirit: A Re-examination of the New Testament Teaching on the Gift of the Spirit in Relation to Pentecostalism Today* (London: SCM, 1970). Dunn, an English Methodist who is sympathetic to Pentecostals but critical of their theology, has mounted the most serious challenge to that theology. Pentecostal scholars have labored to counter the theses presented by Dunn in his monumental work.

or she was asked to state the differing opinion. The six issues were: (1) belief in speaking in other tongues as the initial physical evidence of Spirit baptism, (2) water baptism by immersion, (3) the premillennial return of Christ, (4) divine healing, (5) the rejection of eternal security teaching, and (6) entire sanctification.[58] This attempt by leadership to shore up the language of traditional doctrine appears to be a defensive measure adopted out of fear of losing traditional theological distinctiveness.

Traditional Pentecostal theology affirms the experience of baptism in the Spirit as an experience separable from new birth and accompanied by speaking in other tongues. It supports this belief by recourse to the narrative material of Luke recorded in Acts, particularly the episodes described in Acts 2, 8, 9, 10, and 19. On the basis of these five episodes, Pentecostals have taught that a pattern emerges that is a model for the church of today. Early Pentecostals concluded that what was described in Luke's accounts of early church events in Acts were experiences of people who were already Christian believers. Whatever they were experiencing, it was not new birth because they were already Christians. The language of Luke, employing terms like "falling upon" or "filling," was clearly intended to describe what Luke 24:49 and Acts 1:5 called being "baptized in the Holy Spirit." Pentecostals understood that the purpose of this experience was for empowering believers to extend the church initiated by Jesus Christ (Acts 1:8). They saw this verse capturing the outline for the book of Acts, the expansion of the church.

Besides arguing for a Pentecostal experience distinct from new birth, Pentecostals have sought biblical support for answering how a person can know that he or she has been baptized in the Spirit. Pentecostals saw sufficient pattern in the Acts episodes to conclude that Luke was teaching that speaking in tongues is the normative accompanying sign of Spirit baptism. Although tongues is not specifically mentioned in the Samaritan Pentecost episode of Acts 8, it is understood to be very strongly implied. Again, in the Damascus experience of Saul in Acts 9, tongues is not specifically mentioned. Pentecostals respond, however, by turning to 1 Corinthians 14:18, pointing to Paul's affirmation that he spoke in tongues more than any of the Corinthians! If that is so, then the assumption is that this began in Damascus when Ananias prayed for him. Pentecostal advocates infer this since it fits the other initiation episodes of Acts.

The problem with this "pattern methodology" is that even if it satisfies most Pentecostals, it is not persuasive to many non-Pentecostals, let alone to an

---

58. Doty, conversation with author, April 19, 2000. The data compiled by the statistician is distilled into official annual reports on a timely basis.

increasing number of Pentecostal pastors. AG scholars in recent years have undertaken fresh ways of developing a Pentecostal theology. The core of the problem in earlier years lay in hermeneutics. To deflect criticism from evangelical counterparts, Pentecostals argued for a distinct Pentecostal hermeneutics.[59] An example of the challenge Pentecostals faced is the influence of highly respected British evangelical John R. W. Stott, who rejected the propriety of employing biblical narrative materials for the development of theology unless these were repeated in overtly didactic passages.[60] This effectively diminishes Luke-Acts as suitable for constructing a biblical theology. Since all the initiation episodes of Spirit baptism are located in Acts, this obviously has serious implications for Pentecostal theology. In effect, the hermeneutics of people like Stott undercut the possibility of a valid Pentecostal theology.

A sea change occurred in evangelical hermeneutics in 1970 with the publication of I. Howard Marshall's *Luke: Historian and Theologian*.[61] Marshall, considered the foremost evangelical Lukan scholar of our time, rejected the traditional evangelical limitation on the use of narrative materials for theology, insisting instead that denying narrative for theological purposes seriously diminishes a theological opportunity. Since then, a growing number of evangelical scholars have joined Marshall's bandwagon. This has opened new possibilities for Pentecostals to present their faith in ways more persuasive to evangelicals, since a major hermeneutical chasm has been crossed.[62] Roger Stronstad, Robert Menzies, and Frank Macchia are among a growing number of younger, creative, and articulate spokespersons who are now gaining respectability among evangelical scholars for their fresh approaches.[63] In the

---

59. William W. Menzies, "The Methodology of Pentecostal Theology: An Essay on Hermeneutics," in *Essays on Apostolic Themes: Studies in Honor of Howard M. Ervin, Presented to Him by Colleagues and Friends on His Sixty-Fifth Birthday*, ed. Paul Elbert (Peabody, Mass.: Hendrickson, 1985), pp. 1-14.

60. John R. W. Stott, *The Baptism and Fullness of the Holy Spirit* (Downers Grove, Ill.: InterVarsity, 1964), p. 7.

61. I. Howard Marshall, *Luke: Historian and Theologian* (Grand Rapids: Zondervan, 1970).

62. William W. Menzies and Robert P. Menzies, *Spirit and Power: Foundation of Pentecostal Experience, a Call to Evangelical Dialogue* (Grand Rapids: Zondervan, 2000). This volume presents a Pentecostal apologetic on the basis of Marshall's insights.

63. Roger Stronstad, *The Charismatic Theology of St. Luke* (Peabody, Mass.: Hendrickson, 1984); Robert P. Menzies, *The Development of Early Christian Pneumatology: with Special Reference to Luke-Acts* (Sheffield, U.K.: Sheffield Academic Press, 1991); and Frank D. Macchia, "The Struggle for Global Witness: Shifting Paradigms in Pentecostal Theology," in *The Globalization of Pentecostalism: A Religion Made to Travel*, ed. Murray W. Dempster, Byron D. Klaus, and Douglas Petersen (Irvine, Calif.: Regnum Books, 1999), pp. 8-29.

next years, we should expect to see a new level of discussion between evangelical and Pentecostal theologians.

Conclusion

The modern Pentecostal movement celebrated its centennial in 2001. For eighty-five of these years, the AG has been perhaps the most influential denomination within the larger Pentecostal revival movement. At the prospect of embarking upon a new century and a new millennium, it is appropriate to ponder the prospects for the AG in the coming years. Certainly, the challenges for the AG are for the most part quite different from those of the mainline Protestant denominations. Mainline churches are endeavoring to find ways to stem their losses, while conservative churches such as the AG generally appear to be more vital. Miller has remarked that observers of the American religious scene have been surprised that groups like the AG have attracted a growing number of middle-class citizens, evidently filling a vacuum created by attrition among mainline churches. The denomination has appealed to a sizable number of disenchanted Roman Catholics as well.[64]

One of the factors that may help to explain the well-being of the AG is the continued evidence of a reasonable balance between charisma and organization. There appears to be sufficient elasticity in the denomination to sustain the inevitable ideological challenges it confronts. A variety of structural mechanisms are available to address the theological tensions provided by the rapidly changing religious environment. The bureaucracy, amenable to the will of the people at biennial General Council sessions, is trusted to carry out clearly defined responsibilities. The institutional apparatus seems to be reasonably effective in facilitating the work of the local churches, which is the heartbeat of the denomination. For the most part, pastors seem to feel encouraged and supported in their desire to fulfill their sense of calling. On at least two occasions in the last forty years the AG leadership has thoughtfully reassessed its reason for being and has sought to clarify goals and objectives in terms that are perceived to be biblical mandates. These values have resonated well with the constituency, providing a sense of common mission. The sense of the immanence of God, that God is accessible, is a major attraction in the local churches. The lively, experience-oriented worship and expansive fellowship fit well in the postmodern age. Revival, the seeking of spiritual renewal, is a fairly common

---

64. Donald Miller, *Reinventing American Protestantism: Christianity in the New Millennium* (Berkeley: University of California Press, 1997), p. 8.

thread in the tapestry of AG churches. That the denomination has from its be-ginnings been a strong missions-oriented body likely has been a major cohesive force through its history. Even if there may be differences of opinion on some matters, these tend to be submerged in the greater, common passion to reach the world for Christ. Confidence in the Division of Foreign Missions provides a rallying center for a wide variety of churches within the fellowship.

To be sure, there are areas of continuing concern and unresolved dilemma. Some of the challenges are certainly more significant than others. Ambiguity about the relationship with the charismatic movement is among the more sig-nificant issues to be faced. It is a perplexing question for the evangelical-oriented AG that many in the last generation reporting Pentecostal-type experiences are identified with liberal Christian bodies. Even more difficult to resolve is the mys-tery that Roman Catholics in large numbers claim a Pentecostal experience, whereas AG people have been taught that the Roman Church may be the harlot of Revelation.

Long-cherished doctrines are under assault within the denomination. Core values such as the initial physical evidence of Spirit baptism (speaking in other tongues) are facing fresh challenges. The very success of the modern Pen-tecostal/charismatic movement has produced an immense array of books on the person and work of the Holy Spirit. Many in the charismatic world have written interpretations of religious experience that conflict in various ways with Pentecostal teaching. A bewildering array of diverse teachings has bom-barded a younger generation of Pentecostals. For many years AG leadership seemed to be content with traditional articulations of Pentecostal belief, not giving serious thought to the fresh challenges affecting young pastors and stu-dents. In spite of some recent encouraging signs, the denomination continues to be marked by a degree of anti-intellectualism. This should not be a great sur-prise, since the denomination has featured the work of the Holy Spirit empow-ering people to *do*. Religious activism has therefore marked the denomination. Pragmatism in the fellowship tends to be impatient with theological reflection. More recently, however, the work of younger AG theologians is being respected as a useful service to the needs of the fellowship in a rapidly changing world. Fresh developments in evangelical hermeneutics have opened new dialogue op-portunities for Pentecostal theologians.

Historically, most Pentecostal people have not been greatly concerned with theological matters. Most are quite content with a simple list of core be-liefs. Herein lies a problem, however. Data disclose considerable cognitive dis-sonance within the AG with respect to Pentecostal experience. A significant number of adherents in local churches accept the doctrine of Spirit baptism but have not made the effort earnestly to seek the experience. The leadership of the denomination is addressing this matter as a sobering challenge for the future of the fellowship.

In spite of a slate of continuing challenges, it appears on balance that the AG is poised for continued growth in the near term. Ministers and laypeople seem to be satisfied with the service provided by the national structure for facilitating their local church ministries. The appeal to young people who evidently are attracted to the values of the fellowship is encouraging for the future. As the AG enters the twenty-first century, the present balance between charisma and structure, as long as it can be sustained, bodes well for the near term.

A Short History of the
Association of Vineyard Churches

Bill Jackson

I grew up rooted in historical evangelicalism. My mother was converted to Christ at a Young Life parents' meeting and led me to Christ when I was a boy. I went on to attend Wheaton College in Wheaton, Illinois, and after graduation worked for Youth for Christ. My future in the evangelical stream would have seemed secure except for one unnerving moment at Wheaton's Science Station in the Black Hills of South Dakota. Two friends laid their hands on me and prayed that I would be "baptized" with the Holy Spirit. Within minutes I had an encounter with the Holy Spirit so powerful I was nearly shaken off my bunk. Some weeks later, back at the college, I lay in my bed looking up at the Edmund Chapel steeple and began to pray in tongues.

My new experience of the Spirit was not embraced within my evangelicalism, so I prayed in tongues in private. I also prayed for someone to mentor me in the works of the Spirit into which I so longed to look. Little did I know that all over the world there were people just like me looking for the same things.

It was during my Gordon-Conwell years that my dilemma came to a head. I was still an evangelical theologically, but my hunger for life in the Spirit had led my wife and me to an Assembly of God church. When I explored ordination with that denomination, I was rejected because I was unwilling to adhere to their "initial evidence" doctrine of baptism in the Spirit as evidenced by speaking in tongues. Not dismayed, we tried to pastor within the Evangelical Free Church, but they wouldn't have me because I spoke in tongues. I was between a rock and a hard place until one day, shortly before graduation, I was invited to hear a man named John Wimber teach on healing.

I went to the meeting reluctantly, but was pleasantly surprised to hear a standard lecture on the kingdom of God à la the required readings of George

Ladd for my "Life of Jesus" course.[1] The music was contemporary and directed to God. I liked the beat. Oh, did I mention that no one was wearing a tie? It was when Wimber had a "word," however, about a woman with a deaf ear, that I sat up and took notice. Sure enough, there was a woman there with one ear deaf since birth. John and others laid hands on her and prayed with their eyes open, explaining that they were looking for signs of the Spirit's activity. Then, suddenly, the lady could hear out of that ear. This, I thought, is what I had been looking for since my days at Wheaton.

I give this autobiographical statement simply because I can. The Vineyard is so new that those of us who are in it have lived it. Many of us are evangelicals who have had encounters with the Holy Spirit along our journey, and at some point met John Wimber. It was Wimber who gave us language for what we were experiencing and dared to invite the Spirit into the framework of our evangelicalism.

Church growth expert Peter Wagner dubbed what began to happen to evangelicals in the 1980s as the "third wave" of the Holy Spirit.[2] Wagner saw the birth of the Pentecostals at the turn of the century as the first wave. The second wave swept the world in at least three different forms, primarily in the 1960s and early 1970s. First, there were the neo-Pentecostals, comprised primarily of those out of historic denominations such as the Episcopalians and Presbyterians. Next, there was a strong Catholic "charismatic" movement that impacted Catholicism worldwide. Finally, there was a massive evangelistic net that swept in thousands upon thousands of young rock 'n' rollers known as the Jesus People. The third wave is represented by the events that follow in the next few pages.

It was the second wave that Wimber had come to reject. He was converted to Christ out of the music industry and quickly demonstrated an uncanny ability to lead people to Christ through what he called "intuition." It never occurred to him that these intuitions might be gifts of the Holy Spirit because the Quaker church he attended taught that such gifts were no longer in operation in the present age.

His ability to evangelize and grow churches eventually led Wagner to invite Wimber to be the first employee of the new Fuller Seminary Institute of Church Growth in Pasadena, California. During the years 1974-77, Wimber worked with over twenty denominations in every state in the Union. He saw the church, warts and all. As he traveled, he began to dream of a church that he would like to go to. Despite his dreams, his spiritual life began to dry up. It culminated one night in a hotel in Detroit, Michigan, when God woke him up, say-

1. George Ladd, *New Testament Theology* (Grand Rapids: Eerdmans, 1974).
2. Peter Wagner, *The Third Wave of the Holy Spirit* (Ann Arbor, Mich.: Servant, 1988).

ing, "John, I've seen your ministry (clearly implying that he wasn't too impressed), but now I'm going to show you mine." Wimber wept into the morning, saying to God, "This is what I've always wanted."

While all these things had been happening, Wimber had also begun to review his position on the gifts of the Holy Spirit. His contacts with visiting missionaries at Fuller had filled his mind with amazing stories of church growth accompanied by miracles such as healing and the casting out of demons. Wimber was aided by Wagner, who was also going through a similar "paradigm shift" in his worldview. They both began to realize that their antisupernatural stance had been based more in their modernistic worldview than in the study of Scripture. It was at this point that Wimber began to read the kingdom theology of George Ladd, which gave him the exegetical foundation for the ongoing ministry of the Spirit in the church. Wimber and his wife, Carol, had also been attending one of the churches affiliated with the Calvary Chapel movement where the teaching of Pastor Chuck Smith, on the ministry of the Spirit, was practical and timely.

Joining himself to a group of Quakers that had been meeting on Sunday nights at their house, Wimber began services for a new church on Mother's Day 1977. They affiliated with Calvary Chapel, as Wimber now began to explore the possibilities of seeing the same kind of church growth, accompanied by miracles, as had been attested by the missionaries at Fuller. Shortly after starting the church, they began to study spiritual gifts on Wednesday nights and Wimber began to teach on healing from the Gospel of Luke on Sundays. After teaching on healing for nine months and seeing no one healed, they were ready to quit. God gave Wimber an ultimatum, either teach on healing or leave the ministry. Wimber chose to stay and teach, and before the tenth month they saw their first person healed. From that point the healings began to trickle in, then pour in.

While all this had been happening, one could not say their church was "charismatic." There were no outbreaks of tongues or other overt manifestations of the Spirit — that is, until May of 1980. Wimber asked a young man converted during the Jesus People movement named Lonnie Frisbee to give his testimony. After finishing, Frisbee invited all the people twenty-five years old and younger to come forward. He then invited the Holy Spirit to bring God's power. What happened is now legendary in Vineyard folklore. The young people were filled with the Spirit, began to fall over, speak in tongues and shake. Witnesses said it looked like a battlefield.

Those young people, many of them junior high and high school age, were so lit on fire for God that they began to see their friends healed and brought to Christ from all over town, baptizing them in swimming pools and Jacuzzis. Within months Wimber's church had catapulted in growth, launching what he would later call "power evangelism," i.e., conversions precipitated by healings and miracles.

Since this watershed period essentially launched the Vineyard movement, we need to pause for a moment and give an overall framework for the periods of our history. Most of these periods center around Wimber's quest to find the radical middle between his historic, doctrinal evangelicalism and his desire to have Pentecostal power.[3] In retrospect, he had two primary callings, to found a church-planting movement called the Association of Vineyard Churches (AVC) and to address a deficient pneumatology in the evangelical church. He accomplished the latter through seminars, courses, conferences, and writings, as church leaders hungered throughout the world for an experience of the Spirit within an evangelical framework.

The Wimber/Vineyard history can be broken down into the following periods:

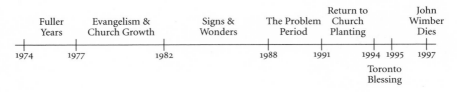

We have already examined the Fuller years and the early years of Wimber's church where he was testing the waters of evangelism and church growth as led by the Holy Spirit. The real beginning of the AVC dates back to that Sunday night experience of the Spirit in 1980 and Wimber's separation from Calvary Chapel in 1982 to align with a fledgling church-planting movement called the Vineyard. We now turn to a brief overview of these events.

The Signs and Wonders Years

After the Spirit was poured out on Wimber's church, Wagner sat up and took notice. Wimber was invited to teach a course at the Fuller School of World Mission called MC 510 (MC stands for "mission class"), "Signs, Wonders and Church Growth." The class not only included lecture, but also a "clinic" time where the Spirit was invited into the room to perform healings and miracles. From the outset, these and other manifestations of the Spirit were prevalent after each class.

---

3. See Bill Jackson, *The Quest for the Radical Middle* (Cape Town, South Africa: Vineyard International Press, 1999).

With Wimber's evangelical prestige as a church growth expert, the word quickly went out. *Christian Life Magazine* devoted a whole issue to the class, and within months MC 510 was catapulted into worldwide visibility. Wimber would teach the class numerous times, eventually opening it up to the public in conference form. Kevin Springer expanded the course syllabus into the book *Power Evangelism*,[4] later followed by *Power Healing*,[5] based on the course syllabus for MC 511.

When Wimber began to heal the sick and pursue the Holy Spirit's ministry in the main church meetings, conflict began with the Calvary Chapel network of churches led by Chuck Smith. Calvary history had been replete with Spirit activity, but it had eventually been relegated to the "back room" where it was less visible. The tension mounted to the point where it was suggested, in a meeting with Calvary leaders, that Wimber's church stop using the Calvary name and affiliate with a young pastor in West Los Angeles named Kenn Gulliksen, who had started a church named the Vineyard. Within a short time, Gulliksen's church had spun off sister churches, all with the Vineyard name. Wimber changed the name of his church to the Vineyard in the spring of 1982. Gulliksen then turned over the churches under his care to Wimber, thus beginning Wimber's leadership over the Vineyard.

With Wimber's catalytic prowess at the helm and the Holy Spirit's wind in the sails, the Vineyard sailed out of safe harbor and out into rapid and stormy seas. By 1986, with the visibility of the MC 510 class and Wimber's aggressive conferencing, people and churches right and left wanted to affiliate with the Vineyard. They, like me, had come aboard to recover the life of the Spirit in the church within the moorings of historic evangelicalism. By the end of 1986, there were 136 Vineyard churches, with twice as many churches projected for the following year.

With growth, however, came severe attack. Fuller put a moratorium on the signs and wonders courses, claiming the "clinics" belonged in the realm of the church, not the confines of an academic institution. Other criticisms came from books and denominational periodicals originating during this period and extending on into the late 1990s. Men such as former Dallas Seminary professor Jack Deere and Wayne Grudem, chair of systematic theology at Trinity Evangelical Divinity School, took up their pens in defense of Wimber's theology and the Vineyard. By the grace of God, the movement was able to negotiate tricky waters and stay the course toward growth.

4. John Wimber with Kevin Spinger, *Power Evangelism* (San Francisco: Harper and Row, 1986).

5. John Wimber with Kevin Spinger, *Power Healing* (San Francisco: Harper and Row, 1987).

The Prophetic Years

All this took its toll on Wimber, however. He suffered from angina, was over-weight, overworked, and by 1988 felt as if he was going to collapse. A remark-able turn in the story appears right at this point. A prophetic minister named Paul Cain began to prophesy with great power to Wimber and the Vineyard, and the movement went into a period of renewal. These years also saw a rela-tionship develop with Mike Bickle, a young pastor of an independent church in Missouri called Kansas City Fellowship. Bickle had gathered a number of pro-phetic figures to his ministry, most notably Bob Jones. Men like Cain and Jones began to regularly minister within the Vineyard with great effect.

Some in the movement were skeptical, however, and wanted to proceed with caution. The messages of Bickle and the prophetic ministers were based in the idea that various gifts of the Spirit had been lost over the ages and were in the process of being restored. The high degree of revelation being received by the prophets was seen as an indication that the prophetic ministry was exceed-ing that of the New Testament (the "greater works" prediction Jesus made in John 14:12). After the prophetic had been restored to the church, next would come the apostolic ministry, which would precede the second coming of Christ.

Wimber bit hard on the prophetic bait, his own son being delivered from drug addiction through a word from Bob Jones. When Wimber's meetings in London in 1990 failed to bring the type of revival expected from a prophecy by Cain, Wimber felt embarrassed and began to distance himself from Bickle and the restorationist thesis. Bickle himself had been embroiled in fighting accusa-tions of false prophecy and aggrandizement. At the time his church had come under the Vineyard banner, becoming Metro Vineyard in Kansas City. He was later acquitted of most charges, and admirably accepted responsibility for the others. When it was all said and done, Wimber led the Vineyard back to its missional, church-planting roots, and Metro Vineyard eventually relinquished the Vineyard name and became Metro Christian Fellowship.

Back to Church Planting

The pastors' conference in Denver in the summer of 1991 moved us away from the revivalism of the prophetic and back to our genetic code in evangelism and church planting. Structures were set in place to proactively plant churches with proper training and oversight. The denominational exception was that the Vineyard was not intending to start its own seminaries and Bible colleges, choosing rather to use traditional evangelical systems of education. The specifics of church planting and leadership were embedded into formalized internships in larger Vineyard churches.

The Denver conference also introduced an expansion into world missions. The Vineyard had always been involved overseas, but usually in the role of renewal. Many of the church leaders in countries inviting the Vineyard to do meetings had asked that there be no church-planting efforts in those countries. During the years 1992-94, the moratorium was lifted as Wimber felt God leading the Vineyard to expand their churches extensively around the globe. As of this writing, we have almost a thousand churches in over fifty countries, seven of those countries having been released to organize self-governing associations of Vineyard churches.

The Toronto Blessing

For one young man the new Vineyard emphasis was not enough. Randy Clark, pastor of the Vineyard on the south side of St. Louis, Missouri, wanted more of God's power in his life. Prophecies given to him throughout his life pointed to more that God wanted to do with him. In a desperate spiritual condition, Clark attended meetings in Tulsa, Oklahoma, in the summer of 1993, led by visiting South African evangelist Rodney Howard-Browne. During ministry after the preaching, Clark went up for prayer again and again. Each time he fell to the floor, overcome by the Spirit of God. He went back to St. Louis a new man. Manifestations of God's presence began to break out in his church immediately. People began to fall, shake, laugh, and receive healing from physical illness.

When he was asked at a regional Vineyard pastors' conference to share what God had been doing through him, the same phenomena were spread to the other pastors. Word of what had happened at this conference reached the ears of John and Carol Arnott, Vineyard pastors of a small church near the airport in Toronto, Canada. Sensing that this was what he was praying for, Arnott asked Clark to come up for a handful of meetings at his church in January of 1994. Little did they know that the St. Louis pastor would not leave Toronto until March 26. Amazing things began to happen at the Toronto Airport Vineyard from the outset of Clark's preaching. Similar phenomena as described occurred in each instance, with the added benefit that people began to receive salvation in Christ. The demonized were freed. Joy emanated from people's faces and the word spread around the country. Suddenly, people began showing up from the States. Before long, planeloads began coming from Britain, then from places in Asia, then from all over the world. Eventually, every continent except Antarctica was represented. The most significant thing was that people who traveled to the

Toronto meetings took the power of the Spirit home with them, almost as if they had taken a fiery briquette with them in their suitcase. Similar things began to break out wherever they went. Before long there were other centers of renewal such as Pensacola, Florida; Pasadena, California; Kelowna, Canada; and London, England. The so-called Toronto Blessing had begun.

Since both main pastors initially involved with the Toronto Blessing were from the Vineyard, Wimber tried to pastor the renewal from a distance. Exotic manifestations were capturing the attention of many, things such as excessive (at least to some) laughter and sounds coming from people being ministered to that sounded like animal noises. Before long Wimber was inundated with requests to put a stop to these things lest the ground gained against the Vineyard critics be lost.

Ever cautious to shut things down prematurely, Wimber wrote corrective articles in his in-house publication called *Vineyard Reflections*. His articles were not enough to keep the "Bible Answer Man," Hank Hanegraaff, from using his radio program and writings to lambaste the Vineyard for what was going on. Vineyard parishioners around the country were shaken to hear the Vineyard being called "a great end-times delusion from Satan." Because of a fear that the Toronto renewal was moving away from the Vineyard genetic code, an emergency board meeting was called where Toronto leaders were invited to interact with Vineyard leaders from around the USA. Upon conclusion, the board published a report offering parameters to govern the renewal.

By 1995 the Toronto Blessing was getting a lot of visibility. Newscaster Peter Jennings did a television special called "In the Name of God" which featured the Vineyard. Phil Donahue had Toronto leaders on his talk show, and investigative reporters from *A Current Affair* were preparing to air their own perspective on what was transpiring. Even this media blitz was not enough to raise Wimber's ire. It was when John Arnott released a book called *The Father's Blessing* that Wimber stepped in. The book featured a chapter attempting to give biblical interpretations to some of the more exotic phenomena of the Holy Spirit. Since Wimber's name was on the back endorsing the book, even though Wimber had not seen this particular chapter, it appeared that Wimber was approving hermeneutical methodology outside of the historical and grammatical exegetical methods endorsed within evangelicalism. It was at this point that Wimber drew the line. An emergency meeting was called in Toronto.

The Toronto leaders assumed Wimber was coming to work through their differences to find middle ground. They were completely taken by surprise when Wimber gave them an ultimatum. Within hours the Toronto leaders affirmed their solidarity with the way they were pastoring the renewal and removed themselves from the Vineyard. For some the separation was a great relief, for others a tragedy. In either case, both the Vineyard and Toronto have moved on, the Vineyard getting "back on track" one more time and Toronto forming its own network of churches. As has historically been true, church rifts resulted in church growth.

The Post-Wimber Era

John Wimber, after suffering for years with angina, cancer, and a stroke, tragically went to be with the Lord on November 17, 1997, after a hallway fall led to a massive brain hemorrhage. The Vineyard had continued to grow throughout John's journey toward God, but many now wondered what would happen to the movement. Would it fracture into old-line Vineyard churches, "seeker" churches, and churches pursuing the renewal? Leadership would be the key.

Acting AVC USA director Todd Hunter, one of Wimber's earliest disciples, was set in place as national director in the spring of 1998 after unanimous approval of the board. All board members voluntarily turned in their resignations to give Hunter the freedom to choose his team. Most of those men have since been retained, having clearly demonstrated faithfulness commensurate with their gifts and callings.

Hunter addressed the "church he would build" at our national pastors' conference in Anaheim, California, in the summer of 1999. He told us he intended to lead us beyond the battles won in the 1980s for intimate worship and the Holy Spirit's presence welcomed in evangelical settings. All over the world people were singing Vineyard songs and laying hands on the sick for healing; Baptists, Lutherans, Presbyterians collaborated side by side with charismatics and Pentecostals, singing the same songs and yearning for the same demonstrations of God's power. He challenged the movement to redefine itself not in ecclesiastical terms as we had done in the past, i.e., the best of evangelicalism and the best of Pentecostalism, but in biblical terms. The Vineyard's challenge was to look forward and define itself as existing for God and the fulfillment of the Great Commission of Jesus (Matt. 24:14). The following organizational case study by Donald Miller and theological essay by Don Williams provide a nuanced analysis of the resources and challenges of faith and leadership that the Vineyard brings to this challenge.

Routinizing Charisma:
The Vineyard Christian Fellowship
in the Post-Wimber Era

Donald E. Miller

In its twenty years of existence the Vineyard Christian Fellowship has been an influential, innovative, and yet oftentimes tumultuous organization. In terms of influence, it has grown to over five hundred congregations in the United States, a rather remarkable achievement in two decades. Equally impressive, there are as many Vineyards outside the United States as within, and in countries as diverse as South Africa and Australia. Secondly, there is little question but what the Vineyard has contributed to creating a new paradigm of culturally relevant churches. Vineyard music is sung throughout the world, and hundreds of non-Vineyard churches welcome the Holy Spirit into their worship in ways that did not occur prior to the renewal conferences of John Wimber. In addition, the Vineyard has been at the forefront of a movement to equip laypersons for ministry, and quite literally to give the ministry back to the people. But thirdly, this innovation has been accompanied by a substantial amount of organizational change and challenge. For example, one of the cofounders of the movement, Kenn Gulliksen, left the Vineyard because he felt it had become too bureaucratic. The other founder, John Wimber — and the person with whom people typically identify the Vineyard — died in 1997 after a prolonged struggle with cancer, leaving a leadership vacuum. Wimber's successor as national director, Todd Hunter, resigned the position after two and one-half years to pursue a calling to plant churches that will minister to Generation X young adults and those with a postmodern mentality.[1]

Of the case studies in this book, the Vineyard is the youngest organization to be studied. But it has had visibility and impact far in excess of its 80,000

---

1. The discussion of the Vineyard movement in this chapter ends with the resignation of Todd Hunter as national director in May 2000.

members in the United States.[2] Therefore several important questions can appropriately be asked. For example, what does the mercurial growth of the Vineyard tell us about how innovation occurs within the Christian tradition? What lessons are to be learned from the Vineyard regarding transitions in organizational leadership? And are there features of the Vineyard's "genetic code" that have application to its ongoing evolution as a Christian movement? The answers to these questions will be drawn from several years of personal visits I made to Vineyard Christian Fellowships in southern California and around the nation.[3] In addition, I will draw on two surveys of Vineyard pastors,[4] along with extensive conversations with both Wimber and Hunter regarding their vision for the Vineyard.[5] In terms of the perspective I bring to this analysis, it is important to note that I am an "outsider" to the Vineyard movement — belonging to a large, politically progressive, noncharismatic Episcopal church in southern California. However, I also have been influenced by doing research in dozens of Pentecostal and charismatic churches in the developing world,[6] as well as by my research on "new paradigm" churches in the United States, and from this research I have learned that divorcing heart and head, mind and body, is often fatal to the Christian mission.[7]

2. The statistics cited in this chapter are drawn from a database compiled in 1998 by the Association of Vineyard Churches. Updated information can be found on their Web site (http://www.vineyardusa.org/index2.htm).

3. Much of the research for this chapter was done in the early 1990s for my book *Reinventing American Protestantism: Christianity in the New Millennium* (Berkeley: University of California Press, 1997).

4. The first survey was conducted in 1992/93 as part of the research for *Reinventing American Protestantism*. The second survey was conducted in 1999 after John Wimber's death, with the specific intention of assessing the views of Vineyard pastors about the status of the Vineyard movement.

5. The conversations with John Wimber spanned several years in the mid-1990s and included one two-day interview period that was very relaxed and informal. The interviews with Todd Hunter were done after he became national director.

6. Ted Yamamori and I have conducted more than three hundred interviews in nearly twenty different countries as part of a project documenting growing Pentecostal churches that have active social ministries in their communities. See our forthcoming *Pentecostalism and Social Transformation: A Global Analysis* (Berkeley: University of California Press, in press).

7. See my *Reinventing American Protestantism*, pp. 6-8, for a discussion of the influence of new paradigm churches on my own thinking.

John Wimber and the Vineyard's Genetic Code

Founders of movements play an important role in setting the genetic code that defines what evolves after their death, and Wimber is no exception.[8] I clearly remember my first impressions of Wimber. The Anaheim Vineyard had purchased a large parcel of land in an industrial park. Work had begun on building a three-thousand-seat auditorium within the walls of a warehouse and office complex. In the meantime, however, the church was gathering under a huge nylon tent structure that had been erected in the building's parking lot. There was a stage/platform at one end of the tent, where an extensive sound system was located, which looked over a couple thousand folding chairs set up on outdoor grass-colored carpet.

For the first thirty minutes or so of the service, the usual soft rock worship songs were sung and people stood, sat, or kneeled as their inclination prompted them, some with their hands held out in expectation and others with hands raised, especially during songs that were praising "the God on high." When the worship period ended, offering baskets were then passed — without commentary — followed by a somewhat overweight man in his late fifties walking up to a bare podium. Wimber read a passage of Scripture and then started to share his interpretation of its meaning, mixed with personal anecdotes. There was no shouting, no dramatic gestures, just an understated sharing of an evangelical message that was filled with a transparent expectation that the Holy Spirit was in our midst.[9]

As the message wound to a close, Wimber invited people to come forward for prayer. To my great surprise, they came by the dozens. In a very informal manner lay members warmly approached each person, and putting an arm around the person — or placing a hand on his or her shoulder — asked the person a few questions and then prayed. When the area around the stage became too crowded, Wimber invited people to raise their hands so Christians around them could pray for them where they stood. No one left the tent. Ministry time was as important as the preaching and worship.

Before long there were little groupings everywhere. Some people were weeping. A few were wailing. Others seemed to be physically touched by the

---

8. Vineyard pastors frequently make reference to the DNA of the Vineyard movement, and I find this biological metaphor very useful in understanding the evolution of the Vineyard church.

9. Many popular understandings of charismatic leadership associate the term with dynamic political expression or even televangelist pulpit pounding and gesticulation. Wimber's charisma was of a different sort, and was much more appropriate to a baby boomer audience that rejected such coercive personality types.

Spirit, and were shaking. What was rather bewildering to me was that all of this was happening without any great emotional hype by Wimber. He had quietly invited the Spirit into our midst. This was nothing like the flame-throwing theatrics of the televangelists. What I was later to understand is that this form of worship was a unique blending of Wimber's heritage in a Quaker church, mixed with deep evangelical convictions, and radicalized by a belief that God is still healing the sick and intervening in people's lives, just as was occurring in the first century.

John Wimber was born in Peoria, Illinois, of hillbilly stock. His route out of this blue-collar beginning was through music, and by age fifteen he was playing his first professional gig at the Dixie Castle in Orange County, California, near where his parents had settled.[10] Before long, however, he learned that he could make more money *managing* bands than he could *playing* in them. During one of my interviews with Wimber before he died, John said he had owned and operated fifty-two different businesses. This business acumen served him well when he later became a church consultant, because it was a small stretch for him to apply his understanding of people and American culture to the growth and decline of congregations.

In spite of the gratitude Wimber felt toward the Friends church which had nurtured him in the faith after his conversion as an adult, he thought their days were numbered. Sitting in his office one afternoon after his cancer surgery, Wimber recounted, "I remember standing shortly after I was converted in the Quaker church, looking at it as a business, out on the front lawn, and thinking, 'This place is going out of business, and I love this place. I met Jesus here. But the building is in the wrong place; it's the wrong kind of building.'" Indeed, he was convinced that many mainline churches had been going out of business for a long time, but they just did not realize it. Only their endowments, in his view, would cushion their collapse.

Hence, when the opportunity came to start his own church, it had a radically contemporary sound. The music drew on the same idiom as the unconverted were listening to in bars and at rock concerts, but the lyrics were different. The revolutions of the 1960s and 1970s had severely damaged propositional theology, but they had also opened the door to pragmatic, experiential verification of truth. In short, there was a new openness to transcendent realities that

---

10. In an interview for the Vineyard publication, John Wimber's widow, Carol, quotes from a *Christianity Today* article that described her husband during his Righteous Brothers period as a "beer-guzzling, drug-abusing pop musician, who was converted at the age of 29 while chain-smoking his way through a Quaker-led Bible study." "The Way It Was: The Roots of Vineyard Worship," *Cutting Edge* 6, no. 1 (winter 2002), http://www.vineyardusa.org/publications/newsletters/cutting_edge/2002_winter/carol_wimber.htm.

resonated with Wimber's Quaker mysticism, and the new worship style of the Vineyard made cultural sense so long as one threw out the fundamentalist's dispensational theology and instead believed that God was in the same business today that he was two millennia earlier.

When teaching at Fuller Seminary, Wimber had encountered the writings of theologian George Ladd, and with this foundation in hand he started telling people they should do the "stuff" practiced by Jesus and the disciples: praying for the sick, casting out demons, feeding the poor and hungry — all of which is the work of the kingdom. If there is no response, believed Wimber, then at least one is following in the footsteps of Jesus, doing the things Jesus counseled his followers to do. The results, in his view, are not up to Jesus' disciples. God is in charge and does things in his own ways and in his own time. We are but his instruments.

From the beginning, the focus of the Vineyard was not on Wimber and his charismatic powers. Wimber saw his job as one of equipping the saints to do the work of ministry.[11] This was to be a people's movement. And it was to be rooted in a clear theology and ideology, not just ephemeral, ecstatic experience. Repeatedly in interviews Wimber told me that he wanted to be a Wesley, not a Whitefield — meaning that he wanted to establish a movement that would endure, not one built around a personality. According to Wimber, "Whitefield came, died, left converts, but we couldn't find any of them anywhere. Wesley came, died, and left a movement. That's what I wanted to do," he said. "So when God gave me the opportunity, I said, 'Okay, Lord.'"

Outsiders to the Vineyard movement oftentimes miss the movement-building component of the Vineyard. They seize only on the spectacular moments of the Vineyard's history, and indeed there are some. Peter Wagner, when he was professor of world missions at Fuller Seminary, invited Wimber to coteach a course that turned into a laboratory for healing and deliverance.[12] In retrospect, seminary is a place to *study* theology, not *practice* the works of the kingdom, and so, amidst great discussion and controversy, Wimber's sojourn as a noncredentialed professor ended. And late in Wimber's life, the Toronto Vineyard erupted with signs and wonders that resembled worship during the Great Awakenings in American religious history. People laughed uncontrollably, made strange animal sounds, and took the presence of the Spirit to heights that worried even the progressive Wimber — and so he eventually sent them packing.[13]

---

11. Not surprisingly, the title of the Vineyard's magazine for many years was *Equipping*.

12. C. Peter Wagner subsequently embraced many of the manifestations of the Holy Spirit that were practiced in this class. Indeed, he has been a primary apologist for what he calls the New Apostolic Movement within Christianity.

13. See Margaret M. Poloma, "The 'Toronto Blessing': Charisma, Institutionalization and Revival," *Journal for the Scientific Study of Religion* 37, no. 2 (1997): 257-71.

Fundamental to Wimber's vision, however, was the desire to give the ministry back to the people. There is no reason for clergy to wear vestments or collars that separate them from their flock. Pastors are not specially endowed superhumans; they sin like everyone else; they have no magical powers. Hence, Wimber used to joke that he prepared for a healing meeting by drinking a diet Pepsi and watching a little TV. After all, he was not the one doing the healing. It was God. In spite of Wimber's charismatic presence, he was an unusually modest and humble person, always turning the glory to God and taking no credit for himself.

If Wimber had a mission in life, it was to ground people in the biblical narratives and train them to do the works of the Spirit. Consequently, Wimber was unusually candid before audiences about his own shortcomings. And he frequently joked during a service, especially when people got too wrapped up in the drama of "signs and wonders," thereby regrounding them in the everyday world. Because for Wimber there was no sacred-secular divide. The kingdom was here, to be enjoyed in the moment.

In his management style Wimber was sometimes autocratic. He genuinely believed that God spoke to him, and that he should be obedient. Hence, it did not make sense to Wimber that he should submit his vision for discussion and democratic vote. According to one of his close friends, this was both Wimber's genius and his weakness. If one didn't like the direction the Vineyard was going, one could bail out. Led by the Spirit, Wimber was a great risk-taker in charting a new course. One of his close associates said that Wimber was willing "to bet the whole farm" on some of the directions the Vineyard took, and it was this quality that enabled him to be a religious innovator.

In hindsight, some of the swings in the Vineyard, by Wimber's own admission, were mistakes. But he was willing to explore new ideas and then, if he was wrong, to confess his sins and boldly move ahead once again. Consequently, the Vineyard was never static. Under his leadership it was always pushing the envelope, exploring new models for expressing the compassion of Christ and the presence of the Holy Spirit.

The one person, however, who did regularly offer him counsel was his wife, Carol.[14] Indeed, some of the core values of the Vineyard are convictions that emerged out of her deep prayer life. The daughter of a physician, Carol Wimber has been an influential and articulate presence in the movement. On more than one occasion God spoke to her in dreams, and indeed, John viewed his wife as a vessel of the Holy Spirit's instructions to him. For example, in 1988 John was pushing hard at a pastors conference to identify the Vineyard as a de-

14. See the interview with Carol Wimber, "The Way It Was."

nomination. In his view it was the rebelliousness of baby boom generation pastors that caused them to resist structure and authority, even though it was precisely this rejection of the institutionalization of religion that had led them to the Vineyard in the first place. Carol Wimber, however, had a vision that caused her husband to reconsider his attempt to denominationalize the Vineyard, and Wimber came away from the conference with a strong feeling that the Vineyard movement should die, and for the next two or three years he did much soul-searching about its future.

The Origins of the Vineyard

The organizational founder of the Vineyard is Wimber, but the person who gave the movement its name and started the first Vineyard church is Kenn Gulliksen. In the early 1970s Gulliksen returned from a stint in the United States Air Force and moved to El Paso, Texas, to lead a Calvary Chapel–associated ministry called the Jesus Chapels. This work grew rapidly, in part because of a migration out of an Episcopal church by people who were attracted to Gulliksen's emphasis on the presence of the Holy Spirit. Viewing himself as a church planter, Gulliksen moved back to southern California after this church was booming and launched the first Vineyard church as a Bible study in the home of Chuck Girard in July 1974. Within months this church also exploded with growth. In an interview Gulliksen said, "This may sound very unhumble and very arrogant, but we fully expected it because the one thing that we learned at Calvary [Chapel] was how to have vision." The methodology was simple: "I played guitar and sat on a stool and led some worship and taught the Bible." At the end of each service, Gulliksen said he invited forward anyone who wanted to receive Christ, and they came forward in droves. In addition to the several thousand people who worshiped weekly at this church, another half-dozen Vineyards were started in the next few years — all under the broad umbrella of Calvary Chapel.

Simultaneously another branch of the Vineyard was forming. In 1963 a jazz musician, record producer, and self-professed heathen was introduced to Jesus. By 1970 Wimber was leading eleven Bible studies a week that included many people who were attending the Yorba Linda Friends Church in southern California. In 1971 he was invited to join the staff of the church, and from 1974 to 1978 Wimber served as a consultant at the Institute of Evangelism and Church Growth associated with Fuller Theological Seminary. While Wimber was still working for Fuller, a group of young adults from the Friends church were packing out the home of one of the members. Wimber began to feel a call to minister to this group, having grown rather discouraged by what he was observing in many mainline churches across the country. On May 8, 1977, a group of 150 people officially declared themselves Calvary Chapel of Yorba Linda, and within a few years the group had grown to 1,500 people, moving from one rented school auditorium to another. By 1980 the Holy Spirit was moving powerfully in their worship, with people speaking in tongues and claiming healing from physical and psychological ailments.

At a fateful meeting in 1982, Chuck Smith, founder of Calvary Chapel, gathered together some of the pastors of the larger churches in the movement, including Kenn Gulliksen, John Wimber, Mike McIntosh, Greg Laurie, Jeff Johnson, and Raul Reis. Several of these young pastors immediately put Wimber on the hot seat for the exercise of charismatic gifts in his church. In spite of Chuck Smith's background in a Pentecostal church, he de-emphasized overt expression of tongues, prophecy, and healing in public worship. In my separate interviews with Smith, Gulliksen, and Wimber, they all shared the same essential recollections of this meeting. After being interrogated by some of the other pastors, Wimber suggested changing the name of his congregation. Smith concurred and noted that Wimber's emphasis on the gifts of the Holy Spirit had many parallels to what was occurring at Gulliksen's Vineyard church. A friendship had already developed between Wimber and Gulliksen, so the match seemed perfect. Thus the Vineyard movement was born in 1982 as an organizational entity separate from Calvary Chapel.

Shortly after this meeting the oversight of this fledgling Vineyard movement passed from Gulliksen to Wimber. In rehearsing the early history of the Vineyard, Gulliksen said he felt like he was on the verge of an emotional breakdown at this time, overwhelmed by the demands of pastoring a large congregation and looking after the new church plants that had occurred. In contrast, Wimber was highly experienced in organizational issues, having run several businesses and, more importantly, having visited some two thousand churches during his years as a church growth consultant.

According to Gulliksen, "John was like a savior in a fat man's body for me at the time. . . . When John came, we had really no organization apart from a deep love for one another and a relationship." Gulliksen had always been a "pioneer," not a "homesteader," and he saw his gift as the ability to plant new churches and then to give them to someone else to tend. In fact, in 1983, the year after Wimber took over the leadership, Gulliksen went to Newport Beach and started another Vineyard, which quickly grew to 1,400 people.

A point of disagreement between Wimber and Chuck Smith is how many Calvary Chapels defected from the movement to join the Vineyard's more charismatic emphasis. Wimber estimates thirty; Smith says as many as a hundred.

Whichever number is more accurate, Gulliksen maintains that these "adoptions" into the Vineyard movement "were pastored by people who were hungry for more of the Holy Spirit in their own churches and in their own lives. They were risk-takers, possibly more pioneering, and they were people who had had previous relationships with John."

The Current Status of the Vineyard

According to the Vineyard's database, in 1998 there were 490 churches. These congregations range from new church starts with a few members to congregations with several thousand members. Although the Vineyard started in southern California, it is important to note that there are currently Vineyard churches in forty-eight states. As one might expect, California far outstrips the other states, with over one hundred congregations. But it is notable that Washington, Texas, Ohio, Florida, and Colorado all have twenty or more congregations.[15]

The largest Vineyard is led by Steve Sjogren in Cincinnati, Ohio, with 3,200 adults and 1,100 children attending weekly. Also in Ohio (Westerville), there is a large congregation with 3,000 adults and 710 children. The "mother" church of the Vineyard, in Anaheim, is third in size, with youth and adults totaling slightly over 2,600. Other states with Vineyard churches ranking in the "top twenty" include Arizona, Idaho, Colorado, Texas, Illinois, Georgia, Indiana, North Carolina, Kentucky, Louisiana, and Virginia.

During the decade after the Vineyard was founded, there were approximately a dozen new church plants each year. In addition, there were "adoptions," or churches that decided to join the Vineyard movement, typically because their pastor and/or people had experienced some type of "renewal" that led them to be more open to the gifts of the Spirit, including healing and direct guidance by the Holy Spirit. Beginning in 1993, the number of new church plants increased, with over forty new congregations added to the movement in both 1996 and 1997.

During the history of the Vineyard, the ratio of new church plants to adoptions has been approximately 3 to 1, although the number of adoptions may decline now that Wimber-led renewal conferences are no longer being held, many of which drew non-Vineyard pastors and members.

---

15. For several graphic presentations of these and the following statistics about the Vineyard, see "Maps and Figures for 'Routinizing Charisma': The Vineyard Christian Fellowship in the Post-Wimber Era," listed under "Donald E. Miller" at http://hirr.hartsem.edu/sociology/sociology_sociologists_of_religion.html#M.

Vineyards seem to grow in all types of soil. Our survey of pastors shows that approximately 30 percent are in cities with a population of over a quarter-million people, 21 percent are in cities of 100,000–250,000, and there are also Vineyards in small cities. The Vineyards are distributed fairly broadly across the United States, although the West Coast has a disproportionate number.

The Vineyard is still not a large movement. The number of individuals attending Vineyard churches on any given Sunday is less than 100,000, which is remarkable given the widespread attention the Vineyard has received. Nevertheless, it is a growing movement and appears to be well positioned to spread its influence given the broad distribution of churches throughout the United States.

By all accounts the Vineyard is a very young movement. According to our survey of pastors, the median congregation was started in 1990. Fully three-quarters of the respondents to our survey are the founding pastors of their churches. The average church has slightly fewer than one full-time paid professional staff member other than the senior pastor. The median operating budget of a Vineyard is $230,000 annually. The median weekly church attendance is 203 adults and 70 children. Comparing data from our survey with one I conducted several years ago, we see that the average Vineyard appears to be growing by about 50 adult members every five years. This is a reasonably strong growth rate, especially if new churches are also being planted each year.

The median age of pastors is forty-five, which places them squarely within the baby boomer category. However, less than 1 percent of the pastors are under thirty years of age, and one in ten is under thirty-five. Hence, the Vineyard is genuinely concerned about its ability to connect with Gen-Xers, even though their clergy population is substantially younger, for example, than Presbyterian pastors, whose average age is fifty-five. Anecdotal evidence indicates that clergy of all denominations tend to draw members that share many of their characteristics. Not only is this true for age, but also for education and background experiences. Hence, it is important to note that a quarter of the Vineyard pastors do not have a college degree, although it is also significant that another quarter have some type of postgraduate degree.

In terms of racial/ethnic background, Vineyard pastors are 95 percent Anglo and the Vineyard is overwhelmingly a "white" church. It is true, however, that a network of twenty-five "La Vinas" is emerging in southern California in response to the substantial increase in the Latino population, and Vineyard-style worship seems to communicate well in this setting. There is also a fairly healthy sprinkling of Asians who have been attracted to the Vineyard, although only 2 percent of the pastors are Asian.

Vineyard pastors are exclusively male, although half of them indicate that they "copastor" with their wives (even though only 18 percent of the spouses receive a separate salary from the church). In terms of church backgrounds, approximately one-quarter of the pastors we surveyed indicated that they attended church less than once a month as an adolescent, and those who did attend regularly were most likely to have gone to a nondenominational church, an Assemblies of God, a Calvary Chapel, or a Southern Baptist church. Once again, these background characteristics have implications for the type of members that the Vineyard will attract.

A Moment of Crisis

On November 17, 1997, John Wimber died of a massive brain hemorrhage. For several years he had not been healthy. In 1995 Wimber had a stroke; in 1993 he was diagnosed with cancer; and before that, in 1986, he suffered a heart attack. Wimber was always struggling with his weight. But he was also the target of substantial criticism by his evangelical brethren who couldn't tolerate the supernatural manifestations that undergirded Wimber's ministry. For a long time Wimber did not respond to these criticisms — he believed that Christians should turn the other cheek — but he felt these attacks deeply, and this uncharitable behavior took its physical toll on him.

The sociologist Max Weber, writing at the turn of the twentieth century, argued that the death of a founding charismatic leader is always a blow to a movement.[16] Sometimes movements simply fold at this point, disappearing after a rather inglorious struggle. In other instances, there is an heir apparent — such as a son or someone who is genetically related — and the mantle is passed to this individual. Other times the charismatic founder appoints his successor, or alternatively, wise persons or magicians are called in to divine the will of the gods. The other option, however, is that the movement begins to institutionalize at this point and a bureaucratic leader emerges, often giving structure and order to a movement that otherwise was ruled by the power of charisma. Indeed, one might argue that in the history of Christianity Paul was the one to routinize the charisma of Jesus, formulating theological explanations of the founder's teachings and presiding over the evolution of ritual development and hierarchical structuring of a fast-growing movement.

Within the Vineyard there were pastors with considerable charisma to

---

16. For a discussion of the routinization of charisma, see S. N. Eisenstadt, ed., *Max Weber on Charisma and Institution Building* (Chicago: University of Chicago Press, 1968). Also see my discussion of charisma in *Reinventing American Protestantism,* pp. 24-26.

whom the mantle might have been passed on the occasion of Wimber's death. The two most likely candidates, however, were no longer around in November of 1997. Tom Stipe, who had left the Calvary movement to join the Vineyard, had subsequently returned to the Calvary fold. And Brent Rue, pastor of another large Vineyard church, had died of cancer at a relatively young age. Knowing that his health was failing, Wimber indicated at a board meeting that Todd Hunter should be his successor, but at the time of his death he had still not laid hands on Hunter to pass the leadership mantle. Hence, when Wimber died there was a leadership void at the top of the Vineyard movement.

According to Hunter, whom I interviewed extensively about this transitional period, Wimber had been waiting for an appropriate moment to officially pass the torch. In the final months before his death, however, Wimber's mental faculties had dimmed, and Hunter says he did not want hands laid on him while in this condition, because people would question the appointment. Consequently, this led to the inevitable: a bureaucratic resolution of the leadership crisis.

In January of 1998 a special board meeting was called. According to Hunter, "I went to that meeting and poured out my heart and said, 'I'm not sure that I'm the right guy. My ego is not attached to this. I would be just as happy pastoring a church.'" But the answer came back, "No, you're the guy . . . we have no questions. You're it." And so Hunter's appointment as the national director was formalized at that meeting, concluding what was a logical bureaucratic transition, since he had been the national coordinator for several years.

Todd Hunter had also been the loyal "son" since early in the movement. He is a relatively young baby boomer who doesn't identify with the hippie movement, having missed the 1960s counterculture. For six months in 1979, Hunter and his wife Debbie served in an apprenticeship role under Wimber's ministry, and then left for Wheeling, West Virginia, where they planted their first church. In America's heartland, they helped start several additional churches, serving also as a regional pastoral coordinator in the Vineyard. Then in 1987 they returned to the Anaheim Vineyard, and for nearly five years Todd served as the senior associate pastor under Wimber at the "mother" church. In 1991 they moved to Virginia Beach, Virginia, where he pastored a Vineyard church and also earned his master's degree in biblical studies at Regent University. In 1994 they returned to Anaheim and Hunter became the national coordinator for the Association of Vineyard Churches.

Todd Hunter's Desire for a Charismatic Moment

According to Max Weber's theory of the routinization of charisma, one would expect the Vineyard to move quickly into a more formalized and bureaucratized mode under Hunter's leadership, because by all accounts, including Hunter's own self-description, he was not a charismatic leader. However, Hunter had read Weber. Also, immediately upon his appointment, he began to consult various management experts, including a disciple of Peter Drucker as well as an experienced denominational head, Paul Sedar, of the Evangelical Free Church. After taking counsel from these "experts," Hunter did a radical thing. In a major policy decision, which is now known as the Columbus Accords, he eliminated all of the middle management in the Vineyard movement. Gone were the regional overseers, the district overseers, and the area coordinators. Instead, he created an extremely flat organizational structure which maintained only the area pastoral coordinators (APCs). There were fifty of them across the nation, and they answered directly to Hunter. There were no middlemen. The motive for this radical move of decentralization was to release what he called the "charismatic moment" in the movement, in which he hoped that a hundred John Wimbers would find their voice and thereby radicalize the Vineyard.

Operationally, Hunter communicated with these fifty APCs through E-mail and electronic distribution of policy and educational materials. Obviously, he was available for personal conversations, but he also believed that many issues and problems could be solved at a local level. If there was a problem with a pastor in one's area, then Hunter expected an APC to call another APC. If a solution could not be crafted, then they should call on a third APC. Hunter's view was that "if three of our best guys can't work something out, what is the chance that I will have the magic answer?" In terms of their job description, APCs were to care, coach, communicate, and coordinate. By *caring*, the APCs were to nurture the ten or so pastors they oversaw, developing deep relationships between and among them. The *coaching* aspect referred to the need to resource these pastors, providing them with information, but also serving as a role model. Their *communication* role was one of ensuring that pastors felt connected to the Vineyard and each other. And the *coordination* function came into play if there were disciplinary problems of any sort.

One of the radical things about Hunter's reorganization strategy was that he allowed pastors to pick their own APC. He sent out a survey to all pastors in the movement and asked them to name two or three people to whom they would like to relate, stressing that these should be people in whom they had confidence and with whom they enjoyed interacting. The process was not entirely democratic because Hunter took the information and made the final decisions so that APCs would each have the same approximate number of pastors to oversee. But in only four or five cases (out of nearly five hundred) did he veto a pastor's choice.

Hunter's strategy — and it was a bold move on his part — was that middle management would get in the way of releasing "spiritual entrepreneurs" (his term). The inevitable tendency is for this intervening layer of bureaucracy to slow down innovation, said Hunter. What he desperately wanted to protect were pastors who would do the new thinking for the movement. And he took this step of decentralizing the Vineyard knowing that some people would oppose him because structure is comfortable. But Hunter's view was that these pastors would not leave the movement. They were not risk-takers. And precisely for that reason, they would also not advance the movement. Hence, he believed that he should not be persuaded by their call for building the pyramid of organizational hierarchy.

The first response to the Columbus Accords was strong affirmation. In the liminal moment of transfer of authority, people typically fear that the new leader will seize control in an authoritarian manner. Hence, the warm reception to the Columbus Accords may have been the result of the movement breathing a collective sigh of relief when Hunter was appointed, precisely because they had gone through such wrenching challenges under Wimber's risk-taking leadership and now it was time to consolidate a bit, building their internal ranks. Initially, Hunter was in a honeymoon period. But the complaints started to come that he had tipped the scale too far in the direction of abolishing structure.

On the survey that was distributed to pastors in 1999, there was a wide range of responses to a question regarding how the Vineyard had changed since Wimber's death. One view was that many leaders had stepped up a notch, assuming more leadership. On the other end of the spectrum were individuals who said the Vineyard appeared rudderless. A common perception was that the leadership was now more decentralized, and that this was a good thing. One respondent said that "there has been a switch from one visible leader to an emphasis on the Vineyard's genetic code/values." Another pastor said the focus had moved away from the West Coast, and this is positive. Another respondent stated, "There is a new release of power; new people have been raised up." There was also a perception that there was now more emphasis on evangelism and church planting and less on "power" ministries of healing and deliverance.

Perhaps not surprisingly, many pastors responding to the survey felt that the Vineyard was changing well before Wimber died. Because of the period of Wimber's illness, one pastor indicated that there had been a progressive shift away from the *man* (Wimber) to the *values and theology* he modeled and taught. On the other hand, somewhat cynically, one pastor said that "for several years before John's death, the Vineyard was in a 'play it safe' mode. It is still there."

Todd Hunter's Resignation

In May 2000 Hunter announced that he was resigning as national director in order to plant a church that would attract Gen-Xers and people with a postmodern mentality. In his place Berten Waggoner, senior pastor of the Vineyard Church of Sugar Land, Texas, was named acting national director. On the Vineyard Web site Hunter was quoted as saying, "If someone is to be an authentic follower of Jesus and pursue the 'pearl of great price,' they may be called upon to risk it all."

When such resignations occur, there is always more occurring than meets the eye (or appears on the Vineyard Web site). My own analysis of the organizational transitions in the post-Wimber era is the following.

Wimber was a charismatic leader, and therefore Hunter had a difficult act to follow. Shortly after Hunter was appointed as national coordinator, a well-known Christian scholar told me that these transitions are always very difficult, implying that whoever was to follow Wimber would probably not last very long. It appears that he was prophetic. It seems that movements, whether Christian or secular, need to chew up and spit out a few successors to charismatic leaders before the followers/members realize that one cannot fill the shoes of the founding leader. Indeed, as Weber argues, many movements fold shortly after the charismatic leader dies. Those that do survive have two options: they can routinize by creating a bureaucratic and rational structure to manage the movement, or they can imbue a new leader with charisma.

Todd Hunter, however, pursued a sociologically novel approach. He did not seek to consolidate personal power by routinizing the movement. Instead, he attempted to remove the layers of bureaucracy that had crept into the movement, and through a radical act of decentralization of authority, he hoped a "charismatic moment" could be created within the movement in which a new level of spiritual entrepreneurship would be ignited, with many pastors in the Vineyard asserting their prophetic call. It was a noble experiment, even though it has seemingly failed. Hence one is drawn to ask why Hunter pursued this course of action.

First, as previously noted, Hunter had read Weber as well as consulted various organizational theorists, and he knew a lot about the deadening effects of routinization. For that reason, Hunter simply refused to go down that route.

Furthermore, as Wimber's protégé, it would not have been faithful to his mentor's vision to be a noninnovative movement overseer. Indeed, the course he is currently pursuing, namely, starting a ministry that targets a new population, is much more aligned with the spirit of Wimber, who believed that Christians must always be adjusting the model to fit the message, taking into account cultural changes that are occurring.

Secondly, Hunter is not Wimber. Hunter is a teacher, not a preacher or prophet. He doesn't like conflict, and usually tries to achieve consensus. Hence, when board members were not willing to bless his vision to start "a movement within the movement" that would tackle the problem of postmodernity — thereby creating a new model within the Vineyard — he chose to resign rather than fight to the end, which is something Wimber undoubtedly would not have done. In fact, Hunter was rather reflective in his comments to me, saying it is the "mad professor," not the university president, who should be thinking radical thoughts about the organization. Clearly Hunter views himself as an innovator and not an organizational manager.

Thirdly, Hunter had started to spell out his vision of a ministry to postmodern youth, and it scared some people within the Vineyard movement, particularly those who lean in a more fundamentalist direction. While Hunter insisted to me that his views remain evangelical to the core, and I have no reason to doubt him, the issues he was confronting in various youth conferences present radical challenges to orthodox models of apologetics because the younger generation is much more experiential in their attempts to validate truth. Evangelicalism is a product of modernist thought, not postmodern culture. Hence, things that Hunter said during these conferences would be taken out of context by individuals who were operating within the rationalistic, foundationalist, modernist approach to theology and apologetics.

Finally, there were individuals within the movement that wanted more structure, not less. They wanted more centralized leadership as well as regional oversight. At one level this is very understandable, since there are many small Vineyard churches led by pastors without much experience who feel lonely in their mission. The idea of further decentralizing the Vineyard organization was therefore not welcomed by them. Some pastors, even if they had denominational roots and had left their churches for the Vineyard because of the breath of fresh air that it introduced into their lives, nevertheless yearned for the good old days when fellow pastors rather than congregational members were their peer group.

Hence, without assessing blame as to whether Hunter was right or the board was correct in accepting his resignation, it is clear in retrospect that the fit was not appropriate. For some of the same reasons that Gulliksen left the

Vineyard, Hunter decided that his spiritual calling was not to be the CEO of a denomination. Hunter is a church planter and a pioneer, seeking to initiate a new model of ministry for a postmodern generation.

Message, Model, and Market

In many ways Hunter is following more closely in Wimber's image by launching a new ministry than if he had chosen the path of being a denominational executive. Perhaps better than anyone in the movement, Hunter understood Wimber's views on the interplay between the *message, model,* and *market* of a religious movement. For Wimber the message was rooted in the biblical narrative and does not fundamentally change over time, although the questions it answers will inevitably be different depending on the issues confronting Christians at any particular point in human history. The model, on the other hand, should always be in flux. There is nothing sacred about clergy dressing in a particular way, or churches playing a particular type of music, or the body of Christ meeting in a certain type of physical structure. Furthermore, both ritual and organizational structures should change with the times. Finally, both message and model should always be responding to the market for Christianity, which is constantly changing as the culture changes.

On the basis of his church-consulting days, Wimber believed that too many churches were trying to apply sixteenth- and seventeenth-century models to the twentieth century. In his view this simply does not work, and consequently it is not surprising that many mainline churches are declining. Instead, one should always be trying to adjust the model to the market, and the message should always be responding to questions being asked in the current context. In fact, Wimber was ruthless in applying this insight to his own movement, believing that the Vineyard was out of sync with many people in their twenties and thirties. Several years before his death he told me: "In my mind the market is moving [referring to the Gen-X crowd]. Let's move with the market. If we don't call it Vineyard, we'll call it Orchard, or whatever other culture-current term there is. I don't care which church it is as long as it teaches the truth of the Word."

During this interview Wimber's brother-in-law, Bob Fulton — who is in charge of the Vineyard's multicultural and international churches — made an astute comment. He said the pastors in the Vineyard and Calvary movements with large ministries have a better, or at least equal, ability to exegete culture as they do Scripture. "They really know how to look at their culture and understand what makes it tick," he said. In Fulton's view, echoing Wimber's insight

Donald E. Miller

about message, model, and market, these pastors "have an instinctual understanding of their culture and their brilliance is in packaging the teachings and the Scriptures in a way that is palatable to their culture." Nevertheless, both Fulton and Wimber acknowledged during this interview that the Vineyard's model and message are geared primarily to Anglo baby boomers and that either the Vineyard will evolve a new style of church that connects with the children of the boomers, or else it will not survive very long into the twenty-first century. Wimber told me somewhat emphatically that the jazz and rock melodies of current Vineyard music sound to Gen-Xers like Bach and Beethoven did to baby boomers. He felt that the current generation of Vineyard leaders had learned a lot about generational change in evolving the movement, and consequently "they won't get caught by change without trying to respond to it."

When I pressed Wimber on what a Gen-X church might look like, he speculated that it will probably have café tables rather than chairs in rows; there will be dancing as part of praise and worship; and the music will be "plugged" (i.e., heavy metal). In probing Hunter about the same issue, he said Xers have a deep hunger for spirituality, but they want it articulated in a way that isn't "slick." Gen-X worship will be "rawer," and more authentic, in his view. It will be very relational as a compensation for the fractured families from which many of these young adults come. And truth will not be propositional. It will be verified experientially: tested by the community for its ability to transform the lives of people who feel lonely, isolated, and frightened by their economic prospects. In our postmodern world, Hunter feels that truth claims by Gen-Xers will be modest, expressed oftentimes in stories rather than propositions or doctrines.

When I pressed Hunter after his resignation about his vision for the church he will start, he was appropriately open-ended but also said it will not look like the 1960s Jesus movement. For example, he suspects that it will be less performance-oriented, with worship being focused not on what is happening on the stage, but in the hearts of the worshiping community. There will be fewer loud screaming guitars, he said, because people will be worshiping God with all the senses, not just that of hearing. In all likelihood, communion will be served weekly. Worship may become more liturgical. Dance, drama, and art will all be important. Indeed, the visual as well as tactile senses may come much more fully into play, and don't be surprised, said Hunter, if you smell a little incense in the worship space or find this gathering of believers meeting in an abandoned mainline church with stained glass windows, thick granite walls, and tile floors.

It is too early to know if the Vineyard will be successful in reinventing itself. A non-Vineyard Gen-X church (Mars Hill) that is booming in Seattle is led by a young pastor who teaches through whole books of the Bible in one sermon, because that is the only way to tell the full-bodied narratives of people encountering God as they wrestle with the problems of lust, greed, anger, and self-interest. In this church, it is interesting to note that candles and various ritualistic elements are being reintroduced to worship, even though its music is a radical blend of contemporary sounds mixed with an occasional Gregorian chant. Culture obviously moves in cycles, and we may witness a revival of practices and spaces that embodied the spirits of ancient times. After all, this is a rootless generation that is seeking stability and connections with the past, however fleeting and individualist these desires may be.

Assessing the Vineyard's Organizational Success

In some ways charismatic leaders get a disproportionate amount of attention in the literature on social movements. While they are often important in launching a movement, the routinization of their charisma is equally important — if the movement is to have any staying power. Bureaucracy is not just a necessary evil. It is essential as movements grow in size. On the other hand, it is also true that movements can get overly routinized — which often happens as they age — and then something dramatic needs to happen to recapture the original energizing insight and passion. Sometimes this occurs with schisms, and at other times a new prophet marches on to the scene and recasts the vision in a way that once again excites the imagination — typically of people who are alienated and not profiting from the existing social arrangements.

The Vineyard has lost its beloved John, its charismatic leader. That's inevitable. Charismatic leaders always die, and sometimes in untimely ways. When this occurs, the challenge is obviously to figure out how to evolve the movement, holding on to the original insight which drew people to it, but also realizing that as people age they often desire structure and comfort. They need more than bread, however — in spite of what Dostoyevsky's "Grand Inquisitor" said. They need to live by *faith,* if the Christian message is going to mean anything at all.

With this as context, it is not all that complicated to figure out why the Vineyard has grown in such a mercurial fashion. The mainline denominations didn't understand the culture, and they created a vacuum into which movements like the Vineyard, Calvary Chapel, and a whole host of other "new paradigm" churches could move. Wimber's several years as a church consultant taught him what was wrong in the mainline. In fact, he probably didn't need to visit two thousand churches as a consultant to inform his analysis. A couple of hundred would have been enough. After all, Wimber was a jazz musician. He knew how to improvise and he knew how to read an audience. In this case the audience was middle-class America. Having been a pagan, he knew how to communicate with non-Christians, and it was in their language — the language of music and understated rhetoric — that he preached the gospel. Charisma for baby boomers did not require shouting and yelling. It meant being honest and vulnerable, and sharing from the gut. It also meant invoking the Spirit, which had all but evaporated in the bottom line of corporate business. And it meant offering a little healing to a generation of people that had really beat themselves up as they destroyed some of our most treasured institutions, such as the family. In this regard, it is no wonder that the Vineyard practiced deliverance. There were a lot of demons to banish, with some of them residing in hurt, wounded, and abused people.

While some people may criticize Wimber for being too authoritarian, it takes a strong, risk-taking leader to break from the chains of the dominant culture. Undoubtedly some people were alienated in the process, because more than a few folks have left the Vineyard — with some of them returning to the safety of the Calvary Chapel fold. But then, there are not too many genuine innovators that don't leave a few bodies in their wake. The path to innovation is seldom a straight one. If it were that easy, more people would figure it out. So Wimber and his ilk of leaders often make mistakes before they get it right, but on the other hand they are willing to break with convention. Cultural innovators march to a different drummer, and Wimber claimed his inspiration to be the Holy Spirit.

The real genius of Wimber, however, may have been fueled by the fact that he was a businessman before the Lord got ahold of him. He understood markets and models and only had to add the message to his repertoire. Hunter, on the other hand, was faced with a different problem. This "son" was wise enough not to try to compete with the father. But he also was a risk-taker, attempting to create a "charismatic moment" within the movement, although, as it turned out, this was even harder than being a charismatic leader.

What does it mean for the Spirit to break through into a movement of five hundred churches? Can there be a hundred mini-Wimbers, all transforming the Vineyard simultaneously? The conventional answer is no. The candle must go out at some point, and the honorable thing is not to postpone the agony, but simply to get on with the second generation of the movement. In short, bureaucratic common sense suggests that one should get more comfortable with the values of the dominant culture, polish up the performative elements of the ritual, make a little money on the CDs, and take longer and more expensive vacations. Hunter, however, puts the situation more charitably. He says the Vineyard is at the "end of the beginning." In his view the honeymoon is over and now it is time to raise the kids, take out the trash, and pay down the mortgage — or whatever is the organizational equivalent of these acts.

Preserving the Genetic Code

When I asked Hunter if the Vineyard was a denomination, he equivocated. In some ways it lacks the traditional markers of a denomination, he said. For example, according to Hunter, the Association of Vineyard Churches does not ordain (this is done at a local level); it doesn't own property (the individual churches do); it doesn't have paid bishops (just area pastoral coordinators, who themselves are pastors); it doesn't have a centralized pension plan (one better have a well-employed spouse!); and there is no centralized health insurance (hopefully some future political administration will solve that one). Nevertheless, Hunter thinks that denominationalism is probably inevitable.

Given his resignation, perhaps the following comments are no longer relevant, because we asked pastors on our survey what advice they had for Hunter. However, the comments may have a prophetic quality to them. One Vineyard pastor said, "Put a few cosmic, spontaneous, visionary, new paradigm brothers at the top." Another said, "Surround yourself with wise, faithful, and dreaming men." And one pastor advised: "Be willing to get out of the boat and walk on the water with Jesus." These admonitions were mixed with sage advice about "keeping the heart of a servant" and maintaining a balance between the "best of evangelicalism" and the "best of Pentecostalism." One pastor clearly thought Todd had been reading too many management books and said, "Stop trying to figure out the right structure and build relationships."

Conclusion

The Vineyard Christian Fellowship represents a different genre of religious organization than do the Methodists or Episcopalians. The Vineyard is part of a "new paradigm" of independent churches and church movements that are deeply suspicious of religious denominations, even though, like the Vineyard, many of these groups are in the process of evolving toward quasi-denominational status. These new paradigm churches prefer to identify themselves as "movements" or networks of affiliated churches.[17] Some of them even go so far as to proclaim that they are part of a postdenominational era in American Christianity, which eschews any centralized organizational structure or control.

In addition to their decentralized organizational structures, these new

17. The first attempt to convene religious leaders representing this movement was by C. Peter Wagner in a conference held at Fuller Theological Seminary, "The National Symposium on the Postdenominational Church," May 21-23, 1996.

paradigm churches are pioneering a revolution in worship style and form. Unlike the reformation led by Martin Luther, the current revolution in American religious practice, which is represented by church movements such as the Vineyard, is challenging not *doctrine* but the *medium* through which the message of Christianity is articulated. Like upstart religious groups of the past, these churches are progressively stripping market share from the mainline denominations. Appropriating contemporary cultural forms, they are creating a new genre of worship music, restructuring the organizational character of institutional religion, and democratizing access to the sacred by radicalizing the Protestant principle of the priesthood of all believers.

The issue facing the Vineyard at the present time is whether it will continue to innovate or settle into a comfortable period of maturation. Hunter is not certain what he will call his new church. He is going to invite the people to name it. And it is not clear to me whether this church pioneer will keep his flock within the corral of the Vineyard Christian Fellowship. After all, the Vineyard needed to separate from Calvary Chapel in order to establish a distinct and authentic ministry. Likewise, a ministry to postmodern people may not fit within the fold of a movement built on the foundation of evangelicalism, which is part of the "modern" as opposed to postmodern culture.[18] Furthermore, it is not clear what the future growth of the Vineyard movement will be — not because it lacks charismatic leadership, but because it has done its job too well, and now there are many Vineyard clones, including not a few within mainline churches. Hence, the distinctiveness of the Vineyard product has been diminished. One no longer needs to sneak out on Sunday evenings to a Vineyard worship service to hear contemporary music or experience the healing power of the Holy Spirit. The spiritual marketplace is more crowded with contemporary worship forms than it was two decades ago. What is only beginning to emerge, however, is a church for the children and grandchildren of the baby boom generation.

18. See the discussion of postmodern religion in Richard W. Flory and Donald E. Miller, eds., *GenX Religion* (New York: Routledge, 2000).

Theological Perspective and Reflection on the Vineyard Christian Fellowship

Don Williams

When Western intellectual history is written, the end of the twentieth century will be remembered as the bridge from the modern to the postmodern age. Among many definitions of the latter, perhaps the best known is by Jean-François Lyotard: "Simplifying to the extreme, I define postmodern as incredulity toward metanarratives."[1] With the collapse of Marxism as a viable worldview and the absence of a rational explanation for the universe, we are in an age where pluralism, multiculturalism, and relativism reign. How will the church cope with this postmodern era? The major denominations' embracing of the modern age, popularly identified as the period from the fall of the Bastille to the fall of the Berlin Wall, makes this question critical. Modernism was the age of the Enlightenment, the age of reason and the triumph of the scientific method.[2] It was the age where mysticism, miracles, angels, demons, and su-

---

1. Jean-François Lyotard, "The Postmodern Condition: A Report on Knowledge," trans. Geoff Bennington and Brian Massumi, in *Theory and History of Literature*, vol. 10 (Minneapolis: University of Minnesota Press, 1984), p. xxiv. Lyotard wrote, "[T]he society of the future falls less within the province of a Newtonian anthropology (such as structuralism or systems theory) than a pragmatics of language particles. There are many different language games — a heterogeneity of elements. They only give rise to institutions in patches — local determinism." While this is increasingly true in the West, it is not true in Africa and Asia, where metanarratives still determine large masses of humankind: animism, Marxism (China), monism (India), etc.

2. Spinoza wrote, "[T]he universal laws of nature are decrees of God following from the necessity and perfection of the Divine nature. Hence, any event happening in nature which contravened nature's universal laws, would necessarily also contravene the Divine decree, nature, and understanding; or if anyone asserted that God acts in contravention to the laws of nature, he ipso facto, would be compelled to assert that God acted against His own nature — an evident absurdity." "A Theologico-Political Treatise," in *The Chief Works of Benedict de Spinoza*, vol. 1, trans. R. H. M. Elwes (New York: Dover, 1951), p. 83.

pernatural interventions were judged naive, the products of childhood fancy. It was the age of demythologizing the Bible.[3] It was the age of humanizing what was left of the "historical Jesus."[4] It was the age of the Constantinian imperial church, informally established in all its forms, adopting large-scale structures with hegemonic tendencies. It was the age of the National Council of Churches, its counterpart, the National Association of Evangelicals, and the World Council of Churches, seeking influence by lobbying Washington. It was the age of the Consultation on Church Union (COCU), where "bigger is better." It was the age of "the Christ of culture."[5] This age, however, is over.

The roots of the postmodern era lie deeper than the "beat generation" of the fifties, the revolutionary sixties, the decline and fall of the Soviet empire, and multinational globalization. Carl Becker asserted in his Storrs Foundation lectures at Yale in 1931:

> What is man that the electron should be mindful of him! Man is but a foundling in the cosmos, abandoned by the forces that created him. Unparented, unassisted and undirected by omniscient or benevolent authority, he must fend for himself, and with the aid of his own limited intelligence find his way about in an indifferent universe. . . . It has taken eight centuries to replace the conception of existence as divinely composed and purposeful drama by the conception of existence as a blindly running flux of disintegrating energy. But there are signs that the substitution is now

3. See Rudolf Bultmann, "Is Exegesis without Presuppositions Possible?" in *Existence and Faith: Shorter Writings of Rudolf Bultmann*, trans. Schubert Ogden (New York: Living Age Books, 1960).

4. With all the continuing quests in the twentieth century, Albert Schweitzer's study is still unsurpassed: *The Quest of the Historical Jesus: A Critical Study of Its Progress from Reimarus to Wrede*, trans. W. Montgomery (New York: Macmillan, 1910). For a scholarly critique of the continuing quest and the Jesus Seminar, see Luke Timothy Johnson, *The Real Jesus: The Misguided Quest for the Historical Jesus and the Truth of the Traditional Gospels* (San Francisco: Harper San Francisco, 1996). For alternative positions on the quest see Marcus Borg and N. T. Wright, *The Meaning of Jesus: Two Visions* (San Francisco: Harper San Francisco, 1999).

5. H. Richard Niebuhr, *Christ and Culture* (New York: Harper, 1951), pp. 83f., wrote, "In every culture to which the Gospel comes there are men who hail Jesus as the Messiah of their society, the fulfiller of its hopes and aspirations, the perfecter of its true faith, the source of its holiest spirit. . . . Such Christians have been described psychologically by F. W. Newman and William James as constituting the company of the 'once born' and 'the healthy minded.' Sociologically they may be interpreted as non-revolutionaries who find no need for positing 'cracks in time' — fall and incarnation and judgment and resurrection. In modern history this type is well known, since for generations it has been dominant in a large section of Protestantism. Inadequately defined by the use of such terms as 'liberal' and 'liberalism,' it is more aptly named Culture-Protestantism."

fully accomplished; and if we wished to reduce eight centuries of intellectual history to an epigram, we could not do better than to borrow the words of Aristophanes, "Whirl is king, having deposed Zeus."[6]

Apart from the intellectual elite, however, it was the sixties, with the arrival of the Civil Rights movement, the murders of John F. Kennedy and Martin Luther King, the burning of the ghettos, anti–Vietnam War riots, psychedelic drugs, the pill, and rock and roll where youth editorialized to youth, that ended cultural continuity.

The new youth culture was, among other things, an attack upon the modern era.[7] Timothy Leary, former Harvard professor and high priest of hallucinogenic drugs, asserted that "reason is a tissue-thin artifact, easily destroyed by a slight alteration in the body's biochemistry." In this context the generations were at loggerheads and all established institutions, including the churches, were under attack. The mainline denominations accelerated their protracted decline, a trend not followed by Southern Baptists and other more conservative groups.[8] Symptomatically, Sunday school enrollment dropped by more than half for many church bodies. The next generation absented itself. Churches grayed without replacements.

Longing for spirituality, the sixties generation turned east. It was led by the Beatles and other cultural icons who found Transcendental Meditation, chanting, and mind-altering mysticism more attractive than the formal liturgies of Christendom.

It is no surprise that, in the midst of this cultural revolution, a new Christian dynamic emerged. The press dubbed this the "Jesus movement."[9] By the late sixties, a significant proportion of the "Woodstock generation" renounced drugs and rebellion and turned to Jesus himself. They brought their counterculture lifestyles of communal living and folk and rock music into the churches that would welcome them. If turned away, they started their own fellowships. Looking for a spiritual high better than drugs, they celebrated Jesus' love and the power of his Spirit, many becoming neo-Pentecostals or charismatics. In

6. Carl L. Becker, *The Heavenly City of the Eighteenth-Century Philosophers* (New Haven: Yale University Press, 1932), p. 15.

7. Theodore Roszak, *The Making of a Counter Culture: Reflections on the Technocratic Society and Its Youthful Opposition* (Garden City, N.Y.: Anchor Books, 1969).

8. Finke and Stark demonstrate that mainline decline has been a long process going back to the Revolutionary War period. Roger Finke and Rodney Stark, *The Churching of America, 1776-1990: Winners and Losers in Our Religious Economy* (New Brunswick, N.J.: Rutgers University Press, 1992), chap. 3.

9. For a scholarly summary, see Robert S. Ellwood, Jr., *One Way: The Jesus Movement and Its Meaning* (Englewood Cliffs, N.J.: Prentice-Hall, 1973).

this context the Calvary Chapel churches exploded under the fatherly guidance of a former Foursquare pastor, Chuck Smith. They were known for their informal style, Bible exposition, evangelistic fervor, and culturally current music born from the "rock generation." They were also known for heavy preaching on the imminent return of Christ and the end of the age. In their "afterglow" services people stayed to be filled with the Spirit, receive the gift of tongues, and be healed or delivered from demons. Powerful manifestations of the Spirit marked the early Calvary movement and prepared the way for the Vineyard's return to these emphases later.

Calvary Chapels were transitional from the modern age. While embracing the fervency of conversion and subsequent experiences of the Spirit, they also held to dispensational theology that chops the Bible up into separate economies for God's dealings with Israel and the church. This is supported by a highly rational hermeneutic that claims to interpret the Bible literally. While Smith continued to validate tongues and other gifts of the Spirit, he soon backed away from what seemed to be the charismatic excesses of physical and emotional displays in public, from lifting hands in worship to falling under the power of the Spirit. A small number of Calvary pastors, however, wanted to continue the Jesus movement's assault on the modern age. As elaborated in the Jackson historical introduction (pp. 132-40) and the Miller sociological case study (pp. 141-62), they gathered around John Wimber, a new charismatic leader who would build the emerging Vineyard Christian Fellowship.[10]

In many respects Wimber was a modern man. He started and managed many businesses. He served on the staff of a growing, evangelical Friends church. He consulted with hundreds of churches across America, becoming an expert in church growth sociological theory and practice. He could look at a church in terms of plant, location, visibility, and parking and make accurate judgments about its future, unrelated to its spiritual life. He had new pastors develop their "five-year plan." When he taught healing, he used his five-step method for praying for the sick. In other ways, however, Wimber at his core was not a modernist. Rationalism had not indoctrinated him. While the modern church tried, it did not socialize him. It burned him out. He kept asking, "When do we get to do the stuff?" By the "stuff" he meant what Jesus did: minister to the poor, heal the sick, cast out demons, and even raise the dead.

10. Biographical material on Wimber includes: David Pytches, ed., *John Wimber: His Influence and Legacy* (Guildford, Surrey, U.K.: Eagle, 1998); Carol Wimber, *John Wimber: The Way It Was* (London: Hodder and Stoughton, 1999); Bill Jackson, *The Quest for the Radical Middle: A History of the Vineyard* (Cape Town, South Africa: Vineyard International Publishing, 1999). See also the autobiographical video by John Wimber, *I'm a Fool for Christ, Whose Fool Are You?* (Mercy Publishing, 1987).

Neither, of course, was Wimber a postmodernist. He probably would not have recognized the term. In fact, Wimber was more like a premodernist, a man at home in the Christian worldview and experience that dominated the church and the West prior to the Enlightenment. Wimber loved the Venerable Bede's *Life of Cuthbert* because he lived in a spiritual world similar to that of this seventh-century Celtic monk. Like Cuthbert, Wimber received prophecies and visions that directly influenced the course of his life and ministry. Like Cuthbert, Wimber healed the sick and drove out demons. Like Cuthbert, Wimber engaged in spiritual disciplines, contending against the devil. Like Cuthbert, Wimber experienced immediate, visible answers to his prayers. Like Cuthbert, Wimber ministered out of the fullness of the Holy Spirit.[11] Like Cuthbert, Wimber was a "bishop" to his parish and itinerant as an evangelist. When Bede says of Cuthbert that great numbers of people came to hear him, "attracted by his reputation for miracles,"[12] this could also be said of Wimber. When Bede says Cuthbert was "spurred on by his heavenly vision of the joys of eternal bliss,"[13] this could also be said of Wimber.

Living much of the time in a premodern spiritual world, Wimber positioned the Vineyard with the potential to minister effectively in the antimodern ethos of the emerging postmodern age. As a young, church-planting movement that also attracted adoptive, like-minded congregations, the Vineyard's theology and practice are uniquely wedded to Wimber's spiritual life. Here, in many respects, biography becomes theology and theology becomes ecclesiology.

What Drove John Wimber and What Drives the Vineyard?

In general, Wimber was driven by his understanding of the kingdom of God. Jesus came in the power of the Spirit to evangelize the poor, heal the sick, drive out demons, liberate the oppressed, and build a people living under his lordship who will reflect his character and ministry in fulfilling his mission to the

---

11. D. H. Farmer, ed., *The Age of Bede*, trans. J. F. Webb (New York: Penguin Books, 1983). Bede wrote that Cuthbert came to release a woman from a demon. "[A]s they approached the house the evil spirit, unable to bear the coming of the Holy Spirit with whom Cuthbert was filled, suddenly departed" (p. 62). Cuthbert laid hands on new converts "so that the grace of the Holy Spirit might come down upon them" (p. 81). Again, "Cuthbert preached twice to the milling crowds and brought down the grace of the Holy Ghost by imposition of hands on those newly regenerated in Christ" (p. 83). The same could be said of Wimber.

12. Farmer, *The Age of Bede*, p. 71.

13. Farmer, *The Age of Bede*, 50. Wimber often said, "I'm just a fat man trying to get to heaven."

nations.[14] In Jesus the kingdom has come and is still coming. It will be consummated at his return. The church lives in a tension between these two realities, the already and the not yet.

Out of his grasp of the kingdom Wimber established a church-planting movement focused on worship (loving God) and compassion (loving the world). But where is the Vineyard today? A survey of pastors, designed by Don Miller and reported in his case study, gives a fairly objective sense of the current Vineyard. A review of the statistics makes it clear that the Vineyard mainstream lives out Wimber's kingdom values. A smaller wing is still committed to the prophetic-holiness emphasis of repentance preceding end-time revival that came into the Vineyard through the Kansas City Fellowship in the early 1990s. A "seeker sensitive" wing downplays overt manifestations of the Spirit in Sunday services, such as speaking in tongues, prophecy, and physical evidence of the Spirit's presence. They do this for the sake of attracting outsiders who would be "turned off" or confused by such displays. In the following review, we will look at what drove Wimber and then at what drives the present Vineyard.

First, Wimber was evangelistically driven. His radical conversion experience in the summer of 1963 and early "discipling" by a lay itinerant evangelist, Gunner Payne, put Wimber on the streets. He identified with the Friends church in Yorba Linda because of its warm fellowship and evangelical convictions. By his report he led hundreds of his friends to Christ over a several year period. Evangelism was always Wimber's passion and also his frustration, since in his view the Vineyard movement never realized its full evangelistic potential during its early stages. When Wimber became an advocate of "signs and wonders," a major reason he focused on the miraculous was that he believed it would reach those outside the church with what he called "power evangelism." If people experienced a manifestation of God's power (say, in physical healing), Wimber believed they would be more open to the data of the gospel message.

Likewise, in the Vineyard today over two out of three churches regularly extend "altar calls" for salvation. The rest do sometimes. Backing this up, about a third of the Vineyards showcased conversions with "salvation testimonies," either regularly on Sundays or at least several times during the past year. Half the Vineyard pastors report "leading someone to the Lord" a few times a year. One in five averages this once a month, and more than one in ten report two to three times a month. When asked about the importance of maintaining a strong emphasis on evangelism, almost 85 percent said it was either very important or extremely important. In sum, the Vineyard continues to be an evangelical movement.

14. See Luke 4:16-21.

Second, Wimber was Word-driven. He held to the absolute authority of the Bible as the standard and test for life. He measured all supernatural events, prophetic words, and ministry activities by the Scriptures. When in frustration a parishioner feared manifestations of the Spirit and asked, "How far is this going to go?" Wimber held up a Bible and replied, "No farther than this." He joked later that his response was not as safe as the man thought. Wimber interpreted the Bible from the vantage point of historical exegesis and evangelical faith. Scripture must be seen in its ancient context and understood in its grammatical sense without rationalizing away its supernatural worldview. George Ladd, professor of New Testament at Fuller Theological Seminary, gave Wimber his kingdom theology grid. Wimber not only taught from the Bible, he listened to the Bible. He avoided the excesses of allegory and, at the same time, heard God speak currently with a "living word" through his devotional use of Scripture.

Like Wimber, most Vineyard pastors hold a high view of biblical authority. Eight out of ten consider Bible study either very important or extremely important. A little over half hear God speak through Scripture weekly or more often, and a little less than a quarter, two to three times a month. Almost 75 percent of all Vineyards devote from thirty to forty minutes to Sunday preaching. Another 15 percent give it forty-five minutes. Two-thirds of the pastors report that half or more of their sermons is devoted to biblical exposition. The Bible continues to have a foundational value in the Vineyard.

Third, Wimber was Spirit-driven. He viewed the mainline churches as "pneumatically deficient." He agreed with Gordon Fee that the early Christians were "Spirit people."[15] Intimacy with God was the heart-theme of his life. The road led through worship, obedience, and surrender to the Spirit. As the Vineyard came into being, Wimber's experiences of the Spirit increased. Power was unleashed as he prayed for people. They were often healed in his living room. Ministry became dynamic and at times unpredictable through the presence of the Spirit. One night at the Anaheim Vineyard, much to Wimber's surprise, the Spirit leveled hundreds of young adults, shaking them and gifting them. Wimber came to see that if Jesus ministered in the Spirit's power, he was foolish to think he could do without it.

Submission to biblical authority and the experience of the present ministry of the Spirit were always in creative tension for Wimber. He even taught a series to his church on raising the dead because this was in the Scriptures. To my knowledge, he never personally saw it happen. What the Spirit did sent him back to the Scriptures. What the Scriptures said sent him seeking the Spirit.

15. See Gordon Fee, *Paul, the Spirit and the People of God* (Peabody, Mass.: Hendrickson, 1996).

More than once he changed course or corrected earlier teaching because of a better understanding of the Scriptures. This, not subjective experience, was his final court of appeal. Like the Reformers, Wimber refused to separate the Spirit from the Word and the Word from the Spirit. He expected to hear the Spirit through the Word and to respond in faith and obedience.

The Vineyard today continues to be Spirit-driven. With reference to the gifts of the Spirit, 98 percent of the pastors report receiving the gift of tongues (Spirit-given prayer language); 80 percent pray in tongues weekly or more often. Prophetic and healing gifts are also reported or implied. With reference to the signs of the Spirit, while about 50 percent report never being "slain in the Spirit" (a Pentecostal marker for being physically overcome by the Spirit), 40 percent experience this a few times a year. Ninety-five percent have experienced physical jerking or shaking from the Spirit. Over 30 percent do so at least a few times a year, and close to 15 percent monthly or more often. Close to 80 percent have either laughed or wept in the Spirit, half a few times a year and a quarter even more frequently. About half the Vineyards experience "singing in the Spirit" (singing with the gift of tongues) either regularly or sometimes. A little over half report rarely or never. Over 40 percent celebrate free-flowing dancing in the Spirit regularly or occasionally. For a little under 40 percent this is rare, and it is absent from about 18 percent of the churches. The Vineyards seem to be evenly divided between more controlled and more spontaneous expressions of worship. When asked if the gifts of the Spirit should be downplayed publicly, over 85 percent either disagreed strongly or simply disagreed. Only a bit over 10 percent would put a lid on such expressions. Almost 86 percent are happy with the corporate expression of the gifts. In sum, most pastors report a dynamic personal relationship with the Holy Spirit, and many report substantial Spirit activity in their congregations.

It is sometimes asked whether the Holy Spirit affects decision making for the larger church. About two-thirds of the pastors responded somewhat and a third responded greatly. This means that more than nine out of ten Vineyards expect some degree of the Spirit's leading in their ministries. Almost one out of three is highly dependent upon the Spirit for guidance. One aspect of being Spirit-driven is openness to change and renewal. As was documented in the Miller case study, a significant event in this process was the Columbus Accords that abolished much of the former Vineyard structure (now restored). When asked whether this was in line with God's will, over eight of ten pastors either agreed or strongly agreed.

Fourth, Wimber was prophetically driven. Although his elders theologically suppressed an early experience of speaking in tongues, Wimber always had an intuitive sense of what God was doing and went with it. Later, when a woman prophet wept before him for half an hour, a frustrated Wimber asked her finally to deliver her message. She replied, "That's it" (i.e., the weeping). He felt as if he had been kicked in the solar plexus. In her tears he saw the tears of Jesus over him. Later God spoke to him, "I've seen your ministry (Wimber felt that it was shaky), now I'm going to show you mine." This launched Wimber into doing the "signs and wonders" kingdom ministry of Jesus rather than simply preaching Jesus' message as a typical evangelical.

Wimber led the Vineyard by hearing directly from God. This was not pure subjectivism. He wanted all he heard to be consistent with Scripture and tested by Scripture. He would change course in a sermon because, in the moment, "God told me to." He would wait for direction from the Spirit as he entered into a personal ministry time of praying for the sick. He operated in remarkable prophetic "words of knowledge," having the ability to identify people God was dealing with in a meeting and knowing surprising details about their lives and needs. He also heard from God in the crisis of making ecclesiastical decisions, often to the dismay of others. Later, when prophets from Kansas City appeared and redirected the Vineyard movement for a season (see the historical introduction), Wimber was ready to receive them because of the stream of prophetic revelation coming to him and moving through him. He was also ready to receive them because of personal issues in his life which they tellingly addressed. His openness to the living voice of God, confirmed with signs and wonders, also made him vulnerable to being derailed by others' agendas for him and the Vineyard. Not wanting to offend God, Wimber was cautious at this point. He often remarked that he let a bush grow to see its fruit before trimming it. That fruit had to be consistent with Vineyard kingdom values, biblically based. It also had to evidence Christlike character and promote the mission of the church in world evangelism. After the prophetic period, which focused on the gifted leader in ministry rather than on the gifted church in ministry, Wimber trimmed heavily. While the Vineyard needed church-planting entrepreneurs, it also needed franchise operators. The time was passing for maverick one-person shows.

The prophetic is still alive and well in the Vineyard. Over eight out of ten churches have prophetic utterances either sometimes or regularly in their services. As we have seen, the Spirit affects the decisions of over eight out of ten Vineyards greatly or somewhat. It is probable that this often comes through some means of prophetic revelation. On the personal level, over 45 percent of the pastors give a public prophecy a few times a year. Another 20 percent do so once a month, over 16 percent two to three times a month, and almost 5 percent weekly or more often. This means that close to 90 percent of Vineyard pastors receive and give prophetic revelation more than once a year. Four out of ten do so at least monthly. When asked to value "a prophetic ministry," over half judged it somewhat important, close to a third very important, and over 5 percent extremely important. Like Wimber, the Vineyard continues to be prophetically driven, with a strong prophetic wing comprising over a third of the churches.

Fifth, Wimber was compassionately driven. He genuinely loved people. He knew how to listen before providing wise counsel. He cared for his family, friends, leaders, churches, strangers, outsiders, and people of all denominations, races, and cultures. He lived simply and opened his home, welcoming people in. He constantly gave ministry resources away. He would remark, "Whatever God has given to me, I want to give to you." He never used his ecclesiastical position to distance himself from pain and need. He poured himself out at great cost to his wife, his family, his time, his energy, and eventually his health. In a simple sense, from his heart, Wimber wanted to be like Jesus in every area of his life.

Compassion drove Wimber's commitment to Jesus' healing ministry. He believed in it not simply because it was utilitarian but because it was biblical. He believed in it because people's pain needed the power and compassion of Jesus, but he also believed in it because it worked.[16] His goal was to marshal the whole church into this aspect of Jesus' ministry,[17] and he personally prayed for thousands of sick and demonized. At the same time, Wimber experienced the strong, powerful presence of the Spirit in his meetings. In his words, he counted on God "showing up." When he taught on healing, he expected God "to back up his act." His concern was to divest the healing ministry from professionalism, emotionalism, hype, and exaggerated claims. When there were physical manifestations of power, he would often become humorous in order to defuse the tension of the moment. He wanted his churches to be "naturally supernatural." Wimber also spearheaded one of the largest relief ministries in southern California. His church in Anaheim served a million meals each year on-site and built a huge food bank to care for the poor and homeless.[18] He insisted that kingdom ministry must be directed to the dispossessed.

Wimber wanted to love the church Jesus loved and expended himself to

16. When I first met John Wimber, he told me that everything he knew about healing he learned from the Dominican priest Francis MacNutt, *Healing*, rev. ed. (Notre Dame: Ave Maria Press, 1999). A careful documentation of healings at Wimber's Harrogate Conference, November 3-6, 1986, is found in David Lewis, *Healing: Fiction, Fantasy, or Fact?* (London: Hodder and Stoughton, 1989).

17. John Wimber and Kevin Springer, *Power Healing* (San Francisco: Harper and Row, 1987), chaps. 11–12.

18. David Pytches, "A Man Called John," in *John Wimber*, p. 28.

renew it. He took his healing seminars to Canada, Europe, Asia, and Africa again and again. His vision was not to be a healing evangelist but to equip the whole church to pray for the sick. His impact was so historic that the *Times* of London editorialized against the "Wimberites" who were undermining the traditionalism of the Church of England. Ironically, these were the very churches that were growing and still continue to grow in the United Kingdom.

In Vineyards today, over one out of five find ministry to the poor extremely important, and almost one out of two find it very important. This is a high value for over two-thirds of the churches. The other third judge this ministry somewhat important. Two out of three churches give 1 to 5 percent of their budgets to social outreach ministry. One in five gives 6 to 10 percent.

The healing ministry also delivers compassion in a kingdom context. Most Vineyard pastors personally pray for the sick. Fewer than 5 percent have never seen someone physically healed through prayer. Over 40 percent report such healings a few times a year, over 20 percent once a month, and a bit less two to three times a month. Over 8 percent see physical healing weekly or more often. No wonder almost three out of four Vineyard churches view praying for the sick as either extremely important or very important. The rest judge it somewhat important. To back up this value, almost 80 percent of the Vineyards had testimonies of healing/miracles in their services in the last year. It is not surprising, then, that almost 80 percent offer healing prayer in their churches regularly, and the rest offer it sometimes. Likewise, almost 70 percent offer prayer for deliverance from demonic influence either regularly or sometimes. Healing is alive and well in the Vineyard. Most churches live out the kingdom through praying for the sick and delivering the demonized. In the Vineyard worldview, when people are healed, Satan's kingdom is undermined and God's kingdom is manifested and advanced.

Sixth, Wimber was theologically driven. He was especially indebted to the kingdom theology of George Ladd at Fuller Theological Seminary.[19] Ladd's primary launch point was that "God is King" and that "Jesus is Lord." As sovereign, God is both creator and redeemer. The purpose of his redemptive work, starting with Abraham and climaxing with Jesus Christ, is the restoration of his sovereignty over a cosmos in rebellion. For Ladd (and Wimber), although Jesus inaugurated the present kingdom in his miraculous ministry, its full consummation lay in the future. Jesus brought a measure of "realized eschatology,"[20]

19. See George Ladd, *A Theology of the New Testament*, ed. Donald Hagner, rev. ed. (Grand Rapids: Eerdmans, 1993).

20. C. H. Dodd, *The Parables of the Kingdom* (London: Nisbet and Co., 1936). Dodd wrote, "The eschaton has moved from the future to the present, from the sphere of expectation into that of realized experience. It is therefore unsafe to assume that the content of the idea, 'The Kingdom

but he also ministered in the eschatological tension of a kingdom come and coming.[21]

Since the kingdom of God battles with the kingdom of Satan, Wimber saw that every convert reduces Satan's kingdom by one. Every healing proleptically restores a bit of God's good but fallen creation. Wimber not only taught about the kingdom, he also ministered to see the kingdom come. Unencumbered by the modern worldview, he wanted a church that would "go for it" in power ministry. In this sense Wimber was a pragmatic American. He wanted a "working theology." However, he always sought to discern whose power was operating. Was it God's Spirit or a demonic spirit? Here the witness of Scripture and the witness of the Spirit in the context of community were mandatory guidelines.

The kingdom, present as well as future, raised expectations that now many would be empowered and gifted by the Spirit, healed, and delivered from demons. This was reason enough for Wimber and his followers to embrace this aspect of Pentecostal or charismatic experience. The future aspect of the kingdom explained why all who were evangelized were not converted, and why all who were prayed for were not healed. Abandoning the triumphalism of much Pentecostal teaching (and its roots in Wesleyan holiness), Wimber moved the Vineyard into "faith healing" based on kingdom theology. Wimber also realized that faith could never force God's hand. He often recounted the statement in John's Gospel that Jesus could do only what he saw the Father doing (John 5:19). Wimber's task was not to command faith but to see what the Father is doing and participate in it or "bless" it. This distinguished his view from an Arminian view of ministry and made him more Calvinistic. It also prepared him for his own bouts with severe illness.

The Vineyard today continues to be evangelical in its theology. When

---

of God,' as Jesus meant it, may be filled in from the speculations of apocalyptic writers. They were referring to something in the future, which could be conceived only in terms of fantasy. He was speaking of that which, in one aspect at least, was an object of experience. . . . Here then is the fixed point from which our interpretation of the teaching regarding the Kingdom of God must start. It represents the ministry of Jesus as 'realized eschatology,' that is to say, as the impact upon this world of the 'powers of the world to come,' in a series of events, unprecedented and unrepeatable, now in actual process" (pp. 50-51). In some respects Wimber would take issue with the word "unrepeatable." "Realized eschatology" is the inheritance of the church.

21. For the structure of the new age intruding into the old age, see Oscar Cullmann, *Christ and Time: The Primitive Christian Conception of Time and History,* trans. Floyd Filson (London: SCM, 1951), p. 141. Wimber loved to use Cullmann's distinction between "D-Day" and "V-Day." "D-Day" established the beachhead for victory. "V-Day" ended the war. In the same way, the ministry of Jesus is "D-Day" and his return is "V-Day." The church lives, certain of his victory, mopping up the opposition.

asked if Christ is the only way to salvation, over 98 percent of the pastors surveyed agreed or strongly agreed. Again, over 98 percent either agreed or strongly agreed that the devil really exists. Most Vineyard pastors hold the foundational truths of kingdom theology. On the issue of authority, when asked whether the Scriptures are "inerrant, literally accurate," almost 30 percent agreed and over 60 percent strongly agreed. Almost 90 percent of Vineyard pastors embrace the most conservative doctrine of biblical authority.

Seventh, Wimber was pragmatically driven. Having become an expert in church growth principles, he applied them directly to the Vineyard movement. He welcomed Calvary Chapel's value of being culturally current through informal dress and contemporary music. Wimber's services adopted a modified rock concert style with an extended set of songs. It was normal for the Anaheim Vineyard, which he pastored, to sing uninterrupted for half an hour.

As a professional musician, Wimber knew that music was a key to reaching and holding the boomer generation. He said, "It is our first priority to give God's love back to him in worship." With this, the congregation became the choir. Often Wimber would start with songs of high praise and conclude with quiet songs, designed to draw people into intimacy with God. Since worship had its own value, it was not used to warm up the crowd. As the worship of God went up, however, Wimber believed that the presence and power of God came down. He expected people to be converted and healed during worship. They were there to meet God in their singing. In my first experience watching this, there was hardly a dry eye around me. People sensed that the Presence was there. Wimber not only led worship from his keyboards, he also wrote some of the most enduring contemporary music in the church and enabled others to do the same. His lyrics often reflected biblical passages and moved from talking about God to talking to him. For example, this text reflects Isaiah 9:6:

> Isn't He beautiful, beautiful, isn't He?
> Prince of Peace, Son of God, isn't He?
> Yes You are wonderful, wonderful, yes You are,
> Counselor, Almighty God, yes You are, yes You are. . . .[22]

In an age of alienation, Wimber also knew the need for family. He knew that a network of small groups meeting weekly could stem migration from church to church. He called them "kinship groups," highlighting the longing for belonging. He taught his leaders to grow the church from "the inside out."

---

22. Wimber's music is available through Vineyard Music Group, 5340 E. La Palma Ave., Anaheim, CA 92807. For historical and critical comment, see Matt Redman, "Worshiper and Musician," in *John Wimber*, chap. 4.

As people commit to relationships and ministry, lasting church growth takes place. Wimber's goal was to make the priesthood of all believers more than Reformation polemic. He told the Vineyard, "Everybody gets to play," not just the up-front leaders and ordained clergy.

At the same time, Wimber was a leader of leaders. His clergy were to "equip the saints [believers] for the work of ministry" (Eph. 4:12) rather than doing it alone as professionals. They were player-coaches. Wimber had clinics and seminars where students learned the theory and then practiced it. The pastoral task was to teach, model, train, release, deploy, and monitor a growing lay army that would do the real work of ministry.

Wimber knew that for any movement to sustain itself it needed decisive leadership (which he provided), structure, authority, accountability, discipline, and continued training and relationship. His young pastors needed direction and vision. His planning methods helped them get organized, learn goal setting, and evaluate success and failure. Wimber was decisive without being autocratic (most of the time). Nevertheless, when he had to remove a pastor for immorality or a church for departing from his authority and direction, he did it. This caused him much pain, and in the case of severing the Toronto airport church from the Vineyard, not a little controversy.[23] It was the cost of leadership and he paid it.

To build leaders Wimber provided a wide variety of books, teaching tapes, videos, manuals, seminars, and conferences. He also encouraged his leaders to follow suit, which they eagerly did, extending the influence of the Vineyard far beyond Wimber himself. He also sustained and expanded his ministry through various profitable business ventures, including music recording and publishing. This is part of his enduring legacy.

What of the current Vineyard? It continues to be pragmatically driven. One in five Vineyards has a noncharismatic "seeker service," a response to the tension built into the Vineyard between evangelism and renewal. No survey is needed, however, to document the central place of worship in all Vineyard churches. This is a given, and Wimber's purposes for it are experienced on a weekly basis. Small-group ministry also continues to be central to the Vineyard. Close to 98 percent of all churches report having small groups, making them one of the highest Vineyard values and practices. Here the real pastoring of the church goes on. Small-group ministry facilitates Wimber's dictum "Everybody

---

23. The Airport church became a center of renewal and the source of the "Toronto Blessing." See Guy Chevreau, *Catch the Fire: The Toronto Blessing, an Experience of Renewal and Revival* (Toronto: Harper Collins, 1995); and John Arnott, *The Father's Blessing* (Orlando: Creation House, 1995).

gets to play," and becomes a central vehicle for worship, teaching, training, and relationship building. Here is where a continuing crop of lay leaders is grown.

Eighth, Wimber was ecclesiastically driven. He often said he loved the whole church. This came, in part, from his work with the Institute of Evangelism and Church Growth, associated with Fuller Theological Seminary. Such a wide exposure to congregations and traditions gave Wimber compassion and appreciation for the church in all its varieties. Being sociologically astute, he knew that successful ministries had to find their market niche. No single expression of faith reaches all. He was a grassroots ecumenicist, uninterested in formal moves toward church union but eager to "bless the whole church" wherever he found it. He often described the unity of the Vineyard as "centered-set." The center is Christ, which leaves the boundaries open on issues like eschatology and the sacraments. Beyond the Vineyard, Wimber welcomed fellowship with all who were centered-set as well, regardless of their labels.

Wimber's commitment to the whole church was especially evident in his worldwide renewal conferences. He taught equipping seminars in worship, healing, and church growth. Those who were raised in modern churches went through a paradigm shift when encountered by the power of the Spirit.[24] The presence of the supernatural became a part of their experience and was incorporated into their worldview. In the early days this resulted in numbers of churches transferring into the Vineyard. This influx was not always compatible with Wimber's passion for evangelistic growth. Through his renewal ministry, Wimber had a substantial impact on the Church of England starting in 1981.[25] John Gunstone, canon emeritus of Manchester Cathedral, writes, "My guesstimate is that Wimber probably influenced to a greater or lesser extent around fifteen per cent of Church of England parishes, though a higher proportion of the clergy, especially the younger ones."[26]

Wimber's concern for the whole church continues to affect the Vineyard to some extent. When asked if Vineyard churches should network outside the Association of Vineyard Churches, over two-thirds of the pastors agreed or strongly agreed. Over one in three churches, however, hold a more exclusive attitude and disagree. One percent strongly disagree. They seem to have missed Wimber's vision here and perhaps his centered-set welcome of all who believe in Christ and follow him.

Ninth, Wimber was missionally driven. He was a "Great Commission

---

24. Thomas Kuhn, *Structure of Scientific Revolutions,* 2nd ed. (Chicago: University of Chicago Press, 1962).

25. Pytches, "A Man Called John," pp. 33f.

26. John Gunstone, "An Anglican Evaluation," in *John Wimber,* p. 225.

Christian," believing that Christ's call to the nations included all ethnic groups. As we have seen, this expressed itself in worldwide renewal conferences for established churches. Wimber wanted to see Christians come alive in the power of the Spirit and enter into Jesus' kingdom ministry by evangelizing their own countries and subgroups. As these seminars multiplied, Vineyard churches materialized outside of North America. Intentional planting began in South Africa in 1982.[27] The first Vineyard appeared in England in 1986.[28] Commitments Wimber made not to plant Vineyards there could not be kept, and he later concluded that they should not be kept. In 1993 Wimber felt released to become intentional in international church planting and adopting existing congregations. His renewal ministry with existing churches had not produced identifiable evangelism. Wimber concluded that if these churches would not take the gospel to the streets, then the Vineyard would. By 1998 there were 370 Vineyards abroad in fifty-three countries.

Following Wimber's lead, most Vineyard pastors are engaged in cross-cultural mission activity, locally or internationally. Almost half participate a few times a year. One in ten does so monthly, and another one in ten is even more active. This means that about three-fourths of all Vineyards are "Great Commission" churches. They also put their money where their mouth is. When asked if 3 percent of the local budget should go to national and international church planting, almost nine out of ten either agreed or strongly agreed.

Tenth, Wimber was devotionally driven. He talked openly, warmly, and passionately about his love for Jesus and expressed this in intimate worship. He lived in the Bible so that he could live like the Bible. He experienced the presence and power and gifts of the Spirit operating in his life. He called these gifts tools for ministry that the Spirit would provide on the job as needed. He referenced again and again an intimacy with God where he heard his voice, received revelation in visions, dreams, impressions, prophetic words, and biblical passages.

Wimber had a conversational or dialogical relationship with God. He often prayed with his eyes open. Out of the calling on his own life and his track record of ministry, he enjoyed tremendous spiritual authority. Wimber described himself as "a fat man trying to get to heaven." This was his way of expressing the reality of the supernatural world in which he lived much of the time, especially in quiet devotion or hands-on ministry. His life was pointed beyond this world. Wimber's radicalism was expressed in his classic statement and question: "I'm a fool for Christ. Whose fool are you?"

Most Vineyard pastors today are also devotionally driven. This is implied

27. Jackson, *The Quest,* pp. 256ff.
28. Jackson, *The Quest,* p. 260.

by their commitment to Bible study, experiences of the Spirit, praying in tongues, personal evangelism, prophetic activity, healing the sick, ministry to the poor, and cross-cultural missions. Wimber defined all of this as life in the kingdom. Pastors engaging in spiritual disciplines also demonstrate a strong spiritual life. Almost 40 percent observe "sustained silence" a few times a year, and close to 20 percent do so once a month or more often. This accounts for about six out of ten pastors. Almost 50 percent of Vineyard pastors spend a day or more in solitude a few times a year; 15 percent do so once a month, and over 5 percent, two to three times a month. Over 50 percent of Vineyard pastors fast several times a year. Close to 20 percent do so once a month, and almost as many do so two to three times a month or more often. Fasting is a part of the lifestyle of almost 90 percent of all polled. Another spiritual index is the hope pastors have for the future. When asked if "the best years of the Vineyard are still ahead," over 40 percent agreed and another 40 percent strongly agreed. Over 85 percent of Vineyard pastors face the future with optimism.

From this review, the conclusion is clear. The values, teaching, and modeling of John Wimber are still at the heart of the Vineyard's life. He has provided the Vineyard's "genetic code." For a large majority, the realized eschatology of the kingdom still defines ministry. Most churches are strong in biblical preaching. Most churches give calls for conversion. Most churches regularly pray for the sick. Most churches expect and experience prophetic ministry. Most churches are structured with small groups. Most churches are active in serving the poor. Most churches are committed to church planting and missions.

The Vineyard perseveres in this style and substance of ministry, despite mixed success and the loss of Wimber through debilitating illnesses. It lives out the eschatological tension of the kingdom come and coming. This cannot be stressed enough. George Ladd's kingdom theology, as interpreted by Wimber, determines both the values and practices of the Vineyard. Wimber succeeded in demonstrating that the church is "the eschatological people of God." This means necessarily that the Vineyard is open to the future, living both in the already and the not-yet. In Wimber's phrase, it is committed to "doin' the stuff."

The Theology of the Vineyard

Wimber's faith was strongly evangelical and, at the same time, surprisingly open. As we have noted, he described the fellowship of Vineyard churches sociologically as centered-set, that is, with Christ at the center. Faith in him held the whole together. This contrasts with churches that are bounded-set, where issues such as eschatology, cultural habits, or liturgical forms define the fellow-ship.[29] While some may object that music is the liturgical form that defines the Vineyard, this is reductionistic. Worship (constantly changing) and kingdom ministry are at the core of its values and practices.

While being theologically open on many issues, the Vineyard does have a statement of faith.[30] It is necessarily a statement rather than a confession. The statement defines the movement's theological position without forcing its members to confess the whole. At the same time, it is expected that Vineyard leadership will be in harmony with it.

The statement is structured by kingdom theology. It is cast in the context of God as King, exercising his reign which, while usurped by Satan, is restored first to Israel and then to the nations. This is effected by Christ, who overcomes the powers of darkness. As we have seen, it is the presence of the kingdom, in the eschatological tension of the already and the not yet, that dominates Vine-yard thought and practice. It also determines the heart of the *Statement of Faith*. What then are its major influences?

First, there is the patristic period. Consider the opening paragraph: "We believe that God is the Eternal King. He is an infinite, unchangeable Spirit, per-fect in holiness, wisdom, goodness, justice, power and love. From all eternity He exists as the One Living and True God in three persons of one substance, the Father, the Son, and the Holy Spirit equal in power and glory."[31] Here the state-ment confesses the classic patristic definition of the Trinity. It later follows with the two natures of Christ: "We believe that in the fullness of time, God honored His covenants with Israel and His prophetic promises of salvation by sending His only Son, Jesus, into the world. Conceived by the Holy Spirit and born of the Virgin Mary, as fully God and fully man in one person, He is humanity as God intended us to be."[32] These quotes clearly place the Vineyard within main-stream Christian orthodoxy. The Vineyard embraces the whole of Christ's church through the generations, separating itself from ancient and modern heresies concerning the doctrine of God.

Second, there is the Reformation. The statement is clear about salvation through Christ alone. It reads: "After dying for the sins of the world, Jesus was raised from the dead on the third day. . . . In His sinless, perfect life Jesus met the demands of the law and in His atoning death on the cross He took God's

29. Jackson, *The Quest,* pp. 244f.

30. See "Vineyard Statement of Faith" at the Vineyard USA Web site: www.vineyardusa .org/about/beliefs/beliefs_index/statement_faith.htm. Subsequent quotations of the statement made within this section refer to paragraphs in that document.

31. "God the King and the Holy Trinity," par. 1.

32. "Christ the Mediator and Eternal King," par. 6.

judgment for sin which we deserve as law-breakers."[33] The statement is also clear that the Bible is the written Word of God, the final authority for the Vineyard: "We believe that the Holy Spirit inspired the human authors of Holy Scripture so that the Bible is without error in the original manuscripts. We receive the sixty-six books of the Old and New Testaments as our final, absolute authority, the only infallible rule of faith and practice."[34] These doctrines distinguish the Vineyard from the medieval church with its teaching of salvation through sacraments and good works and the supremacy of papal authority. The statement employs the phrase "without error" with respect to Scripture in order to define the highest commitment to biblical authority in an evangelical context. This clearly separates the Vineyard from neoorthodoxy and liberal evangelicalism.

Third, there is the eighteenth-century evangelical awakening. The statement speaks of the new birth or conversion: "God regenerates, justifies, adopts, and sanctifies through Jesus by the Spirit all who repent of their sins and trust in Jesus Christ as Lord and Savior."[35] The church is one, holy, and universal, and is made up of "all who repent of their sins and confess Jesus as Lord and Savior" and who are "regenerated by the Holy Spirit and form the living Body of Christ, of which He is the head and of which we are all members."[36] Regeneration then leads to a life of holiness. The statement says, "The Spirit brings the . . . presence of God to us for spiritual worship, personal sanctification, building up the Church, [and] gifting us for ministry."[37]

Fourth, there is the influence of the modern missionary movement. The Vineyard stands under the marching orders of the Great Commission to take the gospel to the nations by planting churches. With John Wesley, the world is its parish, as seen by the Vineyard going international. The statement reads: "[Jesus] is the eternal Messiah-King advancing God's reign throughout every generation and throughout the whole earth today," and further, "The Spirit brings the permanent indwelling presence of God to us . . . gifting us for ministry, and driving back the kingdom of Satan by the evangelization of the world through proclaiming the word of Jesus and doing the works of Jesus."[38]

Fifth, there is the impact of the biblical theology movement. As already noted, Wimber was strongly influenced by George Ladd of Fuller Theological Seminary. Ladd's central teaching was the present/future kingdom of God in-

33. "Christ the Mediator and Eternal King," par. 6.
34. "The Sufficiency of Scripture," par. 8.
35. "The Power of the Gospel over the Kingdom of Darkness," par. 9.
36. "The Church: Instrument of the Kingdom," par. 10.
37. "The Ministry of the Holy Spirit," par. 7.
38. "Christ the Mediator," par. 6.

augurated in the ministry of Jesus. The whole *Statement of Faith* is cast in the framework of the kingdom, from creation to redemption. It is written as historical narrative. Salvation includes leaving one kingdom for another: "God regenerates . . . all who repent of their sins and trust in Jesus Christ as Lord and Savior. By this they are released from Satan's domain and enter into God's kingdom reign."[39] The statement draws to its conclusion by saying:

> We believe that God's kingdom has come in the ministry of our Lord Jesus Christ, that it continues to come in the ministry of the Spirit through the church, and that it will be consummated in the glorious, visible and triumphant appearing of Christ — His return to the earth as King. . . . After Christ returns to reign, He will bring about the final defeat of Satan. . . . Finally, God will be all in all and His kingdom, His rule and reign, will be fulfilled in the new heavens and the new earth, recreated by His mighty power, in which righteousness dwells and in which He will forever be worshipped.[40]

In the *Statement of Faith,* Wimber's evangelical theology is systematized in a kingdom context. It represents the conviction of his mind and the passion of his heart. When it was first read to the National Board, he wept. The statement in tract form is readily available in most Vineyard churches, answering the question: "What do these people believe?" It continues to inform outsiders and newcomers and provide a benchmark for pastors and leaders. It is universally accepted in the Vineyard and appears on many church literature tables.

The Polity of the Vineyard

From its origin in Calvary Chapel, the Vineyard has been a loose confederation of congregations, sharing common faith, common values, and common practices. As a growing network of churches, there is a high stress on relationships. There are monthly area pastors meetings for worship, sharing, and mutual support. Program agendas are clearly secondary. No roll is called. No official minutes are kept. No votes are taken on the local level. Congregations are independent and individually incorporated, usually with a pastor and elders for plurality of leadership. Only the name Vineyard was trademarked by Wimber. Pastoral care and discipline are exercised in a personal way rather than by a judicatory. In comparison to the presbyterian system, there are no courts through

39. "The Power of the Gospel," par. 9.
40. "The Kingdom of God and the Final Judgment," par. 12.

which to appeal rulings. Discipline is enforced by local leadership with the area representative serving as a bishop, just as John Wimber and Todd Hunter served as bishops over the whole movement. This role is now taken by Bert Waggoner, a Vineyard pastor from Texas.

Wimber's ideal was "charismatic leadership," leadership called and gifted by God himself and raised up with a track record of ministry from the local church. Such leadership would be prophetically directed and affirmed by fellow leaders. Building off of Jacob's wrestling all night with an angel (Gen. 32:22-32), Wimber often said, "Never trust a man who doesn't walk with a limp." Wimber earned the trust of his fellow leaders and congregations because of his credibility and vulnerability. He kept them current through all the crises and struggles of his life. While Wimber carried unique authority, he was a churchman and a family man. He loved community; he was never a loner. He was submitted to his wife, Carol. She was his primary adviser and supporter through the years. Once the Vineyard came into being, Wimber quickly formed a national board. He sought to lead by consensus. At the same time, he had the final word. When the board debated adopting a church into the Vineyard, Wimber ended the discussion by saying, "You get into heaven through Jesus and you get into the Vineyard through me."

Unity, training, relationship, and direction for the Vineyard were built and sustained by national pastors conferences. The different phases of the movement and seasons of Wimber's life (church planting, healing, renewal, the prophetic, and missions) can be traced through these gatherings. They showcased the Vineyard, served as minirenewals and revivals, equipped pastors, and recruited new friends into the movement. They also displayed Vineyard values with extensive times of worship, seminars led by a large number of pastors on basic themes (such as evangelism, church planting, building a worship team, how to pray for the sick, building small groups, building children and youth ministries, reaching the poor, missions, etc.), and occasions for pastors to pray and prophesy over each other. Wimber saw these conferences as reunions. What was true for the local church was also true for the movement. Wimber said, "People come for many reasons, but they stay for the relationships."

Wimber resisted the temptation to create an administrative structure separated from the local churches. This kept a high degree of trust and support flowing from the national level to the local level and back to the national level. While the Vineyard networked congregations into area and regional groupings, all leaders must also be pastors. Up until his final years of ill health, Wimber himself functioned as the pastor of the Anaheim Vineyard. On the analogy of the early church, leaders were not professional administrators or therapists. They were bishops.

One basic issue before Wimber and now before the Vineyard has been how to sustain a renewal/revival movement into the next generation. Wimber rejected creating a denominational structure at the pastors conference in 1988. The Vineyard needed to be "free-flowing." Wimber sensed that if the church lost its cutting edge (in sociological terms, if it moved from being a sect to being a church),[41] it would no longer be a force for renewal, innovation, and contemporary, experimental ministry. It would no longer be Spirit-led; it would be law-led. Pastors would no longer be submitted to each other, they would be submitted to the structure. Too much order would quench freedom. Wimber wanted to live in the tension of having enough order to make community possible but also having that order serve the freedom of the Spirit. This, of course, is a classic problem, evidenced in the New Testament itself.[42] It is never fully resolved. Wimber lived in its ambiguity, which is perhaps another way of saying that he walked by faith.

The Vineyard and the Twenty-First Century

How does the Vineyard look as it enters the twenty-first century? We have seen that Wimber's values and practices are largely intact. Vineyard kingdom theology determines kingdom practice. Now these values and practices are confronted by an age of pluralism, multiculturalism, and relativism. The modern age asked, "Is it true?" The postmodern age asks, "Is it real?" Any gulf between head and heart, theology and practice, or intention and action will be lethal for ministry. Any church claim, theology, agenda, program, or leader is subject to deconstruction. In our cynicism and skepticism, we want to know "what is really going on." Years ago Bob Dylan said it was his intention to take off the masks to see what is behind them. In "When He Returns" he asked, "How long will you falsify and deny what is real? How long will you hate yourself for the weakness you conceal?"[43] These are the postmodern questions that the church must answer.

While in many respects John Wimber was a modern man, he also had a core spiritual life which was more premodern. He shared the worldview held by most Christians for seventeen centuries. He took the ministry of Jesus in the Gospels at face value. He refused to explain away the miraculous or relegate it to another dis-

41. Ernst Troeltsch made this analysis in *The Social Teaching of the Christian Churches*. His work is excerpted in J. Milton Yinger, *Religion, Society, and the Individual* (New York: Macmillan, 1957), pp. 416ff.

42. See 1 Cor. 14.

43. On the album *Slow Train Coming* (New York: Columbia Records, 1979).

pensation. He embraced as his own Jesus' preaching of the kingdom "at hand," but he also wanted Jesus' agenda for ministry to be his and the Vineyard's.

A central text for Wimber was Luke 4:16-21, in which Jesus entered the synagogue, read from the Isaiah scroll, and announced that this Scripture is now fulfilled "in your hearing." What Scripture? The Scripture that proclaims the empowering of the Spirit: "The Spirit of the Lord is upon me, because he has anointed me. . . ." This is the Scripture that calls for kingdom ministry: to preach good news to the poor, to proclaim freedom to the prisoners, to proclaim recovery of sight to the blind, to release the oppressed, and to proclaim the year of the Lord's favor. Wimber not only devoted his life to this. He trained his churches to do the same. He insisted on both the message and the ministry of Jesus. The church is to be an instrument of the kingdom, experiencing, however imperfectly, the messianic age to come as it invades the present.

With the grip of rationalism broken, supernatural, biblical faith is competitive within a pluralistic culture when it is demonstrated in practice. Its reality cannot be hyped or faked. It must be seen as "naturally supernatural" and have transparent integrity. The Vineyard is well positioned for the new postmodern openness to the supernatural. It expects God to "show up" in worship and ministry times when the sick are healed and the demonized delivered. The oft-prayed "Come, Holy Spirit" is uttered with a high expectation that the Spirit will visit, sometimes dramatically and overwhelmingly. For the Vineyard the Spirit is not merely imminent but also transcendent, moving with empowering and gifting beyond our control. The Vineyard's theology of Satan and demons equips it to face the dark side of the postmodern world. The Vineyard rejects the illusions of humanistic optimism or inevitable progress. These old myths are dead. Kingdom ministry, however, does not breed cynicism or resignation before the powers of evil. It has its triumphalistic side. Jesus is Lord. His name is above every name. Postmodernism has a lingering idealism, hoping for change. Kingdom ministry meets this hope. Vineyard ministry will credibly reflect this as it touches the sores of society. Praying for the sick and hands-on ministry to the poor, the addicted, and the marginalized point the way to the presence of God's kingdom.

With Wimber's stress on community lived out in small groups, the Vineyard is ready to rebuild fractured family life, heal grief and loss, provide training and discipleship in ministry, and build accountability for the addicted. In our increasingly isolated and technologically sophisticated world, ministry without small groups will be no ministry at all. A challenge for the Vineyard at this point will be to go beyond evangelical individualism and catch a new vision for the church as the people of God. If it does this, it will help to arrest the consumer Christianity so rampant in our culture.

To be postmodern is to have "no metanarrative." Everyone has his or her own unique story and small, fractured community where it is told. Part of the mission of the Vineyard is to subvert this assumption. It will be done not so much on an apologetic level but on the level of the manifest presence of the kingdom. In this "power encounter," my story is intersected by Jesus' story in the proclamation and demonstration of the gospel. Moreover, Jesus' story can be understood only in the context of the whole biblical story, cover to cover.[44] His story then makes sense of mine. Through this (word and deed), I am drawn into the Big Story, the metanarrative of the biblical worldview. Once again, existence is seen to be "divinely composed and purposeful drama" rather than "a blindly running flux of disintegrating energy."[45] Rather than "Whirl is king," Jesus is Lord.

As the Vineyard faces postmodern pluralism, major issues surface. They include the full empowering of women as ordained pastors and church planters,[46] the empowering of the next generation of leaders without unnecessary educational credentialing, American multiracial and multiethnic churches that share Vineyard theology and values but not "Vineyard" (American) culture, and the demand for justice for oppressed minorities. If the Vineyard is locked into seventies' and eighties' white, middle-class ministry and fails the postmodern challenge, it will be apostate from its own mandate to be culturally current. It will also be apostate from its own kingdom theology which sees the Spirit moving and the kingdom coming in and for each generation in time and space. The Vineyard must learn again, as Wimber would say, to "see what God is doing and bless it," and then, of course, jump in with both feet.

Success is always a threat to the Vineyard. One saving grace is that the Vineyard churches are no longer the new kid on the block with the privileged position that this implies. Wimber's eagerness to give away all that God gave him has empowered thousands of non-Vineyards "to do the stuff" and worship Vineyard-style. This forces Vineyards to have kingdom vision for what God is doing in their communities rather than harbor the arrogance of being on the cutting edge alone. Another threat to any renewal movement is familiarity. As Luther says, "What is gospel today becomes law tomorrow." The challenge before the Vineyard will be to break from the familiar again and again

---

44. For a scholarly presentation of this position, see N. T. Wright, *The New Testament and the People of God* (Minneapolis: Fortress, 1992); N. T. Wright, *Jesus and the Victory of God* (Minneapolis: Fortress, 1996); N. T. Wright, *The Challenge of Jesus: Rediscovering Who Jesus Is and Was* (Downers Grove, Ill.: InterVarsity, 1999). For a popular critique of current alternative views of Jesus, see N. T. Wright, *Who Was Jesus?* (London: SPCK, 1992).

45. Becker, *The Heavenly City of the Eighteenth-Century Philosophers*.

46. This is currently the option of each local church in the United States.

and let the fresh winds of the Spirit blow without trying to produce them or control them.

All renewal movements easily accommodate to the mass culture, especially as they get position, money, and temporal power. What will prevent the Vineyard from moving from sect (high tension with the world) to church (low tension with the world)? There is no easy answer. A saving grace may be for each Vineyard leader to repeat after John Wimber again and again, "I'm a fool for Christ. Whose fool are you?"

Anglican Mission in Changing Times:
A Brief Institutional History of the
Episcopal Church, USA

Ian T. Douglas

The Episcopal Church in the United States of America has a curious institu-tional history. With roots in the church of British colonial power, Angli-cans in America struggled to be fully contextualized in form and structure in the early years of the United States. The church's political, economic, and social ascendancy in the late nineteenth and first half of the twentieth century led Episcopalians to believe that they were, de facto if not de jure, the established church in the United States. Radical changes both at home and in the wider world over the last three decades have deeply challenged American Episcopa-lians to shed their own "national church ideal" and live as one among many in a radically multicultural and pluralistic global Anglican Communion.

The settlement of Jamestown, Virginia, in 1607 by the London Company, later the Virginia Company, marked the beginnings of the Church of England in the American colonies. The church slowly grew throughout the other colo-nies up and down the eastern seaboard of what is now the United States, even-tually becoming the established church (i.e., state church) in Virginia, North Carolina, Maryland, South Carolina, Georgia, and the lower four counties of New York. By 1700, more than 100 Anglican churches had been set up from Massachusetts to South Carolina with the majority of Anglicans living in Vir-ginia and Maryland. In these two colonies Anglicans outnumbered other Christian traditions.[1]

The ministry of the Church of England in the American colonies was

---

1. A variety of recent books are available on the history of the Episcopal Church in the United States with excellent attention to the late eighteenth and early nineteenth centuries. See David L. Holmes, *A Brief History of the Episcopal Church* (Valley Forge, Pa.: Trinity Press Inter-national, 1993), and Robert W. Prichard, *A History of the Episcopal Church* (Harrisburg, Pa.: Morehouse Publishing, 1991).

aided significantly by the Society for the Propagation of the Gospel (SPG). The society, founded in London in 1701, came together to advance Anglicanism among the settlers, Indians, and African slaves in the American British colonies. Much of the growth of the Church of England outside of Virginia and Maryland is credited to the work of the SPG and its missionaries. One of the most famous SPG missionaries to the American colonies, although he had a lackluster ministry of less than two years in North America, was John Wesley. Because of the efforts of this venerable missionary society, the Church of England made significant inroads into the predominantly congregational-leaning Massachusetts and Connecticut colonies during the eighteenth century. The colonial Anglican Church, however, was hampered in its efforts to become genuinely American because most clergy were British-born or expatriate missionaries and there was no episcopal (i.e., bishop) presence in America.

The American Revolution of 1776 threw the established Church of England in the colonies into turmoil and confusion of identity. Although many of the country's patriots, including George Washington, Alexander Hamilton, and Benjamin Franklin, as well as more than half the signers of the Declaration of Independence were Anglicans, the matter of loyalty to an English state church was called into question with the founding of the United States. As a result, by the end of the Revolution the Anglican churches in America had become disestablished as well as disassociated from the mother church in England.

Cut loose from the Church of England, these churches at first had no constitutional organization or episcopacy. The first step to secure an American episcopacy occurred in 1783 when ten clergymen in Connecticut met secretly and elected Samuel Seabury as a prospective bishop. Although Seabury had been both an SPG missionary and a loyalist, English bishops refused to consecrate him since he would not take the required oath of loyalty to the Crown. Seabury thus went to Scotland and was consecrated by three nonjuring bishops of the Scottish Episcopal Church. In 1785 he returned to Connecticut and ordained the first twenty-six Episcopal clergy in the new nation. In the same year, lay and clerical delegates from seven of the nine states south of Connecticut met in Philadelphia in the first General Convention of the Protestant Episcopal Church in the United States of America. There they drew up a constitution, drafted an American *Book of Common Prayer,* and devised a plan for the consecration of additional bishops. Two years later Americans William White and Samuel Provoost were consecrated bishops in England without having to swear loyalty to the Crown. The young American church now had enough bishops to guarantee its own apostolic succession, a central tenet of Anglican identity.

Of the early gatherings of the Episcopal Church in the United States, the General Convention of 1789 is the most significant. The *Constitution and*

Canons and the *Book of Common Prayer* agreed to there are the basis of the polity and worship of today's Episcopal Church. For the last two centuries the triennial meeting of the General Convention has governed the Episcopal Church. The convention is made up of two houses, the House of Bishops and the House of Deputies. All bishops sit in the House of Bishops, and the House of Deputies is made up of an equal number of clerical and lay deputies from each diocese in the church. Since 1789 the *Book of Common Prayer* has dictated the patterns of worship for the Episcopal Church, although it has undergone three revisions (1892, 1928, and 1979).

For the last two decades of the eighteenth century and the first two of the nineteenth, Episcopalians were preoccupied with organization and extension of the church within their own states and not with missionary outreach beyond their borders. In 1821, however, the General Convention established both a general seminary for the whole church as well as the Domestic and Foreign Missionary Society of the Protestant Episcopal Church. Unlike the independent voluntary missionary societies of the Church of England, this society was set up under the auspices of the whole church meeting in General Convention. Unfortunately though, the first decade and a half of the Missionary Society saw lackluster results, with only a few missionaries sent to the western frontier and four individuals sailing to Greece.[2]

In 1835 the General Convention took three significant steps to invigorate the mission of the Episcopal Church. First, it declared that the whole world, at home and overseas, was the church's mission field. Second, it stipulated that all Episcopalians, by virtue of their baptism and not their financial contributions, are members of the Domestic and Foreign Missionary Society. And third, it inaugurated the missionary episcopate. The 1835 convention elected Jackson Kemper bishop for Missouri and Indiana, the first domestic missionary bishop. A little less than a decade later, in 1844, the first two foreign missionary bishops were elected, William Boone for Amoy and other parts of China, and Horatio Southgate for Constantinople.

In the footsteps of Kemper and Boone, the Episcopal Church pushed westward across the United States while initiating foreign missions in China, Japan, and Liberia. On the domestic frontier and overseas, the Episcopal Church followed a watchword of "good schools, good hospitals and right ordered worship" all under the episcopal oversight of missionary bishops. In most cases parochial work was reserved for ordained men while women missionar-

---

2. For an institutional history of the foreign mission work of the Episcopal Church, see Ian T. Douglas, *Fling Out the Banner: The National Church Ideal and the Foreign Mission of the Episcopal Church* (New York: Church Publishing, 1996).

ies, who were excluded from ordained ministry, staffed the schools and hospitals. The Woman's Auxiliary to the Board of Missions of the Domestic and Foreign Missionary Society, organized in 1871, became the primary source of financial and personnel support for the church's mission work at home and around the world.[3]

The Episcopal Church also pursued a vigorous ministry in the urban centers of the United States. Individuals such as William Augustus Muhlenberg, rector of the Church of the Holy Communion in New York City, promoted the social outreach of the Episcopal Church. With a labor force comprised primarily of women providing health care, education, and economic assistance to the disabled and disadvantaged, the Episcopal Church was a leader in the Social Gospel movement in the United States.

In the late nineteenth and early twentieth centuries the Episcopal Church became increasingly more unified around a central identity, that of a "national church." The Chicago-Lambeth Quadrilateral of 1888 was held up by William Reed Huntington and others as a point of unity for all non–Roman Catholic Christians in the United States.[4] Motivated by both the social gospel and a romantic desire to reclaim Anglican establishmentarianism, Episcopalians increasingly saw themselves as a unified body whose calling it was to spread the riches of American society and the richness of Anglican tradition at home and overseas. At the same time, the foreign mission work of the church profited from American imperialism and territorial expansion at the turn of the century, and new missionary districts were added in Alaska, Cuba, Mexico, Brazil, Haiti, Honolulu, Puerto Rico, the Philippines, and the Panama Canal Zone. The mission of the church, in the United States and around the world, was not so much evangelization and conversion, but rather social regeneration through Christian moral truths and American democracy.

The General Convention of 1919 revolutionized the structures and strategies of Episcopal mission work. To begin with, the convention ratified a constitutional change that provided for an elected presiding bishop. In addition, it consolidated the church's work in missions, education, and social service under

---

3. The most comprehensive history of Episcopal women's ministries in the late nineteenth and early twentieth century is Mary Sudman Donovan, *A Different Call: Women's Ministries in the Episcopal Church, 1850-1920* (Wilton, Conn.: Morehouse-Barlow, 1986).

4. The Quadrilateral articulated four principles for ecumenical cooperation: the Holy Scriptures of the Old and New Testaments, as containing all things necessary for salvation; the Apostles' Creed and Nicene Creed, as sufficient statements of Christian faith; baptism and Eucharist, as sacraments ordained by Christ; and the historic episcopate, locally adapted. The Quadrilateral, although originally intended as an ecumenical document, has increasingly become the defining marks of Anglicanism.

one national coordinating body known as the National Council. And finally, it instituted a very successful nationwide campaign designed to provide immediate and ongoing financial support for the new council and its work. With a new centralized church structure under the leadership of an elected presiding bishop supported by a nationally planned fund-raising program, the Episcopal Church claimed its coming of age as a "national church."

In the two decades following World War II, the Episcopal Church in the United States came the closest to realizing its ideal as a national church. Under the leadership of Presiding Bishop Henry Knox Sherrill, the National Council broadened its institutional reach in Christian education, social service, and church extension. When missionaries were expelled from China following the Revolution of 1949, the Episcopal Church increased its missionary efforts in Latin America. Bolstered by the American affluence of the 1950s, and following the leadership of Bishops Walter H. Gray and Stephen Bayne, the church emerged as a significant leader in inter-Anglican conversations. With new mission fields, new money, and new leadership, it began to see itself as the preeminent church in the Anglican Communion.[5]

As independent nations and churches emerged during the 1960s in what had been colonies and mission fields of continental Europe and North America, the national church ideal began to be challenged from overseas and within the United States. The Anglican Congress of 1963, made up of ordained and lay representatives from every church in the Anglican Communion, issued the revolutionary document "Mutual Responsibility and Interdependence in the Body of Christ" (MRI) that held up a different vision for mission. The Episcopal Church could no longer be Lady Bountiful dispensing good schools, good hospitals, and right ordered worship to dependent missionary districts around the world. Partnership in mission became the new order for the day.[6] At the same time, the Civil Rights movement, urban unrest, and the social upheaval of the 1960s in the United States resulted in a questioning of the church's calling at home. At the height of this crisis, Presiding Bishop John Hines called on the Episcopal Church to "take its place humbly and boldly alongside of, and in support of, the dispossessed and oppressed peoples of this country for the healing of our national life." In response, the Episcopal Church initiated the General Convention Special Program (GCSP) in 1967 and redirected the national church program and budget to support the poor and those working for social

---

5. See Stephen Fielding Bayne, ed., *An Anglican Turning Point: Documents and Interpretations* (Austin: Church Historical Society, 1964).

6. See Stephen Fielding Bayne, *Mutual Responsibility and Interdependence in the Body of Christ* (New York: Seabury Press, 1963).

justice in our country. The church's commitment to MRI and GCSP represented fledgling attempts by Episcopalians to respond to the realities of a new
world.[7]

Changes afoot in world Christianity, first acknowledged by MRI and
GCSP, have only quickened in pace over the last three decades. Anglican mission scholar David Barrett has documented that in 1900, 77 percent of the 558
million Christians in the world lived in Europe and North America. Today only
37 percent of the close to 2 billion Christians do so. Barrett further predicts that
in less than three decades, in 2025, fully 71 percent of Christians will live in Asia,
Africa, Latin America, and the Pacific.[8]

The Anglican Communion has experienced deeply these radical demographic changes of the world Christian community over the last four decades.
The evolution in contemporary Anglicanism, from a white, predominantly
English-speaking church of the West to a church of the Southern Hemisphere,
is now undeniable. The Lambeth Conference of Anglican bishops, meeting in
1998, pushed church members in the industrialized West to wrestle deeply with
the reality that the Anglican Communion is no longer a Christian community
primarily identified with Anglo-American culture.[9] Anglicans in the West can
no longer rest in the economic and political privilege of colonialism or the
theological and philosophical paradigms of the Enlightenment, which have so
long defined the church.[10]

The Anglican Communion, now a "family" of thirty-eight equal and autonomous churches, is wrestling deeply with the possibilities and limits of new
relationships in a new world. Without a clear, central authority structure (such
as Roman Catholics have) or an agreed confessional statement (as found
among Presbyterians and Lutherans), Anglicans are struggling to discern how
to remain together as the body of Christ, the church catholic. What are the limits of Anglican identity, now that most Anglicans do not share a common lan-

7. See John Booty, *The Episcopal Church in Crisis* (Cambridge, Mass.: Cowley, 1988).

8. David B. Barrett, "Annual Statistical Table on Global Mission: 2000," *International Bulletin of Missionary Research* 24 (January 2000): 24-25. See also a more popular historical presentation of changing global Christian demographics in Philip Jenkins, *The Next Christendom: The
Coming of Global Christianity* (New York: Oxford University Press, 2002).

9. For a wonderful collection of voices from throughout the Anglican Communion, with
a priority on the churches of Africa, Asia, Latin America, the Middle East, and the Pacific, see
Andrew Wingate, Kevin Ward, Carrie Pemberton, and Wilson Sitshebo, eds., *Anglicanism: A
Global Communion* (New York: Church Publishing, 1998). For a discussion of the politics of on-
going Western hegemony in the Anglican Communion, see Ian Douglas, "Radical Mutuality
Still out of Reach: Lambeth Analysis," *Witness* 81, no. 11 (November 1998): 24-27.

10. See Ian T. Douglas, "Authority after Colonialism," *Witness* 83, no. 3 (March 2000): 10-
14, and "Lambeth 1998 and the 'New Colonialism,'" *Witness* 81, no. 5 (May 1998): 8-12.

guage or culture? Where does authority lie in a global church that looks to the archbishop of Canterbury as a titular head, but who has no legislative or canonical power outside of England? These are the questions that lie at the heart of inter-Anglican conversations today.[11]

There are still those in the Anglican Communion who believe that Anglicanism's identity lies in a shared British heritage and history. Such individuals would argue that English good taste, liturgical vestments crafted at ecclesiastical haberdashery shops in London, and allegiance to the British monarch are the defining marks of Anglicanism. For such folk the increasing plurality and multiculturalism of the Anglican Communion is a threat to their Anglo-Saxon sensibilities. In their attempt to reclaim the church of the British Empire, they attempt to draw boundaries and set tight doctrinal controls in order to define who is and who is not an Anglican.

Others emphasize that the marks of contemporary Anglicanism lie less in cultural or doctrinal agreement and more in who gets invited to what meeting by the archbishop of Canterbury. Significant attempts have been made to define "four instruments of unity" in Anglicanism, namely, the office of the archbishop of Canterbury, the Lambeth Conference of bishops meeting every ten years, the annual gathering of the archbishops of the Anglican Communion known as the Primates Meeting, and the triennial meeting of the Anglican Consultative Council that brings together laypeople, priests, and bishops from each church in the Anglican Communion.[12] In addition, there are a variety of international committees and commissions loosely related to, or called into being by, any of the four instruments of unity as well as a host of "official" and "unofficial" networks related to such particularities as indigenous peoples, women, and peace and justice commitments. It must be noted, however, that the making and unmaking of international Anglican meetings, official and unofficial, is subject to the political and economic forces of a new colonialism where those with money often have more power to set the agenda and control outcomes.

Tensions and difficulties across the churches of the Anglican Communion seem to be exacerbated increasingly at the turn of the twenty-first century. The debate over human sexuality, specifically the place and acceptance of homosexuals in the church, once the exclusive preoccupation of churches in the industrialized West, has been globalized across the Anglican Communion.

11. See Mark Harris, *The Challenge of Change: The Anglican Communion in the Post-Modern Era* (New York: Church Publishing, 1998).

12. See "The Virginia Report," in *Being Anglican in the Third Millennium: Anglican Consultative Council X,* ed. M. and Nicola Currie Rosenthal James (Harrisburg, Pa.: Morehouse Publishing, 1997), pp. 211-88.

Whether it be pronouncements by the decennial meeting of the bishops of the Anglican Communion at the Lambeth Conference of 1998 or recent attempts by some primates to ostracize perceived "revisionist churches" in the communion, human sexuality, like it or not, has become a defining issue in contemporary inter-Anglican relations.[13] Even the selection process of the 104th archbishop of Canterbury, the Most Reverend Rowan Williams, has been overly focused on his views toward human sexuality.

As much as some in the press, and in the Anglican Communion itself, would like to put issues of human sexuality at the very center of Anglicanism's life and witness, there are many positive and daring attempts by Anglicans around the world to engage the powers and principalities that control issues of life and death today. The Anglican Communion's united witness in addressing both the evils of international debt and the HIV/AIDS pandemic, specifically in Africa, points to positive and life-affirming actions under way in contemporary Anglicanism.[14] These often underreported efforts by a communion of thirty-eight Anglican churches around the world, comprised of over 70 million members, point to new possibilities for solidarity and action as a global Christian community.

No one can deny that the Episcopal Church and wider Anglican Communion are experiencing profound change. The Episcopal Church in the United States is no longer the church of the establishment bound together by a national church ideal. The realities of the postcolonial, postmodern era have challenged presuppositions about what it means to be an Anglican and have demonstrated that old ways of relating based on inherited structures, nationally and internationally, have lost their efficacy in the new globalized world. Finding new and creative ways for Episcopalians in the United States to order their common life and organize their religious work, both as a local American church and as one Anglican church in a worldwide fellowship, is the order of the day. The Episcopal Church is thus actively wrestling with its mission in the United States and the wider world, particularly given the realities of American society and global tensions after the September 11, 2001, terrorist attacks on the Pentagon and World Trade Center.

The 2020 Movement is one response to a changing world. Initiated at the 2000 General Convention, 2020, as the effort is known, seeks to double the

13. On the latter proposal see Drexel W. Gomez and W. Maurice Sinclair, eds., *To Mend the Net: Anglican Faith and Order for Renewed Mission* (Carrollton, Tex.: Ekklesia Society, 2000).

14. For a discussion of the changing demographics and dynamics of Anglicanism and how the Anglican Communion engages the realities of a postcolonial and postmodern world, see Ian T. Douglas and Kwok Pui Lan, eds., *Beyond Colonial Anglicanism: The Anglican Communion in the Twenty-First Century* (New York: Church Publishing, 2001).

membership of the Episcopal Church in the first two decades of the twenty-first century. Particular attention is paid to people groups historically underrepresented in the Episcopal Church, such as new immigrants from Latin America, Asia, and Africa, as well as the X Generation. Ostensibly, 2020 has a missiological imperative as leaders in the movement emphasize that the Episcopal Church needs to move from "maintenance to mission" if it is to have any future in the twenty-first century.

Responding more directly to the wider contexts of both globalization and the United States's "War on Terror," the bishops have embraced a different vision for the future life of the Episcopal Church. In the fall 2001 and spring 2002 meetings of the House of Bishops, they dedicated themselves to becoming agents of reconciliation both in a church divided over issues of human sexuality and in a world torn apart by terrorism, war, poverty, and disease. The bishops' powerful statement from their meeting of September 2001, fifteen days after the terrorist strikes, charts a future for the Episcopal Church:

> We are called to self-examination and repentance: the willingness to change direction, to open our hearts and give room to God's compassion as it seeks to bind up, to heal, and to make all things new and whole. God's project, in which we participate by virtue of our baptism, is the ongoing work of reordering and transforming the patterns of our common life so they may reveal God's justness — not as an abstraction but in bread for the hungry and clothing for the naked. The mission of the Church is to participate in God's work in the world. We claim that mission.
>
> "I have set before you life and death . . . choose life so that you and your descendants may live," declares Moses to the children to Israel. We choose life and immediately set ourselves to the task of developing clear steps that we will take personally and as a community of faith, to give substance to our resolve and embodiment to our hope. We do so not alone but trusting in your own faithfulness and your desire to be instruments of peace.
>
> Let us therefore wage reconciliation. Let us offer our gifts for the carrying out of God's ongoing work of reconciliation, healing and making all things new. To this we pledge ourselves and call our church.[15]

Time will tell whether the future of the Episcopal Church will be characterized more by the 2020 efforts to double its size or the bishops' commitment to "wage reconciliation." Perhaps its future might even realize a combination of

15. "On Waging Reconciliation," statement issued by the House of Bishops of the Episcopal Church, September 26, 2001, in Ian T. Douglas, ed., *Waging Reconciliation: God's Mission in a Time of Globalization and Crisis* (New York: Church Publishing, 2002), pp. x-xii.

church growth and new realities of reconciliation, since the two visions need not be set in opposition to each other but are best seen as complementary and mutually reinforcing. What is clear is that the leaders of the Episcopal Church know that change is inevitable. American Episcopalians are called to a new life in a new world as the church seeks "to restore all people to unity with God and each other in Christ."[16] The resources for reconciliation and leadership available for this call in the church's theology and national structures are the subjects of the organizational case study and theological essay that follow.

16. Response given to the catechism question, "What is the mission of the Church?" Episcopal Church, *The Book of Common Prayer* (New York: Church Hymnal Corporation, 1979), p. 855.

A Primacy of Systems: Confederation, Corporation, and Communion

William H. Swatos, Jr.

T he phrase "the national church" is among the standards of Episcopalian discourse. One might think, therefore, that its meaning was similarly standardized; that is, that everybody knew what everybody else meant when she or
he talked about the national church. Yet that is hardly the case. "The national
church" refers to several bodies, loosely joined together, some incorporated,
some not, with uncertain ties to dioceses, parishes, and interest networks that in
turn produce uncertainties about the roles to be played by the different levels in
creating and sustaining the mission of the church. Many parishioners and clergy,
as well as some bishops, use the phrase disparagingly, suggesting that "the national church" is out of touch with the actual life of the church nationally, even
problematic to it. Yet, as historian Pamela Darling points out, "[a]lthough most
Episcopalians have little direct contact with these organizational units" that
more or less encompass "the national church" as the phrase is used by most Episcopalians, "the development and implementation of legislation and program at
the national level establishes the framework in which all diocesan and local parish life takes place" — even if that be in setting an agenda for controversy.[1] Thus,
to examine the Episcopal Church at the organizational level denominated by the
phrase "the national church" is to engage a crucial dynamic in the shaping — for
better or worse — of "Episcopalianism" at the turn of the third millennium.

The Episcopal Church per se has no incorporated status. One evidence
for this came in the late 1990s when a group of conservative Episcopalians took
the full historical title, the Protestant Episcopal Church in the United States of
America, and actually did proceed to incorporate and domesticate it across the
United States (hence the "PECUSA, Inc." incident). Although the incorporation

---

1. Pamela W. Darling, *New Wine* (Cambridge, Mass.: Cowley, 1994), p. 3.

effort was subjected to secular adjudication and was thereby foiled, it makes the point with backhanded precision. The official corporate name for the entity to which everyone who speaks of *the* Episcopal Church refers is the Domestic and Foreign Missionary Society of the Protestant Episcopal Church in the United States of America, usually abbreviated DFMS. Although the DFMS today is in effect only a holding company for the Episcopal Church as an unincorporated association, nevertheless by canon "all persons who are members of the Church"[2] are included in the DFMS's membership. The PECUSA, Inc. incident, however, clearly points to conflicts that surround the status of "the national church" and what "the Episcopal Church" means.

After a descriptive exposition of the Episcopalian organizational complex, we will turn to a recent and specific denominational crisis. Here I use the social drama model of Victor Turner both to analyze this crisis and to suggest how the diffuse organizational structures and competing strategic visions of the church actually allowed for creative, healthy resolution of this breach of trust between the church at the national level and its local constituents.[3]

It is surely not the DFMS per se to which Episcopalians refer when they

2. Canon I.3.1.

3. Data for this case study and Jennifer Phillips's theological essay that follows were gathered primarily through fifty-five extended, semistructured interviews with a wide range of leadership in the Episcopal Church, drawn in snowball fashion. About two-thirds of the interviews were conducted by telephone, one-third in person. I conducted all the phone interviews. Most of the interviews conducted in person were done by Phillips and me together. The length of the interviews averaged about an hour, but there was considerable variation. Interviewees were both encouraged to elaborate upon answers to the initial uniform set of questions and also invited to comment on areas they thought were salient but did not seem to be captured in this set.

Subjects included present and retired bishops, particularly those who had served in administrative positions in connection with the Episcopal Church's New York offices, and included both the present and prior presiding bishops. Also included were members of present and past Executive Councils, both clergy and lay; deputies to the church's General Convention (including three presidents of the House of Deputies); and present and past national staff employees, both clergy and lay, from secretaries to chiefs of staff. In addition, we conducted a variety of informal interviews during a meeting of the Executive Council, which we attended in its entirety. This meeting, as well as several visits to the Episcopal Church Center, including one that coincided with a meeting of the presidents (and/or vice presidents) of the church's nine provinces, which I attended in full, also gave us opportunities to observe the actions of virtually all the principals of current Episcopal Church operations in interaction with one another.

We conducted additional informal interviews, both by phone and in person, after the chapters were in their initial drafts. These interviews included consultations with assistants to the presiding bishop and an extended meeting of the research team with one of those persons. We are especially grateful to Bruce Woodcock, who adroitly managed our contacts in this process. Of course, no one other than Phillips and I should be held accountable for the errors that may still be in our work, nor for the conclusions we have drawn.

speak of "the national church." This phrase comprehends much more. For some it is the General Convention, which meets triennially; for others it is the Executive Council, which is simultaneously the Executive Council of the General Convention *and* the Board of Directors of the DFMS; not to be forgotten, however, are the Church Pension Fund and the Episcopal Church Foundation, each of which has been involved at some level in policy, organizational, and financing decisions that have made a contribution to the image of the national church. Each of these groups has some level of staff located in New York City, with everything but the Pension Fund operating out of the Episcopal Church Center, popularly known from its street address as "815." The "program" staff at 815 constitute another image of the national church. Cutting across all these groups, although least so the Pension Fund, is the role and person of the presiding bishop, often referred to as the PB, who not only represents the Episcopal Church officially both nationally and internationally but also is ultimately responsible for the *management* of the bulk of the 815 staff. The work and person of the presiding bishop provide the crucial opening to a window on the national church as it exists today. A pastor of systems, as the present incumbent has described his understanding of the episcopate, is increasingly important in a world of increasingly uncertain organizational ties. The movement from confederation through the difficulties of the corporate into an emergence of a deep communion that is yet to be fully revealed describes the organizational trajectory of the recent history and contemporary reality of the Episcopal Church.

Background

The Episcopal Church is a residual of the American Revolution. That is, when the United States successfully gained its independence from Great Britain, there were still people in the United States who wished to continue worshiping according to the forms of the Church of England, which was established by law in England but disestablished in the United States as a result of the Revolution. Ironically, the American Revolution created the Anglican revolution, because it was as a result of the creation of the Protestant Episcopal Church in the United States of America that the Church of England was in effect denominationalized.[4] In that process the Episcopal Church nevertheless also retained certain distinctive qualities that set it apart from most of its American denominational counterparts. One of these was the historic episcopate; another was a

4. I have discussed this process at greater length in William H. Swatos, Jr., *Into Denominationalism* (Storrs, Conn.: Society for the Scientific Study of Religion, 1979).

transorganizational cultural identity that at least in part includes a tradition of social honor among lay leaders — what Max Weber refers to as *honoratiores* — who stand in a unique relationship to rank-and-file constituents.[5] Some measure of "state-churchiness" remained in the Episcopal Church well into the twentieth century. Ian Douglas refers to this as "the national church ideal."[6]

Like most of the mainline denominations in the United States, however, the Episcopal Church made a transition to its present organizational structure in the early twentieth century. Although the groundwork for the DFMS, for example, was in place by 1821 and the title of presiding bishop was used at the General Convention of 1795 (having been added to the *Book of Common Prayer* by action of the convention in 1792), neither one took on the significance it did after the watershed year of 1919, when the most important changes were made to the Episcopal Church's structure since Independence. First, a National Council, which also simultaneously became the Board of the DFMS, was empowered to carry out the work of the church during the triennium between conventions. Second, the office of the presiding bishop was dramatically altered: the PB was no longer simply the bishop who by seniority presided over the House of Bishops' meeting during General Convention (and such times when it met apart from General Convention), but an elected presiding bishop of the *church* — a title that brought Presiding Bishop Thomas March Clark resounding criticism when, less than two decades earlier, he had slipped and used it for himself.[7]

5. See Max Weber, *Economy and Society* (Berkeley: University of California Press, 1978 [1921]), pp. 1007-64; cf. S. Charles Bolton, *Southern Anglicanism* (Westport, Conn.: Greenwood Press, 1983); William H. Swatos, Jr., *Mediating Capitalism and Slavery* (Tampa: USF Monographs in Religion and Public Policy, 1987).

6. The history of the development of the national organization of the Episcopal Church is covered comprehensively in Ian Douglas, *Fling Out the Banner* (New York: Church Publishing, 1996). Constitutional and canonical issues are assayed with equal thoroughness in Edwin Augustine White and Jackson A. Dykman, *Annotated Constitution and Canons for the Government of the Protestant Episcopal Church in the United States of America Otherwise Known as the Episcopal Church* (New York: Seabury Press, 1981).

7. See Ronald Foster, *The Role of the Presiding Bishop* (Cincinnati: Forward Movement, 1982), pp. 50-51. The presiding bishop issue was filled with ironies. On the one hand, Bishop Clark did favor the idea of an elected presiding bishop of the church, while his successor Daniel Sylvester Tuttle, who was presiding bishop at the time the legislation actually passed, opposed it. Furthermore, there was a lack of clarity in the church generally about what it meant, as witnessed by the fact that for about six months after the passage of the new canons on the presiding bishop and council, *The Spirit of Missions,* the quasi-official Episcopal Church (i.e., DFMS) monthly, began to refer to Bishop Thomas P. Gailor of Tennessee as presiding bishop, whereas Bishop Gailor had been elected pro tempore president of the council to serve until the first elected presiding bishop should take office, since Bishop Tuttle in fact remained presiding bishop. Following Bishop Tuttle's death in 1923, there was a rapid succession of several presiding

William H. Swatos, Jr.

Over successive conventions, two further developments occurred, one with reference to each of these 1919 innovations. First, the name of the council was changed from the National Council to the Executive Council in 1964. While there may have been many motives in this change — some see it simply as a recognition of the internationalization of the Episcopal Church as extraterritorial missionary dioceses were added — Ian Douglas, following Dykstra and Hudnut-Beumler, sees it as a move from the council serving primarily administrative functions to the council as a regulatory agency.[8] Second, the PB's office was enlarged in two ways. In the 1940s the decision was taken at General Convention that the PB should resign his territorial see (diocese). This created a new creature for the global Anglican Communion, since heretofore all archbishops, to which role the PB's office is the closest analogue, also had diocesan responsibilities. In the 1970s the PB was given the authority to enter dioceses for sacramental and preaching ministry, for consulting with bishops, and for related purposes. This extends to the PB *extraordinary jurisdiction* (or "metropolitical authority"), and might theoretically be said to "papalize" the PB's role. In 1982 the PB was also given the title "primate"; however, by no means do all Anglican primates have the extrajuridical authority that pertains within the purview of the PB's office within the Episcopal Church.[9]

At the same time, there is a "flip side" to this increasing concentration of authority; namely, the Episcopal Church continues to be a *confederation* of dioceses, each technically an independent body:

The P.B.'s chair is an honored spot,
But O my friends that seat is hot.
In the House of Bishops you can come to grief.
It's a tribe in which each man is a chief.[10]

---

bishops due to difficulties of the sucession process on the one hand and untimely deaths on the other. The office did not stabilize until Bishop Perry's accession in 1930.

8. See Craig Dykstra and James Hudnut-Beumler, "The National Organizational Structures of Protestant Denominations: An Invitation to a Conversation," in *The Organizational Revolution*, ed. Milton J. Coalter et al. (Louisville: Westminster John Knox, 1992), pp. 307-31; Ian Douglas, "Whither the National Church? Reconsidering the Mission Structures of the Episcopal Church," in *The Future of Theology*, ed. Robert Slocum (New York: Church Publishing, 1999), pp. 60-78.

9. The title of presiding bishop is unique to the Episcopal Church in the United States among the bodies of the Anglican Communion; the primate of Canada now shares with the presiding bishop in the United States a see-less office.

10. Doggerel verse composed by Bishop Richard S. Emerich of Michigan on the occasion of the retirement of Henry Knox Sherrill; see Henry Knox Sherrill, *Among Friends* (Boston: Little, Brown, 1962).

Although claims are often made, for example, that the Constitution of the Episcopal Church is "modeled" on that of the United States, in fact it is less like the Constitution than like the Articles of Confederation.[11] Dioceses accede to the Constitution and Canons of the Episcopal Church, and in so doing align themselves with the General Convention, but in theory any diocese may withdraw from this union. Today there would probably be legal challenges, particularly regarding property rights, the relative success or failure of which would likely be determined by secular courts on a case-by-case basis. Nevertheless, the 1998 Lambeth Conference of the Anglican Communion's bishops again reaffirmed the integrity of diocesan boundaries, hence the centrality of the diocese to the church's characteristic "disbursed authority."[12]

The integrity of the diocese as the basic unit of the American church has been recognized in a number of ways, though it has also been tested and limited. The extraordinary jurisdiction of the PB, for example, is one theoretical incursion across diocesan boundaries. In fact, it is unrealistic to think that a PB could actually successfully intervene in a diocese without a strong base of support within the diocese setting the stage for his action. On the other hand, the right of each diocese to equal representation at General Convention, though often challenged, has never been altered. The relationship between the diocese and the national church is mirrored in that pertaining between each diocesan bishop and 815. The diocesan bishop is strategically placed to filter communications in both directions. Nevertheless, dioceses can — and do — withhold money from "the national church" program, and the national church has no mechanism to force the diocese to pay its assessments. Specifically, there is no *ad limina* in the Episcopal Church that gives "teeth" to the papalization of the PB's office, such as characterizes that of the bishop of Rome.

It is true that there is a system of checks and balances between the diocese and the rest of the American church. Among others, every newly elected bishop must obtain approval for consecration from a majority of both the standing committees (elected bodies in every diocese consisting of laity and clergy) and the current diocesan and coadjutor bishops before the PB can "take order" for that person's consecration. Similarly, errant bishops can be brought, via the PB's office, before an ecclesiastical court of bishops for a process of trial and potential dismissal. It is not clear, however, what power the church at the national level could exercise to enforce these prerogatives if a diocese were determined

11. Presbyterians also like to make the claim that their organizational structure has affinities to the Constitution, and this is more likely accurate.

12. The phrase "disbursed authority" is credited to Edward Norman in a lecture delivered on behalf of the Ecclesiastical Law Society during the 1998 Lambeth Conference; see Dorsey Henderson, Jr., "Lambeth Diary," *Living Church*, August 30, 1998, p. 8.

to obtain or retain a bishop against the national will. That this is so is in some ways a continuing legacy of the historical position of the Church of England as a state church, on the one hand, thrown into juxtaposition with American religious pluralism, hence voluntarism, on the other. In practice, it has never been tested to this point, and church members remain generally compliant with the existing order or choose to exit on their own.

The Presiding Bishop

The life of the Episcopal Church as a national body today is wound, albeit loosely, around the work and person of the PB. The "modern" exercise of the duties of the PB may be dated from the assumption of the office by Henry Knox Sherrill in 1947. Prior to accepting the office, Bishop Sherrill had been bishop of Massachusetts, one of the largest dioceses in the Episcopal Church, hence a diocese that had a history of influential bishops. Each PB from Sherrill forward has served for approximately a decade, with the exception of Arthur Lichtenberger, who followed Sherrill and resigned after only six years for reasons of health. In the past fifty years the PB has been increasingly present throughout the life of the Episcopal Church as a national body.

The nature of the office is such that it carries enormous office charisma (in the Weberian sense), but it is also one in which the personal character of the incumbent can strongly influence the image and function of "the national church" in specific, concrete directions. This is so because the PB has multiple roles to play simultaneously and because "the national church" is diffusely defined. The office charisma of the PB is a unique characteristic of the Episcopal Church among the denominations in the ORW (Organizing Religious Work) study. We find no other denomination where the official head is for example regularly, liturgically remembered *by name* Sunday by Sunday (and weekday by weekday, where there are weekday liturgies, which is a widespread practice in Episcopal parishes) throughout most of the church. Among major Western churches in the United States, only Roman Catholic parishes have a similar practice. Because the PB is elected only by the other bishops, and by them only within certain guidelines, it is virtually assured that the incumbent will be a person relatively skilled in human relationships and gifted in genuine leadership (though that leadership *style* may differ dramatically from one PB to another). It is at the same time virtually certain that no PB will be able to attend to all the potential functions of his office equally, just as will no parish rector.

First, the PB retains the historic role bestowed on the office from 1789 forward of actually presiding over the House of Bishops during sessions of the

General Convention. The PB is thus the president of one of the two houses of the body that makes the rules in which and through which the mission of the church is to be carried forward, including the budget priorities for that. Unlike the House of Deputies, which is composed of clerical and lay deputies from each diocese elected specifically for this event, the House of Bishops continues throughout the triennium.[13] In other words, when a General Convention is over, the members of the House of Deputies are done with their work and go home unless they are appointed members of "interim bodies" (usually called standing commissions), which continue to work during the triennium; lay members are appointed by the president of the House of Deputies, bishops by the PB. The House of Bishops, however, continues to meet as a body through-out these years, usually semiannually. The PB has a considerable role in setting the agenda for these meetings.

In addition, the PB retains the role of "taking order" for the consecration of new bishops, hence at least shepherding the ever changing composition of the house. Although the PB cannot block the consecration of any bishop who has received the necessary consents, the PB can influence the degree of the bishop's participation in the work of both the house and the interim bodies specifically through the power of appointment. "Taking order" for the consecration of bishops does not mean that the PB must consecrate every new bishop, but that the PB has the *right* to do so. Edmond Browning, presiding bishop from 1986 through 1997, who spent almost 80 percent of his time out of the Church Center, made the exercise of this right one of his priorities. The present PB, Frank Griswold, has indicated that he does not intend to exercise this right to the same extent, since the role of chief consecrator is a largely symbolic one. It brings the PB into high ceremonial profile but in itself allows the PB relatively little opportunity for significant conversation (a favorite word of Bishop Griswold) with constituents, including even the new bishop. In this Bishop Griswold is following the advice of Bishop Sherrill given to Bishop Allin, his successor once removed: "Stay at home and run the place."

In a similar role, the PB is also the chief liturgical officer of General Convention. Although the actual liturgical forms and roles are often delegated, the PB has final authority over all the official liturgical observances while General Convention is meeting. This role, like that of chief consecrator, enhances the office charisma that becomes important symbolic capital to the way the PB is able to negotiate other roles, not least the ability successfully to enter dioceses

---

13. Technically the House of Bishops is the "junior house" of the convention, since the 1785 General Convention met as priests and laity, as the House of Deputies (the "senior house") is now constituted.

for more intense interaction with constituents, especially in times of conflict. The PB does not simply come as another bishop but as *the* presiding bishop. The PB is derivatively the chief liturgical officer of the Executive Council when it meets. In any denomination where liturgy is a paramount activity, as is the case in the Episcopal Church, and a liturgical manual is the principal confession of faith, determination of what happens in specific liturgies is an item of no little significance. The symbolic value of liturgical action is likely to be read closely by constituents.[14]

Where the office charisma of the presiding bishop pays the incumbent the greatest dividends, but also sets up the greatest dangers, is in the very uncharismatic role of being the simultaneous chair and president of the Executive Council, and derivatively president of the DFMS. In this role the PB has tremendous power to influence both the church itself and the image of the church on both international and national levels. The agenda for the life of the church that the PB sets is largely the official agenda of the Episcopal Church. This is especially so inasmuch as the PB technically hires every person who works at 815. Of course, much staff hiring is done at lower levels, and while there is no formal tenure system, at the lower levels people tend to be retained from one administration to another (as long as funds hold out).

Some might object that this strong a claim for the PB ignores the role of General Convention — i.e., that it is really General Convention that sets the agenda for the triennium. Such a view of General Convention ignores at least three realities: First, and most simply, General Convention goes home when its meeting ends. Although the Executive Council is strictly speaking the Executive Council *of* General Convention, representing and responsible to the General Convention, it is virtually impossible for the council to oversee the day-to-day operations at 815 because the only place it can reasonably receive information about these operations is from 815. Second, General Convention has had a tendency to put forth so many resolutions, sometimes even contradictory resolutions, that it is similarly virtually impossible to address all of them equally. If we think of General Convention's resolution production as a kind of smorgasbord, it has often been so large that one person after another can go to it, all can come back with their plates absolutely full, and yet some things can be left untouched. The PB can channel resolution consumption patterns. (An effort has been made at recent conventions to correct this resolution glut by, on the one

14. Following the General Convention of 2000, for example, there was an extended series of letters in the *Living Church,* an independent Episcopalian weekly (and the only weekly targeted to Episcopalians), offering conjectures as to the meaning of the fact that during at least one major eucharistic celebration at the convention the presiding bishop wore his stole over his chasuble rather than under it.

hand, requiring more sponsors of resolutions coming to the floor, and on the other, trying to get resolutions and funding more closely tied.) Third, however, no matter which resolutions get passed, the operation of them is put into the hands of specific persons who contextualize and interpret them. These are people the PB hires, retains, empowers, directs, and so on. These people give operational definitions to words like "ministry," "sexuality," "women's concerns," "peace and justice," "stewardship," and "evangelism." Other than legal background checks, there is no formal system of checks on these people and their work except the system the PB decides there should be. During a PB's term, which historically has varied between nine and twelve years (and is currently nine), always thus far followed by retirement, the PB basically has charge over how "the ministry and mission of the Church," or "the work," is conceived and operationalized.

When Your Checks Don't Balance

Nowhere was this dynamic more clearly displayed than in the administrative discord and subsequent scandal that surrounded Ellen Cooke during Bishop Browning's tenure. Cooke was ultimately convicted and jailed for embezzlement, but the embezzlement was really only the tip of the iceberg of the damage the church suffered at her hands. How did it come to be so?

The practice had developed that the incumbent of "the treasurer's office" is simultaneously treasurer of both General Convention and the DFMS. Although formally elected by General Convention, the treasurer is normally an appointee by the PB. This appointment practice is a matter of convenience, but it reveals the peculiar ways in which budgets and funds likewise simultaneously remain separate and commingle, and may be taken at this point as evidence of the relative clumsiness of General Convention as a practical administrative organ of the church. In this specific case, what happened was that coincidentally concurrent with the election of a new PB there was an election of a new president of the House of Deputies with whom, as a matter of fact, the PB did not see eye to eye. Complicating this, both the executive officer of General Convention and the treasurer of General Convention/DFMS retired. The treasurer had served over thirty years. The PB was strongly committed to the ministry of the laity and the ministry of women, and thus was happy to appoint Cooke, with a view toward a tighter operation of the office, upon the recommendation of at least two highly respected bishops for whom she had worked creditably.

What happened thereafter, however, shows the danger of the PB's position. The consensus of those we interviewed for this study was that Cooke began to expand her power, isolate her staff from the program staff, issue reports to the Executive Council that were impossible to understand, and display arrogance toward all who questioned her, but she remained intensely loyal to the PB. He returned the favor, not without support of some commission and committee leaders who were apparently sufficiently impressed by her financial mystifications to excuse her personal offensiveness. In short, critic after critic, questioner after questioner of Cooke was rebuffed by the PB. She took refuge in the women's issue, and he defended her. This became most clear when, after the appropriate body refused to allow her nomination as treasurer of General Convention to go forward at General Convention in 1994, requiring instead a personal nomination from the floor, the PB directly intervened on her behalf with the nominating committee of the convention, and it placed her name on the ballot (as the sole candidate). He did this in spite of the specific dissent of Pamela Chinnis, the new president of the House of Deputies, with whom he was in other respects virtually a soul mate. Only six months later the embezzlement itself came to light. There can be no question that the charisma of the PB's office, combined with his unique executive management role, overrode prudential considerations that questions of fiduciary accountability might have engendered in other circumstances.

A similar, though less dramatic, set of circumstances also prevailed during the primacy of John Hines (1965-74) in connection with the General Convention Special Program (GCSP), a program to channel a relatively massive funding effort directly to community agencies working principally on behalf of ethnic minorities. There is undoubtedly a book to be written on GCSP, but the thesis here is a relatively simple one; namely, that GCSP and Hines's primacy became problematic within the life of the Episcopal Church. This was not because of its focus on minorities, which was already present in the Lichtenberger years, but for two other reasons. First, funds were channeled to local secular agencies without consultation with either diocesan authorities (principally the bishops of the dioceses involved) or church groups already involved in working with minority ministries. Second, the leadership of GCSP eschewed the leadership within the church already working on these issues. Again, this was allowed to occur first because of Hines's personal charisma (often referred to in his case as "prophetic leadership") in generating the funds, principally from the women of the church, and then because of the office charisma of the PB that enabled him to work unchecked.

In both the Cooke and Hines cases, however, brakes were applied. They came not in the first instance from the votes of General Convention but from the "green vote" (greenbacks from the grass roots): dioceses not paying their quota of national church (i.e., 815) support. Here is where the diocese as counterweight comes down strongly: the major source of 815 funding is diocesan budgets. These are indirectly the product of local congregational giving and directly the product of diocesan conventions. Either or both may cause a downturn in revenue received at 815. The bottom line of "staff development" is no money. Two major reductions in staff have been taken in the last fifty years: one in the Hines era, the other (really in two steps) in the Browning era. The green vote, not the "priorities of General Convention," has determined these. Only after the necessary accommodations were made to the crises did General Convention respond — for example, in those portions of the Structure Commission report adopted by the convention of 1997. Nevertheless, even here we can see the continued power of the PB, since the PB determines, directly or indirectly, who will go and who will stay among the staff, hence what priorities and constituencies are ultimately served — and in what ways. Even now, with a new PB and money flowing favorably, decisions about what "work" will continue, who will do it, how it will be done, what will be initiated and what dropped remain ultimately in his hands, regardless of the amount of conversation that takes place in the process.

The PB also has other roles. Increasingly significant and demanding of time is his presence within the wider Anglican Communion and in ecumenical relationships. The other representative role, which can also be controversial, is that of "spokesperson" not only to the church but also to "the world." What this means is that the PB can, if he chooses, make politically charged statements. The canon is ambiguous about whether or not these statements have to reflect directly General Convention positions. While there is little doubt that the PB would be acting wrongly to contradict a specific General Convention position, there does not appear to be any limit on the PB speaking to other issues "as the representative of this Church and its episcopate in its corporate capacity."[15] In this respect the PB may speak to a host of geopolitical and socioeconomic issues in the name of the Episcopal Church. Bishop Browning's stand on the Gulf War, frequently reported still as "opposition of the Episcopal Church to the Gulf War," is an example. Such stands can similarly prove costly in the green vote, though not as costly as those that directly involve funding issues.

The Weberian distinction between prophetic and priestly ministerial roles is helpful in examining these crisis moments in Episcopalian leadership on the part of PBs. It can be plausibly argued that prophecy comes closer to genuine charisma, while the pastoral role makes use of the office charisma that represents a second-order "routinization" of genuine charisma. Weber makes it clear that ideal-typical charisma is not concerned about matters of administra-

15. Canon I.2.4(a, 1-2).

tion or administrative routine. In the strict sense, prophets are not concerned about profits. Given the internal contradictions of the PB's role, the evidence in practice is that when a PB has made the prophetic side of the position's multi-faceted set of expectations a distinct priority, the routine tasks of administration have correspondingly floundered.

In both the Cooke and Hines cases, for example, accountability to church leaders was sacrificed. Given the voluntaristic nature of American denominationalism, this creates institutional costs in a double sense. Curiously, however, the built-in contradictions of the PB's role combined with the competing strategic visions for the organization serve as a counterweight that ultimately rights the sinking ship while simultaneously creating additional mechanisms toward pattern maintenance.

815

What happens at 815? One of our interviewees, a retired staff member with many years of service to the church, told us of a visit she made to a diocesan convention during some of the difficult years of the GCSP era. One woman came up to her during a break, obviously unhappy about how things were going in "the national church," and asked her, "Do staff persons have a parish of your own?" The staff person replied that she did as did others, told the inquirer something about her own parish and involvement in it, but then added, "Frequently if we're out traveling [on Sunday], or since I live in New York City, it's easy for me to go to church or service at 815," trying thereby to make the inquirer aware that the Church Center was also a place of worship with services every morning during the week. The listener was pleased but in a different way: "I prefer the early service myself," she replied approvingly, as if having found a kindred spirit.

When Episcopal clergy speak of "the national church," they are often referring to the staff at 815. Laity are only vaguely aware of 815's existence, possibly associating the church headquarters instead with National Cathedral in Washington, D.C., where the PB does in fact have his "seat." Within the staff at 815 there are three major operating divisions. One of these, largely uncontroversial, is the General Convention staff, whose primary responsibility is to keep the wheels of the convention turning between conventions, as well as to plan and execute the myriad details required to "pull off" a successful meeting. Another division, also uncontroversial until the Ellen Cooke incident, is administrative and involves all the work of the treasurer's office, plus human relations, building services, the mail room and bookstore, and so on. Here one might also put such offices as clergy deployment and the bishop for the Armed Forces, Health Institutions, and Prisons, although these are in some ways quasi-independent functions while in other ways sliding toward program.

The third division of the 815 staff, however, and clearly the most controversial, is the program staff itself, particularly those whose work addresses domestic rather than global constituencies. The program staff is controversial because it is perceived as not related to specific tasks that keep the Center and the General Convention operating as institutions. Program staff are perceived as in themselves "good" people, but sometimes people who are out to create and implement agendas that may not be those of General Convention. These are seen by some as efforts at job preservation. They are also seen by some as ideologically driven by a particular view of the church that is not necessarily shared with grassroots understandings (e.g., evangelism) or even the unique specific constituencies (e.g., Native Americans, Asian Americans) that a specific program "desk" is supposed to serve. These problems are somewhat crosscut by the way some of these positions are funded, which is by either direct or indirect endowment. For example, the position of liturgical officer was at one time close to the ecclesiastical equivalent of an endowed chair in academe, though it has recently been placed into the budget. In other cases endowments may be reinterpreted from their original purpose to an allied intent. For example, endowments given in the 1800s for former slaves or slave children may be incorporated into the funding of the African American desk. Some of these moneys may not be directly a part of the General Convention budget, hence program staff have a greater role in the decision-making processes on how they are spent. Since these are staff of the PB, accountability flows primarily through the office of the PB, as distinct from General Convention.

Staff size has fluctuated considerably across time. At the time we did our interviews, there were 240 total Church Center staff employees, including approximately 70 missionaries in the field.[16] Those in-house are divided between about 60 percent who are support staff, typically paid on an hourly basis, and the remainder, who are program staff. Also in the building are a number of independent but church-related agencies. These involve another 28 people. The staff has numbered over 400 in the early 1970s and as few as 190 later in the same decade, to some extent reflecting church membership decline across the same period.

16. This number has increased since our visits and probably will be increasing slightly over the remainder of the triennium. That increase is unlikely to be more than 10 percent.

General Convention

While the PB and the 815 staff probably represent "the national church" to most clergy, two other interrelated meanings are more likely to be in the minds of laity. One is the most simple, direct literal meaning; namely, the church as it exists spread out across the fifty states (the "domestic dioceses"). In fact, this is the view for which the present PB advocates: "all of us together are the national church . . . this curious but grace-filled house." This use does not refer to a specific organizational structure at all, but simply means something akin to "how we Episcopalians do things across the country." For the majority of laity, this view is likely to be shaped by national secular media and by travel and residential mobility. Given that the Episcopal Church has had one of the lowest levels of member-retention loyalty, it can probably be inferred that there is considerable diversity in the national church defined in this way.[17] (One could also, equally accurately, say there is a high degree of parochialism within the Episcopal Church; the two are not mutually exclusive.)

The second meaning is not unrelated to the first, since it too reflects the idea of the Episcopal Church spread across the nation. This meaning is the General Convention: that time every three years when deputies from all the dioceses — four clerical deputies and four lay deputies, whether the diocese has Massachusetts's 95,000 communicants or Eau Claire's 2,674 — as well as all the bishops,[18] come together to spend two weeks debating "resolutions and memorials," worshiping, adopting a budget that will keep 815 afloat for the coming triennium, and electing persons who will serve on national bodies — most significantly the Executive Council and the Board of the Church Pension Fund. General Convention makes rules to govern the church (the Constitution and Canons) and sets broad guidelines on church policy (resolutions). General Convention also either creates or is connected to the vast majority of other national bodies. One of our interviewees, a national staff member, stated quite directly, "The General Convention is the national church, really."

Another of our interviewees, with a quarter-century of experience as a deputy, aptly described General Convention as consisting of "a representative cross-section of Episcopal Church activists." That is, the General Convention

17. On membership retention, see Wade Clark Roof and William McKinney, *American Mainline Religion* (New Brunswick, N.J.: Rutgers University Press, 1987).

18. The phrase "all the bishops" means not only diocesan bishops, but also coadjutors, suffragans, assistants, and any other bishop, validly consecrated in the Episcopal Church, who has not been suspended or deposed, including all retired bishops. As with issues regarding the equal size of diocesan deputations, efforts are regularly made to change this compositional structure of the house, but again, none has been successful.

hardly reflects the average Sunday churchgoer. General Convention deputies are selected at diocesan conventions, whose membership in turn is selected by congregations. Although dioceses pay for the expenses of their deputies to convention, thus removing a direct basis for socioeconomic discrimination in deputy selection, the duration of the convention itself plus pre- and postconvention meeting expectations — not to mention possible appointment to an interim body — ensure that the majority of lay deputies are likely to be either people with excess leisure time or people with a cause. About one-third of the deputies at each convention are serving for the first time, although others have served as many as ten or fifteen successive conventions.

The convention of 2000 was unique in that over half the deputies were newcomers. The work of General Convention is itself a sufficiently complex process that relatively few first-time deputies have any significant involvement in it. A corollary of this is that among the lay deputies in particular a cadre of repeatedly elected deputies holds significant leadership clout. Some interviewees commented that among the lay leadership the same people are recycled through different committees and commissions, giving at least the appearance of the same group of people being in place who were there twenty years ago.

In theory, General Convention committees receive reports from the interim bodies and church boards and agencies. The interim bodies formally cease to exist during the convention, when legislative committees take over their work. Some members of committees may have been members of their analogue interim bodies or may subsequently be appointed to such bodies. Bishops are appointed to these committees and commissions by the PB, and clerical and lay members by the president of the House of Deputies, though there is normally consultation between the PB and the president, and also between each of them and their respective Councils of Advice. The membership of the PB's Council of Advice is set by canon, while the president may appoint a Council of Advice on a discretionary basis.

Particular note has been taken of the increasing role and presence of the president of the House of Deputies since the election of Pamela Chinnis. From the time Chinnis was elected vice president of the same body in 1986, Bishop Browning sought to include her in an enlarged leadership role, with strong encouragement from the Women's Caucus. For example, she was invited to attend meetings of Executive Council, of which she was not a member. Once Chinnis was elected president, Bishop Browning came close to treating her as a coequal, even inviting her to meetings of the House of Bishops, and having her give an address from the chair at Executive Council meetings (as the PB exclusively had done previously). Bishop Browning justified this as reflecting, again, both his view of the ministry of the laity and his commitment to the ministry of women throughout the church. Her presence in these ways certainly did not go unnoticed, nor was it unremarked that she and Bishop Browning shared a common sociopolitical agenda that was not shared between the PB and her predecessor, Dean David Collins of Atlanta's St. Phillip's Cathedral, the nation's largest Episcopal congregation.

Indeed, over time the House of Deputies has become a somewhat less fluid body. Since the appointment of an executive officer for the General Convention in the 1970s, the house has a more distinct continuing character as a result of more professional administration. As late as the 1950s, for example, deputies (all men until 1970) sat in ganged folding chairs with no printed agenda, while much activity took place behind the scenes among a limited leadership cadre. Virtually all convention officers were volunteers, and many served what amounted to lifetime careers. At the same time, the question is now raised about the relationship between 815 staff and interim bodies, with claims being made in at least some cases that staff write interim body reports and largely direct their activities. Some interim bodies, particularly as related to Executive Council, appear to have a large degree of staff generation. The Commission on HIV/AIDS and the Committee on the Status of Women may both be taken as examples of this tendency to create agendas.

Nevertheless, the power of the General Convention to "set the course" for the Episcopal Church during each triennium is relatively limited, for reasons already cited. It lacks continuing existence, and its resolutions are subject to evaluation and interpretation by the PB and 815 staff on the one hand and the dioceses on the other. A recent move by General Convention to track the resolutions process has created an interesting data set for a statistical analysis of General Convention resolutions. Beginning in 1994, the General Convention office reported on responses from the dioceses to General Convention resolutions "referred to dioceses for action." In 1994 (reporting for the 1991 convention resolutions), before the Ellen Cooke crisis, there were forty-seven such resolutions. Particularly aggressive efforts to obtain data from the dioceses yielded reports from about 90 percent of the domestic dioceses. In this period, for example, all dioceses gave some consideration to resolution A069a, to Promote the Growth of Youth Ministry, but less than a third responded with any action on resolution B048, Commissions for Religious Freedom/Economic Liberty in Eastern Europe. Still, the majority of dioceses gave some form of consideration to 90 percent of the resolutions. By 1997 (reporting for the 1994 convention resolutions) the picture had changed. Only twenty-two resolutions were referred to the dioceses, but without the aggressive efforts employed in 1994 to obtain the data, only 58 percent of the dioceses complied with the reporting procedure. In addition, whereas only 6 percent of the resolutions in 1994 received no action from any of the reporting dioceses, this proportion rose to 32 percent in 1997. It should be noted, furthermore, that these statistics do not measure favorable versus unfavorable action, but merely whether resolutions were considered at all and at what level — i.e., "completed," "ongoing," or "considered." If we take the combination of considered (but not acted upon) and not considered at all, then the negative figure rises to 32 percent in 1994 and 45 percent in 1997.

The low reporting rate for 1997 — barely over half, less than half if the nondomestic dioceses are included — combined with a "rejection rate" of almost half among those that did report suggests a considerable gap between General Convention's priorities and those of the dioceses. This is doubly curious, because the representatives to General Convention are sent from the diocesan level and are canonically bound to report back to the dioceses, while the dioceses are canonically bound to make provision for these reports. Yet in spite of this, it appears that in the majority of dioceses the majority of General Convention resolutions fall on a deaf ear, and that this is increasingly so — in spite of a decrease by over half in the total number of resolutions referred.

The Executive Council

At one level Executive Council is itself an interim body. That is, it meets "for" General Convention and usually thrice annually, during the triennium when the convention is not in session. Its specific "duty" is to "carry out the program and policies adopted by the General Convention." Thus it "shall have charge of the coordination, development, and implementation of the ministry of the mission of the Church."[19] This seems clear enough, and might well be were it not that the same canon that provides this definition for council also allows council during the triennium to "initiate and develop such new work as it may deem necessary."[20] Council meetings can become field days for special interests on the part of either members, staff, or the PB himself.

Executive Council consists of forty members, including the PB and the president of the House of Deputies. Twenty members are elected directly by the General Convention, and eighteen are elected by the nine provinces of the church — geographical units across the country and abroad that consist of between five and twenty dioceses each.[21] Provincial representatives ensure some

19. Canon I.4.1(a).
20. Canon I.4.2(e).
21. Nondomestic Province IX is the smallest of these; however, two domestic provinces have only seven dioceses each.

degree of geographical balance, since this is not required in the General Convention elections. As with General Convention, although Executive Council members have their expenses paid, they still must have the time to contribute a minimum of three weeks per year to the meetings, not counting extra service demands. Some more senior interviewees lamented the fact that longer council meetings and the increasing politicization of elections are bringing more professional (lay) church workers on to council rather than active lay congregants with expertise from secular callings. At the same time, others point to council as now being "more diverse" and "less defensive" than it once was.

The interface between council and staff is one of continuing negotiation, complicated in turn by that between council and the interim bodies. The major source of information that council has about the ongoing work of the staff is the staff itself. Unless a council member chooses in effect to make his or her position something like a full-time job, it is virtually impossible for the member to get an independent read on what's going on. Staff thus both report to council and assist in shaping council's agenda and the interpretation of its goals and priorities. Because council has the mandate to undertake new work, various innovations can be made at any point by anyone on council and indirectly by staff via the PB. Thus whole new areas of concern can be opened up, while original convention mandates may be back-burnered. Like General Convention, council meetings are not merely business meetings, but involve worship, reflection, and possibly various kinds of small-group activities that are not directly attentive to specific details of reports, resolutions, and so on. Council does "visioning" activity as well as fulfill canonical mandates.

Again, the role of the PB with respect to council is crucial and combines charisma of office with routine management functions, even though canons now provide for appointment of an "executive director . . . who shall be the chief operating officer" — apparently of "the mission and ministry of the Church" (the canon does not actually say *of what* the executive director is chief operating officer). The canon makes quite clear, however, that the executive officer "shall serve at the pleasure of the Presiding Bishop and be accountable to the Presiding Bishop" — not to council. Thus the PB's role as having "ultimate responsibility for the oversight of the work of the Executive Council" remains unlimited.[22] The

---

22. Canon I.4.3(a, d). Paragraph a. of this section of the canon says that the presiding bishop, as chair and president of Executive Council, "shall have ultimate responsibility for the oversight of the work of the Executive Council in the implementation of the ministry and mission of the Church as has been committed to the Executive Council by the General Convention." Since the executive director reports directly to the PB and is accountable to the PB, the executive director is executive director and chief operating officer of "the mission and ministry of the Church." This could perhaps be spelled out more clearly and effectively in subsequent legislation.

council is required to report to the General Convention, but for reasons already indicated, it will more likely be accountable to the green vote than to any specific General Convention body. Furthermore, because council members are elected for six-year terms, there is no way for a General Convention in effect to "clean house" if it does not like the way a particular council has behaved during the prior triennium. Furthermore, since 45 percent of council members are not elected by General Convention (nor do they need to be deputies to General Convention), agendas other than those of the convention may well be brought to council. Communication between provincial council representatives and their constituents varies dramatically both because of the varied natures of the provinces themselves and the inclinations of the individuals elected.

The Church Pension Fund

The idea of a dependable pension system for clergy applied throughout the church was innovated in the early years of the twentieth century, largely under the aegis of Bishop William Lawrence of Massachusetts. It replaced a voluntary system, into which the clergy (rather than the congregations) paid, which was then supplemented by grants to needy widows and orphans. Because every congregation with ongoing clerical ministry, hence the majority of Episcopal clergy as well, participates in this system, it also comes to be associated with the phrase "the national church." More than once in difficult times the statement that "the Church Pension Fund (CPF) is the only thing holding the Church together" has been voiced. The CPF is the only major national church agency to which the PB has no statutory relationship, and its offices are physically separate from 815.

The CPF impacts the local congregation because pension assessments are required to be paid for all salaried clergy. The pension adds between 18 and 22 percent to the cost of clergy employment by the parish (depending on whether housing is paid as an allowance or provided in kind). In other words, the local congregation that offers its priest a stipend of $24,000 per year plus occupancy of a home that it owns will pay the Pension Fund about $5,280 in assessment. This assessment is frequently articulated as being paid "to the national church."

Beginning in the early 1990s, however, another CPF agency, the Church Insurance Company (CIC), began to intervene in local congregational affairs in a more policy-oriented fashion. The CIC provides comprehensive fire, casualty, and liability insurance to approximately 70 percent of church properties. The loss of a major sexual misconduct suit in Colorado led CIC to mandate a stringent policy of background checks and training for all clergy and for lay workers who have specific administrative responsibility for activities involving minors

William H. Swatos, Jr.

(e.g., Sunday school superintendents, DCEs, youth coordinators, camp directors), if a congregation wished to continue to receive CIC coverage. Although congregations are not required by national legislation to insure with CIC, the majority do (in some cases due to diocesan requirements), and these interventions within the life of the whole church gave to CIC a new and somewhat controversial prominence as a policy-making agency at the national level. Some of these extracanonical interventions have now been incorporated into the church's canons, but not without continued expressions of dissatisfaction. Clearly one of the agenda items for the Episcopal Church as it faces the third millennium is to develop a theology of risk to complement the putative theology of stewardship that underlay these decisions and others like them (e.g., approaches to church-building security that result in fewer churches being open continuously through the day to "enter, rest, and pray").

The Episcopal Church Foundation

The Episcopal Church Foundation (ECF) is an independent organization founded by Bishop Sherrill during his primacy to provide for long-term development activities on behalf of the church. The PB is the chairman of the board of the ECF, but its self-perpetuating board is composed entirely of laypersons who are accountable to no one except themselves. The offices of ECF are housed at 815.

For many years the primary role of the ECF was grant making — either to churches or to individuals, in the latter case especially for graduate work at the doctoral level. In 1987, however, at the urging of Bishop Browning, the ECF began a new venture known as Cornerstone. This project, which has now developed cooperative ventures that include the Church Pension Fund and 815 clergy development staff, focuses principally on clergy and congregational wholeness or wellness, broadly conceived. Topics include not only physical and spiritual well-being, but leadership development, initiation of new pastoral relationships, and issues of "involuntary termination" in a pastoral relationship. More recently the ECF initiated the Zacchaeus Project, intended as the foundation's fiftieth anniversary "gift to the National Church." The project "explores what it means to be an Episcopalian in today's society and how they renew their sense of identity in communities of faith."[23]

When placed in relationship to the increasing involvement of the Pension

23. *The Zacchaeus Project: Discerning Episcopal Identity at the Dawn of the New Millennium* (New York: Episcopal Church Foundation, 1999), p. 7.

Fund and its affiliates in clergy and congregational life, ECF efforts suggest a newly evolving model of "the national church" — namely, of units apart from the 815 staff taking major responsibilities for organizing and reorganizing church life, particularly as it relates to the local congregation. One could argue that these CPF/ECF initiatives meet a need that 815 program staff has been insensitive toward or else impotent to act on. And the problems the CPF/ECF initiatives have sought to address existed *before* the Ellen Cooke fiasco, though that incident certainly did nothing to solve them. These initiatives throw into relief a long-standing gulf between practical needs at the congregational and diocesan levels and ideological questions, which sometimes appear to drive 815 staff efforts.

How the Executive Council and 815 program staff engage the emerging initiatives beyond their purview will be a major issue in the first century of the new millennium. There are models of successful engagement between 815 and other agencies, in particular the Episcopal Partnership for Global Mission (EPGM) that brings together over forty mission agencies and organizations in the Episcopal Church in relationship with each other and the executive-legislative bodies of the church through the Executive Council. But the uncertain ties that run through the national church may operate here in a proactive way: that is to say, like Cornerstone, the EPGM, and the emerging Episcopal Network for Evangelism, some programs for the life of the church may develop with or without the blessing of Executive Council and with or without the involvement of 815 staff, and yet prove fruitful.

Continuing Issues

"The national church" remains an uncertain term in the life of the Episcopal Church both because of uncertain ties between the parishes and dioceses and the various national bodies, and because of uncertainties about how these national bodies themselves interrelate. The symbolic capital and office charisma of the presiding bishop is the signal point of potential unity holding it all together. This places enormous responsibility on the PB to act on behalf of the whole church and to consider the downside potential of single-issue commitments, no matter how laudable in themselves. It can be seen clearly from past events that the Episcopal Church went into crisis whenever routine accountability was laid aside in favor of ideological commitments. Breach of trust knows no bounds of race, color, creed, sex, or national origin. At the center of the PB's agenda must be structures and processes of accountability that can be easily and fairly applied across national staffing. Serious consideration may need to be given to how many long-term staff members should be continued indefinitely, and how much there should be a clean break with the past. Although the expressions of staff people about the "abuse" from the Cooke years need to be recognized and honored, these wounds may also impede fresh approaches and sap enthusiasm for genuinely new directions.

General Convention remains an odd amalgam of business meeting, political convention, and liturgical celebration. Like much of the public life of the church, it seems dominated by such issues as sexuality, sexual abuse and exploitation, marriage and divorce, women's ordination, and so on. It is not clear that the interface between General Convention and Executive Council is a strong one, in spite of various efforts over the years to make clear the superordinate-subordinate relationship between these two bodies. How much of the work of General Convention is necessary to making the work of the church go forward remains unclear. The present PB reported, for example, that prior to his primacy at least, he experienced General Convention "largely . . . as a free-standing event" apart from the ongoing life of the parish and the diocese. He proposed that a concept of "Jubilee" or "rest" be built into the 2000 convention, so that the convention as "a community of faith" could "enter into a process of discernment rather than decision making." Certainly a corporate body needs to exist to generate representatives to serve on such continuing bodies as the Executive Council and the Board of the Church Pension Fund. Whether this body needs to meet for two weeks and generate resolutions on a wide variety of topics seems debatable. Do these resolutions do any good? Who listens to them, how often, and to what end?

The combined role of Executive Council as custodian of the ongoing work of General Convention, initiator of new ministries, and board of the DFMS gives it a particularly unclear character and focus. Basically anything *can* come before council without any warning. Yet at the same time, council's authority to *do* anything other than issue resolutions, except by the PB's leave, makes it a body uncertainly tied to convention. It is practically impossible for council to act as a watchdog for convention, nor is it clear what would happen if it did. Only in the budgetary process does council have leverage to take definitive action, and that only within limits of relatively large categories. Council cannot in itself hire or fire, nor can it direct the specific operation of task management.[24]

24. Of course, a PB may choose to give this authority to council as a strategic move. This occurred, for example, for a period of years during the Allin administration. What is significant is how easily this may be altered. For example, during Bishop Allin's term 815 stationery read "The Office of the Presiding Bishop and the Executive Council of the General Convention." Bishop Browning changed it to read "The Office of the Presiding Bishop."

The collaborative activities of the Pension Fund and the Episcopal Church Foundation offer much potential, both in themselves and as a model for other bodies. Yet the role of the Church Insurance Corporation also waves a caution flag. Its move into the policy arena — though consistent with insurance practice generally (e.g., health care) — has serious practical and theological implications. At what point is the work of the church driven by considerations of risk avoidance? Does fear rather than faith become the metaphor of incarnational institutional church life? How do we distinguish between damned fools and fools for Christ's sake? For the church to be a hope-full place, it is important that congregations be shown positive alternatives within the body of Christ for accomplishing the historic works of mercy as well as the contemporary cure of souls.

Blest Be the Breach That Bridges

The role of the PB is sufficiently beset by contradictions that it is virtually ensured that the person in it will never please everyone within the church. This is not merely a matter of taking sides on the "hot" theological or sociopolitical issue of the day. Merely by deciding what clothes to wear each day, the PB will please some and disappoint others among his constituents. Yet if the PB were to go to the office wearing a bathrobe, it would in fact create a breach that would be severe enough to get everyone to take notice and begin to ask questions.

Because of the range of internal differences among Episcopalian constituencies, it was possible for systems of interaction both within 815 and between 815 and the larger church to grow unchecked since the upsizing/downsizing years of the Hines administration. It was not that one PB or another avoided criticism, but to a large extent the critics canceled each other out, while the day-to-day activities of parishes and dioceses simply became more removed from "national church" programming and structure. The national Christian education curriculum innovated in the 1950s, for example, was eliminated, and specific target-population ventures came to replace those directed to the broader constituency.

At the same time, the church was generally well served by dedicated volunteers and paid employees, most of whom saw their work as a "calling," even if they differed as to what that calling entailed. A fiefdom system evolved, and leadership circles turned into vertical monopolies characterized most aptly as "silos," which were joined only at the top. This highly bureaucratized, hierarchical system was not particularly effective for outreach and growth, but it had an inherent inertia that also for many years kept its worst possibilities in check.

By coincidence 1986 turned out to be a watershed year for the structure of the Episcopal Church. Simultaneously a new PB, a new president of the House of Deputies, a new executive officer/secretary of General Convention, and a new treasurer of the DFMS/General Convention came onboard within a year of each other. The treasurer's position was particularly critical, because the new appointee would follow an individual who served for over thirty years. This long-term service in an institution characterized by inertia, however, also meant that virtually no one in the system really understood how the work of the treasurer's office was carried out or what kinds of checks and balances had to be in place to see that the work was done appropriately.

As a result, when Ellen Cooke was appointed treasurer on the nomination of at least two bishops, but with no appropriate background checks, the possibilities for misconduct were legion.[25] These were heightened dramatically when the PB's chief of staff resigned relatively quickly, and the PB — acting in part on a consultancy report whose authors were engaged by Cooke — decided not to replace him. Although the PB was supposed in effect to do direct staff supervision, the result was that Cooke, with the PB's unwavering support, aggrandized more and more power to herself, and therein gradually undermined not only whatever effectiveness remained among much of the program staff particularly, but also morale in the Church Center as a whole.

The story of Cooke is only partially comprehended by the embezzlement that is a part of the public record. Much more significant is the effect her conduct had on the structures of the Episcopal Church — 815, General Convention, Executive Council, the office of the PB, statistical and financial record keeping even at the parish level, and on and on. Staff members and others speak of "the hurt," "the pain," and "the tragedy" that resulted through the career of Cooke and the PB's decision to support her for almost eight years in spite of very mixed reviews throughout the church — bishops, laypersons, even the presidents of the House of Deputies.

But to stop the story there is to miss the redemptive role of conflict and the opportunity that has been seized to redress long-standing dysfunctions in the system of action. In this section, using an analytical approach rooted in the work of Victor Turner, I want to show how the Cooke debacle — the *breach* that occurred as a result of the structural nakedness her misconduct uncovered — led the Episcopal Church to reexamine its organizational culture and begin to take steps, some of which may seem amazingly elementary to the outsider, to

---

25. Significantly, through an extensive career of church-related positions, apparently no one ever checked Cooke's credentials. Had there ever been a background check on her, her misrepresentations would have become immediately apparent.

remake itself into a healthier body that may be far better equipped to face the coming century than it might have been without this crisis.[26]

The concept of *social drama* is at the center of Turner's work. Social dramas are units of aharmonic processes that arise in conflict situations. Social dramas represent the time axes of fields. A field is composed of the individuals or "actors" directly involved in the social processes under examination. Typically these show a regularly recurring processional form, or "diachronic profile," and follow an observable pattern of four phases, of which breach is the first. A breach occurs in regular norm-governed social relationships between persons or groups within the same social system. Whereas conflict had been mounting both within and without 815 over issues of administration throughout the Browning primacy as the result of Cooke, only with the public disclosure of her embezzlement can a breach be said to have occurred. Just as if the PB had shown up for work unclothed, so the regular norm-governed social relationships between persons or groups within the Episcopal Church's system of action were completely exposed to public view. The PB was aware of this and rose to the challenge of public disclosure. This situation was different from those that normally confront both his office and the work of 815 precisely because the treasurer's action completely crosscut all party lines. Liberal, centrist, and conservative money was equally in jeopardy.

The second step in the drama is that a period of mounting crisis or escalation follows the breach, unless the conflict can be sealed off quickly. Here the effects may extend to the limits of the parties involved. This second stage is always one of those turning points when a true state of affairs is revealed and hitherto covert and private factional intrigue is exposed — when, in Turner's words, "it is least easy to don masks or pretend that there is nothing rotten in the village."[27] Quickly upon the heels of the Cooke disclosures came calls for the PB's resignation. By his own estimate, 1995 was the worst year of his life, when he "almost lost it." The publicity surrounding the Cooke affair served to heighten the shrillness of the church's conservative factions and also galvanized disparate conservative groups into a more cohesive opposition. At the same time, it was far more difficult for the PB's supporters to defend him. Fortunately, the involvement of external actors — namely, various levels of law enforcement — actually served to slow the process and to introduce impersonal, "objective" processes into the crisis. The external system of action Turner calls

26. See Victor Turner, *Dramas, Fields, and Metaphors* (Ithaca, N.Y.: Cornell University Press, 1974), pp. 37ff. The summary of Turner's position given here is taken from William H. Swatos, Jr., and Loftur Reimar Gissurarson, *Icelandic Spiritualism* (New Brunswick, N.J.: Transaction, 1996), pp. 24-28.

27. Turner, *Dramas, Fields, and Metaphors*, p. 39.

the "arena." It is "the social and cultural space around those who are directly involved with the field participants but are not themselves directly implicated in the processes that define the field."[28] Arena is characteristically the group's culture, but also includes territorial and political organization.

The third stage of the drama takes place as adjustive and redressive action is brought into operation by leading members of the social group. Presiding Bishop Browning addressed the concerns of his constituencies quickly, and a search also was quickly undertaken for a responsible treasurer. After an initially difficult phase, a new treasurer of impeccable integrity was onboard within approximately six months. Various outside agencies, both those associated with the criminal proceedings against Cooke and national accounting firms of high repute, were brought in to assess the damage. Bonding ensured that the financial loss was minimized, and over time a significant amount of the dollar loss was actually recovered through legal proceedings against Cooke and the discovery of procedural errors in the way banks processed some of the fraudulent transactions she had made, hence holding them partially accountable for the losses.

Less quickly healed was the larger damage Cooke's behavior patterns had inflicted on both the Church Center staff and the image of the Church Center on the national stage. Some attempt to redress the latter was achieved through the 1997 General Convention's action in accepting portions of the Commission on Structure's recommendations for canonical changes. These involved more stringent internal and external auditing and the appointment of an executive director to oversee all 815 operations, with direct responsibility to the PB. It thus fell largely to Presiding Bishop Griswold to undertake the task of trust building both within 815 and between 815 and the larger church.

This process is still very much ongoing, but has now reached the fourth stage, in an apparently positive way — namely, reintegration of the disturbed social group, rather than social recognition of an irreparable breach or schism. For Turner this is the moment for an observer to compare relations that preceded the social drama with those following the redressive phase. The scope, range, or structure of the field will have altered. Yet, through all the changes — some crucial, others seemingly less so — certain norms and relations will persist. What can we see?

---

28. Marc Swartz, ed., *Local-Level Politics* (Chicago: Aldine, 1968), p. 11; see Victor Turner, *On the Edge of the Bush* (Tucson: University of Arizona Press, 1985), p. 84.

Networks and Systems

First and foremost, the integrity of the office of the presiding bishop has survived. Beginning with an institutional sermon that stressed conversation, conversion, community, and commitment, Frank Griswold began dialogues with the larger church both through formal consultancy activities and through an interactive download teleconference on the occasion of the first anniversary of his institution. By his personal demeanor, his view of himself as a "pastor of systems," and his intentional spirituality he distinguishes his ministry as oriented to the needs of the larger church. Whereas some bishops less than six months prior to his consecration were saying that schism was a question of "not if, but when," this language seems to have all but disappeared within the episcopate. The very same bishops are in some cases lauding and welcoming the new spirit. Following upon this, conversation *is* taking place. The PB has achieved his own first goal as "facilitator of conversations."

Uncertainty, however, still remains at two levels. There remain the suspicions between the local settings and national agenda that were exacerbated by the kinds of disjunctures that surrounded, albeit with different motivations, the administrations of the Cooke and Hines eras. And much more broadly, there are the changing nature of the world, globalization, and a need for a new organizational style for the new era. These two levels are not entirely independent of each other. The events of the past that created suspiciousness of national program and personnel cannot be separated from an administrative culture — corporate culture, broadly speaking — that in some ways was actually conducive to the dynamic of distrust. The culture of "the organization man" was imported into the denominations without significant theological reflection, and gradually became a culture unto itself apart from spiritual goals or values.[29] As this happened, denominations were decreasingly differentiated from other corporate structures as one after another "business method" was introduced into their operations. Yet the denominations continued simultaneously to articulate patently religious ideology that was inherently incompatible with the ideology of the rational-legal corporation. These two alternative self-expressions of identity created the context for the eruptions of distrust that manifested themselves both in regard to the General Convention Special Program and in the Cooke incident. In the former case, Presiding Bishop Hines attempted to move the Episcopal Church "prophetically" into religious activism without adequate attention to the grassroots core that constituted the "corporation." In the latter case, Ellen Cooke

---

29. See Ben Primer, *Protestants and American Business Methods* (Ann Arbor, Mich.: UMI Research Press, 1979).

traded on the ideology of good will within the culture of the Episcopal Church to manipulate corporate structures for her own gain.

Beginning with the EPGM, the Episcopal Church has begun to endorse a new structural type, whether or not it recognizes it. It is the *network*. Beginning with the work of Michael York and continuing with that of Hizuru Miki, sociology of religion organizational theory has begun to understand contemporary religious innovations as involving networks, rather than corporate organizations as usually conceived.[30] What is happening in the Episcopal Church, at its best, is a move from (in Miki's terms) a traditional authority-oriented organization to a *traditional autonomy-oriented network*. This, as Miki points out, is a type that has no historic exemplars, hence it will of course be fluid, fragile, subject to moving in fits and starts, and extremely threatening to those who have most invested themselves in the corporate structure — or what might more accurately be termed the quasi-corporate structure of ecclesiastical bureaucracies. Not surprisingly, for example, within the narrow "national church" of 815 it is among holdovers from the corporate culture of the Episcopal Church's prior structure that greatest resistance to openness of communication and flow of information continues to manifest itself. Not surprisingly, either, within the larger Episcopal Church across the country it is those who see religion primarily as an authority structure who will most resist the idea of remaining united in a denomination that is an autonomy-oriented network rather than an authority-oriented organization. This is nothing less than the leap from modernity to postmodernity — the religious equivalent of moving from Newton to Heisenberg.[31]

If the present presiding bishop can lead what he has called this "curious but grace-filled house" with a "diverse center" that is the Episcopal Church in and through this process of movement from organization to network, from the authority orientation of a hierarchical church that "tends to foster passivity and blame" to the autonomy-oriented network of "discernment rather than decision making," then it is just possible that this curious but grace-filled house can and will be the model for a new Christian religious expression for the twenty-first century. Precisely the fact that we do not know what "the national church" is, that the definition has remained forever fluid, may be the key to a new beginning, an open system.

---

30. See Michael York, *The Emerging Network* (Lanham, Md.: Rowman and Littlefield, 1993); Hizuru Miki, "Towards a New Paradigm of Religious Organizations," *International Journal of Japanese Sociology* 8 (1999): 131-59.

31. See David Lyon, *Jesus in Disneyland* (Oxford: Blackwell, 2001).

Crisis as Opportunity: Scandal, Structure, and Change in the Episcopal Church on the Cusp of the Millennium

Jennifer M. Phillips

The shipwright who made the Ark left empty a place for a nail in it, because he was sure that he himself would not be taken into it. When Noah went into the Ark with his children, as the angel told him, Noah shut the windows of the Ark along with him as he went into it, and when Noah blessed the Ark the Devil found no other way but the empty hole which the shipwright had left unclosed, and he went into it in the form of a snake; and because of the tightness of the hole he could not go out nor come back in, and remained like this stuck until the Flood ebbed; and that is the best and worst nail that was in the Ark.[1]

L ike a number of other denominational and faith groups in the United States, the Episcopal Church recently weathered a large and notorious scandal. In 1995 national treasurer Ellen Cooke, the wife of a priest in active service, embezzled from the church large amounts of money — in the neighborhood of $2.2 million over five years — and was subsequently discovered, convicted, and jailed. "Don't write about that incident," urged someone at a conference of the Executive Council when my sociologist colleague William Swatos and I were observing and interviewing there. "It was just an aberration, just the behavior of a mentally ill individual." And so we might have concluded at the beginning of our research. After some seventy-five interviews of national staff, bishops, and veterans of General Convention, however, it seemed to us that the malfeasance many referred to as "the Ellen Cooke incident" was some-

---

1. Kenneth Hurlstone Jackson, ed. and trans., *A Celtic Miscellany: Translations from the Celtic Literatures* (Harmondsworth, U.K.: Penguin Books, 1971), p. 304.

thing of a catalyst for structural change and relational change that has helped to reorient the way national church components operate and to set useful directions for further change.

Wherever in the denomination there were already feelings of conflict or mistrust toward "the national church" (however individuals defined this entity), this incident was read as the confirmation that there was some "rottenness at the core." Individuals variously laid the blame at the door of the presiding bishop, the Church Center staff in general or particular portions of it, the ineffectiveness of General Convention governance, or the inadvisability of having any large, bureaucratic central organization in a denomination that is largely a federation of dioceses. Others saw it more as an aberration that showed some weaknesses of a generally sound structure. Others still saw it as no one's fault but Ms. Cooke's own.

The Cooke event still sends shudders through national Church Center staff and brings forth from those recalling it descriptions like "tragic," "shocking," "deeply embarrassing," "heartbreaking," and "knocking us off our pins." As we listened and conversed with church leaders and support staff at many levels, from the past and present presiding bishops to long-term secretarial workers, we began to assess the Cooke incident as not simply an unprecedented disaster for our church but also as the crisis that provided opportunity for new health and growth. One metaphor that arose for us was "lancing a boil," so that much long-standing systemic poison can drain out and the attention of the whole body of the denomination can be focused on the need for better health maintenance and care. It seems well within our Anglican way of thinking to look at a painful episode in the life of the church to discern how God might be acting, even there, for renewal.

Theological Context

The denomination's reactions to the Cooke crisis or any crisis arise from a complex and distinctive heritage. The Episcopal Church, and the Anglican tradition that gave rise to it, was birthed in the Protestant Reformation and the Counter-Reformation of the fifteenth and sixteenth centuries in Europe. Since then, the emerging churches of the Anglican Communion have remained both Catholic and Reformed, refusing to jettison either portion of their heritage in complete favor of the other, and characterized by the tension of holding together disparate extremes and steering a muddy and wavering course down the middle. Anglicans have long spoken of our tradition as the "Middle Way." We consider ourselves catholic with a small *c* as a strand within the braid of the one universal church of Jesus Christ, as though from the perspective of other parts of that church we are schismatic. We retain an episcopacy in the apostolic succession, although some other parts of the church consider us to have breached that succession by the consecration of women bishops. We retain and have strengthened in modern times a baptismal and eucharistic focus of worship and believe that Christ is truly present in the sacrament. We are configured in geographic dioceses in a largely voluntary relationship with one another.

We are at the same time Protestant and Reformed. We rejected the magisterium in favor of making the Scriptures available to all persons in their vernacular languages and recognizing the gift of the Holy Spirit in raising up teachers among all orders of ministry. We developed a synodical form of governance. In the Episcopal Church in the United States, triennial General Conventions receive deputies, bishops, and legislative issues emerging from the dioceses, each with its own diocesan convention. Our bishops expect obedience from their clergy but have almost no power to command obedience from lay members. Their teaching authority depends on the willingness of the membership to receive their words. Our archbishops and primates have limited power to direct the member churches of the Anglican Communion to do anything, and the presiding bishop of the Episcopal Church has less autonomous power than most of his Anglican peers.

On nearly every issue in the Episcopal Church there is a spectrum of opinions and positions voiced. We argue a lot about authority and identity. We do not share a confession as a basis for our life together. Individual conscience, formed and practiced in the praying congregation, is expected "with a meek, candid, and charitable frame of mind" to "consider . . . what Christianity is, and what truths [note the plural] of the Gospel are," and then pass this learning on to others.[2] In recent General Convention legislation, a perceived need to define more clearly our shared authority led to two resolutions declaring that "the Discipline of the Church shall be found in the Constitution, the Canons and the Rubrics of the Book of Common Prayer" and "the Doctrine of the Church is to be found in the canon of Holy Scripture as understood in the Apostles' and Nicene Creeds and in the sacramental rites, the Ordinal and Catechism of the Book of Common Prayer."[3]

The Reformed theological voices among us tend to begin from an empha-

---

2. Jeremy Taylor, "The Great Exemplar," in *Collected Works of Jeremy Taylor*, ed. Reginald Heber (London: Longman, Brown, Green and Longman, 1850-59), 2:1ff.

3. Resolutions A013a and A014a, *Journal of General Convention* (Philadelphia, 1997), p. 784.

sis on Jesus Christ's atoning death on the cross for a fallen humanity within fallen creation as well as the individual's need to accept this rescue by an act of faith. The Catholic voices among us tend to begin with a focus on the whole incarnation — God's love for the entire creation which is renewed and sanctified in Jesus Christ's birth, ministry, death, resurrection, ascension, and gift of the Spirit.

From one set of roots we develop an ecclesiology that tends to see the church as the little band of the elect for salvation called to extend the lifeline of Christ to convert the perishing world, defending the purity of the church and the honor of God against the world's corrupting influences. Into this ecclesiology individuals enter by often sudden and complete conviction of their sin and of the chaos of the world and by an experience of the saving hand of Jesus Christ accepted as Lord and Savior.

From the other set of roots we see the church in images of the inclusive banquet table of God's reign or the hospital of souls where all are invited in and loved, and the church's task is to discern in every life where God is at work calling, forgiving, transforming, and gathering into community. In this view creation still shines with its original, God-manifesting loveliness, though tarnished by sin. The foundational religious experience of this perspective tends to be a gradual enculturation and formation into an awareness of the goodness of creation, despite its being smirched by sin, steadily drawing toward its author as revealed by the saving and nurturing activity of God in Jesus Christ and the Holy Spirit.

Tension between these foundational religious experiences and the differing emphases to which they give rise makes for a church with a lot of argument, a love of debate (though not without fear), liturgical richness, and a tendency to try to resolve differences by what look like very secular means (votes, referenda, collections of position papers, and diverse essays). We have few volumes of systematic theology. We have dozens of little books of essays, poetry, novels, plays, and papers from symposia. Much of our best theology, therefore, is conveyed through the arts (including liturgical forms), which are more spacious and allusive, evocative, and less tidy than theological tomes.

With this strong heritage of flexibility we often find ourselves uncomfortable, and there are regularly calls from the more traditionalist parts of the church to lock down and limit our doctrine and discipline more tightly. So far, these have not received the assent of the majority of General Conventions. We maintain the myth of a "common prayer" increasingly challenged by multicultural currents, still "seeking to keep the happy mean between too much stiffness in refusing and too much easiness in admitting variations in things once advisedly established" — although these days we argue hotly about what was "once established."[4] This is not a new phenomenon. Nineteenth-century theologian Jeremy Taylor wrote, "Such being the nature of men, that they think it the greatest injury in the world when other men are not of their minds; and that they please God most when they are most furiously zealous, and no zeal better to be expressed than by hating all those whom they are pleased to think God hates."[5]

Richard Hooker, arguably our preeminent founding theologian besides Thomas Cranmer, wrote to establish a middle ground between Calvinist Puritans and Roman Catholics, with the Holy Spirit leading human beings into truth primarily through reason. The Bible, he argued, is the first pillar of authority in the church (including the Apocrypha, although these texts hold less authority than the rest). Reason is another pillar, and this understood as an educated, well-formed faculty developed and tested not privately but in the worship and life of the church. Church tradition is the third pillar, with generally the greater authority resting in the more ancient traditions, although Hooker acknowledged that no era was without its errors and excesses. The three together constitute a structure of authority Anglicans have often pictured as a three-legged stool. Our more Protestant members are quick to remind us that the Bible leg is longer and more primary than the others, while our Catholic members insist that even the Bible is apprehended through reason (which contemporary Anglicans tend to define as including experience).

Along with Roman Catholic and Reformed elements, Anglican theology draws upon Celtic and Eastern Orthodox strands of tradition — and the Celtic strand was much influenced by the Orthodox. Both include a rootedness in creation, a domestic piety and asceticism, an anthropology that is optimistic in light of the incarnation, and strong trinitarianism. The persons of the Trinity are seen as conversing endlessly with one another in love, a circle of pillow talk: "see . . . the Father kissing the Son in the white dew," wrote the Welsh poet Saunders Lewis. Into that conversation, humankind — starting with the church — is drawn to listen and to speak. "All around me the most beautiful music plays: the songs of birds, the lowing of cattle, the leaves rustling in the wind, the cascade of the river . . . it is the music of Christ himself, given freely."[6]

Because of this diverse heritage, Anglican theology is always discursive, communicated by a plurality of voices. One might imagine this as a *schola,* a little polyphonic singing school, or perhaps as a jazz combo. Now one, now an-

4. Preface written in 1789 for *The Book of Common Prayer,* still included as preface to the 1979 book, pp. 9-10.

5. Taylor, "The Great Exemplar," pt. ii, sec. xii, 2:329.

6. Saunders Lewis, "Ascension Thursday," in *Selected Poems,* trans. Joseph Clancy (Cardiff: University of Wales Press, 1993), p. 35.

other voice may rise to the fore, or sometimes all may sound equally together. There can be discord as well as harmony, and both are fitting. Leadership may shift with flexibility, though there tends to be a designated head and convener. The music is ephemeral and changeable, but a lasting value is created. Tradition and change are incorporated along with many diverse influences. Rhythm and pace are coherent but not uniform. There is a recognizable aesthetic and ethos that aims to create something beautiful and truthful pointing to a transcendent dimension and drawing its hearers and members into it.

The jazz combo can even have a new iteration in the medium of the electronic, virtual network. Via the Internet, radio, and satellite, musicians from around the world have collaborated to make music together, gathering in sounds from their various corners of creation, along with recorded bits from other times and places, and circulating these back and forth in a jazz performance. This might be a provocative new metaphor for our Anglican performance as church.

Given the pluralism composing the Episcopal Church, it is to be expected that we respond to institutional crises not only with a diversity of voices and movements but also with certain underlying principles. As Christians rooted in the incarnation, we place considerable importance and some trust in the operation of the physical and social world to right itself after a catastrophe. We perceive that God acts through those physical and social remedies and the self-righting tendency of living systems. Just so, God acts through the church structures we create, although they will not always be congruent with God's desire since such structures are rendered imperfect by sin. To maintain our unity, it is essential that our lay and ordained leaders be well formed in this breadth of tradition, especially since the majority of Episcopalians grow up in other religious denominations.

The Incident

There seems to be consensus that over a period of years Ms. Cooke concentrated power and financial information in her own hands, rebuffed questions from fellow staff, estranged herself from colleagues, and exploited the loyalty of the presiding bishop who had committed himself to advancing the ministries of women at every level of the church. She is described as having encouraged the belief that she was the only one who understood the inner workings of the finances of the church and could keep it all in operation. Having "built an empire for herself," she maintained that the presiding bishop knew and approved of her actions. A senior cleric active in the governance of General Convention noted that from her very arrival on the job, Ms. Cooke began to dismantle checks and balances and to displace employees who had continuity and long service.

Ms. Cooke functioned as the volunteer treasurer of the General Convention Office, which manages the triennial governance assembly of the Episcopal Church and its various interim committees and commissions. She also was elected by the General Convention as salaried treasurer of the Domestic and Foreign Missionary Society (DFMS), the incorporated entity to which every Episcopalian belongs (most without knowing it) and which is the core corporation of the Episcopal Church. She was thereby manager of Executive Council's funds. In these roles Ms. Cooke had connections with virtually every part of the Church Center and oversaw the budget for a large part of the national church from the time she was hired in 1986. She managed the committees that oversaw the many trusts managed by the DFMS, committees that depended on their staff support. Many staff describe years of abuse and manipulation at her hands, distorting the ideal of the national staff work as rooted in servant ministry. Some felt Ms. Cooke was doing a tough job tidying up loose financial systems of the past that needed repair, but that she was heavy-handed in doing this. More than a few spoke their concerns aloud despite being scolded for doing so.

The presiding bishop maintained a fierce loyalty to Ms. Cooke through the public announcement of her resignation effective January 31, 1995. By all accounts he was stunned by the revelation of her dishonesty, which was announced in the Episcopal News Service on February 15. He responded to this with immediate honesty and as much directness as the legal process would allow. In a poignant article for the May 16, 1995, issue of *Episcopal Life,* he wrote, "I still believe that, in this world of cynicism, suspicion and disbelief, trust is a necessity. . . . What did happen on my watch was a massive betrayal of trust. Ellen had strong support in many quarters. . . . However, I take full responsibility for hiring Ellen and keeping her on, even when I knew her working style was autocratic rather than the collaborative one I have tried to model." Bishop Browning went on to speak of the clear necessity of prosecution. "We pray for her contrition and repentance," he concluded, "and for our ability to forgive. . . . In the way hardship can bring a family together, I pray that this will bring us together as a church."

Eventually through criminal and civil process, the Cookes yielded most of their liquid assets and personal property. Along with insurance collected and some financial acceptance by banks of responsibility for failed oversight, this repaid most of the loss. Ms. Cooke made a claim in court that a cyclothymic mental disorder caused a memory loss about stealing the funds, but the judge handed down a stiff sentence of five years in prison, noting that stealing from a church resulted in a loss of confidence in an institution "that performs an essential function in the care of the needy" and constituted a "flagrant . . . abuse of trust."[7] The sentence was upheld on appeal. She has not, to date, publicly owned culpability or remorse for the embezzlement.

In the aftermath, changes began to be made at once in business and administrative practices at the Church Center, along with changes in financial personnel, strengthening of the internal auditor, and a thorough outside audit of funds. The internal auditor had been reporting to the treasurer. At first this was changed to mandate reporting to the chief operating officer, and subsequently changed again to mandate reporting to the audit committee. The membership of this committee was modified to conform more exactly to canon. The Presiding Bishop's Discretionary Fund, which had been excluded from audit during the Cooke tenure, was returned to the annual auditing process. Management and communications changes followed as well. Some of these would have likely come as a result of the changing times and climate of institutional structures. The Cooke crisis highlighted the problems and hastened the process.

Administrative Change

Several staff in the Episcopal Church Center, referring to the work of outside consultants, described the administrative structure during the Browning years as "silos." This corporate structure was not uncommon and consisted of vertical columns of relationship, communication, and function within individual program areas or departments that were isolated from one another horizontally. In the words of one staff person, the silo structure was adopted to streamline the former set of "eighteen fiefdoms" under Presiding Bishop Allin. In a silo system, only a few top-level individuals (such as the treasurer and presiding bishop) linked one silo with another, and potentially these few persons had great regulatory power over information, communication, and the flow of resources. The silo system was thought to allow separate areas of corporate function to develop their particular gifts and internal relationships as well as to maximize efficiency, but it is clear from hindsight that such structure lends itself to unchecked exploitation by individuals at the top.

This model did not seem to fit the presiding bishop's espoused model of administration. In Bishop Edmond Browning's public discourse, his most frequent scriptural image for the church was Paul's metaphor of the body and its

7. "Episcopal Church Treasurer Sentenced to Five Years for Embezzlement," Episcopal News Service, July 1997.

members. From his first acceptance speech upon election at General Convention in Anaheim in September 1985, Bishop Browning used this metaphor to support his central declaration of mission, that in the Episcopal Church there would be "no outcasts." Over his years as presiding bishop, he reiterated this conviction in relation to debates over the place of gay and lesbian people in the church, the place of indigenous Indian ministries and other ethnic ministries, his antiracism initiatives, the role of women in the church, care for people with HIV infection and AIDS, his concern for the poor and for migrant and immigrant mission, and his stated commitment that conservatives would not be ignored or marginalized within a generally progressive denomination. Again and again, the church heard him quote, "the hand cannot say to the eye 'I have no need of you,'" "we are all members of one body," and the like.

The more science reveals about living bodies, particularly our human body, the more it is clear that mutual communication and adaptation take place between the many parts and systems of the body on every level, not merely from the brain down to the subsidiary systems and from the systems back again. New research shows that even the lowly cells of human blood vessels adjust to circulatory stress by switching genes on and off, by communicating to other cells to affect clotting, and by moving themselves away from areas of turbulence.[8] Communication flows in many directions. The metaphor of the body therefore may need to evolve with our emerging understandings to correspond with the latest "network" model of structure.

Presiding Bishop Browning's twelve-year term ended at the end of 1997, a bit more than three years after the Cooke crisis. The mood of the church was changed. In his last address to General Convention 1997, Browning described the embezzlement as "one of the greatest personal challenges I have ever faced. . . . We have been touched by the power of Jesus Christ to redeem the most difficult and tragic of situations. . . . We have been wounded and examined our wounds. We have been called to forgive, and asked to be forgiven. . . . Scar tissue, they say, is the strongest tissue there is." Ms. Cooke was not mentioned by name. Browning spoke of laying a new foundation of trust. One notable sign of this new trust was the recommitment of the House of Deputies to being a church in mission, restoring funds and focus for this purpose. Another was the choice of a new presiding bishop who most felt had a good grasp of administration, theological articulateness, a progressive-centrist political reputation, and a pastoral heart.

---

8. Jonathan Knight, "Cunning Plumbing: In the Battle to Stay Healthy, the Complex Twists and Turns of Our Arteries May Be the Best Weapons We Have," *New Scientist* (London), no. 2172 (February 6, 1999): 32.

As a witness to that General Convention, it was my experience that much of the assembly felt chastened by the experience of a major scandal, satisfied that due process had occurred, and ready for systemic change to tighten up oversight and improve the workings of the Church Center. We were also ready to receive the contrition of top leadership and to trust incoming leaders to prevent a recurrence of malfeasance. We were receptive to structural change but not panic-driven toward it.

Management Change

Students of organizational structure are presently intrigued with the discoveries and theories of contemporary post-Newtonian science that suggest some fresh approaches to management and structure. Management consultant Margaret J. Wheatley highlights some learnings from physics and chaos theory in particular that seem of particular significance for Episcopal approaches to structure and which have influenced the management theory of our new presiding bishop.[9] In brief, some of these are:

- An emphasis on the system as system and on the relationships that constitute it, not reducible to bits or to cause-effect phenomena.
- A realization that dissipative processes are not just about decay but that "living systems . . . respond to disorder (non-equilibrium) with renewed life," that chaos and order fluctuate in balance, and that organizations are living systems, conscious entities continuously renewing themselves and having an inherent orderliness beyond their chaotic behaviors.
- Management should be based on a belief that motivation for work comes not only or primarily from extrinsic rewards but also from human longing for community, meaning, dignity, love, generativity, and the joy of the work itself.
- Structures and forms are temporary solutions to changing environments, but within an organism, mission remains congruent over time.
- Leadership should not be about a set group of people muscling chaos into a set order, but about allowing informal leadership to arise as needed, looking for underlying order, facilitating the interconnectedness of people within and beyond a system, thinking and acting quickly rather than investing great energy in rigid long-term plans, improvising, and exercis-

9. Margaret Wheatley, *Leadership and the New Science: Learning about Organization from an Orderly Universe* (San Francisco: Berrett-Koehler, 1992), pp. 9, 11, 13, 16, 21, 39, 105.

ing strong relational skills. "Love in organizations, then, is the most potent source of power we have available."

- "Acting locally is a sound strategy for changing large systems." Small changes can lead to quantum jumps of massive change. Not every member of an organization must understand a change in order for the whole group to change, and one cannot predict just how or when such large change will occur.
- Information is the key ingredient in creating structure and must be continuously generated — the more and the freer-circulating, the better. "Let it procreate promiscuously," and liveliness will result.

The Episcopal pattern of loosely tied task groups that can arise independently to meet particular needs within the organization may be an ideal dynamic system for allowing informal networks of relationship to adapt and solve problems as they arise. Among such groups are the Church Pension Group, the Episcopal Church Foundation, the Prayer Book Society, the Episcopal Women's Caucus, and the Episcopal Council for Global Mission. Rather than trying to untangle and tidy up the complex interrelationships between all our groups and their lines of authority, we might instead expect that their changeable interconnectedness and fluid evolution or demise will be creative and fruitful. The new management of the church expresses a desire to accept and support places of energy for the gospel wherever they arise. Our denominational experience (along with other faith groups) that members prefer to undertake much of their work and invest most of their resources locally rather than centrally might be understood in this cognitive frame as a natural and positive force for change.

Our set hierarchy of leadership may fit Wheatley's insights more uneasily. Our deep tie to and identity in a structure of bishops, priests, deacons, and laity will, I suspect, be with us for the long haul. Even so, change is evident in the redefining of roles, functions, and interrelationships and in the shifting investment in the authority of these roles. Also pointing to change are the experiments in locally ordained non-seminary-trained priests, mutual ministry congregations like those of northern Michigan, and quarrels about whether to allow "flying bishops" and nongeographical dioceses to accommodate Episcopalians who dissent from the majority views on women's ordination, liturgical reform, and homosexuality.

In light of changes consistent with new scientific knowledge and theory, perhaps the most helpful response of leaders may be to remain nonanxious, to lead in as light and noncontrolling a fashion as possible, to allow experiments and reconfigurations and to trust that the inherent patterns of chaos and reordering will be held within bounds by the underlying orderliness of the cosmos and life systems God has created, including the church. The strongest leaders will be those who think on their feet, trust in life and God, and love deeply and responsibly so as to create a climate of love in the systems they pastor. We Americans need to remind ourselves that we are not pursuing a squishy, feel-good, anything-goes sentimentality, but a love that is firm, faithful, brave, respectful, and trustworthy, as Scripture so often describes.

The free flow of communication will ultimately be fruitful and energizing, say scientists. One instance of this might be in looking at the way the least-establishment, most "underground" publication of our recent General Conventions (which are reported out to participants in at least four different print journals as well as by electronic media) has been crucial in generating debate that moves the assembly forward. Instead of greeting new informal information sources with suspicion and restriction, we should trust that the ferment of ideas and opinions will ultimately serve everyone, and that all members and leaders would be well advised to scan information from as many sources as possible, including those from groups with whom they deeply disagree. With the proliferation of information, we must also develop habits of discernment about the source and veracity of information. From congregations to the national church, there are constant complaints of poor communication. Science suggests leaders not worry about formalizing communication channels but open the gates to more unrestricted information (including ambiguous, complex, or apparently useless information) and let it spark new ideas, while attending to the big picture of how information is giving rise to thoughts and new forms.

The Cooke incident may have been a catalyst for a significant change, such as physicists describe. Many small changes in behavior resulted from that incident and are moving the entire organization to a new level and a new self-understanding. That event marked a threshold from which it became clear to people across the church that there could be no going back into old ways but that some new order and structure was emerging.

If there is ambiguity in the minds of most Episcopalians about what the national church actually *is*, with all its parachurch organizations and parts, there is clarity about what it is *not:* a monolithic monument fixed in time and form. It is a living, breathing, dying and renewing, sinning and repenting, metamorphosing community into which God calls us together and into which we invite God to dwell, finding God already delighting to dwell with us as we pray. In the economy of God, our failure and sin is recycled into the unfolding divine design. Our energy for mission springs from the nexus of our gatherings in which the Holy Spirit moves and breathes.

Fiduciary Change

In an effort to make the national budget clearer, the process toward a democra-tized, accessible, transparent, unified budget, funded by a formula producing diocesan requests based on income, had already begun at the 1994 General Convention. Instead of separate budgets — the General Convention Expense Budget (prepared by the treasurer) and Program Budget of the national church (prepared by Executive Council with the treasurer's assistance) — the two were combined by resolution.

In the Cooke era, much of the initial budget refinement process was done by the treasurer herself. She controlled much of the information available to staff and some of what was disseminated to the wider church. The unified bud-get served her ends of controlling information. The treasurer prepared and pre-sented to the General Convention portions of the two-tiered budget, while the Executive Council prepared the program budget, aided by staff and including input from the treasurer. Even matters like parochial reports, from which come the baseline data about the membership and financial contributions of all the congregations and dioceses of the church, were gathered by Ms. Cooke.

During this same period, Church Center staffing performance review was done by the "Hay" system common in corporations, in which the larger the staff and budget under one's supervision and control, the higher one's sal-ary. Ms. Cooke was reportedly willing and eager to take on additional respon-sibilities, expand her staff, and thereby increase her pay. At the same time, ac-cording to denominational executives, the number of people around the senior executive table shrank until it was primarily the presiding bishop, the treasurer, and Diane Porter, the senior executive for program. There were com-plaints about this, according to several staff, about which the presiding bishop chose not to act.

After the shake-up of the Cooke crisis, each body constructing the budget seems to have turned to its task with more attention and less willingness to rubber-stamp decisions. For a number of reasons, there had been a reduction of funds flowing into the national budget from dioceses, although the shortfall was larger in perception than in reality. Some dioceses found their own funds from congregations reduced. Some withheld funds out of anger about the na-tional church's stance on social issues like human sexuality. Some were angry and mistrustful after the revelations about malfeasance at the highest levels of their church. Applying the language of "covenant commitment" to funding re-quests was no quick fix for any of these causes for withholding. Only the grad-ual rebuilding of trust and confidence under new personnel has begun to give flesh to the idea of covenant relationship between dioceses and the national church. Future General Conventions will reveal whether the trend is positive in this regard.

A New Theological Emphasis, a New Presiding Bishop

The belief among many that Presiding Bishop Browning had lapsed in prudent oversight of Ms. Cooke and his other staff and finances prompted a series of questions about the office and role of presiding bishop. Other questions were emerging simply because of changing times and understandings of authority, and because of perceived shrinking financial resources. It is not easy to sort out which questions were prompted by which causes.

The 1997 General Convention asked whether the role of the presiding bishop needed to be clarified. The Joint Commission on the Structure of the Church answered yes, reporting to the General Convention the evolving issues about the presiding bishop's role.

> By Canon the Presiding Bishop is the Chief Pastor and Primate of the Church, and is presently vested with responsibility for leadership in initiating and developing the policy and strategy of the church and with the ultimate responsibility for the implementation of such policy and strategy. Thus, this church has called the Presiding Bishop to be the President of the House of Bishops; the Chief Pastor to the Church, its people, clergy, and especially its bishops and their families; the Church's Primate as to the Anglican Communion, sister Christian churches, other ecumenical bodies, and the world; and to be the church's chief executive, operating officer, and management officer.[10]

The committee quoted commentators from 1926 to the present who voiced concern that the pastoral role of the presiding bishop and indeed every bishop was being weighed down by organizational tasks. The ambiguous expectations of the role were acknowledged, along with the consensus that the presiding bishop *not* exercise archiepiscopal or metropolitical authority over the church and the disagreements over his authority to be a spokesperson for the whole church. The committee's resolutions defined the role and left him free to appoint staff as needed to fulfill it. The General Convention voted to accept the commission's proposal, slightly paring down the presiding bishop's responsibility for implementation of policy.[11] There was debate at the convention over whether a chief

10. *Report to the Seventy-Second General Convention*, p. 484.
11. Resolution A183, *Journal of General Convention*, p. 194.

operating officer should be nominated by, appointed by, and accountable to the Executive Council or the presiding bishop. The convention seemed content to entrust operations management to the good shepherding of presiding bishops, leaving the appointment and accountability in his hands and the Executive Council in a role of advice and consent. In so deciding, they perhaps concluded that the weak area of one particular bishop need not be cause for abridging the prerogative of all presiding bishops to appoint administrative staff.[12]

Should the presiding bishop remain the distinct head of the national church, or should the president of the House of Deputies (alternately an elected lay or ordained person) be a coequal leader with similar staff and salary? The General Convention in 1997 said it is reasonable for the president of the senior house (Deputies) to have a chancellor paid to give legal advice, but did not add an expense line for that position to the budget allotment for the president of the House of Deputies.[13] The church voiced its preference for the presiding bishop to remain in a solo leadership role as a spiritual and administrative head.

Conservative church leaders along with self-avowed liberals seem to agree that the presiding bishop should be a pastor first of all, not a CEO. In March 1998, shortly after the investiture of the new presiding bishop, *United Voice,* the publication affiliated with the conservative Episcopalians United, ran an article by the Reverend Todd Wetzel headlined "The Church Needs Shepherds — Not CEOs." Wetzel decried "consumer Christianity" in which clergy have lost their calling and feel like "employees" and laity like "customers," with bishops functioning as "managers" rather than servants. Wetzel voiced optimism that the new presiding bishop will "help us find more responsive, less expensive, less monarchical ways that free bishops from the vise of the CEO model, clergy from the bonds of the employee mentality, and laity from the grips of consumerism — and into the baptismal covenant of ministry."

While the average Episcopalian may be critical of his or her own bishop and quick to see that person's clay feet, we retain a reverence for the office and charism of episcopacy, although less so than some generations of our forebears. Several laypeople with whom I spoke used similar words: "We need to be able to look to a spiritual leader who in his person reminds us of who and how we are to be." He is expected to incarnate the "Episcopal *us*," to represent in some measure our passions and interests but as centered and balanced in God. Since these are wildly diverse and in tension, he (maybe someday she) must hold this tension together in himself.

12. Resolution A189s, *Journal of General Convention,* p. 193.
13. Resolution A194 (rejected), *Report to the Seventy-Second General Convention,* p. 494.

Presiding bishops have defined their roles and style differently. A bishop interviewed offered the opinion that though the church at large might forget structural debates and changes within a year or two, what most people would remember was the way the personality of a presiding bishop set the tone for his tenure. It has not been uncommon for a presiding bishop to take the lead in issues of social justice, though some have focused more on administration and structure, others have exercised quiet diplomacy, and still others have raised insistent prophetic voices of advocacy for change, as did Bishop Browning.

Implicit in the 1960s to 1980s was a theology that a fully engaged people of God could make substantial strides to building the reign of God on earth, restoring the lost justice of society along the way. There was little talk in that era of the way human beings and enterprises are constantly ensnared by sin and fall short of God's glory. Today, the Episcopal Church seems tired after its decades of wrangling about tough social issues yet to be resolved, sick of destructive partisanship (though not quite ready to stop practicing it), and intolerant of sloppy, inefficient, corrupt systems. In these things Episcopalians share much with American society at large. The Cooke crisis brought to a head some of the frustration and anxiety about the direction of the church, and has played a role in our choice of a presiding bishop with a track record of effective administration and staffing, systems acumen, a theologically reflective and sophisticated mind, and a dedication to prayerful listening and conversation that takes precedence over other issues and partisan concerns. Whether we will be forgiving of his clay feet remains to be seen.

Presiding Bishop Frank Griswold began his tenure in 1998 by offering his favored metaphors for his ministry. They are:

- Pastor of systems. "The whole idea — that within a force field of constantly moving particles there is an underlying order or structure which in time will reveal itself — has taught me to let loose of control and to allow the energy within the system to order itself. This approach has helped me to be much more patient with seeming ambiguity and contradiction."[14]
- A church called at every level to *conversation,* which leads to conversion and communion with careful listening and mutual respect. This is a task of *hospitality,* rooted in the Pauline understanding that we are members of one another.[15]

---

14. Interview in the *Journal of Anglican Musicians,* September 1997.
15. Address to Diocesan Convention, Chicago, 1993.

- A church whose mode of theology is as a contemplative exercise in which prayer corrects tendencies toward being arrogant and self-serving.[16]
- Repairing and rebuilding the church, not as an object or institution to be fixed but as a relationship of communion as "living stones" by baptism into Christ, being "caught up into solidarities we have not chosen" (words of Bishop Rowan Williams) through "a costly and excruciating process of conversion."[17]

Griswold used the living stones metaphor again in his sermon at the Lambeth Conference of 1998 at Canterbury Cathedral, saying about that great building and the church community: "One portion is added to another, and the ever-expanding whole is bonded and knit together through dynamic of stress and counterstress, by one stone pressing against another and thereby producing an overall state of equilibrium and concord."

At a "Future Search" conference in St. Louis in the winter of 1998-99, a lay educator participant said, "We want the PB to lead us out of his strengths," a hope shared, I suspect, by many. Over the years we have begun to have an inkling of how our presiding bishops and other leaders have led us out of their weaknesses in ways just as valuable to the life of the church. The snake in the ark was the worst and the best nail, as the Celtic story maintains.

Other Structural Issues

The usefulness and necessity of changing church structures are inherent in Anglicanism. Richard Hooker wrote in the sixteenth century, "The Church hath authority to establish that for an order at one time, which at another it may abolish, and in both do well."[18] The Commission on Structure stated six general principles for the Episcopal Church that governed its recommendations to the 1997 General Convention:

1. This church is a national church participating fully in the Anglican Communion.

---

16. Sermon at the "Liturgy Unbound" conference, January 1999.

17. Sermon from the Investiture of Frank Griswold as Presiding Bishop, Washington National Cathedral, January 10, 1998.

18. Richard Hooker, *Of the Laws of Ecclesiastical Polity: And Other Works by and about Mr. Richard Hooker,* bk. 5, ed. J. Keble, R. W. Church, and F. Paget (Ellicott City, Md.: Via Media Publications, 1994), p. 33.

2. This church is one diverse community of Christ's reconciling ministry in the world.

3. This church will commit to the dioceses and provinces only that mission and ministry which cannot be accomplished effectively by parishes and congregations.

4. This church will commit to national structures only that mission and ministry which cannot be accomplished effectively by dioceses and provinces.

5. The form of this church will follow function, and the structure of this church will follow ministry and mission.

6. This church must be structured at all levels so that structures do not inhibit deliberate change.

The description of the principles went on to acknowledge the hierarchical nature of the church and its pitfalls in creating "vertical monopolies," and called for the church at all levels to live out the baptismal covenant by fighting evils, spreading the kingdom of God, uniting and reconciling all in Christ, and exercising wise stewardship of creation and ourselves, so that none of these efforts would be compartmentalized.[19] Within this text lies the painful shadow of the silo model of organization that came to an abrupt end in the Cooke crisis.

After the 1998 General Convention, the Executive Council restructured itself to create a Standing Committee on Planning and Development. This group made four- to five-day visits to eighteen selected dioceses, two "dissimilar" ones in each province, to meet with lay and ordained leaders and ask, "What is the mission of the church?" One of the recommendations gathered by this body about the Church Center staff was that staff see one of their primary roles as providing "networking/facilitating and resourcing" to dioceses and congregations, with emphasis on small congregations. From the Diocese of West Virginia they carried back the comment, "Many people are not aware of who the program staff at 815 [the Church Center address in New York City] are or how to contact them . . . of the diocesan linkage person program or its goals." The need for upgraded communications systems was stated by the Diocese of San Diego, and other help with emerging technologies for networking was requested by Upper South Carolina and West Missouri. A more relational General Convention was the hope of Central Pennsylvania. Montana called for "reestablishing and renewing the corporate identity of what it means to be an Episcopalian." Ten out of twelve recommendations focused in some way on

19. Report of the Commission on Structure, in *Report to the Seventy-Second General Convention*, p. 454.

strengthening communications and connectedness.[20] The end of the silo mentality era was clear. The desire for closer contact across the national church was
eloquent. At a time when one might have expected emphasis on accountability,
cleaning up, and discipline from the dioceses, the bottom line was a plea for im-
proved *relationships*.

The Executive Council as a leadership body has also begun to have a redefined role. Bishop Griswold encouraged them beyond just holding administrative, program, and planning responsibility:

> A member of Council is an ambassador . . . of the church, who by virtue of
> participating in the life of the Council is called to be a carrier of the life of
> Council — beyond the sub-basement — back into your province, your dio-
> cese; and conversely, you are to serve as an ambassador from your diocese
> and province back to the Council. . . . [B]e very intentional about that. . . .
> Council is not simply a conduit for information or a body to carry out
> tasks; but also . . . an experience of being the church. . . . Executive Council
> is a fractal. . . . [T]he way we deport ourselves, the way we interact with one
> another, the way we listen to one another, the way we make our decisions,
> the way we give space, the way we pray together, all those things are integral
> to what we carry out of here . . . a very important aspect of our being faith-
> ful.[21]

His intention seems to be that each constituent body of the church view itself as
the church in microcosm. Under his leadership the staff has begun doing just this.
They have a weekly brown-bag lunch together and are urged to attend the Eucharist that precedes this even if they cannot make the other daily services during the
week. He has added a font of holy water and some soft furnishings to the chapel at
815, which serves staff, visitors, and neighbors. A staff member describes finding
the presiding bishop humming to himself, turning out musty old books and vestments from drawers and tidying up the sacristy with relish and delight during his
first week at the Church Center. Worship, conversation, and communal dining
are to be at the center of the staff's life together. Wandering through the offices
and dropping in on staff, wearing blue jeans and flannel shirts when not conducting public events, Bishop Griswold is setting the tone for an episcopate that he
hopes will be accessible and informal, and link parts of the organization to each
other by his visible presence. Although he is required to travel, his aim is that staff
experience him as present at 815 "more often than not."

20. Report of the Executive Council's Standing Committee on Planning and Evaluation
on the Diocesan Consultations, 1996.
21. Frank Griswold, remarks to Executive Council, February 12, 1999.

Jennifer M. Phillips

Risk, Sin, and Discipline

Like other faith groups, the Episcopal Church has been pressed to develop policies and procedures about every kind of professional misconduct by its employees. We have had our share of sexual and financial misconduct trials in many dioceses. As the society around us has withdrawn favored status from churches and become more questioning of people in authority, it has become impossible to continue injurious old practices of moving malefactors from place to place and ignoring complainants. Insurance liability has been a thick stick spurring legislative and behavioral change.

Over the last nine years the Episcopal Church has radically revised its disciplinary canons regarding misconduct by clergy, bishops, and staff, creating a large body of revised canon law at General Convention 1994. Administrative practices have shifted as well. Background checks are now routine at every level of church employment from sextons to bishops, and training on misconduct and on drug and alcohol abuse is required of employees and volunteers with oversight of children. Each diocese bears responsibility for doing this in a way that satisfies the Church Insurance Company or other insurers. Dioceses increasingly press congregations to conform to standard business practices in the handling of money, property, and securities, and to have both in-house and professional audits regularly. Protective policies that substantially change clergy pastoral practice are largely accepted, though not without debate. Such changes in policy are by no means unique to the Episcopal Church and are driven at least as much by insurance requirements as by concern for the care of persons. The Cooke experience added impetus to a movement already under way. It has become increasingly clear to churches that if they did not effectively police themselves, society would impose constraints from outside.

Theological rationales for risk reduction procedures come after the fact, but they do come. We interviewed a self-avowed optimist on the national staff who spoke of "raising the bar of awareness" to "say more positively the ways we can exercise more competent hospitality in using our humanity, our malehood, our femalehood, our frailty, our sinfulness, you name the mix and match of what we are as religious leaders, to be more self-aware and more skilled when we interface with vulnerable people." An interviewee from the Church Insurance Company addressed the issue of risk management as "hospitality, creating a safe place for God's children, which is also good loss-prevention [policy] because when you don't injure people, you don't have law suits."

Traditionally, complaint procedures in cases of misconduct began from the early church practice of first making the complaint privately, then coming to the offender with a fellow Christian, and then bringing a group or the whole community together to put pressure on the offender to answer for his or her behavior (Matt. 18:15-17). This is hardly a sophisticated enough procedure for dealing with the complexities of sexual misconduct or the realities of modern legal systems. There are now provisions for suspending priestly functioning of alleged sex offenders or others accused of professional misconduct or of felonies, while continuing to pay them unless and until guilt is established. There are victims' advocates available as well as judicial bodies within the church for hearing complaints and conducting investigations and church trials. Civil authorities tend to be involved early, setting the conditions under which accused offenders and their victims may communicate.

The Gospel of John's teaching to the disciples, traditionally read as "If you forgive the sins of any they are forgiven, but if you retain the sins of any they are retained" (20:23), may be translated even more aptly as, "Of whomsoever you release the sins, they are released, but of whomsoever you seize/bind the sins, they are subdued." In establishing risk reduction policies, the discerning church must distinguish between those sorts of sins that can simply be exposed, responded to, and released, and those that are so destructive to the fabric of community that they need to be laid hold of, contained, and thoroughly constrained. Of this latter type are sins of professional misconduct, both sexual and financial.

Scripture is replete with testimonies that God cares particularly for the vulnerable, the weak, and victims of injustice. The Gospels add that as we treat the "least of these," Jesus' sisters and brothers, so we treat Jesus himself (Matt. 25:40). It is the great commandment that we love one another as Jesus has loved us (John 13:34), and "love one's neighbor as oneself" (Mark 12:31). Our loving God is inseparably linked to the concrete loving of our neighbors, especially our most vulnerable neighbors. For those vested with special authority and power, "Of those to whom much has been given, much will be asked" (Luke 12:48). Increased oversight, well-boundaried intimacy, and a humble understanding of universal sin and the limitations of our leaders as human beings may balance our Anglican optimism about human nature.

In the contemporary United States, the Episcopal Church included, we seldom quote the scriptural admonition not to sue our fellow Christians in courts of law (1 Cor. 6:1ff.). We may in fact be too quick to assume that the satisfaction of civil justice will accomplish the maintaining of justice, *koinonia*, and reconciliation within the church.

Forgiveness and Reconciliation

The destruction of trust in relationships was the most painful cost of the Cooke era among staff. Not only were relationships with Ms. Cooke injured, but also relationships between persons and departments on many levels, and between staff and members of the wider church. One staff member said, "In our culture there is already a suspicion of large systems which gets escalated by finding out about a large deception that's been going on for many years and is using your resources without your knowledge. . . . It goes right to the heart of what each of us fears and resents."

The national staff met together to do some healing work with each other in the months following Cooke's departure, but four years later the wounds still felt deep to many who remained. The new presiding bishop, Frank Griswold, took senior staff on retreat soon after his arrival in New York, and has continued the forums for working through and healing broken relationships and trust. This has been a slow process.

Ellen Cooke went to prison. A staff person overheard her saying, as she was escorted from the building, "I hate them all." How shall such wounds heal, for her or for others? How do our systems help or impair healing? Certainly not by "forgiving and forgetting"! In an Episcopal magazine, an inmate in California's Vacaville prison wrote eloquently:

> Excusing and mitigating criminal behavior because of a person's background is nearly as dehumanizing, in a subtle way, as the current conditions within our prisons. It sends the message, "You are incapable of rising above your background. We don't expect more from you." Alternately, the system sends the message, "You don't want to change. We expect the worst from you." The first sounds patronizing, the second sounds harsh. Both extremes deny the dignity of accountability and remove the possibility of transformation. To have both justice and mercy, responsibility and reconciliation, we must find a middle ground.[22]

If convicted by civil or ecclesiastical authorities, those guilty of professional misconduct in the church are punished, de-licensed, sent for rehabilitative treatment, and generally end up outside their religious communities completely — informally excommunicated. Sometimes in shame they excommunicate themselves. There they remain, outside. Or perhaps if they can come to terms with their own behavior, they relocate to another part of the church, slide into the back row of a place where no one knows their story, and

22. James R. Tramel, letter to the editors, *Witness* (New York), March 1999.

stay in the shadows. Victims leave their churches almost as often, I suspect, once trust in the structure and its leaders has been shattered.

In all the properly strict new processes for dealing with misconduct, the discourse about forgiveness seems to find little place, even in the church. What the victims' rights movement usefully has taught us is that forgiveness cannot be forced, hasty, or superficial, nor may it keep offenders from the painful consequences of their sin. Where abuse has happened, there are care and counseling to help victims and congregations come to terms with and heal from their experiences. There are public disclosure and censure. All to the good. Forgiveness, however, becomes a private, inner matter for the victims to work out with their therapists if they choose. Some persons find they are stuck in a permanent identity of "victim" in their own mind or the minds of others. Victims are shielded from confrontation with their offenders by regulations designed to protect them. Congregations mend as best they can and go on.

In the Middle Ages, when church leaders strove to set up rules and systems for maintaining order, there were often elaborate procedures for dealing with infractions. Those causing public scandal by notorious sin might indeed be officially excommunicated, and this in a time and society in which most people deeply believed that outside the church one went straight to hell and eternal torment. To be restored after an offense, the sinner had first to confess, repent, and receive instruction. He or she might be required to stand outside the local church for months or years while others went in to worship. Then he or she might progress to kneeling in the church porch while the victim, the injured family, and the community of faith filed in and out. Only after months or years when the priest or bishop deemed penance sufficient would the offender be allowed into the back of the church and finally restored to communion.

History records how King Henry knelt and was scourged at the tomb of Archbishop Thomas Becket as a public penance for murdering him — and as an avenue for the people and the church to forgive him. As a victim, by the time you have walked past your offender week after week kneeling in humiliation in front of God and everyone, I suspect the hardness of heart and anger dissipate to the point that pity and forgiveness can find room. Our Puritan ancestors had a similar experience when they walked past malefactors held in the stocks on the town square.

We Episcopalians have no modern equivalent to such public penance that would enable the psychic and spiritual journey from rage to forgiveness for all those injured, the identified victim, and the offender, and thus allow the communion of the whole body to be restored. Concerning how often to forgive the offending church member, Jesus said, "Not seven times, but, I tell you, seventy-seven times" (Matt. 18:22). We have no idea how to accomplish this Herculean spiritual task. We fear forgiveness as a form of expunging the bad behavior so as to dishonor the wounds of those harmed and deny the reality of the sin and hurt. In his interview with us, Presiding Bishop Frank Griswold spoke of this process:

> There's a distinction between forgiveness and amendment, and my sense is one always proffers forgiveness if it's sought for, and that's one of the difficulties in some of these instances, but there may be . . . historical consequences that then preclude the forgiveness being articulated in a way that simply restores the offender to whatever position they held in the life of the church. . . . The capacity of the community to accept you trustfully again has been so shattered by the historical reality of what happened that you can't [go back into your position again]. Though you can be forgiven and you certainly can be reconciled to the life of the body of Christ, you cannot exercise that ministry of trust and leadership again because of the pain suffered by the community.

Our ancestors in faith were wise in recognizing that there were a series of steps to move from injury to forgiveness, for both sinner and community. For the offender these included admission and confession of sin; contrition — looking backward and seeing the pain of the injury to others and being sorry; compunction — feeling the pain and sorrow of it; commitment to amendment of life; repentance — a willingness to make amends and turn again to Christ; penance — the making of amends by actual or symbolic humiliation, labor, and restitution; and receiving absolution and being restored to full communion in the community. The victims moved from outrage and grief at injury, to receiving restitution and witnessing penance — even to getting *tired* of witnessing penance and having it at last feel like *enough* — to confession of their own wrongdoing or complicity, to allowing the offender back into the margins of their lives to begin to rebuild trust, to final forgiveness and communion. The process took years. It took the collaboration of offender, victim, priest, and community staying in some relationship with each other to accomplish it. The ugly reality stayed right in front of everyone like the image of the yellow-striped, manacled chain gang cleaning up the roadside in a Southern town. I suspect such systems enabled genuine forgiveness in a way that neither our hygienic, politically correct, liberal-psychological systems nor our harsh banishing and executing conservative systems can do.

Twelve-step recovery programs have outlined an effective program for working through a sense of victimization, sinfulness, and the need to take responsibility and act to reconnect with community. One of the strengths of that model, and also of our biblical tradition of universal sinfulness, is that not only the identified offender but also the identified victim and the whole community are called to mutual responsibility and reminded of shared frailty. Disciplinary approaches in our church often assume that the victim is naive, weak, and in need of complete protection, entirely innocent of any responsibility or the need to consider what brought him or her to the situation of victimization. Structures of the church and persons in authority within them tend to be cast in the role of rescuer and savior without regard to their own sinfulness and imperfection. The church community also tends to be regarded as offended against without consideration of its complex role in the shared web of sinfulness that led to an offense. Out of our common plight comes our call to common prayer to the One who is Savior and Reconciler.

On the part of all concerned, it takes courage — that old-fashioned cardinal virtue of fortitude in all its nuances — to accomplish forgiveness and reconciliation. It also first requires grace. We do not get there on our own, for on our own we remain stuck in anger, scorn, alienation, and despair.

In this matter of sin and forgiveness, I maintain that our *Book of Common Prayer* of 1979 needs augmentation. Episcopalians in nearly every Eucharist and daily office make a "Confession of Sin," acknowledging sin in thought, word, and deed, things done and left undone, and (in the language retained from the previous prayer books) that we have "followed the devices and desires of our own hearts." The prayer book also contains two forms for the "Reconciliation of a Penitent," formerly called "Private Confession," which use similar language and allow a penitent to name particular sins to God and a confessor, to receive direction and counsel, and absolution. The rite states that it is the presence of God in the heart and on the lips that makes confession possible. The rubrics for both rites require that the penitent "has given evidence of due contrition." In one form of the rite the penitent must declare, "I firmly intend amendment of life and I humbly beg forgiveness of God and his Church." The other form gives the penitent these words: "I have squandered the inheritance of your saints and have wandered far in a land that is waste. . . . I confess to you [God] and to the Church. . . . I turn again in sorrow and repentance," and requires that penitents "turn again to Christ as [their] Lord" and "forgive those who have sinned against [them]."

What is lacking from these two forms for "Reconciliation of a Penitent" and from public, congregational "Confession of Sin" is a liturgical rite and pastoral practice that acknowledges the breach sin causes in the whole community and moves all the estranged parties through steps of restoration toward communal reconciliation. Episcopalians tend to believe that "as we pray, so shall we live." The omission in our prayer becomes incarnate in a failure in our common life to accomplish reconciliation beyond the private level. Sin is seldom private. It cuts to the heart of community and often needs communal remedy beyond forms our church has provided.

In a teleconference called "Come and See" that was downlinked across the Episcopal Church in 1998, Presiding Bishop Griswold said, "We are for one another's salvation. . . . I need the extension of the incarnation in concrete lives of those I've not chosen but God has given me as fellow members." If we are members of a church that is not a voluntary society but an extension of the incarnation convened by God, then it is a matter of great urgency that we attend to the methodology of reconciliation, "since all have sinned and fall short of the glory of God" (Rom. 3:23) and will surely go on doing so. In a denomination that stresses God's incarnation and atoning work in Jesus, the stories of our scandals and failures must be told as part of the living testimony of God's activity among us. We need not fear them. We would like them to fall into silence and avoid the further embarrassment their airing brings. They are crucial in our history, however, as stories of God's power over sin, stories of the resilience of Christ's body the church, and stories of resurrection and hope.

tructuring a Confessional Church for

e Global Age: Admission to Communion

the Lutheran Church–Missouri Synod

l Marschke

H istorically, the Lutheran Church–Missouri Synod (LC-MS) has restricted admission to Holy Communion to those who are either parishioners of the synod or members of a church body in formal fellowship with it, with some exceptions made for pastoral discretion in particular cases.[1] In 1997 the Florida-Georgia District of the synod affirmed "the right of its pastors and congregations to welcome to the Lord's Table those who, regardless of denominational affiliation, share our confession of Christ and our conviction of what He freely offers in the Eucharist."[2] This resolution expressed the spirit of a prior document circulated in the district, *A Declaration of Eucharistic Understanding and Practice,* namely: "Scripture imposes no denominational requirement on baptized Christians who accept the Real Presence and are able to examine themselves and desire to receive the Body and Blood of Christ offered in the Lord's Supper."[3]

The reasons for the action of the Florida-Georgia District are too com-

1. The Missouri Synod has patterned its policy after that of most historic Christian communions. See August R. Suelflow, ed., *Walther's Letters* (St. Louis: Concordia, 1981), pp. 57-58, 68, and 125, for early treatments of the issue. Synodical convention minutes of 1967 (2-190), 1969 (3-18), 1981 (3-01), and 1995 (3-08) have reiterated the denomination's policy. The synod's Commission on Theology and Church Relations (CTCR) released reports explaining the policy in *Theology and Practice of the Lord's Supper* (St. Louis: Office of the Secretary, 1983) and *Admission to the Lord's Supper* (St. Louis: Office of the Secretary, 2000).

2. The Lutheran Church–Missouri Synod, *Convention Proceedings, 1998* (St. Louis: Office of the Secretary, 1998), pp. 115-16. See Resolution 3-05, "To Reaffirm Our Practice of Admission to the Lord's Supper."

3. Committee for a Declaration of Eucharistic Understanding and Practice, *A Declaration of Eucharistic Understanding and Practice* (Boca Raton, Fla.: Bishop and List Interests, 1996), p. 4.

plex to analyze at length here, but in the main supporters of the resolution were reacting to a whole set of demographic and cultural changes of the past generation which have affected the composition both of their membership and of their Sunday visitors, and which have made a strict application of close communion policy more difficult.

The Florida-Georgia resolution was perceived as a challenge to the doctrinal position of the denomination. Critics thought it asserted an "open communion" policy and threatened the doctrinal unity and integrity of the synod. The church body reacted. The 1998 convention of the LC-MS resolved that the district's resolution was null and void, adding that the *Declaration of Eucharistic Understanding and Practice* was "inadequate" for addressing the question of admission to the Lord's Supper.[4]

Never has the synod so explicitly declared the action of a district null and void. The action of the synod thereby reraises questions about the duality, if not the dualism, in the relationship between the synod and its thirty-five districts. Some worry about excessive centralization of authority at the denominational level. Others fear that decentralization, or at least the rights and freedoms of congregations, has gone beyond the original intent of the synod in its first constitution in 1847.[5] The close communion matter offers, then, a useful case study in applying confessional theology in a pluralistic society. Can a decentralized organization satisfy the need for pure doctrine? Will a persistent emphasis on purity eventually wear away the local initiative which religious analysts consider essential to the vitality of denominations in the new century? Will, in short, duality degenerate into a destructive dualism?

The two essays that follow call our attention to sociological, anthropological, and theological questions that lie beneath the surface of this controversy. David Carlson, in his organizational case study, asks to what extent ethnicity has led this German community to its historic communion policy. The synod has always been a staunch defender of the Lutheran Confessions, but German ethnicity, too, played a powerful role in shaping the synod and its position on fellowship with other denominations. The synod needs to accommodate changing social structural patterns associated with geographical distribution outside the Midwest and with the rise of an urbanized laity. Additionally, the church body needs to consider whether its categorical definition of fellowship

4. The Lutheran Church–Missouri Synod, *Convention Proceedings, 1998*, pp. 115-16.

5. August R. Suelflow, *Heritage in Motion* (St. Louis: Concordia, 1998), pp. 158-89, has the discussion of recent decades, especially the report of Task Force II to the 1981 synodical convention, which tried to resist the temptations to centralization. Lawrence Rast, Jr., cautions about decentralization in "Demagoguery or Democracy? The Saxon Emigration and American Culture," *Concordia Theological Quarterly* 63 (October 1999): 247-68.

— limiting formal relationships to Christian bodies which are in agreement with the synod's doctrinal standards — will continue to be acceptable to clergy and parishioners in the current evangelical era, in which alliances within evangelical denominations work toward common objectives independently of the denominational structure. The synod has a heritage of congregational empowerment which should allow it to engage fruitfully in such debate, but the question is whether sufficient mutual trust remains in the denomination for a healthy discussion to take place. If the leadership tries to impose a solution, the consequences for the existence of the synod could be very serious, Carlson concludes. He believes that the national convention in 2001 may have taken a step toward reversing a recent emphasis upon centralization.

Eugene Bunkowske, drawing on twenty years of pastoral ministry in Africa, brings the perspective of transactional theology, or theology applied to the messy circumstances of life, to his theological essay. He notes that different persons had different and potentially divisive lenses through which they viewed the word "communion" at the 1998 LC-MS convention. Agreement was lacking on the meaning of such basic labels as "close communion" and "open communion." On the basis of his analysis of this convention, Bunkowske concludes that two communion cultures, or "silos," have been dividing the synod. One silo calls for purity of doctrine and separates the synod from other Christians, while the other welcomes to the communion table Christians from other denominations. A third communion culture nonetheless is offering hope for healing the divisions. The "holistic" communion theology values the Lord's Supper as a communal meal and nurtures mutual love and responsibility among members. To regain this holistic view of communion, according to Bunkowske, two models are available as alternative church structures for the twenty-first century. One adapts communal settings of the apostolic age to our own; the other is a vibrant transactional theology like that of Christians in sub-Saharan Africa.

The organizational case study and theological essay are intended to interject fresh historical, sociological, and theological questions into the ongoing debate in the synod about admission to the Lord's Supper. Since they make observations about ethnic and theological lenses and point up the challenges posed by unrecognized worldviews, let me here hazard the rather subjective venture of trying to identify worldviews.

Sixteenth-century Lutherans no doubt shared with many citizens of the age a simple trust that God is at the center of the universe and that each person has a designated place in the universal chain of being. In the hymns of the century, if nowhere else, one finds these bedrocks of faith. The late Reformation period added to these elements of worldview the zeal for confessional faith. Increasingly, the tone of these confessional statements was defensive and polemical, stemming in part from the violence and insecurity of life in the empire in the generation after Luther.[6]

German small towns may have added their particular ideology to basic Lutheran views of the world emerging from the Reformation. Mack Walker, in his study *In German Hometowns*, traces the exclusivity and quiet localism in these towns of 10,000-15,000 residents. The view was that towns beyond 10,000-15,000 residents would surely include more noncitizens as "tolerated residents" than town fathers thought desirable — illegitimate children, Jews, manual servants, or poor people. Towns were kept small to preserve their intimacy of relationships. Town leaders allowed no penetration of outsiders into their internal affairs, resenting in particular the intrusions of distant governments. Walker argues, in fact, that the German conception of freedom was rooted in the local variety and autonomy of the hometowns, rooted in centuries-old customs and history.[7] Their articles of government maintained the small-town climate. Statutes in Nördlingen, for example, included five main articles covering everything from moral and religious questions, through the prohibition of marriage to outsiders, to police and fire regulations. "Now everyone knows how he shall act," the statutes concluded.[8] In the nineteenth century the small-town spirit was used to fight industrialization and the growing bureaucratic structures in the German states. It became a worldview deeply ingrained in the inhabitants of these towns.[9]

The German emigrants who founded the Missouri Synod, consequently, were a tightly knit group. Their community was bonded by zeal for confessional purity, above all, which separated them from other Lutherans and other Christians. The 1854 synodical convention put it with customary Missourian frankness: "Strangers cannot become members of synod unless they can properly identify themselves in respect to doctrine and life."[10]

6. Robert Kolb has an excellent discussion of the confessing period of the sixteenth century in his *Confessing the Faith: Reformers Define the Church, 1530-1580* (St. Louis: Concordia, 1991). See especially chaps. 4–5.

7. Mack Walker, *In German Hometowns: Community, State, and General Estate, 1648-1871* (Ithaca, N.Y.: Cornell University Press, 1971), pp. 17-20. Johann Moser listed 139 towns with their customary rights against princes, taking three hundred pages to describe their rights.

8. Walker, *In German Hometowns*, p. 43.

9. The Biedermeier style left its imprint on the hometown. "Its unique quality among styles, though, was its provincial homeliness and quiet social familiarity. It was a style of withdrawal . . . from the massing of forces and the pervasiveness of change that marked public consciousness of the nineteenth century from its beginning" (Walker, *In German Hometowns*, p. 307). More concisely, Walker refers to the "hometown principle of enclosed familiarity." See chap. 10 for this discussion. For the statistics on the number of towns, see p. 32.

10. C. S. Meyer, ed., *Moving Frontiers: Readings in the History of the Lutheran Church–Missouri Synod* (St. Louis: Concordia, 1964), p. 150.

More generally known than the influence of the German small town is the importance of pietism to the founding fathers of the Missouri Synod. German pietism of the seventeenth and eighteenth centuries, taking a cue from Philipp Spener, emphasized the subjective, experiential dimensions of Christian life above the objective, doctrinal formulations of the church. The early nineteenth century experienced a revival of pietism across Germany. C. F. W. Walther, later to become the first president of the Missouri Synod, but unconverted in his university years, joined a circle of pietist students to pray and read the Bible. Walther acknowledged that the literature in the group was pietist and often legalistic. Wilhelm Sihler, the first vice president of the synod, and F. C. D. Wyneken, the second president, acknowledged close connections with pietism in the Old World.[11]

Pietism contributed to German romanticism. Romanticism in Germany appealed more to the community than to the individual, reinforcing the close community of small German towns. Of particular interest is the fact that German romantics in the early nineteenth century emphasized the fundamental value of the German language, which was more to them than a medium of communication. The German language plumbed the depths of the soul and expressed the deepest elements of human nature. "What is there more characteristic of man, or of greater importance to him," asked Friedrich Schlegel, "than language?"[12] Language was the expression of the psyche of a people and of their culture. It communicated their deepest emotions and traditions.

Not surprisingly, then, the emigrant leaders who later formed the Missouri Synod were adamant about preserving the German language, fearing that the Lutheran faith might not survive without its German doctrinal and liturgical sources. Article 14 of the constitution of Trinity Lutheran Congregation in St. Louis, Walther's parish, called for the sole use of German in worship. Walther fought unsuccessfully to have the article made irrevocable.[13]

Wilhelm Loehe, the Bavarian pastor who supplied the Missourians with German pastors for much of the nineteenth century, was, if anything, more passionate than Walther and his Saxons about the use of the German language. Giving instructions to emigrant clergy commissioned to America, Loehe described the ideal German candidate as one who "recognizes the full importance of the German language for the *German faith* if we, without being misunder-

---

11. Walter A. Baepler, *A Century of Grace: Missouri Synod, 1847-1947* (St. Louis: Concordia, 1947), pp. 42, 54, 76.

12. Koppel Pinson, *Modern Germany,* 2nd ed. (New York: Macmillan, 1966), p. 46.

13. Gerhard Mundinger, *Government in the Missouri Synod: The Genesis of Decentralized Government in the Missouri Synod* (St. Louis: Concordia, 1947), pp. 143-44.

stood, can call the faith of the Evangelical Lutheran Church German. . . . Over there German language and customs are the vanguard of the Evangelical Lutheran faith."[14]

True, there were increasing numbers in the Missouri Synod, laity and clergy alike, who advocated the greater use of English. Walther himself devoted serious efforts to uniting American Lutheranism. Still, one would expect little enthusiasm from the membership for these efforts when ethnic differences remained vivid and the English language was thought to communicate both cultural and spiritual dangers for confessional truth.

By the early twentieth century, largely because of World War I, the tensions aroused by the language question became less overt. Still, the Missouri Synod remained something of a German island in an American sea, and the language accommodation was the tip of the iceberg as this German church struggled to make pure doctrine come alive in the changing, complex circumstances of ministry on local levels. Second- and third-generation German Lutherans on the front lines of mission and ministry had to figure out what was German and what was Lutheran about their witness and work.

The tensions in these matters could often be seen in the way the synod organized itself for its work. A duality of structure emerged, more by accident than by design: centralization in matters of doctrine, decentralization in other matters. When the synod, in 1854, created four districts and tried to explain the distribution of responsibilities between itself and its districts, it retained the role of guarding its doctrine and left to the districts and congregations the specific programs and ministries of the church.[15] Such a division of responsibilities was not explicit nor was it intended — the districts were intended to be extensions of the synod in their geographical areas, not autonomous units — but by the mid–twentieth century districts were quite sure that while the synod in St. Louis focused on doctrine, trained clergy and teachers, and undertook some mission endeavors or other activities that could not be handled well locally, the districts did "the real work" of the kingdom. And what was "the real work" of the church?

Over and over again districts and congregations, and sometimes other independent associations like the Lutheran Laymen's League, took the initiative in ministry, and the synod rather counted on them to do so. For example, Trinity Society in Buffalo, New York, invited youth from around the synod to attend an organizational meeting in 1891.[16] Thus was born in 1893, the Walther League.

14. Meyer, *Moving Frontiers*, p. 99, emphasis mine.
15. Meyer, *Moving Frontiers*, pp. 159ff.
16. Baepler, *A Century of Grace*, p. 210.

The Lutheran Education Society and the Northern Illinois District joined forces to begin a teachers college in River Forest in 1912.[17]

This pattern of decentralization was no more evident than in mission work, both in the United States and overseas. Professor E. L. Arndt in 1912 could hardly contain his chagrin with the synod over the opening of a China mission. He wanted to initiate the work, but synod argued that it should take the lead. Arndt complained: "The history of our synod . . . glitters with enterprises which were first begun in smaller circles and then were taken over by synod. . . . Practically all progress we can record has first been planned and begun in smaller circles. . . . Why should we not rather permit even individual congregations to send out missionaries to the heathen?" Synodical officials gave in and, grudgingly, allowed Arndt to do his work in China.[18]

More often the synod seemed almost relieved to have local units, whether districts or congregations, take the initiative. Districts therefore became more closely associated in the popular mind with congregations than with the national level. The Synodical Survey Commission, created by the 1959 San Francisco convention of the Missouri Synod to study synod-district relations, observed that synod was in absolute control of doctrinal matters. In theological concerns the synod's relation to the districts was rigid; in all other matters it was tolerant. In financial affairs it seemed almost to "bargain" with the districts — it "petitioned" them or "recommended" to them.[19] Given this informal relationship between the national and local levels, the synod did not commit itself to a national bureaucracy until after World War II, some years after other Protestant bodies were organizing themselves on the model of corporate America.

One measure of the centralizing tendencies in the history of the LC-MS is the reliance on executive authority in times of difficulty. The founders of the synod, struggling to sustain their church on the American frontier, not the most congenial environment to doctrinal purity, anchored supervision of doctrine and life in the president's office. It did not hurt that Walther was that pres-

17. Baepler, *A Century of Grace,* p. 224. Very helpful coverage of the centralization-decentralization issue up to 1960 is offered by a series of reports from the Synodical Survey Commission to the synodical convention. See August R. Suelflow, "The District Relations of the Lutheran Church–Missouri Synod in Historical Perspective" (Reports A-C), hereafter cited as SSC. The author worked with a set of manuscript copies rather than printed and published versions. The commission was worried about loose controls of the synod over its districts, which seemed to be more in evidence as they wrote their reports, but on the other hand they did not advocate centralization in St. Louis, either. Their advice was cooperation between the two levels, also with the third administrative level, the circuits within the districts.

18. Meyer, *Moving Frontiers,* pp. 306-7, citing Arndt in his *Missionsbriefe I,* February 1912, pp. 19-23.

19. Suelflow, SSC, Unpublished Report 2B, pp. 53-54.

ident, for he was considered the champion of confessional Lutheran theology by his fellow emigrants. The revised constitution of 1854 again instructed President Wyneken "to see to it" that district presidents and other synodical leaders spoke and worked in accordance with the synodical constitution.[20]

In the second half of the twentieth century, the environment for ministry changed dramatically, and the structure of the church struggled to keep pace. Intertwined with issues of centralization and decentralization was a distinct question of the dual mentalities of preservation and mission outreach. The 1960s were the watershed in synodical history. This decade raised serious moral, social, and doctrinal questions for the synod. The Mission Affirmations (Detroit synodical convention, 1965) questioned the preservation mode of doing Christ's ministry. The mission of the congregation was to send its people out into the world — into that world of drugs and war and murder and civil rights, and above all into the workplace, that is, the places where lay Christians were to live out their Christian vocation.[21] The mentality of pure doctrine needed objective standards and clear assertions with which a closely knit band of Lutherans could sustain itself in a pluralistic society; the mentality of mission work, by way of distinction, was to make doctrine a living, active thing in the hope of rescuing desperate people from the excesses of the postmodern world.

In the 1960s and 1970s the two mentalities of preservation and outreach went to war with each other. President J. A. O. Preus II led the fight to uphold synod's doctrine of Scripture. Ready and willing to exercise his presidential power for the cause, he confronted the faculty of Concordia Seminary (St. Louis), which had been accused for at least fifteen years of being too open, too liberal, and too modern, particularly in its exegesis of Scripture. His blunt presidential style offended moderates in the synod but reassured his supporters. When at the New Orleans convention (1973) President Preus argued that "someone in this church ought to have authority to determine how we today interpret, confess our Lutheran faith," a delegate defended him against his angry critics: "If that's a popish statement, then let Missouri rejoice in such a pope! After all, we don't want any more questions, we want answers — and we're getting them."[22] The synod repudiated the leadership of its prize seminary and, directly or indirectly, limited the initiative of its other educational institutions as well.

Historically, then, one set of voices in the LC-MS has emphasized the pu-

---

20. Meyer, *Moving Frontiers*, pp. 159ff.

21. The Lutheran Church–Missouri Synod, *Convention Workbook* (St. Louis: Office of the Secretary, 1965), pp. 113-40.

22. Suelflow, *Heritage in Motion*, p. 26.

rity of the gospel: only if doctrine is kept pure and sound will the gospel survive. Other voices in the church, particularly in the twentieth century, have given increasing attention to the mission of the gospel, such as the overseas mission, or the mission of mercy among the sick and poor, or evangelistic outreach and witness, or family life ministry. It is the thesis of this essay that the energies being devoted to mission and ministry on the district and congregational levels, and in other synod-wide corporate entities, have unwittingly posed a challenge to the traditional emphasis on doctrine, raising questions for the life and outreach of the church that the dogmas of the church are not designed to answer. This challenge has in turn skewed the debate on centralization and decentralization, as well as on the relationship of the clergy and laity in achieving the purposes of the synod. As they operated after 1965, these two mentalities of preservation of doctrine and gospel outreach — always in tension with each other but rarely in conflict — became more competitive than complementary. The conflict led to increasing debate about the need for greater centralization to control districts and congregations whose "transactional" theology seemed at variance with the goal of pure doctrine.

The heritage and precedent exist in the LC-MS to keep these two mentalities in balance — pure doctrine and mission energy. Both are needed to penetrate a changing culture, and both benefit from the balance between forces of centralization and forces of localism. Walther, in 1848, cautioned that if submission to all synodical orders were the prerequisite for membership in the synod, "the exercise of our power would have laid the foundation for constant dissatisfaction."[23] The trouble, as Walther perceived, is the ease with which duality can degenerate into a hard dualism. Already in 1862, H. C. Schwan, then president of the Central District, observed about the synod that "the greater danger is still in the direction of legalism."[24]

The Missouri Synod has adequate structures in place to carry on its religious work on national, district, and local levels, if it will use effectively and evangelically what it has. The challenge for the synod is to hold in healthy tension the dualities of preservation and growth, clerical and lay leadership, centralization and decentralization. These forces need to breathe into denominational order, if that is possible, a mutuality of spirit and a genuine commitment of members one to another — in short, they need to serve the community of saints. The case study and essay that follow, each in its own way, steer the

---

23. Meyer, *Moving Frontiers*, contains the full text of the address.

24. Thesis 18 of a set of thirty-two theses which Schwan presented to the Central District of the Missouri Synod in 1862, cited in *Forward*, February 1998, pp. 4-5, under the title "Celebrating Synod's Sesquicentennial: Voices from Missouri's Past."

church's conversation about admission to Holy Communion toward the essential task of building community in the church. Luther could not have been more on target for this purpose: "The significance or purpose of this sacrament is the fellowship of the saints, whence it derives its common name, that is, *synaxis* or *communio,* that is, fellowship."[25]

25. Martin Luther, "The Blessed Sacrament of the Holy and True Body of Christ, and the Brotherhoods" (1519), in *Luther's Works,* vol. 35, ed. Theodore Bachmann (Philadelphia: Muhlenberg, 1960), p. 50.

Fellowship and Communion in the Postmodern Era: The Case of the Lutheran Church–Missouri Synod

David L. Carlson

I n the summer of 1834 a young German theologian arrived in Baltimore. Having completed his university education, Friedrich C. D. Wyneken had arrived in North America to minister to German Lutheran immigrants. Shortly after his arrival, Wyneken wandered into a revival meeting. Asked how he liked it, Wyneken is said to have replied: "Whether it is of God or of the devil, I don't know, but it certainly is not Lutheran."[1]

Fellowship and Communion in the Missouri Synod

Wyneken had an understanding of what it meant to be Lutheran, and evangelical revivalism didn't fit that understanding. Wyneken's response and his subsequent ministry clearly indicate that he did not view the participants in that revival meeting as being in fellowship with the body of believers who called themselves Lutheran. To understand his response, we need some understanding of the place of revivalism in American Christianity, but more importantly, we need to understand Wyneken's understanding of what it meant to be Lutheran. Now, at the turn of a new century, it is helpful to ask if the way in which Wyneken and other early Lutheran pioneers understood fellowship is still ap-

1. Erich H. Heintzen, *Prairie School of the Prophets: The Anatomy of a Seminary, 1846-1976* (St. Louis: Concordia, 1989), p. 18.

The author thanks the Lilly Foundation for underwriting this research and the Hartford Institute for Religion Research at Hartford Seminary for coordinating the Organizing Religious Work project. I am indebted to Eugene Bunkowske, Paul Marschke, John Kayser, and especially Ken Schurb for their helpful comments.

propriate. Is it still clear that contemporary evangelicals are not in fellowship with the contemporary body of confessional Lutherans?[2]

Different understandings of what it means to be in fellowship are central to a current conflict within the Lutheran Church–Missouri Synod (LC-MS), one of the two largest synods of Lutherans in America.[3] While differing understandings of fellowship are exhibited in many forms, this case study examines a judicatory challenge to the historical definition of fellowship posed by one of the districts of this body and the reaction of the central judicatory authority to this challenge. The issue is communion, and the conflict is over who ought properly be invited to share the sacrament.

2. Contemporary revivalism is closely allied with evangelicalism. The current revivalistic movement is viewed in this paper, in part, as a response to postmodern relativism. Timothy George, a senior editor of *Christianity Today,* defines modern evangelicalism this way: "Seen historically, evangelicalism is a renewal movement within historic Christian orthodoxy. Its theology and piety have been enriched by many diverse tributaries, including Puritanism, pietism, and Pentecostalism, but its sense of identity as a distinctive faith community, what we might call the evangelical tradition, has been shaped decisively by three major episodes: the Protestant Reformation, the Evangelical Awakening, and the Fundamentalist-Modernist Controversy" ("If I'm an Evangelical, What Am I?" *Christianity Today,* August 9, 1999, p. 62). I am persuaded that a fourth element is instrumental to contemporary evangelical revival. The emergence of relativism, as a dominant cultural force at the close of the century, has spawned a counterreaction that has coalesced around modern evangelicalism. This counterreaction is manifested as a renewed emphasis on biblical inerrancy as an alternative to relativism. In this renewed emphasis on biblical inerrancy, confessional Lutherans and modern evangelicals have found common ground.

3. The Evangelical Lutheran Church in America (ELCA) is the other. The LC-MS for the past 150 years has understood itself to be the more representative synod of confessional Lutheranism in America. While all Lutheran synods are confessional in the sense that they trace their identity to the historic confessions of the sixteenth century, the LC-MS emerged as a self-conscious coalition of Lutherans whose primary mission was the preservation of these confessions. The antecedent synods of the ELCA generally acknowledged this as Missouri's primary mission, and referencing the LC-MS as the primary defender of orthodoxy (often described pejoratively as "dead orthodoxy"), were more likely to define their mission evangelically.

As used in this paper, "confessional" denotes an emphasis that has divided American Lutherans since early in the nineteenth century. "Confessional" denotes a repristination emphasis on adherence to the sixteenth-century symbols of the Reformation. Particular emphasis is given to the Augsburg Confession and Luther's *Small Catechism,* but Missouri Lutheranism also references Luther's *Large Catechism,* the Apology to the Augsburg Confession, the Smalcald Articles, and the Formula of Concord as the confessional symbols of historic Lutheranism. Lutheranism in America has often divided on the issue of the sufficiency of the sixteenth-century symbols. "Confessional Lutheranism" in this sense denotes a more conservative orientation that defends the sufficiency of these symbols as opposed to others who view the historic confessions as more advisory and less binding.

Fellowship and Denominational Affiliation

At its triennial convention in 1997, the Florida-Georgia District of the LC-MS adopted a resolution which recommended that district pastors and congregations welcome to the Lord's Table all individuals who, *regardless of denominational affiliation*, shared the confession of the Eucharist articulated in the historic confessions of the Lutheran church. This resolution was predicated on a position paper produced by the Committee for a Declaration of Eucharistic Understanding and Practice, a group of pastors within the district who had organized to challenge the historical LC-MS practice of "close (or closed)" communion. The following summer, at its 1998 convention, the national governing body of the LC-MS declared that the rationale utilized by the committee to support the resolution was inappropriate. Finding the committee's rationale and the resulting district resolution contrary to synodical resolutions, the delegates to the synodical convention declared the Florida-Georgia resolution "null and void."

This conflict reflects a division within the synodical membership that has multiple implications but one central question: What does it mean to be in fellowship? This case study examines the organizational structure of the LC-MS through the window of this question, and the related issue of how the LC-MS might resolve the issue of who ought to be invited to the communion table.

Fellowship: Categorical Membership versus Collective Conscience

The word "fellowship" means different things to different people. It is a term commonly used in LC-MS polity. Historically, LC-MS directives define fellowship in reference to the body of believers who embrace confessional Lutheranism. More specifically, when used in this context, fellowship generally refers to incorporated bodies of believers. Thus, the LC-MS officially recognizes a number of organized church bodies which are deemed to be in fellowship with the synod. In this sense fellowship is defined categorically. Confessional Lutheranism has been understood by the LC-MS to be a fellowship of believers who have organized to extend the legacy of the Reformation. Fellowship, therefore, is the body of believers who embrace the full exposition of the faith as defined by the sixteenth-century Reformers. More specifically, fellowship implies submission to and conformity with a comprehensive exposition of the Lutheran Confessions. Membership in a congregation affiliated with the LC-MS, or with another organization similarly committed to the preservation of the confessions, has historically been defined as the necessary condition to be considered "in fellowship." Being in fellowship, as so defined, has been viewed as a necessary precondition for participation in the Eucharist. This is the policy of close(d) communion.

It is the above definition of fellowship that is challenged by the Committee for a Declaration of Eucharistic Understanding and Practice's rejection of it as a precondition for sharing in the sacrament. In the process, the committee redefined what it means to be in fellowship, replacing denominational affiliation with a personal understanding of the sacrament as the appropriate criterion for participation in the sacrament.

In rejecting categorical membership as a necessary condition for participation in the sacrament, the committee has in principle redefined fellowship to include all believers who believe they agree with the Lutheran understanding of the sacrament. While retaining the historically Lutheran understanding of the sacrament, the committee's criterion accentuates personal autonomy and subjective association as the primary criterion for fellowship.

It is these differing understandings of fellowship that are at the center of the conflict over communion policy, a policy which historically the LC-MS has called "close (or closed)[4] communion." Using a more individualized and subjective understanding of fellowship, the views of a new generation of Lutherans conflict with a more traditional view of fellowship.

To set the stage for examining this conflict, we need to look at how the LC-MS arrived at its policy of close(d) communion, and to understand this we need to return to 1834.

The Emergence of the Lutheran Church–Missouri Synod

Friedrich C. D. Wyneken would emerge as a key architect of confessional Lutheranism in America.[5] He along with other nineteenth-century German pi-

---

4. The current conflict over communion is reflected in disagreement as to the proper terminology to describe existing policy. Is the existing LC-MS policy one of "close communion" or of "closed communion"? "Close communion" accentuates commonality of agreement with the historical Lutheran doctrinal understanding of the Lord's Supper. "Closed communion" accentuates exclusivity. While the terms are not mutually exclusive, each implies a different emphasis. The former is more subjective, the latter is more categorical. In this sense this contested ground is reflective of the conflict addressed in this paper.

5. "Confessional Lutheranism" is understood here as a doctrinal orientation that embraces the historic confessions of the Reformation church as the foundation for contemporary church polity. Article II of the Confession Constitution of the LC-MS states that

oneers, especially C. F. W. Walther and Wilhelm Sihler, would create a church that would become the LC-MS. For these men, emigrants primarily from Saxony and Prussia, America represented the best, and perhaps the last, hope of preserving confessional Lutheranism. Wyneken and his colleagues had departed a Europe where the Lutheran Confessions were enduring a frontal assault by the state. For these German pioneers, far more was at stake than simply ministering to emigrants to the New World. The foundations of the church itself were under attack.[6]

The emigration was in response to the coerced union of Reformed and Lutheran Christians in Germany into a single state-established church.[7] This unionized church was more Reformed than Lutheran, and the governments of

---

The Synod, and every member of the Synod, accepts without reservation:

1. The Scriptures of the Old and New Testament as the written Word of God and the only rule and norm of faith and of practice;
2. All the Symbolical Books of the Evangelical Lutheran Church as a true and unadulterated statement and exposition of the Word of God, to wit: the three Ecumenical Creeds (the Apostles' Creed, the Nicene Creed, the Athanasian Creed), the Unaltered Augsburg Confession, the Apology of the Augsburg Confession, the Smalcald Articles, the Large Catechism of Luther, the Small Catechism of Luther, and the Formula of Concord.

6. Writing to an American missionary in 1844, Loehe provided this instruction: "A German Lutheran Candidate for the ministry who, like you, is ordained under the circumstances prevailing in North America recognizes the full importance of the German Language for the German faith, if we, without being misunderstood, can call the faith of the Evangelical Lutheran Church German. Therefore you will conclude no union with congregations which would allow room for English in the office of the ministry and in instruction. Over there German language and customs are the vanguard of the Evangelical Lutheran faith" (August R. Suelflow, "Beginnings of 'Missouri, Ohio, and Other States,'" in *Moving Frontiers: Readings in the History of the Lutheran Church–Missouri Synod,* ed. Carl S. Meyer [St. Louis: Concordia, 1964], p. 99).

7. Friedrich Wilhelm III, the Prussian monarch, was a Calvinist, but he governed a people who were largely Lutheran. In an attempt to reconcile the confessional differences between himself and his people, Wilhelm ordered the creation of the United Evangelical Church in 1830. The confessional practice of this unionized church largely reflected the influence of rationalist and idealist principles. In 1830 German nationhood was still emerging from the medieval alliance of Germanic principalities. Prussia was the largest and most powerful of these principalities, and the combined threat of Wilhelm and Napoleon was rapidly fusing a new sense of German nationhood. Thus, rationalism and idealism were largely associated with the Napoleonic Wars and the French Revolution. Emergent German identity embraced the Reformation as the primary German contribution to Western civilization. The Reformation was elevated to the level of a national myth, and Luther was embraced as the principal German hero. A renewed interest in Luther's theology and a desire to preserve this idealized German culture largely motivated Wyneken's, and his cohorts', emigration to the United States (Robert C. Schultz, "The European Background," in *Moving Frontiers,* pp. 55-61).

Prussia and Saxony had denied requests from Lutheran pastors to establish an alternative church. The Lutheran pioneers who would establish the LC-MS came to America to preserve a faith they could not preserve in Germany. Their circumstance was not unlike that of the faithful during the Babylonian exile, and like the Israelites, they would seek to preserve a culture that nourished the faith in the midst of a foreign culture. To understand contemporary conflict within the LC-MS, it is necessary to understand the context from which these early pioneers emerged and the conditions they faced on the American frontier in the early nineteenth century. They brought with them a deep suspicion of emergent church forms and a powerful sense of a German Lutheran identity. This suspicion of religious "unionism" and an accompanying sense of exclusive fellowship have stamped the character of the LC-MS to this day.[8]

The Europe Wyneken had left behind, when he arrived in Baltimore in 1834, was one that knew only established religion. The established church in Germany was more Calvinist than Lutheran, and Wyneken's primary concern was to establish a church in America grounded on the historical confessions of the Reformation. Another way of saying this is that Wyneken's primary intention was to preserve Lutheran fellowship. Fellowship, as he understood it, was both ethnically German and doctrinally Lutheran. Opposition to revivalism per se was not his central concern. He was far more concerned with establishing a church committed to the preservation of the historical Lutheran Confessions than he was with entering into dialogue with evangelicals to resolve doctrinal issues. The Lutheran church Wyneken found when he arrived in America exhibited, for him, too many of the same rationalistic elements German Lutherans had come to associate with Enlightenment thought and Reformed theology. Wyneken wanted to create a church where none of these existed.

Understanding the juxtaposition of German nationalism and Lutheran doctrine, in the creation of this church, is central to understanding the way Wyneken and the other LC-MS pioneers envisioned fellowship. Wyneken, as would Walther and Sihler, championed throughout his life the need to preserve German as the language of discourse within the Lutheran church. Their justification for doing this was the inadequacy of English translations of the liturgy, but these pioneers viewed that which was truly Lutheran as essentially German. For these men fellowship was closely linked to ethnicity. Later Missouri Lutherans might grant fellowship to non-Germans, but they retained the sense that

---

8. The term "unionism" is part of the LC-MS lexicon. As used in the LC-MS, the term originated in reference to the creation of the United Evangelical Church of Prussia, commonly called the Prussian Union. The term is now commonly used to indicate any form of ecumenical cooperation with church bodies not officially recognized as being in fellowship with the LC-MS.

fellowship was categorical. With time, the understanding of fellowship was transformed, although never entirely, from being German to being LC-MS.

Shortly after Wyneken's arrival in America, a cadre of Lutheran clergy would respond to his lead and follow him from Germany to North America. They came to shepherd the growing flock of immigrants, who on the western frontier were often lured from their Lutheran heritage by itinerant evangelicalism, at this time primarily in the form of Methodism. Accordingly, upon arriving in America, Wyneken began an urgent appeal to the church in his homeland to send these missionaries. Wilhelm Loehe would hear of Wyneken's appeal in Bavaria and dedicate his life to recruiting and equipping missionaries for the American frontier. One of these missionaries was Wilhelm Sihler. Over the next several decades Wyneken, Loehe, and Sihler would build a body of believers in North America that would eventually be organized as the Lutheran Church–Missouri Synod.

In Europe the enemy of confessional Lutheranism had been the state. The German Lutheran pioneers faced no such obstacle in America. As they began to build their church on the American frontier, they encountered a new enemy. Roving evangelists were stealing the scattered sheep. The German Lutheran immigrant farmers and tradesmen on the frontier were, in the absence of the "true" church, being gathered by sectarian circuit riders. If we view the Methodist campaign on the western frontier as the nineteenth-century corollary of modern evangelicalism, it can be argued that the LC-MS, to a large degree, emerged as an organized attempt to advance historical confessional Lutheranism in the face of evangelical sectarianism.

The LC-MS emerged out of a desire to preserve and advance a North American church dedicated to preserving the doctrines articulated by the sixteenth-century Lutheran reformers. While the nineteenth-century German Lutheran pioneers viewed evangelical Methodism as the primary opponent to confessional Lutheranism, we must raise the question of the degree to which their opposition to the Methodists was driven by opposition to evangelical worship, and the degree to which it was driven by distrust of a church that was both English and sectarian. This is not to say that worship forms were unimportant to nineteenth-century Lutherans. On the contrary, they were central to Lutheran identity. But Lutheran liturgical forms would emerge as a way of distinguishing the German Lutheran church from its sectarian rivals. This point is key in understanding the current conflict within the LC-MS. It matters whether communion practice emerged as part of liturgical practice intended to demarcate German Lutheran ethnic identity, or whether traditional communion practice is central to the Lutheran confessional understanding of the sacrament.

Contemporary conflict in the LC-MS is now, to a large degree, a conflict

David L. Carlson

between evangelical and traditional advocates within the church.⁹ The LC-MS emerged in a context of sectarian conflict that threatened the very existence of confessional Lutheranism.¹⁰ The LC-MS pioneers, understandably, were militant in defending close fellowship. But for better or worse, the historical context from which the LC-MS emerged has ever since encouraged a culture within the synod that is suspicious of unionism and inclined toward exclusion. Fellowship is not easily granted in the LC-MS, and the conditions for recognizing fellowship have ever since reflected the pioneers' errand on the American frontier.

The motivation of these pioneers is beyond reproach. Their singular errand was to preserve the historic confessions of the Evangelical Lutheran Church and to preserve the legacy of the Reformation. We have no cause to question their motivations, and still less to suggest that their religious zealotry was a cover for jingoism. But for these pioneers Evangelical Lutheranism was

9. While this paper will focus on the purported conflict between modern evangelicalism and historic confessional Lutheranism, the current conflict is being played out in the wake of another conflict. That conflict, which led to a split of the synod in the 1970s, was also over the understanding of confessional Lutheranism and focused on the proper Lutheran understanding of biblical inerrancy. Principals to that dispute differ as to whether those who departed the synod or those who remained were the true representatives of confessional Lutheranism. I will have more to say about this later. While this paper will focus on the impact of modern evangelicalism on the application of the historic Lutheran understanding of the Sacrament of the Altar, this conflict could as well be viewed as an extension of the earlier conflict. That dispute, as well as this, is about disagreement over the meaning of the Lutheran Confessions. At no point should it be forgotten that the communion table is an important battle, but in a much larger war.

10. In the nineteenth century the Lutheran reaction to Methodism was largely articulated as rejection of sectarianism, which is to say, of sectarianism per se. How and to what degree the German Lutheran pioneers were particularly offended by Methodist doctrine is not clear and not particularly important. The LC-MS emerged through the efforts of people who had no concept of anything other than a nationally established church. For these people the Lutheran church was a German church. The pioneers of the LC-MS insisted that German be the language of discourse in the church because, they said, there was no adequate translation of the liturgy available in English. This was probably true, but the preservation of a German Lutheran church was far more than a utilitarian attempt to preserve the best available translations of the liturgy. German identity was at the heart of the emergent church. The Methodists were, of course, largely English. But there is reason to doubt that the conflict with the Methodists was primarily a reflection of doctrinal disagreements. Paul Marschke has observed that there was no similar reaction to the Anglican/Episcopalian church, and offers the suggestion that nineteenth-century German Lutherans were comfortable with the idea of an established English church. The Methodist church was never established. In addition, the Methodists were making converts among German immigrants. One must question to what degree the hostility to frontier Methodism was discomfort with evangelical Christianity per se, and to what degree it was a reaction to sectarianism.

the "German faith," and English transformations were likely vehicles for creeping unionism. They had seen how the erosive tendencies of American Lutheranism had impacted an earlier generation of German immigrants and compromised the integrity of the historic confessions. The LC-MS was born in the midst of an assault which came from two directions. From behind, they were under attack from a church-state alliance in Europe that would replace the historical confessions with Reformed doctrine. At the front, they encountered an alliance of English sectarianism and rationalistic Lutheranism in America. It would be a mistake to minimize the climate of siege, and the resulting sense of urgency to preserve confessional Lutheranism, from which the LC-MS emerged.

Heritage and Ethnicity

The current conflict over who should be invited to the communion table centers, as it always has, on the issue of fellowship. LC-MS fellowship in the nineteenth century was largely ethnic in nature. We are using a concept of ethnicity here that is defined not so much by nationalism as by common identity. "Ethnicity," as used here, refers to the tendency of people in modern societies to define themselves in reference to pools of role opposites when faced with the impersonality of mass society. Andrew Greeley has pointed out that European immigrants embraced religious identity in America because it was a meaningful way of differentiating themselves and thereby establishing their own identity.[11] Given the inexorable connection between ethnicity and religion in Europe, embracing one's religious identity was not instrumental to European identity. But it was in America, and while American denominationalism emerged as surrogate to national identity, denominationalism per se tended with time to become the principal measure of ethnicity.

For the LC-MS pioneers, ethnicity was both German and Lutheran. The singular task of the leaders of the first generation of Missouri Lutherans would be to establish a church that would preserve confessional Lutheranism. They were a community of people dedicated to the preservation of *Reine Lehre* (pure doctrine). This, and this alone, defined who they were. This task differentiated them not only from English sectarians but also from an earlier generation of German Lutherans who, from their perspective, had sullied the historical confessions through compromise with Americanisms.

11. Andrew M. Greeley, *The Denominational Society* (Glenview, Ill.: Scott, Foresman, 1972), chap. 5, "Religion as an Ethnic Phenomenon."

For the first generations of Missouri Synod Lutherans there was little distinction between being Lutheran and being German. The identification of later generations of Lutherans with German heritage tended to inexorably wane, but their identification with confessional Lutheranism held firm. The result was that being Lutheran, rather than being German, increasingly defined who they were. And being a Missouri Synod Lutheran meant not only being dedicated to the preservation of the historic confessions, but embracing a linkage to the historic defenders of the faith. German heritage still remains a nostalgic point of reference for many contemporary Lutherans, but it is dedication to *Reine Lehre* that defines them. At the beginning of the twenty-first century, many in the LC-MS, identifying with long family histories, continue to feel a deep connection to this ethnic heritage. This is a heritage which originated in and continues a singular mission to preserve that which is uniquely Lutheran. This is the heritage which spawned and continues to champion close(d) communion. For these Lutherans fellowship is reserved to those who are similarly dedicated.

A growing body of people within the LC-MS have an agenda that is less bound to this heritage. In our highly individualistic age, for another large and emerging segment of the LC-MS fellowship is not understood in this way. For this emergent group, being Lutheran is no less important, but being LC-MS is not their primary identity. For them Lutheranism is more ontological than categorical. To be Lutheran means to emphasize an understanding of Scripture that is differentiated from that which is Reformed, Arminian, or Roman Catholic. On the surface there is no contradiction between ontological Lutheranism and historical Lutheranism; the traditionalists generally embrace the same ontological distinction. It is emphasis that divides. For Lutherans more oriented to postmodernism, faith is more abstract. They emphasize the invisible church and reflect the postmodern inclination to be suspicious of organizations. Fellowship for those of a more postmodern bent is defined within the contours of the invisible church, and those who are viewed as having a common understanding are viewed as being in fellowship — regardless of denominational affiliation. To understand the current conflict in the church, we need to examine this more postmodern understanding of what it means to be Lutheran as well. But before proceeding to this, it would be well to tell the rest of the story of how the LC-MS emerged.

Polity within the Lutheran Church–Missouri Synod

If the cultural climate of the LC-MS was shaped on the frontier of Ohio, Indiana, and Michigan by the Wyneken/Loehe/Sihler vision, we must look farther

west to find the context from which the polity of the church emerged. To anticipate how the current conflict over communion fellowship will be resolved, we
need now to turn to this context.

From its earliest years Lutheranism in America has been divided between
those who would more deliberately maintain a church organization dedicated to
the preservation of the Lutheran Confessions, substantively articulated during
the Reformation, and those who would construct a uniquely American Lutheran
church. Advocates of "American Lutheranism" differed from the advocates of
"confessional Lutheranism" in their attitude toward Luther's role in the Reformation.[12] The former considered themselves nineteenth-century reformers who
believed the Reformation was a work in process, while the latter were more inclined to view the doctrinal position of Luther as final and authoritative.

American Lutherans and confessional Lutherans have created church
structures that reflect their differing orientations toward the role of the church
in addressing culture and in preserving doctrine. Historically, the advocates of
American Lutheranism were more likely to be earlier immigrants, more likely
to be concentrated in the East, and more directly influenced by the social, political, cultural, and economic currents in the United States. Confessional Lutherans were more likely to be later immigrants, and while there were confessional
Lutherans among Scandinavian immigrants, the pioneering founders of the
LC-MS were almost exclusively German. While the Wyneken/Sihler/Loehe men
and their emergent congregations would provide the largest body of believers
in the establishment of the LC-MS, it was a smaller group of Saxon immigrants
associated with C. F. W. Walther who would be the architects of the organizational structure of the synod.[13]

The history of the Saxon Lutherans, who emigrated to Missouri in 1839, is
central to the emergence of the organizational structure of the LC-MS. This
group had essentially been driven out of Germany because of increasing opposition to their leader, Martin Stephan, and also because they opposed the established union of a combined Reformed and Lutheran church. As such, like the
Wyneken/Sihler/Loehe men, they were already predisposed to organize a
church structure in America that would emphasize doctrine that was uniquely
Lutheran. Paradoxically, however, these Saxon Lutherans had formed a church
in Germany that closely resembled what Max Weber describes as a charismatic
sect, a body bound together by the dominating personality of its leader.

12. Jack T. Robinson, "The Spirit of Triumphalism in the Lutheran Church–Missouri
Synod: The Role of the 'A Statement' of 1945 in the Missouri Synod" (Ph.D. diss., Vanderbilt
University, 1972), pp. 10-19.

13. See Earnest T. Bachmann, "The Rise of 'Missouri Lutheranism'" (Ph.D. diss., University of Chicago, 1946).

The Saxons' charismatic leader, Martin Stephan,[14] had assembled a group that was fiercely loyal to him. Before their arrival in America, the leaders of this group had extended jurisdictional power to Stephan that was not only dictatorial in essence, but which challenged the foundational Lutheran understanding of the priesthood of all believers. This "Declaration of Submission" delegated virtually all authority, both temporal and doctrinal, to Stephan and was signed by all the adult members of the group.[15]

Shortly after the Saxons arrived in Missouri, Stephan was deposed for sexual immorality and financial malfeasance, leaving his flock in a condition of disarray. Stephan had surrounded himself with an inner circle of devoted young clergy and theological students, and in the wake of his demise the people turned their anger toward this inner circle. This circumstance left the laity with a profound distrust of the clergy and an equal distrust of clerical attempts to centralize their authority.

Stephan had attracted a lay following that, while largely rural, included some who were well educated. These lay members of the Saxon immigrants also enjoyed some degree of theological sophistication, and in the wake of Stephan's (and his disciples') humiliation they challenged the essential authority of the clergy.

In the belief that the remaining clergy had forfeited their calling by resigning their parishes in Germany and that therefore no church existed among the Missouri Lutherans, a leader of the laity, Carl Eduard Vehse, drew up six "Theses on the Church" in which he proposed a radical form of congregationalism. Vehse, an attorney, exhibited significant theological understanding which left the young clergy, of whom Walther was the youngest, bewildered.

---

14. Stephan's ministry had attracted a wide following in Saxony. According to Bachmann, Stephan's preaching emphasized two doctrines: the doctrine of the atonement and the doctrine of the ministry. There can be little doubt that it was the first of these that gained him his following. Stephan preached in what Bachmann describes as an anomalous ecclesiastical environment characterized by a "Roman Catholic ruling house, a Lutheran established church, and a cultivated spirit of compromise or indifferentism rooted in the Enlightenment" ("The Rise," p. 88), and his message of God's transcendence via the atonement fell on fertile ground. Walther, for example, when advised by one of his teachers to be wary of Stephan, is said to have responded: "Shall I desert a man who, by God's grace, has saved my soul?" (p. 84). Giving Stephan his due, having communicated the gospel to a wide following, it was his second doctrinal emphasis that was to be remembered as his legacy to the LC-MS. "Stephan asserted that the ministry is the visible embodiment of the Word of God. With the times being confused to the lay mind, he invited his followers to have complete confidence in his counsel and guidance" (p. 87). The reaction to this doctrinal emphasis, following Stephan's humiliation in Missouri, would leave the LC-MS with its congregational polity and an institutionalized suspicion of an ecclesiastical hierarchy.

15. Bachmann, "The Rise," p. 102.

Walther retreated to examine Vehse's argument. Relying on his own biblical understanding and Luther's apologetics, Walther concluded that Vehse was essentially correct, but that Vehse, reflecting a lawyer's tendency to exaggerate an argument for effect, had understated the role of the pastor in providing leadership to a congregation,[16] particularly his role in maintaining the spiritual and doctrinal integrity of the body.

Preparing a counterargument presented in a dramatic public debate in Altenburg, Missouri, in April 1841, Walther won the day. The outcome was a carefully crafted description of the church emphasizing Luther's distinction between the visible and invisible church. Walther's description of the church would become the model for the organizational structure of the LC-MS.[17]

The impact of Walther's triumph on the subsequent structure of confessional Lutheranism in America can hardly be overstated. Having no European precedent for a congregational Lutheran church, Walther's description of the church would become the model for confessional Lutheranism in America. Wyneken and Sihler would embrace Walther's understanding of the church and provide the critical mass for the creation of the LC-MS.

Walther's understanding has two important implications for the current case study. First, the original constitution of Trinity Lutheran Church, St. Louis (Walther's church), would become the model of organization for the LC-MS. In that document it is acknowledged first that "[F]inal authority was vested in the congregation as a whole, for . . . whatever is done or decided by an individual or smaller body on the basis of duly delegated authority can always be brought before the congregation as the supreme court for final decision."[18]

But a proviso was added that, for our purposes, provides a second important distinction in understanding the LC-MS position on congregational authority: "[T]he congregation has no right to make regulations or to decide anything contrary to God's Word and to the symbols of the pure Evangelical Lutheran Church. . . . Should the congregation do this, then all such regulations are null and void."[19] Given that the pastor, by virtue of his training, is in the best position to determine when congregational actions are or are not consistent with God's Word, the clergy has de facto authority to direct congregational initiatives, even while the congregation retains de jure authority to regulate its own affairs.

Organizationally, the Missouri Synod retained the right, via its seminar-

---

16. Bachmann, "The Rise," p. 102.
17. Bachmann, "The Rise," pp. 135-36.
18. Bachmann, "The Rise," p. 145.
19. Bachmann, "The Rise," p. 145.

ies, to authorize ministerial candidates for ordination. And thus the synod, via its capacity to monitor clergy, effectively maintained considerable authority to regulate congregational initiatives. It need be noted, however, that such authority was, and is, indirect. This is to say that the synod maintains considerable authority to monitor the activity of clergy, who in turn have considerable authority to monitor congregational initiatives, but the synod has no direct authority, short of suspension or expulsion, to sanction congregations.

These two circumstances, what might be described as a unique ecclesiastical congregational political structure and a historical legacy of confessional Lutheranism, have produced an organizational climate in LC-MS polity which more or less always paints political issues in doctrinal language. Such language tends to provide a dramatic and often emotional edge to LC-MS politics.

Given that the synod has no direct authority to regulate the affairs of congregations, church doctrine is maintained by the persuasive power of the ordained ministry. LC-MS pastors maintain considerable prestige, both by virtue of their extensive theological instruction and by a historical legacy reflecting the heritage of the Reformation and the German Evangelical Lutheran Church. The German church provided pastors with extensive jurisdictional power, maintained within a cultural context that encouraged lay subordination to authority. An important question, raised by the current case study, is the degree to which this legacy of pastoral prestige and its connection to synodical authority is still recognized by an increasingly urbanized and cosmopolitan LC-MS laity.

Another way of framing this issue is to note that the authority of the synod is largely maintained via trust. Given no formal bureaucratic authority to directly oversee the affairs of congregations, the synod exercises authority primarily through the office of pastor. This authority is extended via the synod's seminaries and an educational system that includes elementary and secondary schools as well as a nationwide university network. This educational system, second in size only to the Roman Catholic system, is commonly referred to as "the System" by church members. The System, at the university and seminary level, is a hierarchy which is owned and operated by the synod, and is jealously guarded by the leadership of the national church.

Elementary and secondary schools, in contrast, are almost always owned and operated by a local congregation. This subsystem of schools was inaugurated in the formative years of the LC-MS and was instrumental in maintaining the organizational integrity of the synod in the wake of the emergent congregationalism sanctioned by the synodical constitution. Congregations were encouraged to establish elementary schools, whose manifest function was to provide newer generations with a well-grounded base of confessional Lutheranism. The schools also provided congregations with a cadre of trained laity under the direct supervision of the parish pastor. The system which emerged to provide trained lay leaders as teachers for the synodical schools is the foundation for maintaining the ecclesiastical element of the synodical polity. The System is the organizational counterpoint that keeps congregationalism in check.[20]

Congregational versus Ecclesiastical Authority

The historical foundation and the operating polity of the LC-MS include a unique and paradoxical mixture of congregational and ecclesiastical elements. The 150-year history of the LC-MS reflects periodic swings between efforts to control both the doctrine and practice of the congregations by national structures, and a tenacious congregationalism within the member churches.[21]

The constitutional structure of the synod virtually guarantees periodic tension between the synodical leadership and local congregations. In the wake of the Stephanite controversy and Walther's response, congregational autonomy became the bedrock of Missouri Synod polity — except that the tradition of confessional Lutheranism was also institutionalized via the means of clergy ordination (and the synod's educational system). One might say that there are two bedrocks of tradition supporting church polity within the synod. One is grounded in the European legacy and is committed to the defense of the historic confessions of the sixteenth century. This tradition demands ecclesiastical authority, which supports a well-established scholastic hierarchy within the leadership of the synod, which in turn provides a high degree of authority to the pastor in the local congregation. The other bedrock orientation is congregational autonomy. This tradition, which is more consistent with the American experience, encourages empowerment of laity and a concomitant distrust of centralized authority.[22]

20. The importance of the school system, maintained by a synodically trained cadre of teachers and administrators, is underscored by synod's certification of properly trained teachers as "ministers." The more or less self-conscious attempt to check the teaching responsibility of unauthorized laity, at least in the synod's formative years, was also evidenced by LC-MS opposition to the emergent Sunday school movement.

21. Carl S. Mundinger, *Government in the Missouri Synod* (St. Louis: Concordia, 1947), and August R. Suelflow, "Church Polity," in *Heritage in Motion*, ed. August R. Suelflow (St. Louis: Concordia, 1998).

22. It should be immediately apparent that these competing traditions portend a unique status for a Missouri Synod parish pastor. He, more than anyone else, must balance his role between these two traditions. On the one hand, he is always in a precarious position with the constant threat of being caught in the cross fire between an aroused laity and ecclesiastical authority. On the other hand, he has the potential to marshal a considerable base of support to assert his will. It is the latter contingency which is at the heart of the current conflict.

David L. Carlson

The constitution of the synod has institutionalized "ecclesiastical congre-gationalism" by vesting final authority in a plenary convention of delegates equally divided between ordained clergy and laity. This balance of ecclesiastical and congregational representation virtually guarantees periodic conflict.[23] There are two factors, however, which portend change in the nature of the con-flict as we enter a new century. The first is cultural, the second is social-structural. The first is associated with fundamental cultural shifts generally as-sociated with what can be labeled a transition from an industrial age to an in-formation age. The second is far less abstract and has been inherent in the pol-ity of the synod from almost its very beginnings. This is the conflict between the central judicatory of the synod, the synodical convention and its elected leadership, and the localized districts. The latter factor is more easily grasped and is more directly central to the focus of this paper. It is there that we turn first.

Districts and Synod

Shortly after its creation in 1847, the synod created districts to more locally co-ordinate the activities of member congregations. From the beginning, some op-posed the creation of these districts out of fear of splintering the synod.[24] De-fined primarily by geography, districts were in more or less constant contact with synodical leadership and were intended to extend the ministerial oversight of the central hierarchy of the synod. They were never intended to be autono-mous governing units. The language employed to describe the status of dis-tricts, as well as congregations, at the time of the creation of the synodical con-

---

23. Alan Graebner, *Uncertain Saints: The Laity in the Lutheran Church–Missouri Synod, 1900-1970* (Westport, Conn.: Greenwood Press, 1975), in his analysis of the history of laity of the LC-MS points out that in spite of the circumstances which shaped the original constitution of the church, lay participation in the shaping of the polity of the synod was largely absent during its formative years. This owed largely to two factors. One was the legacy of clerical aristocracy imported from Germany. The other was the rural context in which the synod emerged. While many of Martin Stephan's disciples, including Vehse and Marbach, were reared in more urban-ized settings and were well educated, the great mass of the early German immigrants were of ru-ral stock and settled in largely agrarian communities. The synod emerged in a context where the parish pastor was often not only spiritual adviser, but business, legal, and social counselor as well. This had the effect of further cementing the authority of the clergy while neutralizing the de facto authority provided to the laity by Walther's interpretation of church polity.

24. August R. Suelflow, *The District-Synod Relations of the Lutheran Church–Missouri Synod in Historical Perspective, 1872-1922*, Report to the Synodical Survey Commission (St. Louis: Lutheran Church–Missouri Synod, 1961).

278

stitution, is revealing. By way of clarifying the understanding that districts are bound to carry out synodical resolutions, the synodical polity emphasized the proviso that "The expediency allowed to congregations does not include Districts."[25] This language indicates that districts were not to enjoy the same kind of autonomy provided to congregations.

This proviso was accentuated in a report recently requested by synodical leadership to help define the role of districts in the governance of the synod. The report was authorized by, and presented to, the Task Force on National/District Relations, a committee whose very existence demonstrates the current concern addressed to this issue. The degree of concern is clearly illustrated by inclusion in the report of fifty-five synodical resolutions, dated from 1962 to 1998, that address the role of districts in the polity of synod. The timing of the emergence of the resolutions, beginning in 1962, is significant.[26] The clear substantive pattern of the resolutions, even more so. The great preponderance seek to assert the subordinate status of the districts vis-à-vis the national synodical leadership.

It is clear that the original intention of the founding fathers of the synod was that districts were to be operative extensions of synod. This is illustrated by the language used to describe district operatives. Each district was further subdivided into circuits, and these circuits were to be directed by "counselors." That the most direct synodical liaison to local congregations was designated a "counselor" underscores the intent of the leadership that the lower judicatories of the synod were to provide continuity of pastoral oversight. Over time, however, this changed. In a 1961 report to the synodical leadership, August Suelflow made this observation about the office of circuit counselor: "What was originally conceived as a highly spiritual office, instituted for the proper supervision of doctrinal and moral standards of the Synod, gradually emerged into that of a synodical agent in the lowest level of the administrative structure."[27]

25. Raymond L. Hartwig, *Report on Pertinent CCM Rulings,* Memo to the Task Force on National/District Synodical Relations (St. Louis: Lutheran Church–Missouri Synod, February 26, 1999).

26. The revolutionary zeitgeist of the 1960s, characterized not only by a pattern of confrontation with political authority but also by a questioning of the very normative standards upon which primary institutions rest, is well documented. The period was particularly traumatic for the LC-MS. The conflict over the appropriate interpretation of biblical inerrancy between the majority of the faculty of Concordia Seminary, St. Louis, and the elected leadership of the synod precipitated a synodical split in the 1970s. John Tietjen, *Memoirs in Exile: Confessional Hope and Institutional Conflict* (Minneapolis: Fortress, 1990), who as president of Concordia Seminary was at the center of this controversy, indicates in his memoirs his belief that existing tension among the seminary faculty, resulting from disagreements over U.S. policy in Vietnam, was a significant factor in igniting the confrontation.

27. Suelflow, *District-Synod Relations,* p. 19.

Circuits were not constitutionally structured to be governing units, but they have become important elements in the governance of synod in that they have become the "precincts" from which voting delegates to the governing national convention are selected.[28]

We have already noted that in recent years leaders at the national level have been increasingly concerned that districts are assuming unintended authority to act as autonomous agents in providing counsel to congregations. The current conflict between the Florida-Georgia District and the national leadership did not emerge as an isolated event and can be viewed as symptomatic of a trend. One may well ask what the larger issue is that portends increased tension between the national leadership and regional districts. There are, no doubt, many issues that encourage this conflict, but generally they are symptomatic of the natural consequences of growth and expansion. Given the increased breadth and complexity of synodical jurisdictions, it is no longer clear that the original intention for which districts were created can be sustained.

Two patterns, characteristic of the larger demographic realignment of the United States, have reshaped the congregational distribution within the LC-MS. The first is a general shift of the population away from the Midwest (and the East) toward other parts of the country, especially the South and the West. This has produced a realignment of the nationwide distribution of congregations. Second, the ongoing pattern of urbanization in the twentieth century has accentuated the growth of urban and suburban congregations at the expense of rural congregations. An important consequence of the increasing urbanization of the synod is the emergence of a laity which is increasingly diverse, better educated, less responsive to traditional authority, and more cosmopolitan. Urbanization has tended to reorient the laity, away from respect for traditional hierarchical patterns of authority and toward increased congregational autonomy. At the same time, geographical expansion has tended to disperse System-trained leadership away from the Midwest. The consequence of these related trends has been to reduce the social distance between the local synodically trained leaders, who are being increasingly confronted by an aroused laity, while increasing the social distance between operatives within the System.[29]

28. The triennial national synodical convention is the chief governing body of the synod. The convention's authority has repeatedly been challenged (chiefly by members of larger, more urbanized congregations) as being unrepresentative of the body of synod at large. The political structure, originally created to facilitate pastoral oversight, effectively gives each congregation, regardless of size, an equal vote in defining church polity.

29. Relative social distance is manifested in a variety of ways. Most immediately, it is reflected in formal administrative procedures. In this case, the ongoing administration of congregations is far more likely to be conducted in consultation with district leaders than with synodi-

A natural consequence of these trends has been for the role of districts to wax, while the role of synod has tended to decline. The more localized judicatories of synod (districts) are governed by leaders elected in triennial district conventions, by the vote of a pastoral and lay delegate from each congregation. In recent years districts have generally been reorganized and have expanded district staffing to provide more direct services to congregations. As the distinct service responsibilities of districts have expanded, interaction between district officials and congregational leaders has expanded. Similarly, direct interaction between the synodical leadership and congregational leaders has been less frequent. This is what is meant, in sociological language, by saying that the social distance between district leaders and congregation leaders has declined while the social distance between congregations and synod has increased. It can be further assumed that the relative social distance between districts and synod will be associated with geographical proximity. One would anticipate that the farther congregations are from the Midwest, the greater will be the social distance between synodical leadership and congregational leadership. This is supported by available data. In recent years, several studies have indicated that the allegiance of church members to their congregations has grown, while identification with synod has greatly diminished.[30]

One of the consequences of the reshaping of the landscape of synodical polity has been the emergence of distinctly different judicatory cultures at the synodical and district levels of administration. Michael Kalmes, a political scientist and a member of the faculty of the Concordia University System of the LC-MS, has observed that the different judicatory cultures can easily be observed by comparing the participants at any given district convention with those at the synodical convention. The prototypical participant at a district convention is the parish pastor and a lay delegate who, as often as not, is a confidant of the pastor. The agenda of district conventions reflects this constituency; that is, it will most directly reflect issues of congregational practice. On the other hand, the prototypical participant at the synodical convention is an individual, whether clergy or lay, who is a recognized "name" within the synod. This is to say that the constituency of the synodical convention is far more

---

cal leaders. But more importantly, social distance is reflected in consciousness of kind and in what could be described as cultural conversation. Reduced social distance tends to frame conversations in a context of greater intimacy with an associated tendency toward like-mindedness. Increased social distance has the opposite effect. One ought to anticipate that any increase in social distance, between congregations and synodical leadership, will be reflected in a tendency to exaggerate differences that will inevitably emerge from time to time.

30. See, for example, *The Charron Report to the Lutheran Church–Missouri Synod* (St. Louis: Charron Research and Information, 1997).

likely to be people who have a long-established reputation within the synod. Not surprisingly, the agenda of the synodical convention will be oriented more toward doctrinal issues.

The conversations, at these two levels of polity, are quite often qualitatively different. Not only will the nature of the agenda vary between these two forums, but the very nature of the language used to frame issues will vary. The following theological essay by Eugene Bunkowske shows that the language used to frame the multiplicity of resolutions relative to eucharistic practice introduced at the 1998 synodical convention varied substantively. One need not look too long to discern that much of the difference follows from differing understandings of what it means to be in fellowship (or community). To anticipate how the synod might respond to the current impasse, illustrated by the conflict between the Florida-Georgia District and the synod at large, we need to examine why at this point in history there is such fundamental disagreement among members of the synod as to the meaning of "community." And here we are brought back to the question of fellowship.

It is also here that we confront the second challenge facing the LC-MS at the turn of the century. If the first challenge is to accommodate the changing social-structural patterns associated with geographical distribution and an urbanized laity, the second challenge is to accommodate the realignment of "community" (or fellowship) associated with the transition from an industrial-based culture to an information-based culture. While a culture shift is less immediately visible than a social-structural shift, the impact may be more far-reaching.

Culture War, the Rise of Modern Evangelicalism, and the Redefinition of Fellowship

The LC-MS emerged in opposition to the dominant culture of the American frontier of the early nineteenth century, a culture that was driven in large part by a fusion of Jeffersonian liberalism and evangelical Protestantism. The synod was forged by leaders who had emerged from a climate of European repression and were on a crusade to preserve confessional Lutheranism in territory occupied by evangelical enthusiasts. This context provided the synod with its prevailing spirit, but over the years the infusion of English, the scattering of the flock from the Midwest, and the diversification of the membership have weakened the center. Emergent cultural forces will soon force the synod to make some difficult decisions. These decisions are likely either to move it to the cultural margins, as the defender of traditional confessional Lutheranism, or to expand a dialogue with modern evangelicalism to produce a new confessional-evangelical Lutheran church.[31]

The larger context for this choice is the emergence of the information age, what some have called postmodernism, and what Alvin Toffler has called the third wave.[32] It is still far from clear how the emergence of an information age will impact either the structure of the LC-MS or other Christian denominations. But a case can be made that modern evangelicalism is a consequence of the emergence of postmodernism (see n. 2 above). A further case can be made that the emergent conflict in the LC-MS over close(d) communion is a response to contemporary evangelical revival. This is not to say that evangelical revival is exclusively a twentieth-century phenomenon. A nineteenth-century version was apparent to Friedrich Wyneken when he walked into that revival meeting at Baltimore in 1834. The circumstances at the dawn of the twenty-first century, however, have recast this historic conflict between evangelicalism and confessional Lutheranism in a new light.

This is not the place to provide a detailed assessment of the impact of postmodernism on American religious life. My purpose here is to highlight two consequences of the third wave that I believe frame the current polity of the LC-MS. The first is the rise of moral relativism and the reciprocal emergence of

31. Advocates of confessional Lutheranism are properly suspicious of attempts to accommodate culture in the organization of church polity. If the synod opts to remain a main player in American evangelical Christianity, one of the primary challenges facing synodical leadership is to define what is essential to preserve a distinctively Lutheran church in the cultural landscape of the information age. Once this is done, culture must be accommodated for the church to successfully carry the Great Commission forward. The problem is always one of preserving the historical confessions in a changing cultural landscape. To provide for a proper application of the Eucharist, Lutheran theologians must discern the Lord's understanding of who is to properly be invited to the meal, and how the Lord intended his meal to build up the body. The question raised here is how the dispersion of authority, and a concomitant acceleration of individualism, conditioned by instantaneous and largely uncontrollable mass communication, will change the way in which postmodern people construct community. How will the church be constructed within the changing contours of this emergent community? It is axiomatic to sociology that people will seek fellowship. How best to accommodate this need for fellowship, while preserving a biblically defined church, is the issue at dispute in the current case study.

32. Alvin Toffler, *The Third Wave* (New York: Morrow, 1980). Toffler has argued that modern civilization has emerged as the consequence of two great technological revolutions. He uses the metaphor of tidal waves to illustrate the power each of these movements had on the transformation of the extant culture. The old cultures were simply swept away as consequences of the emergent technology. The first wave, the emergence of agriculture, swept away hunter-gatherer culture forms. The second wave, industrialization, swept away agrarian forms of social organization. Toffler believes that the third wave, the emergence of an information society, will have similar impact on the existing social order.

modern evangelicalism. The second is the dispersion of authority. We will look at the rise of relativism first.

Wyneken was persuaded that, in 1834, evangelical revivalists were not in fellowship with confessional Lutherans. I have made the case that this was a reflection of the context of his time. At the time Wyneken arrived in the United States, German Lutherans had been forced into a union that imposed upon them a Reformed theology. Wyneken and his comrades were persuaded that, via Luther, Germany was the appointed defender of the true church. And in the early nineteenth century, this church was being held captive. Much like Israel during the Babylonian exile, the German Lutheran pioneers had a task to create and maintain a church in exile. For these pioneers, revivalists and sectarians were rightly excluded from fellowship. Their primary task was not to evangelize the unchurched but to gather the scattered saints.

The foundation of the church these pioneers created was a carefully articulated and jealously defended doctrine that embraced Luther's understanding of the church. The greatest threat to the church, especially in the religious free market of the American frontier, was unionism (see n. 8). While there was no threat of a state-imposed unionism on the frontier, the newly mandated congregational autonomy provided a constant threat of gradualist unionism. Admission to fellowship was strictly guarded and was predicated on individual assent to all aspects of this doctrine. Agreement with Luther's understanding of the sacraments, especially his understanding of the Lord's Supper, was the most visible means of marking fellowship. But it would not be sufficient simply to agree with Luther's understanding of the "true presence" in the meal. It was necessary for those who would participate in the sacrament to be in complete conformity with the Lutheran understanding of doctrine. Given the context of the nineteenth century, it is difficult to quarrel with this understanding of fellowship. The question for the current leadership of the LC-MS is whether full conformity with doctrine is still an appropriate standard for fellowship in the twenty-first century.

It may be more appropriate to phrase the question differently. Should the LC-MS choose to enter into dialogue with modern evangelicalism, seeking common ground while maintaining its commitment to confessional Lutheranism, the appropriate question is: What are the essential standards of doctrinal commitment necessary to maintain a truly confessional Lutheran church? And this in turn raises an equally difficult question: Who should be trusted with the task to decide? These questions presuppose that something is to be gained by seeking common ground with modern evangelicalism. There are many in the LC-MS who see little reason to enter this dialogue. Better, they would say, would be to maintain constancy and continue to present confessional Lutheranism as a clearly demonstrable alternative to the vagaries of contemporary culture.

How ought the LC-MS respond to postmodernism, and to what degree should it participate with evangelicals in this response? Those who would support a more open communion policy are persuaded that the current threat to the church is not so much unionism as it is relativism. The question is: Has the cultural landscape shifted to the degree that confessional Lutherans now have more common ground with contemporary evangelicals than disagreements that divide? To the extent that relativism is a greater threat to the church than unionism, and to the extent that contemporary evangelicalism is primarily a response to relativism, are contemporary confessional Lutherans now largely in fellowship with evangelicals?

The understanding of "fellowship" is now the key issue. The term is loaded with symbolic meaning for many in the LC-MS because it is central to the synod's defining spirit. We could use a less value-loaded term such as "community" and express the same idea, but this would be missing the point. Those Missouri Lutherans who would find affinity with evangelicals understand fellowship more subjectively. They define it in the context of like-mindedness and are more comfortable with shifting constellations of fellowship groups who share at least some common presuppositions. These Lutherans would say that they are no less confessional in their understanding of the historic confessions, but while they use the confessions as their own individual anchor, they are also willing to seek fellowship with other Christians who share certain other common understandings.

This is a profoundly different understanding of the church than the one traditionally posed by the LC-MS.[33] This view significantly accentuates the "invisible church" as the true church, while reciprocally diminishing denominationalism. For the contemporary advocates of the invisible church, the current cultural context accentuates fellowship amongst those Christians who share a belief in the authority of Scripture. More to the point, these Lutherans view those Christians who (regardless of denominational affiliation) share a common understanding of the Sacrament of the Altar as being in community — or fellowship.[34] Lutherans of this bent would view the act of withholding the Eucha-

33. John Kayser, an LC-MS pastor at a rural parish in Michigan, has observed that when Walther articulated his doctrine of the "invisible church," he planted the seeds of the Florida-Georgia communion policy statement. As Kayser puts it: "You cannot believe in the Invisible Church and exclusive communion at the same time if you would be intellectually honest."

34. St. Luke Lutheran Church in Ann Arbor, Mich., for example, views its policy as one of "close" (as opposed to "closed") communion and defines its policy this way:

Holy Communion is divinely instituted. Jesus Christ gives His true (real) body and blood under the forms of bread and wine. We thus hold that the bread and wine are not

rist from those who share a common understanding of it but lack an appropriate denominational affiliation as an act of inhospitality — and even bigotry.[35]

If this view of fellowship defines one camp of Missouri Lutherans, contrast it with that of those who have a more traditional understanding of fellowship. For these people fellowship represents a shared legacy; it is *Gemeinschaft*.[36] For them community/fellowship is objective, not individually subjective. It defines who one is, and just as festival meals are the occasion for reunion of family, the communion meal is the occasion for the gathering of a body of people who share a common history and embrace a heritage of faith. The family meal is the appropriate metaphor here, and while one may invite acquaintances to common meals, the communion meal is a festival meal and publicly signifies the family of believers. Such a meal is not to be taken lightly, and while

---

mere symbols of Jesus' body and blood. When we receive the bread and wine, we receive in fact the body and blood of Christ for the forgiveness of sins.

In Communion we celebrate this forgiveness and receive it through faith, as we eat and drink. In Communion we remember Jesus' suffering and death, His rising from the dead and return to heaven, and the promise of His coming again. In Communion the Good News of full salvation is offered to those who "hunger and thirst after righteousness."

We believe that, as we eat and drink this Supper, God strengthens our faith in Jesus Christ and our love for one another.

Therefore, we invite to the Lord's Table all who:

have been instructed in the meaning of Communion; have been baptized in the name of the Triune God; have received Jesus Christ as their personal savior and Lord; and agree with our confession; are not living in open rebellion against the Word of God, and do not hold willful and persistent hatred, resentment or anger against any other person.

Ann Arbor, Mich., St. Luke Lutheran Church: *Worship Guide*, 2002.

35. I have described fellowship, defined within the context of the invisible church, as subjective in nature. It is subjective in the sense that it is individualized. But even for such subjective, individual choices there are objective criteria that mark this kind of fellowship, i.e., adherence to the authority of Scripture and subscription to belief in the true presence in the Eucharist. This is nonetheless objectivity of a different quality than that designated by formal membership in a congregation with denominational affiliation.

36. Ferdinand Toennies introduced *Gemeinschaft* and *Gesellschaft* into the sociology lexicon over a century ago. The most frequently heard contemporary translations of the terms are, respectively, "community" and "society." A closer literal translation from the German is "natural will" and "rational will." Relationships in a community that are of the first type are binding in the sense that they have intrinsic significance, such as those that bind families and close friendships. *Gemeinschaft* relationships are ends in themselves rather than means to an end. They are rooted in and exhibit such qualities as tradition, shared values, intimacies, and "we-ness." These relationships tend to be comprehensive and long term. They are, in some sense, natural. See F. Toennies, *Community and Society — Gemeinschaft und Gesellschaft,* translated and supplemented by C. P. Loomis, 2nd ed. (East Lansing: Michigan State University Press, 1957), pp. 248ff.

it would be inhospitable not to welcome acquaintances and strangers to public worship, the meal is reserved for those who seek full fellowship with the body. From this perspective, those who express a desire to participate in the Eucharist are being asked to make a life-changing decision. To treat the meal with any less reverence would be to diminish the faith of the believers and to minimize what is being asked of participants.

The language of community, fellowship, and communion is understood very differently by Lutherans of differing bents. While those who employ a more traditional language continue to view unionism as the greatest threat to fellowship, those who employ a more contemporary language view relativism as the greater threat. Each faction, employing its own respective language, views the conflict between the church and the world from a radically different perspective. One perspective is more consistent with modernism, the other with postmodernism.

The Church in a Postmodern World

James Hunter has argued in *Culture Wars* that the emergence of postmodernism has reshaped the nature of denominationalism in the United States.[37] In the nineteenth century denominational boundaries reflected disagreements among people who framed their positions in the context of biblical language. In this cultural landscape, the Bible was authoritative and denominational disagreements were doctrinal in nature. The dialogue between those in fellowship with the church and those not in fellowship centered on appropriate interpretation of scripturally mandated injunctions. There were ample opportunity and considerable encouragement to explore subtlety and nuance in the biblical narrative. The differences that inevitably emerged created, encouraged, and strengthened denominational affiliations.

The result was an expansion of religious pluralism. In an arena where no single denomination could gain a particular advantage, a measure of cultural consensus also emerged. America became, in this cultural sense, a Christian nation. It was in this context that the LC-MS emerged and negotiated its location in the larger fabric of American culture. While, as we have noted, the LC-MS emerged as a uniquely German American synod, it was integrated into an American culture defined largely through the language, ideals, and legitimating myths of a biblical worldview.

37. James D. Hunter, *Culture Wars: The Struggle to Define America* (New York: Harper Collins, 1991).

With time, as pluralism expanded, so did individual and institutional tolerance. The LC-MS, along with an increasing diversity of other denominations, found its place in this arrangement. What emerged was an American religious landscape in which mutual denominational toleration was the rule. The LC-MS emerged as a self-consciously German American confessional Lutheran fellowship. Inclusion in the fellowship required minimally that one submit to congregational authority, which is to say that one was expected to join a church. Those who would aspire to leadership in the fellowship would further be required to submit to the authority of the System, which meant being trained at a synodical college or seminary and/or being certified for ministry by synodically designated authorities. Thus emerged an understanding of fellowship that marked membership by categorical inclusion in the organized church. This system was hardly unique to the LC-MS, and was in fact the general pattern for Christian denominationalism. The larger system of American denominationalism was enabled by a general acceptance of biblical theism that provided the language in which this arrangement was negotiated.

The arrangement worked well enough for the LC-MS until the second decade of the twentieth century. The entrance of the United States into war with Germany, first in 1917 and later in 1941, changed the terms of the arrangement. The First World War, and an accompanying anti-German backlash, accelerated the erosion of the self-consciously German identity of the synod. But while the synod found it increasingly difficult to maintain its German identity after the war, it maintained its categorical integrity by emphasizing its denominational boundaries, especially its emphasis on its mission to preserve *Reine Lehre.*

The Second World War further undermined the German identity of the synod, but Hunter describes how larger demographic trends undermined the overall denominational balance as well. This balance was upset by the further expansion of pluralism, the continued growth of Catholics, and the rapid growth of Mormons, Islam, and New Age variants of religious expression, especially the human potential movement. Particularly important was the growth in the proportion of "secularists" (those who indicate "none" for religious preference) after World War Two. Secularists, as a group, are disproportionately well educated and have had a particularly important impact on redefining religious dialogue in the postmodern era. By 1990 they constituted over 10 percent of the population. This most recent expansion of pluralism signifies the collapse of the long-standing Judeo-Christian consensus in American public life.

As we enter the new millennium, the organizing principle of American pluralism has fundamentally changed. Religious dialogue no longer centers on theological or doctrinal disagreements, but now reflects a more fundamental disagreement over the very sources of moral truth. The result has been an increase in religious anomie. The prevailing source of this anomie is uncertainty about how to reconcile traditional Christian theology with the discoveries of modern scientific inquiry. Theology has tended to adopt the rules of inquiry which define scientific discourse. This "higher critical" methodology has opened the door to a frontal assault on the biblical narrative. As a result, defenders of orthodoxy have mounted an organized defense of the traditional faith. While neoorthodoxy has taken different forms in different faith communities, among Protestants it has focused upon defense of Scripture.

A consequence of the assault on biblical authority has been the expansion of modern evangelicalism, along with the waning of denominational loyalty and the expansion of parachurch organizations — independent agencies, often drawing interdenominational support, organized on behalf of a particular political, social, or spiritual mission. *"When coupled with the weakening of denominational ties, this expansion has actually encouraged the deepening of century-old intrafaith divisions,"* first, because these groups are partisan both in nature and agenda and second, because they tend to coalesce around the opposing ends of the "new cultural axis": orthodoxy and progressivism.[38]

Hunter's observation that intrafaith divisions have been accentuated by increased partisanship reflecting larger cultural trends is directly pertinent to the LC-MS synodical split of the 1970s. To a large degree this experience shapes the synodical landscape in which the current conflict is being played out. More directly, Hunter's observation about weakened denominational loyalties, reflecting emerging new alliances of orthodox and progressive Christians, is an apt characterization of emerging conflict within the synod. These emerging alliances have thrust many Missouri Lutherans, generally younger and more urban, into associations which Hunter describes as a "new ecumenism" in which distinct and separate religions share resources and work together toward common objectives. This new ecumenism "represents the key institutional expression of the realignment of American public culture."[39]

It is this new ecumenism that is at the heart of the division expressed by the current conflict over communion practice within the LC-MS. Those who embrace and participate in the new ecumenism are generally not only younger and more urbanized, they are more likely to inhabit the "saltwater" districts of the synod — those farther from St. Louis and the Midwest. These Missouri Lutherans are far more likely to view emergent religious anomie and moral relativism as the primary threats to the church. They are far more likely to seek fellowship with Christians of other denominations who share common cultural

---

38. Hunter, *Culture Wars*, p. 90; emphasis original.
39. Hunter, *Culture Wars*, p. 98.

objectives. They are far more likely to view themselves as, in fact, in fellowship with these non-LC-MS Christians.[40]

For Missouri Lutherans of a more traditional bent, who tend to be older and are more likely to be concentrated in the Midwest, the new ecumenism is still ecumenism. For them unionism remains the principal threat to the church, and the communion table is the place where union stops.

Conclusions and Options

In the early 1980s I represented my local congregation as a lay delegate to the triennial convention of the Rocky Mountain District of the LC-MS. I shared a room with a man in his seventies who was representing a congregation located in suburban Denver. He related how he had moved as a young man to Denver in the 1930s, and he spoke with pride about how he had helped to build the first LC-MS church in his community. He had literally built his church, as he was a carpenter by trade. Later when his congregation outgrew that first church, he helped build a larger one. He loved his church and he loved the LC-MS. But his countenance visibly shrank as he related how a few years prior to our meeting his congregation had split with the pastor suddenly leaving, taking half the congregation with him. Tears were in his eyes as he spoke of how families who had worshiped together for generations now no longer spoke to one another. What happened? I asked. "It was this Seminex thing," he said.[41] "Something happened at the seminary in St. Louis and our pastor left the Synod. It tore my church apart and I still don't know what it was all about."

40. While this needs to be documented, there is an apparent paradox in the attitude of postmodern Lutherans toward the Sacrament of the Altar. In many emergent seeker-oriented Lutheran congregations, the sacrament is routinely celebrated at all worship services. Thus, even as they have "opened" the policy of participation, they have routinized the practice. Lutherans of a more traditional bent often observe that by routinizing the practice they have diminished the sacrament. Postmodern Lutherans would of course disagree. It could be said that in the relativist, rationalized postmodern age people have an increased hunger for the transcendent, and that the value of mystery of the sacraments is accentuated by the age.

41. In the early 1970s charges of teaching false doctrine were leveled against several faculty members at Concordia Seminary, St. Louis, by the leadership of the synod. The resulting conflict eventually led to the dismissal of the seminary president, resulting in a walkout by the majority of the faculty and the students of the seminary. These faculty and students established Concordia Seminary in Exile (Seminex) — later renamed Christ Seminary in Exile. The conflict produced a synod-wide split that resulted when synodical members sympathetic to the faculty left the LC-MS and created a new Lutheran synod — the Association of Evangelical Lutheran Churches (AELC). The AELC later became part of the Evangelical Lutheran Church in America (ELCA) with the creation of that synod in 1988.

Doctrinal disputes have consequences that spread far beyond convention halls, seminary classrooms, and board meetings. The LC-MS is still reeling from the doctrinal dispute that split the synod in the 1970s. If the current conflict over the communion table produces the kind of animus that characterized the conflict of the 1970s, it is almost certain that the LC-MS will divide again. Another split will predictably relegate the remnants of the synod to a significantly reduced role in shaping Lutheranism in the twenty-first century. This is what is at stake in the current controversy. Given the diametrically opposed perspectives brought to the discussion by the parties on each side, there will be no easy solution to the conflict.

This crisis has been precipitated by different understandings of what constitutes fellowship in the postmodern era. Postmodernism has also complicated the search for a solution. As a consequence of the transition to an information age, the very nature of authority has changed. Hierarchical authority was a product of the industrial age, where institutional organization mandated centralized governance. The age of universal access to information mandates authority based on persuasion. It is incumbent on those in positions of leadership within the synod to deliberately facilitate dialogue if another synodical rupture is to be avoided. Conformity to doctrine cannot be mandated in the postmodern era. There is a paradox here. Lutherans in the postmodern era can increasingly be expected to invoke a Reformation formula to the resolution of doctrinal disputes: unless convinced by plain reason and the Word of God, they are unlikely to submit to authority.

While the task facing the LC-MS leadership is daunting, the legacy of the pioneers of the synod has given the LC-MS a unique polity structure which is well suited to governance in the postmodern era. Missouri's uniquely dualistic governance structure, its congregational ecclesiastical polity, provides an opportunity for inventive governance in the twenty-first century. If, as Francis Fukuyama has argued, governance in the information age will be increasingly localized around *Gemeinschaft* constellations of like-minded peoples,[42] one could hardly imagine a better-suited polity structure than that of the LC-MS. A Reformation-grounded, confessional Lutheran church, one that places governance in the hands of an informed laity that is committed to biblical authority and seeks the guidance of an informed *ecclesia,* can be the model for church governance in the twenty-first century.

The problem is that the LC-MS has never really trusted this political structure. Having laid the foundation of this polity in the middle of the nine-

---

42. Francis Fukuyama, "The Great Disruption: Human Nature and the Reconstruction of Social Order," *Atlantic Monthly,* May 1999.

teenth century, it has tended to rely on the earlier European model of hierarchically imposed ecclesiastical governance. The split of the 1970s is evidence of what will inevitably happen if one faction seeks to impose its will by fiat. Contemporary Lutherans will not abide an imposed solution. The challenge to the synodical leadership is to persuade an informed laity. Governance via trust is the only legitimate authority in the postmodern era. If closed communion is clearly biblically mandated, then the *ecclesia* must make its case. If closed communion is more appropriately understood as a culturally mandated means to resist unionism, then closed communion is unlikely to stand. For contemporary Lutherans, unionism is not the issue.

If, on the other hand, the leadership of the synod is convinced that unionism is still the primary threat to confessional Lutheranism, then it must hold its ground. But the leadership will do well to count the cost. An anti-unionist church will almost certainly be relegated to the margins of American society in the twenty-first century.

Postscript

At the triennial convention of the LC-MS held in July of 2001, there were several essays delivered by seminary faculty in defense of the traditional synodical position on close(d) communion, but nothing was to be heard on the issue from the convention floor. This was because the larger issue of ecclesiastic versus congregational authority took center stage and trumped the conflict over communion. While the parameters of that conflict are the stuff of another chapter, the way this issue plays itself out will largely direct the resolution of the communion issue. The conflict at the 2001 convention centered on the issue of pastoral leadership and was reflected in two of the three most contentious issues debated on the floor.[43]

The first of these two motions affirmed Walther's understanding of church and ministry articulated in the wake of the Altenburg debate and originally affirmed by the synod in convention in 1851. The motion was carried. It effectively reaffirmed the foundation for a church polity that has been described in this paper as "ecclesiastical congregationalism." Debate on this issue was mildly contentious, and the motion was supported by a 72 percent majority.

43. The third issue, which was particularly contentious, was a motion to declare that the synod no longer recognize the Evangelical Lutheran Church in America to be an orthodox Lutheran body. The motion was in response to the ELCA's decision to enter into altar and pulpit fellowship agreements with Reformed and Episcopal church bodies. The convention approved this motion.

The debate was preparatory to a far more contentious debate over pastoral leadership. This issue had been brewing for at least two decades and centered on an emerging critical shortage of pastors synod-wide.

There is not space here to describe the details of this debate. A brief summary of this story is that, via a substitute resolution from the floor of the convention, the delegates rejected recommendations from synodical leaders, largely represented by seminary faculty, and instead authorized lay ministry in congregations. While the circumstances under which a congregation was authorized to provide ministry via "deacons" were nuanced to provide for pastoral oversight, the motion significantly reduced the capacity of the national leadership, particularly the seminary faculty, to monitor ministry in local congregations. The debate on this issue was contentious, and after several parliamentary maneuvers to derail it failed, the motion was supported by a bare majority (less than 52 percent). This issue threatens to undo the delicate balance of ecclesiastical versus congregational oversight of the polity of the LCMS, and will almost certainly take center stage for at least the next decade.

The Theological Meaning and Use of Communion:
The Case of the Lutheran Church–Missouri Synod

Eugene W. Bunkowske

Communion with its configuration of subsidiary meanings has always been an important theological concept in the Lutheran Church–Missouri Synod (LC-MS). Today, the diverging LC-MS practices of communion and the differing theologies behind those practices are giving rise to conflict and confusion in the LC-MS, particularly in the understanding of fellowship. In this essay I will focus on both the meanings (theologies) and the practices of communion. In order to give perspective this essay will document the author's personal understanding of changes in LC-MS communion culture (practice and theology) as they have taken place during the middle and latter part of the twentieth century.

The goals of this essay are several. First, I wish to expose the meaning and practice of communion in the LC-MS especially from a dynamic interactive (transactional) point of view, and to provide a clear picture of how the language of theology orchestrated by communicating people is used to develop, organize, change, and reorganize the meaning and practice of communion. The second goal is to describe the relationship between changes in the meaning and practice of LC-MS communion culture and the changes in the sociocultural patterns of society. The third goal is to present conclusions and recommendations, including examples of how, given the findings on communion culture and sociocultural change, the LC-MS can best reorganize for crisp, clean, and clear proclamation of the good news of Jesus in the twenty-first century. The fourth goal will be to recommend how the proper understanding and use of the language of theology fit into the overall picture of organizing for God-pleasing and productive religious work in the twenty-first century. The final paragraph of the essay offers my personal opinion that Christianity will intentionally reorganize for the benefit of an organic and apostolic movement for congregational multiplication with a focus on Jesus the Christ in order to survive and thrive in the twenty-first century and beyond.

Definitions

To open the way for a useful theological discussion on communion, it will be helpful to define carefully what we mean by theology. A friend once said, "Communion theology is in the pastor's and professor's head, and the practice of communion is transacted in the head, heart, and life of the ordinary Christian." Theology sets forth in a proper arrangement what God has revealed about himself in his word. The dictionary speaks of theology as the language about God, the meaning of God, the study of God, the relation between God and the universe, and the study of religious doctrines. It also speaks of theology as a specific form or system for the study of religious doctrines as expounded by a particular religion, denomination, or individual.

From God's side, with a monotheistic understanding in view, the meaning, knowledge, study, and explanation of God and his relationship to all things will be one, not many. From the human point of view, there are as many theologies as there are religions, denominations, and even individuals involved in doing theology. This is especially true as we focus on theology in the normal transactions of life, "real theologies," as a colleague has called them. In this essay I will designate theology as either formal or transactional.

Formal theology is a system of doctrines proclaimed to be true by a religious group. These dogmas are recognized and passed on from generation to generation. Traditionally this transmission has been done orally. In a good number of cases these doctrines are standardized, formalized, and reinforced in writing. An example of written formal theology for the LC-MS is the 1580 *Book of Concord.*[1] This volume contains the mutually agreed upon confessions of the Lutheran electors, princes, estates, and theologians of the Reformation era. These confessions are still subscribed to by Lutherans, especially Lutheran clergy, who normally make a formal subscription to them at the time of their ordination. Another example of formal theology is a text like *Christian Dogmatics* by Franz Pieper.[2]

Transactional theology is quite different from formal theology. It is something that every member of a religious congregation, judicatory, district, synod

---

1. Robert Kolb and Timothy J. Wengert, eds., *The Book of Concord: The Confessions of the Evangelical Lutheran Church,* trans. Charles P. Arand and others (Minneapolis: Fortress, 2000).
2. Franz Pieper, *Christian Dogmatics,* 4 vols. (St. Louis: Concordia, 1950-57).

or denomination is involved in by virtue of being a member. Transactional theology is interactive. It is theology played out in the lives of people in contact with one another and, at times, in confrontation and even conflict. Transactional theology happens as people informally discuss the merits of evolution and creationism. It happens as people talk and argue through their views on moral and ethical issues. It happens, without words, as one person watches another person receive too much change in a financial transaction and observes that person count the change and accept it without comment. It happens as people profess one thing and do another.

For Christians transactional theology is interacted between themselves, Jesus, and other people. It is living in, with, for, and through Jesus in a messy world. It is Jesus living in, with, for, and through the Christians in his body in and for that messy world. Transactional theology is by definition theology in action. It is informal rather than formal. It is doctrine in practice. It is thought and talked. It is part of almost every idea, word, and act, secular or sacred. It is an understanding of God and how that understanding is modeled and molded in everyday life. Transactional theology is dynamic and real in practical living. It is basic to the organization or disorganization, development or disintegration of religious work in the twenty-first century.

Transactional theology has several functions, but two are especially important. The LC-MS speaks of them as Christian nurture and Christian outreach. These functions can each be carried out positively or negatively. From the nurture point of view positively considered, transactional theology is God embracing us with forgiveness, admonition, and love so that we can likewise embrace others with forgiveness, admonition, and love. It is using the Christian's most holy faith to grow together as a group of believers (Jude 20). It happens when believers stop judging, as they remove the splinter from their own eye before trying to take the sawdust out of another person's eye (Matt. 7:1-5). It happens when Christians show mercy to those who have doubts (Jude 22). It happens when they are sympathetic, kind, humble, gentle, and patient (Col. 3:12). In essence, the positive function of transactional nurture theology is the Spirit of God building up the body of Christ into a place where God lives and moves and has his being (Eph. 2:22). Transactional theology of the nurture variety is carried out negatively, however, when a Christian fellowship emphasizes internal denominational nurture to the exclusion of people that Christ came to seek and save. It also happens when those who have already received that salvation in trusting faith are considered distant or heterodox, or are understood to be second-class Christians because they are members of a different Christian organization or denomination.

From an outreach point of view positively considered, transactional theology moves out from where God already has a place in human lives and embraces others who are seeking and searching for life with God. It has to do with leaving one's comfort zone. It also means embracing those who may not even be seeking and searching but are in need of what they do not even know. Ideally, it is taking a Christian lifestyle and message into the rough-and-tumble world without intentionally alienating others or compromising the truth of God's message. Positive transactional theology of an outreach variety is crisp, clean, and clear when it brings biblical truth to bear upon life in a messy world. This happens when Christians make it a point to interact and make friends with people in physical and spiritual need. It happens when Christians live and share their Christian faith with people from another culture or religious persuasion. It happens as a Christian learns another language in order to communicate in someone else's comfortable frame of reference. It happens as the death and resurrection of Christ saves and secures people and flows through those same people to others who are not yet saved in ways that they can understand in their own terms of reference. Transactional theology of the outreach variety is carried out negatively, however, when the message of Christ's coming to seek and to save the lost (Luke 19:10) is not heard in and through Christians for meaningful understanding.

Transactional theology will be very important in this essay precisely because it is in the rough-and-tumble of doing theology in life in a messy world that questions concerning organization and fellowship cry out for attention. These challenges of organization and fellowship are also being lifted up for careful consideration in a variety of churches as we move into a new millennium with its plethora of uncertainties and challenges.

The LC-MS Culture of Communion

The language of theology connected with communion was an important issue at the 1998 national convention of the LC-MS. At first glance, the problem seemed to be the practice of communion. Delegates expressed their opinions and positions on communion practice in terms of close(d) or open communion, with close(d) communion being defined in ways that excluded people, particularly nonmembers of LC-MS. Open communion was defined in a way that allowed all believers, no matter what their denomination, to participate in communion.

In the convention workbook there were thirty-five resolutions on communion from forty-three different LC-MS entities.[3] When carefully examining

---

3. *Convention Workbook* (St. Louis: Office of the Secretary, Lutheran Church–Missouri Synod, 1998), pp. 153-65.

these resolutions, it soon became evident that beneath the diverging communion practices were significant differences in theology as evidenced in the language of theology being used. In fact, biblical exegesis, meaning, interpretation, and subsidiary meanings were pivotal in how these resolutions were written.

At one point during the convention, I took a closer look at the various resolutions on communion. As I made notes in the margins of the convention workbook, I found that these resolutions had been submitted from all over the United States. They came from 34 of the over 6,200 congregations, 3 of the 35 districts, 2 of the 625 circuit forums, both of the seminary faculties, 1 of the 35 district boards of directors, and 1 of the 35 district pastoral conferences, for a total of 43 entities. Twelve of the 43 came from so-called saltwater districts, those that touch the Gulf of Mexico or the Atlantic or Pacific Oceans. Twenty came from the so-called heartland districts, those that do not touch an ocean or the Gulf of Mexico and are close enough to the triangle formed by St. Louis, Fort Wayne, and Minneapolis to be considered heartland. The remaining 11 resolutions were from areas that are neither saltwater nor heartland districts.

Most interesting was the configuration of meaning in these resolutions and the theological language that expressed that meaning. A simple review disclosed twenty-seven different types of overall communion meaning.[4] Con-

---

4. These twenty-seven types of surface structure meanings of communion are listed below by descending frequency of occurrence. Each type of meaning is followed by brackets containing a number and a percentage. The number indicates how many of the forty-three participating entities used this meaning in their resolutions, while the percentage indicates the proportion of participating entities this number represents.

1. Communion is a method for defining a specific community of believers. [36/84%]
2. There are specific denominational requirements for believers who participate in communion in the LC-MS. [31/74%]
3. Close(d) communion is mandatory in LC-MS congregations. [30/70%]
4. Communion is a key designator of separation from all that are not in altar and pulpit fellowship with the LC-MS. [28/65%]
5. Discernment of Christ's true body and blood is necessary in communion. [22/51%]
6. Communion protocol is to be enforced by the LC-MS national president. [21/49%]
7. Worthy and unworthy reception of communion is a key factor in deciding who should go to communion in LC-MS congregations. [20/47%]
8. Communion protocol is to be enforced by the LC-MS district presidents. [19/44%]
9. The sacramental nature of communion is a key factor in deciding who should go to communion in LC-MS congregations. [18/42%]
10. Open communion is to be rejected in LC-MS congregations. [14/36%]
11. Confusion and contradiction are created in the LC-MS by differences in congregational communion theology and practice. [12/28%]
12. Communion protocol is to be enforced by each LC-MS pastor. [11/26%]

sidering these types was much like looking at the proverbial elephant from a number of different perspectives. Each resolution had its own configuration of meanings. These meanings overlapped with the meanings in other resolutions but tended to lean in one major meaning direction or another. Some but not all of these meanings were put forward for consideration in a given resolution. Some meanings were reinforced by other meanings, while others seemed to contradict other meanings. One insight that emerged is that in the "Whereas" sections of the resolutions, the language of theology was used to push one or more meanings into focus for major consideration.

My intention with these data is to tabulate explicit meanings only. In evaluating these meanings of communion, it is important to recognize that simply because a meaning was not made explicit in a resolution does not mean it was excluded by the framers of that resolution. "Discernment of Christ's true body and blood is necessary in communion" (meaning 5) appeared in 51 percent of the communion resolutions. On the basis of this finding, however, it would be

---

13. Communion is an integrated part of the spiritual care function of LC-MS pastors. [11/26%]

14. Forgiveness of sins is a key factor in deciding who should be admitted to communion. [11/26%]

15. The benefit of communion understood as a totally free gift from God is a key factor in deciding who should be admitted to communion. [9/21%]

16. Uniformity in communion theology and practice is a key factor in deciding who should be admitted to communion. [9/21%]

17. Self-examination in communion theology and practice is a key factor in deciding who should be admitted to communion. [8/19%]

18. The concept of being well prepared for communion is a key factor in deciding who should be admitted to communion. [7/16%]

19. Communion participation as public confession of what is being taught in the LC-MS is a key factor in deciding who should be admitted to communion. [7/16%]

20. There are no specific denominational requirements for believers to participate in communion in the LC-MS. [7/16%]

21. The intention of amending one's sinful life is a key factor in deciding who should be admitted to communion. [6/14%]

22. Discernment of oneness with all believers in Christ is a key factor in deciding who should be admitted to communion. [6/14%]

23. Outward unity with all believers in Christ is a key factor in deciding who should be admitted to communion. [4/9%]

24. Worthiness defined by the desire to participate in communion is a key factor in deciding who should be admitted to communion. [3/7%]

25. Unity with Christ and his goals and purposes is a key factor in deciding who should be admitted to communion. [3/7%]

26. Communion protocol is to be enforced by the national synod of the LC-MS. [3/7%]

27. Close(d) communion is to be rejected in LC-MS congregations. [3/7%]

inappropriate to say that 49 percent of the framers of these resolutions denied that the discernment of Christ's true body and blood is necessary in communion. The point instead is that 51 percent explicitly said they believed it while the remainder did not indicate whether they believed or denied it. The value of these data for this essay is to note which meanings were explicitly mentioned and how they shaped the overall communion meaning of a resolution compared with that of another resolution. Moreover, resolutions that did not mention a certain meaning or firmly contradicted a meaning by choosing its opposite are helpful because they expose the emerging oppositions discussed later in this essay.

These twenty-seven meanings of communion are like the players on a stage. Each meaning can be featured at a variety of positions on that stage: front, center, back, retiring, or retired. Obviously, the front of the stage places the chosen meaning in the spotlight to be most noticed in the communication process. In the process of front-focusing one meaning, other meanings are pushed into the background, given a less noticed or totally unnoticed position rather than being highly recognized on the stage of communication. An example of foregrounded meaning takes place in overture 3-02.[5] The eleventh "Whereas" of that resolution states that "The practice of close(d) Communion was officially and publicly taught and observed by the early church." The first "Resolved" further states "That the LC-MS in its 1998 synodical convention reaffirm its practice of close(d) Communion." This resolution neatly foregrounds "Close(d) communion is mandatory in LC-MS congregations" (meaning 3), while "Close(d) communion is to be rejected in LC-MS congregations" (meaning 27) stands totally in the background.

Shared versus Weighted Meanings

We have already seen that the meanings of communion in LC-MS circles are many. It may be possible for two parties to identify a number of those meanings and even agree that communion includes those meanings and no additional ones. A case in point was a dinner conversation about communion that occurred on the second evening of the 1998 synodical convention. As the conversation began, we agreed to identify communion meanings that were held in common by us all. We very quickly agreed upon meanings that were very similar to thirteen I had noted in the convention workbook.[6] At this point in the

5. *Convention Workbook* (1998), p. 153.
6. These thirteen meanings were types 1, 5, 7, 9, 11, 13, 14, 15, 17, 18, 21, 23, and 25 listed in n. 4 above.

conversation, mutual understanding looked hopeful as more and more points of commonality on communion were shared. When no more common meanings were to be shared, however, the conversation faded. A pregnant pause followed, along with a hesitant search for a way to continue the theological transaction on communion.

One man finally took the leap. As he spoke it became apparent that "Outward unity with all believers in Christ is a key factor in deciding who should be admitted to communion" (meaning 23) was more important to him than all the other meanings. For this man, communion was a way of showing that he was in fellowship with all other Christians. The details of other people's faith were not so important for him as long as those persons desired to participate in communion. A woman in the conversation made it plain that she also gave more weight to one of the meanings than the others. However, her most important meaning was, "The benefit of communion understood as a totally free gift from God is a key factor in deciding who should be admitted to communion" (meaning 15). Her view was that unless people really understood that they were saved by grace alone, they should not participate in communion. She also believed it was the duty of each pastor to see that a person did not participate in communion unless that pastor was absolutely sure the communicant understood and believed in free grace.

So far in this case, we can see that while many of the same meanings may be shared, the weight or importance given to certain of the meanings also counts in doing transactional theology. If this weighting is not given legitimacy in theological conversation, the communication can easily become explosive, producing more emotional heat than intellectual light. The key to success in such conversational contexts is that commonly accepted rules for theological exchange must take the foregrounding and weighting of meanings just as seriously as the matter of which meanings are shared.

We return to the dinner conversation. The participants next edged beyond common meanings of communion to meanings that were not shared by everyone in the group. It was soon evident that these meanings were diagnostic: that is, they gave clear signs of differences in communion practice and theology. A delegate from Iowa related an experience in which his brother came from California to visit and was refused communion in the delegate's local LC-MS congregation. With this in mind, he said that in addition to the meanings agreed upon so far, he would have to add at least one more meaning. This took a form similar to "There are no specific denominational requirements for believers to participate in communion in the LC-MS" (meaning 20). As a result of this additional diagnostic meaning, the conversation on communion became quite animated. A friend of the Iowa delegate, also at table, said, "How can you say that? We all know that there are specific denominational requirements for communion in the LC-MS [cf. meaning 2]. We also believe that going to communion is a public confession of what is taught and believed in the LC-MS [cf. 19]. How can you seriously think that your brother should be allowed to go to communion in your congregation? I know for a fact that he left the LC-MS because he does not believe that the true body and blood of Jesus are present in communion [cf. 5]. In addition to that, he believes that there is no connection between sinful living and going to communion [cf. 21]. That is why we have closed communion in the LC-MS [cf. 3]."

This portion of the conversation reveals that in addition to the overlapping, shared meanings, there are often additional diagnostic meanings that are latent but left unmentioned. On the other hand, with another set of people these latent meanings might always be brought up for reasons of conscience but without any reference to the shared meanings of communion. These latent diagnostic meanings often are opposed to others or are given an opposing slant. Therefore, other diagnostic meanings are viewed as unacceptable and become points of direct confrontation and disagreement. This is exactly what happened between the friends just mentioned. Their friendship has since cooled, and an unhealthy separation has taken the place of regular fellowship.

The transactional differences in communion theology that took place in the halls and restaurants of the 1998 LC-MS convention, together with the differences displayed in the convention workbook, must be taken seriously. Both the transactional and the formal differences have given rise to ongoing strained relationships between LC-MS members, which in turn provide a fertile basis for unkindness, injustice, discord, institutional problems, and organizational disunity and damage. At the same time, with a sincere desire to work toward mutual understanding, transactional communion theology can provide a fruitful forum for intentionally surfacing and consciously recognizing theological diversity. Solutions can then be sought by carrying on the conversation in a context of respectful listening and careful articulation, especially when this communicating is done on the basis of Scripture, the historic practices and confessions of the church, and the study of how positive solutions have previously been reached in similar situations of theological diversity and complexity.

Worldview (Presuppositional) Meanings

Theological meanings, including the crisp, clear, and clean communication of God's law and gospel at the crossroads of uncertain and messy situations of everyday life, are foundational to Christian existence. These theological meanings, including meanings about communion, are the logical linkages that organize and drive rationality and connect human thinking with human actions. In terms of a Christian's understanding of theological reality, they are fundamental and indispensable. In addition, the meanings in transactional theology make possible the consistent communication of deeply held beliefs and values to other human beings.

Since there are different meanings (some foregrounded, others backgrounded, some weighted, some diagnostic), and since they can be assigned different levels of importance by different groups of people, the concept of worldview is helpful. Paul Hiebert describes worldview as "the basic assumptions about reality that *lie behind* the beliefs and behavior of a culture."[7] From my perspective, Hiebert is talking about meaning, saying worldview provides a coherent rationale for arranging and valuing multiple meanings. Worldview is therefore a basic tool for doing theology, and theology is essentially a kind of worldview.[8] It is a way to identify the fundamental importance that certain meanings have in the theological configuration of a person or group. These important meanings also serve as controllers and organizers for a person's or group's way of thinking and living. By way of definition, we can say that a worldview meaning is a single, primary, and foundational meaning that is used to anchor and ground a concept like communion and that serves to shape, limit, and focus the other meanings of a concept like communion.

Because of their foundational nature, worldview meanings are fiercely held. When held in common, they are a powerful basis for vital and united community thought and action. When, however, a fiercely held worldview meaning stands opposed to a worldview meaning dear to another person or group, there is powerful potential for division and conflict. Once people have used the language of theology as an instrument for separating into groups, meaning tends to lose its transferability and, at the same time, clear and unambiguous definitions and helpful clarifications are very difficult to achieve. Such separation leads to stronger insistence upon preferred terms and specified interpretations of those theological terms. People also become rigid about

---

7. Paul G. Hiebert, *Anthropological Insights for Missionaries* (Grand Rapids: Baker, 1985), p. 45, emphasis mine.

8. Theology is a kind of worldview, a basic ingredient of human meaning systems. Theological understandings serve as a primary prism through which people evaluate and arrange other meanings as they conduct their theology in everyday life. Their theological worldview meanings automatically organize and control significant parts of their lives. These theological meanings may be spoken or unspoken, consciously or subconsciously held, but they are ever present guides to how life is thought about, talked about, and lived out in everyday relationships.

foregrounded, weighted, and diagnostic meanings. They tend to use their worldview meanings for evaluation when listening to others, which often leads to almost total inability to understand with an open mind what others are trying to say. At this point in the cycle of communication, we can also see the influence of sociocultural inertia, the human tendency to establish and live in comfortable in-groups at the expense of out-groups that produce discomfort. In such cases the language of theology is no longer a loyal servant but a deceitful troublemaker. It has become a divider and a destroyer of the peace, a tool for demolishing the harmony so important for unified organizational progress in any group, congregation, judicatory, district, synod, or denomination.

It is important to recognize that people are frequently unaware of their personal or group theologies. Even when their theological meanings appear certain and fixed in a hierarchy that is firmly based on a foundational worldview meaning, people are often unable to say clearly which meaning is most important in a particular theological position, let alone name all the meanings in that position. Indeed, at the subconscious level the number and order of theological meanings and the foundational worldview meaning may be quite different from those at the conscious level, especially for a concept like communion.

Silo 1 and Silo 2 Meanings

The intensity of the convention discussion on communion made sense to a number of LC-MS members that I will call either "silo 1" or "silo 2" thinkers. Each group discussed communion on the basis of different foundational worldview meanings.

"Communion is a key designator of separation from all that are not in altar and pulpit fellowship with the LC-MS" (meaning 4) is the foundational worldview meaning for a silo 1 theology. In silo 1 communion is basically a *marker of close fellowship* with those who share their foundational worldview meaning. At the same time, it is a *marker of separation* from all Christians who are not in pulpit and altar fellowship with the LC-MS, no matter what their beliefs about Jesus as Savior may be. For silo 1 thinkers, "Discernment of Christ's true body and blood is necessary in communion" (meaning 5) and "Forgiveness of sins is a key factor in deciding who should be admitted to communion" (meaning 14) are also important. This is not to say that additional communion meanings are never present in silo 1 thinking, but rather that they are rarely if ever explicitly expressed even as middle or backgrounded meanings.

Silo 1 communion culture understands Christian fellowship not from a relationship and reconciliation point of view but primarily as separation from heterodox people. Pure doctrine for this group operates in a splintered theological system that makes it possible to place what the Scripture says about relationships and reconciliation almost totally in the background. It desires to use structures and laws to create unity and eliminate tension. It defines the practice of communion in formal, legalistic, black-and-white terms by shaping, limiting, and organizing worldview meaning. This communion culture sees the LC-MS as the world's best if not only hope for the future of Christianity.

Much of the basis for silo 1 communion practice and theology is exemplified in overture 3-18.[9] The second "Resolved" of this resolution reads, "Resolved, that the Lutheran Church–Missouri Synod in convention reaffirm our stance, [of] continuing to restrict our altars to such as are in confessional fellowship with the Lutheran Church–Missouri Synod." I also vividly remember the times on the floor of the LC-MS conventions in 1983, 1989, and 1998 when silo 1 communion practice and theology was transacted with vigor. This view also regularly comes out in private conversations, as it did during a heart-to-heart talk with a dedicated LC-MS pastor and his wife, who said to me, "Purity of doctrine and practice are what the LC-MS is all about. Surely we cannot have communion fellowship with heterodox people who are not members of the LC-MS. The LC-MS must keep its doctrine pure. If it does not there is little hope for the survival of biblical Christianity in the world today."

The foundational worldview meaning for a silo 2 communion theology is, "There are no specific denominational requirements for believers to participate in communion in the LC-MS" (meaning 20). For this group, communion is basically a *marker of oneness* with all others who believe in Jesus Christ as their Savior, no matter what their denominational affiliation may be. Silo 2 thinking also includes belief in the real presence, salvation through the forgiveness of sins, intent to examine and amend one's sinful life, and the willingness and ability to share a common faith and confession of that faith.[10] Silo 2 com-

---

9. *Convention Workbook* (1998), p. 159.

10. An unpublished document entitled "Celebrate (Pentecost 1996): Who Determines Worthiness at the Supper?" was prepared by a committee as a declaration of eucharistic understanding and practice for a meeting at Boca Raton, Fla. It reflects much of silo 2 communion theology. (Extrabiblical references are to Lutheran confessional documents in *The Book of Concord*, supra n. 1.)

- Christians are to realize that when they come together in the Lord "as church" (1 Cor. 11:18), the responsibility for self-examination and discernment obviously lies with the individual believer (1 Cor. 11:28).
- We believe, teach and confess that those who cherish and honor the Sacrament will of their own accord urge and impel themselves to partake of the body and blood of their Savior. (Large Catechism V.43) The clear words of Christ to remember his

munion culture understands Christian fellowship primarily as relationship and reconciliation. Pure doctrine also operates in a splintered theological system that foregrounds what the Bible says about relationships and reconciliation, while placing in the middle or background other theological issues and doctrinal teachings that emphasize a separation from those that add to or subtract from the Christian faith. This communion culture has a strong focus on context and change, and is increasingly aware of postmodernism in which Christianity is no longer the only culturally acceptable religious alternative. Members who espouse silo 2 are intensely aware that the LC-MS lives amidst those who may seek spiritual things and yet minimize or reject Christ as the Son of God and the Savior of the world. Their fear of relativism pushes them toward open fellowship with all Christians, especially evangelical Christians, for whom Christ is still central to religious beliefs and practices.

Silo 2 communion culture has a bit larger theological circumference than the communion culture of silo 1. This hypothesis is supported by the fact that silo 2 explicitly includes belief in the real presence, self-examination, repentance and forgiveness of sins, intent to amend life, and commitment to share a common faith and confession.[11] This point of view is becoming more popular

---

salvational death are both precept and command which enjoin the celebration upon his people. (Large Catechism V.45) But we are not granted liberty to despise the Sacrament. (Large Catechism V.49)

- We reject and condemn the notion that we are to act distantly toward the Sacrament, neglect it, or grow cold and callous toward it. (Large Catechism V.67)
- We reject and condemn the belief and practice that the congregation, the celebrating pastor, the church body, or the denomination has the right to impose additional restrictions upon the believer and presume the right of examination clearly imposed upon each believer (1 Cor. 11:17-34).
- We believe, teach and confess that there is only one kind of unworthy guest; namely those who do not believe (John 3:18).
- We believe, teach and confess that no genuine believer who retains a living faith will receive the Sacrament to condemnation. Christ gave us the Supper for Christians who are weak in faith, but repentant, in order to comfort and strengthen their weak faith. (Formula of Concord, Epitome, VII.18)
- We believe, teach and confess that the entire worthiness of guests at the heavenly feast consists solely in the most holy obedience and complete merit of Christ, not in our own virtue or preparation. (Formula of Concord, Epitome, VII.18)
- We believe, teach and confess that neither Scripture nor the Confessions impose a denominational or synodical requirement on baptized Christians who desire to confess the Real Presence and receive the body and blood of Christ offered in the Eucharist.

11. These attributes of silo 2 communion culture are exemplified in overture 3-06, *Convention Workbook* (1998), p. 155. The first "Resolved" reads, "Resolved, That we affirm our Synod's position relating to the practice of the administration of Holy Communion, which rec-

in LC-MS circles. I hear it regularly in pastoral conferences and from the students I teach at the seminary.

Two things can be said in summary. First, silo 1 communion theology almost totally backgrounds what the Scripture says about relationships and reconciliation. On the other hand, silo 2 tends to background what the Scripture says about theological issues and doctrinal teachings that emphasize the separation from those that add to or subtract from the Christian faith. The communion theology of both groups is guilty of splintering fellowship within the LC-MS to the extent that these theological systems come into direct and divisive conflict with each other.

Secondly, there is the problem about the language in which transactional theology is done. The Carlson sociological case study (pp. 263-93) has pointed out that "while those who employ a more traditional language continue to view unionism as the greatest threat to fellowship, those who employ a more contemporary language view relativism as the greater threat." ("Unionism" in this quote stands for relationship with the heterodox.) My own research indicates that in doing transactional communion theology, silo 1 approaches employ traditional language while silo 2 approaches employ contemporary language. The result is that silo 1 and silo 2 people often identify each other as the enemy on the basis of language usage alone. The lines are therefore drawn, and conclusions about theological correctness are prematurely made on the basis of the contrast between church language and contemporary language, traditional liturgy and contemporary liturgy, and older Bible translations over against more contemporary ones. In reality, these conclusions are often reached even before the theological issues have been put on the table for discussion.

A Third Group of Meanings

An additional finding that emerged from this study is the existence of yet another very significant group of LC-MS members who bear a third communion culture. This third culture centers on a holistic communion theology. I have seen it most frequently in congregations that are over fifty years old where family members have tended to stay near home from generation to generation, cherishing many of the communion traditions of their ancestors. For this sig-

---

ognizes that the Sacrament is for all Christians who are able to examine themselves and who share a common faith and confession." See also the fourth "Whereas" of overture 3-04, p. 154, which reads, "A practice congruent with Scripture and the Confessions calls for the Sacrament to be shared with baptized Christians who repent of their sins, believe the real presence, and sincerely intend to amend their lives."

nificant but ordinarily quiet and cooperative group, the intensity and ill feelings connected with the communion discussion at the 1998 synod convention were unnecessary, upsetting, disconcerting, and discouraging. Some of these people have already addressed the upset, discouragement, and insecurity by leaving the LC-MS.

In this holistic approach the theology of communion is important and indispensable but not primarily focused on fellowship. Being secure and at peace with fellow congregational members of the same background and tradition is far more important. Communion is not a concept that is consciously defined. Instead, communion is part of what it is to be Christian and Lutheran. It is also not something about which to become exercised, have a bad conscience, or ask too many questions. This third communion culture is best seen as a configuration of fairly equally held communion meanings in a broad field of meaning. It does not focus on just one worldview meaning but rather includes seventeen of the twenty-seven meanings gleaned from the 1998 convention workbook.[12] Most of these meanings were and still are patterned across the stage of communion meanings with no one meaning being foregrounded at the expense of the other meanings of communion. Normally, people who hold this holistic communion theology feel free to configure these communion meanings according to their own preferences.

People within this communion culture have lived with this holistic and comfortable understanding of communion for generations. It is their sociological and relational home. They are not splitters but groupers. They enjoy living in a secure Christian environment. For them, relationships, reconciliation, careful formulation of doctrine, outreach evangelism, and fellowship with all other believers in Christ are important but are not issues to be fought over. They would like to see the traditions of the LC-MS change slowly in a calm and secure context. "Calm and secure" is defined in terms of familiar pastoral care and comfortable ways of doing things, both inside and outside of formal church services.

This third communion culture is expansive. It takes the middle road, overlapping to some extent with silo 1 and silo 2. Neither unionism nor relativism is the major concern for this group. Instead, fellowship is viewed through the lens of peace and unity in LC-MS culture and life. Since the LC-MS has been preoccupied with fellowship from its beginnings, it is significant not only that silo 1 and silo 2 have chosen a worldview meaning that focuses on fellowship, but also that this holistic communion theology is oriented toward fellow-

---

12. These seventeen meanings were types 1, 2, 3, 5, 7, 9, 10, 11, 13, 14, 15, 17, 18, 21, 22, 24, and 25 listed in n. 4 above.

ship. Each group reflects a different perspective on fellowship, however. Silo 1 seeks fellowship with those of the same denomination and especially with the comfortable part of that fellowship, and separation from all those of different denominations. Silo 2 seeks fellowship with all fellow believers in Christ, and implied separation from those who are not Christians, assessed on the basis of the centrality of Christ and biblical infallibility and inerrancy. Holistic communion theology seeks fellowship with all Christians, especially those of the same mind, heart, and tradition, and separation from those who stir up trouble and make life sociologically uncomfortable.

Of special interest is the fact that the number of people affirming holistic communion theology appears to be growing. In addition, people in silo 1 and to some extent silo 2 are becoming more vocal and strident in articulating their distinctive communion theologies. For these groups, their position on communion is most important (sometimes consciously and at times subconsciously) because it is an expression of each group's position on fellowship. The hope of silo 1 is to challenge and confront silo 2 and holistic communion theology by their way of thinking. They hope to bring unity in the LC-MS by convincing others of their doctrinal and intellectual position on communion. The hope of silo 2 has two prongs: first, to bring unity to the denomination by consolidating their communion position with others in LC-MS on the basis of a relationship of reconciliation, and second, to include the unsaved in that growing relationship by reconciliation through Jesus Christ.

For completeness, we should recognize that formal theological niceties on communion are not the main concern for many LC-MS members, including some who are intensely involved in the communion controversy. Their main concern is who is on their side and who is on the other in the fray. As each side transacts communion theology on a daily basis, the most intense adherents of silo 1 speak of doctrinal purity while the adherents of silo 2 focus on openness and respect for all other Christians. Interestingly, the theological meanings of communion that each position holds in common with holistic communion theology will normally be glossed over as each side emphasizes its opposing worldview meanings. We should also mention that in formally written communion theology in the LC-MS, the distinctive worldview meanings of silo 1 (centered on meaning 4) and silo 2 (centered on meaning 20) are either not mentioned at all or are overly magnified. This happens because the reason for formally writing theology is often either to stress one particular position in contrast to another or to gloss over all opposition in the hope of promoting unity.

Doing transactional theology also offers at least two possibilities. One possibility is for helpful breakthroughs in communication. Such breakthroughs happen as constructive theological conversation provides a way for open listening, careful clarification, a variety of communication approaches, and time for open minds and hearts to work toward thought-provoking understanding, which in turn can lead to mutual enlightenment. The other possibility, of course, is for a total or nearly total communication breakdown with a good deal of emotional heat. The point is that when people have misunderstanding, miscommunication, and conflict about communion in the LC-MS, it is not a parlor game or an exercise in debate. Instead, it is an exercise in serious theology, both formal and transactional, rooted in specific kinds of worldview meanings and distinctions focused on understandings about God.

These communion discussions have also led me to notice the conscious and subconscious meanings and the attitudes of harmony, diversity, and divisiveness in relation to worldview meanings. Considering these factors leads to four outcomes that are relevant for this communion situation and other LC-MS organizational challenges in the twenty-first century.

1. When communion meanings operate at a subconscious level among those focused on harmony and unity, there is an opportunity for using transactional theology to discuss constructively the differences of communion theology and practice.
2. When communion meanings operate at a subconscious level among those focused on diversity and especially divisiveness, there is a serious threat to using transactional theology to discuss constructively the differences of communion theology and practice.
3. When communion meanings operate at a conscious level among those focused on diversity but not divisiveness, there is an opportunity for using transactional theology to discuss constructively the differences of communion theology and practice. Such conscious knowledge of distinctive meanings enables helpful clarification and understanding and can lead to enlightened communication.
4. When communion meanings operate at a conscious level among those focused on divisiveness, however, the opportunity for using transactional theology to discuss constructively the differences of communion theology and practice is severely limited. Instead, we should expect escalating disharmony and division because well-meaning but ideologically committed adversaries will use their conscious knowledge of distinctive meanings to create further miscommunication and misunderstanding.

Two broad conclusions can now be noted. First, the silo cultures in LC-MS communion theology are defined by meaning patterns that focus primarily on a single worldview meaning. These primary worldview meanings for silo 1 and silo 2 are strongly foregrounded on the communion meaning stage, with only a few other meanings in the middle or background position.[13] These middle and background meanings, although far less important, do have their place in the overall scheme of things, however. They are often used in the "Whereas" language of formal convention resolutions to pave the way for the truly focal worldview meaning in the "Resolved" sections of those resolutions.

Second, it is important to note that the separation of LC-MS members into a number of communion cultures has enabled oppositions to develop. These opposing communion cultures with their opposing transactional theologies and practices have provided handy lightning rods for divisiveness in the denomination, especially on the subject of fellowship. As fellowship issues are forcefully pushed into the center of LC-MS discussion, the presence of a third communion culture represented by holistic communion theology may well hold the key. This approach may be uniquely equipped to deal positively and evenhandedly with the issues of fellowship as we face the changing fabric of the twenty-first century. By fostering an intentional and unswerving commitment to holistic biblical theology, as well as diplomatic and peace-loving conversation as a key component to life together in the body of Christ, this culture promises to be the most successful at tackling the task of doing transactional theology, including communion theology.

LC-MS Communion Culture over Time

We have already seen that communion practice and theology had a high profile at the 1998 synod convention. The formal convention conversation on this subject and the informal give-and-take in the halls and restaurants did not emerge in a vacuum, however. Instead, discussions about communion were already becoming increasingly focused and controversial during the 1960s and afterward. This happened at least in part because the culture of communion, the way LC-MS members think about and do communion, has changed over time.

Soon after I came back to the United States in 1982 after twenty-two years

---

13. In the classical form of silo 1, meaning 4 takes almost absolute precedence. All other meanings, if present at all, have a much reduced status. The circumference of classical silo 1 communion theology is therefore quite small and can be best represented by a tall but narrow silo. In the classical form of silo 2, meaning 20 takes strong precedence, with any other meanings given secondary consideration. The circumference of classical silo 2 communion theology is therefore somewhat larger than that of silo 1. Even so, it is still a *silo* of meaning(s) rather than a wider field of meanings as evidenced by holistic communion theology.

of missionary service in Africa, it dawned on me that no normative communion practice existed in the LC-MS. It also occurred to me that the fairly common theological understanding of communion that had been in place in 1960 was in the process of fragmenting. This almost immediately involved me in regular conversations with all kinds of people about their practice and understanding of communion. These conversations later became more like informal interviews with LC-MS members in many parts of the United States and elsewhere in the world. In the years since these conversations began, several trends in the practice, modeling, and transactional theology of communion seem to be confirmed.

First, individual LC-MS communion practices and theologies have incrementally moved away from a broad, holistic approach in which a field of communion meanings is more or less evenly emphasized. Instead, the movement is toward a more narrow understanding of communion that focuses on one or at most a few communion meanings. As a result, many of the common communion meanings that have been the historically shared heritage of LC-MS members have been profoundly backgrounded. This reduction of the significant meanings of communion results in a number of separate silos instead of what once was a more unified field of communion meanings, both transactional and formal. Much of the integrative meaning, unifying potential, and supportive strength of communion practice and transactional theology in the LC-MS is therefore being decimated, neglected, mislaid, and even lost.

Second, silo thinking opens the door for additional theological and sociological separations in the LC-MS. In addition to the separation over communion practice, there are the "worship wars," the "church and ministry controversies," and the smoldering divisions over the charismatic movement. This tendency toward silo thinking and splintering gained momentum during the final decades of the twentieth century. In other words, these silos in communion practice and theology are a kind of concentrated instance of the larger in-group/out-group tensions over fellowship that have been with the LC-MS from the beginning. They have also become lightning rods in attempts to identify, develop, continue, and enhance differing ecclesial, financial, and political agendas in the LC-MS.

Third, the diverging worldview meanings that define various communion cultures in the LC-MS are being formalized and spoken about more openly and pointedly. As a result, transactional communion theologies are becoming more radicalized as the discussion about communion differences becomes more strident and unfriendly.

In light of these three trends, we turn now to a more detailed analysis of LC-MS communion culture as it was known in some places fifty to sixty years ago, looking at both the practice and its accompanying theology (transactional and formal). I personally experienced this communion tradition that in many cases has never been fully known by other LC-MS members, especially younger ones. For this reason, I will describe this culture in some detail, recognizing that it has never functioned perfectly and has always been subject to sin in at least some ways.

Fifty to sixty years ago among the so-called "builder" generation, communion was a very public and communal event that occurred four and later twelve times each year. It tended to be special and set apart. It was also pervasive and dynamic. It was not individualized, internally centered grace, but communally oriented, God-centered grace. It was focused on the mystery of Christ for and in his body of believers. It was united with that body of believers who received Christ's body and blood in trusting faith for the forgiveness of sins, life (eternal and earthly), and salvation. The overall metaphor for communion was therefore that of a family meal that offered good health, especially relational health with God (on the vertical plane) and with other human beings (on the horizontal plane).

In many congregations the celebration of communion was much like the celebration of Christmas and Easter. It was a special event to be anticipated and requiring preparation. It was collective in nature and well publicized weeks in advance. There were extensive protocols included in preparation for it, many of which were done in the home and community, as well as a special order of service that set the communion service apart from the ordinary weekly service.

Communion was most often spoken of as the Lord's Supper. At its best, therefore, it clearly reflected union with Christ and the outpouring of God's love and forgiveness in which Christians rejoiced and for which they prepared. Ideally, the reception of Christ's body and blood in the Lord's Supper was strongly anticipated. In such situations communion was practiced with a theology that recognized that it would not be healthy or helpful to hold hidden sins, resentments, and grudges when coming to the spiritually powerful communal meal. It was totally inappropriate and in fact theologically wrong to hold back from others the love and forgiveness of God that each Christian was continually receiving. Instead, overflowing love and forgiveness to others were the expected, although not always perfected, preparations carried out through personal acts of confession, forgiveness, and reconciliation. Joyful participation in the Lord's Supper also tended to be a time in which community life focused on transactional theology, on the powerful and pervasive mystery of God's grace, wrath, love, and forgiveness, as well as on communal examination and reformation.

Communion was an adult reality. It was an adult way of publicly saying, "God is real and God matters in adult life." In the best of times, it was also an adult way of saying to God and to each other, "Please forgive me." It was getting right with God and others. It was receiving the assurance of forgiveness of sins, life, and salvation from God, as well as love, forgiveness, and a strong sense of Christian community from fellow Christians. Typically, children were vitally involved as quiet and thoughtful observers. Communion was a major communal tool for socializing the young into adulthood and into commonsense civility. Often (but not always) this approach successfully taught young people the basics of God's power, love, and forgiveness, and also the appropriate response to the triune God in biblical worship, including private, family, and corporate worship.

When this communion practice was fully integrated, most of the process of communion did not take place in the church building. Instead, it culminated in the church building as the congregation gathered to share in the communion meal after days and sometimes weeks of openness to God's word and Spirit as people were getting right with others in and beyond the family. This process often led to a time of holistic sensitivity in community, a time of confession and forgiveness motivated by God's Spirit, and a time of unloading the sins of the past, both privately and, in appropriate cases, publicly. At its best, this process provided a time of mending fences and taking advantage of family and pastoral counseling and care. At such times communicants also came prepared, with the help of God and the encouragement of their Christian families, friends, and neighbors, to step forward in faith to overcome Satan's temptations, their sinful flesh, and the besetting sins in their lives.

This process often led nonbelievers to look on with interest, awe, and respect. Some were converted because they saw the power, love, and forgiveness of God in communion. One example of this that I recall involved a shopkeeper who was moved by the Spirit of God to receive Christ and be baptized, together with his family, because the father of an LC-MS family had returned stolen goods as a natural part of that family's preparation for and participation in communion.

In this collective communion process, the entire Christian community tended to become involved. By definition, there was an intentional emphasis on the consolation and mutual concern for other people. There was a deep commitment to the fact that faith was demonstrated in life. If a person's life deviated and showed an exaggerated love for money, pleasure, self, and other kinds of antisocial behaviors, there was cause for congregational concern and action. Where such sins showed themselves, it was recognized that there was manifest need for kind encouragement and loving admonition. In such a case, the congregation needed to be involved through its members and especially its elders and pastor.

As God's people responded to God's Spirit, suitable encouragement and admonition were practiced first and foremost by the appropriate people in the family, both nuclear and extended. This normally also included workers attached to businesses and farms as well as their families. It was also practiced in the natural networking of Christian friends. Men, women, and, where appropriate, children (especially older ones) were regularly involved in this communal activity. These activities of mutual encouragement were given strength and impetus as the communion process moved forward toward the spiritually centered communal meal in the gathered congregation of Christians. When the family and friendship networks, plus the natural systems of communication, were not effective in promoting Christian repentance and reconciliation, the church elders and pastor would be called on to be of assistance. Individual communion announcements with the pastor were also an integral part of the process, giving the pastor a natural channel for encouragement and admonition. This was a precious and very personal time with the pastor, a time set apart to discuss life, including the spiritual part of life.

In this intact and integrated holistic model of announcing for communion with the pastor, the announcing was done some days before the service in which the communion meal was celebrated. This happened because if it became evident during the announcement time that the communicant's conscience was burdened by sin that needed to be confessed, there was still time to go and do the confessing, not only to God but also to other persons. The result would hopefully be personal forgiveness and reconciliation. At such times it was often but not always necessary for elders, the pastor, or both to be involved in this essential communication so that Christian care could immediately be available to all parties at the time of confession and forgiveness. This part of the communion process was at times very simple and straightforward, and at other times very complex. Positive completion of complex situations often took several days and occasionally weeks, months, or even years. This was not only because it normally involved several people, but also because it took time for people in conflict, sin, and fear to work through a situation that was often quite entangled.[14]

---

14. This holistic process of communion, including complete preparation, recognized that when communal confession and forgiveness was successfully completed by the power of God's Spirit, it opened the way for needed love, forgiveness, and assurance of freedom from sin and guilt. It also naturally strengthened and fortified the kingdom of God through the building of communal oneness in Christ. All of this happened in the context of receiving full assurance of Christ's love and forgiveness by participating in the reverent mystery of sharing in the communal meal of Christ's body and blood as a body of reconciled believers in Christ. It was in every way a remembering and living in and with Christ as a fundamental part of everyday life until he comes again.

Foundational to all these communion practices was a transactional theology of communion, an understanding of God that made it natural to open oneself in community to the Spirit of God to enhance both the vertical and horizontal relations of examination, confession, forgiveness, and love. The basic idea was that communion should build community with Christ and with fellow Christians.

In many LC-MS situations today, holistic communion is no longer an option because communion has been reorganized in a way that no longer focuses on human relationships. Instead, it is understood to be strictly a spiritual, momentary event rather than a dynamic and divine interpersonal process. For this reason, the communion process leading up to the communal meal in church, once so important in LC-MS personal piety, has been de-emphasized to the point of being beyond the recollection of many.

In studying LC-MS communion thought over the past few decades, I have tried to develop metaphors that describe the two ends of the communion spectrum in our transactional communion theology. The two metaphors that have been most helpful are *communal meal* and *health supplement*. In the interview process, I asked people to identify their spontaneous, uncritical (unmarked) understandings of communion from the point of view of these two metaphors. In my estimation, the majority (although not overwhelming) of LC-MS members chose the health supplement metaphor. Men consistently chose it more often than women, as did the so-called "boomer" generation (especially the younger end of this group, born between 1946 and 1964) and "Xer" generation (born after 1965) than the builder generation (born before 1946).

A significant percentage of the participants say they have never considered the idea that communion builds relationships of loving acceptance and interconnected Christian community by confession, absolution, and forgiveness in the context of God's love and forgiveness. This is especially true of LC-MS members for whom family no longer has a high priority in everyday life. For them the horizontal understanding of the body of Christ, with its associated communal fellowship and human forgiveness, is almost completely backgrounded because there is little communal theology or practical family living to trigger it.

When I have suggested that the metaphors of health supplement and communal meal are overlapping and that both are important in biblical communion, it tends to lead to conversational heat rather than to helpful understanding and light. A good number of LC-MS members today see communion strictly as either one or the other. In addition, a significant minority of those involved in transactional communion feel uncomfortable and at times threatened and defensive when the scriptural roots of communion are introduced into the conversation.

When the discussion turns to the benefits of communion, there is a further spread of meanings ranging from benefits described as forgiveness of sins, life, and salvation to benefits described as the release of internal, personal power. At times this internal power is described as a kind of New Age release of energy rather than as a gift of God's grace.[15] This point of view was most clearly expressed to me some years ago by an articulate businessman who said, "Life is heavy. I just try to get through to another Sunday. I go to church for communion. Communion resets my internal gyro. It clears my mind and activates my flagging get-up-and-go power. It gets me ready for another demanding week." The concept that the word of God is the power of God unto salvation (Rom. 1:16), and that the sustaining promises of God through his Spirit are accessible throughout the week, at any time and place, without some kind of special sacramental infusion, seemed illogical to this man. Also puzzling to him was the idea that without the word of God, communion is ordinary bread and wine.[16]

For such LC-MS members, the authority, meaning, and efficacy of communion do not rest on a Spirit-engendered faith relationship with God based on his words and promises, but on the communion elements and ceremonies themselves. Such people also find church services without communion to be incomplete and of less than full value. The number of LC-MS members that think this way about communion seems to be increasing. All seems well for such people if and when the communion rite is administered by the right person, in the right way, and in the right place. Each of these "rights" will normally be defined individually, independently, and internally. Certainly such people have faith, but their faith seems to be focused primarily on the forms, ritualistic processes, and pragmatic results. In such cases the understanding of communion is not communal but very individuated and personal. It focuses on what communion does for me, my desires, my energy, my attitudes, my credibility, my competence, my ability to do what is best for me, my obligations, and my responsibilities. It is perceived as a pure, potent, personal health supplement rather than as a nutritious communal meal provided by the Lord Jesus Christ for the forgiveness of sins and as a support for Christian community. It is projected as individual and internal, or at best as sacramental, vertical, and personal, rather than as spiritual and sacramental with both a vertical and horizontal dimension and a powerful communal and interpersonal effect.

15. This personal energy moves beyond the idea of help and healing for guilt and sin and the gift of life in this world and the next, to the idea of superior personal performance. This benefit is seen as a kind of superior performance derived from the sacramental power that pushes a person through the activities of the week at a better level.

16. *Dr. Martin Luther's Large Catechism*, trans. John N. Lenker (Minneapolis: Augsburg, 1935), p. 175.

I have tried to chronicle the unraveling and reorganizing of transactional communion practice and theology. This unraveling and reorganizing have placed great collateral pressure on matters of fellowship in the LC-MS, internally and externally, especially during the latter decades of the twentieth century. Because the foundational self-understandings, structures, and practices of the denomination were built on fellowship commitments, these strains in communion theology and practice are significant.

Since the days of the various immigrations of Lutherans to the United States, the Altenburg debate, and the founding of the LC-MS seminaries, there has been tension about how to define and express fellowship commitments. LC-MS fellowship commitments were fashioned out of a fabric of pure doctrine, faithfulness to the confessions and the gospel, and preserving that purity in relation to other theological traditions and the larger society. Today, fellowship issues within the denomination are focalized in communion practice and theology. The present communion confrontations call into question the definitions and the fabric of these same fellowship commitments.

Parallels between Communion Culture and American Culture

In order to understand further how these commitments have been threatened, we examine how sociocultural change in the larger society has contributed to contemporary denominational divisions and conflicts. In particular, I will explore five types of sociocultural change in America and how these compare with recent shifts of understanding in LC-MS communion theology.

From Communalism to Individualism

The first sociocultural change to be compared is the pervasive transition from communalism to individualism. The authors of *Habits of the Heart* document this striking sociological shift by distinguishing between communities of memory and an individualism dominated by separation and utilitarian self-expression.[17] This distinction highlights how Americans have gradually moved from a primary focus on community to a primary focus on the individual. This same individualism dominated by separation has been apparent to me almost daily since returning from communally oriented Africa in 1982. The contrast

---

17. Robert N. Bellah and others, *Habits of the Heart: Individualism and Commitment in American Life* (New York: Harper and Row, 1985), pp. 153-55.

between contemporary American individualism and my youthful memories of mutually supportive community continues to be very strong. My own cousin memorably recalled how, in the 1940s and 1950s, "we shared everything as together we grew into manhood in a cherishing extended family community." In the 1990s, by contrast, a friend from Denver remarked, "I have gotten carried away with the bottom line of profit and loss. I hardly see my wife and children any more because it is early to work and late night meetings to keep the business spiraling upward." When asked why he accepted the responsibility of coming to the 1998 synod convention as a delegate, he said, "I am programmed for personal responsibility and for separation. How else can one succeed?"

There is a striking parallelism in change patterns between the culture of communion and the culture of a society that has moved away from communities of memory and toward separated, utilitarian, self-expressive individualism. During this same period, many LC-MS members have moved away from a communion culture of communally oriented meal toward one of an individuated, health supplement understanding. Similarly parallel change patterns exist with respect to relationships between the denomination and individual LC-MS congregations. One overture in the 1998 convention workbook expressed this trend by saying, "Resolved, that each congregation determine its own practice and procedure for faithfully following the guidance of the Holy Scriptures and the Lutheran Confessions in administering the Eucharist."[18] The Carlson case study speaks of this situation as "conflict between the central judicatory of the synod, the synodical convention and its elected leadership, and the localized districts." This individualistic withdrawal is occurring as the supportive and communal trust relationship that was traditionally part of the LC-MS culture increasingly gives way to a culture of distrust, tension, and separation. This shows itself most clearly between local congregations and districts on one side and the synodical structures on the other side, particularly at the national level.

Separation of Public and Private

The second sociocultural change to be compared is a movement from the overlapping and complementary status of public and private to the growing separation between the two. In the first decades of the twentieth century, people did not make a major distinction between public and private. Religion was a public as well as a private matter. God looked after things very closely, not only in private space but also in the public square (Ps. 139). When my grandfather began

---

18. *Convention Workbook* (1998), p. 159.

his ministry in west-central Minnesota, part of his mission was to be a full-time teacher of the Christian faith in a one-room public school for two months of each school year. (Another teacher was employed to teach the other subjects during the other months of the school year.) In addition, many nonreligious functions were held in the Lutheran church. Private homes in that era were the normal places for births, anniversaries, marriage receptions, birthdays, and the first part of funeral services. Today, these events are most often held in restaurants, hospitals, commercial meeting halls, funeral homes, and churches. At the same time, so-called political correctness dictates that religious sentiments are personal and private and should be expressed only in one's home or in a church, mosque, or synagogue. Personal meditation and prayer is considered appropriate as long as it is not spoken aloud for others to hear. Prayer at mealtime, traditionally very common, is also falling into disuse.

The parallels between this sociocultural change pattern and LC-MS communion culture will be addressed after we have considered the third instance of sociocultural change.

From Spiritual to Secular, Back to Spiritual

The third sociocultural change pattern is a movement from the spiritual to the secular and now back to the spiritual. Traditionally, American culture gave an important role to the spiritual. The middle of the twentieth century fostered a separation of the spiritual from the nonspiritual. It socialized God and the spiritual into a place rather than understanding these as an integrated part of all of life. In this way of thinking, wherever God and the spiritual are, the secular is not, and vice versa. This point of view has been reinforced by a number of Supreme Court decisions, such as those concerning prayer in public schools. In the 1950s the place of the secular increased and the place reserved for God and the spiritual was institutionalized and pressured to give up more and more sociocultural space. For many, God and the spiritual were almost totally marginalized to the point that some wondered whether the spiritual still had a legitimate place in the nuclear family or even in the privacy of the home. Starting in the 1960s, however, this trend began to reverse, until now the spiritual is once again gaining ground in the public square. The secular and spiritual will therefore need to find a way to accommodate each other once again.

The second and third change patterns can be taken together as we consider the parallels between them and the culture of communion. This parallelism is striking. If the sociocultural shift has been from "God and the spiritual in both public and private space" to "God and the spiritual only in private space," the culture of communion for many LC-MS members has moved from "communion focused both vertically and horizontally, encompassing both public and private space," to "communion focused primarily vertically and internally, limited to privatized church building space."

From Holistic to Specialized

The fourth sociocultural change to be compared is the movement from the general and holistic to a sweeping commitment to specialization. Although American culture has always had a plurality of values, certain values and practices were traditionally given pride of place. However, during and since the Second World War, American society has made a continual and sweeping commitment to splitting life into a multitude of pieces, both in terms of practices and values. We have moved from a fairly universal, single pattern to several patterns, some in opposition to others. This movement has included segmentation, separation, and compartmentalization. It is reflected in the division of life into such pairs as home and workplace, work and leisure, white collar and blue collar, and general practitioner and specialist.

As with the previous three shifts, we again notice a close parallelism between this sociocultural trend and the changes in the culture of communion. Both the communion culture and the larger society have moved away from the general and holistic and toward specialization, as well as away from a single pattern and toward several patterns, as their primary way of modeling reality. In communion in particular, this has meant a movement away from a single, holistic type of communion culture with a solid set of shared meanings and toward several narrower, silo-type communion cultures.

From Heteronomy to Autonomy

The fifth sociocultural change pattern to be compared is the movement from heteronomy to autonomy. This shift is seen in the moves from faith in another to faith in oneself, from objective faith to subjective faith, and from Judeo-Christian standards to individual internal standards, sometimes akin to New Age standards. Previously it had been widely accepted that the foundational location of the spiritual was outside of humankind. Christianity located its spiritual understanding in the triune God (Gen. 1:1-2, 27), with salvation in Jesus Christ (John 14:6). As the Enlightenment in its scientific emphasis stressed what one can touch and see, the spiritual with its grounding in God gave way to the autonomously thinking human being. Separated from the spiritual, people increasingly affirmed the rational capacity to know objective facts. The theory of evolution strengthened this faith in autonomy by making it possible and even preferable to speak of the origins and basic structures of life without reference to God or the spiritual.

Even so, the expectation that God and the spiritual dimension of life would shrivel up in the face of such scientific answers has not been realized. Instead, there is an abiding sense of the eternal in people's minds (Eccles. 3:11), and an ongoing search for spiritual reality.[19] In the postmodern age, the growing sociological response has been a decline in organized religion and a parallel increase of interest in what is called spirituality. The question is no longer whether the spiritual will again recover its place, but rather how the spiritual will be understood and practiced among a growing number of people who value spiritual searching over religious certainty. Postmodernism also offers a popular worldview that speaks of each person as the repository of spiritual power, a power that needs to be recognized and released through personal knowledge and ritual manipulation. In such a worldview, personal meditation, exercises, right consumption, crystals, gurus, séances, and channeling are prominent in the media and on the lips of respected individuals. This autonomous way of interpreting reality apart from God is frequently taught in schools and promoted on television. It is the basis for the New Age movement and for many of the popular philosophies and strategies for living and prospering that make sense to many contemporary seekers and searchers.

Again we are confronted with a profound parallelism between these sociocultural change patterns and those in LC-MS communion culture. Communion standards seem to be drinking deeply from the stream of the larger society that is shifting from heteronomy to autonomy, from faith in another to faith in oneself, and so forth. The result is that many LC-MS members are also searching along a kind of trajectory that moves away from biblical standards and toward a mixed pattern combining the word of God with the changing culture and its experimentation. In this regard, I recall a conversation about religion with an LC-MS friend of one of my theological students, who said, "Religious reality is only a matter of education, of learning who I am in relation to the powers of nature within me and how to release those powers for positive and creative personal benefit." I also recall the LC-MS businessman mentioned earlier who said that communion resets his internal gyro, clearing his mind and enhancing his personal power for another week.

---

19. David J. Bosch, *Transforming Mission: Paradigm Shifts in Theology of Mission* (Maryknoll, N.Y.: Orbis, 1991), p. 476.

In all five of these sociocultural change patterns, there is a striking parallelism between changes in the culture of American society and changes in LC-MS communion culture. Voltaire is said to have suggested that people are creatures of the age in which they live, and that very few are able to raise themselves above the ideas of their time. On the basis of my findings, I would have to agree. The shifts in communion theology, so similar to those in the larger society, have appeared in both the practice and theology of communion at the transactional level and are being used extensively as tools for defining opposing positions on fellowship in the LC-MS. Of additional interest is the fact that these understandings in communion theology are now beginning to make an impact at the formal level of communion theology in the LC-MS.

Conclusion and Recommendations

Since the 1960s there has been a movement among younger boomers and especially Generation Xers away from compartmentalized individualism and toward an organic, relational fellowship in the context of emerging postmodernity. This movement has challenged the compartmentalized specialization, impersonal precision, and anonymous rigidity of corporate and institutional structures. At the same time, it has enhanced the likelihood of a more informal, integrated, personal, and contextually rooted communication and community. In this kind of situation, it is unlikely that formal expressions of private theologies will be fine-tuned and perfected. Instead, the coming years will be marked by a blossoming of interactive biblical theology transacted publicly in the messy world of our diverse contexts.

My first conclusion, therefore, is that biblical theology will more likely lean in the direction of transactional theology than of formal theology. As this trend continues into the twenty-first century, there may also be a reawakening of first-century Christianity. This kind of Christianity will show itself in a movement back toward organic structures with a high degree of commitment, risk, and personal integrity in life-giving community. The challenge will be for this reawakened Christianity to avoid being grounded in the egocentricity of the New Age movement, but instead remain firmly connected to the Christ of the Bible, transacting an open expression of what it means to be in Christ on the basis of the revealed and inerrant word of God. As this happens, Christians will increasingly transact their theology in word and deed with other people and with Jesus. This will be basic biblical theology in practice. It will be lived in, with, for, and through Jesus Christ in the messiness of human existence. This same Christ of the Bible will live in, with, for, and through dedicated Christians who bring his body into the confusion and challenges of everyday life. Through them he will continue until the end of time his self-professed work of seeking and saving not only those who are looking for truth, life, and hope (Luke 19:1-10), but also those who are not looking at all but are greatly in need of life without end (John 3:16).

Second, based on our study of the twentieth-century LC-MS communion culture, it is predictable that the patterns for doing transactional theology and organizing religious work in the years to come will typically parallel the changing sociocultural patterns of the larger society. This seems to happen whether the patterns produce success and progress or result in regression and failure. It will take a dedicated intentionality for Christianity, including in the LC-MS, to uncouple the seemingly strong connection between shifting sociocultural patterns and those in communion culture, let alone other religious patterns. I would suggest that commitment to such disciplined intervention can succeed only when people recognize and rejoice in the Spirit of God in their lives. By Christ's authority (Matt. 28:18) and with the power of the Spirit of God (Rom. 8:12-14), alternative ways can consciously be chosen and intentionally given preference over the ever changing culture of society. Two viable models immediately come to mind for doing this kind of transactional theology during the twenty-first century.

One model is available in the theory, theology, practice, and application of the apostolic doctrine and life found in the Old and New Testaments of the Bible. This is not the apostolicity of a hierarchical church, but the apostolicity of the first disciples who saw themselves as brothers and sisters in Christ, witnesses sent by God's Spirit to testify to the Lord Jesus Christ in Jerusalem, Judea, Samaria, and to the very ends of the earth. This apostolic testimony followed a costly pattern that was marked by an intentional sociocultural separation that occasionally led to suffering, persecution, and martyrdom. This model of intensely loving but also intensely truthful Christian transactional theology must receive the same priority in the twenty-first century that it had in the first. When this happens, we will again hear people say, as they did in the first century, that the followers of Jesus Christ have "turned the world upside down" (Acts 17:6). In this regard, it is also significant that many religio-cultural patterns in the first century were not very different from those we see today. The early Christians knew what they believed and how to live. Their way of life was vital and essential, not only in terms of patterns, standards, and organization, but also in terms of the survival of the faith in those early days. The same will certainly be true for Christianity in our own time.

Another, similar model of transactional theology available today is found in the example of earnest and eager believers, many of them new Christians.

Taking the Bible absolutely seriously both in doctrine and in practice, this kind of transactional theology is vibrant among many Christians in Africa, especially south of the Sahara. Their positive Christianity is vitally interested in crisp doctrine that brings clear and clean biblical truth to bear upon nurturing the believers and reaching the nonbelievers. This happens when these African Christians apply the truth of God's word in the political, economic, social, mental, and spiritual settings of their individual, family, community, and congregational lives. As with all Christianity in action, the results are sometimes marvelous and sometimes mixed.

Third, the language of theology should not obfuscate, darken, hide, dull, or confuse meaning. Instead, it should brighten, illuminate, illustrate, and clarify meaning. If the language of theology is to be a helpful servant, it must detect and highlight the subsidiary meanings within an overall meaning. When such language helps to identify the shared (commonly held), differentiating (diagnostic), and worldview (foundational) aspects of an overall meaning like communion, there results a potential for rational engagement and enlightened interaction about God. This approach to the language of theology must consciously and in good faith use available linguistic tools to achieve positive progress in Bible-centered doctrine and practice.

In the twenty-first century, it will not be sufficient to use yesterday's words and patterns to do today's transactional and formal theology. Instead, it will be necessary to crisply, clearly, and cleanly put the pure and unadulterated wine of God's meaning into new wineskins, the words and language patterns of today. This is true not only in Bible translation but also in the transactional and formal theology used in talking and writing about God. The uncritical use of church language obfuscates, darkens, hides, dulls, and confuses. By contrast, the positive use of the common language of the people, free of slang and jargon, brightens, illuminates, illustrates, and clarifies for the sake of accurate understanding. This open and engaging use of the natural expressions of contemporary language will also clear the way for all believers to think and talk about God without fear or embarrassment.

Fourth, the language of theology has the potential to make a powerful and positive contribution to organizing religious work in the twenty-first century by taking seriously the meanings of language and especially of scriptural language. In the LC-MS, this will include careful conversational work on how the meanings of communion relate to fellowship. To be most helpful, the language of theology must not become mired in questions classical or contemporary. Instead, relevant transactional theology will make a positive contribution to the organization of religious work by centering primarily on Christology and apostolicity rather than on ecclesiology. It must recognize the original scriptural definition of apostolic as the image of gathered believers continually being sent to the nations (Matt. 28:16-20; Acts 1:8) as Christ's living body (1 Cor. 12:27). Such an apostolic community is specifically sent into all parts of the world to seek and save the searching and lost ones from all groups, languages, and nations (John 10:16; Rev. 7:9-10). This kind of apostolic church is organic in nature. Centered on Jesus Christ, it focuses its conversation and action on imitating Jesus. It extends the loving, compassionate, seeking, searching, and forgiving life of Christ rather than committing its energy and resources primarily to human traditions and the agendas of institutionalized ecclesiology.

Finally, Christianity will survive and regenerate in quite natural ways in the coming years as God's word, empowered by the Spirit of God, is a light to God's people (Ps. 119:105). This will lead to a reorganized brand of Christianity that is creative and ready for continuing renewal. This will happen as God's people focus on Christ and give organizational priority to God's apostolic movement for multiplication, especially the multiplication of congregations. Beholden to God's apostolic mission that all should be saved and come to the knowledge of the truth (1 Tim. 2:4), this reorganization for multiplication will occur marvelously, successfully, and beautifully.

Bibliography

Babin, Pierre, with Mercedes Iannone. *The New Era in Religious Communication.* Translated by David Smith. Minneapolis: Fortress, 1991.

Bellah, Robert N., Richard Madsen, William M. Sullivan, Ann Swidler, and Steven M. Tipton. *Habits of the Heart: Individualism and Commitment in American Life.* New York: Harper and Row, 1985.

Sanneh, Lamin O. *Translating the Message: The Missionary Impact on Culture.* Maryknoll, N.Y.: Orbis, 1989.

Schwarz, Christian A. *Paradigm Shift in the Church: How Natural Church Development Can Transform Theological Thinking.* Carol Stream, Ill.: ChurchSmart Resources, 1999.

Ward, Ted W., Duane Elmer, Lois McKinney, and Muriel I. Elmer. *With an Eye on the Future: Development and Mission in the Twenty-First Century.* Monrovia, Calif.: MARC, 1996.

How Firm a Foundation?
The Institutional Origins of the
National Baptist Convention, USA, Inc.

Quinton Hosford Dixie

> *You will permit me here to repeat what I have said on former occasions: that the conditions in this country have forced the Negroes to be separate in their churches, associations, and conventions, from their white brethren, and these smaller organizations have, by reason of the same conditions, been forced to form this national society and since we have this National Baptist convention, it is imperative that it have a high and noble object. . . . The National Baptist Convention, in this connection, stands for the complete development of the Negro as a man along all lines, beginning first with his religious life, and ending with the material, or business life.*

> Elias Camp Morris, founding president,
> National Baptist Convention, Inc.

When Elias Camp Morris, president of the National Baptist Convention (NBC), uttered the preceding passage at the 1900 annual meeting in Richmond, Virginia, he was convinced that while the problem of the twentieth century might be the color line, the triumph of the next one hundred years would be the unmatched blessings of Negro achievement. After all, it would be the first century since their arrival in the New World in which African Americans would not be bought and sold as chattel, and even as Jim and Jane Crow gained strength throughout the South, Morris and countless others believed "separate but equal" at least afforded blacks the opportunity to create, develop, and govern their own institutions.

Indeed, the NBC stood as a shining beacon illuminating the way toward Negro progress. After only five short years in existence, this fledgling federation comprised hundreds of congregations from coast to coast and could boast of missionary stations in Africa, the Caribbean, and South America. Moreover, its Publishing Board operated a publishing facility that provided literature to nearly nine thousand Sunday schools across the nation, not to mention the numerous normal schools and colleges supported by local and state associations. Morris seemingly had good reason to be optimistic about the future. However, despite all the NBC's potential for growth and advancement, from its origins it possessed a formula for failure which led one historian to call the group a "frustrated fellowship." Deeply buried in its bosom were contradictory objectives that kept the organization at odds with itself and prevented it from ever becoming what James M. Washington called "the church with the soul of a nation." The purpose of this brief introduction is to chart the history of several of the conflicting ideas behind the formation of the NBC which have led to the present organizational challenges elaborated upon in the following organizational case study and theological essay.

Many of the organizational challenges faced by the NBC are rooted in the tension between Baptist polity and its practical application. Often what seemed to make good theological sense was not the wisest organizational or political course of action. From the onset, the NBC possessed institutional logics[1] that prevented both efficiency and harmony within the ranks. At the core of Baptist polity is the belief that power resides at the base of the pyramid with individual members, and those that govern at the top do so only by the mandate of the people. On the basis of their theological interpretation of church order, Baptists assert that political and theological authority resides at the local level with each congregation, its representatives (deacons and trustees), and its pastor. So, in many ways the establishment of a national denominational organization is futile in that national leadership has no power to enforce measures passed by the corporate body. Neither standards of morality nor standards of accounting may be mandated upon any congregation that belongs to the national organization, regardless what national delegates determine in annual session. By the same token, the national organization is duty-bound to follow the dictates of the delegates, regardless of whether or not it seems to be the most prudent decision.

The tension between congregational autonomy and centralized authority was present from the outset of the NBC. At the NBC's 1896 meeting in St. Louis, just one year after the body was organized, the delegates voted to start a pub-

---

1. By institutional logics, I mean those ideas which provide meaning to institutions. Harry S. Stout and D. Scott Cormode note, "An institutional structure can no more function without an institutional logic than a subject without an object, or a government without a governed." Stout and Cormode, "Institutions and the Story of American Religion," in *Sacred Companies: Organizational Aspects of Religion and Religious Aspects of Organizations,* ed. N. J. Demerath et al. (New York: Oxford University Press, 1998), p. 71.

lishing concern and chose Elias Camp Morris and Richard Henry Boyd to establish the venture. Morris, the NBC president, was the founding editor of the *Baptist Vanguard,* a black newspaper published in his home state of Arkansas. As an advocate for the publication of black Sunday school literature, Boyd also was no stranger to religious publishing. Both men knew it would take more than force of will to create and maintain a competitive venture, and the idea of a black-controlled publishing concern came under immediate attack from black Baptists who wanted to maintain their institutional relationship with the white-controlled American Baptist Publication Society. Boyd doubted they could garner sufficient support from local congregations to be successful, and suggested to Morris that they delay the production of Sunday school literature until they were in a better position to gauge the business's viability. While he agreed with Boyd, Morris felt that denominational polity left them no room to disregard the dictates of the convention. "Our duty is plain," he replied to Boyd, "it is to get out a Sunday School matter by January 1, 1897. This duty has been imposed by the National Baptist Convention, and cannot be set aside by us."[2] Clearly, Morris felt that the authority of the NBC superseded the directives of the organizational leadership and that the wishes of the larger body must be heeded. On the other hand, Boyd saw how useless national mandates were without the support of local congregations. Baptist polity seemed to require their obedience rather than their leadership.

There are many examples from the NBC's recent history that demonstrate the way congregational autonomy often renders the leadership of the convention's president ineffective. In the late 1980s T. J. Jemison, then president of the NBC, USA, Inc., had a vision to create a single headquarters for the denomination. The organization's various boards had a long history of conducting business from the home base (local congregations) of their respective corresponding secretaries. Jemison hoped that once a national headquarters was built, all the various entities that make up the NBC would move operations to Nashville. Rumors ran through the organization that Jemison merely sought to leave a legacy in brick and mortar that might balance his otherwise uneventful tenure. Regardless of Jemison's motives, the establishment of a national office would have some positive unintended consequences. The move would indirectly professionalize denomination administration, for denominational administrators would have been forced to give up the local pastorate in order to conduct the business of their respective constituencies (foreign missions, education, etc.). Moreover, theoretically the denominational entities could be held

2. E. C. Morris, *Sermons, Addresses, and Reminiscences and Important Correspondence* (reprint, New York: Arno Press, 1980), p. 169.

more accountable by the NBC president. In 1989 Jemison opened the $10 million Baptist World Center, but was unable to persuade any of the boards to occupy the facility.[3] Regardless of whether or not the center made sound organizational sense, many people in the NBC believed Jemison overstepped his authority as president and acted on his own accord, because he knew there was no support amongst the membership for such a thing. For in the end, local congregations would be required to pay for the facility. Hence, the institutional conflict over congregational autonomy and centralized authority prevented the NBC from taking the next step in organizational development.

At the heart of Baptist polity's commitment to congregational autonomy is the voluntary principle. Baptists believe that individuals and congregations involved in the formation, development, and maintenance of religious bodies should do so as an exercise of free will and not by coercion or compulsion. Granted, such a democratic principle is noble, but when carried out to its logical extreme, it makes funding a national agenda a rather precarious affair. Throughout most of the NBC's history, a board's ability to meet its annual goals and mandates has been predicated solely on the ability of the corresponding secretary to raise funds. Not only was he or she responsible for raising the entire operating budget for his or her respective board, the corresponding secretary was also responsible for getting the money for his or her own salary and expenses.

Few people were more acutely aware of the fiscal shortage that the NBC ran from one session to another than its first president, E. C. Morris. He never received enough money from the national body to cover all the expenses of his office and often used his personal resources to cover denominational expenditures. At the same time, he consistently made recommendations to the convention that did not seem to take into account the limited resources of the boards and the churches that supported them. As if the expenditures associated with a weeklong trip to the annual meeting were not enough, all five of Morris's recommendations to the delegates in 1912 had substantial price tags attached to them. For example, he advised that the NBC send two messengers to the Second European Baptist Congress in Stockholm; that a committee of three be sent around the world to study "the condition of black people in Africa, India, and the Isles of the sea," and to let the world know the "real condition of the American Negro"; that a committee meet, research, and draft a report on the suffrage rights of blacks for the purpose of pressuring the federal government into either enforcing the Fourteenth and Fifteenth Amendments or reducing the con-

---

3. Charles L. Sanders, "$10 Million Headquarters Signals New Course for National Baptist Convention, U.S.A., Inc.," *Ebony*, October 1989, p. 69.

gressional representation of "those states which have, by proscriptive legislation, nullified those amendments"; and that the 1913 session include a special semicentennial celebration of the black emancipation.[4] Morris had no power to compel churches to meet the expenses for these measures, even if the convention delegates representing these congregations endorsed his initiatives.

Most often, individuals called upon to do work for the NBC did so out of their own (or their congregation's) pockets with the promise that the convention would raise the funds necessary to reimburse them. More often than not, it was difficult to get people to spend money to achieve the goals agreed upon at the annual session. While pastors and NBC laypersons claimed to understand the necessity of a strong national body that could represent their interests in ecumenical and political circles, their financial priorities were usually at the local level. At the same time, asking denominational representatives to raise money to cover their own salary led to a host of financial irregularities. While Morris and most of the corresponding secretaries consistently covered organizational expenses first and paid themselves only on those extremely rare occasions when funds remained, some denominational representatives were known to do the opposite. Hence, the voluntary principle coupled with congregational autonomy and a low level of centralized authority has produced a century's worth of financial problems and mistrust on the part of the laity.

Throughout the NBC's history there has been considerable organizational tension regarding the very nature of the convention itself. Just what exactly was the National Baptist Convention? Was it a traditional denomination that represented a particular cultural interpretation about God's dealings with God's people, or was it simply an annual weeklong church service? Regardless of one's theological or social position on the matter, it was clear that the convention had year-round business that yielded both profit and debt. The question of whose responsibility it was to keep the organization solvent remained, however. Within fifteen years of the denomination's founding, it became clear how badly the NBC needed some system of accountability. The convention was a loose confederation of single-issue organizations called boards which acted on behalf of their own national interests. Membership in the individual boards and the convention overlapped, but each board was responsible to its own board of directors. By the end of 1910 the boards were incorporated indepen

---

4. *Journal of the Thirty-Second Annual Session of the National Baptist Convention,* held with the Baptist churches, Houston, Texas, September 11-16, 1912, pp. 46-47. It is interesting to note that just minutes after announcing it was unfair for the National Baptist Publishing Board, the only solvent entity within the convention, continually to pay more than its share of denominational expenses, Morris proclaimed that he expected the Publishing Board to raise the funds for the worldwide investigation of the condition of the black race.

dently of the National Baptist Convention, with the sole exception of the Home Mission Board. One response to the convention's seeming powerlessness over the boards was to incorporate the parent body. Changes in state and federal policies governing incorporation reshaped the organizational molds of both businesses and religious bodies. Between 1886 and 1898 a large number of states, following the lead of states like New York, New Jersey, and Delaware, made it easier for corporations to own real estate and other assets, both inside and outside the chartering state. The appearance of state general incorporation laws also made it easier for one company to hold stock in another company, and corporate entities gained some of the same rights as individual citizens. One historian notes, "In sum, state legislation and both federal and state judicial construction, from the late 1880s onward, increasingly gave to corporations stronger standing as 'natural entities' with contractual and due process rights of persons."[5]

Although incorporating the parent body seemed like the most logical solution to the problem of accountability and control, the task proved to be far more difficult than it originally appeared. To many members of the NBC, their organization simply was an annual meeting that moved from state to state, held no property, and had no business outside of one week each year. Additionally, the NBC could not order the boards to meet at the annual session, since they were separate bodies operating under separate charters. Most of those charters required the annual meeting of the incorporated bodies to be held in the state in which they were chartered. Therefore, meeting at the NBC annual session was merely a gesture done out of convenience, but not out of obligation.[6] If this was the case, and it certainly appeared to be so, then it meant that the convention could legally exercise no authority or control over the boards.

Moreover, opponents of incorporation of the NBC objected on the grounds that to do so would require straying from New Testament models for church order and organization. They believed there was no formal organizational structure beyond the local community of believers in ancient Christian communities, and as Baptists they were duty-bound to follow that model. For some this was the most cogent argument, for they believed the denomination overstepped its organizational boundaries when it sought refuge in the laws of man rather than God. After all, to many of the delegates and members the annual sessions were little more than a weeklong revival with hymns sung, Scripture read, sermons preached, souls touched, and offerings raised. Yet for others

5. Martin J. Sklar, *The Corporate Reconstruction of American Capitalism, 1890-1916* (New York: Cambridge University Press, 1988), p. 51.

6. *National Baptist Review,* May 21, 1910, p. 8.

the convention was not church, but an entity whose mission went beyond the bounds of individual congregations to speak in various arenas — both secular and sacred — on behalf of black Baptists.

Another institutional irony that historically has been a part of the NBC and is featured quite prominently in the following essay, is the role of women within the denomination. In 1900, National Baptist women proposed that they organize the Woman's National Baptist Convention. Just as the NBC as a whole felt the need to take a stronger stance against the paternalism of whites, black Baptist women felt that having their own convention would ease some of the patriarchal control so apparent in the organizational structure of the denomination. This was not the first time they sought autonomy from the men in the denomination. They made similar proposals at the organizing sessions of the Foreign Mission Board and the National Baptist Convention in 1880 and 1895 respectively, only to be relegated to the organizational margins of the denomination.

Two ideas prevailed among the brethren as to why the women should not have their own organization. One group seemingly was concerned about the implications it raised for governance, efficiency, and accountability, while another group of men explicitly was more interested in women remaining in their place. While the majority of the men opposed the formation of an independent women's organization, they did so on the grounds that the denomination's organizational logic dictated that the women should organize as a board and thereby be kept under the control of the denominational leadership.[7] Nevertheless, the result was the same. Both groups pressed for the women to organize as a board under the control of the NBC. In the end, the women settled on something of a compromise. They organized as the Woman's Auxiliary Convention of the NBC yet functioned in a similar fashion to the other boards. Their work was not limited to their traditional domain of foreign missions, and yet much of what they did remained safely in the realm of "women's work." Although they met in separate sessions during the week the NBC held its annual meeting, they always met in the same city as the convention in the same manner as the convention's boards. This practice remains today. Instead of being integrated into the power structure of the convention, they exercise control over their own separate sphere which has no substantive organizational influence on the denomination as a whole.

Hesitance about the full equality of women is also evident in the NBC's reluctance to adopt an official stance on the ordination of women. Despite decades of dissension in the organization, the churches of the NBC have been in

---

7. Evelyn Brooks Higginbotham, *Righteous Discontent: The Women's Movement in the Black Baptist Church, 1880-1920* (Cambridge: Harvard University Press, 1993), pp. 152-54.

agreement historically in their opposition to the ordination of women. There have been no meaningful debates on the convention floor about the topic, nor any leadership initiatives pushing the denomination toward the inclusion of women in the ministry. Instead, it has been far more convenient to hide behind the bars of biblical precedence and claim that the lack of representation of women as pastors and preachers in the biblical canon prevents twenty-first-century Christians from thinking outside the box. As a result, those women most interested in ordained ministry have fled the NBC for religious organizations that were more supportive of their vocational interests. An additional consequence of women being blocked from most NBC pulpits is that they have no genuine access to leadership positions within the denomination. The organization's upper echelon has been the exclusive domain of pastors, and since most NBC women interested in ministry find it difficult even to get their call to ministry recognized, it is virtually impossible for them to break into and through the old boys' network.

Conclusion

On the surface, it would appear that the NBC's competing institutional logics not only have prevented organizational development, but also have produced a culture of comfort with instability and confusion. I submit, however, that such a surface reading of the NBC's history fails to broaden our understanding of this organization's purposes and how its structure has both helped and hindered its achievements. Therefore, instead of seeing the denominational schisms of 1897, 1915, 1961, and the near split of 1998 as examples of black Baptist disunity and the inability to "get it together," we might learn more by inverting our interpretation. Why is it that black Baptists place such a high premium on dissent? How is this institutional logic built into the organization's structure? To what extent is it unique to this organization? Instead of wondering aloud why the male leadership is patriarchal, perhaps we might question why the women continue to choose their own auxiliary organization over fighting for full participation in the organizational life of the NBC. Of course, I do not claim to have the answers to these questions. It is my role only to provide a historical perspective for some of the organizational challenges facing the NBC in the twenty-first century that will be analyzed sociologically and theologically in the following case study and essay. However, it is my hope that in doing so I have given a description thick enough to muddle any simple conclusions.

One of the true blessings of American democracy is the room it makes for dissent. Individual members of the collective are permitted to vote their own conscience, and are not duty-bound to follow what is popular or what others perceive to be right. By the same token, there is something frightening about majority rule which may disempower those with one less vote. The key to a healthy democracy is not demanding immediate resolution between these ideals, but recognizing that both exist and are, perhaps, necessary to provide some semblance of balance to the political structure. As I have shown, the NBC rests on a foundation of polarized positions constantly in a state of motion. But it rests in the knowledge that its foundation has withstood past tremors, and it can weather future storms so long as its quest for unity is tempered with a healthy dose of respect for dissent.

The National Baptist Convention:
Traditions and Contemporary Challenges

Aldon D. Morris and Shayne Lee

The National Baptist Convention, USA, Inc. (NBC), is over a hundred years old. It is the largest black religious organization in the world with over five million members and thousands of affiliated churches. The NBC reflects the aspirations, contradictions, struggles, and culture of the entire African American community. It is a unique denomination because its constituency is composed of a historically oppressed population that has endured two and a half centuries of slavery and three-quarters of a century of Jim Crow oppression. The legacy of this oppression as well as contemporary racial inequality continue to influence all aspects of the NBC. As a denomination, the NBC cannot be understood outside this social context.

Because of its long history and enormous resources, the NBC is a central institution within the black community. It has the capacity to generate vast economic resources, influence the outcome of political elections, launch and sustain social change movements, and produce cultural innovations. It administers to the inner lives of millions of people troubled by racism and spiritual challenges. Thus, the NBC is an important national force affecting the black community and the nation. Because the NBC has seldom realized its potential, some astute observers have often viewed it as a sleeping giant. In this essay we address the NBC's traditions and contemporary challenges and seek to shed light on whether it is likely to remain relatively dormant or awaken fully and realize its potential.

This study of the NBC is rooted in an organizational, cultural, and gender analytic framework. First, we seek to understand the NBC as a formal organization embedded in complex macro- and microsocial relations. In this connection, attention will be paid to the NBC's internal, structural, and political dynamics and to its organizational environment. Second, the NBC is a profoundly cultural institution concerned with belief systems, moral matters, and interpretive dilemmas. Thus, it has to be confronted as a cultural enterprise. Finally, the NBC is a deeply gendered institution and its gender relations are central to its functioning and will be important in shaping its future. Thus, our efforts to understand the NBC are guided by an analysis of its organizational dynamics, its cultural dimensions, and its gender relations.[1]

Before proceeding, we situate the NBC within the context of the seven major, historically black religious denominations and briefly describe our methodology. The NBC is by far the largest black religious denomination, three times the size of any other. It is a part of the larger black Baptist community that also encompasses the National Baptist Convention of America and the Progressive National Baptist Convention, Inc. The black Methodist denominations include the African Methodist Episcopal Church, the African Methodist Episcopal Zion Church, and the Christian Methodist Episcopal Church. The final black denomination is the Church of God in Christ. The Black Muslim community is also important in this context given its growing significance in the black community. Black Baptist churches are unique in that they function according to the local autonomy principle that grants independence and sovereignty to local congregations. The black Baptist denominations, along with the Church of God in Christ, are the most conservative with respect to gender inequality, especially as it relates to the ordination of women. With the exception of the Black Muslim faith, these denominations differ little in theology, but they do differ in polity, history, and traditions. They all compete for the hearts and souls of black America.

The Autonomy Principle

The power of the NBC rests not at the top of the organization, but comes from below.[2] The NBC's power is anchored in its local congregations, local associa-

---

1. The data for this study consist of open-ended interviews with NBC leaders and scholars of religion knowledgeable of the NBC, as well as organizational documents, participant observations, and numerous secondary sources. While the data do not constitute a representative sample, we believe the diverse data sources enable us to present a balanced view of the NBC. Unreferenced quotes are from the above-noted interviews.

2. See James Melvin Washington, *Frustrated Fellowship: The Black Baptist Quest for Social Power* (Macon, Ga.: Mercer University Press, 1986); C. Eric Lincoln and Lawrence H. Mamiya, *The Black Church in African American Experience* (Durham, N.C.: Duke University Press, 1990). This was also emphasized in our interview with a president of a black seminary and black church scholar.

tions, and state conventions. The NBC has no power to force individuals, churches, associations, or state conventions to join the national denomination. It cannot appoint or ordain local pastors, or determine which churches should form associations, nor can it appoint state presidents. The NBC cannot demand that any of these entities fund the national headquarters. In short, there exist no presiding bishops, elders, or national authorities that can issue authoritative orders to any level outside the national convention. In the black Baptist world, local congregations are autonomous and reserve supreme power to run their own affairs. This is the principle of local autonomy, and each church, local association, and state convention jealously guard it.

The autonomy principle is the regulating guide of the black Baptist church community. A former general secretary of the NBC explained that "Baptist churches are independent . . . we are not connected in the sense that you could talk about the Presbyterian Church, talk about the United Methodist Church. Those are connectional churches. But you have to talk about Baptist churches. . . . So it [power] comes up from the bottom rather than down from the top." Similarly, another NBC pastor explained that the local church is "totally self-sovereign in its own right; we don't have to answer to any bishop. Nobody can come here and tell me what to do. We can change something in the middle of the stream and can't nobody say nothing to us about it." According to church scholar Robert Franklin, the NBC is unique precisely because it "represents something quite extraordinary in the history of the evolution of the Black church in America in so far as it represents the coming together of a vast number of independent institutions and local congregations that willingly and voluntarily decided to convene and cooperate together as a national denomination." Similarly, Lincoln and Mamiya wrote that "the church itself, that is, the congregation, is the supreme governing body."[3]

The autonomy principle enables pastors to function as the main instruments of power. The local pastor is the head of his church family. In most instances he is given the latitude to make major decisions and to set the tone theologically and programmatically. While he may share power with a board of trustees or the deacon board, it is the pastor who usually functions as the dominant actor of the local congregation. Although important checks and balances exist, they usually do not prevent the pastor from determining the outcomes of most financial decisions and delegating authority. The pastor is the head of his religious household and retains power much like the classic charismatic leader. Thus, the office of pastor is paramount in the black Baptist polity and within the Baptist community.

3. Lincoln and Mamiya, *The Black Church*, p. 43.

Rise of Local Associations and Conventions

Local associations and state conventions predated the NBC. The slave pastor realized that he and his church exercised limited power as isolated actors. During slavery and the Jim Crow era, the black church faced enormous challenges. The oppressive institution of slavery needed to be overthrown, and self-help programs were needed for the downtrodden and largely illiterate black masses. Additionally, at the heart of the mission of the black church was the challenge of saving souls for Christ and preparing black people to live Christian lives so that upon death they would pass into the kingdom of God. Black church leaders also concerned themselves with the souls and well-being of blacks in the Black Diaspora, especially in Africa and the Caribbean. They concluded that black churches should establish foreign mission boards through which blacks in foreign lands could be lifted out of barbarianism and elevated into modern civilization while simultaneously embracing Christ.

These were daunting tasks that faced the slave church. Nor did they change substantially with the overthrow of slavery. Following slavery the Jim Crow order was established, ushering in a new system of black subordination. Lynchings, Jim Crowed–public accommodations, excruciating poverty, illiteracy, and a host of other challenges confronted the black church in the late nineteenth and early twentieth centuries. Such problems were too intractable to be solved by individual pastors and churches. A collective response was the only viable option.

During slavery and the early Jim Crow period, local black Baptist churches began forming local associations to address their common problems.[4] They reasoned that they could become more effective by pooling their resources and increasing their numerical strength by creating local associations that united like-minded churches. During slavery these associated churches addressed issues of education, mutual aid, and domestic missions. However, as Washington pointed out, these early associations also functioned as antislavery societies.[5] Black Baptist associations proliferated during the early years of the Jim Crow regime. Thus, early in their history black Baptist churches began evolving local associations to pursue the collective goals of an oppressed people. Because these associations were voluntary alliances, they did not violate the principle of congregational autonomy, for local churches were free to associate and disassociate. Having arisen in the slave period and proliferated throughout the Jim Crow period, local associations became a major structural component of the black Baptist community.

4. Washington, *Frustrated Fellowship.*
5. Washington, *Frustrated Fellowship,* pp. 27-38.

Black ministers are a mobile group, relative to the black population, because of their economic independence and the nature of their profession. During slavery and the Jim Crow period, black ministers traveled across state and regional lines to share pulpits and attend conferences and other religious and social gatherings. The associations facilitated these interactions because they encompassed wide geographical areas that often stretched across state lines. As black ministries solidified these contacts, they began to sense the need to build statewide and even quasi-national organizations. Such organizations provided additional leverage to attack social inequality, to pool resources, to build strong domestic and foreign missions, and to address the needs of the community. During the mid-1800s statewide and regional conventions were organized. These organizations operated according to the autonomy principle at the state and regional levels. Their success revealed that it was possible to build large unifying structures. As a result, state conventions emerged as a major structural unit of the black Baptist community while the regional conventions sparked the interest to organize a national convention.

Between 1880 and 1893 the Baptist Foreign Mission Convention, the American National Convention, and the National Baptist Educational Convention were organized. While each of these aspired to be the national convention, regional and political differences prevented them from attaining this goal. Nevertheless, their presence created the foundation on which a national denomination of black Baptist churches could be built.

Rise and Development of the National Baptist Convention

During the late 1880s discussions pertaining to unification occurred among the leaders of the three conventions.[6] They held a meeting in Atlanta, Georgia, at the Friendship Baptist Church in 1895 to determine whether a merger was possible. These contentious discussions led to a historic merger. Lincoln and Mamiya captured the historic moment: "The merger was accomplished at a meeting convened in Atlanta on September 28, 1895, and attended by over 500 delegates and observers. The resulting organization was the National Baptist Convention USA, with subsidiary Foreign Mission, Home Mission, and Education Boards, to which a publishing concern was added in 1897. Rev. E. C. Morris was elected the first president of the New Convention."[7] The birth of

---

6. See Washington, *Frustrated Fellowship*, pp. 184-85, and Lincoln and Mamiya, *The Black Church*, pp. 28-29.

7. Lincoln and Mamiya, *The Black Church*, p. 28.

the NBC was a culmination of the collective aspirations of black Baptist clergy. With this new organization, they were finally in a position to operate from a national base.

The basic structure of the NBC has not changed in over a century. The NBC encompasses four interconnected structural levels. First is the local church, or congregation, which is its most basic unit. Second are the associations, which are collections of local churches. Third is the state convention, which is comprised of statewide affiliated churches and local associations. The fourth level is the national convention, which encompasses affiliated churches, local associations, and state conventions. The autonomy principle is institutionalized at each level. A former general secretary of the NBC put it this way:

> Baptist Churches are independent but we agree to associate. We associate in local associations, state conventions in terms of our state, and the national. . . . The reason that we associate is that we might be able to share together or benefit from each other's counsel in matters of doctrine and in matters of polity that affect us at our local churches, that affect us at our association or state or national. . . . We associate that we might be able to do together things that would be difficult for us to do individually.

The NBC is often referred to as a "fellowship" among its members to convey the voluntary nature of the national convention.

Thus, the survival and vitality of the NBC depend on the support of its affiliated bodies. Without that support it could not accomplish its major goals of evangelism, home mission, foreign mission, and the production of church literature through its Sunday School Publishing Board. The affiliated organizations provide the NBC with the majority of its finances through membership dues, fund-raising campaigns, and registrations at the annual meeting. The elected and appointed leadership of the NBC is drawn from its affiliated organizations. The state conventions have evolved into major centers of power and resources. In 1998 there existed sixty-one of them, all affiliates of the NBC. No candidate for NBC's presidency can win without the backing of a majority of state conventions. Most NBC presidents have been state presidents because that position provides them with visibility, access to valuable networks, and legitimacy. Moreover, state presidents constitute the majority of NBC's national board, upon which they sit because of their state office. A great part of the funds used to support the national office is raised by state conventions. The state conventions are pivotal sources of power and resources on which the NBC rests.

NBC's Office of President

The presidency of the NBC is the most powerful office within the black Baptist community. As the chairman of the NBC's Foreign Mission Board stated, the president has this power because "He can appoint a certain number of members at large on the board of directors. In most cases he can influence the elections of state presidents, who become members of the board of directors. He has almost complete control over the finances through the treasurer. He can determine the various programs, many by bringing them before the board, and unless it's terribly objectionable we're gonna give it to him."

A former general secretary of the NBC agreed that the "President is able to nominate all of the other auxiliaries and many of the other leaders of the convention so that's a great deal of power in terms of patronage because the convention usually accepts the nomination." Another NBC pastor argued that "the President of the NBC is the leader of the leaders in the African-American Baptist Church. . . . There is no way that we can have this discussion without talking about the absolute authority of the position of president." And another NBC pastor remarked that the presidency "means that you've got one hell of a powerful man. You can get things done. Most of the time the president gets things done his way. He's got power to get money, and he has the power to do what he wants with it."

The NBC presidency allows its occupant to achieve a measure of power in the larger society. A scholar of the black church identified the source of this external power: "For one thing it has symbolic power. To be leader of the largest convention then you serve a representative role. So therefore, just the symbol of that can be translated into cultural capital, political capital, because you can go to the U.S. President and let them know that I represent eight million people, or you can go to a state governor and let them know that I represent eight million people."

The president of the NBC is automatically included in the elite leadership of black America by virtue of the position. Thus, the presidency of the NBC houses internal and external power. As one leader of the convention concluded: "If you're the leader of 8½ million people, everybody will recognize you automatically. Domestically, and afar, you are somebody."

The historical absence of a tenure policy has also contributed to the power that individual presidents have amassed. Indeed, historically NBC presidents have served for extraordinarily long periods of time. This practice was evident from the start when the first NBC president, E. C. Morris, served for twenty-eight consecutive years. Its third president, L. K. Williams, served for seventeen consecutive years. During the modern era, this practice continued when J. H. Jackson was elected in 1953 and served until 1982. T. J. Jemison, who served twelve years before stepping down only when a tenure rule was established, followed Jackson. Such long tenure enhanced the capacity of NBC presidents to become less accountable and to act in a relatively unilateral fashion. A seminary president spoke directly to this situation:

> I think that in the past there has been a kind of laissez-faire attitude in respect to the power of the president. . . . There's a long history from Lacey Kirk Williams to J. H. Jackson, and through Jemison and so leaders who served long tenures who amassed favors, who are able to reward loyalty, who as ambassadors negotiate with other public and secular powers, especially corporations and the government and received certain benefits through those negotiations and are able to again reward their loyal followers. So there's the president with a very strong portfolio that has operated. And that's been the norm in the National Baptist Convention with relatively little checks and balances despite those loose structures that exist that are supposed to exercise some accountability.

The lack of a tenure rule coupled with minimal accountability created what some refer to as the *imperial presidency*. These practices tended to stifle democratic procedures at the highest level of the NBC. They also created room for presidents to become corrupt and to endanger the convention.

Earlier we argued that the pastor is the main source of power in the black Baptist church. The typical pastor operates as the patriarch of his church family. He is often able to maneuver around checks and balances to realize his will. All presidents of the NBC have been pastors, and they maintain their local pastorates during their presidency. As NBC presidents they function as the pastors of the largest church of them all — the convention. They run the convention largely in the same manner as their local church. The members of the convention perceive the president as the pastor of the convention who deserves the latitude and power to administer this large religious family. Moreover, the overwhelming majority of those to whom the president is accountable are also pastors. Thus, they understand the role of a Baptist pastor and are hesitant to subject the president to strict rules and regulations. Thus, the NBC president generally "gets his way" because of the autonomy granted to the pastor.

There are structural limitations and opportunities built into the NBC's presidency that can increase the likelihood that a president will exploit the office. The NBC does not have a pension plan. This can create anxiety about one's financial future and may press the NBC president to use the office to acquire funds for personal security. Additionally, NBC presidents continue to pastor their local church while serving as president, thus holding two full-time jobs simultaneously and receiving the salary from their local church. The presidency itself is also a lucrative position because the incumbent is in high demand for speaking engagements that pay considerable honorariums. Thus, one can leave the office in much better financial condition than when he arrived.

In summary, the office of president is central to the functioning of the NBC. In it resides a great deal of power. Candidates campaign extensively to be elected, because they realize that the office will provide them with considerable institutional influence and personal power. Because of the enormous discretion given to the office, the president plays a central role in shaping the direction, as well as the health, of the convention.

The NBC and the Baptist Vision

The NBC and its affiliated congregations, associations, and state conventions are not held together by structure alone. These enterprises have been developed to produce and disseminate particular religious views. Black Baptist organizational structures, therefore, are energized and given meaning through intense cultural work. They also constitute the main sites where black Baptists engage in continuous and intense activities to realize the goals of their community. Moreover, these sites are also the major historic reservoirs of African American culture. There is a common system of beliefs that drives the NBC and unifies the members of the larger community. In general terms, black Baptists share the basic religious beliefs of the larger Baptist community. Nevertheless, they have appropriated them and fashioned them into a unique faith to deal with the distinctive social conditions of African Americans.

A doctrinal consensus exists within the NBC and the black Baptist community. That consensus is rooted in the articles of faith embraced by the larger Baptist community and adopted by the NBC. Consistent with these articles, black Baptists believe that the Holy Bible is the Word of God and the supreme standard by which human beings are to be judged; that there is but one living God who encompasses the Trinity of the Father, the Son, and the Holy Spirit; that Christ is the Son of God who died on the cross but was raised from the grave and ascended into heaven to reign with his Father; that Christ died for the sins of all human beings, and in so doing, made it possible for all to be saved from sin through the grace of God; that in order to be saved, one must be baptized; that the duty of a Christian is to live according to God's Word and to spread that Word to all corners of the globe; that the pastor has been appointed by God to bring the true Word to the people; that God is just, fair, and forgiving; that Christ will return to earth and gather all Christians, both living and dead, unto him and take them to heaven where they will joyfully dwell in paradise, with God, throughout eternity; and that those, both living and dead, who chose a sinful life will be punished in hell throughout eternity. These are powerful beliefs that unite and inspire black Baptists. They existed long before the articles of faith were enunciated in 1833, but NBC's formal adoption of the articles provides followers with clear-cut guidelines.

Nevertheless, black Baptists were destined not to follow the vision in a rote manner. For one thing, these tenets are continuously debated both theologically and practically. Moreover, the Baptist vision had to be refashioned to address the predicament of a subjugated people. The institutions of slavery and Jim Crow created unique conditions for the black population. They caused blacks to be viewed and treated as an inferior species of humanity. This oppression prevented blacks from building viable institutions through which their interests could be pursued. It also caused high black illiteracy and the lack of opportunities and educational vehicles to reverse these conditions. Thus, slavery and Jim Crow generated the need for blacks to develop the intellectual and material resources required to dismantle these houses of bondage, so that freedom could be achieved.

This quest for freedom shaped black Baptist churches and the NBC. It caused the black Baptist community to weave a creative vision that guided their theology and religious institutions. To be sure, blacks emphasized certain aspects of the Holy Scriptures not central to the vision of white Baptists. Black congregants were drawn to the view that God was a God of justice and fairness. They gravitated to the narratives in the Bible that spoke to the biblical struggles between oppressors and the oppressed. A seminary president highlighted this emphasis: "We as African Americans have tended to think of ourselves as a biblical people, as a people of the Book. In reading the Old Testament we are really reading our story — the pilgrimage from Exodus, from slavery to freedom." Thus, black Baptists have tended to develop an activist theology that put forth the view that God is concerned with earthly justice. Martin Luther King, Jr., emphasized this thrust: "But a religion true to its nature must also be concerned about man's social condition. . . . Any religion that professes to be concerned with the souls of men and is not concerned with the slums that damn them, the economic conditions that strangle them, and the social conditions that cripple them is a dry-as-dust religion."[8] In this view God requires an activism geared toward social change in which he is placed on the side of those fighting for justice.

This activist interpretation of Scriptures has played a key role in the de-

8. Martin Luther King, Jr., *Stride toward Freedom* (New York: Harper and Row, 1958), p. 36.

velopment of the NBC. A central thrust of the convention is its work to uplift the black community. Immediately following slavery the NBC began founding and supporting black schools and colleges.[9] Its churches constituted stations along the Underground Railroad. They have also been key sites of mobilization for resistance movements during slavery and the Jim Crow periods.[10] From the very beginning, the convention has promoted black literacy by establishing a publishing board that supplied churches with religious literature. One of the convention's earliest documents declared that a goal of the denomination was "to encourage our literary men and women, and promote the interest of Baptist literature."[11] Similarly, from the beginning the convention positioned itself as the forum through which the overall interests of the black community could be pursued. Thus, the same document argued that the role of the national convention would be "to discuss questions pertaining especially to the religious, educational, industrial and social interest of our people. . . . To give an opportunity for the best thinkers and writers to be heard . . . [and] that, united, we may be more powerful for good and strengthen our pride in the denomination."[12]

Thus, the NBC developed as an institution that encompassed the political, economic, and social aspirations of an oppressed people. Out of necessity, the NBC fashioned a theology and a belief system that promoted an activist church concerned with the oppression of African Americans.[13]

The NBC has also played an important role in convincing black people that they were "somebody" despite contrary messages espoused by white supremacy. During slavery black churches promoted the idea that blacks were important because they were God's children. This race consciousness was crystallized in the NBC. Prior to its birth and during its early years, members of the black Baptist clergy differed over whether a national convention should exist independent of white Baptists and whether it should conduct business separate from white denominations.[14] The "separatists" won out over the "integration-

---

9. See Lincoln and Mamiya, *The Black Church*, pp. 29-30, and E. L. Thomas, *A History of the National Baptist Convention* (Nashville: Townsend Press, 1999), p. xiv.

10. See Vincent Harding, *There Is a River: The Black Struggle for Freedom in America* (New York: Vantage Books, 1983), and Aldon Morris, "Centuries of Black Protest: Its Significance for America and the World," in *Race in America*, ed. H. Hill and J. Jones, Jr. (Madison: University of Wisconsin Press, 1993).

11. *The 1998 Annual Report, the Record of the 118th Annual Session and Minutes of the 1998-1999 Board of Director's Meeting* (National Baptist Convention, USA, Inc., 1999), p. 19.

12. *1998 Annual Report*, p. 19.

13. See Peter J. Paris, *The Social Teaching of the Black Churches* (Philadelphia: Fortress, 1985).

14. See Washington, *Frustrated Fellowship*, and Lincoln and Mamiya, *The Black Church in African American Experience*.

ists" by arguing that they owed a debt to future generations. E. C. Morris, the first president of the NBC, argued that a Baptist publishing house was necessary because it would provide more "race employment, race development," and business experience.[15] The debt, therefore, consisted of building a legacy of work and independent institutions valuable to future generations.

Thus, the NBC developed as an institution imbued with black consciousness and race pride. It sought to be a shining beacon, championing the message that black people could build their own institutions, produce literary works, erect forums from which the contentious issues of the day could be addressed, advance the freedom agenda, and build God's kingdom. This sense of black pride and consciousness is alive in the contemporary NBC. One of the recent presidents of the Illinois State Convention put it this way: "It [NBC] means a heritage of our race, our denomination. . . . I think the most powerful thing is that out of a hundred years existing, we are still in charge of this one thing that Black people have that we can call ours. . . . Well it's the only thing that white folks can't tell us what to do. It's National Baptists, Black owned, Black run. We operate it. It's ours from start to finish."

The NBC's Foreign Mission Board chairman registered a similar sentiment, declaring that "it is a great source of our history as well as our salvation history of Black people in the United States." The renowned black Baptist pastor Gardner Taylor simply refers to the NBC as the "House of our Fathers."[16]

Given the historic conditions of black people, the NBC was left with little choice but to embrace the political striving and ideological tendencies of the African American community. As a result, the NBC is political by nature and is bathed in black religious nationalism developed by a people seeking a positive sense of self so long denied by the white majority. For believers in the faith and the NBC, a religiously based political view of the world and race consciousness are constitutive parts of what it means to be a member of the black Baptist family.

The Family Metaphor

The idea of family is a cornerstone metaphor of the black Baptist community and the NBC. Members of a black Baptist church view themselves as a church

---

15. Washington, *Frustrated Fellowship*, p. 181.

16. Gardner Taylor, "The President's Message to the Progressive National Baptist Convention, INC., September 1968," in *Black Theology: A Documentary History, 1966-1979*, ed. Gayraud S. Wilmore and James H. Cone (Maryknoll, N.Y.: Orbis, 1979), p. 263.

family. Likewise, NBC members view themselves as the family of the National Baptist Convention. This family metaphor has power because it provides the boundary markers of the community and suggests the types of social relationships members should establish internally and externally. It is not surprising that the church family metaphor has developed given the hostile treatment blacks have received from a white racist society. In many ways the black church has functioned as a warm nurturing sanctuary where people feel safe and are encouraged to develop their gifts and talents. It is a place where dignity is conferred and where each individual matters. Like a family, the black church has sought to be the "balm in Gilead" for black people.

The concept of family conjures up images of deep personal relationships, loyalty among kinship members, obedience to parental authority, trust and nurturance. In America the family concept also generates images of patriarchal authority where the father is the legitimate head of the household. Finally, the family image connotes strict boundaries separating members from outsiders. In fact, "family business" refers to private activities of family members and to the expectation that outsiders are not to interfere in family matters. The family, therefore, is a tightly knit unit where intense personal relationships are privileged.

African American churches usually perceive themselves as church families. The use of the family metaphor is especially prevalent in the black Baptist church. A black church historian spoke to the centrality of the family metaphor: "The sort of ecclesiological image that is used often for a Black congregation is that it's the family of God and we are a church family. The second thing is that with this family metaphor then you [church members] have to try and figure out how do you relate to the power structure. Language of rebellion is used, as rebellion with rebellious teenagers. Languages of the need to follow leadership, sometimes language of obedience is evoked, you need to obey. This family metaphor sets the norm for behavior, cooperating, following leadership, etc." In this imagery the head of the family is the pastor who is almost always a male figure. Sociologist Cheryl Gilkes refers to this imagery as an "ethic of family-hood" that usually relegates the activity of women to a feminine space where influential women are referred to as "mothers."[17]

The family metaphor plays an important role in the life of the NBC. It encourages its polity to operate more like a familial form of social organization than an impersonal bureaucracy. Power struggles within the NBC are re-

17. Cheryl Townsend Gilkes, "The Roles of Church and Community Mothers: Ambivalent American Sexism or Fragmented African Familyhood?" in *African-American Religion,* ed. Timothy E. Furlop and Albert J. Raboteau (New York: Routledge, 1997), pp. 367-88.

sponded to as "family fights" rather than as organizational phenomena. It is difficult to hold those in power accountable according to routine business practices, because family logic dictates that they are treated as parental authorities. Our black church historian argued: "People feel, sometimes, that as the pastor rules or runs the congregation, the president should rule or run the Convention, and that you need to give the president the freedom, the space, to see what he can do, and not try to fight him all the way. Because it is not perceived that the president is a representative image, it is not the image that we have this sharing of power, sort of this democratic model."

The family image mitigates against the establishment of a set of formal procedures to remove an officer — especially the president of the NBC — who fails to execute his duties effectively. One does not remove a father from his family. Moreover, when outsiders attempt to interfere with NBC's leadership, the family metaphor enables insiders to label them as enemies who must be resisted and not allowed to infiltrate the sacred family. That is, the family model instructs insiders that, again quoting the above-noted black church historian: "You don't leave your family, you don't desert your family especially during times of crisis. So when a crisis comes up, that is when you need to be there, and then when people call for change . . . they are seen as being disloyal, they are seen as not following leadership."

The black Baptist belief in the power of grace also supports the family model of social organization in the NBC, because in this view, human beings are inherently sinful and frail. This belief in grace requires that forgiveness be given to a transgressor who repents and pledges to seek the path of righteousness. It enables the members of the church family to remain in the fold and to be given another chance to regain trust despite past wrongdoings.

Finally, the family metaphor makes it easier for black male clergy to transplant patriarchal relations into the churches and the NBC. They argue that the Holy Scriptures demand that the male head of the church should run God's church as he runs his family. Thus, they adopt the instructions to Timothy that the head of the church "must manage his own household well, keeping his children submissive and respectful in every way; for if a man does not know how to manage his own household, how can he care for God's church?" (1 Tim. 3:4-5). The family model allows the convention to have, and project, a patriarchal face of power. In short, one has to be attuned to the power of the family metaphor, for it helps to order the structural and cultural realities of the NBC. As our black church historian put it: "There's a host of other images that could be used but the one that dominates the Black Church is that we are a church family. . . . Once that metaphor is used it begins to take over in certain ways."

Preaching and the NBC

Preaching is the privileged form of communication in black Baptist churches, and in the NBC. Within these communities preaching is the fine art through which the clergy attempt to connect with the church community. Preaching plays a fundamental role in all aspects of the NBC, including its power dynamics, its opportunity structures, and its overall culture. As we argued earlier, the Baptist church emerged to attend to the material and spiritual needs of a collectivity that was largely illiterate and severely oppressed. The denial of educational opportunities during slavery prompted African Americans to develop a rich oral culture. In this context preaching developed as a major black art form that has been refined down through generations.

Moreover, there are theological and religious reasons why preaching has become so central in the black Baptist church. Black Baptists believe that the Bible contains the holy words of God. The Bible is referred to as the Word, and it is believed that ultimately these Scriptures are the pure truths of God. The preacher is viewed as the instrument appointed by God through which his Word is communicated to believers and sinners alike. The preacher is to study and prepare himself to receive the Word from God. However, once he has done this, the act of preaching is thought to be that moment when God uses his lips, gestures, and style to connect people to his divine Word.

Black Baptist preachers are aware of the crucial role that preaching plays in the church and the NBC. One convention pastor captured the power of black Baptist preaching when he stated that "Preaching is at the very heart of what it means to be a Baptist. In addition, of course that is both our commendation as well as our condemnation, because we should not just be about preaching. But that would be very difficult and, matter of fact, almost impossible. . . . You have to be able to lay down the word." Another Baptist minister concluded that "you cannot deny that one of the strongest foundations in the Black church across the board is preaching. I don't care what you preach, if you preach it well enough you'll have a following." The seminary president we interviewed stated that in the black Baptist tradition, "What's going on there is that God seems to select spokespersons, not all of them exceedingly eloquent, some of them with stammering tongues, but clearly those who stand before the people and offer as God's representative a vision of a better life. So that office of the preacher, the eloquent speaker, has been quite exalted and reified in Black church culture. So folks who have some gifts and some abilities can really exploit that tradition. We privilege the pulpit in the Black Church culture over the priest." Preaching is the focal point of worship and politics in the black Baptist church, and that fact greatly affects the NBC.

The way to attain power in the black Baptist church is to become a pastor. The way to gain even more power is by becoming an important pastor in the convention. The ultimate power is gained when one becomes the president of the NBC. That position means that one has become the leader of the largest black Baptist community in the world — the National Baptist Convention. Becoming a pastor at any of these levels requires the ability to preach.

The first leg to a pastorship is receiving a "call" from God to preach. The "calling" occurs when one has a personal experience with God in which God speaks directly to the individual, making him aware that it is God's wish for him to preach the gospel. When an individual is considered for a vacant pastor position, he delivers a trial sermon to the congregation. If the candidate fails to preach well, he is unlikely to be successful. Thus, when Martin Luther King, Jr., was confronted with his trial sermon at the Dexter Avenue Baptist Church in Montgomery, Alabama, he felt the pressure. He wrote that "I was very conscious that this time I was on trial. How could I best impress the congregation? Since the membership was educated and intelligent, should I attempt to interest it with a display of scholarship? Or should I preach just as I had always done, depending finally on the inspiration of the spirit of God. I decided to follow the latter course."[18] Preaching, therefore, plays an important role in gaining a pastorship, which is the ground floor of power in the Baptist church.

The ability to preach generates visibility and chances for upward mobility at the local, state, and national levels. At each level this ability conveys that one has been chosen by God to be a spokesperson. It enables one to connect to vast social church networks and to gain legitimacy as one climbs the pastoral ladder. As one pastor declared, "If a guy can't preach, he can't reach." The overwhelming majority of NBC presidents have been renowned for their preaching ability. A black church historian revealed just how important preaching is to winning NBC's presidency: "When you're running for president and you go to the local circuit — both state conventions, and district, and local churches — when you go on the circuit that's where people meet you. People don't really want to hear what you want to do for the Convention. They're going to invite you there to also deliver a sermon. So if the sermon doesn't go anywhere, then there's no way that they're going to be able to connect with you on that. So it's the power of rhetoric, I think, that is the key." The ability to preach is paramount in determining who moves up the ladder in the black Baptist church and who exercises influence in the NBC.

Preaching is critical in the polity and life of the black Baptist church and the NBC. It is the main device through which charisma is unleashed, and the

---

18. King, *Stride toward Freedom*, p. 17.

major form of communication that connects pastors and congregations. It is the members of the community that are organized into congregations that determine who will be selected as church pastors and who will obtain major offices in the associations, state conventions, and the national convention. They do so through voting or acquiescing to the choices placed before them. The selections are heavily determined by how well the candidates are able to win over large numbers through superior preaching.

Preaching and charisma are intertwined in the black Baptist church. Weber defined charisma "as a certain quality of an individual personality by virtue of which he is set apart from ordinary men and treated as endowed with supernatural, superhuman, or at least specifically exceptional powers or qualities."[19] A person who is able to rule over others because of his charisma possesses charismatic authority. That is, for a person to have charismatic authority and to rule over others, it is crucial that followers recognize that individual as charismatic because "It is recognition on the part of those subject to authority which is decisive for the validity of charisma."[20] The charismatic leader is one who, because of grace, leads through inspiration and a strong magnetic personality. Thus, the charismatic leader is blessed with unique gifts unavailable to the general population. The highly successful black Baptist minister acquires charisma largely through the art of preaching.

The preacher exudes such charisma because his followers believe that God has chosen him as the instrument through which his word is to be delivered. That special gift is on display during the act of preaching. One pastor in the convention explained that preaching is "that epic moment in which the gifts that have been given by God to a particular man all come into focus, all come into perspective; the apex, the moment where people say that [this] truly is the individual that is head and shoulders above the rest. We cannot deny that here is a unique species among ourselves. It is almost assumed and presumed that the gifts automatically equate the favor of the Lord." Another leading convention pastor concurred, stating that "Preaching is words that come from God; God speaks through the Preacher." To be a great charismatic preacher, one has to be a virtuoso of this particular art form. As the Illinois state president stated, "It's not only the Scriptures or what he can say, it's how he says it and the power behind it."

The charismatic preacher is the figure that successfully connects with the audience by evoking and creatively amplifying the shared vision of the black

19. Max Weber, *The Theory of Social and Economic Organization* (New York: Free Press, 1947), p. 358.
20. Weber, *Theory,* p. 359.

Baptist community. As a church scholar argued, "The great preachers bring the followers into the rhetorical world shared by the community of followers." In that rhetorical world, people are able to draw upon messages that resonate with their daily lives. In this regard a leading NBC pastor stated that "Many times people go to church and they're depressed, they have problems that they can't find answers to. The preacher don't know that they got any kind of problems and they just preach, and they leave there relieved because the preacher said something."

Preaching, therefore, is the privileged interaction in the black Baptist church because it resonates with people's needs and culture. Our church scholar put this aspect of preaching in perspective: "People can testify to their lives being changed by the power of preaching. So that it was through the preaching event that they come to be either converted, or come to a new awareness, or that they saw things in a new way. . . . Within the African American Community 'it's my pastor said this, my pastor said that.' So that there's regular quoting of their pastor or regular quoting of some other Black preacher to a higher percentage than they would be quoting their therapist or quoting anybody else — except maybe their mother or father."

Weber argued that the visions and deeds of a charismatic leader have staying power only as long as he continues to prove himself, because "If he is for long unsuccessful, above all if his leadership fails to benefit his followers, it is likely that his charismatic authority will disappear."[21] Black Baptist ministers connect to the welfare of the governed through the act of preaching.

The ability to preach plays an important role in whether a pastor will ascend to a top NBC position and whether he will survive in that position. For example, in order to become an NBC president one must form an election team and excel as a campaigner. He must appear before numerous religious organizations, including powerful state conventions. But it is the ability to preach at such sites that matters. An Illinois state president explained that when he invites an NBC presidential candidate to the state convention, he begins by trying "to read off his resume and they [pastors] get up and say, 'we don't need all of that, if you for him, I'll make the motion right now.' I'm like, well here's these handouts, but they're like, 'we don't need that.' To try to solidify him, I'll bring him in at the annual session and say this is the man, because sight goes better than just a name. Now if he can preach, then he's got everything in there zipped, he just hooked it up."

Maintaining power at the pinnacle of the NBC is a challenging ordeal. Internally there are numerous gifted and ambitious preachers who covet the pres-

21. Weber, *Theory*, p. 360.

idency, while externally there are forces capable of derailing one's presidency. The astute officeholder knows that the ability to maintain office depends in part on his ability to reach believers through preaching. During crises he must fend off rivals through oratory at the pulpit. The Baptist belief in grace is often the rhetorical strategy used at the pulpit by incumbents to neutralize coups and silence rivals. Our black church historian explains that

> The theology of grace . . . recognizes human frailty and imperfections, human finitude; and [it] brings people into a sort of a rhetorical world where "I have failed but we all have failed, and so my mistakes and indiscretions are the mistakes and indiscretions of all humanity because of the sin of Adam." What you're doing is you're going from whatever problems you have with me — then you bring other people in to both acknowledge and affirm their own faults — and then end with "but it's by the grace of God that we are who we are." And so therefore, people are brought into that story, into that world, and they're with you now — what can they say?

Thus, in the heat of a crisis the shrewd preacher mounts the pulpit and fights his battle with the weapons of oratory and charisma. At the heart of this oratorical warfare is the idea of forgiveness.

Baptist preachers are aware of the power of oratory and charisma. An NBC pastor explained that "Preaching can get you out of almost as much trouble that you can get into. People will forgive you for stealing money, they'll forgive for adultery. . . . But they'll forgive you for anything, but if you can't preach, if you can't preach you're in trouble." Joseph Jackson, who served as NBC's president for twenty-nine years, was renowned for utilizing the pulpit to maintain power. The current pastor of Jackson's historic church notes that "Dr. Jackson was a tremendous orator; you'll hear many things about him, but you'll never hear anyone say that he couldn't preach. As a matter of fact there were several elections where organizational coups were afloat, and they were ready to work. And literally the brethren for years said whatever you do, do not let the brother take the microphone and talk." He said one coup attempt was working until "they let him mount the pulpit, and after the Sunday morning sermon, that was reversed and they were excommunicated and the right hand of fellowship was rescinded. There's power there, no one can explain it. Like the Bible says, it's through the foolishness of preaching that God has chosen to confound the wise."

Preaching is the main source through which charisma is able to flow and shape the very structure of black Baptist churches and the NBC. As Lincoln and Mamiya concluded, "from their beginning in the invisible 'institution' of slave religion, African Americans have invested far more authority in the charismatic personality of the preacher than in any organizational forms of bureaucratic hierarchy."[22] This tradition has produced important charismatic leaders including Martin Luther King, Jr., and Jesse Jackson. As we will argue later, it has also produced problems of accountability, inefficiency, and scandals in the NBC.

Above we have attempted to lay bare the cultural underpinnings of the NBC, and the black Baptist community it reflects. Because worship styles and music are also important components of this cultural world, they will be considered when we analyze the NBC and its organizational environment. We turn now to the gender and age hierarchies that are deeply embedded in the NBC.

Gender and the NBC

African American men and women have been the architects of the NBC. However, the relationship between men and women in the NBC has been characterized by deep inequality for well over a century. In the NBC men set policy, exercise power, and lead the convention. Women have functioned in vital support roles that enable the NBC to stay afloat and achieve its goals. Without this support system the NBC would not be able to pursue its multiple goals. Yet gender inequality and occupational-based sex segregation are built into the very structure of the NBC.

Throughout the NBC's history women have constituted its core of infrastructure workers. Lincoln and Mamiya captured the nature of this work: "Women serve in myriad roles in black churches as evangelists, missionaries, stewardesses, deaconesses, lay readers, writers on religious subjects, Sunday school teachers, musicians, choir members and directors, ushers, nurses, custodians, caterers and hostesses for church dinners, secretaries and clerks, counselors, recreation leaders and Directors of Vacation Bible Schools."[23] Fund-raising is another crucial role that women have performed for the NBC.[24] Thus, women have raised the bulk of the money supplied to the NBC's Foreign Mission Board. For example, the executive secretary of this board related that while doing work in Malawi, West Africa, he "found out that five out of ten pregnant women were dying in childbirth and six out of ten babies were dying before they were one year of age if their mother couldn't give them breast milk." The

22. Lincoln and Mamiya, *The Black Church*, p. 14.

23. Lincoln and Mamiya, *The Black Church*, p. 275.

24. See Evelyn Brooks Higginbotham, *Righteous Discontent: The Women's Movement in the Black Baptist Church, 1880-1920* (Cambridge: Harvard University Press, 1993), and Ethel M. Gordon, *Unfinished Business* (Detroit: Harlo Press, 1976).

NBC was challenged to confront this situation because they had a mission located there. A great deal of money was needed to address this catastrophe, and it was the women who generated it. The executive secretary recalled: "I led a group of our ladies over there and the women were so impressed with the need. They said what can we do? I said maybe we can start a hospital or clinic. They said that we'll try to help you raise money, I said alright. We found out that we could build a seventeen bed hospital for one hundred and ninety five thousand dollars. . . . So they gave me the first sixty-five thousand of the one hundred and ninety five thousand dollars it cost and we built the seventeen bed hospital."

Women play dominant roles in executing the programs of black Baptist churches and the NBC. This is true, in large part, because the sexual division of labor in these institutions funnels women into support work. However, it is also the case demographically, because women far outnumber men in black Baptist churches and the NBC. Higginbotham found that as early as 1916, women constituted "more than 60 percent of the NBC's membership."[25] This gender imbalance has increased through time. After documenting this phenomenon in the 1980s, Lincoln and Mamiya concluded: "Any casual observer of a Sunday worship service in the typical black church is immediately struck by the predominance of female members. Depending on the congregation, between 66 to 80 percent of its membership is usually composed of women. In our survey of 2,150 churches male membership averaged 30 percent. There are about 2.5–3 females to every male member."[26] As we will demonstrate, gender segregation and inequality are responsible for women performing support work throughout the infrastructure of the NBC.

Evidence demonstrates that black women continue to perform largely support roles in the NBC. When the major offices of the NBC are examined, it becomes clear that in terms of leadership and power the convention is a bastion of patriarchy. In 1998 there were twenty-one convention officers, which included the president and vice presidents. A woman did not fill any of those positions. The Executive Committee consisted of fifteen positions, and a woman filled only one of those, and that was because she served as the president of the convention's Woman's Auxiliary. Men held all the board positions, including chairman, vice chairman, and secretary. Of thirty-eight board members at large, none were women. The Executive Board consisted of fifty-six members, with only seven being women, because of their position in the Woman's Auxiliary and the Ushers' and Nurses' Auxiliary.[27]

25. Higginbotham, *Righteous Discontent*, p. 166.
26. Lincoln and Mamiya, *The Black Church*, p. 304.
27. *1998 Annual Report*.

The NBC is organized around its major missions, auxiliaries, and congresses. These spheres of activity include the Foreign Mission Board, the Home Mission Board, the Sunday School Publishing Board, the Evangelism Board, the Congress of Christian Education, the Ushers' and Nurses' Auxiliary, and the Woman's Auxiliary. No women occupy positions of power on NBC's major boards, except those segregated along gender lines. This is striking, because historically women have been particularly active in the work of foreign and home missions, and in evangelism and Christian education. For example, while women constitute the majority of Sunday school teachers, none serve on the eleven-member Sunday School Publishing Board. The activities of NBC's Ushers' and Nurses' Auxiliary and Woman's Auxiliary have been viewed and treated as "women's work." Thus, in 1998, nineteen of twenty-three board members of the ushers' and nurses' group were women, including its president. Likewise, women filled all sixteen positions on the Woman's Auxiliary Board. The NBC is permeated with gender inequality rooted in sex segregation. The convention is governed largely by one gender — males.

The root causes of NBC's gender hierarchy are apparent. As we argued earlier, the way to achieve power in the black Baptist community is to become a pastor. This avenue is usually closed to women at the point of entry and in terms of mentoring. Ultimately women are excluded from the pulpit where pastoral power is enshrined.

The overwhelming majority of black Baptist clergy do not believe that God intended for women to be ordained as pastors. That is, they oppose the ordination of women on scriptural grounds. This is the rationale they give. Whether it is the only one or even their main motivation will be discussed shortly. The point here is that this gendered view of ordination is the major barrier erected in the path of women seeking to become preachers and pastors.

Earlier we discussed "the calling" that members of the black Baptist community view as the personal contact God establishes with an individual he wants to preach his Word. The calling is the first rung on the ladder toward a pastorship. Having received the call, the neophyte alerts pastoral authorities of the blessed event with the hope that these elders will set in motion the process through which he can climb to a pastorship. The next step is the trial sermon, where the elders and members of the congregation decide whether the call is authentic based on the preaching ability of the candidate. For the neophyte the event of the calling is a time of great stress and uncertainty. Even in the best of situations one cannot be sure that the call will be judged as authentic.

Women seldom experience this anxiety because their claim will almost certainly be met with skepticism. In fact, women are usually discouraged from pursuing their calling. A female pastor, attorney, and former leader of a major national civil rights organization experienced the call to the ministry. She relates the following: "Certainly women are not given the pastoral option. There's a glass ceiling; it's not even glass, it's a ceiling that you're expected to accept and in due season if you faint not, it will change. Even to acknowledge your calling, there are few men who will at least give you normal encouragement but most you can't even talk to them." She pointed out that when women receive the call, they usually "go to the pastor and try to share this common experience and would be rejected at that level."

Gender inequality at this entry point is substantial. The president of the NBC's Young Pastors and Ministers Department addresses this inequality: "We would take the testimony of a ten year old boy who says he was called to preach; with no experience, no base, no knowledge and put him up with pride . . . and say 'God called him'; and take a woman who's had experience with God, walked with God, has integrity with God and say God can't ever do that. . . . What are we saying?" Similarly, after examining the historical record, black womanist theologian Jacquelyn Grant concluded that "in addition to not being granted ordination, the authenticity of 'the call' of women was frequently put to the test."[28] The result is that many women fail to even consider the ministry as an option.

Mentoring is crucial to landing a pastorship. The neophyte is usually taken under the wings of an experienced pastor and taught the secrets of the trade. One of NBC's leading pastors spoke to the role of mentoring: "I love young preachers, and the reason I love them so much is because I caught so much hell when I was a young preacher. . . . Now I'm appreciative of it and if a young preacher comes in here and tells me, Pastor, I've been called to preach. Alright, I'll find a date to let you acknowledge it and preach your trial sermon." The mentor usually informs the candidate that "if you go to school I'll help you, if a church becomes vacant I'll try to get you in there." However, this mentoring is not available to women when a pastor does not believe God calls them to preach.

The mentoring process also teaches a new round of young male clergy to keep the pastoral doors closed to women. A state president was asked how he would respond to a highly qualified woman who wanted him to serve as her mentor. He replied: "I would tell her she could work under me, but at this time our church and this pastor does not support women ministers." An NBC pastor who mentored and licensed over thirty-five ministers admits that many years ago he licensed a woman to preach, but has since reevaluated his position. He stated, "I don't do that any more nor do I ordain women and there have been

28. Jacquelyn Grant, "Black Theology and the Black Woman," in *Black Theology,* p. 425.

women who left this church because they felt a call and they wanted to be ordained, and I sent them to friends of mine who ordain women." When he trains his male mentorees, he counsels them "that women are not to be ordained into the pastoral ministry." Women, therefore, are usually excluded from the pastoral mentoring process while men are coached and encouraged to keep the club all male. One pastor recalls that he would have had to pay a steep price at his own ordination if he supported women, because "One of the questions on the ordination was 'would I ordain a woman preacher?' All of these old preachers were there. So if I would have said yes, I wouldn't have got my papers."

In many black Baptist churches women are not allowed at the pulpit. Jacquelyn Grant revealed that on one occasion she approached a pulpit to place a tape recorder on the lectern but "was stopped by a man who informed me that I could not enter the pulpit area. When I asked why not he directed me to the pastors who told me that women were not permitted in the pulpit."[29] Similarly, an ordained female minister related that when she accompanied her pastor to a revival, she was reminded of how male ministers prevented women from reaching the pulpit. She recalled that "when my pastor was taken up to the pulpit the pastor of the church told me to sit down on the ground level."

Thus, in the NBC and many black Baptist churches, women are not recognized as pastors and may be blocked physically from entering the pulpit. A leading pastor of the convention put it this way: "Number one, the National Baptist Convention was put together by preachers, men. Women are out of place preaching. Most Baptists . . . do not recognize women as preachers and pastors; I'm one of them, I don't recognize them. . . . If a woman head toward my pulpit up there, ushers would be running from every direction. . . . They don't come up there [to the pulpit]. They ain't got no business up there to do nothing but clean it up. They're not allowed in the pulpit."

The barriers to the pulpit and pastorate function to limit the number of women available to serve as role models. This situation was clearly revealed in our interview with the editor of the *Baptist Advocate*. Below is a portion of that interview:

> EDITOR: I know a lot of Baptist churches do not condone female ministers, do not allow them in their pulpit and things of that nature.
> INTERVIEWER: What's your church's stance on that?
> EDITOR: They're not allowed in the pulpit, they're not recognized.
> INTERVIEWER: So you've never seen in your pulpit a woman preacher?
> EDITOR: Oh no.

29. Grant, "Black Theology," p. 426.

INTERVIEWER: And how long have you been going to that church?

EDITOR: All my life.

INTERVIEWER: So you're telling me that you have never ever seen a woman stand behind that pulpit in a service and say anything.

EDITOR: No.

The NBC is a thoroughly gendered institution. Men wield power. Women follow and engage in support work.

Widespread gender inequality in black Baptist churches is rooted in theological views, the family metaphor, and male privilege. There exists a range of views regarding gender among the Black male clergy. The "ultraconservatives" argue that women are not supposed to preach or pastor churches under any circumstances. The "moderates" argue that, as far as they understand the Scriptures, women are not to be pastors, although they are open to that possibility if a convincing scriptural case can be made for gender equality. The "radicals" argue that men and women are equally qualified to preach and pastor. In their view male clergy are opposed to women pastoring because they wish to protect their own self-interests. In the black Baptist church and the NBC, the ultraconservatives and moderates are clearly the dominant and most powerful groups.

Both conservatives and moderates argue that the Bible and Jesus' behavior demonstrated that women are not to be ordained as preachers and pastors. They embrace Paul's view, which states, "Let a woman learn in silence with all submissiveness. I permit no woman to teach or to have authority over men; she is to keep silent" (1 Tim. 2:11-12). One NBC pastor explained that he is opposed to the ordination of women because "I take Paul literally, that women ought to be silent in the church. . . . It was critical for me to read the Scriptures for myself to be clear about the distinction that God has made as it relates to their [women's] roles." An Illinois State Convention president concurred: "My stance on it is that I don't have Scriptural substantiation that women have a calling in the ministry." Another leading convention pastor spoke clearly about the issue: "You can't find nothing in the Bible that would substantiate their call. The Lord never even alluded to women leading men, and if you're going to preach and pastor you're gonna be in a leadership position so you'll be leading me — women are not supposed to lead men; read your Bible." Another Illinois State Convention president put it this way: "I can speak for the majority of pastors in the Convention that we do not ascribe to women preachers based on the Bible, nothing else, purely the Bible. . . . We cannot find it in the Bible. . . . We feel that it is a divine call of God directed at men."

The perceived gender-relevant behavior of Jesus is also cited as proof that women are unfit for the ministry. That is, some pastors argue that Jesus appointed only men to ministerial positions. Thus, the above Illinois State Convention president continues, "Jesus had a lot of women around him but he never called one of them to be his disciples, he had 12. . . . I mean in his circle, there were 12 men." Another former Illinois State Convention president agreed: "Spiritually, I look back at the New Testament Church which we are a part of. I look at Jesus making his assignments and I look at who he put in leadership; I follow the same trend." The majority of NBC pastors embrace the view that the Holy Word requires that women not be ordained.[30] They feel that Christ led the way by appointing a male regime to preach the Word of God.

This male-centered theology has come under attack. Radical theologians, especially black womanist theologians, argue that there exist biblical texts which suggest that God does not make gender distinctions. According to this view, Jesus was far more liberal than Paul, and he surrounded himself with powerful women who could lay down the Word. A basic challenge confronts the conservative male-centered theology. Namely, there are Scriptures maintaining that slaves should obey their masters. If black male clergy believe only in the literal interpretation of the Bible, why did they employ religion to attack slavery and racial oppression? As the seminary president we interviewed argues, the critics maintain that they want "to critique 1st Timothy and say we need to argue with that Scripture, just as Black male ministers argued that the writings in Philemon and other places that condone slavery — we certainly critiqued those. How is it that we draw a line when it comes to the issue of gender judgments?"

These theological debates, coupled with women's demographic strength, have led some pastors to entertain the possibility that Scriptures can be interpreted to support gender equality. One pastor states: "I guess my problem is I think personally I'm open to it [women pastors]. . . . I would like it to be so; it would be easier for me. I'm having problems with the Scriptures though." Another pastor reflected this wait-and-see attitude regarding gender when he related that "I truly desire to know what is God's will and to do it." Thus, the moderates are open to theological debates on the role of women in the ministry. In the meantime, they practice gender exclusion with respect to preaching and pastoring.

The family metaphor directly affects gender inequality in the black Baptist church. It is relevant to a contemporary sociological fact. In particular, women head a large percentage of African American families. Such households are often viewed as "broken" and are contrasted unfavorably with the "normal" two-parent household usually "headed" by a father. In the black church family there are few broken homes because the father is almost always on the throne.

---

30. See Lincoln and Mamiya, *The Black Church in African American Experience*.

Our seminary president identified the connection between the current state of the black family and the metaphorical church family:

> With the kind of fragility of Black families in the post Slavery era there's been such a yearning for a strong Black male presence that there's been a kind of diffuse cultural appreciation for African American patriarchy and a lot of people, even women surprisingly, are willing to permit that even if it constricted their own leadership aspirations because we all wanted to restore Black families and restore strong Black fathers and Black men. So I think that family dynamic as a kind of psychosocial dynamic is as significant as the biblical textual issues.

Thus, in search of black strength, the religious family "repairs" the frailties of the sociological family, but in so doing helps produce gender inequality in the black church.

In this case the church family metaphor has generated a life of its own. Gender inequality in the church is avoided because of its perceived negative consequences for the black community. This view was vividly stated by a convention pastor when he was asked whether he would support the idea of female pastors. He said, "I mean I could foresee the time where I could have women standing in the pulpit, that wouldn't make me no difference. But I mean when it comes to the family, the household of faith, I just don't see a Scriptural compromise that its O.K. for that family to be represented locally as a dysfunctional female-headed household."

Pastors who advocate complete gender equality in the Baptist church argue that it is male privilege, rather than Scriptures, that constitutes the major barrier to women becoming pastors. These pastors, who are clearly a minority, support the ordination of women, and some have ordained women pastors. They are aware that most male pastors have theological difficulties regarding the ordination of women. However, they maintain that these difficulties are rooted in earthly power structures and vested interests. A former general secretary of the NBC made this case: "I think beyond that, their objections would be influenced by the same thing that influenced folks who owned slaves, to want to read the Bible in such a way that maintained support for slaves because it's not in their economic or positional interests to free folks. And so for men to affirm women in ministry creates a situation where they bring another level of competition for pastorates and leadership positions that they don't have to deal with." This position stresses the role of sexism in the black church.

An elder statesman within the NBC identified the role that sexism plays in the black church. When asked why male clergy resist the ordination of women,

362

he replied, "Because they are not used to accepting women in that vein; real ma-
cho. . . . You have to rise above sexism." He added, "I don't go about trying to
prove it by Scripture, I really don't; I'm just comfortable about it." When asked
how long it would take for ministers to support women's ordination in the NBC,
he concluded that "it's gonna take us a long time. I did my first one 45 years ago."

In the meantime, the NBC is an overwhelmingly patriarchal institution in
which men rule over a membership that is predominately female. The female
pastor, the attorney and civil rights leader we interviewed, summed up the situation: "I have never felt this level of discrimination in any of the professions I
have been in. . . . The ministry is the most oppressive of professions that I have
ever been in."

Age Hierarchy

Elder members largely attend the annual meeting of the NBC. The meeting
convenes the first week of September, when school-age children and their parents are usually unable to attend because it coincides with the first week of
school. This timing is reflective of the fact that convention pastors are relatively
old. In the view of the young pastors, there is a rigid age hierarchy that prevents
them from being heard and making meaningful contributions. One of the
founders of the recently begun Young Pastors and Ministers Department related how young people felt alienated from the convention. When he attended
the annual meeting, he discovered that "Most of the people who were on the
Convention stage were of great senior years. . . . In that same session that we
were being birthed [Young Pastors Department], the AARP was making a presentation — Association for Retired Persons — and they asked 'all the people in
the room who are retired persons or senior citizens to stand.' It looked like 80%
if not 90% of the Convention floor stood. And this was at the President's Annual Address so it was very full." Younger members complain that senior members, nestled within a paternalistic hierarchical structure, govern the affairs of
the denomination.

Young pastors argue that those in NBC's power structures believe that
young people should be silent and patient if they wish to ascend the rungs of
power. The president of the Illinois State Convention stated that the attitude toward young pastors in the NBC is that "you ain't got nothing to say, you don't
know nothing!" Another young NBC pastor said that "if you got up and challenged the King's authority in the meeting, you were almost marked forever." A
respected, senior NBC pastor agreed that young people may not always get a
hearing, but added: "I think it would be logical that it takes time to win the con-

fidence and trust of people. You just didn't do it overnight. A young fellow may be ever so popular in a certain area — but it takes time to make good wine; yes it does." In the NBC the rule is that you must come up through the ranks. This age-graded hierarchy poses a number of problems. They include concerns about whether the institution allows new ideas to enter through younger generations, whether the NBC will maintain a vibrant culture capable of attracting succeeding generations, and whether the convention will be able to make the transitions required of an institution that is part of a world undergoing a technological revolution.

NBC and Its Environment

All major institutions are situated in complex relationships with other institutions and societal actors. The NBC is no exception, for it must interact with the state, the legal system, the media, and financial institutions including corporations and banks. The NBC also interacts with other religious denominations, especially other African American denominations and religious bodies. The institutions and organizations the convention must interact with constitute the NBC's external environment. Indeed, its environment influences the overall status of the NBC significantly. Most complex organizations interact through routine bureaucratic channels, and they employ skilled professionals, who navigate them through their environments. Such institutions operate as organizational actors circumscribed by formal rules of engagement. In contrast, the NBC is a large organization, but views itself as a family. This identity affects how the NBC responds to its environment, which became painfully evident during a major public scandal in 1997. An examination of that scandal, and its aftermath, brings NBC's environment and its internal dynamics into clear focus.

In 1994 the NBC elected Dr. Henry Lyons of St. Petersburg, Florida, as its new president. This charismatic orator ran on a platform of raising NBC's standards. He was the first president to serve under a tenure rule that limits a president to an initial five-year term, followed by another five years if reelected. After the second term, he would not be eligible to run for another five years. Lyons's supporters and critics agree that he instituted significant and progressive changes in the NBC. He is credited with decreasing NBC's debt during the first several years of his presidency, increasing democratic participation, reducing the degree of age discrimination, and instituting programs designed to address critical problems of the African American community. Because of his charisma, the power of his office, and reasons already cited regarding the NBC presidency, Lyons was given the latitude to pursue his vision of the NBC.

In March of 1999 Lyons resigned from the presidency because of a public scandal that threatened to destroy the NBC. The scandal was of Lyons's own making, for he used his NBC office to negotiate bogus deals with corporations seeking to profit from millions of NBC members. These deals generated millions of dollars, some of which Lyons used for personal ends. Lyons also pocketed several hundred thousand dollars donated by the Anti-Defamation League to rebuild black churches. Evidence emerged showing he used funds to finance his own lavish lifestyle and those of several mistresses. He was vigorously investigated and prosecuted by state and federal officials.

In February of 1999 an all-white Florida jury convicted Lyons on state charges of racketeering and grand theft. Initially the federal government leveled fifty-four federal charges against Lyons, which eventually led him to plead guilty to two federal charges of fraud and income tax evasion. On March 17, 1999, Lyons resigned the presidency and was sentenced to jail to serve five and a half years for his crimes. The scandal was especially detrimental to the NBC because it was widely covered in local and national media and debated in religious and secular venues.

NBC's organizational environment was central to the scandal. External corporations, the legal system, and media were all crucial actors in the drama. Corporations (e.g., credit card companies, banks, insurance companies, and funeral homes) are especially interested in the NBC and its presidency because of the purchasing potential of NBC's constituency. A high-ranking pastor in Lyons's administration stated that "the moment a man gets announced that he is president, all your big corporations go after him and try to get him." The dominant actor, who negotiates with corporations on behalf of the NBC, is the president rather than attorneys, accountants, and business specialists. Lyons's general secretary confirmed that "the Convention allowed the president latitude to be the president and to pursue the vision that the president had." As a result, Lyons entered into legally risky deals with corporations in which he received millions of dollars that he was left free to distribute as he saw fit. Structurally, the office of the president provided Lyons the room to generate money for the convention. It was the lack of effective checks and balances that enabled Lyons to use funds to support his own shortcomings.

Despite its familial tendencies, the NBC is a legal entity that functions within a legal context. State and federal agencies investigated Lyons vigorously once the allegations surfaced. Vast resources of the state were utilized to ferret out Lyons's secret bank accounts, forged signatures, and distorted information that he provided to corporations. A state judge set the tone for Lyons's trial, and a state jury was empowered to judge the allegations swirling around the charismatic pastor.

The scandal was good copy for local and national media. The local *St. Petersburg Times* covered the scandal extensively, providing a blow-by-blow account of the embarrassing sex and theft allegations. National print media, including the *Washington Post,* assisted in bringing national attention to the scandal, while national television networks competed for an interview with Lyons to expose the sensational scandal. Thus, the *St. Petersburg Times* reported that "For months, the major networks have angled for interviews with Lyons. Producers from 60 Minutes II and Dateline NBC and the Today Show and Barbara Walters all took turns courting Lyons and his legal team."[31] Two days before Lyons pleaded guilty to the federal charges, he appeared on ABC's *20/20* and confessed that he had disgraced the black church and the black community.

The scandal reveals that the organizational environment of the NBC mattered a great deal. Corporations created the opportunities for the scandal, while the media made it visible for the nation to view. The legal system was the final arbiter, which sealed Lyons's fate and propelled the convention down an uncharted path. However, the NBC's power structure did not surrender voluntarily to the bureaucratic institutions in the NBC's environment. They had a defense all their own.

Internally, the family metaphor provided the lens through which the scandal was understood and Lyons defended. When the details of the scandal emerged, the power structure lined up in support of the president. The view emerged among Lyons's supporters that he had acted no differently than his predecessors. That is, Lyons was viewed as a president who entered into lucrative agreements with corporations to defray debts owed by NBC and to sponsor its programs. If in the process he enhanced his own personal finances, that was not viewed as out of bounds.

The prevailing view of the NBC's board and key supporters, many of whom had been appointed by the president, was that Lyons did not commit any wrongdoings against the convention. Hence, they passionately supported Lyons and urged him not to resign. As his general secretary put it: "The Convention at no point accused Dr. Lyons of any wrongdoing. The Convention never joined forces with the state and claim[ed] itself to be a victim of the leadership. In fact, the Convention voted [in] session in Denver that it did not consider itself to be a victim in any way in relationship to leadership." Similarly, another convention pastor said he "could not think of anything [Lyons] did under their administration that the previous presidents did not have the authority to do. Lyons is free to broker deals with corporations, and is just as free to richly profit from those

---

31. David Barstow, "On TV, Lyons Says: 'Let's Get On with It,'" *St. Petersburg Times Online,* March 16, 1999.

deals." Publicly, the elected and appointed leadership stood behind Lyons during the scandal, viewing him rather than the convention as the victim.

The delicate issue of Lyons's involvement with mistresses was viewed as family business, of no concern to the convention or the general public. A leading NBC pastor summed up this view: "My position is I'm a member of the Convention. Now what he did with his personal life is no concern of mine. . . . That was the general opinion of the whole Convention." Even after he was convicted, some NBC leaders maintained that Lyons should remain as NBC president. Lyons's vice president and interim successor stated that "if he can live with it, I can live with it."

During the trial, supporters argued that Lyons was the victim of a racist white media and a racist justice system. A leading pastor of the convention, E. V. Hill, argued that Lyons was convicted by "an unjust verdict produced by a racist criminal justice system in Pinellas County." Hill then invoked the family requirements of the metaphor when he stated, "when your brother is in the muck and the mire, you try to drop everything to help."[32] Critics of Lyons were viewed as disloyal family members. As a black scholar told us, Lyons's attackers were portrayed as hostile white outsiders, which led the president's supporters to call for a closing of the ranks because "We can't let them tell us what to do. In the sense that this is in-house family business and you don't let strangers come into your family and tell you what to do. No, the family needs to decide what we need to do."

Internally, then, Lyons's supporters promoted the view that the scandal was unjust because Lyons's behavior was consistent with presidential authority. Likewise, NBC's leadership viewed the behavior of the state and the media as hostile attacks on family sovereignty. This familial way of acting even manifested itself in Lyons's legal defense. An NBC-related home page stated that "Rev. Lyons's attorneys posed the defense that the traditions of the Black church gave Lyons an unusually broad range of powers that may seem at odds with larger society. . . . Lyons's supporters argued that the black church simply entrusts their leaders with a broad range of powers that is seldom understood by outside institutions."[33]

The white judge and jury rejected the "special family" defense. The family metaphor could not withstand the power of the state and the glare of the media. Yet, within the church the family metaphor had not lost all of its appeal, for

---

32. David Barstow, "Lyons, Directors to Meet to Consider Options," *St. Petersburg Times Online,* March 3, 1999.

33. Religious Movement Homepage: National Baptist convention, USA, http://cti.itc.virginia.edu/~jkh8x/soc257/nrms/nbc_usa.html.

as Lyons was carted to jail the members of his congregation debated his future role at the church. They decided that he would remain in an honorable position at Bethel Metropolitan Baptist Church. A local Lyons supporter, Rev. Manuel Sykes, explained: "The Church is a family. It is so much more than an organization. . . . The pastor is seen as the father figure of that family, especially when they have been there as long as Lyons has. . . . The work of the pastor is about putting lives back together. When he stumbles or has a problem in his life that is no time to abandon him."[34] The Lyons scandal constituted a pivotal moment for the NBC, forcing both its leadership and lay members to look deep within the convention in order to chart its future.

Contemporary Challenges

Many challenges face the NBC as it struggles to address persistent problems and recover from the Lyons scandal. In his first annual address, newly elected NBC president Dr. William Shaw outlined the problems faced by the NBC following the scandal. After characterizing the scandal as a "mirror moment," Shaw stated:

> And we need to look in the mirror of God's Word and will and when we look there, ours is an unpleasant sight. Behold some of our disfigurements. . . . This administration inherited debt and litigation that have been staggering, $900,000 mortgage past due, unpaid bills and accounts in excess of a quarter of a million dollars plus . . . ; another $100,000 plus through the Congress of Christian Education; more than 5 lawsuits and litigation — that's not a pleasant picture. Structurally, we've been a Convention where units have not met and planned together. We've had financial systems without checks and balances, individuals who have treated their part of the Convention as individual fiefdoms, resisting any authority but their own. What we see is not pleasant.[35]

In this concluding section we address major challenges facing the NBC, including the threat of religious alternatives, its loose organizational structure and imperial presidency, its barriers to democratic participation, its stifling age hierarchy, its problematic environmental relationships, its relative inability to address the social conditions of African Americans, and its gender inequality.

---

34. Twila Decker, "Attorney Says Lyons Will Retain a Role with Church," *St. Petersburg Times Online*, April 2, 1999.

35. William J. Shaw, "A Mirror Moment," Presidential Address, National Baptist Convention, Los Angeles, September 2000.

There are other religious faiths capable of attracting NBC members if this convention fails to satisfy its constituency. This is especially true for other black religious communities whose core beliefs do not differ fundamentally from those of black Baptists. NBC's new president alluded to this threat when he warned: "We grow and have believers birthed who are not fed and do not grow and do not mature, and as soon as any strange movement comes by they come to our place and find ready converts because they don't know where they are and don't know what they believe."[36] Most of NBC's competitors are not strange at all. Indeed, some of them are capable of providing a real alternative to the NBC. This is especially the case if they embrace contemporary music as well as attractive worship styles. Because music and worship style are second only to preaching in the Baptist church, they require examination.

Competition in the religious economy forces institutions to appeal successfully to some segment of the religious market or slide into oblivion.[37] Recent cultural developments endanger the NBC's dominant position among African American Christians. For much of the twentieth century the convention had been the largest black denomination and the largest organization of African Americans in existence. Most NBC officials proclaim its membership to include over 30,000 churches and around 8.5 million members. Lincoln and Mamiya say over 30,000 churches, 29,000 clergy, and almost 8 million members are affiliated with the convention.[38] Because no precise membership data exist, these numbers may inflate NBC's numerical strength. Moreover, the NBC membership may be in a state of decline. During the 1999 annual meeting Virginia's state president Geoffrey Guns described several challenges to the NBC, including negative church growth in rural areas and the gradual movement toward minimal church growth at large. A recent NBC annual report confirms Guns's contention by listing fewer than 26,000 churches that officially registered with the convention in 1998. Though some argue that official registration is not a prerequisite for convention participation, this low number presents a formidable challenge to the convention's claim of 30,000 churches.

Religious institutions must be able to adapt to changes to remain relevant in the religious economy. Some NBC pastors attribute their decline to the convention's inability to adjust to new developments in the African American religious milieu. As one pastor put it: "Historically, the convention had a signifi-

36. Shaw, "A Mirror Moment."

37. See Roger Finke and Rodney Stark, "Religious Economies and Sacred Canopies: Religious Mobilization in American Cities," *American Sociological Review* 53 (February 1988): 41-49; and Finke and Stark, *The Churching of America, 1776-1990: Winners and Losers in Our Religious Economy* (New Brunswick, N.J.: Rutgers University Press, 1992).

38. Lincoln and Mamiya, *The Black Church*, p. 31.

cant role in the lives of Baptist congregants but I think that its role has not changed with time and so it is not relevant to youth and young adults and certainly not to the Baby Boomer generation that I am a part of." Our church historian contended that many NBC churches are locked in a traditional mid-twentieth-century church culture that impedes them from competing with a vibrant neo-Pentecostal style of worship, increasingly popular among African American Christians. Churches that are able to adjust are thriving while others are in decline. As an example, he offered: "Clay Evans moved into some of that [neo-Pentecostal worship style], as opposed to Olivet, Monumental, and Pilgrim who did not, and therefore, Clay Evans sees over a thousand people on Sunday morning but Olivet, Monumental, and Pilgrim, who used to see thousands of people, if they can see a couple of hundred they're happy." Lincoln and Mamiya also contend that neo-Pentecostalism, in mainline African American churches, elicits rapid growth in membership: "The challenge which neo-Pentecostalism poses for the Black Church is real, and the issue of how to benefit from this potential of church growth and spiritual revitalization without alienating the pillars of normative tradition . . . and without producing a crisis of schism is a challenge most black churches must inevitably address."[39]

This challenge to the NBC is evidenced in a recent movement called the Full Gospel Baptist Church Fellowship, founded by its presiding bishop, Paul Morton. Morton was an NBC pastor. In 1993 he developed a fellowship of Baptist churches that are sympathetic to a neo-Pentecostal style of worship, as opposed to the traditional mode that existed at the NBC annual meetings. As another NBC pastor describes it: "It began because there has always existed in the Baptist communion those with an appetite for a more spiritual, demonstrative type of worship style. Historically those individuals have been heavily influenced by the Pentecostal tradition and yet have remained within the Baptist communion and in many respects the worship style has been stifled in the Baptist witness. So Bishop Morton really tapped into kind of a sleeping giant in terms of the vastness that really wanted to move in that particular direction." More than thirty thousand people attended the first Full Gospel Baptist Church Fellowship meeting in 1994. Since then, almost a thousand churches have joined the fellowship, posing a threat to the NBC, which has lost churches to this movement.

The Full Gospel group also attracts younger pastors from the NBC who are frustrated by the age hierarchy that thwarts their full participation in positions of leadership in the convention. When asked if there would ever be an opportunity for a forty-two-year-old like himself to take his energy and ideas on a national level in other traditional black denominations, a Full Gospel pastor re-

---

39. Lincoln and Mamiya, *The Black Church*, p. 388.

plied: "No. That's why the Full Gospel has come together so I won't have to wait until I get old. The Bible says that I'm supposed to serve God in my youth. I still have enough energy to do many things; I'd rather not have to wait until I'm old." The new fellowship offers young pastors the immediate opportunity to lead as national bishops, regional and state bishops, and in other positions of influence, as opposed to the time-consuming process of coming up through the ranks in the NBC.

To thwart the profusion of young pastors defecting with their churches to Morton's new fellowship, Lyons formed the Young Pastors and Ministers Department in 1996. Pastor Steve Bland, Jr., was elected president and has led the new auxiliary as a vital force in the convention, with a current membership of almost 2,100 pastors and ministers. He explained: "We've been building the convention; bringing people back to the convention that have been either idle, or left, and offering things that will help the convention as a whole." However, the future of the Young Pastors Department is uncertain because it is dependent on the prerogatives of the new president.

Lyons's administration was responsible for innovative changes, but his scandal-ended presidency obscures the real positive contribution he made to the religious life of the NBC. The crucial question concerning the NBC's survival is whether or not the newly elected president, William Shaw, will continue to provide the necessary innovation for the NBC to be relevant in a changing twenty-first-century religious climate. As the president of the Young Pastors Department put it: "I believe if it turns its back on [change] now, you will see a death like you never thought it would see before because there are too many movements on the horizon now that can easily take its place."

The Progressive National Baptist Convention (PNBC) is another one of the movements that compete with the NBC for its market share among African American Christians. A cadre of disgruntled NBC pastors founded the PNBC in 1961, with the goal to organize a more socially active black Baptist movement in support of Dr. Martin Luther King, Jr., and the Civil Rights movement. Their recent appointment of Dr. Hycel Taylor as chairman of the Resolution Committee is a strong attempt to put the PNBC's focus back toward its original mission. As he told us: "My challenge to them [PNBC] is that they have gone back to being exactly like the National Baptist Convention — they come and preach and eat and go back home and do nothing. This year we're trying to put the PNBC back into the course of what it came into being for: mainly, as a religious dimension for social action." Although the PNBC's numerical growth does not pose as serious a threat as the Full Gospel Baptist movement, its resurgent progressivism may provide the kind of national exposure that could attract younger pastors away from the NBC.

The enormous popularity of independent African American megachurch ministries like that of T. D. Jakes also poses a severe threat to attendance at national meetings. Jakes is an internationally known pastor and best-selling author who conducts nationwide conferences that draw up to fifty thousand people. The church historian we interviewed said, "Jakes is a phenomenon all by himself; no one has reached his heights. We have not had anyone like Jakes previously." The Black Muslim movement is also a growing threat to NBC because of its recent attractiveness to segments of the black religious community.

Such interdenominational ministries as Jakes's, and other rising independent movements, not only challenge the vitality of the NBC, but they also confirm the prediction of one of the most distinguished black Baptist preachers, of a diminished role for all denominations in the future: "I think convention life among blacks and whites is under assault now. American Baptists are having their problems, Southern Baptists are having their problems; we're in a mood where convention life is not nearly as significant as it once was. . . . I think conventions will continue for the foreseeable future to have a reduced popularity and attractiveness to people."

Musicologist Eileen Southern maintains that the NBC's public endorsement was a leading factor contributing to gospel music becoming mainstream in black churches nationwide.[40] The early leading gospel stars such as Mahalia Jackson, Sallie Martin, the Ward Singers, Thomas Dorsey, Kenneth Morris, James Cleveland, and numerous quartets were Baptists and reached national acclaim by performing at annual meetings. In the 1960s the NBC's dominance in this area steadily declined, while black Pentecostals began to dominate gospel music through the 1970s and part of the 1980s. As Lincoln and Mamiya note: "The Church of God in Christ, more than any other single denomination has pioneered the creation of contemporary Gospel. It produced such performers as the Hawkins Singers, Andrae Crouch and the Clark Sisters, and their influence has been such that every contemporary gospel choir of whatever church is almost inevitably brushed with elements of Pentecostalism through its music and its performance practices."[41] Contemporary gospel music has undergone changes in the past decade, with both the NBC and the Church of God in Christ taking a backseat to independent charismatic/Pentecostal churches.

Gospel music has reached an all-time high in popularity because of artists like Kirk Franklin, who produced an unprecedented three platinum albums. The Full Gospel Baptist Church Fellowship, T. D. Jakes, and other independent ministries like Bishop Carlton Pearson's Azusa Fellowship appear to be

---

40. Eileen Southern, *The Music of Black Americans* (New York: Norton, 1997).
41. Lincoln and Mamiya, *The Black Church*, p. 368.

more successful at drawing young adults than the NBC, by featuring popular black gospel singers including Fred Hammond, Donnie McClurkin, Karen Clark-Sheard, the Winans family, Yolanda Adams, and other leading artists at their conventions. The NBC must also respond to the changing nature of gospel music or lose younger members to smaller independent movements.

As with secular organizations, religious institutions must adapt to cultural changes to maintain their position in the marketplace. Competing forces, like the Full Gospel Baptist Church Fellowship and the rise of neo-Pentecostalism, the resurgent social activism of the PNBC, the enormous popularity of independent mega-ministries like T. D. Jakes, and changes in contemporary gospel, all serve as persistent reminders that the stakes are too high for the NBC not to embrace the necessary changes to remain relevant in a competitive religious economy.

We have produced evidence throughout this essay that a loose form of organizational structure, driven by charismatic agency, characterizes the NBC. Crucial to this state of affairs has been an office of president characterized by unlimited power that is not sufficiently restricted by effective checks and balances. For a century the NBC had no tenure rule, which allowed the majority of its presidents to remain in office for well over a decade. As a result, the charismatic pastor/president figure has governed the NBC like an imperial lord. Under this arrangement some of the talented and influential leaders have abdicated their responsibilities under the doctrine that good Baptists follow their leader. Despite the advantages of this form of governance, it also contributed to fiscal mismanagement, institutional inertia, and most recently, a crippling scandal.

The leadership we interviewed appears ready to institute firm structure into the NBC, and reduce the unchecked power of the presidency by introducing a rigorous set of checks and balances. Indeed, NBC's new president has declared that "We've got to have structure, we've begun the process of developing and implementing systems for effective financial functioning. . . . As we look at auxiliaries, and departments, commissions and committee, let us not permit attachment to the status quo to hinder the changes needed to make our convention structurally and programmatically one."[42] Without such structural changes the NBC risks extinction because it will find itself incapable of dealing with the organizational challenges pervasive in the modern world.

As an institution the NBC has not fostered a democratic climate and a high level of democratic participation. In a sense this is a paradox because its autonomy principle has generated a great deal of democracy between congre-

---

42. Shaw, "A Mirror Moment."

gations, associations, state conventions, and the NBC. Yet because of its loose structure and imperial presidency, a form of tyranny from the top has stifled this democracy. Presidential elections seldom occurred because the president was usually declared the victor following his annual address. Other major leadership positions in the NBC are not subject to a tenure rule. Thus, it is not unusual for these positions to be held by the same individuals for decades. Democratic participation in the NBC is also discouraged by women's lack of access to avenues of power in the convention.

There are signs, however, that increasing democratic winds are beginning to blow in the NBC. A tenure rule pertaining to the presidency was established shortly before the close of the twentieth century. As a result, the last two presidential elections have been conducted in a relatively democratic manner. The last election, following the Lyons scandal, generated a spirited race with the victor winning by a razor-thin margin over two other candidates. Moreover, the election itself was conducted through electronic voting, supervised by impartial professionals. Reflecting on this election, one NBC pastor concluded: "The election itself had never been that democratic in a couple of generations I don't think. . . . It's interesting to see a democratic culture being created among a people and to see the beginning stages of that." Ironically, winds of change have blown in on the wings of a scandal and a newly instituted tenure rule.

The age hierarchy has detrimental effects on the NBC. The absence of young adults and people in early middle age in positions of influence deprives the NBC of important input. Young people have different life experiences and worldviews than older members of the convention. Those views and experiences should be reflected in the life and polity of the NBC. The young people are crucial agents that revitalize and contemporize the music and worship styles of the convention. If their experiences are not reflected in the NBC, young people will pursue religious alternatives where their voices will be heard. Most importantly, the technological revolution has not landed squarely with the NBC. Computers providing access to electronic mail and the Internet are not prevalent in black Baptist settings. The younger generations have grown up in the midst of the electronic superhighway, and many have attained the skills required to navigate within this new frontier. The NBC needs to involve this generation in substantive ways in the life of the convention so that it can fully undergo the technological transformation required of those institutions that will remain relevant in the twenty-first century.

Lyons made an important contribution to the NBC when he embraced the idea to create a Young Pastors and Ministers Department in the convention. Currently that department is thriving because young pastors have acquired some important space in the public sphere of the NBC. As a pastor related, the Young Pastors Department "provides an opportunity for young pastors to have their own little convention and their own structure." However, this pastor warned that this department could become diversionary because it leaves intact an age hierarchy structure while soothing the young. It would be in the long-term interest of the NBC to fully embrace its younger members, so as to insure its future.

The Lyons scandal revealed just how inadequate the NBC was in dealing with its environment. Its business practices proved archaic in the context of corporate America. Its practice of allowing the president to operate as its sole proprietor proved naive in a world where corporate management teams and legal experts protect the interests of their firms. The NBC's view that the church operates as a family also proved naive in an environment where organizations and the state operate according to rational legal bureaucratic principles. Structural changes are needed in the NBC if it is to become an effective actor in its environment. An NBC leader pointed out how the Lyons scandal was revealing in this respect:

> I think it alerts the Convention to the fact that in terms of how it does business and how it promotes itself, that it has to be cognizant of the fact that we are in a governmental and political context where we will not escape scrutiny. And where we will be judged by those standards and if we violate them in significant ways, there will be an effort to impose sanction upon us. . . . We're going to have to re-evaluate how we function in our local communities; how do we relate to politicians, how do we relate to economic entities, and we're going to have to understand that there's no blessing without responsibilities, there's not benefit without obligation, and that it's not always easy to determine who the other "Gods" are that we're supposed to have.

A solution to these problems will require that the NBC make some fundamental structural changes, where experts rather than charismatic pastors have the technical responsibilities of steering the NBC through its environment. Indeed, segments of the NBC's membership are not likely to continue to support the convention if it is rocked by additional scandals. The NBC's current debt is in part due to the falling off of contributions by the rank and file during the Lyons scandal. In the absence of effective checks and balances, and needed structural changes, NBC members may vote with their feet by exiting in droves. In light of the recent Enron catastrophe, it should be clear that highly placed actors left unchecked may yield to temptation and exploit their office. The point is that effective structural mechanisms are needed, even in the NBC, because all human beings fall short of God's glory. However, the NBC will need to reconcile and assess its structural requirements and its guiding family metaphor. The church historian we interviewed pointed to this thorny issue: "I think that metaphor then hinders some of the other changes that are being done structurally and organizationally. . . . It's just that with this dominant metaphor, it makes it [structural changes] more difficult."

The family metaphor has real value because it reflects the culture and needs of a community that is not fully embraced by the larger society. Because of the positive contributions the church makes to the well-being of black people, it is unlikely that the family metaphor will lose its resonance any time soon. To be an effective environmental actor, however, the NBC will need to address the tension between its identity as a family and its structural needs, and make the necessary adjustments.

If the NBC is to be respected, supported, and defended by the black community, it must address its political, economic, and social needs more effectively. The convention has no visible and coherent national program to address the poverty experienced by millions of African Americans. Indeed, each year it dumps approximately $50 million into the economy of the city that hosts its annual meeting. After a century the NBC does not own a hotel chain or other major business that could contribute to the economic uplift of African Americans. Similarly, while the NBC believes in an "intact" two-parent spiritual household, it does not have a national plan to strengthen black families, many of whom are poor because they are supported by the meager incomes of single women. The NBC has no national plan to counteract the burgeoning prison industry, which incarcerates a disproportionate number of African Americans. Because of its loss of respect in the larger society, major politicians have begun to ignore the NBC. Thus, its new president revealed that "Months ago I invited Vice President Gore and Governor Bush to address this body and be heard by us, not in an entrapping way, but in a mutually enlightening way. Neither candidate replied on paper. Neither put us on their schedule."[43] He then raised the troubling question: "Have we been written off?"

NBC churches played a critical role in the Civil Rights movement, but without the support of NBC's top leadership. The autonomy principle of the Baptist church enabled thousands of churches and pastors to back King's leadership and follow him into the streets in pursuit of justice and equality. A question now is whether the NBC will engage in creative and innovative social change activities, aimed at generating social equality. If the NBC fails to func-

---

43. Shaw, "A Mirror Moment."

tion as a social change agent, it may alienate a new generation. A leading pastor of the PNBC put this issue squarely on the table:

> There has to come a new generation of Black ministers who will themselves be new creatures. They will attack the system, even the Black church; they will attack the Black church at the core of itself and will force it to raise new questions about itself. . . . They will ask the question why is it that with all of the things that are happening to us, we sing on Sunday . . . but nothing seems to change, in fact things are getting worse for us? So that generation will ask that question and they will do it with anger, disappointment and disillusionment with the Black church.

To be salient in the black community the NBC will have to return to its roots, where injustice and inequality were dissected and confronted. But even here, the NBC has historically allowed itself to be trapped between an activist stance and an otherworldly orientation that focuses disproportionately on spiritual matters. Contemporary challenges demand that the NBC creatively embrace church activism and spiritual matters, so that the vast needs of black people can be addressed.

Eventually the NBC will have to face the widespread gender inequality institutionalized throughout the convention. Deep rumbles over gender inequality are apparent to those who listen. The lid over this issue will not remain intact for an eternity. Eventually the NBC will have to answer for its unwillingness to step up to the moral plate and empower women. It is true that similar levels of gender inequality exist within the Catholic Church, the Southern Baptist Convention, and several other denominations. However, the NBC has a different calling because it was born out of the need to address the unique problems of a people shackled by the chains of oppression. There were Scriptures in the same Bible Baptists use today that condoned oppression, but the NBC critiqued them and struck out on the journey to uplift and free black people. It is curious indeed that the majority of black male pastors not only refuse to embrace the need to empower women, but stand directly in the path to such empowerment. As a result, the perspectives of women are not heard from the pulpit. There are over fifty thousand pastoral and ministerial positions in the black Baptist church, but women do not have access to them because of gender discrimination in the church and the NBC.

In a classic study of NBC's Woman's Auxiliary, Higginbotham documented the central role that women have played in the NBC historically.[44] Her central argument maintains that women in the auxiliary were often leaders who

44. Higginbotham, *Righteous Discontent.*

pursued their own goals, while fighting racism and sexism simultaneously. While this argument captures important contributions made by NBC women, it fails to reveal the extent to which the Woman's Auxiliary has supported male patriarchy in the NBC proper. Thus, constitutionally the "Woman's Auxiliary operates under the auspices of the National Baptist Convention, USA, Inc. The primary objective of the Auxiliary is to support and supplement the goals and objectives of the Convention."[45] This body, therefore, is not to lead, but to "support and supplement." The current president of the Woman's Auxiliary confirmed that the group was not to lead when she stated that the men "are our pastors. . . . They are our leaders."[46]

The future of NBC's gender inequality is uncertain. There are small minorities of highly visible male pastors who ordain and support women pastors. They constitute important role models of change for those pastors sitting on the fence and for young pastors. However, like "enlightened" slave masters, these role models are reluctant to advocate that their colleagues pick up the cross of women's empowerment. In all likelihood, women will have to revolt in order to change the gender inequality in the NBC and the black Baptist church. Thus, the president of a black seminary argued that "unless there is statistically significant unrest, there is unfortunately no intrinsic engine driving male ministers who are in power to begin to change that model [male domination]." However, because of their numerical superiority, women are in a position to force change. As the female pastor, attorney, and national civil rights leader we interviewed put it, "I mean we could shut down the church on any given Sunday with just a simple 'we're not going, y'all run it without us.'" It would be in the long-term interests of the NBC to empower women rather than be confronted with a revolution later. Without such empowerment, that revolution will come as surely as did those that overthrew slavery and Jim Crow.

The NBC remains the largest black religious organization in the world. It has a long and important history in the black community, the nation, and other parts of the world. It is now challenged to make the necessary change that will enable it to be an important force in the world. Its long history attests to the fact that it has been a survivor. The question now is whether it will have the courage and foresight to implement positive changes. As the NBC's former general secretary put it: "The National Baptist Convention wants to live and so therefore it will do what it has to do in order to maintain life. That means it will have to come to grips with the government, with the cultural ethos, with its own con-

45. *1998 Annual Report*, p. 142.
46. Waveney Ann Moore and Twila Decker, "Women's Role in Male-Led Church," *St. Petersburg Times Online*, September 9, 1999.

stituency and other constituencies . . . and if it doesn't it will die." While rumors of NBC's death are greatly exaggerated, to remain relevant and vital the convention must refashion itself in a manner that will enable it to promote the broad interests of the African American community.

Becoming a People of God:
Theological Reflections on the
National Baptist Convention, USA, Inc.

David Emmanuel Goatley

The story of the National Baptist Convention, USA, Inc. (NBC), is fundamentally a theological story. It is theological because it tells about striving
to become a people of God. This saga is about the formation of community, the
configuration of family, and the affirmation of humanity. The constellation of
community, family, and humanity is "trinitarian" in its mutuality, reciprocity,
and perichoretic nature. Each emphasis is interdependent and flows into the
next. The story is essentially anthropological. What is humanity? Furthermore,
what does it mean to be human — created in the image and likeness of God —
in a context where the dominant culture questions, challenges, discredits, or attempts to annihilate one's community? How do you affirm your humanity
when your context seeks to deny it? In a real sense, this is what the history of the
NBC has been addressing since its formation in 1895. What does it mean to be
"African," "colored," "Negro," "black," "African American," and Christian in the
United States?[1]

A Tedious Journey

The NBC story is richly textured with peaks and valleys, straight and crooked
places, successes and setbacks. The narrative is one in the making without a
definitive narrator. This story has been told, is being told, and will be told by
millions of voices across multiple generations that blend together as the saga

---

1. Each of these terms reflects an emerging consciousness of identity in the historical
movement of people of African history and heritage born in America. The evolution of ethnic
identity points to the ongoing self-identification of a people against the background of opposition for self-determination by majority and dominating cultures in America.

unfolds. The story is like a song in African form. It is a complex blend of poly-rhythmic and polyharmonic beats and sounds that produce compositions that inspire laughter and tears, hopes and fears.

The NBC story is complex, in part, because of the heterogeneity of African American people. While some argue for the clear preservation of Africanisms in contemporary African American culture, one cannot argue convincingly for any sense of homogeneity among the African Diaspora, African Americans, or African American Baptists. In spite of the many shades and hues of sentiment and sensibilities among people who share African heritages, however, the large gathering of African American Baptists who identify themselves with the NBC does share a certain core of experiences and values that produce a sense of siblinghood — a sense of family.

In the words of the spiritual song "I Want Jesus to Walk with Me," the NBC story is that of a "tedious journey." Becoming a people of God is not something National Baptists take for granted. This identity is considered a gift from God, but it is a gift that requires something of the giver. They typically believe that when God offers a gift, the receiver has some obligation to "live into" that gift. National Baptists do not hold an attitude of manifest destiny that is prearranged by the omnipotence of God. It is not inevitable that they will become a special people. God may desire that they become a people with an essential identity, but they must participate and cooperate with God in bringing their identity to fruition. In other words, National Baptists do not consider God to be an "interventionist" when it comes to their peoplehood. The songs, sermons, and prayers of National Baptists do speak of God directly intervening in lives and circumstances (usually personal crises). They do not, however, assume that God is going to create an African American Baptist people of God ex nihilo. National Baptists know that God is an "intentionalist" when it comes to their identity as a community of faith. God intends for them to be a special people that is useful to God and helpful in the world. God even invites them to join God as workers together to redeem the world. National Baptists know, however, they are required to participate actively with God if their identity is to emerge. The struggle to give birth to an identity in which the full humanity of African American people is affirmed is fundamental to the NBC experience.

Emerging African American Christianity

African American Christianity in the United States was forged in a crucible where three powerful forces converged. One of those forces was the survival of traditional African religious concepts. Certain beliefs provided a sense of commonality among the various religious and cultural expressions of enslaved African people and their descendants in America. Among them are:

- Believing in one Supreme Creative Being;
- Understanding the role of beings in the spirit world who serve as intermediaries between the Supreme Being and humanity;
- Discerning the holistic integration of all of life vis-à-vis the bifurcation of alleged sacred and secular aspects of reality; and
- Affirming the essential humanity of all people.

Traditional religious conceptualizations were not obliterated by the horrors of chattel slavery despite inevitable modifications in their understandings. The minds of early Africans in America were not devoid of theological discernment, nor were previous religious conceptualizations annihilated by the dreadfulness of chattel slavery.

Chattel slavery was the second force in the formation of African American Christian consciousness. The brutalities and traumatic physical, psychological, spiritual, and relational horrors have made impacts on the collective psyche of African Americans that are still not fully understood. To be treated as property — inventoried with tools and animals, stripped of inherent and historical identities and languages, and subjected to dehumanizing manipulations and abuse — created cultural realities that informed the emerging identities of African Americans.

Southern evangelicalism as evidenced in the great evangelical awakenings was the third force that helped produce African American Christianity. Elements of evangelicalism like the openness to emotive response to the movement of the Holy Spirit, an emphasis on personal relationships with Jesus, and the opportunity to "testify" — to communicate in public what one's experience with God has done in one's life — were all among new expressions of affirmation. To the contrary, however, manipulating Christian doctrines to justify slavery and to validate it among the slavocracy worked to oppress Africans and their descendants spiritually, mentally, and physically.

These three elements helped birth African American Christianity. African American Christians were particularly attracted to Methodism and the Baptist faith. Among other things, both groups were major players in the evangelical revivals, and both took seriously "heartfelt religion." Today, the majority of American Pentecostalism has roots in African American Baptist life. Further, those who identify themselves as nondenominational today possess essential elements of these two historical denominational streams. The Baptist faith, however, took on a special attraction to enslaved and marginalized Africans in America.

Essential African American Baptist Distinctions

Among the strongest attractions in Baptist life were qualifications for ordination and church polity. The historical qualifications for ordination among Baptists in the South normally consisted of evidence of a call to ministry demonstrated by the gift of preaching and a call by a congregation to pastoral service. Although local geographic associations of Baptists would often organize councils to facilitate the ordination of individuals, local congregations also had the power to ordain persons independently if they chose to do so. This latter freedom speaks to another attractive element of Baptist life for the enslaved and oppressed. Local congregations of believers or churches were autonomous. They believed themselves to be competent to manage their own affairs as they felt led by the Spirit of God in their particular contexts. The criteria for ordination and the autonomy of the local church gave to enslaved and oppressed African American Christians a sense of empowerment and affirmation as people created in the image and likeness of God. The emergence of African American Baptist churches and the eventual evolution of their associations and conventions find root in these two fundamentals of Baptist experience.

The earliest African American Baptist churches developed out of separations from previously integrated Baptist churches. On rare occasions the preacher for the integrated church would be African American. The newly segregated African American churches would sometimes have European American pastors/preachers and at other times African American pastors/preachers. The separations were sometimes considered mutually beneficial, giving African Americans their space to function as they desired while giving European Americans much desired distance from their African American "sisters and brothers." At other times the separations were in protest of the unequal participatory opportunities of African Americans in matters of leadership, governance, and representation on denominational levels.

The emergence of African American Baptist churches happened in a dialectical tension. On one hand, these Christians were seeking to actualize their identities as people of God being called forth by the Holy Spirit to be witnesses to Jesus Christ in their own cultural contexts. Consequently, they were seeking to become what they were being called to be. Those who were not a people (not Africans by birth and not Americans by right) were becoming a people through the call and power of God. On the other hand, they were asserting their identities as human beings created in the image of God. They were unwilling and unable to function effectively in a context of oppression and racism that denied their full humanity and rejected their gifts for ministry. Hence, the African American Baptist church came forward as an expression of call and confrontation. They were accepting God's will for them to be a people of God as well as asserting their rights as creations of God to help make their own destiny.

These two concepts that helped parent the African American Baptist church are also related to traditional theological concepts of grace and faithfulness. God's call to be a people in spite of the efforts to nullify one's existence is, as mentioned above, a gift indeed. It is not a call that is sought or requested. It is undeserved. Therefore, it is especially cherished. It was not inevitable that they would become a people of faith and a community of service. This is the place where the idea of faithfulness applies. One must cooperate with God for God's will to be fully experienced in one's life. The idea that people can do nothing but receive God's will is foreign to historic and authentic African American Baptist life. People must collaborate with God if they are to realize all that God has in store for them. Knowing God's will for one's life is not inevitable. God will call, but people must answer. Hence, this back and forth, this ebb and flow, this receiving and resisting are two critical components of African American theology that helped produce an identity in congregational and consequently denominational life.

The historic experience of the NBC is a story of the making of a people who are responding to God's call upon their lives and rejecting the racism that sought to deny the dignity of African American Baptists. As the organization began to emerge, they sensed that God was calling them to have a unified public witness and platform to facilitate the liberation of their people (advocacy); that God would enable them to develop institutions to develop the heads, hands, and hearts of their constituents (education); and that God was sending them forth as missionaries with the gospel of Jesus Christ (missions).

National Baptist Theological Essentials

Relationships are the ground on which the NBC is built. Using the concept of relationships doctrinally is to honor and emphasize the historical weight given to "family" in African American life generally and in National Baptist life specifically. While National Baptists may not consciously articulate a doctrine of family as their theological ground, it is contextually the place on which they stand and build in practice.

To say that family is the theological ground of National Baptist life connects contemporary National Baptists to their African and African American cultural lineage. Generally, African concepts of family are not limited biologically. Consequently, it is unnecessary for Africans to contrast their family and their extended family. To distinguish the two assumes biology or marriages as normative for determining familial relationships. A more natural way of African articulation of family is to contrast family and constricted family. This language communicates that the normative definition of family is relational, so that a qualifier is needed only when speaking of the narrower constellations more akin to Western concepts.

Defining family based on relationships (which does not, however, exclude biological or marital bonds) continued for Africans in America and their descendants because of the historical, cultural norm as well as the horrors of chattel slavery. The demonic separation of biological families by selling enslaved family members to different buyers necessitated the constituting of family in ways not limited by biology. What would have happened to a child who was "sold" to a different slaveholder than the one who "owned" his or her parent if other enslaved people did not accept and embrace that child? The same concept of family defined by relationship continued through days of segregation and discrimination. People often became siblings, cousins, parents, and children not by biology or marriage or legal adoption. They often became family by relating as family. This way of family life continues today, although perhaps with less frequency.

National Baptist churches, like many African American churches, can be considered families. Relating to each other, encouraging each other, helping each other advance, and even frustrating each other are dynamics of African American church life. They are not like families. They are families. The same is true of NBC life. The glue that holds together the NBC is not programmatic potency, structural sophistication, or adherence to propositions about God. It is not conformity to concepts about modernity versus postmodernity or common assumptions about issues like the immutability of God based on Greco-Roman philosophical constructs. It is not a denomination-specific creed or principles to which one must adhere. The bond that holds the NBC together is a sense of family, of belonging together on a journey through difficult terrain that threatens one's very existence if traveled in isolation. National Baptists are part of the family of God, gathered because of their common response to the salvific work of Christ and empowered by the Holy Spirit sometimes to thrive and at other times to survive. If the family manages to stay together, it can successfully achieve its goal of actualizing God's will to be a people of God.

Classic evidence of this theological embrace of family is seen in the denomination's annual meetings. They are not primarily forums for voting on budgets, articulating resolutions, and engaging programmatic strategy. These things are done, but they are not the principal foci of the event. The annual gathering of the NBC is a family reunion. It is a collection of African American Baptists from around the nation that assembles to offer a collective witness to the testimony of God's provision and protection through the years in the face of threatened eradication at the hands of evil and enemies. It generates an aura of confidence and self-respect of a magnitude rarely matched in other African American venues. When National Baptists gather, they gather for worship, for fellowship, and for networking. They plant and water seeds of collaboration among leaders and churches around areas of interests and strengths.

The family focus of the NBC produces both liability and asset. A liability of this structure is that it fails to facilitate the substantive engagement of issues around polity, politics, and program by the body at large. This approach to de-nomination life also makes it difficult to function efficiently as an organization, as will be seen later. A benefit to this approach, however, is that it can create a large table that has places for many different voices. This doctrine of family upon which the NBC stands makes it possible for so-called liberals, progressives, moderates, conservatives, and fundamentalists to belong together. This does not suggest that the NBC has perfected the concept of family and no fault lines appear. What family has? The family is sometimes functional and at other times dysfunctional. While divisions do occur, however, those who align themselves on either side of difficult social and theological issues generally can find a place to be welcome among the family at the National Baptist table.

In sum, the NBC is more about relations than resolutions. It is more about people than polity. The larger impact of this family dynamic, however, is seen in the implications concerning being related to the larger family of God. The fight for human dignity is related to finding a place at the table of human-ity in spite of those who would deny that place.

Upon the doctrinal foundation of family of God are built three core theo-logical pillars. The theological core for National Baptist churches consists of worship, nurture, and missions. These elements are also intertextual, mutual, and reciprocal. They nourish each other.

Worship

The worship experience is widely appreciated in African American churches. Non–African American cultural groups now embrace elements of worship that have historically characterized African American worship. Praise songs, emo-tiveness, and narrative preaching have gone "mainstream" in vibrant and grow-ing contemporary American churches. Worship has been a hallmark of healthy National Baptist churches. Worship has been the arena in which people have been able to praise God honestly. When the everyday work world humiliates, abuses, and dishonors African American people, the world of worship is the place where God accepts, honors, and affirms them. They can be honest with God about their joys and pains. They can find healing for their hurts. They can gain strength for the next set of struggles they must face. Worship is essential to National Baptist life.

Song and sermon are at the heart of National Baptist worship. Vibrant National Baptist churches are characterized by music and message. Songs belong to the people and convey the range of emotions that connect with life. Just as the Psalms show the pain and praise of the Hebrew people, African American church music reflects depths of grief and heights of joy. Preaching is almost always understood as the climactic moment of worship. While other Christian traditions place different expressions at the center of worship (e.g., the Eucharist), National Baptists normally see the preaching of the gospel as the high point of the worship experience. The preacher is expected to draw the people into the text and bring the text into the experience of the people. The preacher is expected to communicate the gospel in ways that have a real transforming power in the lives of the hearers. National Baptists have historically honored the strong preacher and lifted the preacher to privileged places in the denomination and in the community.

Nurture

The second element at the theological core of National Baptist life is nurture. African American churches create space for affirmation of personhood and preparation for leadership. The African American church has "mothered" people who have held membership as well as many who have had no official connection with the church. It has been a place of rescue and refuge in innumerable ways. The church has provided more than psychological support. It has done that, but it has also provided the family context that affirms and accepts. It consoles and gives confidence. In many cases the African American church has been family in the best definition of the word: not grounded in biology but grounded in relationship. Family members do not have the luxury of choosing only the best. We are brought into family by the actions of others, not by our own actions. And for the church, we are brought into the family by the invitation of God. Like many biological families, the church has had good and bad, successes and failures. National Baptist churches, when at their best, have welcomed the sibling and stranger.

No matter the socioeconomic stratification African Americans may know in the so-called secular world, many have been able to find dignity and respect in the church. African American Baptist churches have historically been places where custodians could be chairpersons of boards, laborers could be leaders, and domestics could be dignitaries. The dominant culture's categories and valuations were modified in the church culture. While churches have never been perfect places and have been influenced by dominant cultures in which they exist, they have improvised and invented new rules and worlds wherein those who were denied dignity on the outside could be honored on the inside. Historically, African American entertainers, politicians, and community leaders have been nurtured and given opportunity for leadership development in the context of the African American church. Nurture has been a hallmark of National Baptist life.

Missions

The third element at the theological center of National Baptist churches is missions. Missiology in African American churches has traditionally been more expansive than many approaches of their European American counterparts. Missions — being sent into the world to touch lives that transform the world — is traditionally integral to the theological core of National Baptist churches. National Baptists have historically understood their responsibility as transforming their communities for good. This explains the historic role of the church in the development of African American businesses during the days of segregation. Banks, insurance companies, funeral homes, schools, and any number of small businesses launched during segregation were supported and strengthened by their ties to the church. Today, progressive African American congregations have regained or retained the historic role of supporting the transformation of lives through for-profit businesses and nonprofit community development corporations. The first national African American denominational entity was the Baptist Foreign Mission Board, founded in 1880 to engage in foreign missions in Africa. Today, National Baptist churches collectively and individually continue to engage in missions in Africa or in countries with substantial African heritage.

This concept of missions is much broader than that in many contemporary American churches. Too often Christians talk about missions in narrow terms of evangelism that "leads the sinner along the Roman road" or that is a means to the ends of church membership. Some mission ministries and agencies appear to make decisions based upon the number of "baptisms per buck." This narrow concept of missions can be found in some National Baptist contexts. The historically normative and currently vibrant National Baptist churches, however, have an expanded concept of missions that reaches to communities in ways that are holistic and transformative, both spiritually and physically.

Theological Tensions

Paradoxically, while National Baptist churches embrace (some more rhetorically than realistically) the essential nature of working in communities (locally and/or globally), many stand accused of being otherworldly. Churches live in a tension of otherworldliness and this-worldliness. Numbers of churches are accused of being "so heavenly minded that they are no earthly good." This charge is made because of an emphasis on heaven and rewards in an afterlife for injustices in this life. While some are extreme in their emphasis on the afterlife, others have moved the pendulum in the opposite direction. A growing number of National Baptist churches are joining other churches of various ethnic backgrounds in the prosperity gospel movement. Proponents of this health-wealth orientation emphasize the accumulation of material goods and physical well-being as signs of God's favor upon faithfulness. This message is being embraced enthusiastically among consumer-oriented classes in the United States and in other countries where Western cultural and economic influence abounds.

Extreme emphases on the temporal as well as the eternal exist in National Baptist life. Most National Baptists, however, live somewhere inside the tension. On one hand, there are times to emphasize the eternal. "This world is not my home" is a sentiment shared by many. On the other hand, there are times to emphasize the temporal. Poverty that is imposed on people because of injustice and exploitation is not piety. Churches must not be duped into believing that accumulation is more important than distribution. A better approach is to embrace the reality that a robust eschatology — a vision of God's goal for creation — is a powerful motivator for an aggressive missiology — radically applying the gospel in ways that transform lives and move creation toward the best.

Another tension in National Baptist life relates to the pastor's role. The principal role of National Baptist pastors is to lead the congregational worship, nurture, and missions. Pastors seek to work effectively in their various contexts through the interdependency of worship, nurture, and missions. The image of the superpastor of the megachurch is an exception to the rule. Most pastors serve fewer than three hundred congregants and are able to relate closely with families and communities in accessible and meaningful ways. Myths abound, however, about the nature of the National Baptist pastor. Some believe that, in general, the pastor presides over his or her own little kingdom. They believe that the pastor can get away with just about anything, that the pastor's power is absolute and that he or she has total freedom to do whatever he or she pleases. Certainly, some pastors seem to avoid any discipline for errors and even near-demonic behavior, but to assume that pastors have carte blanche as the norm seems naive.

National Baptist pastors enjoy a great deal of freedom and authority because the congregations they serve give it to them. Further, just as the congregation gives authority, it can take it away. However, all persons in leadership positions in any organization have the potential to consolidate their power through charisma and/or performance. Consequently, as pastors demonstrate certain relative competencies in the core areas of the church's life (i.e., worship, nurture, missions), they secure more support for their leadership.

The journey toward being a people of God is long and complex. The NBC, however, has a strong theological heart with which to continue its pilgrimage. In order "to serve this present age," the NBC will have to use its strong theological foundation creatively and intentionally to respond to current and future challenges.

National Baptist Challenges: Power, Sex, and Money (Racism, Sexism, Classism)

What are National Baptists trying to become today? National Baptist constituents have participated in Pan-African, nationalist, separatist, and integrationist movements. They are conservatives, moderates, and progressives. It is absolutely clear, however, that the NBC has not essentially sought to become a sociologically, politically, or economically organized unit, although sociology, politics, and economics have informed and influenced their beliefs and behaviors. The challenges of the twenty-first century demand that the NBC reclaim its commitment to a theological anthropology that works to reconstitute, strengthen, and nurture community, family, and humanity. A new, robust, and relevant theological orientation and application will lead the NBC and its churches to engage relevantly the issues of race, gender, and class.

Race

National Baptists have sought to challenge racism and the power questions surrounding it. The most noted civil rights leader of the twentieth century, Martin Luther King, Jr., was a member and prominent leader in the NBC until his meteoric rise in the denomination was thwarted by the then president, J. H. Jackson. King and Jackson represented diverging approaches to the problem of racism in the United States. King was more "progressive" while Jackson was more "conservative." King was more closely aligned with the Democratic Party while Jackson was more closely aligned with the Republican Party. African American clergy in general and National Baptists in particular engineered many of the gains realized through the Civil Rights era. It is regrettable that King and Jackson, as well as other proponents of their respective approaches to a racially just society, could not find ways to collaborate with a "both/and" approach rather than an "either/or" method. To their credit, however, they were seriously engaging the issues of race and justice on the national stage. The NBC has no coherent strategy or policy related to the problems of racism and the distribution of power in society today. Individual National Baptists are often active in their communities and states, but there is no comparable vision for a collective political platform or voice as compared to the vision of the leaders who formed the NBC.

Given the historical role of race in the formation and identity of National Baptist life, one might ask why no comprehensive approach exists today. The heterogeneity of National Baptists works against the development of one approach to race questions. There are regional cultural dynamics such as Southerners versus Northeasterners or rural communities versus urban dwellers that challenge strategy development. Generational tensions between older or more traditional leaders of the civil rights establishment and younger or more innovative advocates for economic empowerment offer another set of challenges. While not making it impossible, these kinds of differences impede the articulation and execution of a contemporary, compelling vision and strategy to address the problems of racial discrimination today. Finally, the complexities inherent in racism and the contemporary sophistication of its expressions suggest that there probably cannot be one universal strategy for its eradication. A multiplicity of approaches and a decentralized line of attack are likely necessary to deal effectively with the twenty-first-century dynamics of the color line(s).

Sex

National Baptists have failed to deal effectively with gender discrimination. The NBC historically has been very attentive to issues of racism while being virtually silent on issues of sexism. Women rarely are affirmed and embraced as preachers and/or pastors. The ordination of women as clergy or deacons is still not the norm in contemporary National Baptist churches. The autonomy principle of Baptist life holds that denominations have no right to interfere in the practices of local congregations. This theological commitment to the autonomy of the local church, however, is no excuse for not challenging the sexism that is rampant in many NBC congregations and the denomination proper. Failure to challenge sexism is to support it. One doubts that those who claim to respect the autonomy of the local church in this matter would choose to be silent about congregations that supported human slavery. In fact, many National Baptists openly criticize European American congregations and denominations that have failed assertively and liberatingly to address racism in their ranks.

Another place many National Baptists turn in their support of sexism in the church is to the New Testament household codes that relegate women to second-class citizenship. Those who turn to Scripture for support of male dominance over females claim that this approach is biblical. They argue that there is no pattern, for example, for women in pastoral leadership in the Bible. This rather literal approach is rife with inconsistency. Again, those who believe that women should be subject to their husbands and/or deny that women should function as preachers and pastors do not believe that slaves ought to obey their masters. A thorough study of how National Baptist clergy use Scripture seems to indicate that the hermeneutic approach of many actually values narrative more than inerrancy. African American preachers seize upon the fictive quality of texts and understand the aesthetic theological approach of entering the text and having the text enter the reader in such a way that neither the reader nor the text can leave the encounter unchanged. The allegation of biblical literalism and conservatism among National Baptists is true for some, but the language used to categorize theological orientations does not always fit neatly in African American life. Theological language is related to the cultural identities of those codifying the language. The language normally used in American theological discussions is primarily born out of and speaks into non–African American cultures and contexts. As a result, African American culture and conscience are not normally considered in the definitions and connotations of the language. Hence, uncritically embracing theological categories crafted without engagement in African American communities is analogous to David trying to wear Saul's armor. It does not fit and it will not work.

Further, some argue that the principal pragmatic reason for blocking women from the pastorate is that the church is the last institution where African American men enjoy the privilege of leadership. The argument alleges that men have been penalized with the loss of opportunities in corporate America and the labor force because of affirmative action preferences for women of color. Therefore, women have been barred from accessing the pulpits and pastors' studies.

Denying women preaching and pastoral opportunities in the local church also denies them access to denominational leadership in the NBC. This is true because the leadership of the denomination is chosen from among pastors. The rationale holds that if the denomination is an association of churches and pastors lead churches, then a pastor should lead the denomination. As a result, until women are welcomed as pastors of local churches on a large scale, the denomination will continue to lose potentially talented and transformative leadership from among its ranks.

Leadership is a crucial dynamic in all communities and organizations today. National Baptist churches need to be more open to all the gifts of the Spirit given to whomever the Spirit has chosen. As more opportunities open on local levels, denominational leaders will do well to be intentional about creating opportunities on national and international levels rather than waiting for a large number of women to move through the ranks in traditional ways. African American men have criticized this ploy in white corporate America for years. More importantly, affirming the full participation of women in ministry is essential to a mature theological anthropology that recognizes the value and gifts of all human beings. Hence, both pragmatically and theologically, the NBC and its churches need to create mechanisms that ensure equality for women as well as men.

Class

One can justifiably criticize the NBC as well as most American churches for a seemingly uncritical adoption of free market, American-style capitalism that disenfranchises the masses of African American people. The efforts to advance social justice for those who are oppressed and to be prophetic on behalf of the marginalized have given more sophisticated analysis to problems of race than those of class. National Baptist churches, which are predominantly socioeconomically working-class to middle-class, are challenged to cross the class divide in order to reach the masses of African Americans who are poor as well as other marginalized groups. Many African American churches have facilities in poor urban neighborhoods but have minimal success in reaching and integrating the poor into the fabric of the leadership and fellowship of the churches. Further, more and more churches are choosing to relocate to suburban areas because of their need for larger facilities to accommodate their growing ministries and memberships. This trend has substantial implications for the urban poor, many of whom are African American.

Charles Wesley's "A Charge to Keep I Have," a familiar hymn in National Baptist life, includes the phrase "To serve this present age, my calling to fulfill." Serving the present age calls for the NBC to help its churches respond theologically and missionally to contemporary challenges of this century. There is a sufficient theological reservoir to support and nourish this phase of the journey. The question is whether there is sufficient will among the leadership to guide the organization to take action for internal change and global impact.

The Call of a Crisis

The final years of the twentieth century were challenging times for the NBC. The largest denomination of African American heritage and tradition was faced with a leadership crisis that focused on its president, Henry J. Lyons. He was convicted and sentenced to prison for activity surrounding fiscal misappropriation in a plan to partner with a corporation that wanted to increase its business with constituents of the convention. The company was to supply funds to the convention in exchange for access to its constituency and affirmation of its business strategy. Lyons deflected large amounts of cash for personal use, claiming they were consulting fees rather than payments to the convention. The period of negative publicity severely damaged the reputation of the organization, the image of pastors, and the witness for Christ.

Many people have criticized the convention for not dealing with its president in some disciplinary fashion early on. Suggested options ranged from reprimand to suspension of duties to removal from office. Media accounts reported that the convention supported its president in spite of the mounting evidence that the allegations of misappropriating funds might be true. While the official actions of the convention or its board of directors did not include disciplinary responses, it is not demonstrable that the convention, as a body, was supportive of Lyons during this tumultuous period. At least three realities must be understood.

First, a majority of members of the convention's board of directors were appointed by the president. Consequently, many of them had political and/or personal reservations about dealing with him harshly. Some trusted their colleague and friend despite growing amounts of evidence. Some tried unsuccessfully to rally support for reprimanding or removing him from office. Further, some argued — true to American-style jurisprudence — that one is innocent until proven guilty, and that since African Americans have had more than their share of experiences with the law that presumed their guilt, potentially premature punitive processes were not warranted. Thus, the board did not bring disciplinary action.

Second, African American Baptists often vote with their money. They give money to support an organization's causes and the visions of their leaders when they are supportive of leadership. The financial condition of the convention during the Lyons years indicates the lack of support given to him as news of alleged misappropriations began to leak. Further adverse fiscal effects were realized as the legal proceedings continued.

Third, many constituents of the NBC reflected a posture that is embraced by large numbers of African Americans. Although media accounts seemed to paint a bleak picture about Lyons's innocence almost from the beginning of the emerging story, numbers of the constituency were determined not to allow the media to dictate the convention's response to one of its own members and especially its chief elected officer. The dominant media in the United States are more often than not hostile to African Americans. Good news is ignored. Bizarre behavior receives excessive attention far beyond proportionate significance. Hints of impropriety are aggressively pursued. Remedies that theoretically may be taken in non–African American communities are proposed as commonsense approaches. What is ignored is that these hegemonic or so-called commonsense responses are supposed to be applied to African Americans with swiftness and severity, while members of dominant communities are often able to escape prompt and unsympathetic punishment, either openly or through confidential negotiations. Consequently, some constituents of the convention took the position that they would allow the justice system to proceed rather than seek remedy within their organizational structures. If Lyons were convicted, then the convention would remove him should he not resign. If he were exonerated, then the convention would have avoided rushing to conclusions based on unfair or inaccurate reporting of alleged facts.

It is important to note that certain issues related to the crisis that arose during the Lyons presidency are not isolated to his tenure. There are structural weaknesses in the convention's governance (such as the presidential appointment of a disproportionate number of board members, the presidents of auxiliaries, and the executive leadership of agencies) that give the office of the president exceptional powers without appropriate checks and balances for accountability. This concept grows from the understanding that a pastor is ultimately accountable to the church body and God rather than to a board or committee writ large.

The latter half of the twentieth century has seen patterns of presidential prerogatives that, when implemented, were accepted or tolerated but not necessarily embraced by the masses of members. The presidency of J. H. Jackson (1953-82) saw the use of power to defeat efforts to enact presidential tenure, promote conservative political and ideological alliances, and block the increasingly popular civil rights leader Martin Luther King, Jr., from denominational leadership. These events all helped precipitate the formulation of the Progressive National Baptist Convention in 1961. The tenure of T. J. Jemison (1982-94) saw the erection of a new headquarters building (the Baptist World Center) in Nashville, Tennessee, that, among other problems, ignored certain Afrocentric aesthetic sensitivities (e.g., a prominently displayed Eurocentric image of Jesus) at a time when this mood was making substantial impact among churches and culture. This emphasis on a massive building project took place on property adjacent to land that held a dilapidated facility for the struggling American Baptist College (the NBC's college). This project demonstrated a lack of sustained programmatic focus on Christian higher education. The Lyons presidency (1994-98) was consumed with debt elimination and economic empowerment schemes. In 1999 the current president, William J. Shaw, began his tenure engulfed in the need to liquidate the mortgage on the Baptist World Center and to resolve numerous outstanding debts and legal issues. Shaw's presidency also began with sweeping leadership changes and organizational adjustments that occurred by decree with the convention being informed of substantial modifications at later dates.

The crises that erupted during the Lyons presidency are symptomatic of other issues in the organization. While the scope of recent problems seems unprecedented, their roots were present long before. The above examples of the privileges of the presidency result from structural vulnerabilities in the governance of the organization that will continue to produce crises unless remedied. More important than structural considerations of the NBC, however, are theological issues that need to receive renewed focus and priority in the denomination's life. Coming to grips with the weaknesses and vulnerabilities of the convention, critiquing them, and refining the convention's theology and practice will help transform the organization from one with great potential to a denominational force that helps congregations recognize, internalize, and actualize a truly liberating praxis to which Christians are called.

The two realities that ground the birth of the NBC (seeking to become a people of God despite the opposition of its dominating culture) still operate today, albeit in sometimes unrecognizable or distorted ways. The effort to become a liberated people through God's call and with human collaboration influenced Henry Lyons to seek economic partnerships for the convention. The Civil Rights movement of the 1950s and 1960s resulted in liberation in terms of legal statutes. The realization of liberation, however, is still a work very much in process. While African Americans have certain legal rights, they are substantially disenfranchised in terms of economic vitality. While more African Americans arguably have greater assets today than ever before, it is also true that substantial gaps separate comparably qualified and experienced African Americans from European Americans, and more African Americans are in poverty than before. As mentioned above, one could argue that the critical test of relevance for the African American church of the twenty-first century will be whether the working-class and middle-class church can effectively minister to and struggle for liberation with the majority impoverished class community among African Americans and throughout the world.

Regrettably, far too many African American churches are primarily concerned with their own institutional survival, thus rendering them irrelevant and endangered. Encouragingly, however, a growing number of African American churches have sought to make economic empowerment an integral part of their mission and ministry. These churches have begun to be more creative and assertive in accessing the capital that others have kept and coveted for too long. Henry Lyons was in touch with the need to utilize the strength and influence of the nation's largest African American organization to leverage cooperation from business communities. It is commonly held that, for too long, European American businesses have profited from African American consumerism and loyalty without African Americans reaping wealth-building benefits of their economic relationships. Lyons saw an opportunity to capitalize on the tremendous economic power of the African American church by negotiating reciprocal investment relationships with corporations. Lyons was not the only denominational leader to seek this path. Almost all the leaders of the historic African American churches collaborated in a business venture during the 1990s in which collective coordinated buying by the denominations' constituencies would allegedly provide economic benefits for pastors of churches as well as the congregations they serve. Many have deemed this effort a pyramid scheme that has produced questionable benefits at best.

Lyons's problems were twofold, one pragmatic and the other theological. First, the kinds of business negotiations required to make large-scale joint ventures successful demand the involvement of people with appropriate business experience, financial acumen, legal counsel, and the like. Even then, deals can and do go wrong. It is the unusual pastor who is equally equipped to shepherd a flock, preside over a large and unwieldy denomination, and successfully negotiate a multimillion-dollar partnership deal with national and international corporations without substantial mechanisms for accountability. Even so, Lyons's failures should not erase the point that he displayed a certain courage and creativity in his willingness to risk a novel and potentially beneficial project for the NBC. Leadership requires taking risks that produce rewards. Unfortunately, Lyons failed personally and professionally.

The second problem that contributed to the NBC public catastrophe was sin. National Baptists take sin seriously. Although they believe in the supreme power of God, they also recognize the significant power of Satan. The result of sin is that we are broken people in need of the continual healing and helping power of God. It is obvious that the wealth, privilege, and entangled relationships that accompany unchecked power overcame Henry Lyons. A thread of sobriety that would surface from time to time during the publicity surrounding the Lyons affair was that all of us are sinners — even those who are saved by grace. Further, there was always the implication that all people have weaknesses.

The temptations that unraveled the presidency of Henry Lyons may not unravel another person's professional practice or divine call. One point must be made emphatically, however: all of us are vulnerable to failure because of our fallenness. The smug self-righteousness of some of Lyons's critics sometimes seemed to be safe because of their inaccessibility to the kind of power and privilege that accompanies the presidency of the NBC. The old adage is probably true: power corrupts and absolute power corrupts absolutely. This perspective in no way lessens the unacceptability of Lyons's actions nor excuses his full responsibility for his behavior. To the contrary, this position challenges the notion that one should demonize a person who obviously was overtaken by a fault.

The theological dimension of sin in the recent difficulties in the life of the NBC naturally introduces another theological issue: forgiveness. Human appropriation of forgiveness is often messy and slippery and is sometimes sloppily handled. Yet the love of God so lavishly poured upon humanity in the atoning event embodied in Jesus Christ demands that we respond positively to the challenge of forgiveness. Here, however, one often has more questions than answers.

- At what point does one graciously and lovingly forgive?
- What are the prerequisites for forgiveness?
- Does saying "I'm sorry" adequately prepare the way for forgiveness?
- What sort of confession is required?
- Is there a need for restitution?
- What does forgiveness look like when given to a leader who has violated trust?
- Can a fallen yet forgiven leader be given the opportunity to lead again, or has the privilege of leadership been forever forfeited?
- What about God's redeeming love?
- Can a leopard change its spots?
- Can Jesus' atoning work melt a heart of stone?

These questions about forgiveness, grounded firmly in the nurturing nature of National Baptist theology, may be the hardest theological questions of all. This may be the case not just because of Henry Lyons's actions as the president of the NBC, but because forgiveness goes straight to the heart of what it means to be part of the family of God that is infected and affected by sin. The quality of the life of the church is at hand in our responding appropriately and faithfully to those among us who have fallen, especially those entrusted with the privileged mantle of leadership. What will the church become if it cannot grow in its ability to relate constructively to those who have sinned? If family is a valid conceptualization of being a people of God, the church's very existence is bound up in its proper execution of forgiveness toward the fallen in the family and the world.

One cannot know in advance how the answers to the questions of sin and forgiveness will play out in relationship to Henry Lyons and the NBC. Neither can one know how the story should unfold. One can be certain, however, that the way the denomination handles this delicate crisis will serve as a model, for good or ill, for its thousands of churches, millions of constituents, and tens of millions of observers, Christian and not. The convention must seek discernment and proceed prayerfully because the matter of sin and forgiveness is crucial for the church. It is at the theological center of what it means to be children of God, disciples of Christ, and people of the Spirit. The NBC has significant theological resources for this phase of its journey. Perhaps, by God's grace, it will discover and utilize these resources to see it through. Hopefully, the NBC will provide constructive models and useful leadership for other denominations with the lessons it learns.

The Reformed Church in America as a National Church

John Coakley

D onald Luidens's organizational case study and Steve Mathonnet-
VanderWell's theological essay to follow reflect on a strong, recent tilt in
the Reformed Church in America (RCA) toward the idea that the very purpose
of the church at the *national* level is to be of service to the church at the *local*
level. Mathonnet-VanderWell analyzes this idea as expressed in the RCA's 1997
Mission and Vision Statement, suggesting among other things that the statement "moves away from traditional Reformed theology and its concomitant
polity." Luidens argues that the trend in RCA congregations over the past half-
century to become more and more preoccupied with their own local concerns
has threatened the very survival of the national agency structure of the RCA.
He interprets this new "localism" of the national church as an emergency effort
to justify that structure and keep it in place. Both authors see the national preoccupation with the local, or at least the extent of that preoccupation, as signaling a new development for the RCA, a new way of thinking of the church as a
national entity.

Here, by way of introduction to Luidens and Mathonnet-VanderWell, I
sketch some of the historical background to this recent change in the RCA's
thinking about itself at the national level. I ask: What is this a change *from?*
How has the RCA conceived of itself as a national entity? How has the "national" been related to the "local"?

To discern the roots of the idea of a national church in the RCA, we do well
to consider first the denomination's Dutch Reformed origins. The earliest of the
congregations that would eventually form the RCA were the Dutch churches of
New Netherland, founded in the mid–seventeenth century on Manhattan and
Long Island and farther north in towns along the Hudson River. After the British
takeover of 1664, these congregations survived and grew in number in colonial

New York and New Jersey.[1] (The greatest concentrations of RCA congregations today are in those mid-Atlantic states and in the states of the upper Midwest that attracted Dutch immigration in the nineteenth century.)[2]

Supervised by the classis of Amsterdam, they remained part of the Dutch church for most of the remainder of the colonial period. This Dutch Reformed Church was a *national* church in the sense of being territorial, that is, coextensive with the territory of the Dutch nation. This fact put the Dutch churches in America, which existed under British sovereignty, in an anomalous position within the Dutch church, and was ironically one reason for their very subordination to the classis of Amsterdam. Thus, in the decades just before the American War of Independence, the requests of the group of American ministers and elders (who called themselves the "coetus") to become a bona fide "classis" (see below) were refused because any such genuine assembly of the Dutch church must be "inseparably connected with the government of this country [i.e., the Netherlands]" — an impossibility in the Americans' case.[3] But even so, there is no question that the Americans belonged to the Dutch church.

The relationship of "national" and "local" levels of the Dutch church was spelled out clearly in its church order, as determined by the national Synod of Dordt, which met in 1618-19. That document designates four types of governing "assemblies," ascending from the local level to the national. The lowest is the consistory, made up of the minister(s) and elders of a local church. The next is the classis (analogous to the Scots' "presbytery"), consisting of delegated ministers and elders from several neighboring churches. Then comes the particular synod, made up of delegates from neighboring classes, and finally the general synod, made up of delegates from the various particular synods. Thus, the general synod could be said to be the only concrete expression of the church at the national level. On the other hand, it is important to understand that the existence of the general synod did not constitute — that is, did not bring into existence — the church as a national entity; the church was constituted not from the top, but indeed from the bottom, in the sense that the preaching, sacraments, and discipline that defined it were by nature *local* actions occurring in the individual local churches. To be sure, this understanding of "church" is pointedly different from that of the Congregationalists, who were coming to

1. The standard account is Gerald F. De Jong, *The Dutch Reformed Church in the American Colonies* (Grand Rapids: Eerdmans, 1978).

2. See the demographic map of the RCA in 1990, in Edwin S. Gaustad and Philip L. Barlow, eds., *New Historical Atlas of Religion in America* (New York: Oxford University Press, 2001), p. 149.

3. *Ecclesiastical Records, State of New York,* ed. Hugh Hastings, vol. 6 (Albany: J. B. Lyon, 1905), p. 3894.

define it not by the presence of word, sacrament, and discipline per se, but rather by the covenant of members with themselves and God — but the point of definition was no less "local" than theirs.[4]

The Church Order of Dordt did not specify the actual tasks of the general synod, and since that synod did not meet again for well over three hundred years, there is little in the historical record to show what they were meant to be. Yet the Church Order states as a general principle that in each of the four assemblies, when considered in relation to its neighbor on the ascending scale from local to national, "no business shall be transacted, except what could not be settled in the lesser Assembly, or such as appertains to the Churches composing the Greater Assembly, in general."[5] Thus the general synod apparently could receive appeals and referrals from the particular synods, but could only originate business that affected the whole national church collectively — the most obvious example being the Synod of Dordt's own definitive formulations of doctrinal standards and church order. The general synod did not *directly* either supervise local churches or address their concerns.

Before we go on, a word is in order about the theological understanding of "church" that underlay this form of church government. The Dutch Reformed Church embraced, as one of its fundamental doctrinal standards, the so-called Belgic Confession of 1561. This document articulates the Augustinian/Calvinist idea of the "true church" as recognizable by two marks: (1) the "pure preaching of the Gospel" and (2) the "pure administration of the sacraments as Christ ordained them," to which the Belgic added (3) "the exercise of church discipline for the correcting of vices."[6] The church's essential task, in such a view of things, was to maintain the purity and correctness of its preaching, sacraments, and discipline. Endeavors such as the conversion of unbelievers, or the amelioration of society in terms of Christian values, were — however worthy — by implication *not* the church's explicit tasks. The church was not, in other words, about changing the world, or at least not directly. Rather it was about preserving a faithful and pure witness to God's revelation; it was not characterized by active enter-

---

4. According to the Congregational "Cambridge Platform" of 1648, the "form" of the church is "the *Visible Covenant,* Agreement, or consent wherby [*sic*] they give up themselves unto the Lord, to the observing of the ordinances of Christ together in the same society, which is usually called the *Church-Covenant*" (chap. 2 sec. 3). *The Creeds and Platforms of Congregationalism,* ed. Williston Walker (New York: Scribner, 1893), pp. 207-8. See the comments on the "essence" of the church in Reformed polity in Allan Janssen, *Constitutional Theology: Notes on the "Book of Church Order" of the Reformed Church in America* (Grand Rapids: Eerdmans, 2000), pp. 221-23.

5. "Church-Order [of Dordt]," article 30, in *Ecclesiastical Records,* 6:4221.

6. The Belgic Confession, article 29, in Philip Schaff, ed., *The Creeds of Christendom* (New York: Harper, 1877), 3:419-20.

prise so much as by steadfastness. Did the Dutch Reformed Church of this period lack a sense of "mission," then? Not necessarily. Certainly the adherents of the Belgic Confession believed that the gospel was meant for the world and that its light was not to be kept under a bushel. But for them, as for the other Protestants of the Reformation, it was precisely the faithfulness and purity of the church's preaching of the Word of God — its steadfastness — that served such mission most directly. This is because the Reformers believed in the active power of the Word of God itself, truly proclaimed, and therefore, as David Bosch has put it, were confident that "it is the gospel itself that 'missionizes,' and in this process enlists human beings."[7] As for the activist work of establishing places for the gospel to be heard, what we would now call "church extension," the Belgic Confession assigned this not to the church per se, but rather to the civil government. It is the magistrates, not the ministers, elders, deacons, or assemblies of the church, who are charged to "promote the kingdom of Jesus Christ and to take care that the word of the gospel be preached everywhere, that God may be honored and worshipped by everyone, as he commands in his word."[8]

When the Dutch Reformed churches in America constituted themselves as a national church in their own right in the years surrounding the War of Independence — the Reformed Dutch Church in the United States (a name employed with minor variations until it was changed to Reformed Church in America in 1867) — they retained the ecclesiology of the Dutch church in most respects. They did make one important change almost immediately, namely, to reject any role for the magistrate in church affairs.[9] But otherwise they embraced the Belgic Confession and the other two Dutch Reformed doctrinal standards (the Heidelberg Catechism and the canons of the Synod of Dordt) as well as, in its essentials, the Church Order of Dordt. Even in their assertion of church-state separation we can discern the traditional Reformed idea of "church." According to the preface to the 1792 constitution approved by the general synod of this new church,

> Whether the Church of Christ will not be more effectually patronised in a civil government where full freedom of conscience and worship is equally protected and insured to all men, and where truth is left to vindicate her own sovereign authority and influence, than where men in power promote

---

7. David Bosch, *Transforming Mission: Paradigm Shifts in Theology of Mission* (Maryknoll, N.Y.: Orbis, 1991), p. 244.

8. The Belgic Confession, article 36, p. 432.

9. The magistrate had the responsibility, as the Belgic Confession put it, "to maintain the sacred ministry so as to root out all idolatry and false worship of God." The Belgic Confession, article 36, p. 432.

their favorite denominations by temporal emoluments and partial discrim-
inations, will now, in America, have a fair trial; and all who know and love
the truth will rejoice in the prospect which such a happy situation affords
for the triumph of the Gospel and the reign of peace and love.[10]

It is true that the envisioning of a "reign of peace and love" here suggests an un-
Augustinian optimism about the future of Christian society that would have
been foreign to much of the early Reformed tradition and that anticipates the
millennialism that would become commonplace in the American Christianity
of the decades to follow. It is also true that the preface presents the very exclusion
of the magistrates from church affairs — without any reassignment of missionary functions to the church itself, or indeed to anyone else[11] — as something
positive and hopeful. The idea here is that the very freedom accorded the gospel
in such a situation would constitute the best condition for the envisioned social
change. But significantly, the preface does not present the church as an *agent* to
bring about that change. Instead it speaks of the church in passive terms, as
something to be "patronised," apparently in the sense that citizens will have access to it for what it has to offer, in the same way, if with greater foreseen success,
as when it was under government protection. What the church offered in that
case was precisely its preaching, and sacraments, and discipline; we find ourselves here still within the realm of the earlier Reformed ecclesiology.

As for the infant RCA's notion of the "national" church, and by implication that of the "local" church, again it followed the Church Order of Dordt
fairly closely. Indeed, the section of the constitution on church order is called
the "Explanatory Articles on the Church Order of Dordt." The same four assemblies are set forth in the same ascending order beginning with the local consistory, and related to each other in the same way as in the older document. The
church is still understood as fundamentally local in its marks, and none of the
assemblies can trump its lower neighbor's proper authority.

Thus, in substance, the RCA remained true to the earlier tradition. But in
its understanding of the work of the church at the national level, a new tone is
discernible in the articles. On the subject of the general synod, they say more
than Dordt had said: "A General Synod represents the whole body. It is the
highest judicatory, the last resort in all questions, which relate to the government, peace and unity of the church. To this is committed superintending the

10. "Preface to the Entire Constitution, Embracing Doctrines, Liturgy and Government,
1792," in Edward C. Corwin, ed., *A Digest of Synodical Legislation in the Reformed Church in
America* (New York: Board of Publication of the R.C.A., 1906), p. vi.

11. Marvin D. Hoff, *Structures for Mission,* Historical Series of the Reformed Church in
America, no. 14 (Grand Rapids: Eerdmans, 1985), pp. 15-16.

interests of religion, the maintaining harmony, and faithfully preserving the churches in principles and practice of their holy religion."[12] Here the general synod is given something of its own to do — maintaining standards of doctrine and practice and also, vaguely but broadly, "superintending the interests of religion." It looks to be, potentially anyway, more an activist body than the old church order envisioned.

The articles go on to say that the general synod has the power of "nominating and appointing Professors of Theology" and holding them accountable to itself, corresponding with other churches, and constituting and receiving appeals from particular synods. They also speak of "deputies" to be appointed to be present at classis examinations of candidates for ministry (presumably exercising the synod's responsibility to maintain standards of doctrine and practice).[13] The drafters of the explanatory articles seem to have been quite deliberate in attempting to envision the functioning of the church at the national level, even if the phrase "superintending the interests of religion" remains somewhat vague.

This activism at the national level would soon be more than merely a matter of tone. Beginning in the early nineteenth century, a new idea of "church" gained currency in the RCA, with important implications at the national level. This was the idea that, whatever the church's commitments to steadfastness and purity in preaching and sacraments, it must also be a zealous agent to bring and apply the gospel to the world, especially through evangelism. It was an idea that was also taking hold in other American churches at the time, and that underlay the new phenomenon of the American "denomination" as (to use Sidney Mead's term) a "purposive" and ecumenically cooperative body aimed at the Christianization of the republic as well as of the whole globe. Typically, American churches expressed this zeal at first by supporting voluntary societies for missions and other Christian initiatives, and then, roughly from midcentury onward, began to form their own respective structures of agencies for these purposes.[14] In the RCA case, after a period of unsuccessful

---

12. "Articles Explanatory of the Government and Discipline of the Reformed Dutch Church in the United States of America," art. 51, in *A Digest of Constitutional and Synodical Legislation of the Reformed Church in America*, ed. Edward Tanjore Corwin (New York: Board of Publications of the RCA, 1906), p. lviii.

13. Corwin, *Digest*, p. lviii.

14. Sidney E. Mead, *The Lively Experiment: The Shaping of Christianity in America* (New York: Harper and Row, 1963), p. 103; Russell E. Richey, "The Social Sources of Denominationalism: Methodism," in *Denominationalism*, ed. Russell E. Richey (Nashville: Abingdon, 1977), pp. 63-84, esp. 166-71. For the processes of agency-formation in other denominations in the nineteenth century, analogous to that of the RCA, see C. Conrad Wright, "The Growth of Denominational Bureaucracies: A Neglected Aspect of American Church History," *Harvard Theological Review* 77 (1984): 177-94.

experimentation in which the general synod attempted to sponsor missionary work through, successively, a committee of its own, a particular synod (that of Albany), and a voluntary missionary society, the general synod created in 1831 its own Board of Missions (renamed in 1844 the Board of Domestic Missions). This was an agency distinct from the synod that eventually had its own staff, and yet also served at the synod's pleasure and entirely under its direction.[15] Insofar as it was thus both discrete from and dependent upon the synod, it established a model for several other boards that soon came into being, all under the synod's direction: the Board of Foreign Missions (1832), the Board of Education (1832), the Board of the Sabbath School Union (1839, abolished 1863), the Board of Publication (1854), the Women's Board of Foreign Missions (1875), the Women's Executive Committee for Domestic Missions (1882).[16]

By forming and directing these boards for the pursuit of various missional purposes, the general synod was not only taking on a new task, but signaling a genuinely new understanding of the church as a national entity within the terms of its own tradition. The Church Order of Dordt had not foreseen such a function, and indeed the activist idea of mission that this function presupposes is patently not the same as that of the early Reformed tradition, as assumed by the old church order that was still enshrined in the RCA constitution. The church indeed recognized this in the late decades of the nineteenth century, and after some years of debate passed a constitutional amendment in 1901 specifying that

> to the General Synod also belongs the power and duty to institute and organize such general agencies as shall best enable the church to fulfill the command of the Lord Jesus Christ by which he has enjoined on all His disciples the duty of teaching all nations and preaching the Gospel to every creature; to maintain, supervise and direct such agencies when erected in the conduct of missionary operations at home and abroad, and to recommend such methods in the church as shall effectively sustain such agencies and tend to secure the largest dissemination of the Gospel.[17]

Thus, the great task of mission came to be lodged officially at the national level of the RCA; and the national entity became — or had already become — the premier expression of the church as missional.

This idea of the national entity as the spearhead of mission remained in place through most of the twentieth century. It found particularly strong expres-

---

15. Hoff, *Structures for Mission*, pp. 20-32.
16. Corwin, *Digest*, pp. 94-96.
17. Minutes of General Synod, 1879, p. 378, quoted in Hoff, *Structures for Mission*, p. 44.

sion in the second half of the century, characterized by a certain sense of urgency about the work of the general synod's agencies and a chronic impulse to reorganize them for greater efficiency and effectiveness — a process influenced by organizational models derived from the corporate business world. In 1952 a Stewardship Council was established which coordinated the agencies' work and presented a single budget to the general synod, in contrast to the previous system whereby each agency had made its own direct request to the synod for funding. Then in 1961 the General Synod Executive Committee (GSEC) was formed to provide a similar focus and coordination for all the other work of the synod. Then in 1968 the General Program Council (GPC) was created to supersede the Stewardship Council, and carried consolidation of program significantly further by literally merging the boards and agencies into a single corporation with its own representative board and staff.[18] The GPC, after some reorganization of its own in 1980, eventually went out of existence in 1992 when a new, single General Synod Council (GSC) took over both its functions and those of the GSEC; and the GSC itself has recently conducted an "organizational audit" with a view to clarifying its own position and tasks.[19] Throughout this long period of reorganization, the professional staff of the national agencies have emerged as important players, especially the general secretary, whose position (given its present name in 1968) evolved out of the old functionary position of clerk of the GS (general synod), to become in effect CEO of the whole structure of national agencies.[20] In all these developments the idea of the church as "purposive" body, intent on effective action, is very much in evidence.

That heightened sense of purposiveness about the national work of the church indeed forms the immediate background of the changes discussed by Luidens and Mathonnet-VanderWell; but before we return to those changes, there is one more element to consider in the historical record. I have suggested that from the nineteenth century onward the national entity took on new tasks. But that does not mean it ceased to be what it had been. We have so far discerned two operative ideas of "church": the older Reformed doctrine that defines it in terms of the purity of its ordinances, expressed within a territorially defined polity, and the more recent idea of the church as inherently purposive, defined by its mission. The more recent idea dominates any account of the national church in the last century and a half. Yet it has not supplanted the older one in the RCA, but has coexisted with it fairly harmoniously. To be sure, concerns were raised in the long debates that preceded the 1901 constitutional

---

18. Hoff, *Structures for Mission,* pp. 92-199.
19. Minutes of General Synod, 2000, pp. 71-72.
20. Hoff, *Structures for Mission,* pp. 121-23.

amendment that making the agencies constitutional altered the traditional polity unnecessarily; and in years of continual postwar restructuring the fear has
been expressed that the agencies would take over the proper responsibilities al-
lotted to the general synod by the ancient Reformed polity.[21] Yet fundamentally, not only the historical polity but also the basic Reformed doctrines remained in place; the RCA has continued to embrace the Belgic Confession and
the other Dutch Reformed doctrinal standards; and its *Book of Church Order*
has continued to maintain, in essentials, the polity of the Church Order of
Dordt. Insofar as the general synod remains in charge of the national agencies,
one might even say that the delegation of missional tasks to the general synod
as specified in the constitutional amendment of 1901 marked an instance of
what the Church Order of Dordt envisioned in specifying a Greater Assembly's
business as that which "appertains to the Churches composing the Greater Assembly, in general." In this sense the national church did not alter, over the
course of the last century and a half of "purposive" action, the basic relationship to the local church it always had. There has been a balance or harmony in
the RCA between its two guiding ideas of "church."

Now let us return to the present and the newly prevailing idea that the
business of the national church is to serve the local church. What precisely has
changed? What has not?

One thing that has *not* changed is the notion of the church as *fundamentally*
local. Often one hears voices of alarm in the RCA that label the new sensibilities
within the denomination as evidence of creeping "congregationalism," as though
the emphasis on the local itself violated the historic presbyterial polity of the
RCA. There may be evidence for this in particular cases (such as the Mission
Statement's characterization of the RCA as a "fellowship of congregations"). But
in the RCA's tradition the very definition of the church as the locus of preaching
and sacrament already construes the church as something essentially local.
Churches with true "congregational" polity have a different way of defining the
church as something local, and they have a different (more voluntarist) notion of
the relationship between the local and national levels of the church. But that does

---

21. *Christian Intelligencer,* November 19, 1888, p. 8; a pastor who was president of the general synod in 1961 wrote in alarm to the stated clerk complaining about the latter's newly enlarged powers: "The role of the Stated Clerk in the Executive Committee should, it seems to me,
be of a truly secretarial nature; . . . the Stated Clerk would somewhat embarrass his position at
church headquarters if he assumes direct responsibility for the 'coordination of the work of the
Boards and agencies of the church' [cf. Minutes of General Synod, 1961, p. 342]. This responsibility should always clearly rest with the Committee rather than the person, whether he be president of the Synod, Stated Clerk or whatever." Norman Thomas to Marion de Velder, November
16, 1961, RCA Archives A/81-1, box no. 3.

not make their conception of church any more "local" than the RCA's — or any less national, for that matter; indeed, Congregationalists (and other churches of congregational polity) have strong traditions of national witness, in many cases rivaling that of the RCA. Strong assertions within the RCA of the local nature of the church do not, in themselves anyway, constitute a breach from tradition.

A second thing that has not changed, at least not since the emergence of the RCA as a "denomination" in the nineteenth century, is the conviction that the church must be "purposive," activist, about its mission. That conviction, which from the early nineteenth century marked a departure from the sensibility of the Reformation, has if anything gained in strength since enshrined in the RCA constitution in 1901; the spirit of the Mission Statement of 1997 is nothing if not purposive.

As for what *has* changed, again I point to two things. One is exactly the balance between the older and newer notions of "church" that derive from the RCA's tradition. I wonder if it will soon be no longer appropriate to speak of such a balance at all. Specifically, I wonder if mission in the "purposive" sense is increasingly being considered as the very essence of the church. As Mathonnet-VanderWell's essay shows, the single-mindedness of the Mission Statement in this respect causes it to obscure or subtly revise elements of the older polity, such that little sense remains of a "territorial" notion of church with its attributes of steadfastness and purity. (In this context it is also worth noting that the practice of infant baptism, historically inseparable from that idea of church, is being seriously questioned in many parts of the RCA.) The provocative phrase in the Mission Statement, "we will not do business as usual, or the usual business," is sometimes invoked in the context of the questioning of existing structures of polity.

In the second place, and perhaps most obviously, the assumption that it is the national entity that most properly has the job of "mission" has come in for severe criticism. That assumption seems to have been so strong in the nineteenth century as not to need any particular argument to justify it; similarly now, the contrary assertion — that the local church is the proper locus of mission — is set forth (as, for instance, in the Mission Statement) as something self-evident. Loren Mead has pointed to this change of emphasis on the broader stage of American Christianity, calling it a paradigm shift, one of those changes that is too profound for people quite to spot or understand it when it first happens; and that characterization seems apt.[22] The following case study and theological essay explore the implications of this, as it has appeared in the national structures of this one denomination, in fascinating detail.

22. Loren Mead, *The Once and Future Church* (Washington, D.C.: Alban Institute, 1991), pp. 8-29.

National Engagement with Localism:
The Last Gasp of the Corporate Denomination?

Donald A. Luidens

> *Forty years ago we asked, What is the purpose of a denomination? The an-*
> *swer: A structure that carries out our mission, builds up institutions, en-*
> *forces procedures, and publishes materials. It seemed the purpose of congre-*
> *gations was to support the denomination.*
>
> *Today we ask the same question. But our Mission and Vision Statement,*
> *adopted by last year's General Synod, provides a different answer: "Our*
> *shared task is to equip congregations for ministry." The denomination serves*
> *congregations.*[1]

Prologue

Initial strokes of the death knell of the corporate structure of the Reformed
Church in America (RCA) were sounded in the early 1950s. Over the next forty
years these peals have grown louder, although they have not rung their last. The
lessons of the last half of the twentieth century have been lessons of the growth
and rationalization of the corporate model, and then of its decline and transformation in this mainline Protestant church.

---

1. Wesley Granberg-Michaelson, "Path to the Twenty-First Century," *Church Herald*,
July/August 1998, p. 17.

The author wishes to thank colleagues Roger Nemeth, Lynn Japinga, John Coakley, Stephen
Mathonnet-VanderWell, David Roozen, Kenneth Bradsell, and Katherine Bawinkel Harmsen
for comments on earlier drafts. Needless to say, the analyses and conclusions are my own.

Introduction

In 1992 Craig Dykstra and James Hudnut-Beumler wrote about the rise and fall of the corporate organizational structure among mainline Protestant denominations.[2] Beginning in the late nineteenth century and reaching its zenith in the 1960s, the mainline's adoption of the corporate model of organization for its national structures paralleled the rise of modern bureaucracies in business and politics. Large-scale programs and objectives necessitated large-scale, highly formalized organizations to carry them out. Moreover, with the large-scale bureaucratic machinery came grand, outward-looking visions. As was happening in big business, so too in the church. Corporate management techniques, which were regularly upgraded and refined in the secular sphere, were systematically appropriated by church bureaucracies as well.[3]

The corporate denomination "metaphor" (their term) seems to be an apt representation of the organizational formula that saw the establishment and routinization of religious communions throughout the United States. The wide-open "religious marketplace" in the post–World War II era accelerated the development of this corporate model. Like competing businesses occupying a growing market niche, Protestant denominations around the country routinely perfected their production processes and marketing techniques. In these early years the level of competition was minimal and "success" was widespread. However, over time the religious marketplace became a crowded one, competition grew and success became more elusive, which accelerated the transformation of the corporate denomination.

Among the defining characteristics of the corporate denomination was a highly evolved bureaucratic structure, often centralized in a "national office" and undergirded by democratically elected synods and boards.[4] This elaborate matrix provided denominations with the administrative and material resources needed for their collective missions. The corporate entity also served as a visible representation of the denomination's success. If it sported a visible bureau-

---

2. Craig Dykstra and James Hudnut-Beumler, "The National Organizational Structures of Protestant Denominations: An Invitation to a Conversation," in *The Organizational Revolution: Presbyterians and American Denominationalism,* ed. Milton J. Coalter, John M. Mulder, and Louis B. Weeks (Louisville: Westminster John Knox, 1992), pp. 307ff.

3. Donald A. Luidens, "Organizational Goals, Power, and Effectiveness" (Ph.D. diss., Rutgers University, 1978), and Donald A. Luidens, "The National Staff in Its Tenth Year," *Church Herald,* October 6, 1978, pp. 13-15.

4. Donald A. Luidens, "Bureaucratic Control in a Protestant Denomination," *Journal for the Scientific Study of Religion* 21 (June 1982): 163-75.

cratic structure, a denomination could take its rightful place in the pantheon of established national churches.

Moreover, reflecting the imperialistic optimism of the age, the corporate model ushered in a worldwide vision for Christian ministry (symbolized in the title of the flagship mainline Protestant journal of this era, the *Christian Century*). For many Protestant churches this vision was also the driving force behind an aggressive "global mission" program, ecumenical and activist in style, evangelical and engaging in tone. The corporate model fueled, and was in turn fueled by, a Christianity that was outward looking and expansionist. While often complicitous with Western colonial chauvinism, this American Christian culture was also redolent with concerns about human needs among the world's most economically and politically disadvantaged.

Thus, in both form (a highly refined growth- and program-oriented bureaucratic structure, complete with centralized authority often residing in "national staffs") and mission (a global vision which necessitated challenging local congregations to move beyond their own limited environments), the corporate denomination was very much a "modern" institution.

The death of the corporate model, according to Dykstra and Hudnut-Beumler, involved both the loss of this outward, expansionist vision and the failure of the large-scale, bureaucratically structured, highly centralized national executive offices. In the wake of this corporate pattern, they suggest, has risen the denomination as "regulatory agency," one which asserts and enforces appropriate conduct and belief on controversial social issues. Concerned with right thinking or acting rather than with building a global and ecumenical community, the denomination as regulatory agency finds itself mired in interminable crises, precariously straddling moral and ethical divides.

The "Corporate Denomination" Comes to the Reformed Church

The history of the RCA has followed closely the pattern suggested by Dykstra and Hudnut-Beumler. As the world mission and Sunday school movements grew during the late nineteenth and early twentieth centuries, the RCA developed ad hoc and largely autonomous institutional structures to promote members' involvement in these enterprises. However, not until after World War II was the full force of the corporate model felt within the RCA. The maturation of a formal bureaucracy — the corporate model — during the 1950s was closely followed by its wane in the 1970s. By the opening of the twenty-first century the corporate structure of the RCA was in uncertain straits, hanging on with a reduced staff to a localist agenda that had considerably narrowed the grand scale of earlier visions. As will be seen below, these stages of the metamorphosis of the denomination were not anticipated — or even desired.

The postcorporate regulatory agency Dykstra and Hudnut-Beumler write about does not fully describe the current situation in the RCA. While the denomination does have a limited prophetic voice (which Dykstra and Hudnut-Beumler associate with "regulator denominations"), this appeal is a vestige of its more prominent, 1960s forerunners. Rather than represent a new departure, taking positions on controversial social policy issues has been routinized as denominational "business as usual," a role the congregations seldom include under their own aegis. However, in recent years the prophetic voice, too, has lost its cutting edge and has been domesticated as an extension of evangelism (for those on the right) or mission (for the remnant on the left). In these capacities, even the prophetic role has been largely absorbed under the rubric of local activism.

It has not been to regulatory responsibilities that the corporate denomination has been yielding its centrality in the RCA. Rather, the shrinking corporate denomination is being overtaken by a hyper-localism characterized by the axial role played throughout the church by individual congregations. In an unprecedented fashion, congregations are coming to see themselves as autonomous actors within the historically "connectional" Reformed Church.

Symptoms of this quest for autonomy include the growing number of congregations that have tried to unilaterally discharge their pastors, a function constitutionally reserved for the classis (the regional judicatory of ministers and selected elders), which "constitutes" the congregations and their relationship with pastors. Moreover, congregations exercise considerable choice in the religious material they purchase, the forms of worship they use, and their contributions to the activities of the denomination's branches. Reformed Church publications, lectionary, and programs are finding a diminishing audience as parachurch groups compete for congregational dollars. Finally, a handful of congregations have in recent years elected to withdraw from membership in the RCA — negotiating separation agreements that entail compensation for property, consideration for ministers' pensions, and other matters. Significantly, churches from both liberal and conservative communities have been involved in this severance. In each case the departing church found the congregationalist pattern of self-governance more to its liking, and has affiliated with Baptist, nondenominational, or United Church of Christ associations. While the number of disaffiliating congregations remains small, each severance creates ripples of discontent and disillusionment. As ideological battles become more frequent, these departures may become more common.

As congregations continue to assert their centrality in the Reformed Church, the corporate denomination finds itself left increasingly out in the cold. In a noble effort to find a productive role in the church, the executives who currently embody the corporate structure have turned to greater engagement with localism as their calling. This appears to be a cause with diminishing prospects, and may prove to be the final gasp of an institutional model that has succumbed to external structural and cultural changes beyond its control and to internal institutional decisions which, often unintentionally, place the corporate denomination in the cross hairs of localism.

Undermining, External Forces

Amidst the euphoria of the post–World War II years, the growth of the institutional church was taken for granted throughout middle- and upper-middle-class America. As Hoge, Johnson, and Luidens have written: "In 1955 *Time* magazine rhapsodized: 'Everybody knows that church life is booming in the U.S., and there are plenty of statistics to prove it.' *Newsweek* dedicated its March 28, 1955 cover story to 'Resurgent Protestantism.' It pointed to 'the vast resurgence of Protestantism' experienced in Sunday schools, lay groups, and seminaries."[5]

The RCA was party to these rollicking good times. Its active communicant membership grew by a third from 168,000 in 1946 to an all-time high of 225,000 in 1967. New congregations proliferated throughout the country, and a variety of levels of the church structure were bent to the task of creating new parishes. Individual congregations "gave birth" to "daughter" spin-offs, classes expanded their boundaries to include new congregations in the West and South, and the denomination engendered many "new church starts" through various funding programs. Particularly energetic in this process were several particular synod (regional) executives. They actively promoted new church starts, working to capitalize on the upward economic mobility and nascent suburbanization transforming the United States (and, to a lesser degree, Canada). In the words of one former staffer, "New churches were cropping up everywhere; we could hardly fund the new churches or find pastors for their pulpits!"[6]

But there were significant, hidden costs to these aggressive thrusts into congregation building, and some of them became apparent only during the late 1960s and early 1970s. The principal cost to the RCA was the advancement of a

---

5. Dean R. Hoge, Benton Johnson, and Donald A. Luidens, *Vanishing Boundaries: Religion of Mainline Protestant Baby Boomers* (Louisville: Westminster John Knox, 1994), p. 1.

6. Rev. Dr. Bert Van Soest, private conversation.

congregationalist subculture throughout the church. As a denomination with a "presbyterial" form of polity, the RCA traditionally based its governance on the collective wisdom of its ministers and elders. Individual congregations are instituted by classes, and they must seek classis approval for the disposition of their property. Ministers are called to local congregations by the classes, whose ranks they then join. In these and other ways the RCA has been a decidedly "connectionalist" denomination, carefully distinguishing itself from churches with congregational or episcopal structures.

In contrast, the newly developing congregationalist subculture was distinguished by its absorption with the local church and its autonomy. Moreover, eschewing historical RCA patterns of growth from within (an approach that became virtually impossible to sustain as birth/baptism rates plummeted during the twentieth century), the new congregations found themselves increasingly seeking new members through "market-driven" recruitment strategies and programmatic offerings to targeted groups (especially young suburban white families). The external focus that had fueled the corporate bureaucracy for over a century, a focus that had been expressed in world mission appeals as well as in urban and social justice ministries, gradually yielded to a form of religious localism and isolationism reminiscent of the "New Federalism" looming on the secular political horizon.

Such a profound change to the course of its history was not new to the RCA. From inward-looking, Dutch-language congregations of the colonial era, dependent upon imported leadership and expanding immigrant membership, the RCA joined the American Protestant mainstream during the nineteenth century. In the process, the prevailing notions of cultural expansionism and structural rationalism — that is, the ideological and organizational foundations for the subsequent corporate denomination — became part of the fabric of the RCA. The introduction in the nineteenth century of these external foci began to undermine the RCA's historic, organic, Dutch ethnic culture (including the Dutch language that was widely used throughout the RCA long beyond midcentury). By the twentieth century, while retaining its Dutch accents, the RCA reflected other mainline denominations with its women's mission board, its burgeoning empire of missionaries, its colleges and seminaries, and its ecumenical commitments (the RCA was one of the founders of the Federal Council of Churches).

A century later the new congregationalism — spawned by changing national demographics and a bureaucracy determined to capitalize on expanding market opportunities while facing competition for reduced resources — was to significantly erode the underpinnings of cultural collectivism that had held the RCA together for over a century. An early warning sign — the initial death knell, as it were — of this impending flood tide was the gradual reallocation of institutional funds away from collective, denominational activities and increasingly toward local, congregational expenses. Per capita giving (in 1990 constant dollars) more than doubled from about $210 in 1946 — a level which had held steady since the 1870s! — to $500 in 1966.[7] Along with much of Middle America, the socioeconomic tide was rising in the RCA as well, and some of the increased disposable income found its way into the church's coffers. For a short time the resources were proportionately shared; as expenses for local congregations grew, so too did funds distributed "upward" to the denomination. Yet, even in the 1950s, an increasing proportion of the RCA's finances was being directed toward new church starts — a largely congregational objective.

However, by the mid-1960s funding in the RCA experienced a dramatic shift. Moneys were increasingly directed away from extracongregational undertakings in order to cover skyrocketing congregational expenses. Until then, roughly 25 percent of money contributed to the church was earmarked for external expenses. By the 1990s that proportion had plummeted to less than 10 percent.

It would appear that several trends were embedded in this changing pattern. For instance, pastors' salaries — long treated as arbitrary matters between congregation and cleric — came under increased regional synod regulation. Compensation levels were pegged to church size, length of ministry, and other "rational" standards, away from congregational wealth or whim. As a result, congregational budgets were taxed in a new way; discretionary funds for extracongregational purposes became more strained.

On another note, the proportion of small congregations (those with fewer than one hundred members) jumped between 1950 and 1990 from 20 to 40 percent of the RCA. Many of these ailing congregations were in eastern synods, which experienced significant out-migration; more and more RCA constituents were migrating away from rural and inner-city parishes and toward suburban ones. Small congregations have always been the least able to generate "surplus" resources from which extracongregational programs could be funded. As the number of small parishes grew, less support flowed to the national church.[8]

---

7. Roger J. Nemeth and Donald A. Luidens, "The RCA in the Larger Picture: Facing Structural Realities," *Reformed Review* 85 (winter 1993-94): 85-113, and "The RCA: A Virtual Denomination?" *Church Herald* 8 (November 1998): 8-11.

8. See Roger J. Nemeth and Donald A. Luidens, "The RCA: A Virtual Denomination" and "Dutch Immigration and Membership Growth in the Reformed Church in America: 1830-1920," in *The Dutch-American Experience: Essays in Honor of Robert P. Swierenga,* ed. Hans Krabbendam and Larry J. Wagenaar (Amsterdam: Vrije Universiteit, 2000), pp. 169-88, and "Fragmentation and Dispersion: Post-Modernism Comes to the Reformed Church in America," in *Reformed Encounters with Modernity: Perspectives from Three Continents,* ed. H. Jurgens Hendriks et al. (Stellenbosch: Media.com, 2001), pp. 125-38.

Additionally, the RCA saw a tremendous shift in its core constituency away from the urban centers of the East Coast to the midsized towns and suburban sprawls of the Midwest and West. In the process, the denomination lost the historic economy of scale which had been present when its largest congregations were urban, "parish" churches. These "tall steeple" congregations — lining the main streets of New York City, Philadelphia, Newark, Jersey City, Albany, Schenectady, and Rochester — had long been the strongest supporters of denominational programs. They had been the chief proponents of a rationalized, bureaucratized, corporate denomination, a model their business and civic leaders had introduced to the church. They had historically contributed a disproportionate amount of their funds to denominational endeavors (often a third of their income went to extracongregational programs) and of their sons to RCA leadership positions. Indeed, so complete was their thrall over the operation of the corporate RCA that their dominance was long resented by their smaller, country cousins.[9]

In their place the suburbs of the Midwest and West have produced a like number of megachurches. However, as market-driven regional niche churches rather than as local parishes, this new brand of large congregation has extremely costly overhead. Constantly challenged to meet rising competition from other niche churches, a megachurch must continually provide new and innovative programs for prospective members. Membership size plays a key role in the survival/success of these churches, so the recruitment and currying of new members becomes the principal preoccupation of leaders and pastors — and an overwhelming demand on the church's budget. As a result, their operating expenses and localist focus have increasingly precluded supporting denominational endeavors. In the RCA today, the largest congregations (those with over one thousand members) contribute to denominational ventures at the same per capita level as the smallest congregations.[10]

As with most mainline denominations, the RCA was also hit during the 1960s with a rapidly declining birthrate. While it had long depended upon replenishing its member losses from within its own ranks, for the first time in its history the RCA found fewer young people in their pews from which to draw. This pattern had a devastating effect on the denomination's confidence in its ability to grow. Indeed, the drop in membership, which has been unabated

---

9. Historian Randall Balmer traces this tension back to rivalries in the seventeenth century between the burghers of New York City and the country folk of surrounding New Jersey and Long Island parishes! *A Perfect Babel of Confusion: Dutch Religion and English Culture in the Middle Colonies* (New York: Oxford University Press, 1989).

10. See Nemeth and Luidens, "The RCA."

since 1967, has led to a variety of efforts to promote church growth strategies —
strategies which themselves reinforced the centrality of congregations over the
denomination. Willy-nilly the RCA found itself a competitor with countless
other denominations for new members in a wide-open religious marketplace.

In each of these ways, structural and cultural changes swirling around the
RCA have buffeted and remodeled the corporate denomination. Each contributed to the diminishing size of the national staff, and each underscored the
growing centrality of the local congregation. Internal forces were at work as well.

Internal, Corporate Decisions

In a number of cases, what were intended as corporation-enhancing decisions
in the RCA contributed paradoxically and inadvertently to the weakening of the
corporate denomination. Some of these decisions were broadly supported at
the time as "rational" and "efficient" choices for the church to make. For instance, the Board of World Missions (BWM) had long been the flagship branch
of the denomination. During the 1950s and 1960s the RCA underwent a period
of considerable "rationalization and consolidation" of its national office structure, as Coakley's historical introduction notes. Much of this restructuring was
at the expense of world missions. The story of the declining role of the BWM
can be told in the fits and starts of bureaucratic decision making, and its ultimate cost has been the inexorable shifting of denominational focus away from
external, global initiatives and toward internal, congregational ones.[11]

In 1952 the RCA established the Stewardship Council (which was formally
staffed in 1956). Its aim was, in part, to systematize the budgeting procedures of
the denomination so that the four competing boards (World Missions, Domestic Mission, Pension, and Christian Education) and agencies would not be (or
be perceived to be) in competition with each other.[12]

As Marvin Hoff, a church historian and erstwhile national staff member,

---

11. In retrospect, historical trends have an air of inevitability. When those trends are the
result of very human decisions, the impression of manipulation or contrivance can be inadvertently implied. Institutional decisions, often made for limited and immediate purposes, can interact with environmental changes to weave patterns of unintended outcomes. So it has been
with the metamorphosis of the national staff of the Reformed Church in America.
Misimpressions of manipulation or malicious intent are hereby disavowed (as are perceived
slights toward individuals). Other persons, in the same positions and faced with similar choices,
would likely have made the same (or parallel) decisions. What has come about is most evident
in retrospect and may have had little chance of being averted.

12. See Nemeth and Luidens, "The RCA."

recounts the process, the Stewardship Council initially divided all undesignated money sent to the denomination on a proportional basis reflecting the designated funds which had also been received.[13] For instance, if the BWM had received 38 percent of the designated funds in a given year, it would receive a similar 38 percent of the undesignated funds. As had long been the case, this board continued to receive the lion's share of denominational funding.

However, by 1958 the council had altered its allocation policy in order to promote greater funding parity among the boards and agencies in the face of their historic imbalance. One component of this policy was a plan to "equalize" funding for the various branches. Hoff cites the 1958 Minutes of the General Synod: "The new plan developed by the Stewardship Council provided that 'at the conclusion of the year all boards which have received more than their askings shall return to the Staff Conference such funds in excess of their askings as shall have come from undesignated funds. These returned undesignated funds, together with other undesignated funds, shall be used to assure all other boards of their full askings.'"[14] By Hoff's calculations, the BWM was the great loser during the next few years, receiving by 1965 barely a third of the undesignated funds that its previous proportion would have garnered.

The rationale for this reallocation of funds was an organizationally sound one: several boards and agencies were having difficulty meeting their basic operating expenses while the mission boards were generally flush with funds at the end of each fiscal year. Why not redistribute the resources so that all would have an operating level of support? Did not the sizable undesignated funds allow such redistribution?

This shift in funding resulted in two incipient wedges being driven between the corporate bureaucracy and the denomination's constituency. First, the allocations were increasingly going to programs and activities that were perceived as less important by the membership. While there was wide support for world and domestic missions programs among RCA members, there was less enthusiasm (perhaps founded on ignorance of the programs involved) for many of the other initiatives being undertaken — such as building the ministers' pension fund or stockpiling resources in the Extension Fund.

The second wedge was that the agencies which were the principal recipients of the enriched funding were precisely the ones that generated localist tendencies among the congregations. The Board of Education and the Church Building Fund were substantially enhanced during this period, and their efforts were explicitly localist in thrust.

13. Marvin D. Hoff, *Structures for Mission* (Grand Rapids: Eerdmans, 1985), p. 104.
14. Hoff, *Structures for Mission*, p. 104.

Hoff writes the following about the impact on the Board of Education of the reallocation of resources into their coffers:

> Providing new financial resources to the Board of [Christian] Education made the greatest program impact on the life of the Reformed Church. The additional funds came as the board was publishing the Covenant Life Curriculum with several other denominations and as American Protestant churches began to provide increasing staff services for the burgeoning educational programs in their local churches. The exceptionally large increase . . . made it possible for the board to increase its staff and provide significant new services to the church. . . . Without the new equalization policy this growth in staff providing educational services to local churches would not have been possible.[15]

While not the intended outcome, this expansion of the Christian Education portfolio resulted in rising expectations — both among congregations and among staff members — that supplying local congregations with services was of a growing premium.

Inevitably, increased denominational funding for new church starts further promoted competition for denominational dollars. New congregations in the Reformed Church were being promoted ex nihilo, as it were. While in the past, most new church starts had been extensions of existing congregations, the new model of church planting involved more generic church growth principles. For three centuries new congregations in the RCA were the organic extensions of existing congregations. With few exceptions (including "new" congregations developed to appeal to migrating RCA families who moved to southern California, Florida, and the American Southwest), new churches grew from established congregations that were commissioned to launch daughter congregations. Whether because of population growth in an existing RCA "enclave" or the migration of entire congregations (such as the move from an inner-city locale to the surrounding suburbs), "successful" new congregations traditionally followed current or former RCA congregants.

In the wake of the redirection of funds to the Church Building Fund, however, a whole new pattern of church planting was initiated. Once again, the rational-bureaucratic decisions made by the corporate leadership led to unintended, localizing consequences. The RCA adopted and adapted more widely established church growth techniques being promoted throughout the country by church growth specialists. Extensive "market research" would be undertaken in a "target community"; potential parishioners in the neighboring area were

---

15. Hoff, *Structures for Mission*, pp. 105-6.

polled as to their preferred religious experience. A ministry would be designed to meet these market-generated expectations. Trained "evangelists" would be supported in these extension contexts, often at considerable denominational expense and for extended periods of time. Sizable resources would be needed to purchase property and set the stage for the construction of a religious facility. In the words of one former church executive, "The RCA has come to plant congregations the same way that Walmart decides where to open a new store."[16]

In many cases — especially in the suburbs of the East and Midwest — this approach was successful. That is, many new congregations were opened (at the same time that others were abandoned, so the denomination's total number of congregations changed very little throughout the postwar years) and new parishioners were being attracted. However, as generic mainline (or, increasingly, conventional evangelical) Protestants, this new constituency of religious shoppers represented a significant change in composition from earlier generations of RCA members.[17] For the purposes of the current conversation, their key commonality was that their involvement in the RCA was incidental to their commitment to the local congregation. If it existed at all, their loyalty to the denomination was very much an instrumental one, seeing it as the source of services rather than as an organic extension of their own church lives. This new breed of congregations came to see itself as the legitimate end source for denominational programmatic and funding attention. The resulting impact on the culture of the Reformed Church was a lasting one, leading to extensive discussions about the identity of the transformed denomination.[18]

The negative effect of the reallocation of funds on world missions operations was a profound one. Its extent is only partially indicated by the decline in the number of persons supported as RCA missionaries (a decline not entirely accounted for by this reallocation of funds). In 1946 there were 132 nondomestic missionaries listed in the Minutes of the General Synod; this number increased with the rising economic tide to a high of 157 in 1966. However, by 1986 the number had fallen below 1946 levels (to 130), and in 2000 there

---

16. Douglas Walrath, sociologist and church executive responsible for new church starts, made this comment in my presence during a conversation in the early 1980s.

17. Donald A. Luidens and Roger J. Nemeth, "'Public' and 'Private' Protestantism Reconsidered: Introducing the 'Loyalists,'" *Journal for the Scientific Study of Religion* 26 (December 1987): 450-64, and "Refining the Center: Two Parties of Reformed Church Loyalists," in *Reforming the Center: American Protestantism, 1900 to the Present*, ed. William Trollinger and Douglas Jacobsen (Grand Rapids: Eerdmans, 1998), pp. 252-70.

18. Donald A. Luidens, "Between Myth and Hard Data: A Denomination Stuggles with Its Identity," in *Beyond Establishment: Denominational Cultures in Transition*, ed. Jackson Carroll and Wade Clark Roof (Louisville: Westminster John Knox, 1993), pp. 248-69.

were only 75 missionaries supported on a full-time basis by the RCA. An additional 39 were World Mission Program Associates, often short-termers receiving partial funding through the RCA. More consequently, the shifting of funds away from world (and domestic) mission programs signaled the waning of a global perspective within the national staff and a redirection of its focus toward national and local issues.

The establishment of the Stewardship Council was followed in quick order (in 1961) by the formation of the General Synod Executive Committee (GSEC, as it was widely known). This body was charged with the daunting task of conducting affairs on the denomination's behalf between sitting general synods. As a result of this charge, it accrued considerable and unprecedented authority. Through the office of the Stated Clerk of the Church, GSEC became the first denomination-wide agent to act on behalf of the entire RCA. Its very raison d'être was to rationalize and systematize the "business" of the Reformed Church — quintessential "corporate denominational" tasks. But the rationalizing and consolidating were not complete. As historian John Coakley has written:

> The Executive Committee found itself charged early on (by the Synod of 1962) . . . to make a study [of] the possibility of further restructuring, which it entrusted to a committee (not insignificantly comprised of lawyers and businessmen) that recommended further consolidation. Their recommendations led to the third major structural change, the formation of the General Program Council in 1968, which carried consolidation of program significantly further by literally merging the Boards and agencies into a single corporation with its own representative board and staff.[19]

Throughout this period of reorganization and consolidation the driving motif was the corporate mandate to increase efficiency and productivity. Coakley points out that the principal actors in much of this were lay leaders. Business executives and lay professionals set the pace of bureaucratic rationalization and served on the restructuring committees which marched this process to fruition. Thus, during the stages that brought the RCA to fully embrace the corporate model, theological reflection was not an integral component, although there was some effort to legitimize the process with theological rhetoric. For instance, it is not accidental that the initial organizational entity in this process was named the "Stewardship" Council, an indication of the implicit theological model that dominated this period. While the rationalization of pro-

19. John W. Coakley, "National Organization in the Reformed Church in America: Some Historical Background" (paper shared with author, July 30, 1998, 26 pages).

cesses and structures was driven by the management paradigms of the business community, its theological legitimation was couched in terms of "stewardship" of the church's resources, the religious equivalent of "bang for the buck."[20] Issues of justice, service, and commitment, all of which had undergirded the early stages of the corporate model and each of which was firmly grounded in Calvinist theological formulations, increasingly gave way to arguments of efficiency and productivity for "stewardship's" sake. While the structures grew more rational, they grew more remote from their constituencies.

Other "rational" decisions inadvertently helped to undermine the corporate model in the RCA. In response to the growing budget crunch mentioned above, and to the membership's growing disquiet about the perceived remoteness of "475" (the national headquarters of the RCA is housed in the Interchurch Center at 475 Riverside Drive, New York City), the General Program Council (GPC) initiated a decentralization venture in 1968. This innovation resulted during the next decade in a general dispersal of the RCA's national staff throughout the regional offices of the denomination.[21] Hoff comments on this decision: "[T]he General Program Council developed its 'centers' proposal which assumed that the resources of the Reformed Church could be more thoroughly released for mission through several decentralized locations rather than through one central office."[22] The consequence was that program agencies were scattered around the country — women's programs in one locale, domestic missions in another; publication and distribution facilities in one city, new church start agents in another. Most dramatically, the world mission staff was divided by region of the globe served — the Middle East executive stayed in New York City; the agent for Far Eastern missions was housed in California; the one responsible for Latin and South America was in Iowa; and so on. Once again, "efficiency for mission" was the legitimating watchword for a step that decentralized the denomination's national staff and thereby diluted the cohesion of the corporate entity. The unanticipated consequence was, once again, the undermining of external programs, as the locus of RCA activity was moved away from external programs and toward local ones.

---

20. When translated to the world mission field, this model of cost accounting spelled doom for mission work in the Middle East, Japan, and the Indian subcontinent. The "yield" in terms of converts to capital expended was lower in these places than elsewhere, such as in sub-Saharan Africa and Latin America. Mission funds were gradually directed away from the former and into the latter. In recent years, funds have been further reallocated toward work in Eastern Europe, widely perceived as a field ripe for a great harvest. Stewardship language lends itself nicely to concerns of bureaucratic productivity and heathen conversion rates.

21. See Luidens, "Organizational Goals, Power, and Effectiveness."

22. Hoff, *Structures for Mission*, pp. 159-60.

Arie Brouwer, the associate general secretary of the GPC (1968-77, and general secretary of the RCA, 1977-83), was instrumental in this process of dispersion of the members of the GPC staff. His experience, prior to becoming associate general secretary, had been exclusively in local parishes. While Brouwer had served for a time on the governing body of the Board of World Missions, his predisposition had always been toward parishes. This inclination is evident in his rationale for the regional centers: "[World] mission cannot be carried out in separation from local mission. The dispersal of world mission staff, missionaries and Christians from other countries across the Reformed Church is an essential part of the center style. I believe it is fundamental to a renewal of our participation in world mission."[23] Looking back on the restructuring from the perspective of 1977, Brouwer reaffirmed this initial intention:

> The development of . . . field services staff [the national staff executives of the respective boards and agencies] and a growing emphasis on the importance of communication between the staff and local congregations gradually led the boards to locate an increased number of their staff out of New York. . . . In 1972 the General Program Council took a further step in this direction by regionalizing its administrative structure and assigning its entire program staff to such regional structures. *This administrative reorganization and dispersion of staff was designed to relate national program services more closely to local congregations.*[24]

It was Brouwer's notion that, by bringing the members of the national staff into closer proximity with congregations, they would serve as leaven to the churches. Indeed, that was the case; national staff members were much more visible in the local judicatories of the denomination and in local congregations. However, by displacing a lively informal network of staff relations (which had existed in "475") and by decentralizing power, this dispersion further undermined the cohesiveness of the historic mission structure and facilitated the weakening of its national and international mission.

With the establishment of regional centers, the leadership of the RCA also shifted dramatically from those who had been highly invested in external programming (principally world and national mission advocates) to those who were primarily engaged in serving congregations (such as Christian Education developers and promoters of new church starts). In the course of barely fifteen years, former missionaries and those who were aggressive proponents of world and do-

---

23. Hoff, *Structures for Mission*, p. 160.

24. Arie R. Brouwer, *Reformed Church Roots: Thirty-Five Formative Events* (New York: Reformed Church Press, 1977), p. 108, emphasis mine.

mestic mission programs virtually disappeared from the ranks of the principal executives. In their place came denominational "team players" — that is, skilled administrators who looked to the smooth functioning of the corporate structure as a whole rather than the promotion of world and domestic missions.[25]

A final illustration of the shifting culture of the corporate denomination is buried in the publication history of the denomination's journal, the *Church Herald.* Beginning with volume 1 in 1944, the *Church Herald* was intended to provide the denomination with a single forum for discussion and reflection. During the heyday of the corporate denomination, the fortunes of the *Church Herald* soared. By the mid-1950s it boasted more than 50,000 subscribers. Regular features attested to the world mission program of the church, and the editorial thrust championed American evangelical themes. Operating under an independent board, the *Church Herald* was reluctant to be drawn into the denomination's growing corporate structure, a lure which was unrelenting as the corporate structure solidified.

The independence and success of the *Church Herald* was not to last. Subscriptions continued to rise until 1969, peaking at over 78,000 (these and subsequent subscription data were published annually in the Minutes of the General Synod). Gradually at first, subscriptions began to fall off; by 1984 fewer than 44,000 subscriptions remained. As a result, the *Church Herald* began to cut back from its weekly publishing schedule. From 1962 to 1973, summer issues came out biweekly. Beginning in November 1973, the paper further reduced its publication rate so that it appeared biweekly throughout the year. In 1982 the summer issues became monthly ones, a harbinger of things to come.

In January 1989 the editor, John Stapert, announced "A New Beginning" for the *Church Herald.* Attributing rising costs to postal rate changes, Stapert revealed that the *Church Herald* would now appear on a monthly basis: "You won't be getting a *Church Herald* as often this year as last — just twelve times, once a month, rather than the twenty-two times you received it in 1988. But

---

25. The author sat in on a (representative) Administrative Council meeting during the general synod of 1976. The council was headed by the executive secretary — the "chief operating officer" under the general secretary's more public "chief executive officer" role. In addition, there were three staff members responsible for "operations" or "interpretation" of the denomination's program, and three who were regional secretaries, responsible in part for interacting with their regional judicatories. None of these officers had been a missionary — although one had spent a short term overseas (his denominational portfolio had nothing to do with mission work, however). Moreover, while the regional secretaries were charged with oversight of some aspect of world or national mission, their personal experiences and immediate-past responsibilities had been on the local level — serving congregations through the development of Christian education material or through church extension projects.

with twice as many pages in each issue, and twice as long to read, reflect on, and react to, its contents, we hope this *Church Herald* will be the helpful and challenging denominational magazine the RCA needs as it nears the last decade of the twentieth century."[26]

While postal rates were indeed escalating, that was not the whole story for the contraction of *Church Herald* publication. Subscriptions — which had been voluntary throughout the history of the journal — were significantly reduced. On the eve of the "New Beginning" initiative, only 41,000 subscribers were still on the rolls. While striving to remain independent (the board continued to be independently selected) and reflect the interests of lay members, the *Church Herald* suffered from growing competition from outside publications, the decline of denominational loyalty among parishioners, and general malaise about extracongregational matters. Significantly, the quality of the publication, the editorial rigor, and its commitment to the RCA were extremely high, belying the weakening subscription pattern.

By 1993 the circumstances surrounding the publication's financial status were so acute that major transformations were required to sustain it. These came about, in part, through muting the independent voice of the *Church Herald*. As recounted in the 1992 report of the General Synod Executive Committee to the General Synod:

> In an earlier study GSEC indicated that the relationship between the *Church Herald* and the General Synod "should be closer and more mutually enhancing." . . . The *Church Herald* should create a sense of identity, build community for the denomination, and provide news and information of what is happening throughout the RCA. There should be more emphasis on material about and from within the RCA, even if it reduces the number of articles of a generic nature about topics relating to Christian living. The editor should be allowed to retain a high degree of editorial discretion *in order to further the work and witness of the denomination.*[27]

In exchange for being incorporated into the "assessment" structure of the general synod (each congregation would be assessed subscription rates based on its membership), the *Church Herald* was made available to every RCA family. On the recommendation of its incumbent president, the 1992 General Synod adopted the following measures: "To send the *Church Herald* to every household of the Reformed Church in America as a benefit of membership in the denomination, beginning in 1993; and further, to set the General Synod assessment for

26. John Stapert, "A New Beginning," *Church Herald*, January 1989, p. 4.
27. Minutes of the General Synod, 1992, vol. 72, p. 72, emphasis mine.

the *Church Herald* in the 1993 General Synod operational budget at $4.87 per active-confirmed member; and further . . . to urge every RCA congregation to submit its membership list to the *Church Herald* by September 1, 1992."[28] After having long resisted absorption by the corporate structure, the *Church Herald* is very much a part of that apparatus today. Financial constraints and the impetus for consolidation and constriction have had a profound impact on this journal.

Thus, at the very time the RCA was most fully incorporated as a bureaucratized organization, the stage was being set for its further transformation and shrinkage. Indeed, the very rationalizing processes that marked the bureaucratic ethos were instrumental in undermining the corporate model.

The Final Thrust

The corporate model in the RCA is not yet buried; while it has shrunk significantly in size, it has resorted to displacing its outward-reaching objectives. Its most recent step has been the transition from an agency acting *on behalf of* congregations to one acting *on* congregations — the national structure fully engaged with local matters. While the groundwork for this transition was laid during the 1960s and 1970s, the decisive stages began in the 1980s under the leadership of Edwin Mulder (1983-94) and came to full fruition under Wesley Granberg-Michaelson (1994-present), the most recent of the general secretaries of the RCA. For the former, the change in focus was a gradual and reluctant one. As the paragraphs at the outset of this chapter attest, the latter has embraced the new order and has seen in it a viable thrust for the corporate denomination.

The Mulder Years

In the words of Kenneth Weller, then president of Central College, an RCA-affiliated college in Iowa, and a lifelong friend of Mulder, the touchstone of Mulder's service as general secretary was his pastoral approach. Witness Weller's comments at the time of Mulder's retirement: "In Ed Mulder's case, his remarkable success clearly derives from the fact that deep at the core of his being beats a pastoral heart. He has been a pastor to me for thirty-five years, as he has been for countless others. But in a very real sense he has been a pastor to all of us as members of the Reformed Church in America."[29]

28. Minutes of the General Synod, 1992, vol. 72, pp. 198-99.
29. Kenneth Weller, "The Pastor as Leader," *Church Herald*, June 1994, p. 19.

Despite his relational and pastoral predisposition, Mulder was not blind to localism's challenge to the corporate denomination. The matter of finances provided several instances of this challenge. At the end of 1991, the General Program Council found itself in considerable debt. Breaking from long-standing practice, the elected members of the GPC (through the staff) decided to appeal directly to "friends" for financial support. Pastors, missionaries, and other denominational leaders — active and retired — were solicited for donations to sustain the corporate structure. Some of the shortfall was covered in this way, but it was clear from the responses that parishioners (and Mulder himself) were uneasy about this direct encroachment on the autonomy of local congregations. Mulder wrote in his monthly editorial in the *Church Herald:*

> The year-end appeal has again raised the issue of direct solicitation; that is, the denomination contacting individuals directly rather than through the local congregations. There are those who feel that this undermines congregational giving. In no way does the General Program Council want to diminish giving to the local congregation. . . . Somehow we have to find a way to provide RCA members with an opportunity to become informed about the mission of our denomination and to support it, without taking away from the local congregation. After all, we are part of one body.[30]

While some people saw this issue as a matter of congregational autonomy, Mulder felt it was one of denominational integrity. Despite Mulder's plea that the unity of the denomination and its congregations be honored, the issue of finances would continue to plague the corporate RCA.

A year after this episode Mulder directly addressed the issue of localism (what he called "congregationalism") in his monthly editorial: "One of the trends in religion today is an expanding spirit of what is called congregationalism. It means simply that each congregation considers itself autonomous; that the final authority for decision-making is in the assembly of the local congregation. . . . It comes as a surprise to some people that Reformed Church congregations are not entirely autonomous. No RCA congregation is at liberty merely to do its own thing. We are a connectional church."[31]

This issue clearly troubled Mulder. In the next month's editorial he returned to it, challenging congregationalism's implicit religious isolationism as an affront to the denomination's Reformed heritage. He concludes: "The ways denominations defined themselves in the past are becoming increasingly blurred. There was a day when churches — even our church — defined them-

---

30. Edwin Mulder, "A People Who Respond," *Church Herald*, April 1992, p. 11.
31. Edwin Mulder, "The Reformed Connection," *Church Herald*, February 1993, p. 11.

selves in over-against terms. Today the emphasis is on the experiential. We stress our similarities rather than highlighting our differences."[32]

Mulder then considers the 1992 article by Dykstra and Hudnut-Beumler (cited above) and its implications for the RCA: "I ask myself, Who is the denomination? Is the General Synod the denomination? The General Program Council? The seminaries? The denomination is us [sic]. It is 967 congregations comprised of 340,000 members. It encompasses our history, liturgy, standards, polity, programs and institutions."[33] His solution to the growing dilemma? "We must close the gap between individuals, congregations, and the denomination. We are all members of one body. In unity there is strength. There is much that needs to be done. We need to be about God's mission in the world."[34] For Mulder the pressing issue of his tenure was the headlong rush of the congregations of the RCA into isolationist enclaves. He brought to bear the diminishing resources of the corporate structure to advance this unity; but it was a frustrating struggle.

By the final year of his service, Mulder had come to recognize that the corporate denomination's future focus would have to be on congregations — although he was loath to relinquish the denomination's prophetic responsibility to challenge congregations to look beyond themselves: "The denomination exists primarily to serve congregations and to enable congregations to do what they cannot do for or by themselves. In a consumer age, denominational leadership must listen to what the church says it needs, while calling the church to be and do more than it asks. A general secretary is required to be both pastoral and prophetic."[35]

The Granberg-Michaelson Years

The tension between congregationalist demands and the connectional, ecumenical, and worldwide focus which had historically characterized the corporate Reformed Church has continued to intensify. While Granberg-Michaelson has a well-deserved reputation as an ecumenist, he signaled early in his tenure as general secretary his intention to focus the corporate denomination's attention on the local congregation. In his inaugural interview with the editors of the *Church Herald*, he responded as follows:

32. Edwin Mulder, "Constantly Being Reformed," *Church Herald*, March 1993, p. 22.
33. Mulder, "Constantly Being Reformed," p. 22.
34. Mulder, "Constantly Being Reformed," p. 22.
35. Edwin Mulder, "Gee, Ed, What *Do* You Do?" *Church Herald*, December 1993, p. 16.

Q. The search committee in its material reported about your "clear commitment that the local church is at the center of the mission of Christ in the world." What does that mean to you?

A. It means that mission takes place in every congregation and that the life of the church comes in response to God's mission in the world. Mission is not something that happens "out there" or "over there" but that happens from the local congregation.[36]

In this initial conversation, Granberg-Michaelson echoes Mulder's concern with those who would see the local congregation as the final expression of "church":

Q. How do you understand the relationship between local congregations and a denomination?

A. No local congregation can live successfully unto itself and be biblically faithful. Even the way in which we frame these questions, we still have this feeling that it's the denomination out there and then local churches. . . . The denomination is all of us; when we begin to function out of a we/they mentality, it reveals a premise that is finally going to fail. The church simply can't exist as only a local congregation. . . .[37]

Granberg-Michaelson then lays out his vision for the role of the denomination: "[F]irst, the denomination becomes that mechanism that links local congregations to each other, links them together in local situations. . . . Secondly, the denomination becomes the means by which the local congregation makes real, in concrete ways, its belonging to the church global, to the body of Christ throughout the world. Finally, a denomination becomes a means for taking the full diversity of members of Christ's body and bringing them into interaction with one another."[38] As this list of denominational responsibilities suggests, in his first year as general secretary Granberg-Michaelson struggled with the tension between inward-looking endeavors and outward-reaching ones.

However, by February 1995 he had clearly come down on the side of inward endeavors. At this time he prioritized "the denomination's" (that is, the national corporate structure's) efforts in a significantly different way:

36. Wesley Granberg-Michaelson, "Taking a Closer Look," *Church Herald,* July/August 1994, p. 15.

37. Granberg-Michaelson, "Taking a Closer Look," p. 15.

38. Granberg-Michaelson, "Taking a Closer Look," p. 15.

First, the denomination exists to strengthen the life and ministry of the church in each local place. That means our 968 RCA congregations and also each of our forty-six classes. Strengthening such local ministry should be the focus of the denomination's resources, training opportunities, and educational efforts. . . . But then we are called to be part of the church global. Here, the facilities of the denomination exist to make specific connections between the local church and its global identity. Our world mission efforts, for instance, can be understood largely in this way.[39]

In this quotation the primacy of the corporate leadership's focus is unmistakably on the local congregation.

The impressive array of initiatives that have been directed at local congregations in the last decade makes obvious the ascendance of the localist focus for the corporate denomination. For instance, through the introduction and establishment of such denomination-wide programs as an elaborate training and structuring of diaconal ministries (soon to be followed with similar programs for elders); a biennial gathering of ministers and spouses for rest and religious rehabilitation; the financing and promoting of a unified computer network to connect all congregations;[40] the development of an extensive "urban ministry" enterprise to be carried out by local congregations;[41] the promotion of "vision statements" for local judicatories and congregations, statements which reflect the denomination's vision statement;[42] and a call for including some form of worship in all congregational meetings, the denomination's corporate engine has effectively interposed itself in the life of the local congregation on many levels.

Perhaps the most powerful and telling of these initiatives has been the reconceptualization of the congregation from principally a community of worship and renewal (foci which are still affirmed) to one that has an activist, "missional" priority. "Congregation as mission agent" is the watchword of this new image, and it serves as the principal corporate entrée into the lives of local congregations. As Granberg-Michaelson has written, "In the future, each con-

39. Wesley Granberg-Michaelson, "No Christian Is an Island," *Church Herald*, February 1995, p. 11.

40. Wesley Granberg-Michaelson, "A Chip off the Old Gutenberg," *Church Herald*, November 1996, p. 14.

41. Wesley Granberg-Michaelson, "New Opportunites for Ministry," *Church Herald*, March 1997, p. 19.

42. See Mathonnet-VanderWell's article in this volume; also, Granberg-Michaelson, "New Opportunites for Ministry," p. 14, and "Vision from the Mountain," *Church Herald*, June 1997, p. 22.

gregation in the RCA should come to see itself as a mission outpost."[43] While congregations have long been involved in their local communities in a vast array of programs, it is only with this new corporate thrust that these programs have been stoked by denominational support and configuration.

At the present time, the focus of considerable denominational corporate effort is an urban ministry thrust, one being urged on congregations regardless of their particular social environments. With the support of several branches of the national staff (including the "minority councils" and the "urban ministries team") and of regional judicatories engaged in urban ministry, this program is drawing congregations from throughout the RCA into new and creative efforts in cities.[44]

The earliest signs of the corporate crisis in the RCA were the diminishing of financial resources, a shrinkage that came with the shift during the 1960s away from extracongregational programs to local ones. The march of this financial erosion continues apace.[45] In recent years, numerous measures have been taken to stem the tide: individual missionaries are now required to engage in fund-raising for their own support (as clear a signal as any that "the goose that laid the golden egg" has been institutionally cooked); "area secretaries" — historically charged with overseeing global mission efforts in Asia, Africa, South America, and elsewhere — are now uniformly entitled Coordinator(s) for Mission Stewardship, a title not shared with nonmission executives and one indicative of their added fund-raising responsibilities; consolidation of classes has begun (particularly in the California and mid-Atlantic regions) and will continue; the utility of regional synod judicatories has been brought into question, and there are concerted efforts to disband or radically reconfigure them; staff in the corporate offices have regularly been "restructured" (a church structural euphemism for the secular euphemism "downsized"), and retirees have been reluctantly replaced.

There are also proposals on the table to reduce the representative apparatus of the denomination (although these have been resisted at the most recent general synods). It has been formally proposed that the general synod gather biennially and that standing boards and commissions meet less regularly than they currently do.

---

43. Wesley Granberg-Michaelson, "Four Key Issues in RCA's Future," *Church Herald,* September 1995, p. 17.

44. Granberg-Michaelson, "New Opportunites for Ministry," p. 19.

45. Wesley Granberg-Michaelson, "Sharing Our Common Gifts," *Church Herald,* March 1995, p. 10.

Epilogue

Along with other mainline Protestant denominations, the Reformed Church in America found itself increasingly drawn into institutional rationalization that accompanied the rise of large-scale mission and Christian education work in the late nineteenth century. The resulting "corporate" structures in the RCA — embodied in a "national staff" initially located in New York City headquarters and focused on promoting and orchestrating foreign and domestic mission work — reflected the unique interests of the denomination's membership. However, when the post–World War II church growth occurred, there was a vast reordering of priorities among parishioners. Local concerns became increasingly paramount, and the historic connectional underpinnings of the corporate model were significantly eroded.

As the national entity began to shrink, it sought a variety of ways to sustain itself. Almost as a final resort, it has turned its focus to the local congregation, directing much of its attention and resources on these bodies. In a real sense, the denomination has come full circle from the early-nineteenth-century experience. At that time the denomination was an ephemeral entity, vaguely charged with church discipline and order, and the local congregation was the focal point of all RCA activity.

What does the future bode? That is a tantalizing question. Perhaps Ingham and Mulder got it right, and we are on the verge of a twenty-first-century renaissance of denominationalism with a new face:

> In 1928, the tercentenary year of the RCA, the Rev. John A. Ingham made this observation: "There are some today who seem to cherish the notion that a discarnate religion, one without organization, creeds, ceremonies, in short without embodiment of any sort, would be preferable to the concrete realities with which we are familiar. Of course such an altogether vague and misty church, if it could be called a church at all, would be entirely free from bureaucracy and 'organizationalism,' if we may coin a word. And it would likewise be as ineffective and inert as the fog. If one could lay off his body he would presumably be rid of rheumatism, toothache, and sundry ills that flesh is heir to, but it would be at the cost of life itself." Ingham was saying sixty-five years ago that we have this treasure in earthen vessels. He was saying we need certain structures through which we do the work of church.[46]

46. Mulder, "Constantly Being Reformed," p. 22.

Donald A. Luidens

References

The Acts and Proceedings of the Annual Session of the General Synod of the Reformed Church in America. Appears annually.

Balmer, Randall H. *A Perfect Babel of Confusion: Dutch Religion and English Culture in the Middle Colonies.* New York: Oxford University Press, 1989.

Brouwer, Arie R. *Reformed Church Roots: Thirty-Five Formative Events.* New York: Reformed Church Press, 1977.

Coakley, John W. "National Organization in the Reformed Church in America: Some Historical Background." Paper shared with author, July 30, 1998. 26 pps.

Dykstra, Craig, and James Hudnut-Beumler. "The National Organizational Structures of Protestant Denominations: An Invitation to a Conversation." In *The Organizational Revolution: Presbyterians and American Denominationalism,* edited by Milton J. Coalter, John M. Mulder, and Louis B. Weeks. Louisville: Westminster John Knox Press, 1992.

Granberg-Michaelson, Wesley. "Taking a Closer Look." *Church Herald,* July/August 1994, p. 15.

————. "We've Got Something People Want." *Church Herald,* January 1995, p. 13.

————. "No Christian Is an Island." *Church Herald,* February 1995, p. 11.

————. "Sharing Our Common Gifts." *Church Herald,* March 1995, p. 10.

————. "The Safest Place You Can Be." *Church Herald,* April 1995, p. 13.

————. "Four Key Issues in RCA's Future." *Church Herald,* September 1995, p. 17.

————. "A Chip off the Old Gutenberg." *Church Herald,* November 1996, p. 14.

————. "New Opportunities for Ministry." *Church Herald,* March 1997, p. 19.

————. "Grasping 'the Vision Thing.'" *Church Herald,* April 1997, p. 14.

————. "Fleeting Thoughts about Classis." *Church Herald,* May 1997, p. 17.

————. "Vision from the Mountain." *Church Herald,* June 1997, p. 22.

————. "Unfolding the Vision." *Church Herald,* July/August 1997, p. 17.

————. "Correcting the Focus." *Church Herald,* September 1997, p. 17.

————. "What Is the 'Main Thing'?" *Church Herald,* January 1998, p. 12.

————. "Path to the Twenty-First Century." *Church Herald,* July/August 1998, p. 17.

Hoff, Marvin D. *Structures for Mission.* Grand Rapids: Eerdmans, 1985.

Hoge, Dean R., Benton Johnson, and Donald A. Luidens. *Vanishing Boundaries: Religion of Mainline Protestant Baby Boomers.* Louisville: Westminster John Knox, 1994.

Luidens, Donald A. "Organizational Goals, Power, and Effectiveness." Ph.D. diss., Rutgers University, 1978.

————. "The National Staff in Its Tenth Year." *Church Herald,* October 6, 1978, pp. 13-15.

————. "Bureaucratic Control in a Protestant Denomination." *Journal for the Scientific Study of Religion* 21, no. 2 (June 1982): 163-75.

————. "Between Myth and Hard Data: A Denomination Struggles with Its Identity." In *Beyond Establishment: Denominational Cultures in Transition,* edited by Jackson Carroll and Wade Clark Roof, pp. 248-69. Louisville: Westminster John Knox, 1993.

Luidens, Donald A., and Roger J. Nemeth. "'Public' and 'Private' Protestantism Reconsidered: Introducing the 'Loyalists.'" *Journal for the Scientific Study of Religion* 26, no. 4 (December 1987): 450-64.

————. "Refining the Center: Two Parties of Reformed Church Loyalists." In *Reforming the Center: American Protestantism, 1900 to the Present,* edited by William Trollinger and Douglas Jacobsen, pp. 252-70. Grand Rapids: Eerdmans, 1998.

Mulder, Edwin. "A People Who Respond." *Church Herald,* April 1992, p. 11.

————. "The Reformed Connection." *Church Herald,* February 1993, p. 11.

————. "Constantly Being Reformed." *Church Herald,* March 1993, p. 22.

————. "In Their Time of Need." *Church Herald,* June 1993, p. 17.

————. "Gee, Ed, What *Do* You Do?" *Church Herald,* December 1993, p. 16.

Nemeth, Roger J., and Donald A. Luidens. "The RCA in the Larger Picture: Facing Structural Realities." *Reformed Review,* winter 1993-94, pp. 85-113.

————. "The RCA: A Virtual Denomination?" *Church Herald,* November 1998, pp. 8-11.

————. "Dutch Immigration and Membership Growth in the Reformed Church in America: 1830-1920." In *The Dutch-American Experience: Essays in Honor of Robert P. Swierenga,* edited by Hans Krabbendam and Larry J. Wagenaar, pp. 169-88. Amsterdam: Vrije Universiteit, 2000.

————. "Fragmentation and Dispersion: Post-Modernism Comes to the Reformed Church in America." In *Reformed Encounters with Modernity: Perspectives from Three Continents,* edited by H. Jurgens Hendriks et al., pp. 125-38. Stellenbosch: Media.com, 2001.

Stapert, John. "A New Beginning." *Church Herald,* January 1989, p. 4.

Weller, Kenneth. "The Pastor as Leader." *Church Herald,* June 1994, p. 19.

No Longer Business as Usual:
The Reformed Church in America
Seen through Its Mission Statement

Steve Mathonnet-VanderWell

The adoption of a Mission Statement at the 1997 General Synod of the Reformed Church in America (RCA) is emblematic of the transitions and new directions within the denomination. For the first time, the widest annual assembly of the RCA endorsed a statement that attempts to convey the mission and vision of this church.[1] Neither the structures nor the polity of the RCA was changed by the Mission Statement. It brought no new organizational flow-charts or restructured committees. However, its adoption and ensuing popularity provide a useful glimpse into the state of the RCA, especially how its structures are perceived and how they function.

The theme of this volume is "organizing religious work." What I will attempt is not a comprehensive explanation of the organization and various structures within the RCA. Instead, the Mission Statement will be used as a snapshot of the denomination — its trends, themes, and theology. This will not be a "close reading" or line-by-line exegesis of the Mission Statement. Some lines and phrases from the statement will be mentioned. However, the broader ideas represented by the words and tone will be more important than a narrow focus on specific words. The overall symbolic value and impact of the Mission Statement will be the primary focus.

A closer look at this snapshot will display, I believe, an attempt to portray the work of the church in energetic, result-oriented, inspirational, and accessible terms. The picture focuses on the local congregation. According to the Mission Statement, the local congregation is to be the recipient of denominational resources. Its activities are defined as "mission." At the same time, however, there seems to be an unresolved ambivalence about everything pointing toward

---

1. A complete text of the Mission Statement is found in the appendix to this chapter.

the congregation. Is there something perplexing about a document with a local, grassroots view of the church being produced and adopted by the widest national assembly of that church? There seems to be a concerted effort to release the local congregation and celebrate the ministry of the local congregation, yet present the denomination as a vital resource for that local ministry. The document's warm, spiritual tone is applied not only to the local church but also to the wider assemblies of the RCA, and even their staffs are now portrayed as having more spiritual and less administrative influence. If the congregation is the focus of the church, then what is the basis for the relationship between the congregation and the wider denominational bodies? Is it voluntarist, based on the resources received, or is it integral to the entire notion of a connectional church?

When first seen through a more theological lens, this attempt to rework the connection between the local congregation and the wider denominational assemblies appears to move away from traditional Reformed theology and its concomitant polity. The Mission Statement's lack of classic theological terms may be attributed to its efforts to use accessible language. It may also suggest the faint presence traditional doctrine actually has in today's church. Yet neglect of theological terminology produces not an "untheological" document but one with an unspoken, modified theology of its own. Is this theology, however, better or healthier theology for the church?

Quick Turnaround

The process that brought about the adoption of the Mission Statement already conveys some of the impetus and ethos of the statement. To amend, alter, or adopt new portions of the RCA's constitution is a long and painstaking task.[2] The process involves approval at a general synod, followed by ratification by two-thirds of the denomination's classes (the RCA's terminology for the most

---

2. The constitution of the RCA consists of three parts. It has been compared to a three-legged stool by Daniel J. Meeter, *Meeting Each Other in Doctrine, Liturgy, and Government: The Bicentennial of the Celebration of the Constitution of the Reformed Church in America* (Grand Rapids: Eerdmans, 1993), p. 159. The doctrinal leg consists of the three historic ecumenical creeds (Apostles', Nicene, and Athanasian) and the three Reformed "doctrinal standards" (the Heidelberg Catechism, the Belgic Confession, and the Canons of Dordt). The liturgical leg is represented by the various approved liturgies, especially the liturgies for the sacraments. The governance leg is expressed in the *Book of Church Order: Including the Government, the Disciplinary and Judicial Procedures, the Bylaws and Special Rules of Order of the General Synod, and the Formularies of the Reformed Church in America* (New York: Reformed Church Press, 2002).

local church assembly), and finally approval again by the subsequent general synod.

Every general synod receives a great many reports and overtures on which it may act immediately. The overtures are usually generated by the classes. Various standing committees and commissions of the RCA submit the reports. The Mission Statement came before the general synod as a part of one of these reports, specifically in the report from the General Synod Council. It was voted on and approved by a single general synod. Because it is not a change in the denomination's constitution, it did not require any further approval. There is absolutely nothing irregular or devious about these procedures. Unlike the usual pattern, however, a major document and new direction were initiated in very short order.

To say that its adoption was a short and relatively simple task is not to say it was put together in a hasty and haphazard manner. Its roots have been traced to a 1994 meeting of the RCA's General Synod Council that approved the nomination of the Reverend Wesley Granberg-Michaelson as the general secretary (highest executive officer) of the RCA. In the following years, according to Granberg-Michaelson, that group began "creating space for working with vision, goals, and long-term direction rather than simply micro-managing the details of programs and budgets."[3] By early 1997 the General Synod Council had drafted a mission statement, but then instructed a group of eight church leaders (the general secretary, annual general synod officers, and several RCA pastors) to go "up a mountain" to do the final wordsmithing of the document. Its actual adoption at the 1997 General Synod was still, however, short and relatively simple.

This process for adopting the Mission Statement is already suggestive of a climate in the RCA, especially about attitudes toward structures and constitutional documents. Recall that to delete an inconsequential semicolon from the *Book of Church Order* (the denomination's polity statement of church government, which is part of the RCA's constitution) requires a lengthy and often tedious procedure. By contrast, the Mission Statement, which has received widespread attention, great publicity, and almost creedal status throughout the RCA, was adopted by a single general synod.

This suggests a variety of intertwined attitudes in the RCA. First, it signaled that the way to change, move, or motivate the RCA was not through changing its constitution or restructuring its agencies and offices. Second, the Mission Statement could be adopted and then circulated quickly. Third, its adoption conveyed a rapid, activist, pacesetting approach. By contrast, constitutional change is perceived not simply to be wearisome but also to accomplish

---

3. Wesley Granberg-Michaelson, "Why a Mission Statement?" (lecture delivered at New Brunswick Theological Seminary, February 2, 1998), p. 4.

very little. Adopting a mission statement rather than changing the constitution or reorganizing the denominational structures seemed to convey fatigue, impatience, and even distrust of what is frequently perceived as parliamentary posturing, bureaucratic burdens, and tedious procedures associated with the denominational constitution. It does not seem too much to assert that the Mission Statement voiced what was widely known but never before stated so clearly: the constitution of the RCA — its doctrinal standards, liturgy, and polity — has a very weak grasp on the average congregation of the denomination. The impetus for the Mission Statement and its relatively uncomplicated procedure for adoption are themselves symbolic of one of its most memorable phrases, "We will no longer do business as usual, nor our usual business."

Activist and Optimist

In 1978 a thoughtful and complete statement of faith entitled "Our Song of Hope" was adopted by the RCA. Although it does not have status equal to the RCA's "doctrinal standards," it is well regarded as a contemporary expression of Reformed theology. However, "Our Song of Hope" has had very limited impact and received little attention in the RCA, despite efforts to adapt it for use in worship. In the late 1980s there was a denomination-wide effort to discuss and discover a denominational identity. A short "Identity Statement" which rang with a creedlike tone and held the possibility for use in worship emerged from this focus on denominational identity. However, that statement also received little attention and was quickly forgotten. Currently, the Theology Commission of the RCA is attempting to develop a short expression of the Reformed faith for use in worship and publicity. While the assignment is not an easy one, the low profile given to the project and the slow response from the commission seem to indicate that it is not seen to have great urgency. Given the lackluster reception of recent attempts at creedal statements in the RCA, perhaps this is no surprise.

What accounts for the less-than-energetic response to these attempts at theologically weighty statements? Perhaps it is because they did not arise from a crisis or a timely and heated theological controversy. There was little sense of groundswell or urgency behind them. Instead, they come largely from the impetus of individuals: theological professors or annual denominational presidents. It is likewise difficult to perceive any large popular demand or crisis-moment that gave rise to the Mission Statement. This statement was also largely the brainchild of denominational presidents and a new general secretary. Why, then, has it received more recognition and acceptance?

Obviously, it is not intended to be a genuinely creedal document. There is

no attempt to state afresh the nature of the Trinity or explicate in modern idiom the nature of Christ. As a mission statement, it is more a plan of action
than a statement of belief. Not surprisingly, then, its overall tone is pragmatic
and task-oriented. Words like "equip," "unleash," "alert," "front lines," "transformed," "engaging," "risk," "dream," "proactive," and "celebrate" give the document an energetic and eager quality. This activist, pragmatic tone seems to connect with congregations and pastors in a manner that more doctrinal
statements do not. If the brief process for the adoption of the Mission Statement suggests fatigue with wrangling over polity, then the precedence it has
taken over statements with more doctrinal emphasis may suggest a similar fatigue with doctrine. Just as constitutional and polity changes are viewed as
cumbersome and irrelevant, so fresh theological conversations apparently are
not considered timely or productive.

The vigorous and enthusiastic tone of the statement distinguishes it from
voices frequently heard in American mainline Protestant literature today.
Terms and images like "post-Christian," "relinquishment," "resident aliens,"
and "exile experience" have been commonly used to express both the pain and
the potential resulting from the erosion of mainline Protestantism's influence
in American life.[4] The Mission Statement shows little or no connection to this
line of thought. There is an air of vitality and confidence in it.

This is not to say that it has a naive or outmoded perspective on American society and the church's place in that society. The statement describes the
world as "lost and broken." Indeed, the very idea of a mission statement implies
that there is much for the church to do. Yet the church seems up to the task before it. The Mission Statement may express some exasperation toward past
church practices ("consistories selected more for ministry than management"
or "no longer do business as usual, nor our usual business"). However, the
themes of exile, weakness, and relinquishment common elsewhere are not
found here. Are these themes too dismal and debilitating for the statement?
Does their absence convey a belief that the RCA is distinct from American
mainline Protestantism and exempt from its plight? Whatever the reason, the
Mission Statement opts instead for a more energetic and optimistic approach.

From where does this confident, activist tone arise? In his book *Dutch*

---

4. Well-known examples of this post-Christian exile theme include much of the work of
Stanley Hauerwas and William Willimon, especially their joint effort, *Resident Aliens: Life in the
Christian Colony* (Nashville: Abingdon, 1989), or Willimon's more recent collaborative effort
with Martin B. Copenhaver and Anthony Robinson, *Good News in Exile: Three Pastors Offer a
Hopeful Vision for the Church* (Grand Rapids: Eerdmans, 1998). Walter Brueggemann's work,
such as *Cadences of Home: Preaching among Exiles* (Louisville: Westminster John Knox, 1997),
often carries similar themes.

Calvinism in Modern America, James Bratt classifies the nineteenth-century Dutch Reformed immigrants to the United States into four categories. Although attending primarily to the RCA's sibling denomination, the Christian Reformed Church, Bratt labels the Dutch immigrants who became part of the RCA in the American Midwest as "outgoing, optimistic pietists." In contrast to other Dutch Reformed immigrants of the time, this group was more open to American influences and was more "moralistic, genteel, willing to submerge strict 'Reformed-ness' in general Protestantism in order to spread the faith over the entire nation." Their faith "induced a life of service . . . and service was *the* end of religion."[5]

The roots of the RCA Mission Statement may be found here. The optimistic spirit of American can-do-ism and service is evident throughout it — for example, "a thousand churches in a million ways doing one thing," "laity and pastors unleashed," "alert to opportunities around them," "eager and equipped to serve," and "classes that are empowering and proactive." The adoption of the Mission Statement can then be viewed as evidence that this strand of late-nineteenth-century immigrant optimism and activism has gained ascendancy within the RCA.

Postmodern Bricolage

After looking for some connection between the Mission Statement and nineteenth-century Dutch immigrants, it may seem odd for us to speculate that the document also shows influences from postmodern theology. Granted, the term "postmodern" is notoriously slippery and overworked. In this context, however, it is intended to convey a pragmatic, nonsystematic, more emotive than rational endeavor. The pragmatic agenda of the Mission Statement itself is clear. The church needs to be about doing, engaging in activity, and achieving results. Failure is understood as a lack of results or imagination, not theological heterodoxy. "What works" is given priority over how it is held together or systematic consistency. Besides the attention to pragmatic outcome, clearly the statement intends to inspire rather than explain. Its use of the terms "vision" and "imagine" along with the activist, enthusiastic rhetoric indicates that it is hoping for people to "catch a vision." The use of the rubric "imagine" throughout the document suggests that the intention is for people to dream and to be caught up in the moment.

5. James D. Bratt, *Dutch Calvinism in Modern America: A History of a Conservative Subculture* (Grand Rapids: Eerdmans, 1984), pp. 44-45.

It could be argued that the Mission Statement is a fine example of theological "bricolage." This term, most commonly associated with Claude Lévi-Strauss,[6] comes from the French word for handyman, jack-of-all-trades, or *bricoleur*. The *bricoleur* is not a master builder, or to shift to more theological language, not a systematician or encyclopedist. This person is able to piece together available resources in a workable, "good-enough" fashion. With bits of string found in the pocket and other readily available odds and ends, the *bricoleur* gets the job done. Likewise, the RCA Mission Statement draws upon familiar, accessible language, bits of string pulled from various pop-culture lexicons. This colloquial accessibility may account for the wide and popular notice it has received.

Other than the terminology for RCA assemblies (consistories, classes, and synods), there seems to be no denomination-specific language in the Mission Statement. Likewise, it is difficult to detect any "classic" themes of Reformed theology in it, such as sovereignty, election, guilt, grace, and gratitude. It is fair to say that this could be the mission statement of almost any American Protestant denomination. This observation need not be understood as a criticism. Yet the statement's generic quality does seem to be a long way from earlier efforts of the 1980s to find that which was unique about the RCA, the search for a denominational "identity" or "glue that holds us together." It recalls Bratt's claim that the optimist-pietist strain of nineteenth-century Dutch Reformed immigrants displayed a willingness to submerge "Reformed-ness" into a more general American Protestantism.

The Mission Statement's pragmatic, nonsystematic approach indicates that if there is a denominational glue, it is neither a common heritage nor classic theological confessions, but mission activity in the present. Unity and identity are found in a common purpose and activity. What unites the RCA is being engaged in mission. This mission activity is a positive, challenging, and generally uncontroversial theme. By drawing attention to a shared task and activity, the denomination can focus less on doctrinal questions or hot-button social issues that inevitably bring division and splintering.

Polity and Assemblies Redescribed

If the Mission Statement is not very denominationally specific in tone, the frequent references to the various assemblies and structures of the RCA make

---

6. Claude Lévi-Strauss, *The Savage Mind* (Chicago: University of Chicago Press, 1962), pp. 17-22.

plain the Reformed connection. Terms like "congregations," "consistories" (the governing body of the local congregation), both "pastors" and "ministers of Word and sacrament," "classis," "synod," "staff," and "denomination" are found throughout. The two main portions of the document, entitled "The Vision" and "Living Out the Vision," move through the different assemblies, organizations, and offices of the RCA, beginning with the local congregation and concluding with the denomination as a whole. A brief look at the statement's description and portrayal of these various assemblies and structures may be instructive.

In the RCA's presbyterial polity, the classis has been described (semi-accurately) as a "corporate bishop." The authority and role of a bishop are placed in a collective gathering of ministers and elders from local congregations. The classis is the body to which both congregations and ministers are accountable. The Mission Statement describes it as a community of "nurture and vision." The word "accountable" is used twice in conjunction with it. However, the stronger emphasis of the statement seems to view the classis as the place of "living in communion" where collegiality, relationships, and support are found. This is not an entirely new understanding of the role of the classis, but this relational emphasis is clearly in line with the document's warmer, supportive tone.

The RCA has both regional synods and a general synod, but the Mission Statement does not distinguish between them. In one reference synods are grouped with the classis. In another place the synod is grouped with the staff. When placed alongside the classis, the synod receives a description similar to that just noted for the classis: community, nurture, and accountability. When the synod is placed with the staff, more programmatic and institutional themes emerge in phrases such as "connected to the larger church" and "funnel resources." A tension or ambivalence seems present in the description of the synods. Are they "communities of nurture," or do they have institutional, programmatic functions? Can they do both? Should they do both?

The curious inclusion of staff among the different RCA assemblies merits some discussion. Staff is an interesting and somewhat incongruent addition since it is obviously not a term of RCA polity such as consistory or synod. Staff includes those persons employed by classes, regional synods, and general synods. While the various assemblies such as classes or synods come together temporarily, take on their business, and then disperse, the staff continues to implement the actions of the assembly.

The mention of staff in the Mission Statement may indicate the arrival or recognition of a somewhat new polity in the RCA. In a very real way, of course, the staff has come to be more associated and identified with the synods (regional and general) than with the occasional convening of the assembly. Although the Mission Statement was primarily drafted by local ministers of the RCA, it originated in the General Synod Council to which all denominational staff report and serve as resource persons. The mention of staff alongside the various assemblies suggests that the staffs of the synods are viewed as a significant power and presence in the RCA. They are accorded status equivalent to the assemblies of RCA polity. On one level, this may not be overly important or surprising. Perhaps the Mission Statement is simply recognizing and voicing what has long been acknowledged. Regular employees, like the staff of synods, cannot help but have considerable, long-term influence. On the other hand, it may also suggest that staff were an important impetus behind the Mission Statement itself. There is a certain irony that in a document that focuses strongly on the key role of the congregation (as we shall soon see), the staff plays such a prominent role and now seems to join congregation, classis, and synod as an important institution and factor in the RCA.

The Funnel Connection

The Mission Statement uses the image of a funnel to describe the connection between the local church on one side and the synods and staff on the other (e.g., "synods and staff that funnel resources to the local church"). Note the direction in which the funnel flows. The synods and staff funnel the resources to the local church. The funnel flows to the congregation. The congregation is to receive from the synods and staff, which are to serve and focus on the congregation. They exist "to equip congregations."

There is no mention in the statement of the congregation funneling resources to the denomination. The connection between congregation and denomination is now portrayed as based on and presumably justified by the resources provided to the congregation. Congregations maintain their connection to the denomination because of these resources. There is no indication of the denomination setting any terms or parameters for the congregation's connection to it. One wonders what happens should congregations not be pleased by the resources flowing to them through the funnel. Moreover, the Mission Statement seems to overlook the fact that all resources assemblies and staff have at their command were originally funneled to them from the congregations.

The funnel therefore becomes the image whereby the denomination is now asking for entrée into the congregation's "mission," promising to funnel and provide resources of some sort. To switch metaphors, rather than trying to keep congregations marching in line behind it, the denomination is now asking if there might be room in the congregation's parade and agreeing to be a beneficial band member.

This attention to the congregation as the focal point and even the raison d'être of the staff, synod, and entire denomination should not come as a complete surprise. In the Mission Statement's own words, the RCA is a denomination that is "locally-oriented." The classic doctrine of the church in the Reformed tradition has always had a local weighting. The church is where the Word is preached, the sacraments celebrated rightly, and Christian discipline exercised. However, this notion of the congregation as the target of the denominational funnel is new. The other assemblies of the denomination have traditionally been understood to have different tasks beyond the abilities or reach of congregations. While these other tasks may indirectly benefit the congregation, these assemblies have not previously been articulated as funneling resources toward the congregation.

Of course, countless observers have noted the ascendancy of the local congregation throughout American Protestantism and a corresponding decline in denominational strength and loyalty. Denominational staffs and assemblies have clearly recognized the importance and influence of this trend. However, an acknowledgment of the congregation-centered denomination has usually been mixed with subtle and not-so-subtle warnings and disapproval from denominational loyalists. For example, Edwin Mulder, general secretary of the RCA from 1983 to 1994, wrote in 1993, "It comes as a surprise to some people that Reformed Church congregations are not entirely autonomous. . . . We are a connectional church."[7] By contrast, the Mission Statement seems to grant approval, apparently without reservation, to the congregation as the "front lines of ministry" and the target of the denomination's funnel. To reiterate, the swing toward the centrality of congregations has been noticeable for quite a while and has generally received some denominational recognition and tepid acceptance. In the Mission Statement, however, the tepidness becomes noticeably warmer.

This is arguably the biggest change represented by the Mission Statement. Instead of being threatened by a lack of denominational loyalty, the statement recognizes, permits, and even blesses the connections that congregations have made on the local level. Furthermore, it commends these connections and activities with the esteemed mantle of "mission." Supporting the Young Life chapter at the local high school, cooperating with a neighboring Methodist congregation on a soup kitchen, or holding joint Lenten services with the Lutheran

---

7. Edwin Mulder, "The Reformed Connection," *Church Herald: A Publication of the Reformed Church in America*, February 1993, p. 11.

congregation down the street are the ground-level reality for typical Reformed congregations. According to the Mission Statement, these activities qualify as mission. In a denomination in which foreign missions have long been the favored child, conferring this mantle of mission to the congregation is no small happening, and is in fact quite the compliment. The activities of the local congregation are now described as mission, yet the activity most commonly associated with that term — denominationally supervised missionary work undertaken by full-time, commissioned professionals — is never explicitly mentioned in the Mission Statement.

The RCA is described as "locally-oriented, globally connected." This hints at some recognition of those broader concerns that have traditionally been viewed as the denomination's role: world missions, formal ecumenical ties, and theological education. As alluded to earlier, before the congregational focus of the funnel image, the broader assemblies of the RCA had generally been understood to carry out different tasks than a local church, often those beyond a congregation's reach. None of these broader, denominational tasks received more attention in the RCA than foreign missions.

In telling congregations to do mission and affirming their present activities as mission, the Mission Statement keeps before congregations what the denomination does best and what has received the most support and appreciation. If congregations are to be about mission, does it follow that part of that mission must include denominational foreign missions? If there has been an unspoken funnel in the past, it has carried the dollars of congregations to support these visible and popular denominational ventures. In the RCA, foreign missionary activity has traditionally taken a lion's share of denominational monies. The view from the pew has been that if the denomination does anything, it should be missions. The phrase "globally connected" in the Mission Statement may be a subtle argument that the front lines of ministry are not entirely at a congregational level, and that some dollars must continue to flow through the funnel in the reverse direction.

Are We a Fellowship?

Probably no word in the Mission Statement has generated more discussion and concern than "fellowship" (e.g., "the Reformed Church in America is a *fellowship* of congregations"). Fellowship has not previously been a part of either historic Reformed ecclesiology or RCA parlance. Traditionally, it has implied a more independent understanding of the church than the more organic connectionalism of the RCA. Its inclusion in the Mission Statement may simply be an example of bricolage at work, drawing from accessible and common language. Others, however, suggest that fellowship terminology indicates a significant and troubling turn in the understanding of Reformed ecclesiology.

Fellowship, it is argued, conveys a much more voluntarist notion of church than has been the classic Reformed viewpoint. It implies like-minded persons coming together of their own accord. Just as fellowship can arise spontaneously and informally, it can also dissolve easily and without lasting consequences. According to critics, this lacks an awareness and appreciation of the formal, enduring bonds that undergird the Reformed understanding of the church. Fellowship terminology fails to take seriously the covenant relationships within a congregation and between congregations in the RCA, replacing them with passing, subjective compatibility. A variety of derogatory labels has therefore arisen in reaction to the fellowship terminology of the Mission Statement. A closetful of Reformed bogeymen appear, and critics seem to apply the one that scares them most.

"Congregationalism" is the most frequent slur. This denunciation has a long history in the RCA and is seemingly used whenever denominational loyalty is in jeopardy. When used in this way, the word implies the supremacy of the congregation over the denomination. Every congregation does what is right in its own eyes. Congregationalism is, of course, a historic, recognized, and formalized church polity, albeit not the RCA's presbyterial polity. Its hallmarks have generally included decision making on a local level and congregational independence. This accusation, then, fails to appreciate that historic congregationalism is not congregational in the same sense as the Mission Statement's understanding of the local church as the target of the denomination's resource funnel. Many congregations within denominations with a congregational polity would likely be surprised to hear themselves described as the targets of the denomination's funnel.

"Sectarian" is another favorite Reformed aspersion used by critics of the Mission Statement's fellowship terminology. Drawing on the well-known work of Ernst Troeltsch, the term is a correct description to the extent that it conveys the same quality of a voluntarist, believer's church as does "fellowship." When Reformed critics use it disparagingly, they are generally attacking a perceived withdrawing, quietist, or separatist understanding of engagement with culture — Christ *against* culture, to borrow H. Richard Niebuhr's familiar phrase. There is little indication of this sort of sectarianism in the Mission Statement. Given today's culture wars and ongoing debates about the most appropriate form of Christian engagement with culture, the label sectarian is likely to be misunderstood and to serve only to confuse matters.

"Localism" has been offered as another criticism of the statement's perspective. The use of the funnel image certainly suggests a strong local leaning. Nonetheless, as mentioned earlier, classic Reformed ecclesiology has a similar impulse toward localism — the Word is preached, the sacraments are celebrated, and Christian discipline is practiced on the local level. None of the three RCA doctrinal standards mentions the wider church. Of course, to say a Reformed understanding of the church has always had a localist inclination is not to say that this has been at the expense or neglect of wider church assemblies. The denomination's doctrinal standards may not make explicit mention of the wider church, but certainly it was always implied. Dordt, for example, was itself a synod where doctrinal standards were adopted. That monumental synod stipulated the activities and purview of the broader assemblies as those things that the more local assembly could not address. "In those Assemblies, ecclesiastical matters only shall be transacted, and that in an ecclesiastical manner. A greater Assembly shall take cognizance of those things alone which could not be determined in a lesser, or that appertain in the churches or congregations in general, which compose such an assembly."[8] While localism may be intended as a criticism of the Mission Statement's funnel focus on the congregation, there is a sense in which it is an appropriate and fair description of Reformed views of the church.

"Congregationalism," "sectarian," and "localism" all have shortcomings as critical descriptions of the use of "fellowship" in the Mission Statement. No more accurate or appropriate term of critique will be proposed here. Yet acknowledging the deficiencies of these critical labels does not mean that the thrust behind the criticism is incorrect. Despite their inadequacies, these three flawed terms do serve as points that can help to circumscribe the disconcerting position implied in the statement. There is no doubt that Reformed ecclesiology has had a fuller sense of the church being a lasting, interrelated union than is conveyed by the term "fellowship."

More significant is whether "fellowship" connotes a shift in the source and initiative of the church. The Heidelberg Catechism (question and answer 54) says of the church, "the Son of God through his Spirit and Word, out of the entire human race, from the beginning of the world to its end, gathers, protects, and preserves for himself a community chosen for eternal life and united in faith." The church is formed and sustained by God's activity of gathering and preserving. The church is not primarily a human endeavor. It is not a group of like-minded individuals who come together by choice. As is the case with so

8. Articles of Dort (1619), article XXX, *A Digest of Constitutional and Synodical Legislation*, ed. Edward Tanjore Corwin (New York: Board of Publishing of the Reformed Church in America, 1906).

much of Reformed theology, God is the one who takes the initiative. In this sense "sectarian" may be the most accurate description of the Mission Statement's fellowship terminology despite the unintended undertones of cultural quietism it often implies. The church in Reformed theology is neither a voluntary association, a humanly generated institution, a fellowship of believers, nor a group of people involved in mission or other laudable activities.

This indicates that the use of the term "fellowship" in the Mission Statement is an aberration, a break (intended or not) with Reformed ecclesiology. At the same time, it must be noted that almost immediately after it uses the term, the statement describes the fellowship as "called by God and empowered by the Holy Spirit to be the very presence of Jesus Christ in the world." "Called by God" resounds with the Reformed tradition. If critics maintain that fellowship terminology implies a "lower" ecclesiology than the traditional Reformed position, here a "higher" and more traditional Reformed ecclesiology seems to be articulated. Moreover, "the very presence of Jesus Christ in the world" sounds like a much higher ecclesiology, almost Roman Catholic in tone, than a Reformed perspective. Do these higher and more traditional descriptions of the church balance and mitigate the Mission Statement's use of fellowship, or are they symptomatic of an inconsistent and muddled ecclesiology?

Recalling the earlier discussion of bricolage may be instructive at this point. It may be too much to ask for a consistent and clear ecclesiology from a denominational mission statement. This one uses an assortment of terms that may not reliably fit traditional theological categories. "Fellowship" may simply be a familiar and popular term that carries no great implications to the vast majority of persons and is not viewed as distinctively different from Reformed beliefs. Discomfort with its use may signal our misunderstanding of the statement's audience and intent. A finely honed, theologically precise document it is not. Accessible theological bricolage may be a more accurate description of it.

Intentional or not, however, the use of the word in the statement still reveals a significant development. True, it is a pragmatic mission statement, not a precise doctrinal creed. However, the choice and use of language and terminology matter and will have serious long-term implications. The use of fellowship terminology introduces an unfamiliar element into the Reformed lexicon. Consciously or unconsciously, this sort of bricolage will change the theological vocabulary over time. That an average audience is more familiar with fellowship terminology only confirms that today's society holds a non-Reformed, voluntarist understanding of church. The Mission Statement's usage may simply be a reflection of that perception. Yet by recognizing and conceding this situation, it also results in the sanctioning of the situation.

From Description to Prescription

If up to this point the attempt has been primarily to report on the RCA Mission Statement, this final section will move more overtly to analysis and critique. This analysis will attend to two basic themes. First, despite the attention given to congregational activities in the Mission Statement, it also gives expression to a new conception of the synods and their staffs. These groups are framed in more spiritual and visionary terms. The statement seems to build the relationship between denominational structures and the congregation on the basis of some sort of spiritual authority. Yet at the same time, that relationship is built upon more market-driven images of consumer and provider. Second, we must ask how Reformed ecclesiology is altered in a variety of ways, small and large, by the statement. The most significant of these alterations implies that the initiative for the church is found in human activity. This attention to the church doing mission is likely intended to be motivational but finally may place such high expectations on these activities as to lead instead to weary and disillusioned congregations and Christians.

I believe the Mission Statement has gained widespread attention and influence in the RCA and, to that extent, has been a success. Even if one totally discounts its substance, the broad recognition of it throughout the RCA suggests that the ability of a denomination to publicize and promote themes or causes is stronger than might be imagined. After its adoption, a copy of the document, impressively printed on parchment-like paper, was sent to every RCA congregation. Thousands more copies were requested by individuals, congregations, and other church bodies. Over two-thirds of the RCA's congregations accepted a videotape and study guide for the Mission Statement. The statement has appeared prominently in the denomination's annual "plan calendar." It has been frequently cited in denominational reports and literature. A phrase from it now appears on the bottom of RCA letterhead.

Given the consensus that denominational loyalty has unraveled in recent decades, the statement appears to stand as a counterexample of a denomination being quite successful in bringing its project to the attention of congregations. Although talk of denominational weakness is widespread in the United States, the RCA Mission Statement demonstrates that a denomination's power to publicize and even persuade, its capacity for dissemination, and its ability to secure the attention of congregations should not be underestimated.

The attention the statement has received, however, should not be accounted for totally by the RCA's capacity to publicize. Its content and substance must also be given credit for the interest it has garnered. Its eager, activist rhetoric, its accessibility, and its can-do pragmatism all likely account for its impact.

Most importantly, I would argue that it is perceived less as an attempt to foist a denominational agenda or doctrine upon congregations than most items approved by a general synod. This is the genius of the Mission Statement and the most significant change represented by it. Rather than somehow trying to marshal, mildly chastise, or rein in congregations, it is perceived as freeing and empowering them. They are exhorted to do mission. In turn, they appreciate that the denomination recognizes and sanctions their activities as being mission. Instead of feeling threatened by a lack of denominational unity and allegiance, congregations are given the impression that the denomination acknowledges and accepts its secondary status in congregational life and simply wants to be a useful partner in congregational mission.

Yet what appears to be a denomination willing to relinquish some prominence is described by Don Luidens in the accompanying sociological case study (pp. 410-35) as "managing localism." This may seem strange after the previous discussion of nascent congregationalism or sectarianism. Is the denomination taking a more hands-off approach, or is it attempting to manage and invade the local congregation? Paradoxically, some have even accused the Mission Statement of representing "creeping episcopalianism." In this case "episcopalian" refers to a polity with bishops and not the Anglican tradition. Nonetheless, after just reporting that some of its critics accuse it of being too congregational, how then can it also be episcopalian? Perhaps this is overheated rhetoric, but it gives voice to the concern that, despite initial appearances of blessing a congregation's local activities, the statement really establishes a new and intrusive link directly between the general synod and congregations.

Resolving the Paradox

While the Mission Statement seemingly signals a new appreciation for the local nature of the church and a genuine unleashing of congregations to move creatively in mission, it also can be seen as a new and more overt flexing of denominational power. Instead of taking responsibility for underappreciated but necessary tasks like ecumenical relations, administration, and theological education, or being viewed as the outside enforcer attempting to foist its program and conformity upon congregations, the statement sets the denomination up as the inspirer, the vision caster, the fresh breeze in the congregation's sails.

This is the perplexing ambivalence that drifts through the Mission Statement. It sets the congregation free for mission and yet portrays the denomination as an essential inspirer of this mission rather than its unobtrusive administrator. It celebrates the grassroots church and yet was generated by a denominational council, adopted by the widest denominational assembly, and vigorously publicized by denominational structures. It focuses on the local church and yet synod staffs receive mention and are granted an almost official status within RCA polity. It gives the wider church assemblies a warmer, more relational, and spiritual gloss and yet uses the denomination's promotional machinery to advertise this spiritual approach. In the Mission Statement we see the denomination attaching itself to congregations through a document that suggests congregations are almost voluntarily less attached to the denomination.

Of course, denominational structures have often tried to generate excitement among congregations. What is new or now more obvious is the denomination attempting to play the role of spiritual nurturer. This warmer, more collegial connection would have been associated with the role of the classis in RCA polity. Perhaps it is this change that gives rise to accusations of creeping episcopalianism. There is no need to suggest that this more relational, spiritual presentation of the denomination is a Trojan horse, a sinister conspiracy intended to gain easier access to congregational coffers. It does, however, indicate that the denomination realizes it must establish its relationship with congregations on new and different grounds.

The Mission Statement clearly is an attempt to move the denominational structure away from the rational, corporate model and toward a warmer, spiritual connection. While RCA polity has never implied that the denomination's task is to mirror corporate business methods, generally there has been a sense that the denominational structures are more functional than spiritual. Less than forty years ago the title of the top officer of the denomination was still "stated clerk," a title that may convey slightly more than a bean counter but hardly suggests any sort of great spiritual authority or charisma. Certainly few if any would expect someone called a stated clerk to develop or advance a mission statement. Granberg-Michaelson recognized this in saying, "the expectations . . . for the RCA's general secretary . . . are almost schizophrenic. They move in two different and often competing directions: to be the chief executive and administrator . . . and to be a pastoral presence and servant-leader."[9]

The Mission Statement's move toward a warmer, spiritual tone and away from a rational, corporate approach appears at the same time to be a move away from traditional Reformed doctrine and polity. While bricolage from pop lexicons may partially explain the absence of Reformed themes from the document, the absence also suggests a deep ambivalence about the viability of Reformed theology in the future. Reformed themes and doctrine have been

9. Granberg-Michaelson, "Why a Mission Statement?" pp. 2-3.

lumped together, it seems, with a perceived corporate bureaucracy under the label of "denomination." Antipathy toward the latter has bled over to the former. Defending bureaucracy is a task few would want to undertake. However, a hallmark of Reformed theology has been that vocations and tasks such as businessperson, lawyer, executive, or administrator are very capable of providing service to God's kingdom. Trying to put a more spiritual, pietistic gloss on the activities and assemblies of the church may inadvertently shrink the sphere of influence of God's kingdom and narrow the perceived tasks and ways one may serve in the church.

The optimistic, activist tone of the Mission Statement further contributes to the lack of appreciation for a theological heritage. Looking to the future, the statement's exuberance seems to slip into impulsiveness and impatience. Terms associated with the past are perceived as impediments that must be discarded. Yet its popular, contemporary vocabulary seems to bode a very short life span. It leaves the RCA with fewer roots from which to draw for the next mission statement or similar project.

The desire of the denominational structure to cast visions and exert spiritual authority suggests disquiet about the ability of those structures to continue to make a case for themselves and their designated functions. Knowing its support is eroding, the denomination appears eager to recast itself in new terms and tasks. If "administrator" was perceived instead as "bureaucrat" and "theological voice" was understood as a distant doctrinal "enforcer," then "inspirer" and "equipper" become the new, preferred, and necessary tasks. It is still an open question whether these new tasks and roles will successfully rally denominational attitudes or whether the denomination has jettisoned so much of its past as only to hasten greater erosion.

It is a legitimate concern that the Mission Statement fails to appreciate and make a case for the necessity of those unglamorous tasks that denominational structures must do, regardless of the manner. Traditional missions and missionaries continue to require support. Denominational pension and insurance plans must still be maintained. The need for providing theological education remains. Ecumenical relationships may take new forms but are also likely to continue on any denominational agenda. Yet has the Mission Statement made any explicit or effective case for these tasks? Will any denomination and its staff be able to continue these tasks while also attempting to be a warm inspirer and resource provider? It seems improbable.

Along with inspirer, the Mission Statement also makes the denomination into equipper. The synods and staff must funnel resources to the congregation. In a rather unexpected turn, the spiritual tone here takes on a much more economic, goods-and-services quality. These days, of course, mission statements are a common part of the corporate world for small businesses, industrious executives, and huge corporations. Moreover, this greater spiritual authority of the denomination still relies on a vigorous promotional blitz. Is the funneling of resources to congregations by the denomination truly a basis for some sort of inspirational connection or is it just plain consumerism? If the RCA wants to base its connection to the congregations on its ability to fill the funnel with good resources, can it really provide them? A recent study done for the RCA said,

> Consistories are most likely to desire assistance from classes, regional synods, and the general synod with issues that concern them and with their primary goals for congregations . . . recruiting new members, managing facilities, developing outreach programs. . . . Unlike more traditional denominational services . . . [these] are issues that are usually idiosyncratic, issues that "play out" differently from one congregation to another. They are ultimately local issues that must be addressed locally.[10]

Conclusion: Who Establishes the Church?

Although the RCA Mission Statement is not part of the RCA constitution and does not attempt to be a confessional document, it carries all sorts of implicit theology closely related to an understanding or definition of the church. As previously noted, its tilt toward localism is not entirely new or unfamiliar to Reformed theology. It is, however, more pronounced in this document. The congregation is now the target of the denominational funnel, as opposed to the more traditional, mutual to-and-fro that occurred between congregations and the broader assemblies. There may be, however, an even more fundamental shift in the notion of what constitutes the church.

The attention to doing in the Mission Statement — inviting, growing, renewing, directing resources, feeding the hungry, engaging the world — gives the impression that the church is established and maintained by human activity. The activities the statement holds up are certainly laudable and worthwhile. They do not, however, constitute the church. A Reformed perspective proclaims that the church is "called and gathered" by Christ.

The activist, pragmatic tone of the statement presents a church that is a grassroots endeavor. The statement attempts to counter the prevalent and neg-

---

10. *1998 Consistorial Reports: Significant Events, Concerns, and Goals of Reformed Church Consistories, Prepared for: The Task Force on Responsibilities and Purpose of Regional Synods and Classes* (Holland, Mich.: Carl Frost Center for Social Science Research at Hope College, 1999), p. 76.

ative "top-down" impressions of the denomination by focusing on congregational action and directing the denominational funnel toward the congregation. Actually, the different assemblies in Reformed polity — classis, regional synod, and general synod — have traditionally been considered wider assemblies, not higher ones. Decisions made at a synod, for example, come from a broader base but not from the top down. In order to counter this top-down misperception, however, the Mission Statement shifts to a more grassroots tone. The difficulty with this grassroots understanding of the church is that, in a very real theological sense, the church from a Reformed perspective is a top-down endeavor. It is top-down not in the sense of hierarchical, heavy-handed, or bureaucratic structures, but because the initiating and sustaining of the church are of God. In Christian theology, of course, God's top-down initiatives are frequently manifested on a grassroots level, as the incarnation so tellingly reveals. In trying to correct a hierarchical, bureaucratic view of the various denominational assemblies and elevate the congregation, however, the Mission Statement instead stumbles toward a voluntarist notion of the church. The church is considered to be constituted by human mission activity rather than the call of Christ. As one person quipped of the Mission Statement, "It is all immanence with no transcendence."

In claiming that the statement leans toward a voluntarist basis for the church, I am not trying to be a doctrinal purist, maintaining the Reformed tradition simply for its own sake. Nor am I attempting to sound holier-than-thou, ridiculously claiming that the statement leaves God out of the church. A grassroots church, however, is always going to be measured by the state of the grass rather than by trusting in the initiative of God, the call of Christ, and the sustenance of the Holy Spirit. Although the Mission Statement is meant to energize, motivate, and unleash, might it not instead lead in the long run to frazzled, disheartened, and anxious congregations who falsely believe that the church rises and falls with their success and failure in mission?

Appendix: Reformed Church in America

Our Mission

The Reformed Church in America is a fellowship of congregations called by God and empowered by the Holy Spirit to be the very presence of Jesus Christ in the world.

Our shared task is to equip congregations for ministry — a thousand churches in a million ways doing one thing — following Christ in mission, in a lost and broken world so loved by God.

The Vision

Imagine . . .   laity and pastors unleashed, hungry for ministry; congregations mission-minded and inviting, authentic and healing, growing and multiplying, alert to opportunities around them.

Imagine . . .   classes and synods as communities of nurture and vision — accountable, responsible, sustained by prayer, alive to the Spirit.

Imagine . . .   a denomination, locally-oriented, globally connected, that prays in many languages and beholds the face of Christ in every face; a denomination renewed and renewing, raising up leaders, always directing its resources toward the front lines of ministry.

Imagine . . .   hurts being healed, the lost being found, the hungry being fed, peace healing brokenness, hope replacing despair, lives transformed by the love of Jesus Christ.

Imagine . . .   the Reformed Church in America, engaging the world.

Living Out the Vision

The vision will be lived out . . .

By congregations focused on ministry — creative, confident, healing, and radically attentive to the world outside its doors.

By consistories selected more for ministry than management, attuned to the Spirit, eager and equipped to serve.

By ministers of Word and sacrament open to dream, prepared to lead, willing to risk.

By classes that are empowering and proactive, living in communion, each accountable to all, and all to Christ.

By synods and staff that funnel resources to the local church and keep us connected to the larger church.

By all people of the RCA, a network of relationships, a fellowship that celebrates its gifts and confesses its failures, and where the ministries of all are valued and cherished.

To live out this vision by consistories, classes, synods and staff, our decision-making will be transformed by a pervasive climate of worship, discernment, and biblical reflection. We will no longer do business as usual, nor our usual business.

The United Church of Christ:
Redefining Unity in Christ as Unity in Diversity

Barbara Brown Zikmund

T he Christian church has struggled with questions of diversity and unity for over two thousand years. In the first century questions revolved around how Christian converts from outside the Jewish community could become part of the church. After considerable debate, Christian leaders decided that anyone could become a Christian without converting to Judaism first. God, concluded the first-century church, was in Christ reconciling the *world.*

As Christian history unfolded, however, the church was often more pre-occupied with preserving its orthodoxy than with reconciling the world. Creeds and doctrines developed to ensure that no error or heresy from secular philosophies or other religions distorted or diluted the gospel. Indeed, early Christianity was extremely skeptical about diversity and feared syncretism, the blending of religious ideas. Yet, even as the church sought to define and protect the purity of Christianity, key Greco-Roman ideas intruded into and reshaped its Hebraic origins. From its very beginnings, Christianity has been a mixture of eternal truths and diverse cultural values and contexts.

Early Christian history is filled with efforts to keep Christianity pure. In the fourth century the Greek churches and the Middle Eastern churches divided over how Christians understood the relationship of Jesus to God in what historians came to call the "Arian controversy." In the eleventh century the Greek and the Roman churches divided over questions of ecclesiastical authority, icons, and interpretations of the Holy Spirit. In the sixteenth century the Western Roman Catholic Church further divided over ecclesiastical corruption and the role of Scripture, resulting in various Protestant denominations. By the twentieth century the Christian church had fragmented into hundreds of groups, each trying to be faithful to God by promoting its particular understanding of the gospel in faith and practice. Instead of embodying Christian unity in a world of diversity and pluralism, the Christian church had become a prime illustration of the ways in which diversity and pluralism erode human community.

In the eighteenth and nineteenth centuries, as the economically dominant cultures and peoples in the Northern Hemisphere sought to share their worldview (or impose their ideas on everyone else, depending upon one's perspective), the proliferation of Christian churches and denominations began to disturb many Christians. Jesus had promised unity, yet his church was shamefully divided. For various theological, social, cultural, and historical reasons, Christians began to look for ways to reclaim their lost commonalities and overcome the fragmentation of the "body of Christ." The search for Christian unity generated an "ecumenical movement" which encouraged mergers and reunions of related ecclesiastical bodies throughout the early part of the twentieth century.

The United Church of Christ (UCC) is rooted in this history. It brings together a wide variety of traditions with deep commitments to Christian unity. Its particular story begins in the sixteenth-century European Reformation. By 1550 some of the Reformed followers of Zwingli and Calvin had found each other in the Swiss Rhineland and embraced a generous interpretation of their Reformed faith in the Heidelberg Catechism. In the eighteenth century descendants of these German Reformed people settled in the American colonies. There they further enriched their confessional life and nurtured a lively appreciation for liturgical tradition and pre-Reformation traditions.

A bit later, other Lutheran and Reformed groups became involved in a grassroots spiritual movement that focused upon personal faith and practice. Known as Pietism, it inspired Lutheran and Reformed believers to support mission work among all Germans settling on the American frontier.

Finally, by the mid–nineteenth century various new groups of German immigrants brought a different kind of German church experience to America. These newcomers, mostly from northern Europe, had overcome many of the historic animosities between Lutheran and Reformed Protestants in a Prussian "unionist" movement. They arrived in America with a keen appreciation for the shared legacies of Lutheran and Reformed faith and practice. They called themselves German Evangelicals and nourished a practical irenic piety with special sensitivity to wider social movements.

By the early twentieth century these two groups of German immigrants, rooted in German church history and American frontier patterns, embraced a growing ecumenical spirit. In 1934 the Reformed Church in the United States and the Evangelical Synod of North America came together to form the Evangelical and Reformed Church (E&R).

459

The UCC also draws upon radical reform movements within English church history. In seventeenth-century England, Puritans and Separatists did not believe that Anglican reforms of Roman Catholicism went far enough. Deeply influenced by the Reformed theology of Calvin, some English radicals fled to the Netherlands and eventually to America — others migrated directly to establish a Puritan commonwealth in New England. In their zeal for religious freedom they developed an ecclesiology based on the centrality of the local congregation. Although in practice early Congregationalism could be extremely self-serving and unyielding, Congregationalism eventually developed important principles for dealing with religious change and diversity. By the 1930s the Congregationalists merged with a very small denomination known as the "Christians."

The Christians resisted being known as a denomination. They were the product of anti-ecclesiastical and antidenominational thinking which flourished during the American revolutionary period. As American patriots, the Christians believed they were part of a new democratic experiment in politics and religion. They were impatient with old religious ideas and practices, rejecting all schools of thought and traditional denominational or party labels. They were free spirits inspired by frontier revivals and very suspicious of hierarchy and confessions. "Just call us 'Christians,'" they insisted.

For over one hundred years the Christians went their separate way. However, by the early twentieth century they too began to worry about the fragmentation of the Christian church. They discovered that they had a great deal in common with the Congregationalists, cultivating an understanding of the church as a voluntary association of disciples gathered and bound together through covenants. In the 1930s they merged with the Congregationalists to create the National Council of Congregational Christian Churches (CC). Although many local congregations were only vaguely aware of this alliance, the collaborative educational and mission work of the Congregational Christian Churches was impressive.

The E&R and CC came into being in the early twentieth century, but their antecedent groups had all participated in the global mission movements of the nineteenth century. They wondered out loud how the spectacle of a divided church could give hope to a divided world. They were influenced by historical-critical biblical scholarship which invited them to read and interpret Scripture in dynamic ways. They were deeply committed to overcoming the internal divisions created by the historical circumstances of class, race, language, and culture within their churches and in twentieth-century society. And they participated in some of the early ecumenical meetings which led to the formation of the Federal Council of Churches, the World Council of Churches, and the National Council of Churches. Through ecumenical fellowship experienced in worship and service, the E&R and CC denominations discovered that they had more in common than they imagined.

Louis Gunnemann, longtime historian of the formation of the UCC, points out that in the premerger conversations there was a theological assumption that "Christ's will and the believer's duty" coalesced in the act of church union, leading to the "subordination of doctrinal differences to the goal of Christian unity."[1] As a consequence, when the UCC was formed in 1957, two things happened. The new UCC neglected and even avoided formal theological or ecclesiological questions about its identity as a church; and second, the UCC embraced social activism without developing a "clearly articulated theological grounding." Leaders and members of the new UCC consistently failed "to articulate the faith foundations, theologically identified, of the social responsibility they so devotedly espoused." In the end, according to Gunnemann, the new UCC came of age in the social ferment of the sixties and was overwhelmed with tasks, coming up short on the "vision, time and energy for sustained theological reflection."[2]

Ironically, although the subordination of doctrinal differences to the goal of Christian unity was later recognized and criticized, at the time it was celebrated as a turning point in American Protestantism and in the ecumenical movement. People rejoiced that two very different church traditions had been able to consummate union precisely because they deliberately downplayed doctrinal concerns (or, as Shinn argues in his following theological essay, sought to embody a "calculated ambiguity"). They also downplayed differences in polity and structure, a fact that years later led increasing numbers to think that the UCC had, right from its inception, a dangerous "ecclesiological deficit."

From the standpoint of history there are many reasons that the leaders of the CC and E&R stepped into the unknown to create the UCC. The Congregationalists drew upon their longtime sense of civic responsibility and commitment to local participatory decision making unencumbered by hierarchy. They honestly believed that God was creating a new thing and that their involvement in a new united church was consistent with their Congregational principles. The Christians reaffirmed their judgment that denominational factions were unnecessary and unity a given. The German Reformed tradition had developed a new appreciation for the pre-Reformation church and the shared witness of all Christians, based on the work of key nineteenth-century Reformed thinkers

---

1. Louis H. Gunnemann, *United and Uniting: The Meaning of an Ecclesial Journey* (New York: United Church Press, 1987), pp. 26-27.
2. Gunnemann, *United and Uniting*, pp. 27-28.

at their Mercersburg Seminary in Franklin County, Pennsylvania (subsequently moving to Lancaster, Pennsylvania). And the German Evangelicals reclaimed their practical piety which had always insisted "in essentials unity, in non-essentials liberty and in all things charity." Buoyed by the earlier successful mergers of the 1930s which created the CC and E&R denominations, inspired by a growing global ecumenical enthusiasm, chastened by two world wars, and bound together through new biblical scholarship and extraordinary theological leaders, these four traditions took the risk. Jesus prayed for his disciples in the Gospel of John, "that they might all be one," and for a time in the 1950s national leaders rooted in Congregational, Christian, German Reformed, and German Evangelical histories believed that God was calling them into a new form of church.

As with most human organizations, however, the new grew out of the old. The merger was a blend of two very different patterns of church order. On the one hand the E&R Church had a presbyterial or representational structure. Things were centralized and decisions made by the national general synod, or other national offices were binding on local congregations. Budgets were dependent upon a modest but regular flow of local congregational support.

On the other hand the CC churches had a decentralized past. Congregationalism did not even have a national structure until the mid–nineteenth century, over two hundred years after its arrival in New England. Instead of a national organization, Congregational Christian mission outreach was fueled by local initiatives in partnership with a variety of special interest national boards and affinity groups loosely connected to the National Council — a board for church extension, a board for homeland mission, a board for Christian education, etc. By the 1960s these national "boards" formed by the Congregational Christian churches had merged and pooled their rather sizable endowments. And after 1957, when the national CC boards merged with parallel entities in the E&R Church to create the United Church Board for Homeland Ministries and the United Church Board for World Ministries, they were careful to protect their independence. In 1961 the new UCC constitution stated that the homeland and world mission boards were "recognized instrumentalities" of the United Church of Christ. Recognized instrumentalities agreed to serve as national agencies of the new denomination, but they were not subject to the direction of the general synod. All other entities, created and funded by the general synod through voluntary contributions flowing from local congregations, were known as "established instrumentalities."

This arrangement was a creative compromise. The two "Big Boards" were zealous to protect their resources. New ideas were often layered on to old assumptions and limited by old habits. At the same time, the autonomy of the Big

Boards with their sizable endowments allowed them to do very creative and prophetic things unencumbered by the need for national votes or synod budgets. It is important to note that much of the vitality of the UCC during the 1960s and 1970s flows out of this unconventional denominational structure.

The United Church of Christ was created in 1957, but in retrospect many feel it is more accurate to say that "the merger" was voted on in 1957, but the theological and structural integration was still not fully consummated. Forty-plus years later, an increasingly unequal resource base among national instrumentalities stimulated the denomination to correct the imbalance. Membership losses and declining revenues from local congregations had caused general synod budgets to shrink, while prudent investing had given the Big Boards more and more financial power. In one sense, it is possible to say that the 2000 restructuring of the UCC described in the Barnam/Chaves sociological case study and the Shinn theological essay is an attempt to finally complete the merger.

Restructuring, however, has also caused the UCC to recast its understanding of its ecumenical vocation. During the ten-year process leading up to the 2000 constitution, UCC leaders examined the so-called ecclesiological deficit. Rather than going back to a classic ecclesiology (thinking about the church), they chose to focus upon missiology (thinking about the church as an agent for God's mission in the world).

Drawing upon the traditions which flow into the UCC from its antecedent denominations, and recognizing its commitment to diversity since 1957, this most recent restructuring is motivated by at least two agendas, as shown by the following case study and theological essay. First, it seeks to change the relationships between the organizational units of the church so that they reflect a more balanced and just distribution of money and power. This is done so that the church can be more effective as God's mission. And second, it presses the UCC to understand its long-standing ecumenical calling in some new ways. The history of the UCC shows that there have always been remarkable diversity and openness in its various expressions. Although there have been times when an unexamined "historical orthodoxy" has limited its horizons, there have also been times of remarkable prophetic solidarity with diverse peoples and traditions.

Historians of the ecumenical movement like to distinguish between those Christians that focus upon unity issues related to faith and order and those who define and explore unity through shared life and work. The UCC, as it moves into the next stage of its life, seems to be suggesting a third (different) vision of Christian unity, *one rooted in who makes up the church, not in what it confesses or even what it does.* As the case study and theological essay note, when contemporary UCC leaders are asked about the ecumenical vocation of the UCC, more and more of them find themselves defining ecumenicity in terms of the union of diverse persons.

This understanding of ecumenicity in terms of diversity has not been claimed overtly; rather it has come about somewhat indirectly. It is a product of the ecumenical life of the UCC since the early 1970s. At that time the UCC was involved in a wider ecumenical venture known as the Consultation on Church Union (COCU). In COCU initial efforts were made to craft a plan of union for denominations even more diverse than the UCC by focusing upon differences related to faith, worship, and ministry. If they could develop a theological basis for the mutual recognition of members and ministries, the various church leaders in the COCU denominations felt that union might be possible. Eventually, however, COCU concluded that the contemporary ecumenical agenda was more complex. COCU, and the UCC within it, came to see that there were certain nontheological issues which were "church dividing." The issues of racism, sexism, institutionalism, and exclusivistic congregationalism kept the church from its unity in Christ. Until these nontheological issues were confronted, the COCU leaders argued, Christian unity was in jeopardy and the Christian church in danger of continuing to contribute to the erosion of human community.

Since the early 1970s the UCC has lived with this assumption embedded in the early work of COCU. The findings of the case study and theological essay show that there is a new understanding of church unity emerging in the national setting of the UCC when key leaders no longer define ecumenical identity and activity in terms of efforts to heal divisions between different religious or confessional camps. Rather the focus has shifted to define the oneness of Christ as that which results when the church is able to "bind in covenant faithful people of all races, ethnicities and cultures."[3]

Some observers suggest that the UCC has lost its ecumenical nerve and is no longer as committed to Christian unity as it was. It may be, however, that UCC ecumenical passion has not waned, it is simply being defined differently. The merger that created the UCC in 1957 paid little attention to resolving doctrinal divisions. It was preoccupied with structure and overcoming cultural differences. At its inception the UCC merger surprised people. Ecumenical observers wondered how two such different traditions and cultures could merge — Germans and English, confessional and nonconfessional, congregational and presbyterial, rural and urban, professionals and blue-collar workers, etc.

---

3. "Statement of Christian Conviction of the Proposed Pronouncement Calling the United Church of Christ to Be a Multiracial and Multicultural Church," *General Synod Minutes 1993*, 39-40.

From the standpoint of history, therefore, to define the ecumenical vocation of the contemporary UCC in terms of creating a "true multiracial and multicultural church" is not a new way of being the church for the UCC, although it may be a new way of speaking about ecumenism. The recent restructuring of the UCC simply stretches classic definitions of church unity, based on a new vision of theological and organizational oneness. In these times the UCC has moved from speaking about a unity in Christ which calls Christians into closer relationships with other Christians, to a commitment under Christ to be a new people cultivating a "oneness of community embracing diversity." If the church is ultimately "the body of Christ," then this vision of the UCC as a multiracial, multicultural church is merely a new answer to Jesus' prayer "that they may all be one."

Strategy and Restructure in the United Church of Christ

Emily Barman and Mark Chaves

T he United Church of Christ (UCC) is in the midst of a major restructure, one that culminates a decade-long planning process. The new structure was approved in summer 1999, with implementation beginning in 2000. Given the recentness of the implementation, the focus of this case is the structure as approved. Although the primary goal of this chapter is descriptive — simply providing an account of the key features of UCC restructuring and the factors that appear to have prompted it — we also discuss restructuring goals in light of social and organizational realities within the UCC.

The chapter has three sections. The first provides a brief and basic description of UCC organizational structure. A second section — the main body of the chapter — describes the two major goals of restructure. We identify the ways in which particular aspects of restructure are intended to further these goals, and we also place these goals in the context of larger social and organizational realities in the UCC. A third section reviews the factors that seem to us to be producing this restructuring effort. Throughout, we examine documents that were produced as part of the long planning process for this restructure, we employ financial reports, and we draw on interviews with national executives, regional executives, and local clergy within the UCC.[1]

1. Most of the documents we use were produced by the UCC during the restructure process. These include policy statements, financial reports, annual reports, internal surveys, and theological writings. We also conducted interviews with twenty-four senior executives at the national setting of the UCC. In these interviews we asked our respondents a variety of questions about their work, as well as about their understanding of restructure and its goals. We also draw on surveys of and interviews with UCC conference executives and on interviews with UCC clergy from other Organizing Religious Work (ORW)–related studies. The former were conducted by Adair Lummis as part of a larger study of regional executives (Adair Lummis, "Sum-

The United Church of Christ

The United Church of Christ was formed in 1957 from a merger between the Congregational Christian Churches and the Evangelical and Reformed Church. The denomination exists organizationally, to use UCC language, in four manifestations: twelve (before current restructure) instrumentalities located in Cleveland and New York City; thirty-nine regional conferences, in turn composed of 200 more local associations; and approximately six thousand congregations. UCC congregations spent $684.7 million in 1996, $18.1 million of which went to the national setting. The national instrumentalities also received $33 million in income from other sources in 1996, primarily from their endowments.[2]

The UCC's polity is "congregational" in that, as stated in its constitution, no other parts of the denomination may impair the autonomy of any local church in the management of its own affairs. Neither regional nor national organizations exert any administrative, religious, or financial authority whatsoever on any local operations, and all contributions that flow from congregations to the regional units are voluntary. As one conference executive put it, "There is no hierarchical function between [the national offices] and this conference. Nothing that is done up there is binding [on this conference] and nothing in the conference is binding on the local church."

The conferences and associations of the UCC are bodies organized on a territorial basis, each holding a distinct set of responsibilities. Associations hold some religious authority in the UCC in that they grant congregational and ordained ministerial standing in the denomination and can remove congregations from the denomination.[3] Even this authority, however, is less than absolute, since congregations are not obligated to employ clergy with ordained standing in the UCC. Conferences provide counsel, resources, advice, and in-service training for ministers. They also conduct conferences and workshops at the regional and local settings, including preretirement seminars for clergy, evangelism training, and awareness training on mission and justice issues. Conferences serve as a conduit for funds between local churches and the national setting, and they retain a portion of the resources coming from congregations, usually 40 to 60 percent, for their own work.

mary of UCC Results from the ORW Regional Judicatory Survey" [Hartford Seminary, 2000]). The latter were conducted by Nancy Ammerman as part of a larger study of congregations (Nancy Ammerman, "Summary of UCC Results from the ORW Congregational Survey" [Hartford Seminary, 2000]).

2. *Annual Report of the UCC* (Cleveland: United Church of Christ, 1997).

3. Executive Council for the United Church of Christ, *Constitution and Bylaws of the United Church of Christ* (Cleveland: United Church of Christ, 1997), p. 5.

The representative national body of the UCC is the General Synod, which meets every two years for seven days. Postrestructure, the General Synod will consist of delegates chosen by the conferences and ex officio delegates. Ex officio delegates include the elected officers of the UCC, members of the Executive Council, and the moderator and assistant moderator of the General Synod. The total number of elected delegates from conferences ranges from 675 to 725 at a General Synod. Each conference sends 3 or more delegates, depending on the number of persons who have membership in their local churches. The criteria for conferences' delegations are clearly specified in the UCC's constitution: each delegation must be made up of at least 50 percent laypersons; must display racial, ethnic, and gender diversity; and should consist of at least 50 percent persons under thirty years of age.[4]

The General Synod possesses various responsibilities within the denomination. It oversees and financially authorizes the work of the UCC, authorizes changes to the constitution and bylaws, calls or nominates and elects General Synod officers and the boards of directors of those ministries whose election is vested in it, determines the relationship of the UCC to other ecumenical and interdenominational bodies,[5] and pronounces upon social issues of the day.

Although the General Synod sets denominational policy, it has no administrative or other authority over regional bodies — conferences and associations — or congregations, as stated in the constitution. The General Synod possesses more formal authority over the national expressions of the church than over local or regional ones. Even the national instrumentalities, however, enjoy a fair degree of autonomy and are able to exercise considerable control over their own internal operations. This is especially true of the national agencies that are older than the denomination.

The Restructure

The UCC's restructuring was formally approved in the summer of 1999, and began to be implemented in 2000. The restructure planning process formally began in 1987, when the General Synod's Executive Council appointed an Advisory Commission on Structure. This commission evolved into a Committee on Structure, which presented a final report to the 1995 General Synod. This report

4. Constitution and Bylaw Revision Team, "Working Draft #4 of Revised Constitution and Bylaws of the United Church of Christ" (February 6, 1997, memo), p. 27.
5. Constitution and Bylaw Revision Team, "Working Draft #4," pp. 8-9.

was accepted as "providing a sufficient basis for restructuring the national setting of the church."[6] The 1997 General Synod approved the proposed amendments to the constitution, and with two-thirds of the regional conferences approving these changes, the 1999 General Synod ratified a final document. The implementation began in 2000.

Several different outcomes were considered along the road to restructure. The report of the initial Advisory Commission on Structure recommended seven areas for further study: ecclesiology, coordination, ecumenicity, office of the president, funding allocation, relationship between and among conferences and national bodies, and proliferation of structures.[7] By the 1991 General Synod, the General Synod Committee on Structure had looked at three outlines of possible structure for the UCC. These models shared many features: a strengthened office of the president, a "management team" at the national setting, a reduced number of offices, a significant reconfiguration of the assets of the recognized boards, and conference representation in the management team.[8] These three models differed in the importance of the president to decision making, that is, the degree to which the national level should be governed by the principle of hierarchy rather than covenant. As an ecclesiology of covenant became articulated, the two outlines of restructure based in hierarchy were abandoned and the third model was formally adopted.

UCC restructuring was intended to achieve multiple goals, but the major goals can be grouped into two broad categories. First, restructure was intended to establish new relationships among the various organizational units of the denomination. Second, restructure was intended to push the UCC further in the direction of emphasizing and valuing diversity of various sorts. These goals are complex. In some ways they represent continuity with the UCC's history and identity; in other ways they mark a departure from the status quo. In this section we take a close look at these goals and how they are addressed by various concrete changes brought about by restructure. We also discuss these goals in light of relevant social and organizational realities within this denomination.

6. *Report on Restructure to the Twenty-First General Synod of the United Church of Christ* (Cleveland: United Church of Christ, 1997), p. A-2.

7. *Report of the General Synod Committee on Structure to the Eighteenth General Synod* (Cleveland: United Church of Christ, 1991), p. 1.

8. *Report of the General Synod Committee on Structure to the Eighteenth General Synod,* p. 4.

Emily Barman and Mark Chaves

New Relationships among Parts of the Denomination

One major goal of the restructure is changing the relationships among the various organizational units that constitute the UCC. Three intended changes are key. One is structural and obvious: national setting agencies are to be fundamentally reorganized toward greater simplification and ease of use. The other two key changes are cultural and more subtle: national agencies are to be reoriented toward better serving congregations, and the restructured relationships are to follow a theology of organization — an ecclesiology — rather than the political and functional pragmatism that undergirded the prior structure. We will consider each of these in turn.

National Reorganization

The most dramatic consequence of UCC restructuring was that twelve national instrumentalities became four covenanted ministries. Figure 1 on page 471 shows the prerestructure national agency structure of the UCC. The size of each box in this figure roughly represents the relative income of each national unit in fiscal year 1996. As indicated by the three columns, these units are of three different types: recognized instrumentalities, established instrumentalities, and executive offices. The two recognized instrumentalities predate the UCC itself. The United Church Board for Homeland Ministries is concerned with social ministry and social justice. To that end it provides programs, training, and financial support to other settings of the denomination. The United Church Board for World Ministries focuses on the work of the church abroad, providing evangelism, education, and social services.

Before restructure, although each of these units was formally responsible in some degree to the General Synod, the recognized instrumentalities (colloquially known as the "Big Boards") had much more autonomy than either the established instrumentalities or the executive offices. Indeed, there have been several occasions when representatives of the Big Boards argued that these boards are completely independent of General Synod directives.[9] It also is worth emphasizing that the various national units have been autonomous with respect to each other, and even with respect to the president's office, which had very limited administrative authority.

Established instrumentalities have been formed for a variety of purposes since the UCC's inception. They were created by and are funded primarily by the General Synod, to which they are also accountable. They consist of agencies

9. R. Shinn, personal correspondence with authors, 1999.

470

Figure 1. UCC Pre-Restructuring National Bodies

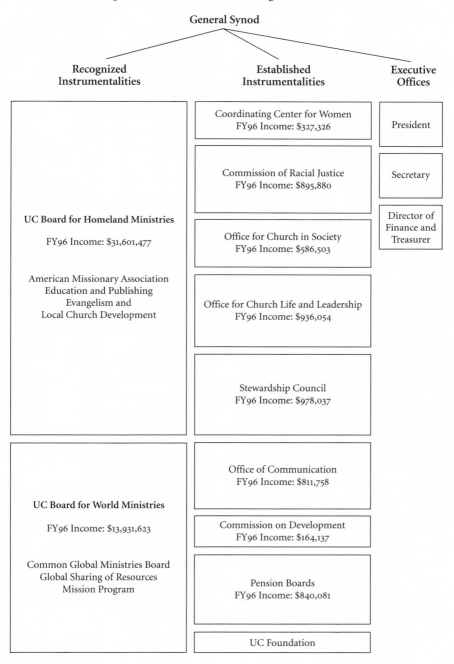

General Synod

Recognized
Instrumentalities

Established
Instrumentalities

Executive
Offices

Coordinating Center for Women
FY96 Income: $327,326

President

Commission of Racial Justice
FY96 Income: $895,880

Secretary

Director of
Finance and
Treasurer

UC Board for Homeland Ministries

FY96 Income: $31,601,477

American Missionary Association
Education and Publishing
Evangelism and
Local Church Development

Office for Church in Society
FY96 Income: $586,503

Office for Church Life and Leadership
FY96 Income: $936,054

Stewardship Council
FY96 Income: $978,037

Office of Communication
FY96 Income: $811,758

UC Board for World Ministries

FY96 Income: $13,931,623

Common Global Ministries Board
Global Sharing of Resources
Mission Program

Commission on Development
FY96 Income: $164,137

Pension Boards
FY96 Income: $840,081

UC Foundation

serving constituencies within the UCC, providing financial and administrative assistance for UCC clergy and other staff, as well as those offices pursuing social justice within the denomination and elsewhere. The executive offices provided a measure of financial and administrative oversight, although duplicate administrative offices existed within several of the instrumentalities. These offices also managed ecumenical affairs, but without any formal authority. They also were creations of the General Synod and, again, were accountable to and funded primarily by it.

Restructure was intended to enhance efficiency and coordination at the national level by simplifying this structure. As shown in figure 2 on page 473, it establishes four new ministries that centralize functions previously spread across the numerous prior units. The Wider Church Ministries continues the overseas mission and ecumenical work of the denomination. The Local Church Ministries focuses on the religious and fiscal life of congregations in the United States. The Justice and Witness Ministries gathers together the social justice offices, and the Office of General Ministries will be strengthened to provide spiritual, ecumenical, and financial oversight for the entire national structure of the denomination.

The restructured national church also contains two new structures, the Collegium of Officers (consisting of the executive ministers for each of the three new ministries, the general minister and president, and the associate general minister) and the Mission Planning Council (composed of the above-listed officers and the leaders of the principal subunits of the four new ministries, the Pension Boards United Church of Christ, and the United Church Foundation). These two new entities are meant to coordinate the activities of the new ministries. They, in turn, are responsible to the General Synod. The Pension Boards and the United Church Foundation hold a separate status under the direct supervision of the General Synod.

Restructure thus entails a fairly radical reorganization of the national agencies, one meant to achieve a certain rationalization and simplification of national setting structure. This interpretation of restructuring is evident in the discourse of senior UCC executives. When asked about the purpose of restructuring, these executives talk quite a lot about more efficient allocation of resources, reduced costs, less overlap in functions, more efficient warehousing of products, and so on. One executive said, "What in part [the restructure] is meant to accomplish is a leaner, more transparent, more understandable, programmatic structure for the national setting of the church." Another explained that restructure "should result in less redundancy and therefore less expenditure at the national level for administrative type things."

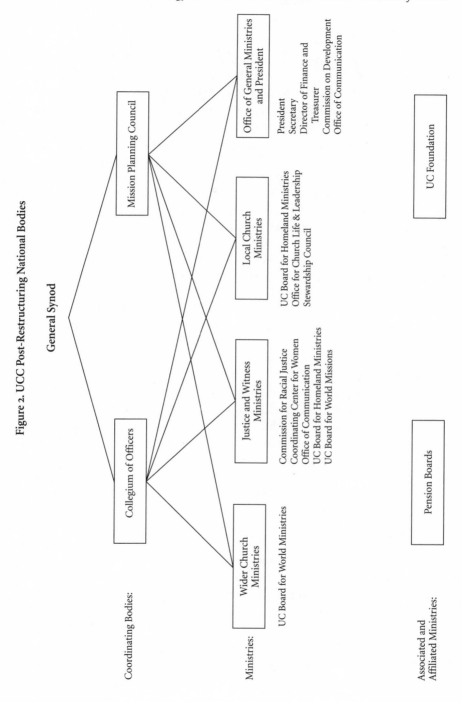

Figure 2. UCC Post-Restructuring National Bodies

General Synod

Coordinating Bodies:

Collegium of Officers

Mission Planning Council

Ministries:

Wider Church Ministries

UC Board for World Ministries

Justice and Witness Ministries

Commission for Racial Justice
Coordinating Center for Women
Office of Communication
UC Board for Homeland Ministries
UC Board for World Missions

Local Church Ministries

UC Board for Homeland Ministries
Office for Church Life & Leadership
Stewardship Council

Office of General Ministries and President

President
Secretary
Director of Finance and Treasurer
Commission on Development
Office of Communication

Associated and Affiliated Ministries:

Pension Boards

UC Foundation

Focus on Congregations

The reorganization of agencies and offices represents an attempt to do more than simplify UCC agency structure. It also is intended to reorient the national setting of the denomination toward servicing and resourcing congregations. It is important to note that the national-setting agencies always have provided services and resources to congregations. The national instrumentalities, however, also possess missions that are unique to their setting, including a commitment to social justice, social witness, and ecumenicity.

Postrestructure, the national agencies will continue to seek to meet congregational needs in areas such as curriculum development and production, clergy certification and placement, fund-raising, endowment management, clergy pension fund administration, building loan funds, and so on. The reorganization of the national church, however, is meant in part to enable the ministries to do all this better by creating a national structure that can be more easily understood and accessed by local congregations. One executive summarized the restructure as "honoring the various parts to become a more accessible partner to the other settings of the church, a more coherent and easily understood partner." Another senior executive put it this way: "As we restructure, the prayer is that the national offices will be more effective in relating to the local churches and better assist the associations and conferences by having single points of contact."

Another aspect of this emphasis on congregations is that the postrestructure national agencies, especially the recognized instrumentalities, will in theory have less autonomy than before relative to bodies representing UCC congregations. It is important to note that while national agencies will be reoriented toward conferences/associations and congregations by the restructure, they will continue to pursue the missions unique to their settings. They will now do so, however, with enhanced participation from other settings of the church. Prerestructure, the recognized instrumentalities possessed their own endowments, and they were largely independent and unsupervised by any other unit of the denomination. With the restructure two main changes occurred. First, the General Synod gained increased formal authority over the national ministries, with the Collegium of Officers, for example, elected by the General Synod. We return later to why the recognized instrumentalities gave up their power, financial resources, and autonomy. Second, the financial independence historically exercised by the Big Boards has been replaced by the new covenanted ministries. For the new structure the Board for Homeland Ministries divided up its assets and transferred control of all its endowment to the new Local Church Ministries, Justice and Witness Ministries, and Office of

General Ministries. The Board for World Ministries keeps its endowment in the new form of the Wider Church Ministries, but gives up a portion of its income for the other three new ministries.

Restructure also increased the number of conference representatives present on the boards of directors of the four new ministries. In addition, one staff member in the Office of General Ministries is dedicated to working with conferences, a position that did not exist in the old structure. All of this is meant to increase the accountability of the national ministries to the General Synod, to conferences, and ultimately to congregations. Not coincidentally, the commitment to meaningful involvement of conferences in national activity is evident in the day-to-day practice of national executives as well as in the formal changes brought about by restructure. We asked national executives to tell us whose support would be most helpful to secure if they had an idea for a new programming initiative. About half included conference ministers in their lists.

Is this refocusing of the national units on congregations evident to people at the regional and local settings of the UCC? The picture is mixed. On the one hand, it appears that the conference-setting executives interpret this aspect of restructure in ways consistent with the intentions expressed in official documents and by national executives, and it appears that they do in fact perceive heightened integration between the regional and national settings. Interviews with conference ministers across the country suggest that many of them are aware of the restructure and see in it an effort to emphasize the local church and a relationship of covenant. One conference minister summarized the restructure as not "a top-down but more a bottom-up model . . . the old paradigm is gone." Interestingly, some conference ministers see restructure as primarily a matter of "downsizing" the national setting. This downsizing will mean that responsibility, previously filled by national instrumentalities, for providing some resources and services to congregations will devolve to the conferences, and some expect this shift to result in more vital conferences. One conference minister, responding to the ORW (Organizing Religious Work) regional judicatory leader survey, noted that "as the national church reconfigures and goes through major staff and structure changes, the conferences are assuming a more proactive role and the Council of Conferences is becoming stronger."[10] This general perception is quite widespread among UCC conference ministers: 88 percent of surveyed conference executives replied that the "relative importance of conferences compared to our National Church offices and agencies has increased" over the last five years, while only 12 percent believed it had remained the same.[11]

---

10. Lummis, "Summary of UCC Results from the ORW Regional Judicatory Survey."
11. Lummis, "Summary of UCC Results from the ORW Regional Judicatory Survey."

If those at the regional setting see things in ways consistent with restructuring objectives, the views expressed by clergy in local churches suggest that it will not be easy for national agencies to break through the widespread indifference among UCC congregations to activities of the national office. One clergyperson summarized the feelings of his laity toward the larger denomination by saying, "The people in this congregation are members of the First Congregational Church, UCC. But the UCC is a parenthesis, a tag on, or punctuation mark, a lengthy punctuation mark . . . their self-perception is that they are part of this particular church, not that they are part of a group of Congregational churches which are in association with a greater body called the UCC." This sentiment is fairly typical. A 1985 survey, for example, asked focus groups from 289 UCC congregations, "What does it mean for you/this church to be part of the UCC?" The modal group response (characterizing almost a third of the groups) was "nothing."[12]

Overall, congregational leaders express an alienation that results from two central issues: the regulatory-sounding nature of the General Synod's pronouncements and a perceived lack of congregational attention from other settings of the denomination. Over the last two decades the General Synod has voted on a number of high-profile issues, including approving the ordination of gay or lesbian people into the ministry, passing a resolution that recognizes abortion as a viable option, and proclaiming the UCC to be against welfare reform. These types of regulatory acts, as Russell Richey has noted, come with certain costs for the overall health of the denomination.[13] In each case, although UCC polity is clear that the General Synod pronouncements speak to, not for, other church units, and that they are only for the *consideration* of other units, some clergy perceive these actions as attempts to speak for them and their congregations without their consent. One minister offered just such an explanation for his congregation's feelings of alienation: "When the church synod makes a pronouncement like that it comes across as — local congregation you should agree with us, we're your voice. The local church feels like, you took my voice away."

Of the congregations surveyed for the ORW project, a sizable minority of UCC congregations consider themselves to be more politically and theologically conservative than the General Synod, leading to further alienation. Fur-

12. W. M. Newman, "The Meanings of a Merger: Denominational Identity in the United Church of Christ," in *Beyond Establishment: Protestant Identity in a Post-Protestant Age,* ed. J. W. Carroll and W. Clark Roof (Louisville: Westminster John Knox, 1993), p. 302.

13. Russell Richey, "Denominations and Denominationalism: An American Morphology," in *Reimagining Denominationalism,* ed. Robert B. Mullin and Russell Richey (New York: Oxford University Press, 1994).

ther, some congregational leaders believe that the General Synod's pronouncements are not only too progressive, but also oriented at a global setting that has little relevance for the lives of their laity.[14] One minister expressed his sense as follows: "I think people also associate the denomination with global concerns and they can't relate to that. Other than that the denomination doesn't mean much at all."

An apparent majority of ministers interviewed for this project also proclaim that they have little contact with and receive little support from the other settings of the denomination. One minister noted that "we send ten percent of our income to the conference who once a year sends us a form letter that says thank you. The rest of the year we never see a conference person around here." While the regional setting may be aware of and support the UCC's restructure, congregations appear to have little interest in this or any of the denomination's activities. If the larger goal behind the reemphasis on local congregations is to change the perceptions of denominational usefulness among local congregations, it would appear that severe challenges lie ahead.

A Developing Ecclesiology

The Advisory Commission on Structure concluded that there was "a lack of clarity and common understanding about the nature and purpose of the new denomination."[15] Accordingly, part of the planning for restructure involved the development of a theology of organization — an ecclesiology — for the UCC, and the initial General Synod Committee on Structure commissioned two "study papers," one on mission and another on ecclesiology.

Drawing on these papers, the Committee on Structure concluded that the ecclesiology of the UCC is grounded in two central premises: that the purpose and identity of the UCC is mission — at all settings of the church — and that relationships within the church are based in covenant. The notion that UCC ecclesiology is based on covenant is not new with restructuring. UCC historian Louis Gunnemann, writing in 1979, characterized UCC polity as "a covenanted relationship of autonomous units in church life."[16] Covenant, as expressed in the new article III of the UCC constitution, is defined in the following way: "Each expression of the church has responsibilities and rights in relation to the others, to the end that the whole church will seek God's will and be faithful to

---

14. Ammerman, "Summary of UCC Results from the ORW Congregational Survey."

15. "Advisory Commission on Structure" (report, 1988), p. 32.

16. Louis Gunnemann, "Order and Identity in the United Church of Christ," *New Conversations* 4, no. 2 (fall 1979): 15.

God's mission. Decisions are made in consultation and collaboration among the various parts of the structure. As members of the Body of Christ, each expression of the church is called to honor and respect the work and ministry of each other part. Each expression of the church listens, hears, and carefully considers the advice, counsel, and requests of others."[17]

In a covenantal relationship no party has formal authority over another, but all parties pledge to respectfully and seriously engage and listen to each other. Covenantal decision making is characterized by communication and shared information. One national executive defined a covenant as "wanting to provide as many modes of connection and participation of persons when decisions are being made as possible." This principle is meant to apply not only to relations among national agencies but also to relations between national units, on the one hand, and conferences, associations, and congregations on the other hand. As another executive put it, covenantal relations are meant to generate the awareness that "we are all members of one church."

Several aspects of restructuring can be seen in light of the intention to generate the understanding that UCC organizational structures and relations in all settings of the church are manifestations of covenant. The simplification of national structures as well as the rededication of national ministries to regional and local concerns are part of the attempt to make the national setting of the denomination live out this ecclesiological commitment to covenant. National executives seem more confident, however, that covenantal relations can be fully lived out within and between the national covenanted ministries than they can between the national and the regional or local settings of the church. One national executive noted that "day to day, I think one of the things that's really a part of who I am and what I've [wanted] this office to be, is that we're in relationship with other people in this building, other officers in this building. And that affects what we do, how we do it, decisions we make. And it's always important to be mindful that we're just one part of the whole within this building."

In discussions of relations between the national and the other settings of the denomination, however, more wariness is evident. A general theme among national executives seems to be that the efforts of the national units to live out covenantal organizational relations are not always matched by efforts at the regional or local settings. One executive put it this way: "I think one of the great weaknesses of our church is that . . . there isn't a general understanding of what it means to be covenantal with one another. . . . Many of our churches believe primarily that what covenantal means is that you leave [us] alone and we do

---

17. Constitution and Bylaw Revision Team, "Working Draft #4," p. 2.

what we want." Another executive noted, "I see the national church making changes but I don't see the same kind of change occurring at the other levels." Still another questioned how a restructured denomination would address the discrepancy between stated denominational priorities and the priorities of local churches that in the past have not followed and presumably will not follow denominational pronouncements on issues such as the affirmation of gay and lesbian lifestyles. From the perspective of some national executives, the responsibilities of covenant seem a bit one-way: national organizations are bound by covenant to regional conferences and local congregations, but regional conferences and local congregations are not bound by anything. This basic asymmetry in the meaning of covenant and its implications for ecclesiology are rooted, of course, in the UCC's tradition of regional and congregational autonomy. It is difficult to see how restructure could effect much change in this arena.

A Multiracial and Multicultural Church

A second major goal of the restructure is to move further in the direction of becoming a more diverse church. This goal reaffirms a long-standing aspect of UCC corporate identity, but in new ways that represent significant long-term change in the meaning of "diversity" within the UCC. Since its inception the UCC's motto has been "That they may all be one," and the UCC always has been committed to the ideal of unity amidst diversity. Recent years, however, have seen a change in the meaning of this ideal from one that emphasizes religious diversity to one that emphasizes various social diversities, especially those of race, class, gender, and sexual orientation. Restructure is intended to move the UCC further in the direction of becoming a multiracial and multicultural church.

The UCC has long been engaged with the ecumenical movement, and this engagement has been central to the UCC's history and identity. The denominations that came together to form the UCC, the Congregational Christian Churches and the Evangelical and Reformed Church, worked together in the ecumenical movement long before they merged to form the UCC. The UCC's first "full communion" agreement with the Evangelical Church of England was made over thirty years ago, and the UCC has committed to special partnerships with a number of other denominations across the globe. A continuing commitment to ecumenicity is apparent in a number of recent developments. The UCC is in full partnership with the Christian Church (Disciples of Christ); it has established full communion with the Evangelical Lutheran Church in America, the Presbyterian Church (U.S.A.), and the Reformed

Church of America; and it is involved in approximately thirty partnerships with other denominations in overseas mission work.

Restructure assures continued emphasis on ecumenicity by carrying over into the new structure a staff position titled Assistant to the President for Ecumenical Concerns. Ecumenical work is mandated for each of the four new covenanted ministries, as proposed in the new constitution of the UCC.

We asked each national executive we interviewed to read three theological statements about ecumenism, all drawn from UCC documents:

> We are a church that seeks to portray in its life and witness the unity and koinonia of the Holy Trinity, the Trinity whose diverse persons become an icon for the unity and diversity the ecumenical movement hopes to embody.

> We believe that God gives the Church its unity and, by the Holy Spirit, leads and empowers the Church to manifest that unity.

> The longing for Christian unity is at the core of our identity. We lose it at our peril.

We asked the executives how these themes inform their day-to-day work, if at all, and how they are reflected in restructuring, if at all. The idea was that executives' interpretations of these passages would provide some insight into how they understood ecumenicity as it currently informs national-setting work in the UCC.

Several interesting patterns emerged in the responses to these texts. First, half the national executives explicitly responded only to the first passage — the one that expresses ecumenicity in terms of the union of "diverse persons." Second, there were two distinct types of responses to these texts. On the one hand, executives whose jobs included significant interaction with other religious groups discussed ecumenism in the traditional sense of cooperation among such groups. These executives also expressed some dissatisfaction with what they saw as the relatively low priority given to ecumenism in the restructure. One national executive commented, "I think that ecumenism has gotten the shorter shrift. It's in there, and at times I have said to myself, I think why it has the shorter shrift is [that] it's assumed by many in a way that the multiracial-multicultural is not, hence more attention is needed [to the latter]." Another claimed that "one of the things that restructure has not addressed is the whole issue of ecumenism."

The other executives — the majority — related ecumenism to diversity based on gender, race, class, and/or sexual orientation rather than to diversity based on religious or denominational affiliation, and they did this no matter which of the three texts they were discussing. As one put it, "I look at diversity and talk about the inclusive church in terms of those with different sexual orientation. Those that are physically challenged or handicapped. I think about gender issues. And one issue . . . I feel missing to the unity of the body of Christ and the UCC expression would be the ecumenical poor." Many executives used the same concepts and terms to discuss both the theology of ecumenism and the theology of becoming a multicultural and multiracial church. While these executives considered ecumenism to be important in their day-to-day work, they had in mind an ecumenism different from the traditional ecumenism that cuts across religious divisions. Not coincidentally, the relatively low salience of ecumenism is not unique to the national setting of the UCC. In a 1985 survey that asked focus groups from 289 UCC congregations, "What does it mean for you/this church to be part of the UCC?" only 10 percent listed ecumenism.[18]

This changed meaning of ecumenism within the UCC is part of a larger concern that is very important for this denomination at this time: the commitment to become a "true multiracial and multicultural church." The UCC is officially committed to becoming a church that "confesses and acts out its faith in the one sovereign God who through Jesus Christ binds in covenant faithful people of all races, ethnicities and cultures," one that "embodies these diversities as gifts to the human family and rejoices in the variety of God's grace."[19] This goal predates restructure, but it is built into restructure in several concrete ways.

One way this commitment was manifest even before restructure is in the ethnic diversity evident among national staff. This was often mentioned by national executives. One said, for example, "I think there is an almost constant reminder, because our staffs are so inclusive that we often call each other on either a language or decision or style we don't see to be inclusive." Another noted that "this is one of the few places where you see a real diverse group of people coming in and out to work together and they're anywhere from executives to the mailroom."

Relative to the ethnic composition of the denomination's membership (more than 90 percent white), people of color are indeed very substantially overrepresented among the national-setting staff. One executive estimated that only about half the national staff people are white. This is not just a matter of

18. Newman, "Meanings of a Merger," p. 306.

19. *Calling the UCC to Be a Multiracial and Multicultural Church,* General Synod Pronouncement (Cleveland: United Church of Christ, 1993), p. 1.

filling in the lower ranks of the agencies with minorities. Of the twenty-four senior executives we interviewed, fourteen are European American, six are African American, and four are Hispanic American or Asian American.

The boards of directors of UCC national agencies, elected by the General Synod from nominated ministers and laity, also reflect a serious commitment to diversity. We examined the prerestructure ethnic and racial makeup of the boards of directors for the two Big Boards, and found one-third of the directors to be African American and another third to be Asian American or Hispanic American. To put this in context, consider that a 1996 study of trustees of fifteen types of nonprofits in six U.S. cities found that only 9 percent are African American and only 5 percent are Hispanic American or Asian American.[20]

It also is relevant to note that even though the UCC is 90 percent Anglo, it does not appear that the substantial minority presence among senior executives has been achieved by hiring outsiders directly to senior positions in the national agency structure. The average length of full-time professional service within the UCC is about twenty years for both white and black senior executives. The average for the few Asian American and Hispanic American senior executives is slightly less, but still substantial: twelve to fourteen years of full-time service to the denomination.

Restructure attempts to further the goal of becoming a true multiracial and multicultural church in several concrete ways, all of which significantly enhance minority group representation in the national church. First, the Council for Racial and Ethnic Ministries will have a voting member on each of the boards of directors of the three new ministries that had boards of directors. Second, someone from each of eight "historically underrepresented constituencies" will be on the board of directors for each of the three new ministries that had boards. The eight are the Council for American Indian Ministry, Council for Hispanic Ministries, Ministers for Racial and Social Justice, Pacific Island and Asian American Ministries, United Black Christians, United Church Coalition for Lesbian/Gay Concerns, Committee on Persons with Disabilities, and Council for Youth and Young Adults. Third, "More than half of the members of the Board of Directors of Justice and Witness Ministries" — one of only four national ministries in the new structure — "shall be persons of color and more than half shall be women."[21] Fourth, the new Office of General Ministries will contain "desks" for each of the four "historically underrepresented" ethnic and racial minority constituencies in

20. R. Abzug, "The Evolution of Trusteeship in the United States: A Roundup of Findings from Six Cities," *Nonprofit Management and Leadership* 7, no. 1 (1996): 101-11.
21. *Report on Restructure*, p. G-13.

the UCC: African Americans, Asian Americans, Hispanic Americans, and Native Americans. The first three of these changes are built into the new UCC constitution.

The ongoing effort to become a multiracial and multicultural church extends beyond minority presence in the covenanted ministries and their governance structures. The national ministries also will continue to support the founding of new minority congregations, assist in recruiting minority clergy to the denomination, and conduct diversity briefings in conferences, associations, and congregations. One executive said her main priority is to "work directly with conferences, associations, and local churches as they seek to work for racial justice in their own places. And much of what we do is trying to serve them and to help them to do their work in their own places."

This recently enhanced emphasis on becoming a multiracial and multicultural church seems to have been perceived clearly by regional executives. When a sample of UCC conference ministers was asked whether the denomination has become more or less effective over the past five years in attracting ethnic minority members, almost 60 percent of the UCC regional executives said that effectiveness has increased in this arena. When regional executives in other denominations were asked this question, only about a third (or fewer) responded that their denomination's effectiveness had increased.[22] The pattern was similar when the same question was asked about efforts to attract ethnic minority clergy.

These efforts also seem to have met with positive results at the congregational setting. Ninety-one percent of UCC congregations founded before 1986 are predominantly white, but only 57 percent of post-1986 congregations are predominantly white.[23] There also is some indication that the UCC's reputation as a diversity-embracing denomination is attractive to some unaffiliated minority congregations. One national executive observed that "more and more of the different racial/ethnic/immigrant communities come to us . . . because we are a very open kind of church." The pastor of a predominantly Latino congregation confirms this observation when he recounts why his church joined the UCC: "The UCC told me, 'Our church is like a rainbow. A rainbow has different colors. If you become a part of us, you don't have to be like us. You add your own color to our denomination.'" He concludes, "That really impressed me. I've never seen that in working with other denominations."

Minority congregations in the UCC also are growing at a faster rate than are the denomination's European American congregations. Only 15 percent of

---

22. Lummis, "Summary of UCC Results from the ORW Regional Judiciary Survey."
23. *State of the UCC* (Cleveland: United Church of Christ, 1997), p. 72.

the latter have grown by 10 percent or more from 1991 to 1996, compared to over 25 percent of the former. In all, European American membership in the UCC has declined by almost 15 percent in the last decade, while racial and ethnic minority membership grew by 10 percent.[24] Thus, in both rates of founding and growth, ethnic and racial minority congregations are outpacing European American congregations.

Still, some on the national staff are skeptical about the likelihood of many congregations becoming multiracial and multicultural. One national executive stated, "I think we've come a long way [regarding diversity] in the national setting, but in the conference settings and in the local church settings, I've become painfully aware, it's not so." And another executive summarized: "There are, however, times when we find ourselves in a different place than a local church or a conference or association about racial justice and those have tended to be times of tension in the life of the church, where we've had to be prophetic in particular areas." Such pessimism is not baseless. Despite the increased number of congregations that are composed of ethnic minorities, the vast majority of UCC congregations are ethnically homogeneous, and the vast majority remain homogeneously European American. Churches where the largest racial/ethnic group is non-Hispanic white represent 90.8 percent of UCC congregations, followed by African American churches (4.7 percent), Asian/Pacific Islander churches (2.8 percent), and Native American/Other churches (0.4 percent).[25] Even if the trend toward more predominantly minority UCC congregations continues, it appears that it will be much more difficult to create diverse congregations than to create diverse national staffs or a diverse General Synod.

Explaining Restructure

Why is the UCC restructuring at this time, and why does the restructure take the form it does? Five factors seem to be driving the restructure.

First, national-setting reorganization can be seen as the late-in-coming culmination of the 1957 merger that created the UCC. Unlike most mergers between Protestant denominations, the UCC merger joined two disparate traditions and organizational structures. It merged two denominations with different social compositions, with the Congregational Churches being composed primarily of long-settled Americans and the Evangelical and Reformed Church made up of

24. *State of the UCC*, p. 73.
25. *State of the UCC*, p. 71.

more recently immigrated German and Swiss populations.[26] The two denominations also possessed different polities, congregational versus presbyterian.[27] The Congregational Churches had devised a church government in which each church was autonomous from other denominational settings. In contrast, the Evangelical and Reformed Church had a connectional polity system.

As a result of these differences, important issues of organizational coordination were left to be resolved until after the merger. This view is expressed in historical accounts of the merger,[28] and it continues to inform both official and informal discourse about organizational issues in this denomination. The Advisory Commission on Structure, for example, concluded to the 1993 General Synod that "the present structure is a result of the compromises reached for the merger."[29] One regional executive recalled that "when we were formed in 1957, they decided it was more important that we come together and work together than to figure out how two structures would work together," and a national executive explained that "this is the first restructuring, because when the UCC came into being, we weren't able to organically merge things, the politics weren't right for it, we had to be forty-five-years-old before we could do this." In short, the politics of the 1957 merger were such that a governance structure that clearly delineates a division of responsibilities, tasks, and authority among the national units was never established. Further indication of the long-standing organizational issues left unresolved by the original merger is that the current restructure represents the third time the UCC has attempted to reorganize the national setting. Both previous attempts occurred in the 1960s. The first call for reorganization, by a General Synod–appointed Committee on Structure in 1967, was defeated by the organized resistance of the Big Boards. The second attempt, two years later, resulted in the establishment of a new instrumentality, the Office for Church Life and Leadership.

The national organizational scene being further complicated over the years by the ad hoc and unsystematic addition of new national instrumentalities was a second factor driving restructure. As new voices and issues rose to prominence within the UCC, offices representing these identities or addressing these issues were added on to the existing structure, resulting in a multiplication of agencies, greater organizational complexity, and increased demand on

26. Louis Gunnemann, *The Shaping of the United Church of Christ* (New York: United Church Press, 1977).

27. See this volume's three pieces on the Reformed Church in America for an elaboration of the difference between congregational and presbyterian polity.

28. Gunnemann, *The Shaping of the United Church of Christ*.

29. *Report of the General Synod Committee on Structure to the Nineteenth General Synod* (Cleveland: United Church of Christ, 1993), p. 6.

resources available to the national structure as a whole. These offices included the Commission on Racial Justice and the Council for Racial and Ethnic Ministries. This process culminated with the formation of the Coordinating Center for Women in 1987, after which discussions about restructure began. Thus, the fact that the merger left the details of rational organizational consolidation and design for "later," combined with unplanned and unsystematic growth at the national setting, generated a chronic set of perceived organizational inefficiencies. This accounts, in part, for why restructure occurred, and for why it took the form of rationalizing and simplifying functions and offices.

These long-term factors do not explain, however, why restructure occurred when it did. Why did it take forty years from the time of the merger for these underlying structural problems to be addressed? Two additional factors, working in concert, seem particularly relevant. The first is the severely unequal resource bases among national units. The two recognized instrumentalities had charters that predated the denomination, and they had their own endowments and constituencies that gave them a measure of wealth and independence. This financial autonomy was not enjoyed by the other national instrumentalities and the executive offices established by the General Synod and wholly dependent on whatever financial support came to them from the mission benevolence giving of local UCC congregations. Of the $13.9 million received by the United Church Board for World Ministries in 1996, less than half — $5.3 million — came from congregations. Even more strikingly, less than 5 percent of the 1996 income for the United Church Board for Homeland Ministries came from congregational donations; the rest — more than $30 million — came from other gifts, publications, and endowment income. In contrast, the 1996 income of each established instrumentality was, on average, $692,472, virtually all of which came from congregational donations. This amount constitutes approximately 2 percent of the total income of the United Church Board for Homeland Ministries, creating vast financial disparities between the various national instrumentalities of the UCC. The Big Boards not only had more resources than the other units; they were far less dependent on congregations for those resources. Furthermore, the salary scales for people doing comparable kinds of work were noticeably different within the Big Boards than within the rest of the national instrumentality staff.

This inequality among the national units was, perhaps, less stressful on the national structure as a whole as long as significant sums continued to come from congregations to support the unendowed instrumentalities. A very important impetus behind restructure, then, is the dramatic decline in monetary resources coming to the national organizations from the congregations. In 1969, $10.1 million was given by congregations to support the national structure. In 1969 dollars, 1996 annual basic support from congregations to the national structure, not including special collections, was $2.6 million.[30] In real terms, the national agencies of the denomination receive today from congregations only about 25 percent of what they received in 1967. In part, this diminution of funds results from the changed flow of resources through regional conferences. Within the UCC, congregations' donations are immediately sent to conferences, which retain a portion before sending the rest on to national structures. Over the past decade, as reported by one national executive, the proportion of congregations' donations kept by the conferences has increased from approximately 40 percent to approximately 60 percent, resulting in less money for the national setting of the UCC. (This reallocation of resources from national to regional settings apparently is present in other denominations as well.)[31]

It seems plausible to suggest, then, that the monetary dependence of the national instrumentalities — except for the Big Boards — on congregations, coupled with substantially declining support from this source, generated increasing political support among the national leadership for a restructure that reduces the resource dependency of the national organizations on congregations. It is not surprising, in this context, that the privileged position of the Big Boards would seem increasingly unjustifiable, and that an ecclesiology of covenant — including the notion that all denominational organizational manifestations ought to be equal — would emerge. Similarly, it is not surprising in this context of dramatically declining contributions from congregations that restructure would emphasize more than ever before the ways the national organizations can better serve the needs of congregations.

Membership loss is a fifth factor playing a role in UCC restructure. Obviously related to declining resources coming from congregations is the fact that, from a high in the mid-1960s of just over two million members, the UCC had by the time of restructure lost over a third of its members.[32] At the same time, the growing minority populations in the United States have not gone unnoticed. As one denominational handbook notes, "by the year 2050, people of color — Native Americans, Asian Americans, Pacific Islanders, Hispanic Americans, African Americans — will be approximately fifty percent of the U.S. population."[33] The UCC 1997 annual report explicitly connects membership loss with the new emphasis on becoming a multiracial and multicultural church. In

30. *Annual Report of the UCC* (New York: United Church of Christ, 1970); *Annual Report,* 1997.

31. Richey, "Denominations and Denominationalism," p. 89.

32. *State of the UCC,* pp. 17-18.

33. *Case Studies in Becoming a Multiracial and Multicultural Church* (Cleveland: United Church of Christ, 1996).

that report the UCC Board for Homeland Ministries stated that its work "is particularly challenging in a time when traditionally mainline denominations continue to experience membership declines."[34] It immediately continues by saying that the UCC's commitment to becoming a multiracial and multicultural church resulted in a "strategy of new church development among different racial and ethnic communities." The commitment to multiculturalism and multiracialism, then, in part represents a response to membership loss and a strategy for growth in the face of perceived demographic change.

More generally, the UCC's commitment to multiracialism and multiculturalism is intended to position the denomination in a new and changing world. This sentiment was voiced by one national executive who said, "[Restructuring] is meant to be a more faithful expression of the UCC for the twenty-first century. It's trying to address what we think the church ought to do in the twenty-first century." Another pointed out that "the very basic purpose of restructuring is to seek to more faithfully embody God's mission in an emerging new time."

Conclusion

We have described UCC restructure, focusing on two major goals of that restructure and noting five factors that seem important underlying causes of it. Rather than recapitulate this material, we conclude with five additional observations about national-setting organization in the UCC.

First, it is striking that two of the national agencies — the Pension Boards United Church of Christ and the United Church Foundation — remain largely outside the more unified national structure created by this organizational change. There was discussion about whether or not to bring these two agencies under the General Synod umbrella, but this did not come to pass. We think it is worth asking: Why not? Although we have no evidence to draw on here, we venture the speculative hypothesis that national agencies operating in solidly institutionalized secular arenas will be better able to maintain autonomy from other denominational units and will be less vulnerable to efforts aimed at simplifying or rationalizing national structures. The management of pension funds and endowments entails technologies and standards that are well institutionalized in the secular world, and conformity to these technologies and standards is enforced both by regulatory authorities and by legal, accounting, and financial professionals who do the core work of these instrumentalities. We think the

34. *Annual Report, 1997.*

deeper embeddedness of these organizations in secular institutional fields — deeper than any of the other national UCC instrumentalities — accounts for their relative immunity from restructuring agendas. There is an irony here. If one major goal of restructuring has been to rein in national units perceived to have been too autonomous from the rest of the denomination, it is striking that the two agencies that are probably the most autonomous are also the two that remain largely untouched by restructuring. This line of thinking implies that the available options for national denominational organization will, in general, be strongly influenced not just by characteristics internal to the denomination, but also by characteristics of the institutional fields within which the various denominational units operate.

Second, it is interesting to note that the UCC's new form of commitment to diversity is of a piece with recent developments in the corporate world. The professional management literature of the 1990s pays substantially more attention to diversity than did the literature of the 1980s, and today it is relatively common for corporations to endorse diversity in their mission statements, provide diversity training for employees, and develop diversity "action plans."[35] Even the explicit attention within the UCC to growth through appeal to minority groups seems similar to corporations that promote developing a more diverse workforce as good business strategy. This corporate logic, as adopted by the UCC, appears to have altered the denomination's historic equation of diversity with justice. Diversity is now pursued not only because it is just but also because it is good organizational strategy. We suggest that denominational organizing or reorganizing often will incorporate prevailing norms and models from the business world, and the study of how religious work is organized ought to focus in part on the perhaps unintentional ways in which religious organizations mimic corporate models of organization.

Third, although we have not systematically assessed the strength of the connections among the three main structural expressions of the UCC — congregations, regional conferences, and national ministries — it seems to us that UCC conferences are fairly closely tied to the national organizations. It also seems that, although the ability of conference offices to maintain a presence with congregations often is constrained by conferences' limited (and often declining) budgets and staffs, congregations are more strongly connected to conferences than to the national agencies. This pattern suggests that denominational organizations, and perhaps federalist structures more generally, are

---

35. Lauren B. Edelman, Sally Riggs Fuller, and Iona Mara-Drita, "Legal Environments and Managerial Rhetorics: The Construction of Diversity in the Post Civil Rights Era" (School of Law, University of California–Berkeley, 1999).

characterized by what we might call the intransitivity of connectedness. That is, it seems that one can have a national setting that is fairly well connected to the regional setting, and a regional setting that is fairly well connected to the local setting, but this does not mean that the national setting will be well connected to the local setting. If this intransitivity holds, then strengthening connections between the national and the regional settings of denomination organization may not have any effect at all on connections between congregations and the national denomination. The complex connections among local, regional, and national units of denominations warrant more attention.

Fourth, UCC restructuring, to an unprecedented extent within this denomination, has placed real organizational power in the hands of historically underrepresented groups. We wonder what effects, if any, this aspect of restructure will have on identity politics within the UCC. Will new groups or identities emerge to challenge the constitutional privileges granted to the eight historically underrepresented groups? If that occurs, how will those privileged by restructure respond? More generally, will those traditionally on the outside become the entrenched powers and conservative defenders of the organizational status quo? Will promoting diversity come to be associated with defending, rather than challenging, current organizational practices? It will be interesting to see if the UCC's institutionalization of its commitment to becoming a multiracial and multicultural church has unintended consequences for intradenominational politics.

Fifth, UCC restructure should be understood in part as an expression of loyalty to and confidence in the UCC as a collective identity. Recall that UCC restructure could not have occurred without the cooperation of the Big Boards; indeed, it was opposition from those boards that effectively prevented earlier efforts at restructuring. We have argued that declining resources coming to the national setting from congregations enhanced the inequality between the Big Boards and the other national units, and that this altered the political dynamics in the whole church in ways that made restructure more attractive, but it seems unlikely that this is the whole story. In a sense, the central fact about UCC restructuring is that two more or less autonomous and healthy organizations gave up a considerable degree of autonomy and control over their resources and transformed themselves into subordinate units of a new organization. According to historical and personal accounts of this transition, the heads of both of the recognized instrumentalities voluntarily led their agencies into closer union with the rest of the denomination. Neither of the Big Boards had to do this for any compelling pragmatic reasons, and we close this case study by suggesting that this action should be understood, in part, as an expression of the continuing significance of denominational identity at the national setting.

Denominational identities may be of declining significance in some senses and in some contexts, but UCC collective identity apparently continues to be strong among those most actively involved with the denomination's national organizations. Perhaps it is more generally true that, at this juncture, the primary carriers of denominational identities are the staff, trustees, and other individuals directly associated with national-level denominational organizations. From this perspective, part of the religious work conducted at the national setting is the maintenance of denominational identity itself.

References

Abzug, R. 1996. "The Evolution of Trusteeship in the United States: A Roundup of Findings from Six Cities." *Nonprofit Management and Leadership* 7.1 (1996): 101-11.

"Advisory Commission on Structure." Report. 1988.

Annual Report of the UCC. New York: United Church of Christ, 1970.

Annual Report of the UCC. Cleveland: United Church of Christ, 1997.

Calling the UCC to Be a Multiracial and Multicultural Church. General Synod Pronouncement. Cleveland: United Church of Christ, 1993.

Case Studies in Becoming a Multiracial and Multicultural Church. Cleveland: United Church of Christ, 1996.

Constitution and Bylaw Revision Team. "Working Draft #4 of Revised Constitution and Bylaws of the United Church of Christ." February 6, 1997, memo.

Constitution and Bylaws of the United Church of Christ. Cleveland: Executive Council for the United Church of Christ, 1997.

"Draft of Revised Constitution and Bylaws of the United Church of Christ." Report. 1996.

Edelman, Lauren B., Sally Riggs Fuller, and Iona Mara-Drita. "Legal Environments and Managerial Rhetorics: The Construction of Diversity in the Post Civil Rights Era." School of Law, University of California–Berkeley, 1999.

General Synod Committee on Structure Report. Cleveland: United Church of Christ, 1995.

Gunnemann, Louis. *The Shaping of the United Church of Christ.* New York: United Church Press, 1977.

———. "Order and Identity in the United Church of Christ." *New Conversations* 4, no. 2 (fall 1979).

———. *United and Uniting.* New York: United Church Press, 1987.

Missio Dei: The Report of the General Synod Committee on Structure to the Nineteenth General Synod. Cleveland: United Church of Christ, 1993.

Newman, W. M. "The Meanings of a Merger: Denominational Identity in the United Church of Christ." In *Beyond Establishment: Protestant Identity in a Post-Protestant Age,* edited by J. W. Carroll and W. Clark Roof. Louisville: Westminster John Knox, 1993.

Report of the General Synod Committee on Structure to the Eighteenth General Synod. Cleveland: United Church of Christ, 1991.

Report of the General Synod Committee on Structure to the Nineteenth General Synod. Cleveland: United Church of Christ, 1993.

Report on Restructure to the Twenty-First General Synod of the United Church of Christ. Cleveland: United Church of Christ, 1997.

Richey, Russell. "Denominations and Denominationalism: An American Morphology." In *Reimagining Denominationalism,* edited by Robert B. Mullin and Russell Richey. New York: Oxford University Press, 1994.

Shinn, R. Personal correspondence with authors, 1999.

State of the UCC. Cleveland: United Church of Christ, 1997.

UCC Constitution and Bylaws. Cleveland: United Church of Christ, 1997.

Zikmund, Barbara Brown, ed. *Hidden Histories.* Vol. 1. New York: United Church Press, 1984.

———. *Hidden Histories.* Vol. 2. New York: United Church Press, 1987.

Faith and Organization in the United Church of Christ

Roger L. Shinn

W hat is the relation between the faith of the United Church of Christ (UCC) and its changing organizational structures? When does organization make faith effective in the world, and when does it smother or distort faith? Why is the UCC now modifying its structure? This essay, relying on the Zikmund historical introduction (pp. 458-65) and the Barman/Chaves sociological case study (pp. 466-92), explores the theological meanings of the reorganization now taking place. This present look into the relations between faith and organization in the UCC is an invitation to this whole church to participate in a continuing venture.

Five Assumptions

My focus is on the UCC today — on this specific fragment of the universal church at this particular time. However, none of us looks at our own time with eyes innocent of past experience. I begin, therefore, with five assumptions that have come out of centuries of experience. Such assumptions do not take the place of empirical investigations of fresh evidence, but they can help us to understand and interpret current evidence.

♦ **Christian faith generates community, and community requires organization.**
From the New Testament onward, Christian faith has constantly created community, and community has then generated organization. Intimate communities have slight formal structures. The family does not need a written constitution and bylaws, but it develops role distinctions, patterns of mutual

493

responsibility and authority, habits of living together and using money. Larger communities need more elaborate organization. Although the church through most of its centuries lived without *Robert's Rules of Order* or checking accounts in banks, it had organizational structures. The arguments between Peter and Paul, recorded in the New Testament, are both theological and organizational. The church from its beginning was organizing religious work.

♦ **When faith generates organization, organization then reinforces or distorts faith.**
Ideally, the organization expresses the faith. Organizations quickly exhibit their own dynamics and survival impulses, however. The popular suspicion of "organized religion" shows that there may be friction between faith and organization. As William James put it, "the spirit of politics and lust of dogmatic rule" are "apt . . . to contaminate the original impulse."[1] The budgetary processes of churches, for example, are never based solely on the Sermon on the Mount.

♦ **Christian faith historically has worked itself out in many forms of organization.**
Think of the diverse locations of authority. There are the papacy, Orthodox *sobornost*, "scripture and right reason" (Martin Luther), the Quaker common mind, biblical fundamentalism, Pentecostal inspiration by the Holy Spirit, democratic structures, and personal conscience. Advocates of each of these appeal to the gospel for its grounding, but others challenge that claim because the New Testament itself shows diversity. In addition, changing times bring new opportunities and new temptations. The New Testament says nothing about pension funds and Web sites. For better or worse, church organizations are products of human ingenuity.

♦ **Constant partners of all churches are the cultures that surround and infuse Christian communities.**
Churches are shaped by culture, usually more than they realize. Language, as an example, is a product of culture, carrying its own weight of meanings. Throughout Christian history many cultures influenced the church. Some obvious cases are the Roman Empire, feudalism, European nationalism, racial arrogance and prejudice, the Enlightenment and the rise of democracy, the industrial revolution and the rise of capitalism and socialism, imperialism and liberation movements, the impulse to indigenize the church in many societies,

---

1. William James, *The Varieties of Religious Experience: A Study in Human Nature* (New York: Longmans, Green, and Co., 1902), p. 335.

and contemporary globalization. Culture gives churches new opportunities, and it can enslave them.

♦ **A continuous process in religious communities is "the routinization of charisma."**
The term is modern, invented by the eminent German sociologist Max Weber (1864-1920), but the process is as old as human society. It operates in all religions. The Christian church begins as an innovative, freshening movement initiated by Jesus of Nazareth, who both draws strength from and challenges a tradition. Charisma — the initial enthusiasm, spontaneity, and Pentecostal fervor — marks its first generation. Then quickly the church begins to routinize its practices. Charisma, if not routinized, dissolves or gets lost in the second and third (maybe even the first) generation. However, routinization can also stifle the innovative power of charisma. Church organization and reorganization is a constant process of routinization, frequently challenged by attempts to recover the original charisma.

Theological Unity and Diversity in the UCC

The theology of a church is a consensual theology from which its members, with all their diversities, find guidance or deviate. To discover the theology of a church — local, denominational, national, ethnic, or ecumenical — is a perplexing task. There are varieties of theology within every church, as there are in the New Testament. The formal theology of a church, as of an individual, may differ from the implicit theology of its worship, its hymnody, its organizational structures, its processes of decision making, and perhaps especially its budget. All these express the beliefs of the people. The implicit theology is likely to be more powerful than the formal theology.

In 1949 the Evangelical and Reformed Church and the Congregational Christian Churches adopted a *Basis of Union* that guided their formation of the UCC and still reverberates in its life. That agreement included this statement: "The faith which unites us and to which we bear witness is that faith in God which the Scriptures of the Old and New Testaments set forth, which the ancient Church expressed in the ecumenical creeds, to which our own spiritual fathers gave utterance in the evangelical confessions of the Reformation, and which we are in duty bound to express in the words of our time as God Himself gives us light."[2]

2. Louis H. Gunnemann, *The Shaping of the United Church of Christ: An Essay in the History of American Christianity* (New York: United Church Press, 1977). See pp. 207-25 for the complete text of the *Basis of Union*.

The *Basis of Union* called for the preparation of a Statement of Faith, to be "regarded as a testimony, and not a test, of faith." That statement was adopted by the Second General Synod in 1959, even before the enactment of a constitution in 1961. It has since been twice revised, without any change in its structure, in order to achieve a gender-neutral language. The most recent version follows:

> We believe in you, O God, Eternal Spirit, God of our Savior Jesus Christ and our God, and to your deeds we testify:
>
> You call the worlds into being, create persons in your own image, and set before each one the ways of life and death.
>
> You seek in holy love to save all people from aimlessness and sin.
>
> You judge people and nations by your righteous will declared through prophets and apostles.
>
> In Jesus Christ, the man of Nazareth, our crucified and risen Savior, you have come to us and shared our common lot, conquering sin and death and reconciling the world to yourself.
>
> You bestow upon us your Holy Spirit, creating and renewing the church of Jesus Christ, binding in covenant faithful people of all ages, tongues, and races.
>
> You call us into your church to accept the cost and joy of discipleship, to be your servants in the service of others, to proclaim the gospel to all the world and resist the powers of evil, to share in Christ's baptism and eat at his table, to join him in his passion and victory.
>
> You promise to all who trust you forgiveness of sins and fullness of grace, courage in the struggle for justice and peace, your presence in trial and rejoicing, and eternal life in your realm which has no end.
>
> Blessing and honor, glory and power be unto you. Amen.[3]

The Statement of Faith evokes clashing responses. Robert S. Paul has said, "[T]he thrust of that biblical faith was beautifully expressed in what is still the best and briefest of all twentieth-century creedal statements, our own Statement of Faith." Thomas C. Reeves disagrees: "Written in unisex language, it omitted the historic triadic form of the Trinity, skimmed over traditional doctrinal matters, eliminated many references to miraculous events in the Bible accounts, and rejected the exclusiveness of Christian truth."[4]

---

3. This is the revision of 1981, affirmed by the Fourteenth General Synod. For all three versions, see the UCC Web site: www.ucc.org/faith/faith.htm.

4. Robert S. Paul, *Freedom with Order: The Doctrine of the Church in the United Church of Christ* (New York: United Church Press, 1987), p. 51; Thomas C. Reeves, *The Empty Church: The Suicide of Liberal Christianity* (New York: Free Press, 1996), p. 177.

From its beginning, the UCC has recognized a responsibility both to its heritage and to new opportunities. Its declared faith is the faith "set forth" in the Scriptures and expressed in traditional creeds and confessions, but which we "are in duty bound to express in the words of our time as God Himself gives us light." The Bible is basic to the faith, but there is no hint of "verbal inspiration" or "inerrancy." Traditional creeds "express" the faith, but contemporary testimony is not only permitted — it is a "duty." Our contemporary testimonies, like those of the past, are not final. Future generations will recognize their duties to express the faith "set forth in Scriptures" in the words of their time.

On the official UCC Web site under the link "Faith" is found the following introductory statement:

> The United Church of Christ embraces a theological heritage that affirms the Bible as the authoritative witness to the Word of God, the creeds of the ecumenical councils, the confessions of the Reformation. The UCC has roots in the "covenantal" tradition — meaning there is no centralized authority or hierarchy that can impose any doctrine or form of worship on its members. Christ alone is Head of the church. We seek a balance between freedom of conscience and accountability to the apostolic faith. The UCC therefore receives the historic creeds and confessions of our ancestors as testimonies, but not tests of the faith.[5]

Linked to this introduction are the texts (usually complete, sometimes abridged) of sixteen documents. These include three excerpts from New Testament epistles (all expressing "high Christologies"), the Apostles' Creed and the Nicene Creed, documents of the Protestant Reformation and later history, the Barmen Declaration, and recent declarations of the UCC.

These statements appear to point to an intensely theological church with deep roots in tradition, yet alert to the contemporary world. The introductory statement itself is entitled with that characteristic phrase, "Testimonies, but not tests of the faith," and appears under the main heading "Testimonies of the Faith." All of this is clear evidence that none are regarded as definitive, final declarations. They embody a calculated ambiguity, rising out of the "balance between freedom of conscience and accountability to the apostolic faith," as stated in the preface to them all. The UCC chooses to live with that deliberate ambiguity rather than presume to solve it by grasping one pole of the ambiguity, either a final definition of doctrine or a looser, rootless faith. The continuing struggle with those problems, with all its exhilaration and perplexity, affects the current reorganization of this church.

5. See www.ucc.org/faith/index.html.

Roger L. Shinn

There is a further irony in the theological situation of the UCC. Although the Web site represents a church of deep theological concern, former UCC president Avery Post wrote in 1987 of the "apparent theological dormancy" and of "an ecclesiological deficit" in the UCC.[6] Initially the UCC had a Theological Commission, but it disappeared early. In 1998 the theological seminaries of the UCC, concerned about the neglect of theology, initiated the semiannual journal *Prism: A Theological Forum for the United Church of Christ.* The irony deepens with the realization that during its formative years, the membership of the UCC included three theologians who belong on almost any shortlist of the most eminent of their time: Reinhold Niebuhr, H. Richard Niebuhr, and Paul Tillich. How can we account for this gap between theological intensity and dormancy? One reason is that the church's polity, with its great emphasis on congregational freedom, can lead inadvertently to a neglect of theology. Another reason is that the implicit theology that guides decisions sometimes differs from the declared theology.

The Two Big Issues in the Current Reorganization

The UCC is now completing major organizational changes. As the Zikmund introduction and Barman/Chaves case study have shown, these fall into two groups: problems inherent in the original constitution, and revised concepts of Christian mission in response to historical challenges during the over forty years of the UCC.

Problems in Constitutional Structures

The initial constitution sought to enact a "balance between freedom of conscience and accountability to the apostolic faith," to quote the official denominational Web site. One outcome is the distribution of responsibilities and powers between the UCC, nationally and ecumenically, and the local churches. Here theology and polity interact.

For any Christian church the ultimate authority is divine. This does not mean that a "big boss in the sky" simply dictates doctrines and commands. It means that the Creator has built into the creation characteristics that human caprice cannot neglect. Truth and morality are not merely our preferences. In scriptural terms, Christ taught with authority (Mark 1:22 and Matt. 7:29) and acted with authority (Luke 20:1-8).

6. Avery D. Post, foreword to *Freedom with Order,* by Robert S. Paul, pp. v-vi.

Then the arguments begin. Some churches see authority flowing from God through a hierarchy reaching down to the people. Others, notably the UCC, understand God to reach out to God's people, who respond by choosing officials to lead, organize, and perhaps correct the activities of the people. Neither of these models is an unalloyed system. The most hierarchical church sometimes hears voices of unaccredited prophets. The most democratic church expects leaders to call it to faithfulness and new opportunities. The constitution of the UCC shows a concern for the balance of freedom and fidelity to apostolic faith. An ironic reader might observe that the constitution follows the maxim, sometimes attributed to Yogi Berra but probably older: "When you come to a fork in the road, take it."

The preamble to the constitution declares:

> The United Church of Christ acknowledges as its sole Head, Jesus Christ, Son of God and Savior. It acknowledges as kindred in Christ all who share in this confession. It looks to the Word of God in the Scriptures, and to the presence and power of the Holy Spirit, to prosper its creative and redemptive work in the world. It claims as its own the faith of the historic Church expressed in the ancient creeds and reclaimed in the basic insights of the Protestant Reformers. It affirms the responsibility of the Church in each generation to make this faith its own in reality of worship, in honesty of thought and expression, and in purity of heart before God. In accordance with the teaching of our Lord and the practice prevailing among evangelical Christians, it recognizes two sacraments: Baptism and the Lord's Supper or Holy Communion.[7]

That paragraph roots the UCC firmly in Christian tradition. It is not a naive faith in *vox populi, vox Dei,* but it surely is not a reliance on human hierarchies. The next paragraph of the preamble refers to "the free and voluntary relationships which the Local Churches, Associations, Conference and ministers sustain with the General Synod and with each other."

Lurking in the preamble are problems that emerge throughout the constitution. A tangled history complicated the problems. A long (1949-53) and tortuous legal action sought to block the formation of the UCC on the grounds that it interfered with the autonomy of local congregations in the Congregational Christian Churches. The challenge was eventually rejected by the court, but it led to a dogmatic formulation of the rights of congregations. The consti-

---

7. All citations of the constitution are from the amended edition of 1999, available on the UCC Web site. The wording is identical with the original edition of 1961, but the articles and sections have been renumbered.

tution (art. V, sec. 10) defines the local church in terms consistent with the preamble: "A Local Church is composed of persons who, believing in God as heavenly Father, and accepting Jesus Christ as Lord and Savior, and depending on the guidance of the Holy Spirit, are organized for Christian worship, for the furtherance of Christian fellowship, and for the ongoing work of Christian witness." However, a later paragraph (art. V, sec. 18) says in sterner, legal language:

> The autonomy of the Local Church is inherent and modifiable only by its own action. Nothing in this Constitution and the Bylaws of the United Church of Christ shall destroy or limit the right of each Local Church to continue to operate in the way customary to it; nor shall it be construed as giving to the General Synod, or to any Conference or Association now, or at any future time the power to abridge or impair the autonomy of any Local Church in the management of its own affairs, which affairs include, but are not limited to, the right to retain or adopt its own methods of organization, worship and education; to regain or secure its own charter and name; to adopt its own constitution and bylaws; to formulate its own covenants and confessions of faith; to admit members in its own way and to provide for their discipline or dismissal; to call or dismiss its pastor or pastors by such procedure as it shall determine; to acquire, own, manage and dispose of property and funds; to control its own benevolences; and to withdraw by its own decision from the United Church of Christ at any time without forfeiture of control of any real or personal property owned by it.

Christians who distinguish sources within the Bible sometimes try similar source criticism on the constitution. They guess that section 10 was written by theologians and section 18 by lawyers. Theologians, with an eye to eternity, hesitate to prescribe for "any future time." Lawyers may do that. The legalistic language of section 18 is followed by the moralistic section 19: "Action by, or decisions or advice emanating from, the General Synod, a Conference or an Association, should be held in the highest regard by every local church." The prohibitions are enforceable; the softer moral advice ("should be") is not.

One early and frequent hope was that the UCC might be "a united and a uniting" church. The logo of the UCC with its biblical slogan, "That they may all be one," expresses a yearning for Christian unity. However, ecumenical conversations show suspicions that section 18 may prevent inclusion of the UCC in any larger union. In the negotiations that recently led to mutual recognition of ministries among several denominations (see the Zikmund introduction), there was apprehension that the UCC was excluding itself by its constitution. Some asked, "Can a church with such sweeping congregational autonomy give any assurance that it is a 'Christian' church?" Nonetheless, the conversations continued with sufficient trust that the UCC squeaked in on the new agreements.

The current organizational changes rely on the words "covenant" and "covenanted ministries" to describe the mutual relations within the UCC. Simultaneously, several other denominations included in this study, with no evidence of collusion, are using those terms. In its biblical history, covenant involves fidelity and moral responsibilities far beyond any that are enforceable in human courts.[8] It is especially significant for the UCC, which values it as an alternative to creedal requirements or rigid definitions of "apostolic succession."

Thus major organizational problems of the UCC follow from the relation between a theology of covenant and a polity of congregational autonomy. Other issues also appear in the merging of the structures of the uniting denominations. Any joining of elaborate organizations jeopardizes old bureaucracies. Competition over prestige and turf leads to wins, losses, and compromises. This is a truism in corporate mergers, openly discussed in the business pages of newspapers. In churches the situation is both better and worse. Church leaders do not flaunt their ambitions and jealousies as they defend their interests. They declare higher goals than profit and power. They pledge to subordinate their own good to a larger good. Yet precisely because of that commitment, they may overlook the mixed human motives that lurk in all communities. They may identify their responsibilities and powers with the good of the church while their rivals do the same.

Thus the constitution led to a kind of caste system, as the Zikmund introduction and Barman/Chaves case study have shown. Ironically this anti-hierarchical church developed a hierarchy (although that offensive term was never used) of three levels: "recognized" instrumentalities that had long prior histories and substantial financial endowments (principally the Board for Homeland Ministries and the Board for World Ministries, often called the "Big Boards"), "established" instrumentalities dependent on the budget adopted by the General Synod, and lesser "bodies" which might be commissions, committees, or offices. Thus the constitution became an invitation to competition and empire building.[9]

---

8. See William A. Hulteen, Jr., "United Church of Christ Covenantal Polity," *Prism: A Theological Forum for the United Church of Christ* 12, no. 2 (fall 1997): 43-53; Yorke Peeler, "Some Thoughts on Covenant and the United Church of Christ," *Prism* 14, no. 1 (spring 1999): 95-102.

9. For the sake of full disclosure, I should state that I was the first president of the United Church Board for Homeland Ministries — not a full-time paid job. The chief executive officer was the innovative and forceful executive vice president, Truman Douglass. Personal experience inevitably covers these paragraphs, but the data in them are verifiable from publicly available sources, including minutes of the General Synods.

The Big Boards, under imaginative and energetic leadership from their executive vice presidents, were often ahead of their times, initiating progressive policies that the General Synod later adopted. They were also jealous of their powers, resisting attempts of General Synods to direct them. Over the years, as the Barman/Chaves case study has shown, financial stringency meant that the budgets of the Big Boards relied increasingly on their own endowments, a fact that provoked resentment from other agencies that were entirely dependent financially on the General Synod.

In this complex picture, the presidency of the UCC was a constitutionally weak office. One reason was theological resistance to location of authority in any person. A less theological reason was the political negotiations in which the Big Boards defended their powers. Competent presidents through their personal gifts exercised considerable influence, but only by persuasion, not by constitutional authority. Veterans of the process understood this. So did successive presidents, sometimes to their near despair. Delegates to the General Synod often learned, to their surprise, that the president they elected actually had little constitutional power.

Over the years there were attempts, usually ineffective, to meet these constitutional problems. The current changes are more far-reaching than any proposed in the past. It is easy to see their intention, harder to predict their results.

Responses to Changing Historical Challenges

From its beginning, the UCC sought to respond to historical challenges. Often identified in the public press as an activist church, it addressed contemporary issues: human rights, racial justice, economic justice, war and peace. Its Statement of Faith gave far more attention to demands of contemporary discipleship than classical creeds. Both uniting communions had developed energetic agencies for social action, and the UCC strengthened and expanded these interests. Two examples are significant.

The first is racial justice and appreciation. The two uniting churches had commitments, conspicuous in the climate of those bygone times, to racial justice. At least sometimes, Congregationalism had advocated on behalf of slaves before the Civil War, as in the famous case of the rebellion of the Africans on the slave ship *Amistad.* Later it established schools and colleges for the emancipated slaves. The Evangelical and Reformed Church (originally German and Magyar) had a smaller African American membership, but its social action agency included an African American leader and vigorously advocated racial equality. However, changing times brought recognition of the vestiges of paternalism that lurked in traditional white advocacy of black causes. If old white liberals sought to be color-blind, new developments sometimes required a heightened awareness of race in order to overcome past habits and institutions. New questions arose. When did genuine equality require affirmative action to repair inequalities? What did it mean to recognize black Christians, not as objects of white efforts for justice, but as active leaders in the formation of policies and programs? Such issues arose in the early General Synods.

A second example is the participation and leadership of women. The UCC was, by traditional standards, progressive. Both uniting denominations had ordained women at a time when many churches did not. Even so, the original leadership was overwhelmingly male. The early history showed signs of expectation that the leadership would continue to be primarily male, not by design but by habits that were scarcely recognized. Hymns, liturgies, and the original Statement of Faith echoed linguistic habits that soon became offensive.

New sensitivities required organizational changes. General Synods added more organizations to the "instrumentalities" and "bodies" already defined by the constitution. Those new agencies sometimes worked effectively to the benefit of the whole church. They had two limitations, however. First, although emergent groups won their own fiefdoms, places where they were really in charge, they were not necessarily powerful among the makers and shakers of the larger church. Second, the new bodies added to the overlapping and competing organizations in an already chaotic structure. The organizational issue, then, was to find ways to incorporate formerly neglected groups intimately within the whole church without letting them get lost there. The UCC responded with a recognition and celebration of diversity, to be embedded openly and firmly in its structures. Did this mean affirmative action? Yes. Did it mean quotas? Again, yes. That word, frightening to many people in the church and the public, was affirmed. There was resistance, sometimes silent, sometimes expressed, but the new policies swept the day.

Inevitably there were questions about the ways to relate diversity to the original aim of the UCC inscribed in its logo, "That they may all be one." The Barman/Chaves case study has referred to a theology of unity amidst diversity that has been the core of the UCC since its inception. The authors quote the declared goal of a church that "confesses and acts out its faith in the one sovereign God who through Jesus Christ binds in covenant faithful people of all races, ethnicities and cultures." This is surely a worthy goal. Harmony is richer than simple melody. Harmonies that include dissonances can be more stirring than those that express only sweetness and calm. Dissonance is not inevitably good music, however.

The Christian church in its nature includes diversity, as the Zikmund introduction has shown. Such diversity is evident in the New Testament. A church without diversity is not an authentic church, but diversity does not make it a church. There is more diversity in any New York subway train at rush hour or in the body politic of any city than in any congregation of the UCC or in the national staff. Diversity — the diversity to which the UCC aspires and which it has partly achieved — refutes all those naive claims to unity that are really efforts of a dominant group to impose its version of unity on others. It requires a digging deep for the sources of unity, and that is a continuing task for the UCC.

Friendly questioners and less friendly critics have pointed out that the UCC did not initiate the movement for diversity at this time in history. The whole society was talking about, quarreling about, and sometimes acting on diversity. Critics therefore ask whether the UCC, in championing diversity, is acting out of its faith or simply riding the crest of a cultural wave. Many protest groups — ethnic, economic, feminist, gay and lesbian, and the physically handicapped — force diversity on the attention of society. Arguments about equal opportunity, discrimination, and quotas engage the Congress and state legislatures, the courts, business management, labor unions, country clubs, television networks, and the press. The churches could not have avoided the issue if they had tried.

That does not refute the theological authenticity of the commitment to diversity. The biblical prophets point to the activity of God in secular processes of history. Second Isaiah hears God say to the pagan Cyrus, "I arm you, though you do not know me" (Isa. 45:5). The church has often been nudged by secular forces to appropriate the insights of its own faith. Only after many centuries did the church realize that its faith required the end of human slavery, an institution taken for granted even in the New Testament, while that same Scripture destroyed its justification.

The church must try to discern those tides and storms of history that it should encourage and those that it should resist. The UCC today acts on the belief that secular movements of human liberation are theologically valid. Of course, not all rhetoric of liberation is divine. The same sin that infects tyrants can infect protestors and revolutionaries. Embedded in the Christian gospel from the beginning, however, is the impulse to appreciate outsiders. Think of Jesus and Samaritans (Luke 17:11-19 and John 4:7-30), of Paul and the Gentiles.

If the UCC is therefore prodded through a widespread cultural movement to recognize impulses inherent in its own faith, it can thank God for that prodding. It can also thank God that its own history has pointed it toward the present moment. Even while it recognizes its own participation in the sins of racism, sexism, nationalism, and predatory economic practices, it also gives thanks for its historic actions in relation to slavery and injustice. It can with honesty say it is carrying into practice theological convictions it has recognized (often too dimly) in its past.

One evidence of the appreciation of diversity is the presence of interest groups within the UCC. Any member with a few friends can start such a group. It needs no approval from above. It generates its own programs. The General Synods encourage such groups by giving them "voice without vote," a privilege that they exercise effectively. They form networks of communication and issue publications (self-financed). The General Synod helps them schedule meetings concurrent with the synod. As evidence of diversity, we can consider the remarkable list of twenty-three groups granted voice without vote at the General Synod of 1999.[10] Other self-initiated voluntary organizations that did not seek voice at the General Synod include "Confessing Christ," and *Colleague: A Journal of Theological Reflection by Pastors of the United Church of Christ,* and the aforementioned *Prism.* At recent General Synods a self-initiated group has produced and paid for *Balaam's Courier,* an opinionated and often satirical daily commentary eagerly grasped by delegates who chuckle over it or complain about it.

Deep into its processes, the Committee on Structure prepared the document "Missio Dei" for the General Synod of 1997. Although brief, it was written as a biblical and theological base for the new structures. It does not entirely quiet suspicions that when the church makes practical organizational decisions, theology may be an afterthought. Now and then, in the National Council of Churches or a denomination, a committee has developed a proposal, completed a draft, and then said, "Now let's get somebody to write a theological basis for this."

It may be that a theological preface, even though written late in the game, verbalizes commitments that informed the whole game. Thus, an implicit theology becomes explicit. Still, the suspicions do not quite die. The interviews

---

10. On this list were: Association of United Church of Christ Intentional Interim Ministers; Association of United Church Educators; Biblical Witness Fellowship; Christians for Justice Action; Council for Hispanic Ministries; Focus Renewal Ministries; Housing and Community Development Task Force; Ministers for Racial, Social and Economic Justice; National Committee on Persons with Disabilities; Network for Environmental and Economic Responsibility; Pacific Islander Asian American Ministries; Spiritual Development Network; Student Ecumenical Partnership; United Black Christians; UCC Coalition for Lesbian, Gay, Bisexual and Transgender Concerns; UCC Chaplains in Health Care; UCC Expression of Marriage Encounter; UCC Fellowship of Reconciliation; UCC Friends for Life; UCC Military Chaplains; UCC Parents of Lesbians and Gays; UCC Office Support Staff Network; and UCC Urban Ministries Network.

conducted by Barman/Chaves show that denominational staff often talk more easily about diversity than about theological convictions. There are reasons for theological reticence. Some diversities are identifiable and measurable. Theological convictions are harder to verbalize and quantify, above all in a church that declares its fundamental theological statements to be "testimonies, not tests" of faith.

In addition, theological discussion, especially as it seeks common ground beneath diversity, easily lapses into platitudes. The Christian gospel is not platitudinous. It originated in a startling declaration that was good news to some and a threat to others. In the routinization of charisma, however, the old words became familiar and lost their sting. Theological extravagance has hurt the church as often as theological restraint. It is therefore understandable that church members, whether in congregations or in General Synods or on national staffs, should show restraint in their theological expression.

Yet theological commitment remains important. It is the subtle but persistent element in the question so often asked in the UCC: Just what is our identity? The union that formed the UCC meant a realization that some old identities were inadequate. Evangelical and Reformed people had long celebrated — sometimes well, sometimes too provincially — their descent from German and Magyar Lutherans and Calvinists, an identity worth remembering but too limited ethnically. Congregationalists had long celebrated — sometimes well, sometimes too proudly — their descent from New England Pilgrims, an identity also worth remembering, but too limited to Anglo American people. In enlarging those traditional identities, the UCC is asking how to avoid dissolving into an amorphous association. It constitutionally "acknowledges as its sole Head, Jesus Christ, Son of God and Savior." How does it relate diversity to that unity? In its continuing search for its identity and mission, the UCC will not find the answer in a theological formula. Its answer, however, cannot avoid theology.

Institutionalizing Change

Three prominent issues emerge in the current organizational changes.

Simplification of Structures

I have earlier and untactfully referred to the chaotic multiplication of agencies with overlapping and competing responsibilities. Because the number of such agencies is now reduced, some observers talk of centralization. Rightly, I think, the Barman/Chaves case study prefers the word "simplification." Another word might be "democratization." Now, for the first time, all the major officers of the UCC are elected by the General Synod. The Big Boards have voluntarily given up their independence, and their successors have accepted accountability to the General Synod and to the whole church. At the same time, they have gained greater participation in the larger life of the denomination. Similarly, smaller agencies have been incorporated into larger ones, with a reduction of free-wheeling independence but, again, greater access to the big decisions.

The changeover, though bumpy enough to produce some painful bruises, showed many evidences of generosity and good will. The key word in much of the negotiation, I have said earlier, was *covenant*. Obviously, no structures can guarantee covenant in its deeper biblical and spiritual meanings. Yet in the complex relation between faith and organization, some organizational structures support and some subvert covenantal responsibility. There is now hope that the new structures may encourage both democratic participation and wise, courageous leadership.

Continued Exploration of Diversity

The UCC has resolved to be an interracial, interethnic, and multicultural church. Of those three terms, it has hesitated to define "multicultural." The intention is fairly clear. An interracial and interethnic church should welcome the richness of cultural traditions within its covenantal fellowship.

One expression of this commitment is *The New Century Hymnal* (1995). It draws on the resources of many cultures. Some of its hymns come from ancient Greek and Latin sources. Many are the well-known hymns of Western traditions, both Catholic and Protestant, and a few are Jewish. A considerable number are contemporary. Many are African American and Hispanic. Others are Filipino, Japanese, South African and Ghanaian, Moravian, American Dakotan and Lakotan. One is Hindu in origin. Some of these appear in their original languages as well as in translations. There are a few old-fashioned "gospel" hymns that were thought too sentimental and individualistic for predecessor hymnals in the UCC. Worship at the General Synod, including music and dance from various cultural traditions as well as the music from this hymnal, has widened the horizons of worshipers, often in exhilarating ways.

The new inclusiveness naturally requires exclusions. In its rejection of gender and ethnic bias, the hymnal more rigorously excludes or modifies hymns that show such bias than do other "new wave" denominational hymnals. Its modernization of language sometimes upsets rhymes and versification, so that a slight change (e.g., from "thee" to "you") may set off a chain reaction throughout a whole hymn. These verbal changes, advertently or inadvertently, sometimes bring major theological changes.[11] A wistful and often expressed hope was that all hymns would be "hymns that everybody can sing" — really an impossibility in a large hymnal emphasizing diversity. Some worshipers occasionally say silently, "Dear God, please understand that I sing this not because I believe it but because I want to join in the worship of a covenantal community."

Multiculturalism is surely enriching the UCC, but some members ask what cultural inclusiveness does about cultural traits that are hostile to Christian faith. In a famous saying of Paul Tillich, "Culture is a form of expression of religion, and religion is the substance of culture."[12] I am not entirely convinced that he was right, or even that he agreed with that all the time, but he pointed to a tough issue. Some religions and some cultures, Tillich knew well, are idolatrous. Some cultures endorse slavery, some practice polygamy, some enforce caste distinctions, some require female genital mutilation, some foment holy wars, and some bless predatory economic practices. Christian faith has historically expressed itself in many cultures. It has been captured and distorted by some. Thus the Christian faith must maintain some leverage against culture, some courage to reject cultural habits — including, in the first place, habits of the culture in which it has made itself at home.

The church has worked on this issue through long centuries. Early in the fifth century, Saint Augustine pointed out that the church calls people out of all nations and languages with their diverse "manners, laws, and institutions." Rather than abolish these diversities, the church "preserves and adapts them." That is multiculturalism, even though the word had not been invented. But Augustine put a limit on the appreciation of diversity: the point at which it injures "faith and godliness." Here the church must dissent to the point of provoking "anger and hatred and persecutions."[13] The worldwide church still faces persecution in some cultures. In American culture it is more likely to be seduced

---

11. United Church of Christ, *The New Century Hymnal* (Cleveland: Pilgrim Press, 1995). For theological discussions of the hymnal, see Arthur G. Clyde, "*The New Century Hymnal:* A Theological and Liturgical Expression," *Prism* 10, no. 2 (fall 1995): 27-35; John Ferguson, "*The New Century Hymnal:* A Review," *Prism* 10, no. 2 (fall 1995): 36-41; and Richard L. Christensen, "What Language Shall We Recognize? A Critique of *The New Century Hymnal*," *Prism* 10, no. 2 (fall 1995): 42-52. See also articles by fourteen authors in Richard L. Christensen, ed., *How Shall We Sing the Lord's Song? An Assessment of "The New Century Hymnal"* (Centerville, Mass.: Confessing Christ, 1997).

12. Paul Tillich, *What Is Religion?* trans. James Luther Adams (New York: Harper and Row, 1969), p. 73.

13. Augustine, *The City of God*, trans. Marcus Dods and George Wilson (New York: Random House, Modern Library, 1950), bk. XIX, chap. 17.

than persecuted. The UCC must ask when multiculturalism is a faithful openness to varieties of culture and when it is a too comfortable accommodation to moods of the time.

The intent of multiculturalism certainly accords with Christian faith, but its sloganizing may be too hasty. For some people the reliance on parliamentary procedure in the General Synod appears to be the imposition of one quite specific culture upon a multicultural church. To most of us conditioned by Western culture, it is a reasonable way to conduct meetings with respect both for majorities and minorities, and with some blend of discipline and freedom. Due to the expansion of international organizations, it is extending its influence around the world almost as fast as Coca-Cola and McDonald's. It is a distinctive product of cultural history, developed only in recent centuries. In some cultural contexts, it is strange and alien.

A continuing issue for the UCC will be a closer examination of multiculturalism with all its unexplored possibilities. Here the UCC may be wise to consult that classic book *Christ and Culture*, written by one of its eminent theologians, H. Richard Niebuhr. Are UCC policies unintentionally drifting into his description of "the Christ of culture," modified to include the several Christs of diverse subcultures? Are they ignoring the possibility of "Christ against culture" or, more important, "Christ transforming culture"?[14] These questions, which have troubled the church throughout its history, have new resonance in the pursuits of multiculturalism.

Declining Membership and Budgets

A big issue not accented in the current reorganization but always present, is declining membership, a characteristic of all the so-called mainline denominations. The Barman/Chaves case study reports the basic information for the UCC. With declining membership come financial troubles that require organizational changes. The exercise of trimming budgets is one clue to the values of any organization, whether family, business, or government, as well as church. It is not a totally reliable clue because whatever the most ardent priorities of faith, some bills must be paid immediately. Roofs leak unexpectedly. A church cannot renege on contracts or on promises to pensioners. The mission of the church requires an infrastructure, and a democratic church requires a costly General Synod or some comparable body. The peril is that sustaining the infrastructure can dominate the budget while the purposes of the church get undernourished.

14. H. Richard Niebuhr, *Christ and Culture* (New York: Harper and Brothers, 1951).

Every day, members and leaders of the UCC are asking what changes must be made to keep budgets in balance. If the answer is not at first glance theological, it soon reaches theological depths.

Theological Reflections

In a broad sense, every page of this essay has been theological. However, the approach to theology has usually been oblique, moving from political-legal-organizational actions to the beliefs they express or contradict. It is now time to lift up theology for more direct examination. In doing this, I shall continue to focus on the UCC, but its concerns will frequently merge with the generic concerns of other churches responding to the same historical problems and opportunities. No church can isolate itself from the wider culture. That may be especially true of the UCC, since it does not rely on the identifying marks of some other churches: a firm doctrinal formula, a carefully cultivated liturgy, a prescribed form of apostolic succession, or an enacted discipline. Seven themes deserve attention here.

Theological Roots and Beliefs

The UCC is intentionally a mini-ecumenical movement uniting several theological and ethnic traditions (see the Zikmund introduction), with the great exceptions, we must not forget, of Catholicism and Orthodoxy. The churches that united to form it had roots in the Protestant Reformation. The Evangelical and Reformed tradition was a synthesis of German Lutheranism and Calvinism with a strain of Magyar heritage. The Congregational tradition was originally Calvinist (via English Puritanism), greatly liberalized in polity. "The Christian Church," which united with the Congregationalists in 1931, brought elements of Methodist, Baptist, and Presbyterian traditions, adapted to the eighteenth-century American frontier. As these traditions interacted in the UCC, they maintained the Calvinist commitment to influence the world — the whole secular world. As one eminent Roman Catholic historian writes, Calvin "inspired Protestantism with the will to dominate the world and to change society and culture."[15]

Calvin's Geneva is often described, with reason if not with strictest accu-

---

15. Christopher Dawson, *The Judgment of the Nations* (New York: Sheed and Ward, 1942), p. 45.

racy, as a theocratic state. New England Pilgrims wanted their communities to resemble the biblical "city set upon a hill," as Governor Winthrop quoted the New Testament. Congregationalism was the state church in Connecticut until 1818, in New Hampshire until 1819, and in Massachusetts until 1833, well past the adoption of the United States Constitution and Bill of Rights.

That Calvinist impulse experienced many reinterpretations as it moved through the Enlightenment, the American Revolution, the antislavery movement, the Social Gospel, and postmodernism. Although the Social Gospel endorsed separation of church and state, its foremost theologian, the Baptist Walter Rauschenbusch, still sought to "Christianize the social order,"[16] a language that sounds strange in the pluralistic sensitivity of our society. Today the UCC, along with other churches, is experimenting with appropriate methods of influencing the whole body politic, not only by guiding its own members but also by organizing efforts to persuade Congress and public officials.

To use the terms made familiar by Ernst Troeltsch, the UCC knows well that it is neither "church" nor "sect." That is, it cannot and does not want to be the traditional territorial church shaping the whole society. And it has no desire to be a sect, a self-conscious faithful minority avoiding involvement and entanglement in the society's political processes. It wants, within the blessings and disciplines of a pluralistic society, to influence public life.

Exemplifying this experimental venture are the resolutions on public policy adopted by every General Synod. These are sometimes satirized as "resolutionary Christianity." Even friendly critics point out that the General Synod adopts in a few days resolutions that would strain the competence of its members even if they had weeks to work on them. The influential social ethicist James Gustafson has objected to "the intellectual and academic flabbiness of most of the 'pronouncements,' whether by church agencies or by individuals."[17] He clearly has the UCC, though not it alone, in mind. The UCC is not likely to take the opposite path of maintaining silence on public issues of moral import. The General Synods have been gradually limiting the number of resolutions and enhancing the process of their review by large committees prior to the action of the synod. This is not a retreat from the public sphere. Sociologist Robert Wuthnow points out that several Protestant denominations are judging that a concentration on few issues may be a better strategy than trying "to keep all pots simmering at once."[18] There will be no final answer to questions about the

16. Walter Rauschenbusch, *Christianizing the Social Order* (New York: Macmillan, 1912).

17. James M. Gustafson, *Ethics from a Theocentric Perspective,* vol. 2 in *Ethics and Theology* (Chicago: University of Chicago Press, 1984), p. 318.

18. Robert Wuthnow, "The Moral Minority," *American Prospect* 11, no. 13 (May 22, 2000): 33.

church's involvement in public issues, but the UCC will not give up its conviction of a God-given responsibility to public life.

Law and Gospel

The relation of love and law has been a perennial theological issue from the New Testament until today. Two popular slogans express the divided mind of American society. One response to social wrongs is, "There ought to be a law about that." A contrary saying is, "You can't legislate morality." Neither slogan ever silences the other. To those who say morality cannot be legislated, the answer is that almost every law legislates morality — quite obviously laws against murder and theft. True, there is no way to legislate love or mercy or forgiveness, but some of the requirements of love, including some measure of justice, can be legislated.

In the theological traditions of the UCC, Martin Luther drew a sharp distinction between law and gospel. He remembered Augustine's summary of Christian morality, "Love, and do as you please," with the awareness that if you truly love, what you please will please God. Calvin was more likely to say, "Love, and enact love through moral laws and structures." If you say that that makes too simple a contrast between Luther and Calvin, I agree, but as a rough description it will do. The UCC draws on both traditions but inclines toward the Calvinistic.

Therefore the UCC enacts quotas. A pure society might need no quotas of representation for women, ethnic groups, and youth. However, if we were to wait for the conquering of all prejudice, much of it unconscious, we would have a long wait until the day of fair representation. This reliance on quotas has its costs. Law, whether in the Bible or in today's world, is a routinization of charisma, which runs the risk of inflexibility and legalism. In current practice the UCC gives great authority to nominating committees. Nominations from the floor risk upsetting the careful distribution of offices that a nominating committee can manage. We hear occasional protests that the power given to nomination committees is undemocratic. We hear questions about the wisdom of telling a conference, "You must elect to the General Synod a set percentage of clergy and laity, of women, of African Americans, and of youth." So far, the UCC meets those objections partly by creating large nominating committees that represent many interests, then giving those committees great power. At this time in its history, the UCC is choosing a few legalisms rather than risking the perpetuation of the fruits of prejudice.

Will these legalisms be helpful in an unforeseeable future? We cannot now know. Laws designed for a historical situation are not eternal. The UCC is not inclined to repeat the grandiosity of its constitution, which forbids certain actions "now, or at any future time." Reorganization is a continuing process.

Revised Understandings of Mission

Every change in organization reflects some understanding of the mission of the church, but many modifications of mission operate subtly within structures. The UCC frequently revises and restates its beliefs about its mission. We cherish the phrase "New occasions teach new duties," from a stirring hymn by James Russell Lowell. One example of such change in recent years is the way we have reconceived the meaning of world mission in the church.

A missionary hymn, written by Mary Ann Thompson in 1870 and well known to our older members, contains this stanza:

> Behold how many thousands still are lying
> Bound in the darksome prison-house of sin,
> With none to tell them of the Saviour's dying,
> Or of the life He died for them to win.

The Pilgrim Hymnal (1958) omitted that stanza, and *The New Century Hymnal* (1995), for all its inclusiveness, excludes the entire hymn. The stanza emerged at a time when the purposes of "foreign missions" gave a prominent place to converting the heathen.

Gradually the aim of conversion diminished. Nobody talks any more of "the evangelization of the world in our generation," the famous slogan of John R. Mott. We have become more aware that Christian missions were too often the accomplices of Western imperialism, military or economic. (I say "too often," but not always. Militarists and expanding industrialists frequently saw Christian missionaries as their enemies.) Today, world missions, while still supporting Christian communities around the world (as partners, not as dependent clients), are more likely to seek interfaith conversations than to proselytize.

There are at least two reasons for this change. One is the plain evidence that several world religions are tenacious and resurgent. The more theological reason is the awareness that missions, as in the hymn just quoted, have too often made judgments that only God can make. The changing attitude need not lessen Christian loyalty to Christ. The church may wish that all people would know the story of Christ, then in freedom make their own decisions of faith. The church also may realize that all religions express the experience and aspirations of people from whom we can learn something. Finally, it may realize that, though the traditional biblical warnings against idolatry are still real and urgent, our primary responsibility may be to expose the hidden idolatries of our own society, sometimes of our own churches, before taking on the idolatries of the whole world.

The UCC is not likely to revise its constitutional affirmation of "Jesus Christ, Son of God and Savior," as its "sole head." Its Statement of Faith declares: "In Jesus Christ, the man of Nazareth, our crucified and risen Savior, you [God] have come to us and shared our common lot, conquering sin and death and reconciling the world to yourself." This belief does not, however, presume to set limits to God's ways of reaching out in liberating and reconciling action. Evangelism is still a good word in the UCC, but it is not immediately equated with proselytizing. Here is a theological opportunity to reconsider historic ideas of evangelism and foreign missions, relating belief in Christ to the pluralism of the modern world. If the Theological Commission of the early years of the UCC should be revived, it might find this responsibility worthy of its efforts.

Changing Ecumenism

In its early days, I have already said, the UCC hoped to be "a united and uniting church." Now that hope appears a little too triumphalist, too expectant of top-down ecumenism. The union that formed the UCC did not become a center for other unions. Some things happened on a larger scale. In its document *Baptism, Eucharist and Ministry,* the Faith and Order Commission of the World Council of Churches reached consensus that had gone unrealized for centuries.[19] In addition, the more recent agreement of several American denominations on mutual acceptance of ministries (see the Barman/Chaves case study) is a real achievement.

More influential in local churches has been the growth of an ecumenical spirit among people who may not know how to pronounce or spell "ecumenism." Across the country, churches (Protestant and Catholic), synagogues, and sometimes mosques work together to help the needy, to open opportunities for youth, or to solve other local problems. More cautiously, they worship and pray together. Some traditional barriers simply fade away. That fading may be a sign of maturity. It can also be an enervating indifferentism. The respected scholar

19. *Baptism, Eucharist and Ministry* (Geneva: World Council of Churches, 1982), a document adopted by the Faith and Order Commission of the World Council of Churches in Lima, Peru, 1982.

Randall Balmer sees particularity dissolving into a bland good-natured loss of cutting edge. He believes that "the fashionable currents of inclusiveness and ecumenicity," though "noble impulses," have "exacted a price."[20] His words deserve attention, but his own data show the perils of static provincialisms.

Meanwhile, new antagonisms appear. Religious conflicts erupt over homosexuality and abortion. If Christian social action was formerly a "liberal" movement, the political activism of the Religious Right makes for new polarization. Religious fault lines, and not always the old ones, still can cause earthquakes.

In the UCC the Biblical Witness Fellowship frequently challenges the church, suspecting doctrinal laxity and easy accommodation to the secular culture. The denomination, if rarely convinced by this fellowship, has come to realize that a church that celebrates diversity should listen appreciatively to dissents from within. *The New Century Hymnal,* I have mentioned, has restored some hymns that express the "old-time religion."

As ecumenical trends rub out old differences, churches ask what happens to their historical heritages. Are they to be erased in a new cosmopolitanism? The denominations that formed the UCC have traditions cherished even in these latter days. Some older members remember when German was a language of worship in Evangelical and Reformed churches. Others feel the power of the Mayflower Compact and the Pilgrim tradition, still preserved in hymnody and in names like Pilgrim Fellowship and Pilgrim Press. The Magyar Synod continues the Hungarian Reformed tradition. In all these cases, the particularity is freely acknowledged, not imposed by others.

African American particularity is radically different. One hymn long cherished in the UCC begins, "O God, beneath thy guiding hand, Our exiled fathers crossed the sea." For most of us, it was never literally true. Our fathers and mothers crossed the sea long after the Pilgrims who are celebrated in the hymn. That did not matter, because we adopted the Pilgrims as ancestors, just as we adopted Abraham and Sarah as more distant ancestors, and so we rejoiced in the hymn. Black people know, however, that their fathers and mothers crossed the sea in slave ships. They were bought and sold, often beaten, deprived of education and opportunity. Even so, many of them found in Christian faith resources that inspired their struggle for freedom. They contributed their spirituals to Christian worship. Their churches became both compassionate and tough communities. When white men bossed plantation, industry, and government, black churches developed their own leadership and style. Whatever the future of a multicultural and multiracial church, it must not rub out the gifts of those churches.

20. Randall Balmer, *Grant Us Courage: Travels along the Mainline of American Protestantism* (New York: Oxford University Press, 1996), p. 5.

In a short but classical work of 1954,[21] W. A. Visser 't Hooft distinguished between Stoic equality, based on the sameness of all people, and Christian equality, which cherishes particular historical heritages. More recent history has confirmed his insight. People want to be appreciated not only in their common humanity but also in their differing histories.

Nobody quite knows what historical particularities will mean organizationally. We are fumbling for answers. *The New Century Hymnal* includes more spirituals than past hymnals and excludes celebration of exiled fathers who crossed the sea. More radically, it excludes all patriotic hymns with two possible exceptions. It uses James Weldon Johnson's "Lift Every Voice and Sing," often called the Negro National Anthem — a hymn worthy to grace any American hymnal. The second is a radically rewritten "America the Beautiful." The editors clearly wanted to avoid national idolatry and militarism. Should they have heeded the call of Kenneth Boulding, the great Quaker and pacifist social scientist, who called for "a redeemed nationalism" that keeps alive particular historical memories?

Structurally, the Magyar Synod persists even though the UCC intended to wipe out ethnic judicatories. The new structures prescribe specific representation of African Americans. They designate representation of eight "historically underrepresented constituencies," listed in the Barman/Chaves case study. Looking ahead, we may ask whether African Americans will want to preserve churches that, without exclusion of others, continue meaningful styles of worship and fellowship. How can they contribute to a multicultural church without being simply absorbed? Even an unimaginably sinless church might find perplexities here; a church that confesses sin finds more.

The Gap between Leaders and Members at Large

The Barman/Chaves case study reports a distance (an "indifference," "wariness," even "alienation") of local churches from denominational leadership. The avowed diversity, so evident in the national staff, has had scarcely a ripple of effect on most local churches. The larger Organizing Religious Work study shows that this distancing is frequent across denominations. The American culture just now shows a broad distrust of big government and bureaucracies, a distrust curiously fostered both by libertarians on the far right and by the recent New Left. That distrust seeps into churches. The problem is especially dis-

21. W. A. Visser 't Hooft, *The Ecumenical Movement and the Racial Problem* (Paris: UNESCO, 1954).

turbing to the UCC, whose constitution declares, "The basic unit of life and organization of the United Church of Christ is the Local Church." What should a church do about the distance that separates its duly elected officials and top administrative staff from the general membership in congregations spread across the country?

If the gap is typical of many denominations, it has some distinctive characteristics in the UCC. For example, the General Synod, largely elected by the conferences, comes from local churches but is usually in tune with national leadership. To take a significant case, the General Synod has said for several years now that homosexuality should not be a barrier to ordination, in contrast to Methodist and Presbyterian positions. Practically, however, it is sometimes a barrier (although certainly not always) because a candidate for ordination may be denied the required endorsement of the local church. It also is a barrier, hidden or open, to a call to ministry in some local churches.

The congregational polity means that the membership at large may simply ignore national policies. If a local Presbyterian church objects to national policies, it is likely to fight back. The local UCC congregation is more likely to go its own way undisturbed or simply drop out of the denomination. The loss of congregations has been one cause, though not a major cause, of declining membership in the UCC.

The gap between leadership and constituencies, traceable to many causes, raises a deep theological issue. What kind of leadership does a church committed to Jesus Christ really want? Surely leaders should not merely echo popular opinion. Leaders often aspire to be prophetic, and any church with biblical roots will appreciate that. Can prophetic leadership become elitism, however, a little too confident in its own superiority?

Why does the General Synod differ so much from the popular attitudes of church members? This is partly because, although elected, it is a highly select group. Only the more committed members, especially if they are hardworking business and professional people, will give up a week of vacation to go to General Synod. Beyond that, something happens to people at the General Synod. Frequently a delegate is heard to say, "I don't know how I'm going to explain this vote to the folks back home." Gunnar Myrdal, the famous Swedish social scientist employed by the Carnegie Foundation to study the racial problem in America, wrote, "When the man in the street acts through his orderly collective bodies, he acts more as an American, as a Christian, and as a humanitarian than if he were acting independently."[22] It is even more likely that delegates to Gen

---

22. Gunnar Myrdal, *An American Dilemma, Twentieth Anniversary Edition* (New York: Harper and Row, 1994, 1962), p. 80.

eral Synod, highly conscious that they are acting for the church, reminded by daily worship about who they are, think and feel differently from the way they think and feel day in and day out.

The General Synod of 1999 adopted a policy that encourages congregational study of proposed resolutions and guidance to the General Synod, without inhibiting the responsibility of delegates to vote their own consciences under the influence of the deliberations at the synod. This is a practice observed only occasionally in the past. Will it mean a dulling of the General Synod, a radicalizing of congregations, or a deeper education of the church at large? We do not yet know.

Changing Patterns of Membership

I have already commented on loss of membership as one stimulus to the reorganization of the UCC. What is the theological meaning of this loss, typical of many Protestant denominations? A common habit refers (a little too easily) to mainline churches as the so-called "seven sisters": the United Methodist Church, the United Presbyterian Church, the Evangelical Lutheran Church in America, the Episcopal Church, the American Baptist Churches, the United Church of Christ (and its predecessor churches), and the Christian Church (Disciples of Christ). These seven have been important for their stability, their educational levels, and their influence on society. All American presidents except Abraham Lincoln came from these churches, until the elections of Roman Catholic John F. Kennedy and the Southern Baptists Jimmy Carter and Bill Clinton. These denominations experienced remarkable growth in membership in the years following the Second World War, but went into major decline in the 1960s.

In 1972 Dean Kelley, on the staff of the National Council of Churches, published *Why Conservative Churches Are Growing*. He described the decline in membership of "major church groups." In terms intended to disturb, he used the word "dying." He attributed the loss to a neglect of concern for "the ultimate meaning of life" and argued that "strict churches" were growing while undemanding churches were shrinking. Kelley stirred many controversies but reaffirmed his argument in successive editions of his book.[23] The most thorough discussion of his work, involving thirty researchers, showed that the losses were

23. Dean M. Kelley, *Why Conservative Churches Are Growing* (New York: Harper and Row, 1972, 1977; with a new preface for the Rose edition, Macon, Ga.: Mercer University Press, 1986).

largely due to a failure to attract young people and not to the social action of the churches.[24] Roger Finke and Rodney Stark argued in 1992 that throughout American history, denominations have declined to the degree that they "rejected traditional doctrines and ceased to make serious demands on their followers."[25] Wade Clark Roof in 1993 produced data to show that the biggest exodus from "mainline Protestantism" was to conservative Protestantism, among people who wanted "stronger moral guidance" and "a deeper Christian faith." He found that more than half the Protestant baby boom generation "feel that the churches have lost the spiritual part of religion."[26] Thomas Reeves in 1996 used the data for a polemic against "liberal Christianity."[27] But Nancy Ammerman, after a detailed study of congregations, concluded that "congregations that do *not* try new programs and new forms of outreach when they are faced with environmental change are not likely to survive the life spans of their current members."[28]

Membership statistics do not measure depth of faith, but the reasons for membership growth and decline may have theological significance. As the UCC first became aware of declining membership, one (although certainly not the only) response was, "That means we must be doing something right." There could be a grain of truth in that guess. Both the Bible and the history of the church show that faithfulness is often unpopular. Mass evangelism is often related to a biblical literalism that the UCC for the most part rejects. Religious television, offering religion on easy terms, may become a substitute for church participation. Such reasoning certainly does not justify complacency, however. One challenge to the new Local Church Ministries will be to ask what membership loss means, not simply to the budget and program of the UCC, but to its theology.

The Stimulating yet Seductive American Culture

Most Americans are aware of cultural changes that affect all persons and organizations within the society. Scholarly books, the press, and television often de-

---

24. Dean R. Hoge and David A. Roozen, *Understanding Church Growth and Decline: 1950-78* (New York: Pilgrim Press, 1979).

25. Roger Finke and Rodney Stark, *The Churching of America, 1776-1990: Winners and Losers in Our Religious Economy* (New Brunswick, N.J.: Rutgers University Press, 1992), p. 1.

26. Wade Clark Roof, *A Generation of Seekers: The Spiritual Journeys of the Baby Boom Generation* (San Francisco: Harper, 1993), pp. 177, 236.

27. Reeves, *The Empty Church.*

28. Nancy T. Ammerman, *Congregation and Community* (New Brunswick, N.J.: Rutgers University Press, 1997), p. 323.

scribe them. Here I can refer to them only briefly and only as they infiltrate churches.

One clue is the decline of denominational loyalty. The usual estimate is that upwards of 30 percent of Americans switch denominations during their lifetimes. Most of these changes are from one Protestant denomination to another, but some are between Protestantism and Catholicism (both ways) and between Judaism and Christianity (again, both ways). Some amount to religious conversions, but more do not. Some are occasioned by marriage. Others come when families move into a new area and look for a new church home, often with less attention to denomination and formal belief than to convenience, congeniality, and styles of music and preaching. In part, we can cheer these changes. There are gains when church membership is freely chosen, not just perpetuated by habit. There are gains in the appreciation of differences, replacing old dogmatisms. There is also some evidence that "those who choose a religion typically are more committed than those who were born into the same religion."[29] Yet we may wonder about the fading of old commitments. When is it indifference over matters that really are important? When is it relaxing old covenants and acquiescing to looser, less demanding associations?

In their influential *Habits of the Heart,* Robert Bellah and his associates discerned a "cancerous" individualism with an accompanying decline in social organizations, whether labor unions, parent-teacher associations, or bowling leagues. Many church leaders, who have trouble persuading members to teach in Sunday schools, get to choir practice, or attend evening meetings, are surprised with Bellah's claim that the organizations that most successfully resist this trend are churches.[30]

Peter Berger's important book, *The Sacred Canopy,* made a strong case that the development of modern economies permeating all social institutions has put churches in a consumer-oriented society where religion must be marketed: "It must be 'sold' to a clientele that is no longer constrained to 'buy.' The pluralistic situation is, above all, a *market situation.* In it, the religious institutions become marketing agencies and the religious traditions become consumer commodities. . . . Now, the religious groups must organize themselves in such a way as to woo a population of consumers, in competition with other groups having the same purpose."[31] Berger set loose a torrent of literature on

29. Wade Clark Roof, *Spiritual Marketplace: Baby Boomers and the Remaking of American Religion* (Princeton: Princeton University Press, 1999), p. 153.

30. Robert Bellah et al., *Habits of the Heart: Individualism and Commitment in American Life,* rev. ed. (Berkeley: University of California Press, 1996).

31. Peter L. Berger, *The Sacred Canopy: Elements of a Sociological Theory of Religion* (New York: Doubleday Anchor, 1990, first published in 1967), p. 138.

the same theme. In 1992 Finke and Stark referred exuberantly to "an unregulated religious economy" and quoted nothing less than Adam Smith's 1776 *The Wealth of Nations* on the advantages for religion of operating in a competitive economy.[32] Two years later, Laurence Moore published *Selling God: American Religion in the Marketplace of Culture*.[33] In 1996 Thomas Reeves's *The Empty Church* included a chapter entitled "Consumer Christianity." In 1999 Wade Clark Roof, more restrained than Finke and Stark but more cheerful than Berger, entitled his book *Spiritual Marketplace: Baby Boomers and the Remaking of American Religion.*

In this cultural environment, churches are frequently described as competitors in a consumer-oriented economy. Pastors are likened to entrepreneurs trying to maintain a share of a market. In a *New York Times Magazine* column entitled "God Is in the Packaging," writer Michael Lewis told of a study by the Harvard Business School of a booming church in Illinois. Only in America, I suppose, would an elite business school do such a study of a church. Lewis's own conclusion from the study was this: "One of the miracles of modern capitalism is its ability to stimulate demand for the most banal products (bottled water, for instance) simply by crafting it a new image. Something like this appears to be behind the revival in demand for Jesus Christ."[34]

Anybody can find evidence to qualify though not necessarily refute that judgment, yet it must make churches uneasy. When compared with traditional established churches, often coercive both physically and spiritually, the current freedom and tolerance of competitive churches have virtues. A culture in which individuals shop for their churches in a free market has lost something, however, when compared with churches that are covenant communities, asking members for commitment and loyalty. We may hope that in their current attention to reorganization the UCC and comparable denominations will recognize the profound theological concerns that underlie institutional forms.

Anticipation

"By the time you have grown up, the church's form will have changed greatly." Those famous words were written by Dietrich Bonhoeffer for the infant baptism of his grandnephew, namesake, and godson. They came out of Tegel

32. Finke and Stark, *The Churching of America*, p. 52. They cite Adam Smith, *The Wealth of Nations* (New York: Modern Library, 1937), pp. 740-41.

33. R. Laurence Moore, *Selling God: American Religion in the Marketplace of Culture* (New York: Oxford University Press, 1994).

34. *New York Times Magazine*, July 21, 1996, pp. 14, 16.

prison, where Bonhoeffer was held under suspicions — accurate, in fact — of complicity in a plot to kill Adolf Hitler. As his imagination leapt into the future, Bonhoeffer hoped for "something quite new and revolutionary," for "conversion and purification."[35] He was too wise to make predictions, however. As it turned out, the church had more stamina (or was it inertia?) than he expected. Changes there have been, though not all of them could be called "purification." More changes there will be. We cannot foresee them with any certainty. Most of us did not expect the resurgence of world religions, the global appeal of fundamentalisms, the wars in which religion was a cause or a pretext. Nor did we expect the events in which a hidden grace brought hope into confusion and strife.

Without presuming to predict, we can stretch our minds by asking a few questions about the future:

- Will Christians become a self-conscious minority in lands that once thought themselves Christian? Will "conversion and purification" restore a high commitment to faith in Christ?
- Will the tides of secularism sweep through cultures, overwhelming biblically illiterate churches?
- Will the movement of "Evangelicals and Catholics Together" (1994) reshape the religious scene in the United States?
- Will the commodification of religion continue with churches becoming support communities, theologically indifferent but useful to people who crave self-esteem and community in a fragmented world?
- Will the center of Christian population shift from the Northern Hemisphere to the Southern and from the West to the East, with consequent changes in the understanding and practice of faith?

Such questions, although unanswerable, may widen our horizons. One task of theology is to enlarge the context within which we face our day-to-day decisions. In the momentous changes of our time, denominational reorganizations are slight events, but they may be signs of faithfulness and readiness to respond to the challenges of a tumultuous history. Those who believe in the freedom of God and of God's human creatures will expect surprises in times of hope and peril. Yet planning, both venturesome and prudent, is consistent with readiness for surprises.

---

35. Dietrich Bonhoeffer, *Letters and Papers from Prison: The Enlarged Edition,* ed. Eberhard Bethge (New York: Macmillan, 1972), p. 300.

Methodism as Machine

Russell E. Richey

O ver machinery — the central, executive, decision-making apparatus of the denomination — American Methodists have *gloried* and *agonized*, from the very beginning. The agonies focused initially on the power and authority exercised by the appointive office:[1]

- by John Wesley, founder of the movement, in his directives from Britain;
- by his assistants in the colonies, Thomas Rankin and Francis Asbury; and
- by the superintendents (bishops), Thomas Coke and Francis Asbury, after the church organized in 1784.

Methodists later agonized over the episcopal surrogates known as presiding elders (now termed district superintendents) who functioned regionally with much of the power of episcopacy but, as themselves episcopal appointees, lacked the authority, affirmation, and legitimacy enjoyed by the elected bishops. Recently, agonies focus on the boards and agencies, the topic of the organizational case study and theological essay which follow. Over the machinery, Methodists have agonized. In it they have also gloried. This essay charts the history of that ambivalence. The following case study and theological essay explore the present United Methodist patterns and stratagems that grow out of that ambivalence.

---

1. The meaning of the phrase "appointive office" will emerge in the course of this essay. It refers to the power in Methodist episcopacy or superintendency — power first exercised by John Wesley — to assign preachers.

Russell E. Richey

Schism over Machinery

The power and prerogative of the decision makers prompted Methodists to fight and even to divide, again and again. Other traditions experience turmoil over doctrine or liturgy. Such matters certainly do figure in Methodist squabbles. However, authority, its form and exercise figure even more prominently. For instance, the schisms of Methodism's first century all concerned the superintending powers and authorities, typically those of bishops and presiding elders. The more important divisions include the following:

- the Fluvanna schism of 1779-81 that preceded the organization of the church;
- the separate organization of African Methodists, traditionally dated from 1787;
- the 1792 walkout of James O'Kelly and supporters to form the "Republican Methodists" and the coalescence of a Primitive Methodist movement around William Hammett in Charleston the same year;
- the New England–based Reformed Methodists organized by Pliny Brett in 1814;
- the Stillwellite and African Zion movements of the 1820s, both launched in New York City;
- the Methodist Protestants whose reform efforts traumatized successive general conferences in the 1820s and divided Methodism at its heart, in the border states (1830);
- the exiting of abolitionists to form the Wesleyan Methodist Church in 1842;
- the split of the Methodist Episcopals in 1844, north and south; and
- the emergence of the Free Methodists in the late 1850s (formally organizing in 1860).

All of these divisions turned one way or another on the central decision-making power, typically that exercised by bishops or their surrogates, the presiding elders.[2]

---

2. These divisions figure prominently in virtually every history of Methodism. For a short review of the issues and actors, see my "Is Division a New Threat to the Denomination?" in *Questions for the Twenty-First Century Church,* ed. Russell E. Richey, William B. Lawrence, and Dennis M. Campbell, United Methodism and American Culture, vol. 4 (Nashville: Abingdon, 1999), pp. 105-16.

Machinery as Missional

American Methodists also gloried over their organization, over the template sent them by John Wesley, over their improvements thereon, and over what they could and did achieve through its instrumentality. And they explicitly compared Methodism to a machine. Bishops Thomas Coke and Francis Asbury claimed their own role and that of the presiding elders "to preserve in order and in motion the wheels of the vast machine — to keep a constant and watchful eye upon the whole — and to *think deeply* for the general good."[3] Editor Nathan Bangs, Methodism's spokesperson for his generation and the "inventor" of Methodism's early agency apparatus, did not use the *M* word for Methodism. He spoke instead of "system," but he gloried in the machinery nonetheless. His panegyric also functions as a good description, well worth quoting at length:

> Let us now, that we may discover at one view the symmetry of the whole plan, glance at the different parts of the system. In the first place, there are the classes, consisting of from twelve to twenty members, under the inspection of leaders, who are responsible for their official conduct to the preacher from whom they receive their appointment. These meet together weekly for mutual edification and comfort, and to pay their weekly dues for the support of the poor and the ministry.
>
> Secondly: — There are the stewards, who take charge of the class, quarterly, and sacramental collections, and disburse them to the poor and the ministry, and are responsible to the quarterly meeting conference, from which they receive their appointment, on the nomination of the preacher in charge of the circuit.
>
> Thirdly: — There are the exhorters and local preachers, who, together with the leaders and stewards and travelling preachers on the circuit, compose the quarterly meeting conference, from which body exhorters and local preachers receive their license to officiate, and who recommend preachers to the annual conferences to be received into the travelling connection.
>
> Fourthly: — There is the travelling ministry, consisting of licensed preachers, deacons, elders, and bishops; and these compose the annual conferences, who have the power of receiving preachers, of trying their own members, of hearing appeals of local preachers, and of carrying into execution the rules of discipline, in relation to spreading the gospel by means of an itinerant ministry.

3. "Section V. *Of the Presiding Elder, and of their Duty,*" in Thomas Coke and Francis Asbury, *The Doctrines and Disciplines of the Methodist Episcopal Church, in America* (Philadelphia: Henry Tuckniss, 1798), p. 52, the only annotated version of the Methodist *Discipline.*

Fifthly: — The general conference, which assembles quadrennially, and is composed of a certain number of travelling elders, elected by the annual conferences. This is the highest ecclesiastical body known in the Methodist Episcopal Church. Under certain restrictions which were imposed upon this delegated general conference at the time it was organized, in 1808, they have the power of revising the discipline, of electing the bishops, the editors and agents of the Book Concern, of hearing appeals from the decisions of annual conferences, and of reviewing the whole field of labor, whether it be included in the general work, or in the missionary department.

In the sixth place: — the bishops who derive their official existence from the general conference, superintend the whole work, preside in the annual and general conferences, perform the ceremony of ordination, and appoint the preachers to their several stations.

In addition to this regular work, in which we behold a beautiful gradation of office and order, from the lowest to the highest, there is the book establishment, which has grown up with the growth of the church, and from which are issued a great variety of books on all branches of theological knowledge, suited to ministers of the gospel, including such as are suited to youth and children, as well as those for Sabbath schools, and a great number of tracts for gratuitous distribution by tract societies, Bibles and Testaments of various sizes, a quarterly review, and weekly religious papers. This establishment is conducted by a suitable number of agents and editors, who are elected by the General Conference, to which body they are responsible for their official conduct, and, in the interval of the General, the New York Annual Conference exercises a supervision of this estimable and highly useful establishment.

In the last place, we may mention the Missionary Society of the Methodist Episcopal Church, which was organized in 1819. . . .

In the work of Sabbath schools, in the establishment of academies and colleges, though the latter have been but recently commenced with any thing like a determination to persevere, this church has taken an honorable stand among its sister denominations. . . .

This is a general outline of the system, the different parts of which have grown out of the exigencies of the times, suiting itself to the mental, moral, and spiritual wants of men, and expanding itself so as to embrace the largest possible number of individuals as objects of its benevolence. I may well be suspected of partiality to a system, to the benign operation of which I am so much indebted, and which has exerted such a beneficial influence upon the best interests of mankind; but I cannot avoid thinking that I see in it that "perfection of beauty, out of which God hath shined," and that emanation of divine truth and light, which is destined, unless it should unhappily degenerate from its primitive beauty and simplicity "into a plant of a strange vine," and thus lose its original energy of character, to do its full share in enlightening and converting the world.[4]

George Cookman, British born, member of the Philadelphia Conference, chaplain of the Senate and fervent abolitionist, viewed Methodism as a machine the flywheel of which was itinerancy.[5] Employing the vision of Ezekiel, he conceded some of Methodism's agony over machinery but warranted its providential design:

> The *great iron wheel* in the system *is itinerancy,* and truly it grinds some of us most tremendously; . . . Let us carefully note the admirable and astounding movements of this wonderful machine. You will perceive there are "wheels within wheels." First, there is the great outer wheel of episcopacy, which accomplishes its entire revolution *once* in *four* years. To this there are attached *twenty-eight smaller wheels,* styled *annual conferences,* moving around *once a year;* to these are attached *one hundred wheels,* designated *presiding elders,* moving *twelve hundred other wheels,* termed *quarterly conferences,* every *three* months; to these are attached *four thousand wheels,* styled *travelling preachers,* moving round *once a month,* and communicating motion to *thirty thousand* wheels, called *class leaders,* moving round *once a week,* and who, in turn, being attached to between *seven and eight hundred thousand wheels,* called *members,* give a sufficient impulse to whirl them round *every day.* O, sir, what a machine is this! This is the machine of which Archimedes only dreamed; this is the machine destined, under God, to *move the world, to turn it upside down.* But, sir, you will readily see the whole success of the operation depends upon keeping the *great iron wheel of itinerancy* in motion. It must be as unincumbered and free as possible.[6]

4. Nathan Bangs, D.D., *An Original Church of Christ: Or, A Scriptural Vindication of the Orders and Powers of the Ministry of the Methodist Episcopal Church* (New York: J. Collord, 1837), pp. 348-51.

5. Itinerancy or itineracy, the hallmark of Methodist ministry, was the system designed by John Wesley of appointing preachers, of putting them traveling on a circuit of preaching places, and of moving them periodically from circuit to circuit. The long quotation above from Nathan Bangs describes this system, as does the following statement from George Cookman. The best way to view the itinerant system is by reading the journal of a traveling preacher, and those abound. See, for instance, David L. Kimbrough, *Reverend Joseph Tarkington, Methodist Circuit Rider: From Frontier Evangelism to Refined Religion* (Knoxville: University of Tennessee Press, 1997).

6. George G. Cookman, *Speeches Delivered on Various Occasions* (New York: George Lane for the MEC, 1840), pp. 127-37.

Writing during the Civil War, when northern Methodism threw its machinery into gear for the Union cause, the historian and apologist Abel Stevens found his image for Methodist machinery not in the scriptural type but in the contemporary antitype. Looking forward rather than backward, he identified two engines that conquered the new world, the steam engine and Methodism. Stevens began his four-volume history of American Methodism with an imagined meeting in 1757 of John Wesley and James Watt in Glasgow. Watt, "the young artisan of Glasgow University, gave to the world the Steam Engine." Wesley fabricated a system, providentially suited, Stevens argued, for the new world, comparable in delivery of morality, values, belief, and commitment to that other engine and establishing a religious economy with its own factories, rails, steamship lines, and infrastructure. Stevens then described the Methodist system, showing how each feature of its machinery suited the American situation. By the conceit of the imagined meeting of Watt and Wesley, Stevens gloried in Methodist machinery: "Watt and Wesley might well then have struck hands and bid each other godspeed at Glasgow in 1757: they were co-workers for the destinies of the new world."[7]

Structuring for Accountability and Efficiency

On the eve of the war, the southern bishop, James O. Andrew (whose slaveholding, it should be noted, had occasioned the church's 1844 division), observed that Wesley's machine had over time acquired a complexity that now challenged the authority structures of the church — episcopacy and conference. Much of the change, particularly the establishment of institutions and agencies, had occurred during his career: "When we first visited an Annual Conference, the most we had to do was to examine the characters of the preachers, take the numbers, attend to the finances, (a very small business about those times,) read out the appointments, and go home. We had no schools or colleges, no Tract, Missionary, or Sunday-school Societies, to manage. We had not a dozen associations whose complicated machinery requires several days to adjust and keep in proper order."[8]

What Andrew viewed as a challenge, the northern church (Methodist

7. Abel Stevens, *History of The Methodist Episcopal Church in the United States of America*, 4 vols. (New York: Eaton and Mains; Cincinnati: Jennings and Pye, 1864-67), 1:16, 18, 26-28, 45-46.

8. James O. Andrew, "Bishop Asbury," one of a series of review biographical statements in commentary on Thomas O. Summers, *Biographical Sketches of Eminent Itinerant Ministers*, *MQRS* 13 (January 1859), pp. 10-11.

528

Episcopal Church, or MEC), by the end of the war, began to recognize as a problem. The machinery, remarkable as it was, could run out of control. In particular, agencies set up as voluntary societies to manage the church's enterprises in publishing, education, missions, freedmen's aid, church extension, Sunday schools — several of these with female counterparts — could operate remarkably independently. A committee set up to study the matter reported to the 1872 General Conference (MEC) on the problem with the whole voluntary organizational plan:

> The members of the Board are elected by members of the Society, and the members of the Society are those persons who become such by the payment of twenty dollars or more to its fund.
>
> The General Conference has no legal connection with the Society, except only that by the charter it is provided that the Corresponding Secretaries of said Society shall be elected by the General Conference. . . .
>
> But as the whole management is vested in the Board elected by members of the Society, the Corresponding Secretaries are powerless to represent any interest of the Church or of the Conference independent of the will of the Board. It is evident, too, that the multitude of members of the Society, scattered widely in all parts of the country, either cannot or will not participate in the election of a Board of Managers. It is equally evident that local combinations are liable to be formed each year to change the management of the corporation, and obtain control of its great resources. We do not express or intimate any doubt of the judicious and faithful management of the Society, but it is high time to close the door against the possibility of danger in the future. . . .
>
> The General Conference, as the supreme legislative authority of the Church, and having in charge all its great interests for the diffusion of Christian civilization, should have a controlling power in all the missionary operations carried on in the name and behalf of the Church.[9]

So the northern church, the MEC, in 1872 and the southern, the MECS (Methodist Episcopal Church, South), in 1874 acted to amend the charters of and reincorporate societies so as to make them denominational agencies, accountable to and with boards elected by General Conference.

Over the next century Methodist bodies sought various other efficiencies in machinery, as for instance, centrally determined budgets for all agencies and

---

9. "The Report of the Special Committee on the Relation of Benevolent Institutions of the Church to the General Conference," *Journal of the General Conference* (Methodist Episcopal Church), 1872, pp. 295-99.

apportionments allocated to the annual conferences, as the MEC bishops advocated in 1912:

> As the head of a family anticipates and provides for the incoming year, as a business man estimates the capital required for his contemplated improvements as well as for conducting present enterprises, so should the Church forecast her needs and consolidate her estimates for all connectional demands — not by the uncertain process of five or six boards and committees sitting apart and acting independently, if not competitively, but by a competent connectional board or commission — in which or before which all interests may be represented — and with final authority to fix the aggregate budget and properly apportion the total amount among the Conferences.[10]

In the 1939 union that brought together the two Methodist Episcopal churches and the Methodist Protestants, directors acquired the prerogative of selecting agency heads (general secretaries). And the 1968 union of the Methodist and Evangelical United Brethren churches, drawing on the experience of the latter denomination, established a program-coordinating agency, the General Council on Ministries, to work alongside the General Council on Finance and Administration.

Wrenches in the Works

By the late twentieth century the machine no longer enjoyed Methodist fascination. Steam ran fewer and fewer engines. The railroads clung on with subsidies. Factories folded and slunk off to the Third World. The industrial age gave way to that of the computer, electronics, media and communications. Machinery in human affairs, bureaucracy, and red tape, Americans disdained and denounced. George Wallace launched a presidential bid running against federal machinery and pointy-headed bureaucrats. And subsequent campaigns for House, Senate, and the presidency, both Democratic and Republican but especially the latter, ran on Wallace's ticket. The same script worked famously on the regional and local levels where candidates campaigned against state government or city hall.

So also in religious affairs, what had once been Methodist glory — national standards, centralized production, efficiencies of scale, common resourcing, proportional fiscal obligations, unified decision making, coherent

10. "Episcopal Address," *Journal of the General Conference* (Methodist Episcopal Church), 1912, pp. 198-202.

denominational policy, easily recognized packaging, familiar products, dependable quality — became Methodist-pillory. Bureaucracy has become a slur word.

That negative reading surfaced powerfully after the 1960s — after the Civil Rights and antiwar campaigns and, for United Methodists, after the 1968 union and 1972 restructuring. It has continued ever since. One of the early denunciations came from two of my colleagues, Paul A. Mickey and the late Robert L. Wilson. Their *What New Creation? The Agony of Church Restructure*[11] looked at bureaucracy and denominational reorganization efforts in the American Baptist, Episcopal, Presbyterian, United Presbyterian, and United Methodist churches. What they found were crises, engulfing the denominations as a whole and focused on their agencies.

Their findings or indictments have become something of a litany. National bureaucracies had been dismantled, reassembled, reshuffled, physically relocated with attendant chaos, confusion, and lowered morale among executives and staff. Funding had dropped as membership plateaued and fell, or as congregations withheld monies in anger over policies. Grassroots anger had indeed focused on a number of controversial and high-profile initiatives, programs had been cut, and distrust toward national and regional offices grew. Such pointed attacks on bureaucracy, sometimes concretized in term limits or other thinly disguised punitive efforts, produced morale problems in the agencies. Caucus attempts to gain footholds on boards and in their staffs intensified the political struggles by which leadership identification took place. Agencies evidenced confusion and unclarity about purposes and goals. The entire connectional scheme seemed in crisis, a crisis Mickey and Wilson insisted derived from underlying crises of denominational belief and purpose.

Since Mickey and Wilson wrote, we have witnessed a whole industry grow up producing books diagnosing the problems in mainline Protestantism and prescribing various antidotes. Many of these treat bureaucracy as a problem and echo the Mickey-Wilson indictments, if not always their vivid conspiratorial style. For instance, two of the volumes in the General Council on Ministries series "Into Our Third Century," *Images of the Future*, by Alan K. Waltz, and *Paths to Transformation: A Study of the General Agencies of the United Methodist Church*, by Kristine M. Rogers and Bruce A. Rogers,[12] treated anticentralization attitudes more as problem than norm, but they recognize the same problematic. Richard Wilke, in *And Are We Yet Alive? The Future of the United Methodist Church*, found plenty of blame to spread around but certainly called

11. (Nashville: Abingdon, 1977).
12. (Nashville: Abingdon, 1980) and (Nashville: Abingdon, 1982).

for overhaul, stripping down, streamlining, and reorienting our structures.[13] Longtime church researchers Douglas W. Johnson and Alan K. Waltz, in their volume with the colorless title *Facts and Possibilities: An Agenda for the United Methodist Church,* pointed to the lack of coordination at the national level among the Council of Bishops, General Conference, and general agencies, *and* this lack of coordination despite the existence and efforts of two coordinating agencies, the General Council on Finance and Administration and the General Council on Ministries.[14] And then a decade ago, the whole Council of Bishops waded in with their prophetic study and episcopal letter, *Vital Congregations, Faithful Disciples: Vision for the Church: Foundation Document.*[15] They too treated central agency structures as problems.

New Machinery for a New Millennium?

The critics of Methodist bureaucracy sound as if they oppose all machinery. However, to view their activities rather than listen to their tirades, one discovers in many of these apparent Luddites incredible institutional ferment, experimentation, creativity, and energy. They denounce old machinery to make space for new — assembled from below; freshly purposive; digital, technological, and media-reliant; highly adaptive; and packaged for business. These Methodists glory over more local or adaptive machinery as they agonize over still-official national structures. This ambivalence runs deep in the Methodist psyche. It derives from habits and patterns and practices that Methodists are much better at doing than explaining.[16] The appointive machinery around itinerancy operationalizes a missional principle, namely, that ministry is sent, commissioned, missionary in character. The superintending or episcopal machinery, at its best, concerns itself with the kingdom, the deployment of each for the good of the whole (earth). The conferences, which Methodists still regard as the basic body of the church, are now being reclaimed as "means of grace," a phrase Wesley himself applied to the conferencing tasks — conversations about growth in holiness for the whole body. And boards and agencies, even they display, as do these other systems, deep Methodist conviction that connecting in the work of

13. (Nashville: Abingdon, 1986). See especially pp. 57-64.

14. (Nashville: Abingdon, 1987).

15. (Nashville: Graded Press, ca. 1990).

16. On the following themes, see the several volumes in the United Methodism and American Culture series. My introductory essay in volume 1, *Connectionalism: Ecclesiology, Mission, and Identity,* ed. Russell E. Richey, William B. Lawrence, and Dennis M. Campbell (Nashville: Abingdon, 1997), pp. 1-20, informs this paragraph.

God is the church, that the church is connectional, that the connection displays God's will.

The *United Methodist Discipline* reads like a book of order or constitution, and that it is. But it derived from a series of conversations that Wesley conducted in conference about how to follow the path to holiness. This counsel about discipline the Americans decided to call *Discipline*. Over time discipline as calling, as response to the divine initiative, as a way of living into God's future has yielded power, structure, and process. Its instrumental value has tended to obscure its missional, gracious, ecclesial character. Nevertheless, the machinery that the *Discipline* describes and for which it calls, Methodists have typically established as an act of discipline. And from time to time they have seen fit to renew or refresh or augment their discipline by adding to or altering the *Discipline*. So their machinery has evolved over time, the acts of discipline over which one generation glories becoming the agonies of a later one.

Connectional Reform?

Agonies over machinery — the central, executive, decision-making apparatus of the denomination — led the general conference, over the last two quadrennia (1992-2000), to commission various studies and task force inquiries into national connectional structures and processes. It is this organizational work and parallel initiatives by the Council of Bishops that are the foci of the following case study by James Wood and theological essay by Pamela Couture.

Leadership, Identity, and Mission
in a Changing United Methodist Church

James Rutland Wood

E ntering the twenty-first century, the United Methodist Church (UMC) faces dramatic changes destined to redefine the role of the denomination's leadership, reshape its identity, and refocus its mission. These changes are driven by social forces in the church's environment and by a vigorous value struggle these forces have precipitated within the church. Contested values include the locus and form of organizational control, the meaning and priority of biblical authority, and the nature and scope of the church's mission. This chapter describes ways the UMC is changing, discusses social forces underlying those changes, elucidates some of their wider implications, and interprets the process of change sociologically as an organization adapting to its environment and theologically as the movement of the Holy Spirit.[1]

Overview of the UMC Structure

A brief overview of the UMC's current structure will provide background for the consideration of changes and proposed changes. For most of the twentieth century the UMC and its Methodist predecessor groups have been characterized by highly centralized bureaucracies. Programs developed by boards and leaders at

1. Data for this chapter include a survey of delegates to the 1996 UMC General Conference, formal interviews with ten UMC bishops (including one from each jurisdiction) and conversations with an additional dozen bishops, interviews with the chief executives of two United Methodist boards, United Methodist responses to the General Social Survey (a national poll), minutes of the 1996 General Conference and other documents related to restructure, and observations of one meeting of the Connectional Process Team and four meetings of the Council of Bishops.

the national level have been implemented in a top-down fashion. Ministers tell the story of one pastor who said, "If by Friday I haven't heard from the District Superintendent or one of the national boards and agencies, I go ahead and choose my own theme for my Sunday sermon." This often-repeated story only slightly exaggerates the way the denomination has attempted to have all of its churches at the same time implementing the general church's programs and promoting its causes. This coordination was accomplished by a leadership hierarchy and a structure that largely duplicated the national structure in each annual conference, district, and local congregation. Since the national structure has included more than a dozen general agencies — including those treating Christian unity, church and society, communications, discipleship, finance and administration, global ministries, higher education, religion and race, status and role of women and United Methodist men — the structure of a local congregation could become quite complex. Though there may always have been some unanticipated costs of this complexity — such as clergy and lay burnout and neglect of some causes of local concern — much was accomplished by this structure. Health and educational institutions were built, home and overseas missions were supported, new churches were started. But people and society are changing, and so is the church. A new type of organization and a new type of leadership are emerging from the UMC's stormy quest for identity and its response to United Methodists' demands that the church's mission impact their lives and their communities.

Leadership and Control

Whether with pride or dismay, most United Methodists acknowledge that their denomination is highly centralized. But it is not easy to identify the center of power. The UMC has no presiding bishop, president, or moderator. The General Conference — the official lawmaking body — is the final authority. This conference is made up of about five hundred clergy delegates and an equal number of lay delegates elected by their annual (regional) conferences. About eight hundred of these delegates represent the annual conferences in the United States, and about two hundred represent United Methodist (UM) churches in other countries.

The Discipline (the UMC's book of laws and policies) states that "No person, no paper, no organization, has the authority to speak officially for The United Methodist Church, this right having been reserved exclusively to the General Conference under the Constitution."[2] But the General Conference

---

2. *The Book of Discipline* (Nashville: United Methodist Publishing House, 1996), p. 277.

meets only once every four years. Where is power centered in the interim? There is no consensus on the answer to this question, and the answer probably varies over time as particular people and entities of the church exert leadership. The evolving role of bishops and the Council of Bishops is a major focus of this chapter. Bishops, individually and collectively, may be emerging as the key power wielders of the early twenty-first century.

Individually, bishops wield a great deal of power in the annual conferences over which they preside as well as within the boards and agencies where they also preside. Here is where much of the significant structural change is occurring. *The Discipline* describes a number of aspects of the bishops' leadership role: it is through their appointing of ministers in their annual conferences that the connectional nature of the UM system is made visible; they are to enable the gathered church to worship and to evangelize faithfully; they are to facilitate the initiation of structures and strategies for the equipping of Christian people for service in the church and in the world; they are to guard the faith, order, liturgy, doctrine, and discipline of the church. Moreover, "The Church expects the Council of Bishops to speak to the Church and from the Church to the world and to give leadership in the quest for Christian unity and interreligious relationships."[3]

G. Bromley Oxnam (1891-1963) may be the best modern example of a bishop who enabled strong collective leadership from the Council of Bishops, especially in the areas of civil rights and international policy. Presently the bishops' initiative on children and poverty represents a major collective effort of the Council of Bishops to shape the identity and mission of the UMC.

Some Widely Shared Concerns

My interviews and conversations with bishops and my observations of four Council of Bishops meetings in 1998 and 1999 show that bishops are well informed about a number of concerns felt throughout the church. One bishop told me, "There has been a sense at all levels that the present organization simply is not getting the job done. The structure is burdensome without serving mission. This has led to a great deal of soul-searching about who we are and what we should be doing."

Some bishops point to pressures within the UMC that are driving the change process. United Methodists are aware that the size of the membership and, possibly, the influence of the denomination have declined. In 1997, for ex-

3. *The Book of Discipline*, p. 266.

ample, 9 percent of the U.S. population gave "Methodist" as their religious preference, compared to 14 percent in 1974.[4] This decline has occurred despite a national climate congenial to religion. Fifty-seven percent of Americans continue
to believe that religion is relevant to contemporary society, and George Gallup,
Jr., reports a "new surge of interest in spirituality" among Americans in recent
years.[5] Against this background, many United Methodists began to believe that
the UMC needed to undertake serious self-examination. As an indication of the
grassroots push for change, one bishop I interviewed emphasized that the new
UMC mission statement, "Make Disciples," "came from pulpit and pew, *not*
from the general church or the bishops." According to this bishop, part of the
dynamic behind a new mission statement was rank-and-file United Methodists
feeling the "need to make a difference." Another bishop was a bit more specific:
"I thought it was interesting that the impetus for change came from across the
theological spectrum. It was one of those places where I saw the left and right
really joining hearts and voice. It has to do with both. Although they see mission and ministry differently, both see and saw the mission of the church being
thwarted by the way in which the church is structured at this time. It is as if our
more bureaucratized way of being is hindering the Spirit." When asked how the
mission statement got to the General Conference, the same bishop replied:
"Well, it came though the traditional route, in General Conference work. It
came from annual conferences and from individuals. It was empowering, some
of it came from the right, the left. In 1996 the Willimon group came in with a
highly polished piece. Others would represent a different theological take saying the same thing. The petition process was used."

The bishops' accounts reflected concerns widely shared by the 1996 General Conference delegates I surveyed. Many of the delegates responded in light of
1996 General Conference legislation that was beginning to meet those concerns.

Asked "What action taken by the 1996 General Conference do you think
has the most significance for the United Methodist Church?" just over a quarter
of the delegates mentioned some aspect of restructure at the annual conference
or national level. Twenty percent mentioned new flexibility of the local church
structure. Also related to the local church, 32 percent mentioned approval of
the changes in ministerial orders. Many saw this as an important structural
change that will bring about, in the words of one delegate, "a new involvement
of the laity in ministry." Those who rate themselves conservative in religious

---

4. Princeton Religion Research Center, *Emerging Trends,* vol. 20, no. 7 (September 1998),
p. 2.

5. Princeton Religion Research Center, *Emerging Trends,* vol. 20, no. 10 (December 1998),
p. 4.

matters and those who rate themselves liberal are about equally likely to mention each of these structural changes as significant.

Delegates' comments about actions of the 1996 General Conference show how leadership, identity, and mission are interrelated. One strong theme is how flexibility in structure and a broader leadership base impact mission at the local level: "It puts us in charge, not the annual conference or the General Conference! Makes it possible to organize for mission and ministry within parameters of the needs of the community." "This helps regain our sense of mission, moves from an authoritarianism which is stifling, and opens the possibility for addressing ministry in a servant fashion." "If taken advantage of, the options have the potential to encourage local churches to analyze their mission and to determine how to meet that mission, thus inspiring action." Another theme links United Methodists' identity as God's people with flexibility of structure that makes room for the Holy Spirit. "It allows each group to be more visionary and creative about the ministry each church feels God is calling them to do." "Allows for flexibility and for conferences to follow where they believe the Holy Spirit is leading them." "We need room for the Holy Spirit to move within the more flexible structure." "It is time to trust God and allow the spirit to freely move — not control it with structure." "Churches need to organize to fulfil their primary mission of making disciples." Delegates also have a keen sense of the relation between lay empowerment and mission: "This empowers the laity in the local church with a sense of involvement in shaping mission response." "[Changes in ministry] could encourage and free persons to be in ministry other than ordained, thus broadening the leadership base." "We have entered a new partnership of ministry for clergy and laity and we have returned to a more biblical and understandable system of ordained ministry." Delegates also applaud the recognition of the distinctive mission and ministry of a diversity of local churches: "This is the beginning step in changing the focus from the general church to the local church." "The small membership church is affirmed in its own special ministry." "This may be seen as responsive to concerns and needs of smaller churches and help alleviate their sense of being ignored." Delegates affirmed the need for the church to frame its message in ways relevant to the contemporary world: "In order to reach the next generation, we must be willing to put forth the same old message, but in new and different ways. We don't yet know what those ways are, and we don't yet know what all the hurts and needs will be. However we will be able to have enough flexibility to respond." "For the church to be viable for the next century, it is necessary to restructure. To empower laity to be in ministry, to bring clergy and laity closer together. The church must be relevant for the next generations." Many see restructure as a matter of good stewardship — putting the money where the mission is: "Downsizing is very much needed and significant. We need more money for missions and evangelism." "The general church agencies do very little for the local church other than cost it money. And trust has eroded from local to general."

Contested Values

There are two processes of change within the UMC. One process is a noisy, visible, occasionally disorderly and uncivil struggle over the fundamental identity of the church. The other process, discussed in more detail later, is more regular and orderly as duly appointed representatives go about redefining the church's mission and redesigning its structure to carry out that mission in the contemporary world.

The first process centers on the meaning and priority of biblical authority and, consequently, on the nature and scope of the church's mission. At one pole are those who are confident that the Bible provides clear guidance on the issues that face the church today. For them the church's failure to follow these clear mandates undercuts the authority of the Bible. These United Methodists typically focus more on individual salvation than on societal reform and place more emphasis on individual morality than on social justice. At the other pole are those who, though they may acknowledge the authority of the Bible, believe that some of the culture-bound injunctions in the Bible contradict some of its most basic teachings about love and justice. These United Methodists often focus principally on societal reform and social justice with little emphasis on personal salvation. Since both these groups of United Methodists are sincere and passionate about their views, it is sometimes difficult for them to dialogue with each other.

If United Methodists in general were this polarized, the church's unity would certainly be in jeopardy. It is likely, however, that those at the poles do not have the followers they imagine. James Davison Hunter, observing the "culture wars" in the general society, discovered that the intense feelings are more of the leaders than of their followers — that the vast middle of the society is not passionately involved in the struggle over values.[6] It is quite possible that most United Methodists, drawing on their rich Wesleyan heritage, have a great deal in common with both groups described above, hence cherish a diversity that encompasses both poles. Still, this struggle over values hijacks the agenda and consumes the energy of the church.

My study of the bishops and the Council of Bishops shows that the bish-

---

6. James Davison Hunter, *Culture Wars: The Struggle to Define America* (New York: Basic Books, 1991).

ops are well aware of these two processes of change and want to address the concerns that stimulate them. Whether the emerging power of the bishops will be equal to that task remains to be seen. Clearly, bishops are caught up in the controversies that are roiling the church. Diverse groups are challenging bishops' and other leaders' control as a means of gaining influence over the identity and mission of the church. Here is an excerpt from a speech by one conservative leader: "I believe most people within our denomination support the high calling of episcopal leadership in the United Methodist Church. We want our leaders to lead. We want our leaders to guard, maintain, and teach the doctrine of our church. We want them to defend the discipline of the United Methodist Church. In fact, we are so serious about it, we believe it is of such crucial importance, that we are no longer willing to allow our bishops to exploit the episcopacy to pursue their narrow ideological agendas."[7]

But bishops are also challenged by their liberal constituencies, who see changes driven by conservative theology as "narrow ideological agendas." For example, the Methodist Federation of Social Action (MFSA) was concerned that the mission statement adopted in 1996 — "The mission of the Church is to make disciples of Jesus Christ" — will be too narrowly interpreted. They proposed expanding that statement by adding the following sentence: "discipleship means continuing Christ's world-changing work of offering God's gift of salvation, healing relationships, transforming social structures and following in the way of love and service."

Here we see the same value conflict that led conservatives dissatisfied with the General Board of Global Ministry (GBGM) to form their own mission society in 1984. At that time, one advocate gave the following as one rationale for forming a new society:

> Consider the annual report for 1982 by the President and General Secretary of the GBGM. In this report it is very difficult to find any clear indication that the evangelistic mandate of calling people to personal, saving faith in Jesus Christ is an urgent part of the program and priorities of the board.
>
> The report says that "we are called to understand ourselves as sharing in the cosmic events of this era," that "mission has moved from the perspective of territorial conquest to one in which the arena is one of spirit and mind," that "mission is a slow, tedious struggle with principalities and powers in the force of evil," that "we must implement the Gospel without fear," and that mission is "being in the frontiers of race, of economic structure, of

---

7. Scott Field, member of the board of directors of Good News, in an address to the national conference of the Confessing Movement, September 1999.

political reality or of cultural difference." What the report does not mention is that *faith* is also a frontier where we are called to witness.

Nothing in this annual report suggests that it is a matter of any special concern to our GBGM that 120 million people in this country and 68 percent of the world's population do not have saving faith in Christ.[8]

In recent years the homosexuality issue has become the symbol of the struggle over the church's identity. Though the bishops have been sharply divided on this issue, and are very much caught up in the controversy, we will see that they feel that facing the controversy has brought them closer together, forging a unity that empowers their leadership.

Still, the church may be growing more polarized as United Methodists at both poles of the liberal/conservative field more forcefully press their views. For example, compare the response of the Confessing Movement with that of the Reconciling Congregation Program to the California/Nevada decision to bring no charges against sixty-eight pastors who, disregarding *The Discipline*'s prohibition of such action, jointly celebrated the union of two women. The Confessing Movement said, in part:

> It is our deep conviction that Bishop Melvin Talbert, the leadership of the California/Nevada Conference, and the 68 pastors who performed the same-sex union have broken covenant with their colleagues in the rest of United Methodism. Our covenant is not restricted to Conference boundaries, but includes the whole of the connection. It is obvious that the decision of the California/Nevada Conference is in violation of Church Law. The question is, will Bishop Talbert and his colleagues in the Conference be held accountable? This arrogant usurpation of power and disregard for the action of General Conference and the decision of the Judicial Council cannot be allowed to stand. To do so would surely bring a division in the United Methodist Church. One would wonder if this is the intent of Bishop Talbert and his colleagues in the California/Nevada Conference.[9]

The Reconciling Congregation board's response to the decision said, in part:

> This ruling is positive in that it reflects the diversity within The United Methodist Church (UMC). The California-Nevada Conference of The

8. Gerald H. Anderson, "Why We Need a Second Mission Agency," an address to UM clergy in Dallas, Tex., October 1983.

9. "Confessing Movement Response to California/Nevada Decision to Bring No Charges against 67 Pastors," *We Confess: A Newsletter of the Confessing Movement within the United Methodist Church* 6, issue 2 (March/April 2000): 2.

UMC has a long history of inclusiveness of gay, lesbian, bisexual and transgender people, dating back to 1964 when San Francisco clergy founded the Commission on Religion and Homosexuality. In 1985 their Annual Conference adopted a resolution commending the Reconciling Congregation Program to all churches and in 1987 they voted to become a Reconciling Conference.

As much as the previous Nebraska ruling that defrocked Jimmy Creech is an interpretation of the UMC Discipline, this California-Nevada decision is equally of the church. Within the book of Discipline, there are contradictory statements on sexual orientation. These rulings highlight the conflict between recent language that restricts celebrations of "homosexual unions" and core statements that reflect our Wesleyan heritage and charge the whole church to be broadly inclusive.[10]

Going beyond statements, United Methodists at one pole have encouraged civil disobedience, such as that of the California/Nevada pastors, while those at the other pole have assembled a legal staff to facilitate the process of holding pastors and churches accountable to the discipline.

Where this will end is not clearly discernible, but already the high-profile civil disobedience on the one side and the policing of local churches on the other have dramatically changed the climate in which the UMC does its work.

Changes in the UMC

Many changes and proposals for change have occurred as United Methodists, individually and in groups, have sought to influence the identity and mission of the church. The current official change process began when the 1992 General Conference directed the General Council on Ministries (GCOM) to "lead the church in a time of discernment, reflection, and study of its mission and its structural needs as it moves into the twenty-first century. The Council will do this by consulting groups across the church, conducting appropriate research, and developing and utilizing resource materials."[11]

As discussed above, drawing on the results of this four-year "connectional issues" study, the 1996 General Conference passed legislation giving considerable flexibility to local churches to restructure themselves to fit the needs of

10. "Reconciling Congregation Board Responds to California-Nevada Conference Decision on 'Sacramento 68'" (press release by the Reconciling Congregation Program, February 11, 2000), p. 1.

11. *Daily Christian Advocate: Advanced Edition* 1 (1992): 537.

their ministries. For example, for the local church the number of required committees was reduced, and though several mandated emphases remain, "every local church shall develop a plan for organizing its administrative and programmatic responsibilities . . . so that it can pursue its primary task and mission in the context of its own community."[12] It appears that delegates also expected that considerable new flexibility for annual conferences would follow ratification of a constitutional amendment to "allow the Annual Conferences to utilize structures unique to regional aspects of their mission, other mandated structures notwithstanding."[13] But when several annual conferences either enacted or proposed such new structures, the Judicial Council (the UMC's Supreme Court) ruled that such changes could not occur until a future General Conference passes appropriate enabling legislation.[14]

The Connectional Process Team

In addition to these actions, the 1996 conference established a Connectional Process Team (CPT) "for 1996 to 2000 to manage, guide, and promote a transformational direction for The United Methodist Church."[15] In February 1999 the CPT released its penultimate report. Though, as we will see below, this report underwent extensive revision as a result of feedback invited by the committee, discussion centering on the report provides an important window on contested values within the UMC today. The report paints a picture of a struggle to clarify the church's identity, to refocus its mission, and to shape its structure to reflect both identity and mission.

The CPT report defines UMC work to reflect the church's identity as Spirit-centered, diverse, global, and focused on mission. It is anchored solidly in biblical theology, especially Jesus' commission to "make disciples of all nations, baptizing them in the name of the Father and of the Son and of the Holy Spirit, and teaching them to obey everything that I have commanded you" (Matt. 28:19-20). This Great Commission is reflected in the UMC's new (1996) mission statement: "The mission of the Church is to make disciples of Jesus Christ. Local churches provide the most significant arena through which disciple-making occurs."[16] The report

---

12. *Book of Discipline*, pp. 136-37.

13. "Judicial Council Offers Guidelines for Conference Restructure at Present," United Methodist News Service, October 31, 1997, p. 1.

14. See, for example, Judicial Council Decision No. 831. http://www.umc.org/interior_judicial.asp?mid=263&JDID=871&JDMOD=VWD&SN=801&EN=900

15. *Daily Christian Advocate* 3, no. 6 (April 22, 1996): 252.

16. *Book of Discipline*, p. 114.

also draws attention to the *Discipline's* statement of the process for carrying out the church's mission:

- Proclaim the Gospel, seek, welcome and gather persons into the body of Christ;
- Lead persons to commit their lives to God through Jesus Christ;
- Nurture persons in Christian living through worship, baptism, communion, Bible and other studies, prayer, and other means of grace;
- Send persons into the world to live lovingly and justly as servants of Christ by healing the sick, feeding the hungry, caring for the stranger, freeing the oppressed, and working to have social structures consistent with the gospel; and
- Continue the mission of seeking, welcoming and gathering persons into the community of the body of Christ.[17]

The CPT then asks one central question of "all of the activities, functions, and structures of the church today: Will this help us invite, nurture, and empower disciples of Jesus Christ through local congregations and faith communities throughout the world?" (p. 6).

The report presents eleven "transformational directions" congruent with this question. The first five embody the CPT's central concern with spiritual leadership — listening, caring, serving leaders whose spiritual life is nurtured by "spiritual disciplines" that have sustained Christians throughout the ages:

- Place spiritual formation at the center of our work.
- Invigorate the ministry of the church.
- Call forth spiritual leaders.
- Create a Covenant Council of spiritual and prophetic leaders.
- Empower the ministry of congregations and faith communities. (pp. 7-9)

Five other transformational directions reflect various aspects of the UMC's identity as a global, connectional, ecumenical, theologically diverse, and inclusive church. The remaining direction expresses the intention that general agencies exist "to support congregations, faith communities, and annual conferences" (pp. 10-11).

Moving from definition to structure, the CPT recommends a number of

17. Connectional Process Team of the United Methodist Church, *Transforming: A United Methodist Church for the Twenty-First Century* (February 1999), p. 5. Page numbers in the following text refer to this document.

structural changes throughout the UMC. The heart of the recommendations is summarized in a paragraph headed "Create a Covenant Council of Spiritual and Prophetic Leaders."

> We propose that The United Methodist Church center on a Covenant Council of spiritual and prophetic leaders, a new form of organization. These leaders will come together to hear the call of Christ, discern the will of God for our ministry in the world, nourish each other spiritually, and support each other in carrying Christ's message into the world. As an organization, we often go to extremes in segmenting our resources and energies into task-related, discrete components. In local congregations these take the form of burgeoning committees and fragmented responsibilities for staff. The same is true in districts and in annual and central conferences. In the general church, the clearest manifestation of this is the vast array of general agencies. This segmentation has confused our understanding of our common mission and our expression of the connection. It has muffled our message as a united church. We recommend creating in each part of the church (local congregation, annual conference, central conference, and Global Conference) a Covenant Council where spiritual and prophetic lay and clergy leaders will gather for discernment, discussion, decision-making, and disciple-making. (p. 8)

Thus the CPT, expanding on the flexibility already granted to annual conferences and local congregations, proposes a simple, fluid decision and control structure that reflects the church's mission "to make disciples of Jesus Christ."

The most controversial recommendations coming from the CPT stem from the reconstitution of the General Conference — the denomination's highest legislative body — as the United Methodist Global Conference and the creation of a United States Central Conference. To illustrate the impact of this change, consider the proposal for balance in global representation. CPT recommended "that no single continent (North America, Europe, Africa, or Asia) have more than 50 percent of the total number of delegates in the Global Conference" (p. 24). For comparison, the 2000 General Conference will have 830 delegates from the United States — 84.5 percent of the total delegates. The CPT was not timid in recognizing the implications of these changes. "This transformation requires a shift from a model in which the United States' perspective dominates a highly structured organization to one where the global perspective supports a rich variety of United Methodist ministries and missions around the world" (p. 21).

Those parts of the proposal related to the Global Conference were highly contested. One reason for this is the power and turf struggles of boards and agencies that have been observed in other efforts to change the UMC bureaucracy.[18] One bishop told me, "If you look at legislation and *The Book of Discipline*, it is written primarily to protect a certain area of the turf and not primarily to engage the church in mission in the world. . . . Agencies have become defensive. They have spent a lot of time preserving themselves and are not interested in change unless they can control that change." Some delegates to the 1996 General Conference perceived the Board of Global Ministries' lobbying effort to keep that conference from moving the board out of New York City as an example of such resistance to change. By contrast, the top executive of the General Council on Ministries seemed willing to accept the demise of his agency provided a new structure continues the essential functions of the GCOM.[19]

This proposal in addition challenges some of the vested interests of various regional entities. One bishop reflected: "To move us toward a more global church and allow other areas of the world to participate on a more equal footing and to deal with the reality of a huge amount of the money still in the United States, how does that play out in terms of these issues around power?" It seems likely, for example, that those called on to pay the bulk of the additional cost of the Global Conference will have less representation than in the current structure. The widely read *United Methodist Reporter (UMR)* observed that "U.S. United Methodists make up 88 percent of the church numerically but will have only a maximum of 50 percent of the representation in the denomination's highest policy-making body." The editorial strongly criticized the proposed global structure for unfair representation, "distancing congregations even farther from their leaders," increased cost that would be borne disproportionately by U.S. churches, and "massive centralization that runs counter to our era of decentralized networks."[20] In subsequent issues of the *UMR,* reader reaction revealed considerable ambivalence toward the global structure. One retired bishop called the editorial "nothing but a rehash of paternalistic and parochial ideas — not to mention 'colonial' attitudes and practices." In sharp contrast, a retired United Methodist missionary to the Philippines sees "the idea of a global structure as detrimental to the movement toward an indigenous church in the Philippines." He believes that "our overseas United Methodist brothers and sisters . . . are eager to share

18. See Paul A. Mickey and Robert L. Wilson, *What New Creation? The Agony of Church Restructure* (Nashville: Abingdon, 1977).

19. See "Council Wants Functions Continued, Regardless of Reorganization," United Methodist News Service, April 29, 1999, p. 1.

20. "Does the UMC Really Need a Global Structure?" *United Methodist Reporter,* February 26, 1999, p. 4.

their faith more effectively at the local level without being under the control of a global hierarchy."[21]

A specific problem for the proposal of a Global Conference was posed by the, then current, crisis over homosexuality, discussed above. A 1999 Judicial Council ruling that the blessing of homosexual unions was against church law was followed by several such celebrations as acts of civil disobedience and by subsequent church trials. A major concern of both liberals and conservatives was where such issues as the blessing of same-sex unions could be decided in the new structure. Since some of the strongest opposition to the acceptance of homosexuality came from outside the United States,[22] conservatives would likely want this issue settled at the Global Conference, liberals at the central conference level. Meanwhile, amidst the furor over same-sex unions, continued pressure to hold the first Global Conference in 2004 as first proposed by the CPT would have increased the danger of a schism. Of course, the kind of spiritual leaders the CPT envisions might have been able to find creative compromises to preserve unity.

The final CPT report, released on December 1, 1999, differed significantly from the preliminary report. Perhaps most significant, the preliminary report proposed that the 2000 General Conference be the last — that it be supplanted by the Global Conference beginning in 2004. The CPT later recognized that the legislative process cannot move that rapidly. They then proposed that the General Conference approve the report in principle and create a group that would prepare needed legislation and propose constitutional changes for the 2004 General Conference. Apparently this seventy-five-member Transformation Implementation Council would replace the present GCOM. The interim council's membership would be 60 percent laity and 40 percent clergy. "The body would include bishops, representatives from the five regional jurisdictions in the United States and central conferences in other countries, the top staff executive and one voting member for each of the 13 churchwide agencies, and two representatives from affiliated autonomous Methodist churches in Asia and Latin America. A category of additional members is also proposed to guarantee diversity."[23]

The proposed Transformation Implementation Council appeared to answer some of the major concerns of a GCOM task force that felt the original CPT report would have the effect of asking the boards and agencies to restruc-

21. "Letters to the Editor," *United Methodist Reporter,* March 26, 1999, p. 4.

22. Though two bishops from Africa told me that they were willing to live in a larger church that left such issues to local discretion so long as their conferences were not pressed to accept homosexuality.

23. "CPT Completes 'Transformational Direction' Report," United Methodist News Service, September 21, 1999, p. 2.

ture themselves. Whether this and other changes would be enough to ward off competing proposals at the 2000 General Conference was doubtful.

Whatever the fate of the CPT's preliminary proposals, they did address a number of values and concerns that were and remain prevalent in the church. In the first place, the report was responsive to needs perceived by United Methodists and reflected in my earlier quotations from General Conference delegates. Referring to the flexibility already granted by the 1996 General Conference, one delegate said, "The General Conference listened to the annual conferences, local churches and membership and responded to their desires and understanding." This can also be said of the CPT.

There was wide participation in the planning process that led to the CPT proposal. From 1992 to 1996 the Connectional Issues Study employed a wide variety of means to sound out all levels of the church on the UMC's mission and its structural needs. Just a few of the means used are a survey of nearly 35,000 annual conference delegates, telephone interviews with leaders of three to five vital churches in each annual conference, and two meetings of a forum of thirty-two persons representative of the total church. All these data were made available to the CPT. In addition, the CPT sent listening teams to visit United Methodists in various parts of the world and invited all United Methodists to give advice. The February 1999 report, which was mailed to a cross section of United Methodists, included a comment form and the invitation to give the committee feedback before they wrote the final report. The report and comment form were also placed on the CPT's Web site!

Many of the changes proposed by the CPT had already been tried at the annual conference and congregational level. For example, in responding to a question about whether local congregations have taken advantage of the new flexibility, for example, collapsing some committees, one bishop stated:

> Yes, the interesting thing is in [our region] we were already there before the General Conference acted. Some people were acting as though the Discipline was preventing but, when people would bring that up, I would just say, "Nothing in the Discipline prevents you from doing what you want to do." I discovered that people were . . . not using all the flexibility that was there. So as we began to get a sense of freedom and move in that direction, some were already going there. But with the General Conference acting the way it did, it kind of blessed what we were about and it has been more intentional on the part of some.

A final strength of the CPT's proposals was that they maintained a certain kind of continuity with Methodist tradition. One delegate, speaking of the

General Conference, said, "We followed Wesleyan heritage by adapting the tradition of ordination to fit the current time." The CPT was intentional in its commitment to continuity: "We celebrate the historic commitment of The United Methodist Church and our Methodist forebears to serve the world as an instrument of God's will. A transformed church builds upon this history by seeking to become a global church of disciples of Jesus Christ who are connected in mission and ministry throughout the world."[24]

It could be said that the covenant councils of spiritual and prophetic leaders — the centerpiece of the CPT proposals — are an adaptation of Wesleyan holy conferencing. The early Methodist conference served as the spiritual center of Methodism.[25] Describing the early conference, Richey concludes, "It should not be surprising that conference continued to nourish revival, that the spirituality within the fraternity would spill outwards."[26] Applying this Wesleyan heritage to the present time, Richey reflects, "No one organization or structure guarantees the Spirit's presence. But to be the body of Christ must not the church be gracious in its style, in its way of doing and being, in its way of conducting business? Must not ends and means link closely? Indeed, must not means be proximate ends? Must not our forms operate spiritually/Spiritually?"[27]

The CPT, quite possibly influenced by Richey's work, clearly attempts to infuse into contemporary UMC organization the gracious style of early Methodist conferencing.

Other Sources of Proposals for Change

As the result of the CPT's information-gathering strategy that cast a very wide net, the CPT report brings together in one document many of United Methodists' ideas, experiences, and movements related to structural change. However, even those consulted were not uniformly appreciative of the report. For example, though bishops had been consulted by the CPT and kept updated (and four bishops were on the committee), bishops were highly critical of the February 1999 draft when they dialogued with committee representatives at the Council of Bishops (COB) meeting later that year. One bishop even asked the committee to consider withdrawing the report. At that time committee representatives seemed confident that the final draft of their report, profiting from the criti-

24. Connectional Process Team, *Transforming*, p. 21.
25. Russell E. Richey, *The Methodist Conference in America: A History* (Nashville: Kingswood Books, 1996), p. 17.
26. Richey, *The Methodist Conference*, p. 40.
27. Richey, *The Methodist Conference*, p. 202.

cism, would be accepted. Since that time, and after the final draft was made public, the report has drawn fire from both the liberal and the conservative caucuses.

The Good News caucus's legislative agenda for General Conference called upon delegates to reject the CPT report. Reasons to do so included the time, energy, and resources it would cost to add another level of resources in a United Methodist Global Conference; that the massive restructure plan would divert attention from the local church; and that much of what is envisioned in covenant councils is already happening and does not require restructure to make it happen. The creation of a Global Conference would remove decision making yet another step away from local churches, and serious theological questions are raised by references to interreligious dialogue with Jews, Hindus, Buddhists, Muslims, and others.

The Methodist Federation of Social Action, a liberal caucus, also opposed the adoption of CPT's recommendations. It encouraged "a church-wide participatory study of important issues raised by the report." And it wanted the church to "provide resources to each Annual Conference and local church to proceed with study and prayerful reflection on such changes and the future of our church."[28]

Meanwhile, there were several other sources of potential proposals to the General Conference. Though the CPT was often conversant with and may have shared members with these sources, they could have produced independent proposals for redefining mission and for restructure that emphasized their particular ideas and concerns. When bishops were asked where to look other than the CPT for models of change, their answer was the annual conferences. They were talking about their own annual conferences as well as others they knew about.

Annual Conferences

One bishop told of being part of a group of more than a dozen bishops exploring the "Quest for Quality" process under the guidance of the General Board of Discipleship. In this process one assumes that the current system is designed to produce the current results. If those results are undesirable, it is necessary to change the whole system rather than to tinker with the parts. Vitality and creativity result from drawing together diverse people and giving them the free-

---

28. Methodist Federation for Social Action, "General Conference Information: Summary of Petitions to 2000 General Conference" (undated information sheet), p. 2.

dom and the challenge to design a system that will produce the results they want. In this bishops' conference liberals and conservatives alike agreed that the primary task of the conference was to provide spiritual leadership. The conference has removed current conference legislative prohibitions for most of the agencies, and it is now working in leadership groups to talk together about how to provide a structural base to undergird the newly defined task — providing spiritual leadership.

Another bishop described how he chose a "vision team" of about forty persons, clergy and laity. The team met seven times, on Friday nights and the following Saturdays, the first year. The team articulated its vision as "challenging and equipping churches to make disciples of Jesus Christ by taking risks and changing lives." According to this bishop, once the annual conference adopted that vision, "then I turned loose these creative minds and said you have a blank piece of paper. There's nothing on your paper and do what you think would be creative." One result was the formation of six implementation teams formed around missional goals such as new congregations, youth, children, "servants like Jesus," and communications. The original intention was to have these implementation teams replace the traditional organization of the annual conference. But because Judicial Council decisions prevented that, the conference had parallel structures as they looked toward clarification at the 2000 General Conference. This bishop sees his conference as exemplary in its articulation of its vision prior to any discussion about structural change and in its willingness to start with a blank page in redesigning its structure.

Still another bishop described the new structure in his annual conference that was struck down by the Judicial Council. The central idea was to centralize resources and decentralize decisions to deploy them. They put into a common pot all the resources of districts, and the conference committees, agencies, and institutions. Then the Executive Steering Team that managed those resources turned to people at the grassroots level for knowledge and advice on how best to use those resources.

General Boards and Agencies

The diverse initiatives at the annual conference level have in common a drive to involve people from diverse backgrounds and at all levels of the church in defining mission and to give freedom and flexibility that will allow mission to happen. This drive is also found elsewhere in the UMC. Another possible source of alternative proposals is related to the GCOM, which is mandated by *The Discipline* "to encourage, coordinate, and support the general agencies as they serve on behalf of the denomination."[29] Most of the UMC's boards and agencies are in theory accountable to the GCOM between General Conferences. Since many leaders believe that appropriate structure will be achieved only after mission and ministry priorities are clear, the GCOM's major contribution to restructure may have been through its efforts to achieve and articulate a common vision — shared by the various boards and agencies. These efforts included consultations that drew together diverse elements of church leadership from across the church.

Evaluating the consultations, the Conciliar Forum, made up of officers and board members of the GCOM, affirmed the need for United Methodists from across the church to sit at a "common table" to discern the appropriate missional direction and organizational framework for the UMC. According to the document affirmed by the group, any new organization for the UMC must have a place "where all the church's vast programs and ministries can be known and information about them known and obtained."[30] A year later the Conciliar Forum received from a fourteen-member GCOM Implementation Task Force a proposal for a Ministry Resource Conference that could take over many of the functions of the present GCOM.

This conference would have 100 to 125 members, including "bishops, individuals from each of the function teams, members of local congregations and annual conferences across the church, caucus representatives, people from affiliated and autonomous churches of the Methodist family, and others to ensure that 'all parts of the church connect and communicate with the whole church.'"[31] Though members were not of one mind as to whether this should be an independent proposal to the General Conference or whether the CPT should be urged to incorporate it, many felt a major strength was that the proposed conference would be a more representative group for transforming church structures during the next quadrennium. The February 1999 CPT report, in contrast, called for churchwide leaders to transform church structures. In addition to the activities already described, staff members of GCOM consulted with annual conferences and groups of local congregations pursuing changes that could serve as models for reorganization. As mentioned above, the General Board of Discipleship had done similar consulting. Networks of large congregations could also have been a source of independent proposals for changes within the UMC.

29. *Book of Discipline*, p. 449.

30. "Group Proposing 'Common Table' for Future Decision Making," United Methodist News Service, July 28, 1998, p. 1.

31. "Another Proposal Emerging for United Methodist Reorganization," United Methodist News Service, August 3, 1999, p. 2.

Social Forces Underlying These Changes

Many of the significant structural changes and proposed changes may be viewed as adaptations to broad societal forces in the surrounding environment. The UMC and its predecessor bodies have undergone continual changes in organizational structure reflecting societal changes. On occasion such changes have been dramatic. Most dramatic was the split of the Methodist Episcopal Church in 1844, creating the Methodist Episcopal Church, South. Reunion did not occur until 1939. The gradual lessening of organizational support for the anti-alcohol movement is a less dramatic example of adaptive change.[32] Some of the societal changes worth exploring as possible sources of adaptive change in the UMC include education, mass communication, the growth of caucus groups within the church, social mobility, the erosion of authority, growing acceptance of homosexuality, receptivity to spirituality, consumerism, the dramatic increase in the number and diversity of nonprofit organizations, and some businesses' concerns with human welfare.

Social Forces Affecting Leadership and Control

In his classic work on leadership, Robert Michels argued that the disparity in education between leaders and members and the resulting apathy by members was a primary source of leaders' control of an organization's policies and resources.[33] In this light, there is little wonder that United Methodists are challenging the authority of their leaders and calling for less centralized decision making. There has been a marked increase in the level of education of the general population since Michels was writing in the early years of the twentieth century. And that trend continues. For example, the percentage of United Methodists with more than twelve years of education increased from 45 percent in 1984/86 to 53 percent in 1994/96.[34] Increased education of United Methodists

32. See James G. Hougland, Jr., James R. Wood, and Samuel A. Mueller, "Organizational 'Goal Submergence': The Methodist Church and the Failure of the Temperance Movement," *Sociology and Social Research* 58, no. 4 (July 1974).

33. Robert Michels, *Political Parties* (New York: Free Press, 1962).

34. I generated these cross-tabulations and the figures reported in the following two paragraphs from data files of the General Social Surveys. See James Allan Davis and Tom W. Smith, *General Social Surveys, 1972-1996* (machine-readable data file), principal investigator, James A. Davis; director and coprincipal investigator, Tom W. Smith, NORC ed. (Chicago: National Opinion Research Center; distributed by Roper Center for Public Opinion Research, University of Connecticut, 1996), one data file (35,284 logical records) and one codebook (1,295 pages). I was also able to obtain preliminary data from the 1998 poll.

negatively affects willingness to follow leaders without question. Also, new information technology, including the Internet, directly impacts apathy, making it possible for followers to be instantly informed of events and developments related to church policies. For example, when one Chicago pastor celebrated a holy union service for two men, the story made the front page of newspapers within two days. The proceedings of the subsequent church trial of this pastor were summarized hourly on the Internet.

Increased societal mobility also negatively affects members' willingness to give unquestioned control to their leaders. Fifty-eight percent of United Methodists don't live in the same city they lived in at age sixteen. This mobility means that many United Methodists grew up in other, more congregational polities. (It also means that United Methodists uprooted from their birth communities may be available for recruitment into other faith communities.) As it turns out, 30 percent of United Methodists were not raised as United Methodists, and about 10 percent were raised Baptist! It seems likely that those raised in a congregational polity might be less willing to accede to the directives of a more centralized polity.

There may be a more direct way that shifting public sentiment has influenced perceptions of leaders. There has been a general erosion of authority in our society. Witness the widespread notion, for example, that taxes are bad — that great pains should be taken to avoid paying money to the government. In 1994/95, according to the General Social Survey, 5.4 percent of United Methodists had "a great deal" of confidence in the executive branch of the federal government and 4.7 percent had such confidence in the legislative branch. Though their confidence in the leaders of organized religion was greater by comparison, only 29 percent had a great deal of confidence in such leaders.

Today's United Methodist leaders also must operate in a climate that includes well-led and well-funded caucus groups, both liberal and conservative. These advocacy groups, several of which were discussed above, are formed of dedicated United Methodists who are passionate about their causes and views.[35]

These and other changes in the contemporary world have necessitated a shift toward leadership that assumes members' awareness of the issues and their ability to thwart policies they oppose. One adaptive response to this situation is to empower the laity and to localize decision making where feasible. Another is for leaders to adopt a more persuasive, educative, participatory style of leadership. As we have seen, both kinds of responses are occurring in the UMC.

---

35. Some United Methodists are concerned about the funding of conservative caucuses by the secular right. For example, UMAction is a part of the Institute for Religion and Democracy, which draws much of its funding from conservative foundations.

Social Forces Affecting the UMC's Identity

Several of the social forces just discussed have helped to precipitate a severe identity crisis within the UMC by making it possible for United Methodists at both poles on contested issues to press their views at least as effectively as official United Methodist leaders can press more moderate views. In addition, two societal trends or cultural drifts are also major forces — the decrease in our society of biblical literalism and the increase in acceptance of homosexuality. The percent of Americans believing the Bible is to be taken literally decreased from 39 percent in 1983 to 31 percent in 1995.[36] From 1984 to 1998 biblical literalism among United Methodists decreased from 35 percent to 26 percent.[37] At the same time, the American public has become increasingly accepting of homosexuality. For example, recent polls show that 61 percent of Americans (71 percent of those aged eighteen to twenty-nine) think high school education courses should not "tell students that homosexuality is immoral."[38] These two trends have contributed to the identity-defining value struggle within the UMC. United Methodists on one side fear that the first trend foreshadows a loss of belief in the authority of the Bible with a resulting loss of an absolute moral standard, as exemplified (for them) in the second trend. Those on the other side see the demise of biblical literalism as an opportunity to teach and experience a culturally aware biblical faith which sets a high standard of morality for all human relationships, and they believe that some same-sex unions can pass this test of biblical morality. As one can see, there is a common ground here — biblical faith — but at the turn of the century those at the poles on these issues seem not to be looking for common ground.

Social Forces Affecting the UMC's Mission

Some societal changes, by curtailing resources or presenting competing causes, put constraints on the church's ability to implement mission. For example, consumerism in our society has developed to the point that many families perceive as necessities things that would have been seen as luxuries even a decade ago. The result is that, from the perspective of these families, there is little or no "discretionary" income to support the church's mission.

The multiplication of alternative ways that people can pursue various

36. Princeton Religion Research Center, *Emerging Trends* (April 1996), p. 2.

37. Davis and Smith, *General Social Surveys.*

38. "Sex Education," ABC News Nightline Poll, February 17, 1995, pp. 2-3.

purposes poses another challenge to the church's mission. Take for example the fact that many public utility companies now work with voluntary organizations in watching after elderly or homebound persons in their homes — a task that was, until recently, primarily in the domain of the churches. Moreover, the efforts of various nonprofit organizations and the media are making it easier for people to perceive the dramatic needs close at hand in any community, hence making them less inclined to send their funds to a central program agency.

But another societal trend may be good news for the church's mission. Many in society have become more receptive to spirituality. Sociologist Wade Clark Roof, describing the baby boom generation, says, "This search, in an increasingly pluralistic moral and religious setting, produced a new salvational dilemma, namely, that of finding one's own spiritual path in the midst of so many alternatives. Fundamental questions, such as 'Who am I?' and 'What am I doing with my life?' took on fresh meaning. Religion — like life — was something to be explored. Old cultural and religious scripts had lost power over them, forcing them to think through anew their religious and spiritual options."[39] This engagement with spirituality poses a challenge to institutional religion, yet many United Methodists find within their Wesleyan heritage both the deep spiritual experience and the social relevance many people outside the churches want. Roof's findings may also suggest a receptive climate for the spiritual leadership the CPT celebrates.

The Leading of the Holy Spirit

All the reasons for changes discussed above seem plausible sociologically. But bishops gave far more weight to another explanation for changes in defining and organizing the work of the church: these changes are manifestations of the movement of the Holy Spirit. Social scientists are better equipped to show the influence of societal forces on organizational change than to discern the workings of the Holy Spirit. Yet I can report the enthusiasm with which bishops credited the Holy Spirit with stirring up change in the UMC. One bishop told me: "It's clear for me in our conference that the change is coming because we are guided in what we think by the spirit of God working within us." Another bishop said, "What is motivating the church today? I believe God is stirring this up. And God is helping us remember that the core center of our life is a body of faith and transformation which is ongoing. Change is not just any change. It's

---

39. Wade Clark Roof, *A Generation of Seekers: The Spiritual Journeys of the Baby Boom Generation* (San Francisco: Harper, 1993), p. 59.

ongoing transformation where you are radically becoming a new thing. If we could discover again the spirit of transformation and know that that's life giving — the core identity of who we are, and if our leaders could live out of that and articulate that, then I think we have new life." Yet another bishop put it this way: "The quest for hands-on mission, the search for meaning. Those issues do not seem to be addressed by the denominational structure, and oftentimes we get caught in perpetuating the work of the form of the church and the dynamic has gone somewhere else. My own judgment is that some (not all), religious or non-religious, judge us as irrelevant as to where the Spirit is moving us."

Another bishop sees in a new way of relating to one another the practical consequences of the movement of the Spirit:

> I see a turning to be more open to God's guidance in the way that we do our work in The United Methodist Church. We are far from enacting that in General Conference. But there's a lot of laity and a lot of clergy and with many people in the council of bishops this really heartfelt yearning not so much what do I want or what does this caucus want or that caucus want or even this annual conference or that annual conference but what does God want. What does God want of The United Methodist Church? And how can we become more open to the direction that God is leading rather than all these things that we have already made these decisions about?

Bishops I talked with clearly believe that the Holy Spirit is actively present in the process of change in the UMC today. One of the major implications of this study (discussed below) is the challenge it presents to the traditional sociological approach to claims for divine guidance. But before turning to the wider implications of the study, let us consider a few sociologically informed cautions about some of the proposals for change.

Some Sociologically Informed Cautions for the UMC

The sociology of organizations and institutions suggests several cautions for those shaping UMC restructure.

Unanticipated Consequences

Often participants in organizations make emotional decisions based on the organization's values without thinking through the long-term consequences. One example comes from the Civil Rights movement of the 1960s. Several southern-based denominations that were cooperating with other denominations in the National Council of Churches made decisions that may have been appropriate for the northern-based denominations but arguably impeded the eventual implementation of the civil rights goals in the southern-based bodies. They lost much revenue, many members, and some congregations. Sociologists call these unwanted consequences "unanticipated" consequences not because they cannot sometimes be foreseen, but because they are out of line with the outcomes sought. Historian Russell Richey has identified just such a situation within the CPT. It appears that the strong desire to be global, heightened by the strong presence of members of the CPT from outside the United States (almost one-third of committee members), may have allowed the CPT to propose a new global structure that is not a realistic means of achieving globality, or at any rate they may have failed to look at more feasible ways of implementing that value. Richey argues that true affirmation of the global mission and outreach of Methodism will not be found in making the UMC a global denomination in the manner the CPT has proposed, but rather in appropriate participation with and ties to other Methodist denominations, especially through a strengthened World Methodist Council: "By using the World Methodist Council as a global expression, United Methodism embraces all the churches that share our Wesleyan and EUB heritage, including those with a British background, those now in united churches (e.g. India, Australia, Canada), those in the holiness tradition (who have believed so deeply in our Wesleyan values that they have had to dissent from the MEC/MECA/MC/UMC accommodation to the world), and particularly with the AME, AMEZ, and CME, with whom we have entered into conversation about a common future."[40]

Richey's point gained strength with the World Methodist Council's September 1999 approval of membership for the Church of the Nazarene.

Dangers of Congregationalism

There are important implications of moving toward congregationalism. As one delegate put it, "[Restructure] may be a step moving us toward congregationalism which would lead to a very different denominational understanding." There are advantages to maintaining a strongly connected formal polity. It is true that in our society, steeped in traditions of grassroots democracy, even the

40. Russell Richey, "A Global Connection: Some Questions about the CPT Report," *Circuit Rider,* September/October 1999, pp. 25-27.

strongest polity must also rely on persuasion — more so in the aftermath of the general erosion of authority that started with traumatic events in the 1960s, the revelations of Watergate and the disaster of the Vietnam War. Leaders need to gain compliance primarily by appealing to members to live out the implications of the fundamental values of the church. The new definition of leaders as listening, serving, caring individuals, strengthened by the spiritual disciplines, may facilitate this type of leadership. Still, the formal polity strength derived from the control of appointments and property provides a context that allows the persuasive process time to work.[41]

There are risks implicit in the emerging model of a national structure that merely resources the local church, which, seen as primary, is empowered to shape its own ministry. The local churches may well "provide the most significant arena through which disciple-making occurs,"[42] as the new UMC mission statement affirms, but the history of the struggle for racial justice shows that local churches sometimes need a bit of pressure from the national church. Moreover, a theology that places the local church at the center may, as Harrison found with the Northern Baptists, impede the development of the kinds of structural checks and balances that prevent national leaders from appropriating illegitimate power. Still, members are often more energized by projects which they have helped to design, especially local projects. The challenge is how to provide permission for local churches to shape the ministries that fit their talents to the community yet maintain a polity strong enough to maintain a collective identity and mission.[43]

Though watchfulness is necessary to be sure structures do not stifle spiritual enthusiasm, structures and institutions are essential for carrying out the church's mission. Speaking of the Methodist conference, Richey observes: "This expansive mission, this spirituality, required order. Indeed, spirituality and order, the freedom Methodists found through conversion and the discipline to which they subjected themselves and others, represent two sides of the evangelical impulse. . . . So conferences began to devote more exacting attention to their own political structure, to polity."[44] Spiritual leaders within spiritual covenant groups may be an effective adaptive structure given certain social forces

41. For a more fully developed treatment of the model of leadership implied in this paragraph, see my *Leadership in Voluntary Organizations: The Controversy over Social Action in Protestant Churches* (New Brunswick, N.J.: Rutgers University Press, 1981).

42. *Book of Discipline,* p. 114.

43. Many United Methodist churches have been influenced by William M. Easum's concept of the "permission-giving church." See his *Sacred Cows Make Gourmet Burgers* (Nashville: Abingdon, 1995).

44. Richey, *The Methodist Conference,* p. 76.

affecting the church today. Yet at some point that leadership needs to be insulated so that it can foster precarious values and enforce contested policies.[45]

Implications of the UMC Case Study

This case study has implications both for United Methodists and for social scientists. For United Methodists, one clear implication of the emerging definition of work in the UMC is the recovery of a fuller spectrum of spiritual/social action. Conservatives have pushed for more spiritual emphasis, and liberals, though they find it unnecessary to endorse classical theology in order to recover spiritual resources, have responded by becoming more spiritually aware. As a result the church is cutting through the false polarity of changing individuals versus changing culture.

Here are relevant comments from two bishops:

> You know you've got people [who see] the job of the church is to change individual lives and then you let individual lives change, and other people that said — and this is probably more prevalent in a lot of leadership in the 60s and 70s — our job is to change the culture and the culture will change life, well, I think that's a false polarity. It's much more of both, that we're doing all of this together. I want us to take a more holistic approach.

> I think one of our difficulties, we have tended, by virtue of where we are theologically, to major in one or the other. And so, if we were more liberal, we were more missional but forgot the life of prayer, intimate small-group theologizing. What was done by our conservative folk did not show in the world. For me, the consistent theology, the money where the mouth is, the rubber to the road, is where those two are in confluence, where there is both/and.

Another bishop reminds us that spiritual leadership and administrative leadership are not opposed to one another:

> I think within CPT there are some folks who see spiritual leadership as different from administration. That is not my view because I think one of the biggest places I exert spiritual leadership is in the appointment process. There is a lot of administration in the appointment process. So I think there was a heresy back in the early church sometimes that separated the

45. On insulating leaders in order to safeguard precarious values, see Philip Selznick, *Leadership in Administration* (New York: Harper and Row, 1957).

temporal from the spiritual and I think that the temptation today is to keep that split and I think what's happening culturally is that it is all coming together. . . . When I make an administrative decision, I am making decisions about people's lives. And about congregations' lives and their own future and that to me is a very spiritual matter. It's about God in the midst of life. So when I am answering mail, I am dealing with people's souls. And the issues of their relationship with God. That's not a task that is void of spirituality because it's administrative. . . . When I think of the church, if we try to pull bishops out of what is perceived to be administrative work of working with the boards and agencies, the church, the boards, and agencies will lose life because those boards and agencies have to be infused with spirit and that work needs to be set in the context of the vision and mission which is a spiritual matter. But we as a denomination still have work to do around that issue. We don't have clarity. I think we hunger for the spiritual and somehow we've got it over against administrative rather than seeing it in the midst of the administrative.

One liberal bishop talks more personally about spiritual leadership:

We have assumed that programs will save people's lives. That just has not worked. We talk now of process, not of program. Go back and live different lives. Be different, listening, learning leaders. The vision emerges from the people — their deepest yearning and desires. As we listen to them we cast that vision. We never stop listening but at the same time listening to what God is saying. The UMC needs transformational leaders who discern God's will. CPT doesn't need to change the structure of the bishops' office, but we need to change the minds and spirits of bishops so that they will function differently in the office. I proudly identify myself now as the spiritual leader. I had to get past some of the hang-ups I had with spiritual leadership.

Researching the Role of the Holy Spirit

This study challenges the traditional way social scientists have researched claims of divine influence. The usual sociological tack starts from the assumption that whatever is defined as real, by particular individuals or groups, is real in its consequences, for those individuals and groups. Two members of the UMC research team for the ORW (Organizing Religious Work) project, both together and independently, have observed real changes in the ways bishops relate to one another as well as the kinds of activities they are undertaking together. Witness this excerpt from one bishop's sermon at a 1998 meeting of the COB.

I went home after my first COB meeting and said to . . . my spiritual director "The COB is the strangest Christian community I've ever experienced. It is rife with anger and suspicion and distrust. They can't seem to talk about what is dividing them." She counseled what she has counseled so many times before, "Pray and wait."

This is my fifth COB meeting. In each of these five meetings, we have spent more and more time practicing the presence of God. Individual prayer. Covenant groups. Community prayer. Prayer interwoven through the day. The practice of prayer is drawing us together at a deeper level. We are spending more time in Biblical and theological reflection about underlying issues. The practice of studying the Scriptures and doing theology together is knitting us together. We are asking questions of discernment — what does God want this COB to be and to do? What will we have to let go of? The practice of discernment is helping us to lay aside our individual wills and search for God's will, and it draws us together. . . . The Episcopal Initiative on Children and Poverty may be changing this Council more than it is changing the world — at least for now. It is uniting us in a common mission. Our genuine appreciation for one another's gifts appears to be enlarging. Is it possible that the practice of "bearing one another in love" — even a little humility, patience and gentleness — is uniting us? . . . If Christ's love can transform us, can it not transform the United Methodist Church?

Later another bishop underscored for me an indication of dramatic change within the COB. At the time of the 1996 General Conference in Denver, the COB was polarized and filled with anger by the actions of fifteen bishops who held a press conference to announce their disagreement with UMC policies relating to homosexual persons. Yet this spring in Chattanooga, the COB unanimously elected one of those fifteen bishops as their new ecumenical officer who will represent the UMC to other denominations and ecumenical groups throughout the world!

The transformation of the COB is certainly an interesting sociological phenomenon. There is evidence that most bishops go beyond merely using spiritual language to describe what happened after the fact. They describe individual bishops and groups of bishops in the midst of deep, hurtful conflict, seeking the guidance and power of the Holy Spirit and intentionally opening themselves to the possibility of transformation of their own attitudes and ideas.

Sociologist Rodney Stark cautions against assuming that revelations do not actually occur:

Unfortunately, as Ralph Hood (1985) has pointed out, even the most unbiased social scientists typically have been unwilling to go further than to grant that the recipients of revelations have made honest *mistakes*, that they have *misinterpreted* an experience as having involved contact with the divine. This is taken as self-evident on the grounds that any real scientist "knows" that real revelations are quite impossible. I fully agree with Hood (1985, 1997) that while methodological agnosticism represents good science, both methodological atheism and theism are unscientific. We do not know that revelations are impossible; it is entirely beyond the capacity of science to demonstrate that the divine does not communicate directly with certain individuals.[46]

Psychiatrist Robert Coles gives a moving account of how an eight-year-old girl he treated while in psychiatric training helped him and his supervising doctor to see the importance of taking seriously the reality of God in the lives of their patients. The account ends with a quotation from the supervisor's summary of progress in the case: "This girl has begun to settle down in treatment. Her use of her Catholic faith has been both a stumbling block and an opportunity for her doctor and me. We have stopped trying to take on her faith clinically! She has built her own version of that faith, and we have let her tell us all about it, and learned more about her. For her God is quite alive; He's a big part of her life. We're hoping He'll be of further help to her — and to us, too."[47]

A major strength of the CPT proposal, which reflected the dynamic going on in several annual conferences and in the COB, was that it appealed not just to a transcendent purpose, but to God who wills and empowers that purpose — to the movement of the Holy Spirit. Theologians may best decide when God's influence is real, but even the traditional social scientist knows that if something is perceived as real, it may be real in its consequences. In my interviews with bishops and observations of their meetings, those consequences were palpable.

Conclusion

There are loud voices warning that the UMC is in imminent danger of schism. They may be right. People at the poles have strong differences that they perceive as irreconcilable. Those who believe the God of the Bible is directing them to be and do something that is incompatible with what others believe the God of the

46. Rodney Stark, "A Theory of Revelations," *Journal for the Scientific Study of Religion* 38 (June 1999): 288.

47. Robert Coles, *The Spiritual Life of Children* (Boston: Houghton Mifflin, 1990), p. 19.

Bible is calling them to be and do may decide to leave the church, individually or collectively. Such a truncation of the diversity within the church would dramatically change both the identity and the mission of the UMC.

There is a more hopeful scenario for the UMC. Perhaps the value struggle will be won not by the extremes, but by the middle. There is strong traditional support for diversity within the church, and only 21 percent of delegates to the 1996 General Conference agreed that "The UMC has become too diverse."[48] Moreover, in the past several years there have been exciting theological diversity dialogues throughout the church. Imagine that, as these dialogues continue, United Methodists discover not only that they can understand and tolerate the views of those with whom they differ, but also that they have more in common with the holders of those views than they had thought. And imagine that the bishops — who, divided among themselves, were forced to form covenant groups and to adopt a discernment process of decision making — imagine that these bishops in their new kind of spiritual leadership discover the power to unite the church in mission. There's a drama for the twenty-first century![49]

48. These statistics are from my survey of the delegates to the 1996 General Conference of the UMC. For more details of the survey see James Rutland Wood, *Where the Spirit Leads: The Evolving Views of United Methodists on Homosexuality* (Nashville: Abingdon, 2000), especially p. 137.

49. See General Commission on Christian Unity and Interreligious Concerns, *In Search of Unity: A Conversation with Recommendations for the Unity of the United Methodist Church* (New York: General Commission on Christian Unity and Interreligious Concerns, 1998).

Practical Theology at Work in the United Methodist Church: Restructuring, Reshaping, Reclaiming

Pamela D. Couture

O ne of the deepest motivators for change in the United Methodist Church (UMC) may be a widely shared sense that the theological values and norms expressed by United Methodists behaviorally and organizationally and the church's verbally articulated theology have gotten significantly out of sync. This felt dissonance between practice and articulated theology suggests that practical theology can help to interpret the United Methodist struggle for change. Practical theologians understand theology to be more than a verbal articulation of beliefs, doctrines, and principles. Practical theologians pay attention to what is said verbally about theological beliefs, but they also watch practices, habits, patterns of behavior, and ways of organizing group life that nonverbally express belief. A special concern for the practical theologian is the way these three aspects of practical theology — articulating, practicing, and organizing — may or may not be consistent with one another.

An interactive practical theological process that pushes and pulls among articulated theology, organizational forms, and practices, habits, and patterns of behavior has deep, and perhaps distinctive, roots in Wesleyanism. In the present struggles, this practical theological process assumes different forms in different projects of the denomination. In this article I will examine the practical theological process of the Connectional Process Team (CPT), so well described in Wood's sociological case study (pp. 534-64), and compare it to practical theological process at work in the Dialogue on Theological Diversity (Dialogue) and the Bishops Initiative on Children and Poverty (Initiative). These three projects have different explicit emphases. CPT has a unique emphasis on organizational structure, what I am calling "restructuring theology," that is not found in the other two projects, though that is not all it is about. The Dialogue has a unique concern for articulated beliefs, what I am calling "reclaiming theology," though again, that is not all it is about. The Initiative has a primary concern for changed practices, what I am calling "reshaping theology," though, as we will see, that concern is not unique to the Initiative. In all three projects we find aspects of restructuring, reclaiming, and reshaping interacting with one another in the practical theological method of the denomination. Each of these ways of doing theology, or expressing the denomination's understanding of the divine-human relationship, has deep roots in Wesleyanism and earlier theological and philosophic traditions.

Wesleyan Theology: Restructuring, Reshaping, Reclaiming

Modern theology is understood to be a thought process that yields verbal reflection, usually in the form of written texts. Such texts present logical, reasonable truths that should be convincing to those who read them, having veracity equal to that of a scientifically proven hypothesis. Practical theologians, however, suggest that scientific and theological arguments have embedded in them undeclared norms, values, and metaphors that express ultimate values and understandings of God. In human action, cognitive processes yield expressions of the divine-human relationship that may not be fully articulated in verbal constructions of theology. To understand theology more fully, an examination of practices is necessary. The idea of restructuring, reshaping, and reclaiming theology further expands this definition of theology by isolating three categories of practices: restructuring, reshaping, and reclaiming.

Restructuring Theology

The idea of "restructuring theology" is that the creation of group life, the connections of groups with one another, the process by which these groups are reformed and re-created, and the way the whole of the organizational web is held together reflect values commonly held or in conflict with one another and facilitate theological practice and theological language that express, nonverbally and verbally, our experience of the divine-human relationship. The struggle with structure as a form of theology may be one of the most distinctive characteristics of Methodist theological life. Russell E. Richey, in *The Methodist Conference in America: A History*, has demonstrated that early North American Methodists took seriously the idea that structure was an expression of their theological values. As they developed the Wesleyan movement beyond the life of its founder, John Wesley, and in a land and political situation very different from his, early North American Methodists transferred Wesley's personal authority for the Methodist movement to the "conference." Analogous to the experiment with governmental structure for the United States that was emerging simultaneously, this experiment with structure as theology had trials and errors in its evolution. These experiments clarified that Methodist theology could not be expressed in a more centralized council of a few elite members but needed the "conference" with broad membership, an expression of North American struggles for egalitarianism. The conference, however, was more than a structure. It was a time of retreat for worship, celebrating sacraments, examining the spiritual life of the Methodist leaders, and determining their proper relationship to the body as a whole. It provided time for clarifying theological beliefs (such as ecclesiology and sanctification) and ethical practices (such as freeing slaves). Richey summarizes the conference "as a/the distinctive [American] Methodist manner of being the church, a multifaceted, not simply political, mode of spirituality, unity, mission, governance, and fraternity that American Methodists lived and operated better than they interpreted."[1]

Reshaping Theology

Already in Richey's description of "conference" we see the Methodist propensity to take seriously, as theology, the various practices or patterns of behavior, habits, attitudes, and sensibilities that Methodists believe form the spirit and the soul. In this process, belief systems are also reshaped and new practices emerge that reflect reconstructed belief systems that interpret the divine-human relationship. The idea of Methodist practices as distinctive to Wesleyans actually created the name "Methodist," originally a derisive term for the Oxford Holy Club that surrounded the Wesleys at Oxford University. The name scorned the early Wesleyans' methodical examination of their spiritual life and the practices of caring for the poor and the outcast that arose from it. When the movement developed in North America, the name became an attribute of identity, as did various spiritual and social practices associated with it. As Methodism developed, some of the original spiritual and social practices were retained and others were rejected. In some cases the rejection of early practices or adoption of new practices led to schism. In current philosophical, theological, and ethical discussion, this Methodist emphasis on practice merges easily with the surge of interest in character ethics for which the idea of practice is central.

1. Russell E. Richey, *The Methodist Conference in America: A History* (Nashville: Kingswood Books, 1996), p. 14.

Character ethicists and theologians argue that we become who we are (e.g., we become courageous) by engaging in various practices (e.g., courageous acts). Although the Wesleys themselves seem to have had little direct intellectual contact with the Aristotelian tradition from which character ethics emerges, Wesleyans such as Stanley Hauerwas and Gregory Jones draw heavily on the character tradition.

Reclaiming Theology

"Reclaiming theology" retrieves theological heritage, critically reflects upon it, and makes connections with contemporary concerns and faith expressions. When we reclaim theology, we articulate the grounding of our understanding of the divine-human relationship for our faith and the values of faith that give rise to theological practices. "Reclaiming theology" may be less unique to Wesleyan tradition than restructuring or reshaping theologies. In fact, evidence suggests that Wesleyans have an ambivalent relationship to their theological inheritance, as they do to the spiritual and social practices it originally entailed. Still, "reclaiming theology" distinguished the Wesleys and marks recent trends in Wesleyan theology. The Wesleys themselves searched the then extant theological thinking in Anglicanism, Puritanism, and Pietism to clarify their thought, but they also reclaimed writers of the early church, as Randy Maddox has argued in *Responsible Grace: John Wesley's Practical Theology*. Part of the struggles for development of a religious movement in North America involved the displacement of some of Wesley's theological beliefs. Using Wesley's New Testament notes and sermons as authoritative, Americans were able to pick and choose among aspects of Wesleyan ethics, many times conveniently ignoring aspects such as those that argued against any practice of slavery and criticized mercantilism's systematic exploitation of the poor. In recent decades Wesleyan theologians such as Albert Outler, Theodore Runyon, Theodore Weber, and Theodore Jennings have specifically reclaimed Wesley much as Wesley reclaimed the early church fathers. In so doing, they have given new life to social justice concerns as distinctive within the Wesleyan tradition. Some Methodist scholars argue that the church should not reclaim Wesley but the sources that Wesley himself reclaimed.

In their present struggle for change, United Methodists do not necessarily invoke these traditions of restructuring, reshaping, or reclaiming, nor do they particularly call upon the early or recent Wesleyans who have continued to give life to these three aspects of the process of Wesleyan practical theology. This method of practical theology, however, is so deeply embedded in the Wesleyan way of life that Wesleyans engage in it without being aware of it. Albert Outler once identified Scripture, tradition, reason, and experience as an embedded method that was distinctive of Wesleyan verbal theology. Restructuring, re-shaping, and reclaiming may be similarly distinctive to methods of Wesleyan practical theology, as they become increasingly important given the concerns of the postmodern era.

In what follows I will ask, "What's the problem that change in the UMC is trying to address?" The three denominational projects mentioned earlier offer different solutions to the problem. They have differently articulated aims, yet in each project we will see that these three aspects of "doing practical theology" interact with each other. In fact, when looked at through the lens of this method of practical theology, persons and groups in different political locations in the UMC end up in strange sorts of companionship.

What Is the Problem Motivating Change?

Are practices, organization, and articulated theology too far out of sync with each other in the UMC? Interviews with seven bishops suggest that this question might offer a window through which to view the problem motivating change in the UMC. They report symptoms of dis-ease: practices of the faith do not produce meaning, organization is burdensome, and consensus around theology cannot be found. The fragmentation of the UMC becomes particularly apparent when it attempts to relate practices, organization, and theology.

What is the bishops' understanding of the motivation for change that emerges from the episcopal interviews? The motivation has to do with searching beneath the symptoms for ways that God is at work. The summary of repeated themes in the bishops' interviews can be concise. The UMC needs a different way of doing things that is driven by the presence of God. Change is occurring because the Spirit of God is working within us. The need for change that is God-centered is coming from local levels of the church, clergy and laity. It is something upon which liberals and conservatives can agree, although they may disagree on what the changes should be.

Several cultural and social trends are contributing to the need for change. Not only throughout the church but also in society globally and culturally, human beings are in transition from a modern to a postmodern way of being human. Organizations are organic, not mechanistic. Rather than being structures with interchangeable parts, they function as a whole while addressing individual needs. A portion of the human need that the modern, mechanistic organizations have produced and that postmodern, organic organizations must now address is spiritual hunger: an active need for God, religious identity, and making a difference in the world.

United Methodists struggle with this change as a denomination because in different regions United Methodism is in different stages of the decline of Christendom. For example, in the northern and midwestern United States, United Methodism is in a post-Christendom era. The dominance of Christianity is over; Christians are a minority and need to focus on quality of mission rather than quantity of membership. The southeastern and south central states have not made this transition and still minister within the ambiance and resources of Christendom.

These trends make a difference in mission. Some are more inclined toward localism. Where Christendom enables the church to have easier influence and access to resources, persons may be inclined to argue that mission is only local or that mission to the world can be done from the local congregational base. Where Christendom is dead, mission needs to be local but it also needs national and international networks to sustain an informed ministry about the relationship of the local congregations in the United States to Christians elsewhere in the world. Problems with present structure and practice are deeply apparent within this change; problems related to theology are more ambiguous.

What's the problem with structures? Both liberals and conservatives agree that the church is being thwarted by present structures. People feel burdened by organization that does not deliver missional objectives. They want structure that empowers and enables them. People don't experience the resources of the church meeting particular needs. For example, the church's finances and its theology don't meet. The church needs to be a process, not a fortress. It needs to move with the work of the Spirit, not prop up forms of church that the Spirit has left.

The local, churchwide perception that the denominational structures aren't working for mission leads to a struggle between decentralization and centralization that mirrors processes in other public and private institutions. A pressure to decentralize comes from localism, from a lack of trust in systems and leaders of systems, and from the need to develop flexibility to do different things in different places. A pressure to centralize comes from the desires to reduce committees and bureaucracy and to gather resources and be able to deploy them. The tension between decentralization and centralization emerges over the enormous economic resources of the denomination. A central question is whether it is possible to distribute economic power within the church so that the church can inspire people to share economic resources at the same time as enabling the autonomy of local and indigenous people to determine how those resources are spent in mission to their wants and needs.

This tension creates a crisis of authority: how to create authority in an age of democracy that thwarts the emergence of strong leaders such as those who emerged when the denomination was in a more trusting mood. Within such tensions, is it possible to create structure that allows the denomination to discern and enable the movement of the Spirit of God?

Though the bishops ask these general questions about denominational structure, they do not for the most part offer generalized answers to the problem of denominational structure, except where their role in restructuring discussions requires them to do so. But many bishops do enthusiastically describe solutions to the problems of structure they have created in their own episcopal areas. These stories of restructuring theology in episcopal areas must be told one by one and relate directly to tensions in the denomination over national structures that have, until lately, mandated that each annual conference replicate national structures. Furthermore, the bishops' questions about structures yield questions about practices. Part of the struggle for language in the UMC is a struggle for language where structure and shaping intersect.

What's the problem that calls for reshaping practices? The bishops characterize culturewide and churchwide spiritual hunger: a quest for meaning, a search for ways that faith can yield ways of living, and a desire for hands-on mission. This characterization knows no regional boundaries, but has a different quality as reported by bishops of different regions: there is a special urgency about the need for a renewed spiritual vitality in the regions where Christendom has declined. In those regions bishops are more specific about the qualities they think the church should promote. According to one bishop, the church needs people who are willing to be out on the edge, who will take risks, who will be vulnerable, who are able to take "chops" and stand strong. The church needs preachers, teachers, persons who can develop preventive care networks, persons who are comfortable with ambiguity, paradox, and their theology. The church needs people who can nurture, do, and feed simultaneously. It needs people who can build bridges to the poorest and wealthiest segments of society. In recent decades the church's need for security and for maintaining its forms has often sent such people away. Therefore, the church has a crisis of leadership.

The issues of practice and structure intersect in a concept for which some bishops have adopted the language of "spiritual leadership." Spiritual leaders are pastors, lay leaders, and bishops whose lives are centered on God. They can help the church to be sensitive to the leadership of God and the Holy Spirit and to bring this leadership to complex ethical, moral, justice, and faith issues. The language of spiritual leadership is ambiguous, however. For some it resonates deeply. For others it is newly and somewhat uncomfortably adopted. For still others it is unclear what spiritual leadership is beyond the obvious claim most church leaders would make that their lives are centered on God.

God-talk is pervasive when bishops talk about structure and practice: the presence of God, the example of Jesus, and God's Spirit are frequently invoked. Bishops make some claims that are explicitly theological, such as, "What's needed? Helping people practice and live the faith — not by being a good officer in the church but by helping people to live day by day, to grow in their love of God and neighbor and live their lives in the way that is pleasing to God." However, in our interviews, despite the fact that we invited specifically theological reflections, the bishops usually answered with language of spirituality and religious experience that was interwoven with practical situations. Other than language of pneumatology or Christology, doctrinal language was not used.

It would be a mistake, however, to think that these bishops do not think theological issues are important to the UMC's present struggle for change. Their sparing use of doctrinal language may be reflective of their sensibility for the ecumenical dictum that "doctrine divides, practice unites." In the view of one bishop, an enormous struggle for power over the denomination gets articulated around moral and theological issues. The moral issue is "same-gender sexuality"; the theological issue is "classical Christian theology." Beneath this articulation of moral and theological standards is a struggle for power and control over the denomination. This bishop believes that in cataclysmic struggle the denomination will find itself structurally and spiritually.

This reticence to use the language of doctrinal theology is not evident, however, in the three projects of the denomination whose practical theology we will now examine: the attempt at restructuring offered by the Connectional Process Team, the focus toward reshaping evident in the Initiative on Children and Poverty, and the reclaiming theology that marks the Dialogue on Theological Diversity.

Practical Theology in the CPT: Restructuring Theology

The Connectional Process Team was established at the 1996 General Conference to continue the work done by the Connectional Issues Study of the General Council on Ministries and the Global Nature of the Church, work that held implications for restructuring in the UMC. The CPT mandate was to "manage, guide, and promote a transformational direction for the UMC." The specific directives given to the CPT asked in part for proposals for restructuring and were popularly understood to be substantially *aimed* toward restructuring. The CPT's work involved questions about restructuring in a way that the Dialogue and Initiative do not. In preparation for the 2000 General Conference, the CPT published a lengthy report.

As a committee widely understood to be developing a restructuring proposal for the denomination, the CPT is distinctive in that it rejected restructuring as the primary mode of organizing religious work in the UMC. Early on it decided that restructuring had to follow, not precede, the reconstruction of United Methodist identity, relationships, and ways of providing information.[2] Therefore, the document says at least as much about reshaping practices and reclaiming Wesleyan identity as it does about structure. Its first three major sections follow a general pattern of recommending a set of practices and then proposing structures that will support those practices. It deviates from this pattern when it reclaims theology and Wesleyan tradition at key points. The last two major sections are more directly about structure. The pattern of the document itself shows the subtlety and complexity of the transformation that the team recommends.

In the introduction the "restructuring" expectation of the CPT is clear: "In light of our study, conversations, and prayer, we have examined all of the *activities, functions, and structures* of the church today by asking one simple but central question: Will this help us invite, nurture, and empower disciples of Jesus Christ through local churches and faith communities throughout the world?" (emphasis mine).[3]

Between the statements that focus the aim of the task and the aim of the work, however, the CPT specifically relies upon "reclaiming" language to elaborate the definition of a "transformational direction." A "transformation," according to the report, only occurs through the work of God's love, creating, sustaining, guiding, redeeming, and perfecting. This love is apparent through the person of Jesus Christ, the presence of the Holy Spirit, and the community of the church, where practices of preaching and sacramental life enable the church to reach out to the world. Therefore, the team bases its recommendations on its discernment of the work of the Holy Spirit. It recommends five "transformational directions": (1) "Center on Christian Formation," (2) "Call Forth Covenant Leadership," (3) "Empower the Connection for Ministry," (4) "Strengthen Our Global Connections and Ecumenical Relationships," and (5) "Encourage Doctrinal and Theological Discourse." In discussing these five transformational directions, the team makes recommendations for structural overhaul of the UMC. The fuller story of this work is described in Wood's case study. Ultimately, the 2000 General Conference in May 2000 affirmed the transformational directions but rejected

---

2. Based on interviews with Bishop Sharon Brown Christopher and Eileen Williams. These three ideas were taken from workshops provided to the Board of Discipleship by Margaret Wheatley.

3. All quotations within this section are from "Connectional Process Team Report," *Daily Christian Advocate, Advance Edition: Journal of the General Conference of the United Methodist Church* 1, sect. 1 (2000): 5-21.

the restructuring proposals that went with them. Even though its specific structural proposals were rejected, the document is interesting for its practical theological method and the subtleties of the solutions it actually proposes.

As a document about structure, the CPT report responds to many of the concerns about structure reported by the bishops. Its primary *structural solutions* to the UMC's discontents propose emphasizing leadership development, streamlining committee structures, reducing bureaucracy, creating flexible networking structures, replacing legislative and legal procedures with discernment and consensus, and displacing the centrality of the United States as the hub of ministry throughout the world. The CPT's attempt to respond to these concerns show that a number of questions remain. Leadership development is qualified by the adjectives "spiritual," "prophetic," "covenant," and "servant," distinguishing the church leader from the leader in general. However, are these kinds of leadership synonymous, and if not, how are they related to one another? Streamlined committees become "councils," and membership in councils is reduced in number. While streamlining addresses the contemporary concern for overburdening apparatus, how would such councils enact the traditional values of broad participation and egalitarian representation in decision making through large membership conferences? Bureaucracy may be reduced by reorganizing the size and number of general boards, agencies, and commissions, but does such reorganization also dismantle a decade-long construction of influence of United Methodism in the world? Discernment and consensus building attempts to eliminate the win/lose quality of the legislative process and aims toward the direct recognition of God and neighbor in decision making, but does it provide a means through which genuine conflict can surface? A Global Conference with equal representation from around the world distributes the political and economic power broadly, but does it de-contextualize and standardize the legal and economic decisions by which Methodists in different parts of the world would then be required to live? As a part of its concern for the practice of justice within its church life, the denomination has relied on specific representation and regularized procedures to guarantee a balance of power in decision making. But have United Methodists attended too little to the wisdom that determines that some problems can't be solved without certain people in the conversation? In others words, they may think their structures are burdensome as they attempt to live values deeply embedded in their tradition. As discontented as they are with that overgrowth, when given the opportunity for change they may also be aware that new structures bring equally vexing new problems while eliminating the solutions to the former problems. Were United Methodists not convinced that the new structures would have carried the strengths of the tradition as well as the present structures do? Or would new structures have diverted the power battle at work in the denomination, a power battle in which many General Conference delegates are heavily invested? It is easier to battle for power in a denomination when familiar structures are firmly in place.

The primary concern in the document is the development of clergy, lay, and episcopal "spiritual leaders." The clearest definition of a "spiritual leader" appears in the section recommending the development of "lay servant leaders in local churches":

> A spiritual servant leader, through God's love, brings the hope of transformation to people's lives and then walks with them on their journey. Spiritual leaders reach out to persons in the servant spirit of Jesus whose love knows no barrier of race, culture, gender, class, or other human circumstance. These covenant leaders are open and listening to God and to all with whom they connect, calling upon us to see God's direction and purpose rather than our own.

How are these spiritual leaders to be developed? Through "reshaping," through practices of spiritual formation that reinvigorate early Wesleyan practices that aim to form believers toward personal and social holiness. These practices create "inward and outward spirituality" through "acts of devotion and acts of compassion." They reclaim Wesleyan tradition in that they were present in the early Wesleyan class meetings and in the Wesleyan outreach based on Wesley's proclamation that "the world is my parish."

How important is "reshaping theology" to the CPT document? The first "transformational direction" it recommends is "Center on Christian Formation." It begins by "reclaiming" Christian formation as "grounded in God's grace" and focuses the goal of Christian formation on salvation, justification, and sanctification through Jesus' sacrifice on the cross and through God's gracious activity in our everyday lives. However, it immediately recommends that "persons develop and nurture *the practices that shape them* into the image of Christ" (emphasis mine). A significant portion of the remaining document specifically outlines practices that aim at this kind of reshaping experience, connecting the reshaping practices to groups within the organizational network of the denomination.

What kinds of groups and practices does the document recommend?

- Methodist followers who do "acts of devotion (prayer, Bible reading, inward examination) and acts of compassion (the simple things we do out of kindness to our neighbor)";
- Methodist followers who do "acts of worship (the ministries of word and

sacrament that we exercise together) and acts of justice (ministries that implement God's righteousness and denounce justice)";

- local churches that create "cluster groups, and classes that provide mutual support and accountability in ministry" that ask traditional Wesleyan questions that inquire diligently about the well-being of each other's souls and bodies, such as "Is it well with your soul? Are you engaged in fasting and prayer? What are you doing to reach out to others? How are you witnessing in your home and workplace? Are you well economically? Are you without work? Are you hungry? Are you facing a crisis?";
- covenant groups that engage in mutual care and support in groups that form around common interests;
- clergy orders that participate in common Bible study and prayer, sharing both good and difficult experiences, responding to current challenges, and exercising mutual accountability;
- spiritual leaders who "practice the disciplines, point to God's saving grace, gather persons for the study of Scripture, teach and model the teachings of Jesus Christ, help persons discover their potential to serve in the name of Jesus Christ, and walk with them on their journeys";
- local covenant leaders who teach, visit the sick, preach, do works of compassion and justice, prophesy the vision of God's reign;
- bishops who "guard the faith, order, liturgy, doctrine and discipline of the church . . . who provid[e] prophetic spiritual leadership, [gather] the community of faith for worship and sacraments, and le[a]d the church to seek Christian unity and justice for all people";
- bishops who "focus their time and energy on spiritual and prophetic leadership within their annual conferences and in the world. Spiritual leadership is supported by the disciplines of prayer, Scripture study, private and public worship, fasting, and Christian conferencing. Prophetic leadership includes listening to the world, to human suffering and sin, and raising the voice of justice and hope";
- seminaries that "stress piety and learning in their mission/vision statements . . . to emphasize Christ-centered preaching and dynamic worship . . . and . . . moral and ethical values";
- councils of "spiritual and prophetic lay and clergy leaders who will gather for discernment, discussion, decision-making, and disciple-making" working in "mutual trust and respect, the style of which will be collegial, Spirit-driven, and responsive to the common purpose of making disciples and serving God's world . . . model relational community and practice the spiritual disciplines and Christian conferencing";
- ministries of the church that include "proclaiming the gospel, worship-

ing, teaching, studying, and nurturing. Disciples are sent to share the Good News, to be present with the poor and marginalized, to care for the creation, and to work for peace and justice";

- annual conferences that "discover, recruit, train, certify, appoint, supervise, sustain, and support accountable servant leaders";
- a Global Christian Conference that includes "connecting, renewing, discerning, and deciding"; and
- covenant councils that involve "openness and a willingness to listen to others and to God as we seek God's direction and purpose rather than our own."

One of the most dramatic structural proposals of the document, the restructuring of the general boards and agencies of the church, in part follows the model of reorganizing around practices. Presently, the general boards and agencies include Global Missions, Church and Society, Higher Education and Ministry, Discipleship, and Finance and Administration, and general commissions include Status and Role of Women, Religion and Race, Christian Unity and Interreligious Concerns. Under the CPT proposal these general boards, agencies, and commissions would be asked to redesign and align their work with attention to Nurture, Outreach, and Witness Ministries; Leadership Development; Congregational Development; Administration and Finance; and Communication and Interpretation. The latter four are described by general areas of work, but Nurture, Outreach, and Witness Ministries are described by the following practices:

- Nurture: "The Biblical Foundations of the Christian faith, our Wesleyan/Evangelical heritage, and acts of piety and devotion are central to this area. The nurturing ministries of the church shall give attention to the educational, worship, and stewardship components of ministry."
- Outreach: "Acts of mercy and compassion and social holiness are central to this area and include local and larger community ministries of compassion and advocacy, church and societal issues, global ministries concerns, health and welfare ministries, Christian unity and interreligious concerns, religion and race, and the status and role of women."
- Witness: "Fully living out our discipleship by embracing the stewardship of all of life, proclaiming the good news of Christ to the world, and providing hospitality to all persons is central to this area. It includes evangelistic outreach to persons, membership care, spiritual formation, communications, lay speaking ministries, and witnessing through the sharing of personal and congregational stories of Christian faith and service."

Furthermore, these proposals for reorganizing this work, so closely connected to reshaping, also reclaim explicitly theological language. The theological language is not developed as it would be in a doctrinal or systematic article or pastoral letter. Even so, appeals are made to a wide variety of theological themes: God's love, grace, justification, sanctification, regeneration, salvation, revelation, the image of God and the image of Christ, God's reign, the church, covenant, the ministry of all Christians, and acts of mercy, piety, and compassion. Moreover, a major section of the document, a "transformational direction," is entitled "Encourage Doctrinal and Theological Discourse."

This document teaches much about the relationships among restructuring, reshaping, and reclaiming theology. The relationship among these three aspects of practical theology is consistently strong where the document is most concerned with Christian formation through "works of piety." It is consistently strong where the primary proposals refer to the restructuring of the denomination in ways that most affect the church in the United States. But it is equally interesting to note the places where restructuring, reshaping, and reclaiming become disconnected. The CPT intended to convey the idea that spiritual leadership is created by an interdependent, integrated practice of the means of grace, traditionally understood as piety and mercy.[4] The document falls short of conveying this integration, however, in specific ways. The reshaping language refers to practices of piety such as prayer, Bible reading, etc., very specifically. It refers to practices of compassion, mercy, or justice in the more general, conceptual language of "ministry." In other words, the document tells us more about the actual practices related to "piety" that form spiritual leaders and less about practices related to "mercy" that form spiritual leaders. In fact, the use of the phrase "spiritual and prophetic" leader leaves one thinking that one is either a spiritual leader or a prophetic leader rather than recognizing that spiritual leaders are prophetic leaders (and vice versa) and suggesting a series of concrete practices that equally shape the "prophetic" aspect of leadership. The reshaping language that refers to explicit practices is thinnest in places where the document speaks of nonsexist, nonracist, ecumenical, interfaith, and global relationships. To emphasize the interdependence of piety and mercy in spiritual leadership, the document would have had to specify a series of practices that are parallel to practices of piety, traditional Wesleyan ministries such as visiting prisoners, the poor, and the sick; providing education and economic relief; and doing this in face-to-face relationships rather than through agencies.[5] Instead,

---

4. This intention was strongly expressed in the interview with Christopher and Williams.

5. See Manfred Marquardt, *John Wesley's Social Ethics: Praxis and Principles,* trans. John E. Steely and W. Stephen Gunter (Nashville: Abingdon, 1992).

the document relies more heavily on restructuring to carry these relationships rather than suggesting an equally concrete set of practices that move the church toward these aims. Similarly, the reshaping language is thin when the document recommends theological and doctrinal discourse. The document suggests in what structures such discourse might be done, but does not offer a concrete set of practices that help the church do a better job at talking out its theological differences. That, however, is the explicit task of the Dialogue on Theological Diversity.

Two difficulties identified in our interviews with the bishops were apparent in CPT discussions that led to the CPT report. The struggle for power that was alluded to by the bishops appeared in the CPT process as a difference of opinion over the most reliable way of distributing power. Over several decades United Methodists have developed a system for distributing power across geography, racial/ethnic groups, and gender groups. This system insured a diversity of heretofore absent voices that could represent the concerns of various denominational groups. The system was deemed to provide the best grounds for making just decisions. Some have wondered whether this system both burdens the denomination with bureaucracy and fails to bring into the conversation all persons who really need to be present. As more streamlined systems were implemented in some annual conferences and became a part of the CPT report for restructuring, many anxious voices were raised about the potential failure of a streamlined system to guarantee diverse participation.

Furthermore, the struggle for language that was identified in the interviews with the bishops also appeared in the CPT discussion, especially around the use of the words "global" and "table." For some the word "global" had expansive connotations. The "global" church is a sign of United Methodist interconnection across the world. For others the word brought associations of colonial religion and imperialist economic exploitation. Likewise, the word "table," as the place where conversation among diverse elements of the church could occur, had eucharistic associations for all. For some, making the connection between the practice of Eucharist and table conversation was positive, taking worship into life. For others such a connection contaminated and cheapened the notion of Eucharist and needed to be avoided. The difficulty over the language of "global" reflects similar problems in discussions of theology and the social sciences. The tension over the language of "table" reflects difficulties in the discipline of theology itself, where some persons reserve "theology" for systematic reflection on practice and others see theology being done and communicated in practice.

The "transformational directions" that the CPT recommends and that were considered by the General Council on Ministry in its work through 2004

Pamela D. Couture

are not just recommendations for restructuring, but recommendations for reclaiming practices that are distinctive to the Wesleyan tradition and are deeply rooted in Wesleyan theology. It will be interesting to find out whether the next stage of work on these directions recommends specific, concrete practices in areas where the CPT report is not as full. Building on the CPT's recommendations, the council might in the next stage develop a model of spiritual formation that engages the practices involved in the wide range of traditional and emerging ministries in the UMC.

Practical Theology in the Dialogue on Theological Diversity: Reclaiming Theology

The Dialogue on Theological Diversity was conducted under the auspices of the General Commission on Christian Unity and Interreligious Concerns. The Dialogue brought together twenty-four leaders "chosen for their competence in reflecting on the doctrine of the church and its contemporary theological task." The leaders also represented the range of theological viewpoints found in the UMC. In addition to a number of working papers, it produced a document entitled "In Search of Unity: A Conversation with Recommendations for the Unity of the United Methodist Church."[6]

The letter that introduces the document addresses the "reclaiming" aim of the Dialogue by saying, "Controversies over social issues have led to the realization that a deeper layer of tension exists concerning the role and authority of Scripture and divine revelation." The implications for "restructuring" follow: "Today, some persons suggest that a split could occur in The United Methodist Church because of the depth of the conflict and the disturbing choices people feel compelled to make." The document appeals at several points to "reshaping" in two forms: the reshaping of the person's dispositions toward unity by the Holy Spirit, and the reshaping of United Methodist discourse about theological differences toward civility. In fact, the most widely adopted part of the document may be its "Guidelines for Civility in the United Methodist Church," an "action step" that works toward reshaping the practices and attitudes of people engaged in conflict in the church. Furthermore, the Dialogue itself took place in a context of worship, a setting where an explicit appeal to the Holy Spirit for the shaping of hearts toward the Spirit's guidance could be made.

"In Search of Unity" is framed in the "reclaiming" language of ecclesiology. It begins with the ecclesial claim: "The church is a gift of the Triune God

6. This section was written in consultation with Bruce Robbins.

580

through the working of the Holy Spirit." This doctrinal statement leads to an immediate intersection between reclaiming and reshaping: "[T]he Holy Spirit works in our hearts to create a disposition to seek unity." The church is a gift of God not to be taken for granted. The search for unity in the church emerges from desires and dispositions, created by the Holy Spirit, that yield practices and ways of living together that could foster unity rather than disruption. This beginning is significant. It implies that human beings cannot do their work for unity through rational theological argument alone. Unity-friendly dispositions, habits, and practices are required.

The document describes a church whose strengths include its practices of worship, sacraments, and ministries of love and justice; its theological heritage; and its structures of conference and itinerancy. These strengths meet three categories of challenges. Again, we find an intertwining of doctrinal theology and reshaped practice. The first category of challenge, "Challenges Stemming from the Fall from Original Righteousness," identifies a series of relational problems in the church, beginning with "our impatience with one another, our tendency to believe rumor and innuendo." The second category, "Challenges to the Quality of Our Existence Together," provides a list of ecclesial disagreements, beginning with "our inability to agree on how to relate our commitment to justice and to God's sovereign purposes for creation to the task of making disciples." The third category, "Challenges That Harbor the Danger of Explicit Disunity or Schism," outlines differences in reclaiming theology, such as "the nature of the Trinitarian faith," that usually lead to differences on divisive social issues, particularly "homosexuality as illustrative of our divergence." The theological themes identified as those most disagreed upon are "authority of Scripture and divine revelation." The document implies that any one of these categories of differences may provide the soil for discord, but differences in reclaiming theology as they are connected to divisive social issues are seen as significantly more threatening than interpersonal differences.

The document seems to argue explicitly that theological differences are most threatening. However, despite the benefit of working papers developed prior to the document, it does not outline the nature of the doctrinal theological differences at any length. Rather, it concentrates on a practical ecclesial problem, originally listed as one item in "Challenges to the Quality of Our Existence Together," in which the potential for schism lies. The problem is "a lack of agreement on the boundaries of assent and dissent." It describes "incompatibilists" or "compatibilists," each of which may be found in conservative and liberal wings of the church. Incompatibilists believe that the boundaries of the church do not allow for dissenting viewpoints related to theology and homosexuality. Compatibilists believe that the church should allow disagreement. This honest description of the conflict that could lead to schism suggests that the knottiest problem is not interpersonal crabbiness or theological difference but instead a conflict about how much homogeneity the church should require. If that is true, the greatest problem is not one of reclaiming theology (even when it reclaims ecclesial statements about the nature of the church that all might agree upon in the abstract) or of reshaping theology (a disposition toward unity and practice of civility), but of restructuring theology (how we are organized and what that organization communicates about our understanding of the divine). Though the aim of the Dialogue is doctrinal discussion, this honest description of the conflict is perhaps its most insightful and original contribution. Furthermore, the deep belief in the necessity of theological practices in the midst of conflict is evident. God must be invoked through reshaping practices so that human beings can be their best selves with one another through "persistent prayer, fasting, rigorous thought, and compassion through Christ-like dialogue. This is not a pious comment but a lasting judgment derived from our conviction that it is God who holds us together in the church and not we ourselves." Only then is genuine discernment about the way forward possible.

Clearly, this Dialogue is, as the document states, a first step. At least three of the series of action proposals were acted upon prior to the 2000 General Conference. As requested, the Council of Bishops did enter its own theological dialogue. In fact, it spent the majority of its plenary time during the last quadrennium conducting its own dialogue and practicing the "Guidelines for Civility," which has been widely distributed and used in the church, and moreover, sent to the CPT for consideration in its discussion. General Conference 2000 recommended that similar Dialogues continue in a variety of venues, indicating that many other recommendations of the Dialogue may find life in the next quadrennium.

What are the implications of the Dialogue in relation to the CPT report? It coheres nicely with the emphasis on devotional practice in the first three sections of the CPT report and specifies particular practices that are important to theological dialogue, practices that might have made the fifth portion of the CPT, "Encourage Theological and Doctrinal Discourse," more consistent with its whole. By placing this fifth section alongside "In Search of Unity," an interesting question comes to the fore. The CPT report specifically calls on theological schools to help to clarify the thought of the church, but "In Search of Unity" shows that clear, abstract, theological thinking is not enough. Instead, to entertain doctrinal differences groups need to be equally schooled in processes of dialogue that are in conflict with academic discourse in the twenty-first century. In academia, including the theological academy, a student often learns that "clear and critical thinking" is created by offering a few appreciative comments about another person's theology and then attacking any weakness in the argument with a vengeance and producing one's own correct, reasoned position with which any other "reasonable" person would agree. "Clear and critical thinking" rarely means genuinely understanding and appreciating a person whose viewpoint differs, finding the strengths in that person's position as well as in one's own position, and finding ways toward a third collaborative alternative of which neither side was previously aware. "Clear and critical thinking" often concentrates on understanding why the other side is wrong, not why the other side is right. Classroom combat is about ideas. One can always reconsider on the following day, though one rarely does. The academic model allows for classroom combat to be followed by sociability away from the classroom. As students spend less time with one another away from the classroom, however, the academic model of combat and conviviality deteriorates. This kind of academic formation may not serve us well in the setting of the church, where the combat is not just about ideas but about personal integrity, ultimate faith claims to live by, and economic resources. The Dialogue suggests that, as the abstractions of doctrine are debated, specific sets of practices of civility that support dialogue across theological difference may be an important aspect of the "formation in spiritual leadership" that theological education has to offer.

Practical Theology in the Bishops Initiative on Children and Poverty: Reshaping Theology

Part of the function of the office of the bishop in the UMC is teaching. An "episcopal initiative" results when the Council of Bishops decides that a particular subject is so important to the life of the church that it will collectively study and teach about it over a period of years. In recent decades the environment and congregational life have been subjects of episcopal initiatives. The Bishops Initiative on Children and Poverty was launched in 1996 and continues as an initiative through at least 2004. Previous initiatives worked toward producing a study guide for the church. The method of this initiative was different: it produced a short "foundation" document in 1996 and then sought to support the efforts of bishops to organize the Initiative as they saw fit in their local episcopal areas.

"Reshaping" is the first of three specific goals elaborated in the foundation document:

> The crisis among children and the impoverished and our theological and historical mandates demand more than additional programs or emphases.

> *Nothing less than the reshaping of The United Methodist Church in response to the God who is among "the least of these" is required.* The evaluation of everything the Church is and does in the light of the impact on children and the impoverished is the goal. The anticipated result is the *development of forms of congregational and connectional life and mission* that will more faithfully reflect and serve the God revealed in Jesus Christ. *Communities of faith shaped by God's presence with the most vulnerable represent alternatives to the values and visions of the prevailing culture.* (emphasis mine)[7]

The kind of "reshaping" that is envisioned is elaborated in the foundation document. The document begins with a social scientific description of the global situation of children and poverty. It is to this situation that United Methodists are asked to respond in imitation of the acts of God. The document demonstrates why they are called to respond to children and poverty by tracing the theme of God's response to children and the poor through the Old and New Testaments and in early Methodist mission and ministry. It returns to the contemporary situation, arguing that for the first time the world has the resources to solve the problem of poverty and that the lack of desire to do so is a spiritual problem. The document imagines people and a church who are "reshaped" by ministering in and among the children and the poor.

The practices it commends are intertwined with the theology it reclaims. The primary theological issue, the document asserts, is the nature and action of God. The primary practice it recommends is the imitation of this God. The second section of the document, "Theological, Historical, and Missional Mandate," portrays the character of the biblical God as one who defends the vulnerable, particularly the widow, the orphan, and the resident alien; who considers practices of justice, compassion, and mercy toward the poor to be more important than cultic practices; who requires tithing as a means of caring for the poor; who in Jesus Christ associates himself with the outcast and declares that "what you do to the least of these is what you do to me."

The document then shows the continuity between this biblical God and the God Wesley worshiped, preached, and imitated. In so doing, it stresses the practices of the original Wesleyan movement. Wesley practiced, as required of his preachers, regular visiting of the poor; design of facilities that welcomed the poor; instruction for the poor and for children in religion, worship, fasting, and academics; spending time with children; and providing holistically for the edu-

---

7. All quotations in this section are from the original foundational document for the Bishops Initiative on Children and Poverty, "Children and Poverty, an Episcopal Initiative: Biblical and Theological Foundations," in Deb Smith, *Community with Children and the Poor: A Guide for Congregational Study* (Nashville: United Methodist Publishing House, 2003).

cation, health, and economic sufficiency of the poor and children, for the freedom of slaves, and for compassion for prisoners and the condemned. Implicitly, it recommends that Wesleyans find contemporary practices that parallel these early Wesleyan essentials.

The document claims that the failure of vision and moral will to solve the crisis of children and poverty is a spiritual crisis. The symptoms of spiritual crisis are the church's and the society's sense of powerlessness; boredom; poverty of vision, community, and hope; and the attitude that wealth is "mine" rather than a trust from God. The practices of building care and community with children and the poor are a means of grace. Therefore, they lead to a spiritual answer to the crisis. What can be gained spiritually by such reshaping is articulated in a "reclaiming" statement early in the document:

> The statistics alone do not tell the full story of what is happening to the world's children. Children are victims of many poverties. Spiritual poverty is more difficult to measure, but its devastating effects on the affluent and the impoverished are evident. To be deprived of love, hope, and transcendent meaning is to be robbed of the abundant life that Christ intends for all. All children have a basic need and right to know that they are loved infinitely by God and that God seeks for them a life of joy, hope, and meaning. Children need to experience their identity and worth as both recipients and means of God's grace. What is happening to the world's children represents a sinful devaluing of God's gracious gift of life and a thwarting of God's justice for all humanity.

Like the CPT report, the Initiative foundation document diagnoses the church's problem as a crisis in its spiritual life. It recommends a series of practices that are equally aimed at the creation of spirituality, but very different from those recommended by the CPT. Where the CPT is strong on practices that aim toward building a relationship with God and with neighbors within the life of the church, the Initiative emphasizes building a relationship with neighbors within and especially outside the church in order to find a relationship with God. Just as "In Search of Unity" offers a set of practices that broaden the fifth section of the CPT report, the Initiative offers a set of practices that could broaden the practices recommended for the creation of "spiritual/prophetic/servant/covenant leadership." Like "In Search of Unity" and unlike the CPT report, the foundation document is more a launching document after a first stage of discussion than a document of recommendations. Practices that might build global, ecumenical, and interfaith community are implied by the way the issue of children and poverty is described in the first section of the document; they are not recommended. However, the practices recommended in this document and in documents that succeeded it, including "Hope for the Children of Africa" and "A Church for All God's Children," provide further interpretation of the kinds of practices that might enrich the fourth section of the CPT report and its understanding of spirituality and leadership. The same is true in reverse: acts of compassion and acts of devotion are not linearly related (though for Wesley, when they temporally conflict, the demands of mercy allow the believer to put aside devotional practice). They are organically and integrally connected with one another; each depends upon the other. Since interconnected practices of mercy and piety informed both the development of doctrine in the early church and the Wesleyan movement, one wonders how a fuller reshaping of spiritual leadership through common practices of mercy and piety might inform the new communities that will be created by additional dialogues on theological diversity called for by the 2000 General Conference.

Though the Initiative foundation document does not recommend restructuring per se, it calls for evaluation of the organization of the church as it responds to God who is among the children and the poor. Where the structure of the church blocks such a response, it would need to be restructured. Since the Initiative is the work of the Council of Bishops, it is not surprising that its implementation reflects some of the bishops' structural concerns. Reflecting their concern for "burdensome organization and bureaucracy," it created no new programs of organizations. Respecting the growing need for contextualization, it relied on each bishop to implement it as he or she saw fit in his or her episcopal area. It focused simultaneously on advocacy and meeting particular needs.

Its struggles and its successes also reflected conditions in the UMC. At some points the Initiative was criticized for being "just another social action program," at others for being "apple pie — who can be against it?" Persons in the church whose programs had long advocated for children against poverty were at times miffed by the bishops' involvement in their "turf," and others distrusted the bishops, doubting they would continue the Initiative until real gains were made. According to the bishops' own evaluation, the hardest problem the Initiative faces is creating practices with the poor, middle class, and wealthy that build community across class boundaries. In that sense the work of the Initiative reveals the fragmentation of postmodern society. But it also works against fragmenting trends in that it represents an unusually collaborative project among the Council of Bishops, the general boards and agencies of the church, faculty from theological schools, agency consultants from within and beyond the UMC, and local groups and congregations.

Conclusion

A close reading of the restructuring, reshaping, and reclaiming aspects of each of these practical theological projects shows that these three aspects are integrally related to each other, even when one aspect is the ostensible aim. It also shows that the most creative theological energy seems to be not in the arena of structure or doctrine but in reshaping the United Methodist way of life through a variety of practices that are related to spiritual development. No one project, however, has a full articulation of what these practices are. The practices recommended by these three projects in the UMC complement one another. Furthermore, a study of the practices enjoined in additional projects (e.g., little is said here about the practice of the arts in a practical theological project) might be necessary for the church to grasp holistic theological practice and spiritual development. The practices that emerge as "spiritually quickening" in these three projects, however, offer a broad vision of a devotional, compassionate, and articulate spirituality of faith and works toward which the UMC might be developing.

Bibliography

"Children and Poverty, an Episcopal Initiative: Biblical and Theological Foundations" (original foundational document for the Bishops Initiative on Children and Poverty). In Deb Smith, *Community with Children and the Poor: A Guide for Congregational Study* (Nashville: United Methodist Publishing House, 2003).

"Connectional Process Team Report." *Daily Christian Advocate, Advance Edition: Journal of the General Conference of the United Methodist Church* 1, sect. 1 (2000): 5-21.

"In Search of Unity: A Conversation with Recommendations for the Unity of the United Methodist Church" is available from the General Commission on Christian Unity and Interreligious Concerns, United Methodist Church, 475 Riverside Drive, Room 1300, New York, New York 10115.

Maddox, Randy. *Responsible Grace: John Wesley's Practical Theology.* Nashville: Abingdon, 1994.

Richey, Russell, ed. *The Methodist Conference in America: A History.* Nashville: Kingswood Books, 1996.

National Denominational Structures' Engagement with Postmodernity: An Integrative Summary from an Organizational Perspective

David A. Roozen

S ignificant changes in religion typically come, historians tell us, during times of momentous social change. As suggested in the introduction to this volume, there is a pervasive literature across a wide spectrum of disciplines that indicates we are indeed in the midst of a major social transition. It is a transition driven by a constellation of technical, social, demographic, and culture changes. It is transforming the very nature of human association, cognition, psychology, and knowing. It is also changing the way organizations function.

Literally hundreds of books have been written describing the characteristics, consequences, and proper labeling of this change. For present purposes I am uninterested in the arguments over the label — I will use "postmodern"; and it is beyond the constraints of this essay to present more than a cursory list of characteristics. Given the general thrust of my analysis which identifies the politicization of national denominational structures as a major concern, let me present here only the following modest list, taken from different sections in N. J. Rengger's *Political Theory, Modernity, and Postmodernity:*[1]

- axial shifts in the material basis of industrial societies associated with the enormous technological advances in communications, information technology, and computing;
- the globalization of financial markets and the transformation of the global political economy; the globalization of consumerism and computer networks; the spatial and temporal shrinking of the globe;
- institutionalized pluralism; variety, contingency, ambivalence, and complexity;

1. N. J. Rengger, *Political Theory, Modernity, and Postmodernity* (Oxford: Blackwell, 1995).

- the scrambling of traditions; de-traditionalization, understood as the routine subjection of traditions to critical interrogation; and
- an increasing sense of personal responsibility for the possibility of choice and the kinds of choices made.

Continuing in the current literature on political science, one finds the further suggestion that these changes are having a pronounced effect on civil government. Although articulated in a variety of ways, the general ideal is captured in the following: *Diversity supported by emerging electronic technology erodes strong power pyramids, erodes singular ideologies, and erodes confidence in the political process and traditional forms of political participation.*

Given the often perplexing unsettledness of our transition to postmodernity, how could someone interested in the human carriers of religion in the United States not be interested in the interrelated questions of how this change is affecting the identity, purpose, and structure of denominational systems, and how denominations are trying to respond? These were the interests that stimulated this book. The following essay is an attempt to provide a general and integrative answer to the questions by putting the contributions to this volume into dialogue with each other and with the broader organizational literature. Before turning to this, however, let me alert the reader to my major conclusions.

The Challenges of Unsettled Times: An Overview

Paraphrasing the above statement about civil government, the most significant long-term effect of postmodernity on religious institutions is the emerging and evolving de-traditionalization and pluralization within the broader society that seeps down into denominational systems. Once inside, it challenges the cohesion and strength of denominational identities, of authority and power in national denominational structures, and of the loyalty and commitment of constituent congregations and members.

The severity of these challenges in some denominations notwithstanding, it is clear that the situation of national denominational structures is one of transition, not demise. To reiterate what was stressed in the introduction, the issue for American denominations as they move into the new millennium is not death, but rather how they can and how they are trying to faithfully and effectively carry their particular legacies into a changing future. The issue is not death, but rather how denominations think anew about God and then structure that thinking into organizational identity and practice. Those who use the banners of death and demise typically do so to advance a political agenda of their own. Nevertheless, the challenges of the current social-cultural transition should not be taken lightly. They are organizationally corrosive. They can be explosive. Some denominations appear up to the challenge, some struggle to cope. All are affected.

To understand and appreciate the challenges, it is important to keep in mind several characteristics of all denominations that follow from those already discussed in the introduction. By its very nature as a national, organizational carrier of a religious tradition, a denomination is intrinsically segmented into a variety of different and potentially different constituency groups. These include national staff and local congregations, large congregations and small congregations, new converts and tenth-generation pillars, traditionalists and innovators, Gen-Xers and pre-boomers, and called clergy and graduate-educated clergy, to mention just a few. By its very nature as a historical and human institutionalization of a religious tradition, a denomination also is, necessarily, theologically compromised. Takayama reminds us that more than any other social system, religious organizations are the repository of "ideals," that is, of truth, symbolic value commitments, and aspirations.[2] Yet they are equally subject to the conventional rules, norms, and procedures that make orderly, human interaction feasible and enable an organization to affect people and stay viable. Convention and ideal seldom coincide, and intraorganizational strains arising from the discrepancy between ideal and actual are ubiquitous, pervasive, and systemic.

Difference and theological imperfection always contain the potential for tension and conflict. Additionally, the ultimate worldly authority for all American Protestant denominational systems is their national assemblies, all of which act through some form of participatory democracy. That is, their decision-making process is intrinsically political. Still further, American denominationalism is constitutionally voluntary. The theoretical meaning of this was discussed in the introduction. One of its more important implications, Johnson reminds us, is that there is no formal denominational system of taxing individual members.[3] Most denominations, however, have a formal or informal apportionment system, which, in Johnson's words, "allocates national and regional denominational budget quotas to the local congregations." Nevertheless, "It is possible for a congregation to ignore these requests and not pay its 'fair

2. K. Peter Takayama, "Strains, Conflicts, and Schisms in Protestant Denominations," in *American Denominational Organization: A Sociological View,* ed. Ross P. Scherer (Pasadena, Calif.: William Carey Library, 1980), pp. 298-329.

3. Douglass W. Johnson, "Program Dissensus between Denominational Grass Roots and Leadership and Its Consequences," in *American Denominational Organization,* pp. 330-45.

share' to the denomination or to send only partial payments."[4] Indeed, this is operative in several of our denominational case studies. It is what the author of the Episcopal case calls the "green vote."

What happens when you put together the broad and pervasive social-cultural transition to postmodernity with national organizations that are intrinsically segmented, theologically compromised, voluntary, and political? Three consequences, all evident in the contributions to this volume, are critical, and all are pointed to in the civil government paraphrase. First, some of the postmodern forces external to a denomination find their way into it. Generational differences in music preferences and understanding of authority are classic examples. The result is increased segmentation and intensification of the political nature of the formal and informal negotiations across segments. Second, at least some specific value issues or movements that are widely and vehemently contested outside of a denomination attach themselves to existing segments within it and turn otherwise manageable internal tensions into major crises for the denomination. Sexuality issues provide a ready and pervasive example. Third, the impact of such externally reinforced crises depends to a large extent on the strength of a denomination's identity. To oversimplify, in strong identity denominations an external threat is much more easily manageable. There is typically sufficient clarity about the group's theology to name the threat as "deviant," and sufficient agreement to either sanction the deviance or at least minimize any political organization of it.

The consequences could not be more dramatically opposite in weak identity groups. These groups tend to be theologically diffuse, precluding a definitive theological assessment, often even to the point of contesting whether an issue is a grace-filled movement of the spirit or an aberration of the gospel. Without a consensual theological case the contestation of any issue becomes visibly political. It is not untypical for already contesting segments to take on a new issue as further fuel for their internal political mobilization. Still further, accountability, much less sanctioning, is already too weak in these denominations to mitigate the corrosive potential of American individualism and voluntarism. Still further, a moderate middle, with its potential mitigating presence, is difficult to organize because of the middle's lack of strong, effectual ties to a core group and identity, which fosters indifference to national fights or preoccupation with one's own, often locally and segmentally diffuse, interests.

The unique challenges of weak identity denominations notwithstanding, it is important to recall that there are stress and unsettledness caused by increasing internal diversity and fragmentation of identities in all eight of the de-

4. Johnson, "Program Dissensus," p. 333.

nominations studied. The severity of stress, however, varies considerably from "annoying but manageable" in denominations that retain stronger identities to "perplexing and paralyzing" in denominations whose identities have significantly eroded. Increasing diversity and the fragmentation of identity creates stress and unsettledness because it escalates the contested politicization of all decision making — including "decisions" about identity. Of special note (and perhaps irony) for groups that advocate pluralism is that increasing diversity and fragmentation is often due to minority viewpoints claiming and organizing their "voice," although oftentimes this gets mixed with the infiltration of "new" viewpoints.

The above conclusions lead to the more foundational observation that the "problem" is foremost a matter of identity, and only derivatively a matter of the role and process of a denomination's national structures. Such a conclusion is reinforced by the fact that one can find struggle and paralysis, as well as at least some moments of vitality, across the full spectrum of polities. Focusing the diagnosis on identity raises two intriguing questions: the first is addressed in part below, but the second is yet to be studied. The first question is: The loose connection between strength of identity and structure notwithstanding, can some kinds of structure help strengthen identity? Second: Who or what within a denomination has major responsibility for sustaining and developing identity, and how does this identity work get infused across the denomination as a total system?

In response to, and arguably in proportion to, the stress of increasing diversity and fragmentation, national denominational structures are giving increasing emphasis at this time to their more internally focused economic (e.g., resourcing congregations), political, and fellowship functions, as can be seen in the preceding case studies and essays. Conversely, their more externally focused, goal-seeking (evangelism, social mission), and accountability functions receive increasingly hesitant attention because they are becoming increasingly more problematic.

Consistent with the above point, structures that optimize the participatory and relational work of working across diversity tend to be more adaptive at this time than structures that optimize efficiency and control. Correspondingly, schism (or other means of reducing diversity) may be a good thing for denominational systems that place a premium on the purposeful action of nationally directed mission or purity of identity.

Liturgical and Pentecostal traditions appear to be more adaptive than more Calvinist or cognitive traditions, at least at the scale of national structures, to the conditions of the emerging postmodern period. There are several reasons for this, all having to do with the ability to handle the ambiguity and politicization of grand narratives. Liturgical and Pentecostal denominations tend to have more distinct and stronger identities. They also tend to give priority to noncognitive bases of religious authority and practice. And they tend to give priority to "being" with its strong relational predisposition rather than "doing" with its strong task orientation.

Within relatively established denominations, the intentional pursuit of denominational narrative practices appears to be a more effective method of strengthening and sustaining denominational identities than the effort to create or maintain high boundaries. The centrality of parish clergy both in sustaining denominational connections and in producing and reproducing denominational identity is reinforced by their role expectations, training, and financial investment. Strategic thinking about strengthening denominational connections and identity, therefore, must give serious attention to such related things as, for example, theological education and the balance of lay, parish clergy, and nonparish clergy representation in national and regional denomination structures.

The Challenges of Unsettled Times: A Deeper Conversation

The introduction to this volume concluded with a brief review of the literature on American denominations. I draw upon it without repeating it here, so one interested in that may want to make a slight detour in one's reading to freshen one's familiarity with it. In doing so one will note that the recent, reflective literature is dominated by a focus on oldline Protestantism and a virtual consensus about the notion of "the declining significance of denominations." One will also recall that I basically agree with this assessment for oldline Protestantism, and that while I believe most denominations in America are challenged by the same sources of stress affecting oldline Protestantism, I also believe the strength of identity typical of denominations outside the oldline mitigates against the corrosive effects, at least in the short term.

Implicit in the review of the literature is the fact that there are two somewhat distinct streams of literature. One is dominated by sociologists and stresses the corrosive effect of diversity and individualism on a sense of connection. The second stream is dominated by historians and stresses the loss (more appropriately, the erosion) of purpose and identity, especially of a denomination's theological center. Both are critically important and intimately related. Indeed, diversity and identity are my two major diagnostic points, and I elaborate on them in the immediately following two sections. Following that are four sections that deal with how denominations are responding or might respond.

David A. Roozen

They include the priority of internal over externally focused functions; the adaptive advantage of noncognitive sources of religious authority; the intentional pursuit of narrative practices; and the undervalued role of clergy in sustaining denominational identities.

1. Diversity and the Intensification of the Political Process

The best resource I have found for helping church leaders understand and appreciate the political dimension of religious organizations is Bolman and Deal's "political frame."[5] Among other things, Bolman and Deal succinctly summarize the political perspective in terms of the following five propositions:

- Organizations are coalitions composed of varied individuals and interest groups.
- There are enduring differences among individuals and groups in their values, preferences, beliefs, information, and perceptions of reality.
- Some differences are irreconcilable, and limited resources preclude the resolution of others.
- The combination of enduring differences and scarce resources makes conflict central to organizational dynamics, and power the most important resource.
- Organizational goals and decisions emerge from bargaining, negotiating, and jockeying for position among individuals and groups, i.e., from the competition of the political process.

Many religious leaders are hesitant, at best, about the nature of politics. Accordingly they will be especially ambivalent about Bolman and Deal's assertion that more than occasionally present, *politics is always present in organizations,* including the church. But I have to agree, as Gustafson noted nearly half a century ago, that whatever else the church is as an earthen vessel, it is also a political community.[6]

It is important to note that the political frame does not attribute politics to individual selfishness or incompetence, but rather to the fundamental organizational properties of interdependence, enduring differences, and scarcity.

5. Lee G. Bolman and Terrence E. Deal, *Reframing Organizations* (San Francisco: Jossey-Bass, 1991). For a summary of Bolman and Deal's political frame and its application to a case study oriented to church leaders, see my on-line "The Political Frame," at http://hirr.hartsem.edu/bookshelf/roozen_article2.html.

6. James Gustafson, *Treasure in Earthen Vessels* (New York: Harper and Brothers, 1961).

Politics, most fundamentally, involves the mediation, coordination, and ordering of difference, and therefore will be present in any and every organization regardless of the individuals involved. It is also important to note that the political frame does not view politics or power as "bad," although both can be used for exploitation and dominance. Both also can be a means of creating vision and reaching collective goals, and channeling human action in cooperative and socially valuable directions. However, Bolman and Deal are absolutely clear that politics dominates the scene under conditions of diversity and scarcity, and when power is diffuse.

I accept it as axiomatic that by its very nature as a national, organizational carrier of a religious tradition, a denomination is intrinsically segmented into a variety of different and potentially different constituency groups. I also suspect that most readers will have a special awareness of (and most likely a self-interest in) one or more such intragroup differences. To borrow a scriptural description — in today's world they are legion. One of the more prominent in the "declining significance of denominations" literature is the difference between national leaders and the local church. More specifically, the contention is that national leaders are out of touch, and the contention is universally advanced as a negative. In our case studies, for example, one of the major goals of the UCC restructuring was to make the national setting of the church more responsive and accessible to the local setting of the church.

Powell and Friedkin identify several tendencies internal to the functioning of national leaders that push toward a national/local gap.[7] Perhaps the most familiar and general of these is Michel's "iron law of oligarchy" — namely, the tendency of national leaders to focus energies on self-serving rather than organizational, goal-directed activities.[8] Indeed, in several of our case studies one even finds significant "turf" wars between national agencies, let alone between national and regional or local. But as Powell and Friedkin also point out, one can find many examples in which national staff are significantly more intense in their advocacy of and commitment to organizationally espoused goals than are other settings of the church. Without denying that there are inevitable organizational dynamics that constantly push toward a national/local gap, I believe that our case studies, especially in conjunction with the regional judicatory and local church findings of the broader ORW (Organizing Religious Work) project, are more supportive of Johnson's hint from nearly a quarter-century ago,

---

7. Walter W. Powell and Rebecca Friedkin, "Organizational Change in Nonprofit Organizations," in *The Nonprofit Sector: A Research Handbook,* ed. Walter W. Powell (New Haven: Yale University Press, 1987), pp. 180-92.

8. Powell and Friedkin, "Organizational Change," p. 181.

that the problem lay in shifting sensitivities and goal expectations between and among both national staff and church members within other settings of the church.[9]

Writing in the same volume as Johnson over twenty years ago, Takayama succinctly describes what was and remains a generally accepted sociological generalization about one of the major differences between national staff and local congregations.[10] He begins by reminding us that religious organizations are, ideally, "purposive." Accordingly, the major incentives for participation should derive from the stated purposes of the organization's theological tradition. He continues by noting that in contrast, local congregations are in practice predominantly "solidarity" or communal organizations — that is, organizations whose dominant inducements are things such as socializing, congeniality, and a sense of group identification — that they are covertly, not overtly so; and that as such they are predominantly oriented toward harmony, not toward issues and causes.

With this as background, Takayama then turns to what for present purposes is the critical point. The existence of two such different incentives, solidarity and purpose, within a denominational system is inevitably a source of strain and potential instability. More specifically, he argues that denominational executives (as well as, he notes, seminary professors and other church professionals) not only give priority to the purposive, but work in settings unfettered by community constraints that give them the freedom to do so. Not surprisingly, this can make them appear to the grass roots as excessively "independent" and "authoritarian." The reverse is, of course, also true, according to Takayama. Specifically, the communal constraints of local congregations can make them appear to denominational executives as overly passive, if not downright resistant to the denomination's purposeful goals.

The communal orientation of local congregations is of course at the heart of sociologist Stephen Warner's new paradigm for understanding religion in America described in the introduction. Central to his perspective and our argument is his emphasis on the new group vitality he sees in American religion and the fading of national denominational structures and the rise of "de facto congregationalism," the latter grounded in the growing prominence of "affectively significant associations under local and lay control." Given that Warner's "new" paradigm was published thirteen years after the above-cited work by Takayama, one wonders what is so new about it. Certainly it is not the communal nature of local congregations. Perhaps it's the acknowledgment by a leading academic

---

9. Johnson, "Program Dissensus," p. 338.
10. Takayama, "Strains, Conflicts," pp. 306-7.

that, especially in the context of increasing diversity, a communal orientation could be a significant cause of congregational vitality. I return to the issue of what might be new about a national/local gap in a moment.

That the communal side of the equation may not be the total story of today's surge of attention to congregational localism is suggested by the second "new paradigm" reviewed in the introduction. It is the perspective of church consultant Loren Mead, and it shares with Warner the sense that the vital center of American religion has shifted from the national to the local. But the reason given is different. For Mead it is because the mission field is no longer some national frontier or international adventure. Rather, it is the community right outside each local congregation's doors. Vitality has shifted to the local congregation because the locus of mission has, according to Mead, become local. It is not lost on at least some observers, consistent with Takayama's argument, that the difference in perspective between the two new localism paradigms may be related to the fact that the author of one is a church professional and the author of the other is a sociologist.

One thing that does appear to be clear, however, is that any national/local gap and related tension between the national structures of a denomination and its local congregations is not new. It is a major theme, for example, in Johnson and Cornell's *Punctured Preconceptions* of the 1970s, and the extensive church survey work conducted a half-century before them by the Institute for Social and Religious Research, during the 1920s, prompted the same conclusion.[11] If not new, could it be that the social and cultural changes related to postmodernity exacerbate the tension and even push the balance of attention back toward the local? I believe that this is precisely the case, with several identifiable factors contributing to it.

Many readers will recall the 1950s mantra of "mass society" and its business equivalent, "mass marketing." Today these have been replaced by the now taken-for-granted presumption of diversity and market niches. Even theologians and missiologists currently take the contextual nature of interpretation and ministry for granted. Different situations and settings require their own unique approaches, particularly at the strategic level, the latter being of greatest urgency for local congregations. Accordingly, local settings appear better positioned to understand and respond to their particularity than some planning office a thousand miles away with a half-dozen staff trying to serve five thousand congregations. The pluralistic nature of the emerging postmodern situation

---

11. Douglas W. Johnson and George W. Cornell, *Punctured Preconceptions* (New York: Friendship Press, 1971). H. Paul Douglass and Edmund deS. Brunner, *The Protestant Church as a Social Institution* (New York: Harper and Brothers, 1935).

David A. Roozen

emphasizes and heightens our awareness of difference, and consistent with
Warner's new paradigm, pushes the locus of vitality toward the local. For those
with theological investments in mission, this emphasis includes the local's responsibility for mission, à la Mead's new paradigm, especially in denominations that for financial and other reasons have de-emphasized national and international mission programs. When national staff can no longer assume a
singular model of the local congregation, nor even any simple set of congregational models, it becomes much more difficult for anyone in the system to be
aware of the needs and aspirations of congregations across the multiple contexts, much less develop the necessary diversity of resources for them.

One consequence of the lack of diverse denominational resources is that
many congregations are turning to sources outside of their national denominational structures for ministry resources, and fewer and fewer congregations restrict their search for ministry resources to those produced by their national denominational structure. The trend away from an automatic reliance on
denominational resources is reinforced by several additional factors. First, the
judicatory and local congregational studies conducted as a part of the larger
ORW project are consistent with two proprietary surveys of congregations conducted by the Hartford Institute for Religion Research. They all indicate that in
most ministry areas congregations rate the quality of denominational resources
lower than that of extradenominational resources. The only two exceptions appear to be international ministry and clergy support. Second, although I am
not aware of hard data that proves it, it is a common perception in the field that
there are more persons and organizations providing ministry resources than
ever before. Third, electronic technology has provided even remotely located
congregations direct access to a vast array of resource options. Accordingly,
even if there are in fact no more providers of congregational resources, congregations are certainly much more aware of the options available to them.

The more people and organizations are aware that they have and have to
make choices, the more they become attentive to and aware of their selves, and
correspondingly, of their differences with others. Such a reality, in turn, reinforces and is reinforced by the pervasive societal shift to expressive individualism discussed in the introduction and the general trend toward an increasing
acceptance of pluralism as both a valid descriptor and social value. Why? Because both expressive individualism and pluralism place a premium on difference and thereby serve to legitimate the self-interested pursuit and development of one's difference — whether as an individual or subgroup. Link this
back to Bolman and Deal's framing of the essence of politics, and there should
be little doubt why the current period is one characterized by the intensification of the political.

For many denominations, especially those within oldline Protestantism, financial pressures further escalate the general intensification of internal politics resulting from the increased awareness and legitimacy of difference. The reader will recall that one of Bolman and Deal's presuppositions about the political arena is that scarcity is a prime cause of conflict. Unfortunately, particularly oldline Protestantism has had a continual run of numerical decline since the mid-1960s. As congregations feel economic pressure, they tend to send less money "up" to their regional and national denominational bodies.[12] One result has been several rounds of downsizing of national staffs, beginning in earnest in the early 1970s. As Takayama put it in 1980, "denominational environmental contexts of the 1950s and 1960s were characterized by the 'politics of abundance,' in that adequate economic resources allowed denominations' dominant leaders to pursue organizationally initiated programs without much visible conflict. Since the end of the 1960s, however, the 'politics of scarcity' has been set in motion."[13] Presaging Bolman and Deal, Takayama then quotes a 1970 article by Zald to make his point perfectly clear. "Organizations changing in a system of scarcity are likely to experience greater conflict and discontent than those in an 'economy of abundance.'"[14] Takayama then adds two important nuances to Zald's general conclusion. He first notes that during periods of scarcity, actions and programs "invisible" in the past become "visible," and formerly uninterested and apathetic groups and individuals become concerned. Relatedly, power balances shift "as different groups within the denomination assume greater or lesser salience as a point of reference for leaders' decision making."

The case studies in this volume describe the situation of national denominational structures in the late 1990s, a period of relative financial stability for most denominations, including those of the oldline. Scarcity, therefore, is not a dominant theme, although it does appear as a subtext in a couple of the cases (e.g., RCA, UCC). Unfortunately, especially for oldline Protestantism, "scarcity" has been more the norm than the exception over the last quarter-century, and the downsizing of national staff an all too frequent reality. I am not aware of hard statistics that compare the size of national denominational staffs today with what they were in the 1950s, but one denominational executive told me that the number of their national staff had dropped from around five hundred

---

12. See, for example, *Church Membership Statistics: 1970-1980* (Washington, D.C.: Alban Institute, 1983). This is research from the Hartford Seminary Foundation and the Alban Institute.

13. Takayama, "Strains, Conflicts," p. 314.

14. Mayer N. Zald, *Organizational Change: The Political Economy of the YMCA* (Chicago: University of Chicago Press, 1970), p. 227.

in the 1950s to a current number around fifty. I suspect the drop is not quite as dramatic in most denominations that have downsized over the last fifty years, but there is seldom any less sense of pain and unsettledness. One of the few comments I hear as consolation in light of the recent downsizing is: "Perhaps we are finally reaching the point when we will acknowledge that we can no longer do the same work with fewer people, but rather need to change the way we work and what we do." Most executives who hear this nod their agreement.

Scarcity intensifies tension and conflict. One wonders if it also intensifies the mean-spirited and aggressive nature that most observers see in current denominational conflicts. How the often personalized, bitter, and negative character of today's conflicts compares with those of previous generations is a judgment I will leave for the historians. That it is present seems undeniable. Indeed, it is not uncommon for religious commentators to draw parallels to the broader, highly partisan "culture wars" being waged in American politics. For example, a recent issue of the *Review of Religious Research,* a sociologically oriented, academic journal, contains an excellent four-article case study of the homosexual ordination conflict currently consuming the Presbyterian Church (U.S.A.).[15] Not only does it present a nuanced picture of the interrelationship of social, political, and theological factors. It also provides a solid sense of the emotional pitch of the seemingly no-win debate;[16] and at the same time provides what strikes me as a healthy critique of those with a vested interest in "culture war" rhetoric.[17] One of the more helpful reminders about denominational conflict at the turn of the millennium is the following from Weston's contribution to the set: "Struggle in the church (and other institutions, too), is usually described as 'left' and 'right' in conflict, or perhaps in dialogue. What really goes on in a church fight, though, is less a conflict between two parties, and more of a competition between two extreme minorities for the vast middle. The two extreme parties have few direct relations with one another, and rarely win one another over. All the action, for good or ill, decline or renewal, comes in the movement of the middle."[18]

Wellman's introduction to the above set of articles also reminds us that the homosexuality debate in the Presbyterian Church (U.S.A.) is appropriately understood as only one manifestation of recent tensions within the wider field

---

15. *Review of Religious Research* 41 (December 1999).

16. The contributing authors all played a role in the ideological discussions within the denomination.

17. See, for example, James K. Wellman, Jr., "Introduction: The Debate over Homosexual Ordination: Subcultural Identity Theory in American Religious Organizations," *Review of Religious Research* 41 (December 1999): 184-206.

18. William J. Weston, "The Presbyterian 'Fidelity and Chastity' Competition as Loyalist Victory," *Review of Religious Research* 41 (December 1999): 207.

of American contemporary culture.[19] This is a prime example of the prior observation that value issues and movements that are widely and vehemently contested outside of a denomination can attach themselves to existing lines of fragmentation within it and turn otherwise manageable internal tensions into major crises for the denomination. The observation is based on the case studies in this book, but was previously noted by Takayama, who elevates it to the following taken-for-granted axiom about schisms: "In our view, a structural change in a denomination will result from the dynamic interplay of *both* internal and external uncertainties (strains), not just internal uncertainties alone. In other words, *internal strains themselves are not likely to cause splits of denominations.* Rather, *external environmental changes act as catalysts to internally generated and unresolved strains,* producing crises."[20] Building on Takayama's further analogy to the effect that semipermeable membranes surround denominations, I would qualify the above axiom with the following. The degree to which environmental changes and tensions penetrate denominational boundaries varies with the strength of a denomination's identity, weak identity denominations having more easily permeable boundaries.

I especially commend to the reader the above-noted *Review of Religious Research* articles on homosexual ordinations because I believe that gender and sexual issues, tending to split along relatively traditional "liberal/conservative" lines, will likely remain the major fault lines within oldline Protestantism until one or another of the contesting extremes leaves or goes underground. The retention and enforcement of boundary-maintaining and distinctive practices (e.g., closed communion in the LC-MS, initial evidence in the AG) will likely continue to define the major fault lines within conservative Protestantism.

Increasing diversity, especially when coupled with increasing fiscal constraints, intensifies the intrinsically political nature of denominational structures. The infiltration of new perspectives from outside a denomination is one source of increasing diversity. Popular seeker and growth-oriented evangelism appears to be one of those "new" viewpoints infiltrating and finding vocal supporters in all Protestant denominations. Not only is it highly visible throughout American culture, especially in its megachurch clothes,[21] but it is also touted by many of the most visible church consultants. Clearly this popular or pragmatic evangelicalism is present in all eight of the denominational case studies in this volume, although somewhat less prominent in the LC-MS, Episcopal, and UCC

---

19. Wellman, "Introduction," p. 185.
20. Takayama, "Strains, Conflicts," p. 311.
21. See, for example, the multiple on-line articles about megachurches by Scott Thumma: http://hirr.hartsem.edu/about/thumma_writings.htm.

cases. Donald Miller's *Reinventing American Protestantism* presents a particularly thorough and relatively objective analysis of the phenomena. It is a particular challenge for denominational structures and those with a doctrinal bent because in these "new paradigm" churches, "pragmatism substitutes for bureaucratic and procedural oversight."[22]

The internal diversity and fragmentation that characterizes today's Protestant denominations prompts Scherer to remind us that, organizationally speaking, the majority of denominations are federations, with most others being more loosely structured coalitions. He further reminds us, consistent with our findings, that "because of the lack of consensus and the amount of uncertainty built into such organizations of organizations, coalitions and federations can be very fragile — constituent members can withdraw at any time and pull out staff and funding overnight. This means such organizations are essentially political (like state or federal legislatures) and can involve constant negotiation." He then wonders "if it is true that organizations today are having more and more to deal with a changing environment, if the internal order which results is more and more only a temporary 'negotiated' one, how can we characterize various kinds of organizations in terms of their internal unity, their looseness or tightness?" He wonders this specifically in terms of structure and for organizations in general, but makes the point especially poignant for religious organizations by noting that they generally, "because of their voluntary character, are more centralized than business or government." He finally solves his own puzzle by concluding that religious organizations "are held together less by structure and apparatus, and more by sentiments and commitments of members and by organizational ritual and ideology ('faith')."[23] I agree, but only with the qualification that one can find more or less coherence in the latter (sentiments, etc.) within Protestant denominations and that those denominations with more tentative and loose identities have nothing to mitigate the fragility of loose structures, especially in a politicized world.

2. The "Problem" Is Foremost a Matter of Identity

In their history of the brief history of social scientific research about congregations, Stokes and Roozen note that it is an unfolding story of pragmatic prob-

---

22. Donald E. Miller, *Reinventing American Protestantism: Christianity in the New Millennium* (Berkeley: University of California Press, 1997), p. 141.

23. Ross P. Scherer, "The Sociology of Denominational Organization," introduction to *American Denominational Organization*, pp. 14-15.

lem solving. That is, one can trace the changing emphasis of congregational studies to the changing sense of what was the primary challenge being faced by local congregations. They argue that from the turn of the century through the 1960s, researchers examined the local church from *without*. They viewed its challenges in terms of the demographic changes of the social context.[24] The challenges were threefold, all missional: evangelism, social mission, and social justice. Continuing their history, they note:

> Following the 1960s and parallel to the broader cultural turn from social idealism to self-fulfillment/realization/actualization in the early 1970s, contextual studies of the congregation gave way to examining the local church from *within*. "Renewal" became the new metaphor, and researchers began to view a congregation's challenges as issues of internal *process* and *program*. It was a time, as the title of James Anderson's book announced, *To Come Alive!* (1973), and congregational studies focused on planning, conflict, leadership, stewardship and a host of other organizational dilemmas.[25]

Writing in 1991, Stokes and Roozen then note the current turn to identity:

> Issues of context, process and program continue to draw the attention of both churches and researchers. But today, as congregations struggle with problems of *identity* in a world increasingly secular and pluralistic, a more holistic research approach is beginning to emerge. . . . It is in many ways a response to the challenge of the multiplicity of social and religious forces that erode a congregation's unity of vision, and it is an affirmation that a congregation's inherited and confessed, formal and informal, web of symbolic meaning, values, and commitments — that is, its culture — always consciously or unconsciously informs pragmatic choices made among the diverse alternatives of program, process, and context with which every congregation is continually confronted.[26]

Denominations have not received nearly the social scientific attention that congregations have, and to the best of my knowledge there is no formal history that traces denominational studies' possible coherence as a field of study or its possible evolution. But if one takes Niebuhr's *Social Sources of Denominationalism,* published in 1929, and Carroll and Roof's 1993 *Beyond Es-*

---

24. Allison Stokes and David A. Roozen, "The Unfolding Story of Congregational Studies," in *Carriers of Faith: Lessons from Congregational Studies,* ed. Carl S. Dudley, Jackson W. Carroll, and James P. Wind (Louisville: Westminster John Knox, 1991), pp. 184-85.

25. Stokes and Roozen, "The Unfolding Story," p. 186.

26. Stokes and Roozen, "The Unfolding Story," p. 186.

tablishment: Protestant Identity in a Post-Protestant Age, one sees striking parallels to the evolution that Stokes and Roozen note for congregational studies.[27] Perhaps equally telling about a deepening concern about organizational identities beginning roughly in the 1980s is the emergence during this period of a significant secular literature about "corporate cultures."[28] Increasingly, organizational analysts were coming to the realization, as we have, that the "problem" is foremost a matter of identity.

Denominational identity properly understood, as noted in the introduction, is a property of a denomination as a total system, not solely nor in some instances even primarily the privileged domain of a denomination's national structure. Nevertheless, as a central part of the overall system, a denomination's national structures are intimately linked to, sometimes as cause and sometimes as beneficiary (or victim) broader identity issues. Building on the secular literature about corporate culture and recent studies of religious organizations, I understand denominational identity to be the unique combination of salient characteristics about the denomination's people, polity and structure, practices, theology and purpose that makes the particular denomination identifiably distinct and denominated (nameable) to its adherents. Note that in such a perspective any one of these possibly constitutive elements, not just beliefs or doctrine, can provide the linchpin of distinctiveness. Indeed, the eight denominations included in this volume provide a broad range of examples, including the Dutch ethnicity of the otherwise mainline Presbyterian RCA; the role of the gifts of the Spirit in the theology and practice of the AG among Protestants, and the role of doctrine and Scripture in the theology of the AG among other Pentecostal groups; the priority of mission within the UCC in contrast to the National Association of Congregational Christian Churches' focus on fellowship. During settled times, identity is a group's taken-for-granted but deeply formative understanding of "who we are" and "how we do things around here."

Such a conceptualization of corporate identity is relatively standard in both the secular and religious organizational literature. Equally standard in this literature is the presumption that a "strong" identity is "better" than a "weak" identity. Unfortunately, there is no clear, much less consensual, answer in the literature about how to define the strength of an organization's identity. There are only, and typically implicit, hints. But since our analysis suggests that denominational identity can become problematic for a variety of reasons, I be-

27. H. Richard Niebuhr, *The Social Sources of Denominationalism* (New York: Henry Holt and Co., 1929); Jackson W. Carroll and Wade Clark Roof, eds., *Beyond Establishment: Protestant Identity in a Post-Protestant Age* (Louisville: Westminster John Knox, 1993).

28. See, for example, Terrence E. Deal and Allen A. Kennedy, *Corporate Cultures: The Rites and Rituals of Corporate Life* (Reading, Mass.: Addison-Wesley, 1982).

lieve it is important to specify the distinct, although clearly interrelated, components of identity strength. Building on the hints in the existing literature, I suggest conceptualizing "strength of identity" in terms of the extent to which the above-noted combination of characteristics (1) is explicit and widely shared, (2) invokes commitment that provides group loyalty and cohesion, (3) has consequences discernible in the organization's strategies for action, and (4) provides distinguishable boundaries.[29]

Unfortunately, hard survey data do not exist that would allow ranking the strength of identity across denominations using this full conceptualization. However, there are two recent surveys, each including a diversity of denominations, from which we can obtain an objective, albeit more limited, read on the strength of identity across the denominations examined in this book. One survey is the Faith Communities Today (FACT) national survey of 14,000 congregations in forty-one denominations and faith groups, conducted in 1999 and 2000.[30] The second survey was conducted in 1998 for the Protestant Church-Owned Publishers Association (PCPA). It surveyed 2,209 congregations in twenty-nine Protestant denominations.[31]

The FACT survey asked a congregation's key informant the extent to which the congregation expressed its denominational heritage. Scores could range from a low of 1 = not very much, to a high of 5 = to a great extent. The PCPA survey asked congregational leaders how important they felt their denomination was to them personally. Table 1 on page 606 presents survey results for several denominations. The reported figure for the FACT survey is the average response to the denominational heritage question, using a five-point scale with five being the highest. The reported figure of the PCPA is the percent of congregational leaders who said their denomination was very important to them personally. Denominations in bold are the focal denominations of this book. The other denominations are included for comparison. The denominations are listed in the table from strongest to weakest identity according to the FACT measure. At least two observations about the table are noteworthy. Despite the very different questions asked bearing on denominational identity, the rank order of the denominations in each survey is nearly identical. The only

29. See, for example, Fred Kniss, "Ideas and Symbols as Resources in Intrareligious Conflict: The Case of American Mennonites," *Sociology of Religion* 57 (1996): 7-23; and Nancy Ammerman, "Religious Identities and Religious Institutions," in *Handbook of Sociology of Religion,* ed. Michele Dillon (Cambridge: Cambridge University Press, 2003), pp. 207-24.

30. Detailed information about the survey as well as access to several survey reports can be obtained at the FACT Web site: http://hirr.hartsem.edu.

31. Reginal W. Bibby, "The PCPA Congregational Resource Study: Summary Report" (June 1998).

David A. Roozen

Table 1: Strength of Denominational Identity

Denomination	FACT†	PCPA‡
Lutheran Church–Missouri Synod	*	**74%**
Church of Jesus Christ of Latter-day Saints	4.53	60%
Historically Black Baptist Denominations	**4.17**	*
Episcopal Church	**4.10**	**58%**
Evangelical Lutheran Church in America	4.00	51%
Assemblies of God	**3.93**	**43%**
Church of the Nazarene	3.61	65%
United Methodist Church	**3.47**	**40%**
Presbyterian Church (U.S.A.)	3.35	40%
United Church of Christ	**3.15**	**43%**
American Baptist Churches USA	3.13	40%
Reformed Church in America	**3.11**	**40%**

† The numbers in this column measure the respondents' assessment of the degree to which their congregations express their denominational heritage, on a scale from 1 (= not very much) to 5 (= to a great extent)

‡ The numbers in this column measure the percent of respondents who said that their denomination was very important to them personally.

* Did not participate in the survey

major divergence in order is that both the Church of the Nazarene and the United Church of Christ ranked relatively higher using the "importance" question in the PCPA study than they did using the "denominational heritage" question in the FACT study. Second, in both studies one finds that the more sacramental and liturgically oriented Episcopal Church and Evangelical Lutheran Church in America rank considerably higher than their more Calvinist-oriented counterparts among oldline Protestant denominations; and that the latter — from United Methodist to Reformed Church in America — have a monopoly on the bottom of the rankings.

That the erosion of denominational identity is most pronounced within oldline Protestantism is certainly consistent with both the argument of this book and prior research. However, the need for distinguishing among different dimensions of denominational identity becomes evident when one considers the various factors pointed to as the primary "problem." The leading explanation in the literature appears to be that oldline Protestant denominations have lost their distinctiveness because their embrace of the pluralism of the broader American culture has eroded their boundary with the secular. Roof and Carroll's *Beyond Establishment* and Wellman's perspective on the conflict over homosexual ordination in the Presbyterian Church (U.S.A.) are representatives of this position. In contrast, my argument is closer to that of Wuthnow's *Restructuring of American Religion,* in my concern with internal diversity and the intensifying effect when internal and external factions and movements merge.[32] Such an explanation merges concerns about distinctiveness with concerns about fragmentation and cohesiveness.

Another major explanation offered for the declining significance of denominationalism is the weakening ability of identity to invoke commitment. Weeks's study of national Presbyterian executives makes this point through a surprising twist.[33] He discovered that even an explicit and distinct denominational identity might not be the primary religious identity of those seemingly most invested in the denomination's national structures. Specifically, he found that even though the executives he interviewed for his study were articulate and largely in agreement about the specifics and distinctiveness of Presbyterian identity, most of them felt "that family, congregation, and general Protestant and/or Christian identity have become personally more important for them and, they speculate, for others in recent years. Presbyterian identity *per se* is less important."[34] That the executives Weeks interviewed in the early 1990s may have overestimated the distinctiveness and explicitness of Presbyterian identity is however suggested by Moorhead's study of the evolving Presbyterian national structure during the early twentieth century. He notes, for example, that at the very time the denomination was centralizing its national administrative functions, it decentralized its control over theological questions, one result being a steadily growing "confessional inclusiveness."[35] Turning his attention to a comparison among oldline Protestant denominations in his conclusion, Moorhead further asserts: "In each instance, reorganization pushed questions of distinctive theology and tradition into the background in the name of efficiency."[36]

Unsettled times highlight and focus attention on identity and values. It

32. Robert Wuthnow, *The Restructuring of American Religion: Society and Faith Since World War II* (Princeton: Princeton University Press, 1988).

33. Louis B. Weeks, "Presbyterian Culture: Views from the Edge," in *Beyond Establishment,* pp. 309-26.

34. Weeks, "Presbyterian Culture," p. 320.

35. James H. Moorhead, "Presbyterians and the Mystique of Organizational Efficiency, 1870-1936," in *Reimagining Denominationalism,* ed. Robert Bruce Mullin and Russell E. Richey (New York: Oxford University Press, 1994), p. 277.

36. Moorhead, "Presbyterians," pp. 282-83.

appears that strong identities are more capable of weathering these storms; diffuse identities struggle because identity itself becomes politically contested. One of the intriguing insights in Bolman and Deal's *Reframing Organizations* is that serious conflicts about most things in organizations are ultimately appealed to the organization's values, culture, and identity. They are silent about what happens when there is conflict over the organization's values, culture, and identity.

It is our observation in the case material, as already noted, that denominations with stronger identities appear to be better able to handle the crises they face. It also appears that while strong identity groups clearly have tensions, ambiguities, and strains, they seldom have real crises. If I am correct about crises occurring when external tensions and threats attach themselves to internal strains and segmentation, then the suggestion of these cases that stronger identity groups are less likely to have crises is consistent with Coser's observation that strength of identity is a mitigating factor regarding outer conflict and inner cohesion.[37] Specifically, for strong identity groups an external threat tends to breed internal solidarity (e.g., our NBC case study), but in weak identity groups external threats exaggerate or inflame already existing strains of internal disunity.

However, not everyone writing about denominations agrees that the major problem is identity. Takayama, for example, argues that mainline denominations have been relying more on structure than on ideology since at least the 1960s, and that with an ecclesiastical and theological deficit this is probably exactly what they have to do.[38] Our rejoinder is that the reliance on structure did not work particularly well for the oldline in the 1960s, nor has it worked particularly well in the nearly half-century since! Reifsnyder, in perhaps the most detailed study to date of the changing organizational nature of an oldline Protestant denomination, makes our case most directly and simply.[39] After several paragraphs of abstract argument, Reifsnyder seals his disagreement with Takayama by quoting C. Daniel Little, executive director of the Presbyterian General Assembly Mission Board (GAMC) during the early 1980s. The quote is from Little's final report after seven and a half years of struggling with restructuring. Little said: "The essential assignment given to the GAMC was a spiritual one — that of searching for a strengthening of the bonds that tie the whole church together. The Mission Council was born in an atmosphere where it was

37. Lewis Coser, *The Functions of Social Conflict* (New York: Free Press, 1956), p. 93.

38. Takayama, "Strains, Conflicts," p. 313.

39. Richard W. Reifsnyder, "The Reorganization Impulse in American Protestantism: The Presbyterian Church (U.S.A.) as a Case Study, 1788-1983" (Ph.D. diss., Princeton Theological Seminary, 1984).

assumed that those bonds were managerial. A principal learning has been that helpful as management tools are, they are tools and not the actual bonds which hold the church together."[40] The problem was, according to Little, that the people disagreed on what the church should be doing, not on how it should be doing it.

3. Functions, Structure, and Cohesiveness

One of my favorite pieces on the kinds of work organizations do and how work is best structured is Dennis Young's unpublished "Strategic Vision as a Determinant of Association Structure." Its appeal to me is simple: it is the only piece I have seen in the literature on nonprofit organizations that relates particular strategic purposes of "national umbrella organizations" to optimal structures via the necessary transactional interactions required to carry out the strategy.[41] Because of relatively comfortable parallels to the existing literature on denominations, I use his framework to frame my reflection on denominational functions. Young's framework includes the following, with my sense of denominational parallels added.

- The *goal-seeking system* relies on hierarchical authority and command and control (e.g., the corporate structure that denominations developed to optimize their purposeful missional activities).
- The *economic system* relies on reciprocity and exchange among sovereign participants who use the associative umbrella as a collective device to meet their individual resource needs (e.g., the contractual implications of servicing congregations).
- *Systems of accountability* are based on checks and balances between different parts of the overall system based on information flows and distributed authority, which range from "bottom to top" systems optimized by central organizations overseeing local members through participatory processes of standard setting and certification to "top to bottom" systems dependent upon an effective governing board that is responsive to local membership.
- *Polities* are forums for political discourse among members that have a common set of interests but diverse approaches to addressing these interests, structurally dependent upon persuasion and consensus building

---

40. Reifsnyder, "The Reorganization Impulse," p. 426.
41. Dennis R. Young, "Strategic Vision as a Determinant of Association Structure" (1998).

(e.g., the covenant ideal among UCC structural levels; the federal structure of many contemporary Reformed structures; the con-federal structure of the Episcopal Church).

To Young's four "ideal types" I would add, given this essay's denominational interests, *fellowship systems,* the purpose of which is identity-intensifying, social
bonding that produces relational capital and a sense of belonging to a greater
whole. Pastoral, hospitable, and covenantal processes and practices tend to optimize the fellowship system.

Within this framework, several points jump out of our case studies. First,
national denominational structures currently and historically have typically
served all five of these purposes, although with different emphases and priorities across denominations and time. In our essays there is evidence of increasing emphasis being given at this time to the economic (e.g., resourcing congregations), political, and fellowship functions, with the goal-seeking and
accountability functions becoming more problematic. The ascendance of an
internal focus following the external "mission" focus of the recent "corporate"
period of America's denominations is consistent with the long history of such
cycles of inward and outward attention documented in Richey's morphology of
denominations and denominationalism.[42]

Second, given that different purposes tend to have different optimal
structures, it should be immediately evident that any single denominational
structure will have less than optimal structures for some functions.

Third, if I am correct about which functions are on the ascendance and
which are increasingly problematic, then it would seem that structures that optimize the participatory and relational work of working across diversity are
more adaptive than structures that optimize efficiency and control. Correspondingly, one could argue that schism (or other means of reducing diversity)
may be a good thing for denominational systems that place a premium on the
purposeful action of national directed mission or purity of identity.[43] Unfortunately, it appears that during unsettled times there is a trade-off within weak
identity denominations between unity and mission. Both demand significant
resources, and the more you direct resources to one, the less you have for the

42. Russell E. Richey, "Denominations and Denominationalism: An American Morphology," in *Reimagining Denominationalism,* pp. 74-98.

43. A recent study of 175 Baptist, Lutheran, Methodist, and Presbyterian and Reformed
denominations between 1890 and 1980 found an average of more than one schism every two
years during this period. Robert C. Liebman, John R. Sutton, and Robert Wuthnow, "Exploring
the Social Sources of Denominationalism: Schisms in American Protestant Denominations,
1890-1980," *American Sociological Review* 53 (1988): 343-52.

other. Relatedly, the trade-off becomes more severe when a declining resource base compounds the situation.

Given my initial thoughts about the primacy of identity, the possibility that structure may help maintain or strengthen stressed or eroding identities is an intriguing idea. And again because of my current hunches regarding the increasing politicization of national denominational structures and that government may present the best organizational parallels to such structures, I find the political science literature providing helpful perspective. For one thing, one finds a general agreement in the literature that diversity erodes strong power pyramids, erodes singular ideologies, and erodes confidence in the political process and traditional forms of political participation.

But even more interesting is that one finds basically the same set of prescriptions for curing this erosion in the constructive theorizing of political scientists and in the recent restructuring of national denominations. There are two broad families. The first is an attempt to increase participatory democracy, both in inclusiveness of diversity and in direct participation. There are a positive and a negative plank to this argument. The negative is that existent representative forms of democracy at the national level typically are not working because the representatives and the bureaucracy the representatives support are too distant and unrepresentative of those they represent, and because the process of electing representatives does not provide a strong enough mechanism of accountability. The positive side is that direct participation increases ownership and commitment. Because of the scale of national structures, most political scientists taking this position combine it with some form of voluntary associationalism. The result is that national structures become a representation of networks of other voluntary associations. Participatory process is of course a fundamental of liberal Protestantism in general. It should not be surprising, therefore, that its strategic role in trying to stem the erosion of denominational identity is evident, for example, in the new national structure of the UCC.

The second general prescription found in the political science literature for stopping the corrosive effect of postmodernity is sometimes referred to as communitarianism. As the name suggests, it gives priority to communal commitments, with individual rights being derivative. Unfortunately, the majority opinion seems to be that communitarianism is antithetical to the late modern or postmodern situation. Except at a very small/local scale, any effort in a communitarian, ideologically singular direction requires strong measures of control. On the religious scene one immediately thinks of the Southern Baptists;[44]

---

44. Nancy Tatom Ammerman, *Baptist Battles: Social Change and Religious Conflict in the Southern Baptist Convention* (New Brunswick, N.J.: Rutgers University Press, 1990).

and among our cases one sees some evidence of this dynamic in the LC-MS and to a lesser extent in the AG.

There is also, unfortunately, considerable skepticism among political theorists regarding the long-term efficacy of the participatory/associative response in a postmodern world. Such skepticism takes its cue from the reminder that procedural democracy is really an adversarial process. Recent evidence suggests that increasing diversity, especially accompanied by the postmodern emphasis on difference over unity, erodes the layers of tolerance that in earlier times soothed the aggressively imperialistic edges of any competition. With the erosion of tolerance each election becomes, the skeptics observe, increasingly plebiscitarian in character, the popular vote determining which party or coalition of parties shall have the exclusive control of the state machine for the next several years. Again, the Southern Baptists and the LC-MS come to mind.

If there is great skepticism among political scientists concerning associative communal responses to the erosive effects of postmodernity, what is one to think? There are at least two additional responses in the current dynamics of national denomination structures, one with some parallel in the political science literature, the other uniquely religious. To the extent that political science skeptics have any constructive thought concerning postmodernity's erosion of political process, it goes something like this: "We'll muddle through somehow, in part because our functional economic interdependence is a more critical factor today than is our political process."

The allure of economic codependence can be seen in our national denominational structures today in what, as noted above, has become the pervasive mantra of "servicing congregations." Consultants like Loren Mead and Lyle Schaller have made the primacy of the local congregation an article of taken-for-granted practical wisdom; sociologists like Steve Warner and Mark Chaves have attested to its reality; and theologians from a wide variety of traditional polities have given it their normative blessing.[45] Combining such awareness with a search for a new reason for being, many denominations (see, for example, the RCA and UCC case studies in this volume) have hit upon the idea that their primary business now should be servicing congregations. In many respects it represents a movement from covenant to contract as the basis of solidarity.

Only time will tell whether contractual interdependence is a viable path to national denominational vitality. However, there are any number of reasons to be skeptical. First, several congregational surveys suggest that a denomination's resources are just not as good as nondenominational resources.

45. See, for example, Darrel Guder and Louis Barrett, *Missional Church: A Vision of the Sending of the Church in North America* (Grand Rapids: Eerdmans, 1998).

Second, there is what Jane J. Mansbridge calls the paradox of parochialism.[46] The paradox is that on the one hand the efficiency required of economies is best exercised in centralized institutions, but centralized institutions seem to erode meaningful participation. On the other hand, the participation most vibrantly exercised in local institutions seems to sap national identity and resolve. One sees a parallel argument in Farnsley's observed tension in the Southern Baptist Convention between increased organizational coordination and the demand for democratic voice.[47] Third, there are several kinds of theologically valued mission that are most appropriately dealt with through nonlocal structures. Fourth, servicing congregations seemingly reinforces a consumerist mentality among congregations that further erodes any lingering semblance of covenantal loyalty. And fifth, especially for those groups that believe in humankind's propensity to sin, a service orientation radically reduces any accountability that congregations have to any external referent. So, while servicing congregations is a pervasive, new "big idea," we will have to wait and see whether it in fact proves to be a good idea.

The final response to the corrosive effects of postmodern fragmentation on national structures that I see being attempted in many denominational structures today, but without parallel in the political science literature, is the attempt to de-emphasize the national structures' visibility or role in traditional forms of decision making. These efforts take one of three forms. One is to emphasize worship and celebration in a denomination's national assemblies and, correspondingly, to minimize business. A second is to call a moratorium on contested decisions. The third, and most interesting to us — both because of its intrinsically religious nature and its direct response to the postmodern philosophical challenge — is the effort to move from rational legal decision-making procedures to a process of spiritual discernment. Modernity's gift (or curse) of rational legal procedures stresses, of course, human agency. In contrast, discernment means to see and acknowledge what already exists by God's will and initiative.

Group discernment processes require time, patience, and a sustained intimacy, suggesting that discernment would be a particularly challenging process for most denominational national assemblies — strangers coming together for one week every two to four years. It is not surprising, therefore, that one sees in our cases experimentation with discernment at the national level only within

---

46. Jane Mansbridge, *Beyond Adversary Democracy* (New York: Basic Books, 1980).

47. Arthur Emery Farnsley II, *Southern Baptist Politics: Authority and Power in the Restructuring of an American Denomination* (University Park: Pennsylvania State University Press, 1994).

episcopal systems in which bishops have a continuing, mutual history. Nevertheless, the more recent experience of the RCA and the longer-term experience
of the Disciples of Christ with discernment approaches to decision making will
enable future research to judge the viability of such alternatives in more Calvinistic traditions.[48]

4. Does Theology Make a Difference?

Organizing religious work is a theological task. By devoting the entire concluding chapter in this book to theological reflection, we seek to appropriately give
that task the final word. Nevertheless, the empirical effect of theology on organizational adaptiveness as viewed across the eight cases in this volume is so distinct as to warrant note here. *Liturgical and Pentecostal traditions appear to be
more adaptive than more Calvinist or cognitive traditions to the conditions of the
emerging "postmodern" period, at least at the scale of national structures.*

Why this is the case is not entirely clear, but the following two related factors are strongly suggestive. First, as previously noted, liturgical and Pentecostal
denominations in our study have more distinctive and stronger identities.
Strong identities help mitigate the corrosive influences of postmodernity, at
least in the short term. Second, and more directly theological, liturgical and
Pentecostal traditions tend to give priority to noncognitive bases of religious
authority and practice. Indeed, there is a growing body of literature that shows
that at this time in the United States expressive forms of religious expression are
more vital than cognitive. Based on his extensive study of new movements on
the Pentecostal side of the expressive, liturgical-to-Pentecostal spectrum,
Miller's *Reinventing American Protestantism: Christianity in the New Millennium* provides the most extended discussion of why this appears to be the case.
Two quotes, the first from the perspective of individuals and the second from
the perspective of organizations, cut to the core of his argument.

> The faith of new paradigm Christians is empirically based. The Bible seems
> to assume authority for these individuals as they practice what it says and
> have prayers answered, see people healed, watch people being transformed
> morally, and experience the "leading" of the Holy Spirit in their lives. Rea-
> son plays a secondary confirming role as these Christians attempt to inter-

48. The RCA has contracted with church consultant Chuck Olsen for guidance in its experiment with denomination-wide discernment processes, and his book, *Transforming Church
Boards into Communities of Spiritual Leaders* (Washington, D.C.: Alban Institute, 1995), provides a good introduction to his approach.

pret what God is doing in the world. Few of them claim to be able to prove God's existence through abstract arguments. It is one's "relationship" with God, they believe, that brings certitude.[49]

New paradigm churches are experimenting with organizational change. They have latched onto the model of first-century Christianity, and it has provided a powerful point of reference for critiquing the institution of the contemporary Christian church. But new paradigm Christians have not only been critics, they have also accepted [corporate leadership guru Peter] Drucker's challenge to innovate. In my opinion they have created a form of human community that addresses many of the crises of our late-twentieth-century postmodern culture, and they have also established a perspective that endorses change in their organizational structure. Drawing on their vision of the role of the Holy Spirit, they have transferred authority from the socially constructed institution of the church to a divine presence, who can take them in unpredictable directions. . . . For new paradigm Christians, little is sacred except God. They are living out the "Protestant principle," which relativizes all human claims to absoluteness, thus allowing for bold and entrepreneurial experimentation.[50]

The juxtaposition of unmediated encounter with God and testing with Scripture that Miller finds in new paradigm churches redefines the interrelationship between freedom and tradition, providing both openness and coherence. It is perhaps not surprising that the parallels are stark between Miller's "new paradigm" and the discernment processes noted above with which several oldline denominations are currently experimenting. Also not surprisingly, both the Vineyard and AG case studies in this book provide glimpses into Miller's new paradigm dynamics.

My own analysis of the Faith Community Today survey data from 14,000 congregations adds the liturgical side of the expressive vitality equation to Miller's Pentecostal and Holiness perspective. In appraising the shift in religious authority and vitality from "WORD to SPIRIT," I divide the forty-one denominations and faith traditions participating in the national study into those that give priority to expressive sources of religious authority and those that give preference to cognitive sources. I then look at the vitality of congregations first within oldline Protestantism and then again within conservative Protestantism. In both instances the analysis shows higher levels of congregational vitality among the more expressive denominations (e.g., Episcopal within oldline Prot-

---

49. Miller, *Reinventing American Protestantism*, p. 133.
50. Miller, *Reinventing American Protestantism*, pp. 155-56.

estantism) than among the more cognitive (e.g., Presbyterian and UMC within oldline Protestantism).[51] One finds further evidence for and commentary on the current shift from WORD to SPIRIT in, for example:

- The "seekership" in Wade Clark Roof's baby boom monograph, *A Generation of Seekers.*[52]
- In Marler and Roozen's use of the two Gallup surveys of unchurched Americans to connect the societal shift from an objective to a subjective locus of authority to the increasing phenomenon of "church as choice."[53]
- In the worry of evangelical Christian scholars about a shift from God as judge to Jesus as friend.

It is evident in these references that before becoming a foundational tenet of postmodernism, the societal shift to more expressive, experiential, and subjective forms of authority was prominent in the literature on the broad cultural shifts carried to prominence during the late 1960s and 1970s by the baby boom generation. Although a bit jaundiced in its appreciation of the change, Robert Bellah and associates' engaging elaboration of the rise of "expressive individualism" in their well-known *Habits of the Heart* remains one of the classic treatments of the potential profundity of the change.[54] Indeed, from today's postmodern vantage point one can only wonder how profound this change will be. Reifsnyder suggests that "ecclesiology" was the central focus of twentieth-century theology, including an intensity of analysis about the nature and purpose of the church unmatched since the Reformation. More importantly, he argues that this analysis was accompanied, particularly within oldline Protestantism, with a radical shift in understanding about the purpose of the church. It was a shift "from viewing the church as the body of Christ in history to viewing it as an event, a movement of the pilgrim people across time and space to participate in the mission of Jesus Christ."[55] The former gives priority to "being" and resonates with the geographically and monopolistically oriented parish

51. David A. Roozen, "Four Mega-Trends Changing America's Religious Landscape" (paper presented at the Religion Newswriters' Association Annual Conference, Boston, September 2001, available on-line at hirr.hartsem.edu/about/roozen_articles.htm).

52. Wade Clark Roof, *A Generation of Seekers* (San Francisco: Harper, 1993).

53. Penny Long Marler and David A. Roozen, "From Church Tradition to Consumer Choice: The Gallup Surveys of Unchurched Americans," in *Church and Denominational Growth,* ed. David A. Roozen and C. Kirk Hadaway (Nashville: Abingdon, 1993), pp. 253-77.

54. Robert Bellah et al., *Habits of the Heart: Individualism and Commitment in American Life* (New York: Harper Collins, 1988).

55. Reifsnyder, "The Reorganization Impulse," p. 381.

forms of religious organization that are the historical legacy of most colonial American Protestant denominations. The latter gives priority to "doing," which, as noted in the introduction to this book, was the strategic vision that gave rise to the "corporate" organization of most large American Protestant denominations today. The affinity between expressive forms of religious expression and postmodernity leads one to wonder if we currently live in the midst of another radical shift in understanding about the primary purpose of the church — a shift from "doing" to "experiencing." Organizationally, such a shift would seemingly require a related change from asking how we best structure ourselves for doing mission to how we best structure ourselves for providing experiences of God.

5. Narrative Practices and Denominational Identity

The challenges of postmodernity make "identity" problematic. Relatedly, one finds increasing scholarly attention being given to the issue as it relates both to the construction and reconstruction of individual identities, and to corporate cultures or identities. One recurring theme in the sociologically oriented literature on the subject is the importance of narrative and narrative practices. Arguments like the following are not untypical: "The reflexive project of the self . . . consists in the sustaining of coherent, yet continuously revised, biographical narratives,"[56] and "[A]ll of us come to be who we are (however ephemeral, multiple, and changing) by being located or locating ourselves (usually unconsciously) in social narratives."[57] From such a perspective, it should be no surprise that those denominations in our study that give priority to narrative practices over text, doctrine, and belief have stronger identities. Indeed, in her congregationally focused ORW complement to this book's focus on national denominational structures, Nancy Ammerman finds that social practices that allow denominational narratives to become part of the ongoing life of a congregation are the most important factor in tying a congregation to its denominational tradition.[58] The 1998 PCPA survey of congregations discussed in section 2 above reinforces her conclusion. When congregational leaders were asked to specify what their denominational publisher's role should be, they

56. Anthony Giddens, *Modernity and Self-Identity: Self and Society in the Late Modern Age* (Stanford, Calif.: Stanford University Press, 1991), p. 5.

57. Margaret R. Somers, "The Narrative Constitution of Identity: A Relational and Network Approach," *Theory and Society* 23 (1994): 605-49, here 606.

58. Nancy Ammerman, *Pillars of Faith: American Congregations and Their Partners* (Berkeley and Los Angeles: University of California Press, 2005).

most frequently said producing resources that reflect their denomination's identity![59]

Critical in both the Ammerman and PCPA findings is the recognition that identity or narrative never exists in the abstract. Rather, it takes life as it is embodied in some resource and used in some practice. In fact, the importance and nature of *carriers* of a denomination's culture is the focal concern of Carroll and Roof's *Beyond Establishment*. Limited to oldline Protestantism, the book examines closely such carriers as fellowship ties, church school, ritual, hymns, retreat centers, church-related colleges, campus ministry, theological education, and ordination processes. Unfortunately for the oldline, the various chapters in the volume present a relatively consistent and negative picture. The picture is of the erosion of each carrier's vitality and its viability as a vehicle of denominational culture.

Carroll and Roof's conclusion presents a strong, even passionate argument for the importance of strengthening and sustaining oldline Protestant identities. It also includes a short list of possible ideas for strengthening denominational identity. But in the absence of any evidence that it was realistic to expect a denomination to turn the ideas into workable strategies, the book is anything but optimistic. Indeed, when one connects the seriousness of the situation for oldline Protestantism as described in *Beyond Establishment* with the broad historical perspective of Richey's documentation of an alternation between an internal and external orientation in the evolution of oldline Protestant denominational purposefulness, one loses some of the hopefulness that cyclical perspectives such as Richey's hold out.[60] The severe erosion of oldline Protestant denominational identities and their respective carriers of identity presents a strong argument for why the oldline's future today might not include a turn or return to missional vitality as it did the last time the denominations turned introspective (during the post–Civil War period).

In contrast to the abstractness and skepticism of the immediately preceding reflections, one of the major findings in Ammerman's congregationally focused ORW complement to this book's focus on national denominational structures presents at least a hint of strategic hopefulness. As suggested above, her analysis leads her to boldly conclude that

> Among both conservatives and mainliners, denominational citizenship is strengthened by intentional congregational practices that link local life to the denomination's narratives. Telling stories about denominational mis-

59. Bibby, "PCPA Congregational Resource Study," p. 78.
60. Richey, "Denominations and Denominationalism."

sion, missional accomplishments, singing the songs of the faith and otherwise emphasizing its distinctive worship practices, teaching children and adults from denominationally-produced materials — these narrative practices are by no means universal, but where they are present, congregations are more likely to describe themselves as strongly aligned with their denomination.[61]

But more importantly she further finds: "The likelihood of engaging in these pro-denominational practices is highest among those that have been drawn into regional denominational participation."[62] At least one remaining, viable carrier of denominational identity is the participation of congregations in regional organization, which in turn strengthens the participating congregations' intentionality about narrative engagement. The "regional" core of this relationship is underscored by the further, and somewhat surprising, finding in Ammerman's study that congregational participation at the national level produced no such boost in sense of connection to a congregation's larger tradition. It also is consistent with our earlier note about the ascendancy of relational tasks in those denominations best adapting to the pressures of postmodernity.

Judicatory leaders and staff are the face of their denomination at the regional level. In anticipation that they and their regional level of organization were integral to denominational systems, the larger ORW project also included a study of judicatories in the project's eight focal denominations. It was directed by Adair Lummis.[63] Her findings show that judicatories are very aware of, and indeed very much experience, the stress on denominational identities highlighted in this book's study of national structures. They are also by and large aware of their critical role in mediating denominational identity. And many appear to be doing it relatively well. But not all are doing it well. Judicatories are challenged by the same corrosive effects of the postmodern world as

---

61. Ammerman, *Pillars of Faith,* chap. 7.

62. Ammerman, "Voluntary Citizenship: Denominational Institutions and Religious Identity," March 2001, p. 32.

63. See Adair T. Lummis, "Brand Name Identity in a Post-Denominational Age: Regional Leaders' Perspectives on Its Importance for Churches" (paper delivered at the annual meetings of the Society for the Scientific Study of Religion, Columbus, Ohio, October 2001); "The Art and Science of Subtle Proactivity: Regional Leaders and Their Congregations" (paper presented at the Religious Research Association Annual Meetings, Columbus, Ohio, October 2001); "The Role of Judicatories in Interpreting Denominational Identity" (paper presented at the annual meeting of the Religious Research Association, Boston, 1999); and "Judicatory Niches and Negotiations" (paper presented at the annual meeting of the Association for the Sociology of Religion, San Francisco, 1998) (Adair T. Lummis on-line articles and books: http://hirr.hartsem.edu/about/lummis_articles.htm).

are national structures, and many observers believe that the range of vital experiments notwithstanding, they are just as weak a link in the overall system as are national structures. To further complicate the matter, at least from the perspective of strategic options for national structures, as demonstrated in the UCC case study in this book, a strong link between national structure and the judicatory does not necessarily result in a strong link between congregation and national structure.

Lummis does nevertheless point to a clear consensus among the judicatory leaders she studied about another potentially concrete ray of strategic hopefulness concerning the strengthening of denominational identities. It is the judicatory officials' consensus that the most important thing they did related to promoting denominational identity and covenant relations among and with their congregations was helping congregations find good pastors.

6. Are Parish Clergy the Major Linchpin in Sustaining Denominational Identity?

Robert Wuthnow, certainly the most prolific academic analyst of the current restructuring of American religion and arguably the most insightful, makes the following blunt assertion about oldline Protestantism: "[T]he guardians of denominationalism will increasingly be the clergy. Perhaps it has always been so, but now the clergy must take on the additional responsibility of caring for the bureaucratic structures built up over the past century."[64] His suggestion that it may always have been so is undoubtedly a recognition of two facts, one historical and one organizational. As church historians remind us, denominational structures in colonial America originally emerged as associations of congregations, represented primarily by their clergy leadership. They emerged for purposes of fellowship. But additionally, because of the distance that separated these American congregations and clergy from their home country judicatories, the associations were necessary "to resolve problems, adjudicate moral and theological disputes, and identify, train and authenticate leadership."[65] Organizationally, clergy are typically heavily dependent upon denominational systems for, for example, career opportunities, insurance and pension plans, and the denominational policies that govern their clergy standing.

But the key point behind Wuthnow's insight is that clergy will *increasingly*

---

64. Robert Wuthnow, *Christianity in the Twenty-First Century: Reflections on the Challenges Ahead* (New York: Oxford University Press, 1993), p. 51.
65. Richey, "Denominations and Denominationalism," p. 79.

become the guardians of denominationalism because the religious identity of laity is increasingly local and personal. Accordingly, national denominational identities and related structural issues become less important to increasing numbers of laity. If such national matters are to receive attention at all, therefore, it will be, by default, from clergy. Wuthnow does not miss the irony in the juxtaposition of this clergy reality and the years of effort by most oldline Protestant denominations to increase the inclusion of laity in their connectional system. Indeed, he fears that two likely outcomes are an increasing separation between clergy and laity, and an increase in levels of anticlericalism.[66]

Unfortunately, Wuthnow does not comment on whether such an increasing clergy investment in national denominational structures is likely to strengthen the identities of those oldline Protestant denominations currently unsettled by weakened cultures. Other analysts of the clergy situation in oldline Protestantism give us reason to be doubtful. The Gilpin and Holper contributions to Carroll and Roof's collection of essays on carriers of denominational identity are particularly stark in this regard. Gilpin begins his essay by noting that "A century ago, in the 1880's, the theological school played a central role in forming denominational identity."[67] He then proceeds to document the "marked contrast" found in the present situation: "In sum, at a time when the mainstream churches are actively seeking new avenues for reestablishing the vigor of denominational identities, they find the seminaries generally sympathetic but not much help. The reason, it seems, is that seminary faculties have given little systematic consideration to the formative tasks involved in the transmission of denominational cultures within their own sphere of work."[68] More critically, he concludes, "The possibility and appropriateness of denominational identity has itself become a question. In other words, the seminaries may be said to have entered the contemporary context lacking a critical 'ecclesiology of denominations,' an understanding of church that would make the case for the formation of denominational identity as an appropriate and integral feature of theological study."[69]

Holper's contribution presents us a double gift. One is its analysis of how changes in ordination policies affected the strength of denomination identity in the specific instance of the Presbyterian Church (U.S.A.). Equally important is the frame used in the analysis, specifically Holper's wonderfully rich, textured articulation of the tension between "discipline" and "democratization." Ori-

66. Wuthnow, *Christianity*, p. 51.
67. W. Clark Gilpin, "The Theological Schools: Transmission, Transformation, and Transcendence of Denominational Culture," in *Beyond Establishment*, p. 188.
68. Gilpin, "The Theological Schools," p. 189.
69. Gilpin, "The Theological Schools," p. 201.

ginally elaborated in Harrison's now classic *Authority and Power in the Free Church Tradition* in a case study of the American Baptist Convention in the mid-1950s, and more recently revisited and refined in Farnsley's case study of the early 1990s' restructuring of the Southern Baptist Convention, maintaining a faithful and vital balance between tradition and democracy is one of the continuing and pervasive challenges to American denominationalism. It is also one of the challenges most affected by the dynamics of postmodernity.[70] Using more specifically Presbyterian language, Holper articulates the challenge as maintaining the tension "between the tradition's Reformation-era commitment to the church as a disciplined, boundaried community whose identity (gift), mission (task), and order (means) are God-given . . . and a more sociologically defined model of the church as a democratic, voluntary society whose identity, mission and order are determined by the free choice of those who associate themselves with Presbyterian congregations."[71] Using the window of changes in ordination policies, he concludes that at least within the Presbyterian Church any balance in the tension has given way to a dominance of democratization, and that the "democratizing trends — entrepreneurial leadership, professional identity, specialization of tasks, constituency-based understandings of representation, and the strategic embrace of government entitlement programs as the primary means for providing social services — has resulted in an increasingly less boundaried and disciplined community of faith and witness."[72]

Several contrasts among denominations in the eight case studies in this book provide support for the above contentions about the critical role of clergy in mediating denominational identities, and the critical role of the certification and training of clergy that strengthens this role. For one thing, theological education is mentioned, even if merely in passing, only in the case studies of denominations with stronger identities. This clearly fits with my broader experience that suggests that overall, the national structures of strong identity denominations have a closer relationship with, and indeed more control over, the denomination's mechanisms of clergy selection and training than is the case in weaker identity denominations. Indeed, from this perspective, one of the regrettable consequences of the fiscal strain experienced by most oldline Protestant denominations over the past quarter-century is that it has prompted national structures to reduce their support of theological education. In a similar vein, the democratiza-

---

70. Paul M. Harrison, *Authority and Power in the Free Church Tradition: A Social Case Study of the American Baptist Convention* (Princeton: Princeton University Press, 1959); Farnsley, *Southern Baptist Politics.*

71. J. Frederick Holper, "Presbyterian Ordination Practice as a Case Study in the Transmission of Denominational Identity," in *Beyond Establishment*, p. 207.

72. Holper, "Presbyterian Ordination Practice," p. 217.

tion pressures that have increasingly reduced national control of ordination policies and processes are much more evident in weak identity denominations, most likely contributing to a downward spiral of cause and effect.

One also sees a link between the denominations in our case studies that best represent Miller's paradigm movements and the above argument for the critical role of clergy in sustaining denominational identity. Specifically, one sees that both the Vineyard and AG have mixed presbyterian and congregational polities. They are presbyterian with regard to clergy and congregational with regard to congregations. Among other things, this means that while congregations are formally independent of national and region control, clergy hold their denominational standing at the regional or national level. In such structures it is unavoidably clear that the clergyperson is the primary mediator of a denominational connection. Indeed, it is not uncommon for a congregation in such traditions to change its denominational affiliation if it happens to call a pastor from another denomination. It is hardly surprising, therefore, that the national structures of these denominations give the high priority they do to their connection to local clergy. One also sees a similar polity and similar priority to clergy in the case of our strong identity, but hardly new paradigm, LC-MS case.

Conclusion

Expressive individualism, congregational localism, increasingly diverse and divisive constituencies, and the fragmentation of grand narratives are among the more pervasive and significant challenges that the postmodern leanings of today's society present to America's denominations. Some denominations appear to be up to the challenge, some are struggling to cope. All are affected.

More specifically, the analytical conversation contained in this summary chapter between the case studies and essays contained in this volume on the one hand and the broader denominational and organizational literature on the other hand pointedly shows that those denominations that are most effectively negotiating the postmodern challenge are those denominations

- with strong identities;
- with strong, personal, relationally dense, crosscutting, connectional networks; and
- with strong noncognitive sources of religious authority.

Additionally, the analytical conversation suggests that these three primary factors are in turn enhanced by priority attention to:

- a denomination's narrative practices, especially the identification and telling of stories that connect the larger denominational identity to the primacy of local identities while at the same time diminishing "the particularism of its various local, regional and national histories";[73]
- the identification, education and training, and ongoing nurture and support of the denomination's ordained, congregational leadership;
- engaging and adaptive forms of worship;[74]
- acute political sensitivities; and
- a dynamic balance being maintained between the disciplined anchoring of the tradition and the potentially renewing and inevitably segmental, incremental, and local impulses of the Spirit.

If there is a single, primary, and integrative banner among all these key factors, my coeditor and I clearly agree that it is *identity.* Accordingly, if there is only one thing that practitioners responsible for national denominational structures take from this book, it is my hope that they ask of every decision they face about denominational policy, program, and practice, *What are the implications of this (policy, program, practice) for maintaining and enhancing the denomination's identity?*[75]

This being the case, let me conclude with just one example of how this question might radically change the character of a conversation. As I write this conclusion many, particularly oldline Protestant denominational executives, staff, and boards, face the painful reality of budget deficits. The two immediate paths of response are begrudging, structural downsizing and the call for evangelism campaigns. In contrast, a focus on identity changes the question from larger size and smaller size, to the question of *right size.* What is the right size of our national structure in this time and place to maintain and enhance the theological identity we carry? Perhaps providentially, the notion of "right size" fits the niche and segmentally diverse reality of a postmodern world.

73. Wuthnow, *Christianity,* p. 49.

74. See, for example, Miller, *Reinventing American Protestantism,* and C. Kirk Hadaway and David A. Roozen, *Rerouting the Protestant Mainline: Sources of Growth and Opportunities for Change* (Nashville: Abingdon, 1995).

75. This is the same primary hope that I have for scholarly study of denominations. My primary hope for organizational scholars is twofold. First, that they attend to the importance of ideas and identity. Second, that the complex interplay of internal and external dynamics in the postmodern world requires an equally complex interplay of organizational perspectives (e.g., the new institutionalism, old institutionalism and resource dependency) in their analysis (see, for example, Powell and Friedkin, "Organizational Change in Nonprofit Organizations").

The Theological Work of Denominations

James R. Nieman

Are denominations really *theological?* The answer to that question probably betrays what one imagines *denominations* really are, especially at the national level. For some, denominations are simply large-scale organizations bent on their own survival. For others they are the scandalous residue of ethnic or class interests, or the bearers of other profanely derived values. For a few they are elite cliques of religious bureaucrats manipulating resources and ideas. For still others they are program-driven structures located far from the actual lives of the faithful. When denominations are seen in these ways, cynicism about the place of theology in them is a natural result. Such depictions keep theology at a distance from the real work of denominations. In such a view, theology serves only an additive rather than an integral role, a later rationalization for decisions made by other means, or perhaps a persuasive warrant that renders denominational work legitimate and palatable.

One of the chief unheralded insights from the theologians who joined in the Organizing Religious Work (ORW) project was their repudiation of the basis for such cynicism. This insight did not, however, emerge from naive optimism or untested ideals. With simple realism these theologians fully recognized the many other forces, roles, structures, and principles that shaped the work of their own denominations. Yet this same realism also led them to see that, at the national level, theological work was truly a crucial activity, often vastly more so than appearances might first suggest. Beyond this, their study showed the true dimensions and contours of this work and what it might mean for denominations to be yet more deeply theological in their efforts.

To venture into these conclusions, however, is to move prematurely to the end of a journey of discovery. My intent in this essay is to retrace that journey on the basis of the evidence gathered by the project theologians. Doing this requires selecting a cross section from the entire collection of articles in this book, focusing mainly upon the eight theological essays in order to summarize and analyze what theology illumines about the work of denominations today. The journey itself has five stations. First, I will explore how the task of examining theological work was conceptualized at the national level of the research. Second, I will review the results of the eight project theologians, with special attention to the themes, methods, genres, and concerns they surfaced. Third, I will use these results to revisit a general claim about the place of theology within denominations. Fourth, I will explore specifically how this theological work seems best to be done at the national level. Finally, I will suggest what this might imply for the resiliency of denominations and their enduring theological purpose.

Conceiving the Task

When the ORW project began, the theologians at the national level of the study were invited into a task whose course was largely uncharted. To be sure, their work could have remained rather conventional. For example, they might simply have taken the events and issues presented in the sociological case studies of their respective denominations and judged them against the overt doctrines, creeds, and belief statements of those same groups, looking for instances of consistency or deviation. This approach would have preserved the traditional notion that "theology" is the same as "systematic theology."[1] As such, it becomes primarily a *speculative* enterprise, an engagement with cognitive ideas that are then subject to academic reflection. Moreover, in the specific setting of a denomination, this sort of theology would then serve a largely *regulative* role in which such ideas are applied to establish rules for behavior, boundaries for the group, and legitimations for action. The problem with this approach, however, was its failure to bring to light the many other ways the project theologians knew that theologies were expressed within denominations. Worse still, it tended to distort and exaggerate the actual way official theologies work within these complex organizational ecologies.

As a result, the theologians plotted a different course. Instead of beginning with explicit doctrines or focusing their attention solely on trained theologians, they looked at how various activities, procedures, rituals, habits, and structures revealed the operative theologies of a denomination, or at least illus-

---

1. Gerben Heitink, *Practical Theology — History, Theory, Action Domains: Manual for Practical Theology*, trans. Reinder Bruinsma (Grand Rapids: Eerdmans, 1999), p. 108.

trated an important dimension of that group's work. Their aim was to gesture at the broadest sense of the theological character of the entire group in its primary actions, rather than the much narrower use of approved documents, acknowledged experts, and intellectual labor that functions mostly at a secondary level of remove. In this way they conceptualized theology as a *practical* enterprise, deeply attuned to the concrete, theory-laden actions of a group.[2] Within the specific setting of a denomination, this sort of theology serves a profoundly *discursive* role, a "telling" or public account of God's ways with humankind and the whole creation. This account then operates as the basis for the pivotal group work of orienting, explaining, and discerning. It is important to notice that this conceptualization of the task locates theology mainly in its ecclesial rather than academic home. Theology so conceived is the native language of the church as "ekklesia," the people who have been called into being by God and who then speak of (discourse) the one who so calls them.

The implications of this conceptual shift were immense, and immediately affected the breadth and depth of the research facing the theologians. Instead of limiting themselves to the customary and comfortable components of theology, they turned to several important and frequently unappreciated dimensions of theology within their denominations. Four of these are particularly significant to notice at the outset. As implied above, theology came to be seen in and through *practices*. Influenced by and contributing to the recent rich discussion of practices, Rebecca Chopp has spoken of practices as "socially shared forms of behavior that mediate between what are often called subjective and objective dimensions. A practice is a pattern of meaning and action that is both culturally constructed and individually instantiated. The notion of practice draws us to inquire into the shared activities of groups of persons that provide meaning and orientation to the world, and that guide action."[3] To discern these patterns the theologians therefore learned to listen for the implicit, subtle, and unofficial discourses carried by a range of actions, rather than only for the explicit, obvious, and formal expressions of theology. The latter were surely not ignored but took their place within an overall pattern of meaning and action, being seen as one of many kinds of theological practices.

This practice-centered dimension also called for appreciating that theology was vitally *social*. At heart this meant that greater attention was given to the work of groups as the agents of theology, rather than simply to the efforts of in-

---

2. Donald S. Browning, *A Fundamental Practical Theology: Descriptive and Strategic Proposals* (Minneapolis: Fortress, 1991), p. 7.

3. Rebecca S. Chopp, *Saving Work: Feminist Practices of Theological Education* (Louisville: Westminster John Knox, 1995), p. 15.

dividual, isolated actors. Beyond this, it also meant that theology was assessed within the dynamics of interaction, rather than being limited to rare opportunities for private thought and abstract deliberation. The theologians became keenly aware that theologies emerged inductively, required mutual effort for their maintenance, were borne by interpersonal relationships, and might reflect the contested social situations in which they developed.[4] All of this demanded the careful, rigorous use of social research tools in the course of examining theologies at the national level, which often resulted in an essential partnership between theologians and sociologists on the various denominational teams.

Given its dynamically social quality, theology was also recognized in its *multiplicity*. This was partly the natural outcome of the many practices and groups within even the national level of a denomination, so that no one theological assertion could possibly encompass them all. At another level, however, this reflected the fact that theology was being deployed strategically to address practical concerns and particular situations, rather than operating abstractly where standards of consistency or coherence might rank more highly. The lack of a solitary let alone constraining theology did not however disintegrate into confusion or relativism. Instead, the project theologians came to the paradoxical realization that several theological strands could still somehow hold together and serve the larger purposes of the group.

Closely related to this, theologies in denominations retained the capacity to exert a significant kind of *particularity*. As a discursive activity, theology could offer a "denominated" telling that operated bilingually, both within and beyond the group. Within the denomination theologies provided a recognizable, relatively stable sense of identity that enabled adhesion to the group by its own members. Beyond the denomination theologies conveyed a range of distinctions that highlighted not only differences from other groups but also the very means for interaction or even collaboration with them. Such particularity in theology thereby gave the denomination an adaptive fluidity that might be useful in diverse situations.[5] Because this kind of particularity suggests how theological work might be more fully grasped and carried out in denominations, I will return to it several times in what follows. For now it is enough to note that these four dimensions of theology (as practical, social, multiple, and particular) redefined the work of the project theologians and led them into new insights and emerging challenges.

---

4. George Casalis, *Correct Ideas Don't Fall from the Skies: Elements for an Inductive Theology* (Maryknoll, N.Y.: Orbis, 1984), pp. 36-41.

5. Robert Bruce Mullin, "Denominations as Bilingual Communities," in *Reimagining Denominationalism: Interpretive Essays,* ed. Robert Bruce Mullin and Russell E. Richey (New York: Oxford University Press, 1994), pp. 168-70, 173.

Overview of Results

When the inquiry into theologies at the national level of denominations was conceived more broadly, these theologians began to surface a bewildering array of particular observations. When all eight of their essays are read as a group, however, certain trends are noticeable throughout this body of research. These have been organized below in terms of the several *themes, methods, genres,* and *concerns* that cut across the entire collection. As each of these areas is explored in turn, I will also highlight what they suggest about any future efforts to study the theologies of denominations in this fashion, with special attention to those places where sociological approaches were valuable or could be exploited further.

Themes

A wide range of focal themes can be seen across the entire collection of theological essays, a matter that was already made clear in the précis to those essays found in the introduction to this collection (pp. 1-34). For example, some treated a practice as an important theme, such as the LC-MS essay's examination of communion and the Lord's Supper or the UMC essay's attention (in part) to care for children in poverty. Procedural themes were more dominant in other essays, notably with UCC efforts toward restructuring the national level of the denomination, a theme that also occupied a different portion of the UMC essay. One essay used a document as the central theme, namely, the recent RCA mission statement. Other essays were drawn more toward themes that showed emerging challenges to the denomination, such as maintaining the distinctiveness of the AG or losing the founding leader of the Vineyard. Still others looked more closely at crises, such as the presidential scandal treated in the NBC essay or the treasurer scandal mentioned in the Episcopal essay.

This bare sketch of the thematic focus for each essay in no way subverts the earlier claim that denominational theology came to be recognized in this research project by its multiplicity. Instead, each essay actually incorporated several subsidiary themes that were thoroughly intertwined around its more central focus, thereby revealing the multifaceted theological character of the denomination in question. The RCA essay, for instance, looked beyond the content of the new mission statement to the procedures for its creation and the practices for its acceptance. Similarly, the public scandals presented in the NBC and Episcopal essays were closely tied to procedures for decision making in the denomination as well as practices of confession and forgiveness. The UMC essay began by exploring three distinct themes in separate sections (care for children in poverty, organizational restructuring, and theological unity in the denomination) that were drawn together at its conclusion. By contrast, the AG essay initially offered a more interwoven narrative of procedures, practices, and documents that were then deployed in facing successive waves of challenges to denominational distinctiveness.

This thematic analysis therefore suggests that the effort to convey the theological character of a denomination requires incorporating several interacting areas, each of which offers a glimpse of a larger picture. Strikingly, none of the essays merely reduced the theological portrait of the denomination to a simple core of overt, ideational theological claims. Instead, a multiplicity of theological expressions was oriented around an identifiable core instance (practice, procedure, document, challenge, crisis) that the theologian felt would best convey the theological character of the entire denomination. These themes or core instances pretended neither to be comprehensive (encompassing the entire theological reality of the denomination) nor archetypical (a timeless pattern slavishly reproduced throughout the whole). Instead, they functioned more like a synecdoche (a part that gestures to a sense of the whole) or a prototype (a primary instance that generates recognizable variation). As such, these themes carried within themselves a web of relationships to other theological themes, offering a way into the network of overlapping and crisscrossing features that constituted the theological "family resemblance" of the denomination.[6]

The risk in using such themes, of course, is whether they accurately and plausibly convey the sense of the whole as fully as they implicitly claim to do. Treating a theme as a theological synecdoche or prototype begs the question of whether it truly holds representative significance across the denomination, and for what period of time. By what means might this be assessed? The theological essays would likely have been strengthened in this regard had there been adequate occasion to compare their respective focal themes with other strong instances of theological activity or expression within the denomination. A broader cross-checking might have been conducted not only at the national level of the denomination but also at its judicatory and congregational levels. This would have required a higher degree of cooperation and interaction with the sociologists on the denominational teams than the project allowed. More importantly, this points to the need for such collaboration in future studies of denominational theology.

6. Ludwig Wittgenstein, *Philosophical Investigations*, trans. G. E. M. Anscombe, 3rd ed. (New York: Macmillan, 1958), pp. 32-34.

Methods

The social quality of theological practices in denominations meant that the project theologians became more attuned to groups of actors in their relationships and interactions. This called for using methods that were more appropriate to that social object, instead of classic theological approaches better suited to isolated academic reflection. These newer strategies were evident in both the gathering and analysis of research materials. In gathering information, personal interviews were perhaps the most frequently used social research method. At times this included formal contacts, as in the structured discussions with Episcopal leaders, but at other times this simply involved informal conversations, as in the casual chats with LC-MS convention participants. Some attention was also given to group observation, a strategy seen most extensively in the UMC essay that relied on attendance at various meetings of decision makers. Even the examination of written records had the potential to lead into interviews or group observation, as when the RCA and UCC essays used a close reading of documents as the catalyst for exploring the group procedures leading to the development of those documents.

In analyzing information, socially oriented methods again were evident. That is, analysis was rarely the private work of a lone scholar arranging research results into abstract ideational categories for comparison and assessment. More typically, it had the character of a collaborative, team effort of review. This team effort in turn sought the social and experiential frameworks within a denomination that might best clarify what had been gleaned during the research phase. For instance, the commonly understood historical challenges of the past provided that framework for the AG materials, while widely felt present and future challenges did this in relation to the UCC materials. In the Vineyard and NBC essays, interpersonal relationships and close social bonds were the larger structure in which particular theological practices seemed to make the most sense. Similarly, shared culture and ethos offered an orienting configuration for interpreting information gathered by the Episcopal team.

All of this can be summarized in two conclusions. First, when the focus of theological attention is a social reality, a more socially oriented research method is required not simply in gathering information but also in analyzing it. Second, because the focal themes of the essays incorporated a range of related theological themes, multiple social research methods adequate to the density and complexity of those themes must be planned from the start. The UMC essay is but one example of how the method of group observation led into personal interviews and record examination strategies, all of which then required analysis by being placed within a widely known social framework of Wesleyan theology and recent challenges facing that denomination. From beginning to end, therefore, discerning theology within denominations calls for diverse research methods that are thoroughly social.

At the same time, although many different methods for gathering and analysis of denominational theologies were used in this project, one particularly important strategy was underutilized. Ethnographic, participant observation approaches would likely have been quite fitting even for a short- or medium-term study of the operative theologies at the national level of denominations or with occasional groups associated with that level. This kind of rich, ongoing, grassroots approach to qualitative data gathering would have significantly complemented the other methods used in the various theological essays, giving yet another test for the significance of the focal themes they highlighted. Although the literature in anthropology and sociology is replete with practical guides in this area,[7] adapting these methods to the group settings of the national offices and staff of a denomination, for instance, has yet to be explored fully.

Unexpected complications in the ORW project sometimes made it more difficult for the theologians and sociologists on denominational teams to work together as closely as had originally been hoped. However, the strong record of those teams that were able to plan together from the start and remained committed to this interaction throughout the research augurs well for such cross-disciplinary work in the future. This is simply to underscore James Gustafson's observation, made over forty years ago, that theology and sociology need a much closer cooperation in order to interpret what actually happens in churches, regardless of the organizational level.[8] The lingering issue, however, comes in respecting what each discipline stands to offer the other in order to be mutually enriching. As already noted in this discussion of methods, sociology stands to offer theology a disciplined and multifaceted approach for paying attention to the particular groups in which theological practices are evident. At the same time, theology stands to offer sociology a way of more fully appreciating the distinctive discourse native to the church as church, i.e., theology itself. For the purpose of further research into denominations at all organizational levels, the partnership between these two disciplines therefore seems essential and worth exploring further.

---

7. For but one concise resource in this area, see John Lofland and Lyn H. Lofland, *Analyzing Social Settings: A Guide to Qualitative Observation and Analysis*, 3rd ed. (Belmont, Calif.: Wadsworth, 1995).

8. James M. Gustafson, *Treasure in Earthen Vessels: The Church as a Human Community* (New York: Harper and Row, 1961), pp. 99-112.

Genres

It was somewhat fitting that the range of focal themes and the range of research methods were also matched by the range of literary genres in which the theological essays were finally presented. In this instance, "genre" means simply a conventional and repeatable pattern of language that, by virtue of that pattern, conveys meaning for a particular audience. It achieves this by establishing a set of expectations that are themselves meaningful and may then be satisfied or subverted to evoke still further meaning. A familiar example is the conventional narrative genre of "religious conversion." Its predictable pattern traces the life of a character from negative conduct through epiphanic encounter to reformed behavior. The pattern itself creates the expectation of such a journey regardless of the specific character involved or the particulars of the conversion. If this genre follows its usual plan, then our expectations about conversion are satisfied and the meaning is reinforced. If, however, this plan is interrupted or later negated by backsliding, then our expectations of the genre are subverted and we are left to puzzle anew about the meaning of conversion. Genres are a way of recognizing that the way material is presented contributes to its meaning as much as does the substance of that material.

The theological essays used many different kinds of stock genres in order to present a fuller sense of the operative theology in denominations. In both the NBC and AG essays, the genre of history provided a basic framework through which more recent theological issues were to be interpreted. Presentations of the Episcopal scandal or a crucial UMC meeting exemplified an episodic narrative genre, retelling how a more narrowly delimited event actually unfolded. The Vineyard essay was distinctive for deploying the genre of biography, using the life story of founder John Wimber as the key to that denomination's theological self-understanding. The genre of commentary typified both the RCA essay's analysis of a mission statement and the LC-MS essay's examination of convention resolutions. Descriptive reports of practices, such as congregational worship in AG or national level decision making in UCC, showed yet another genre for conveying denominational theology. Even the simple genre of list or categorization was useful, as with the theological commitments of the Vineyard.

Although each of the theological essays was often governed by a primary genre, it is important to note that they were never limited to just a single pure genre. Instead, essays freely and fluidly used several literary approaches in often surprising combinations. The move from biography to categorization in the Vineyard essay provides but one striking example of this. In other words, minor or subsidiary genres, useful in presenting some particular aspect of denominational theology, were then nested within an overarching and dominant genre that provided a more coherent structure to the entire essay. If an essay at its broadest level is imagined as a kind of theological narrative, then the use of subordinate genres implies that multiple literary strategies are needed to tell that overall narrative more fully.

This attention to genres also suggests that their value is much greater than being merely a stylistic convenience for the essays. Instead, they actually seem to point to something quite theologically significant and previously undervalued in other discussions of theology in denominations. In intriguing ways the project theologians used genres that themselves reflected the theological character of the denomination. Just as the substantive themes of the essays pointed to a larger theological reality, so the genres suggested a customary technique by which the denomination might express itself theologically. Moreover, these genres might also hint at the thought patterns one should adopt to reason theologically as the denomination natively does. In using particular genres well-suited to the groups in question, the theologians seemed to say, "If you want to understand this denomination theologically, then you not only need to know *about this theme,* but you also need to experience it *in this way.*"

Concerns

One final trend across the collection involved the basic concerns to which each essay pointed. Among the essays, what were the places of deepest theological anxiety or the sources of greatest theological energy evident through the various themes, methods, and genres? Overall, two related theological concerns consistently occupied the attention of the national level of these groups. First, all the essays presented some sort of ambivalence about or even outright disjunction between two or more theological claims being asserted within the denomination at this time. Sometimes these differing claims were embodied by separate subgroups, such as the two or possibly three factions of LC-MS communion theology. More often the claims reflected the gulf between older and newer theological dispositions or commitments, which threatened eventually to splinter into separate subgroups. Attitudes toward congregationalism in the RCA were one example of this, while tensions between the Pentecostal and evangelical orientations of the AG were another. Yet another kind of ambivalence or disjunction involved different theological strategies called upon in stable versus extraordinary times. The Vineyard essay expressed the classic challenge of moving from the charismatic founder toward the ongoing maintenance of the movement, a challenge reflective of two distinct theological strategies. The Episcopal essay also suggested a strategic tension within a liturgical theology that was ordinarily quite potent but seemed ineffective amidst a scandal. Of course, many other particular concerns were exhibited in these essays, worries about schism, purity, diversity, compassion, and mission, to name a few. Even so, these specific topics were usually more accurately understood when assessed against the horizon of the most basic and contested theological claims seen in competing subgroups, dispositions, or strategies.

Closely related to this was a second concern evident across the collection, the question of which theological account or temperament would finally center and orient denominational identity. Virtually every essay argued at some level for resolving this concern over identity by embracing a component of the denomination's theological heritage more strongly or applying it more thoroughly and consistently. In quite different ways the AG and UCC essays called for reclaiming a prized core value within the denomination in order to address present and future organizational concerns. A similar appeal was made in the LC-MS and RCA essays, but here it was by reemphasizing and drawing from explicitly theological documents and confessions of faith. The Episcopal and UMC essays asserted that the recovery of certain key practices could guide and direct the denomination, while the NBC and Vineyard essays argued that a comparable aim would be better met by rehearsing the group's founding narrative.

With both concerns — competing claims and orienting accounts — it is significant that the fundamental work of the denomination was understood to be theological identity formation. Naturally, the specific character and substance of these theological identities differed widely among the groups included in this collection. Despite these obvious differences, however, the essays represent something of a consensus that the work perceived to be most crucial at the national level has less to do with matters of structure, resources, or programs than with foundational responsibilities for clarifying and reinforcing theological identity. This does not mean that focusing on identity was promoted as an adaptive response to challenge or crisis. Imagining that internally shaped culture can effectively solve externally generated problems has rightly been critiqued elsewhere.[9] Instead, the essays imply that theological identity is simply a sine qua non of any denomination and its core project at the national level, regardless of circumstances. Through the range of situations presented by the project theologians, it became clear that their denominations cared deeply about the distinctive discourse of the church (theology) and saw the national level as uniquely equipped to engage this discourse. If these essays truly reflect

---

9. Donald A. Luidens, "Between Myth and Hard Data: A Denomination Struggles with Identity," in *Beyond Establishment: Protestant Identity in a Post-Protestant Age,* ed. Jackson Carroll and Wade Clark Roof (Louisville: Westminster John Knox, 1993), pp. 257-65.

the character of their respective groups and trends among others, then theological identity becomes a far more significant organizational task for denominations than has previously been realized. It is to this task at the national level that we now turn more directly.

Theology in Denominations

Both in the anxieties they surfaced and the successes they retold, the theological essays repeatedly indicated that denominations were at their best when a strong and distinctive theological orientation was deeply owned by members, congregations, and other parts of the organization. Put another way, the very challenges and crises certain denominations were facing arose precisely from a corrosive contest over this same core identity. That active adherents and parties were willing to fight at times, committing significant resources and resolve to such conflict, only proves how important theological identity remains in denominations today. Taken seriously, then, what does this suggest about the work of the national level of denominations? Despite the many imaginable tasks at this level, such as providing resources, governance, regulation, connections, and so forth, there seems little to support the notion that national attention to any of these tasks would, by itself, contribute positively to denominational vitality. Far more significant in our study was the way the national level could ground, clarify, and reinforce a theological identity that catalyzed the denomination, to which other matters of structure, administration, planning, or program were but attendant considerations.

It is important to underscore at this point that the identity work we are describing is distinctively *theological* in nature. This is because theology, the public account of who God is and how God acts in relation to us and all creation, is the particular discourse native to the church as church. The kind of identity work needed at the national level is therefore not that of offering religious justifications for the cultural character of a denomination (such as ethnicity or class), as if this were of ultimate significance. Nor is it to be confused with doctrinal rationalizations for organizational preservation, program continuation, or strategic planning. Finally, it is not limited to the realm of ideas, as if theology were simply a matter of rediscovering and reasserting certain cognitive claims. Instead, the central identity work denominations can engage in is a rich, deep sense of the distinctive beliefs unfolding into, borne by, and manifested through a wide range of practices, such as the use of symbols, histories, narratives, habits, behaviors, words, and structures. At heart, theological identity in a denomination publicly declares in recognizable forms who these adherents are as a group and what they do in light of a specific understanding of God's ways in the world.

Although denominations have historically displayed various organizational aims, from group cohesion to shared action to bureaucratic efficiency to more recent instances of loose networking, the essays pointed to a more basic recognition that theological integrity truly grounds structural considerations of unity, polity, or purpose. Formal aspects of identity are surely important, such as having a recognizable character over time, distinct values open to multiple interpretations, and flexible strategies that adapt to diverse situations. Yet these formal aspects would matter in the identity work of *any* group. What theology gives to a denomination is the *substantive* aspect of identity work that runs far deeper than any formal aspects, important as those may be. In other words, while formal aspects of organizational work do indeed contribute to denominational identity, they best derive from rather than drive the substantive aspect of identity that theology offers.[10] Two reasons for this deserve special mention.

The first has to do with the theological assumptions built into *how denominations come into being.* Since there is no historical blank slate, each denomination by its very founding concedes that it emerged from and was related to a larger and longer theological tradition of which it was neither the originator nor the sole franchise. Its authority and authenticity was negotiated and sometimes contested with an ecclesial reality beyond itself, thus stamping its nascent identity in a deeply theological way. Following upon this, each denomination must then legitimate itself as a valid expression of the church while at the same time granting at least some measure of ecclesial legitimacy to other denominations. The presumption of pluralistic toleration so basic to the American religious scene carries immense theological weight that further shapes every denomination, barring both sectarian tendencies and any wholesale repudiation of other religious groups. Finally, each denomination manifests collective action, using cooperative and translocal efforts both within and beyond itself. This commitment to being connected is not simply a result of how groups must function in a voluntaristic society but is also a serious theological claim about the church as group work rather than individual piety or abstract ideals, a claim that is once again at the very core of denominational self-understanding. In terms of its *founding, development,* and *cooperation,* then, each denomination

---

10. The relation between Presbyterian organization and theology was noted in David B. McCarthy, "The Emerging Importance of Presbyterian Polity," in *The Organizational Revolution: Presbyterians and American Denominationalism,* ed. Milton J. Coalter, John M. Mulder, and Louis B. Weeks (Louisville: Westminster John Knox, 1992), pp. 279-306.

already bears a profound theological identity that cannot be ignored without distorting the very nature of that group.

The second reason the substantive aspect provided by theology is so basic to identity has to do with *how denominations account for themselves publicly.* At heart, each denomination gives voice to its own understanding of God, connection to Christ, and experience in the Spirit. More than merely a cultural or functional task, this identity work overtly declares a transcendent relationship. To be sure, such an account need not be comprehensive and may not be very clear or coherent, but it does represent at least a shared version that the denomination treasures and wants to retain and assert. Building upon this, each denomination as a cooperative and translocal entity stands as a sign or metaphor of how all people can be affected by this divine encounter. Precisely in this group particularity, it makes an argument for a diversity and difference essential to Christian witness in the world. This sort of identity work is how a denomination claims its space in, as, and for the church in a way that enriches the ecclesial whole rather than being a sinful or schismatic embarrassment. Finally, each denomination at its best holds these divine and human accounts in tension, thereby allowing for the critique and adaptation of its own identity. That is, the public account of a denomination's theological identity includes the standards for discernment and examination both within and beyond itself. Therefore, struggles over which theological account would orient denominational identity (repeatedly noted in this collection) can actually indicate a vital denominational energy instead of a deadly drift and decay. In terms of its *transcendent, ecclesial,* and *critical* dimensions, then, every denomination shows an unmistakable theological identity in the ways it renders a public account.

Since theological concerns are already contained within any denomination's origins and accounts, this substantive aspect becomes vastly more significant for denominational identity than its formal aspects. This in turn leads to one of the most promising insights from this entire study, that *the effectiveness of a denomination's work (embodied in its structures, decisions, activities, and so forth) should be gauged chiefly in terms of serving its theological identity.* This assertion rests on a basic recognition that denominations exist first and foremost as expressions of the church and for the sake of that mission. If the church is primarily theological in its discourse and identity, then the question for any denomination as church is whether its organizational forms enhance that theological character or risk frustrating and subverting it.

I would go so far as to claim that every theological essay in this collection is concerned with whether organizational forms finally support or supplant theological character, lest the very identity of the denomination itself be compromised. This was not some clever way for those writing about ailing denominations to avoid accountability and thus excuse ineptitude and torpor. Essays about healthy and growing denominations raised the same issue in their own way as those about churches facing crisis or decline. The real issue concerns the assessment of denominational vitality and effectiveness. On the one hand, assessment by comparison to extrinsic values risks producing organizational success at the cost of denominational soul. Can such a group be deemed effective when it no longer retains the story it alone can tell? On the other hand, assessment rooted in theological identity provides an intrinsic standard based upon a denomination's own particular discourse. That distinctive story makes sense of all other work, even and perhaps especially during periods of stagnation and struggle when paradoxically it may become most valuable and sustaining.[11] Taken as a whole, then, this study supports the view that denominational vitality and effectiveness should be understood and assessed as more of a theological question than an organizational one.

Bearers of Identity

To be realistic, most adherents in denominations are formed in their theological identity primarily through congregations. Aside from those few who are shaped by regular contact with specialized church institutions or judicatory and national offices, the rest are molded in local circumstances through regular contact with fellow members and clergy. Thus, while one might agree that the central, substantive work of denominations should be theological identity, it is quite another thing to presume that this should include the national level to any serious degree, let alone how. For some the national level even seems an impediment to identity formation, distant from the lives and concerns of ordinary believers. Therefore, we must be quick to note that theological identity work in denominations varies according to at least two interacting factors. First, the character of the identity work itself can be an important consideration. For example, an understanding of "belonging" is generally embodied more through local theological practices than through regional or national efforts. Yet second, the character of a denomination can also affect where a theological practice is

---

11. Of course, comparison within certain limits can map alternatives that clarify internal values and strategies. This is especially true when looking at other branches of one's theological family (RCA among the broader Reformed tradition) or groups sharing similar scale, regional orientation, or historic challenges (NBC among the historic African American denominations). In the same vein, the turn to an intrinsic standard is misguided if it presumes or contributes to separation and insularity. Adequate identity discourse never remains isolated. A denomination best explores identity by both knowing itself and staying in contact with others.

situated in denominational structures. In the example above, it is clear that belonging is a much more nationally attuned identity work for members of the NBC than for those in the UMC, while those in the LC-MS have shifted over the past half-century from a national to a regional and even local sense of belonging. Given these variations in how denominations attend to the work of theological identity, what significant role can the national level actually play?

The answer begins with a basic claim that the congregation, although an actual instance of the church, is not coextensive with the entire church and stands as church only insofar as it exists for witness in the world. Genuine formation in theological identity through a congregation therefore depends on a sense that an adequate witness includes other times and places. It is just this kind of scope that the national level of a denomination is distinctly able to offer. It can guard local efforts against the myopia and tunnel vision that insulate theological identity from the larger church and world, let alone even the local setting itself. Regardless of its structures or processes, a denomination at its best is able to do this work for four reasons. First, it *conserves the memory and hopes* of a particular theological identity far beyond the historical and geographic limits of any one congregation. Second, it *offers a range of connections* between congregations themselves and also with other religious and voluntary groups, all of which imply the globally embedded concern of the church. Third, it *presents a wealth of resources* that enable congregations amply to carry out the local work of forming members in this core theological identity. Finally, it *retains a diversity of voices* due to its national perspective, one that constitutes a broad theological identity rather than its reduction to narrow interests or monaural expressions. By lending an expansive horizon of history, connections, resources, and diversity to theological identity formation, the national level is uniquely positioned to promote those practices by which this identity can be gained and reinforced, including (and not least of all) the patient resolve to maintain that identity even amidst challenging and corrosive circumstances.

If this accurately suggests the opportune position of the national level of a denomination, then what kind of practices actually promote theological identity, and how are they deployed? Once again, this is where the overall study offers another valuable insight, that *the national level is most effective when using mediating mechanisms that indirectly contribute to multistranded identity narratives.* Before explaining the key terms of this insight, we need to remember that the national level can neither supply a theological identity fully formed for congregations nor supplant the efforts of congregations required for identity formation. Indeed, occasional attempts by denominations to provide and enforce such work explain the reluctance in some quarters even to employ a denominational label, reacting against the perception of centralized regulatory control. Any efforts by the national level must be grounded in the ecclesiological affirmation that no form of the church (i.e., level, segment, organization, or other institutional expression) has primacy over another, since each has a distinct calling and gifts. It is no more satisfactory for the national (or judicatory) level to be seen as a resource supplier for congregations than for congregations to be seen as branch offices for a denominational brand name. Reciprocal respect between all forms of the church is essential here, along with a willingness to risk receiving what another expression has to offer. Our focus is necessarily limited here to but one dimension of that complex interaction, what the national level can bring to the mutual and open-ended process of theological identity formation.

Returning to the insight above, let us first explore these "mediating mechanisms" that are so important to what the national level of denominations can do. Simply put, they are the concrete means by which different levels of a denomination mutually interact to construct theological meaning. In form they are produced with resources originating at one level of the organization, but their predominant site of implementation is elsewhere. They aim therefore to connect different levels in some fashion by expending rather than conserving the mechanism itself. In substance, mediating mechanisms bear the potential to become theologically significant practices. The focus is therefore not on the mechanism itself but on what it does and the meaning it unfolds in action. To make the foregoing somewhat less abstract, consider the familiar case of a denominational hymnal. Although a hymnal often originates from human and material resources at the national level of a denomination, its primary purpose is to be used for congregational song at the local level. In that very use, a bond between denominational commitments and local capacities is forged. Without such use (for example, if it remained an untouched artifact), the hymnal would fail in its reason for being. The entire aim of a hymnal is that its contents are actually brought to particular enactment, and through this enactment theological claims sponsored by the denomination are voiced and claimed anew.

The existence of mediating mechanisms (although not using this specific term) was explored over a decade ago in several of the essays in *Beyond Establishment*.[12] Looking at denominational resources as varied as church schools, camps, women's groups, fellowship events, hymns, ordination liturgies, and histories, the authors noted how denominational cultures were transmitted within and beyond locales. Although theological purposes were important in several of these examples, a consistent effort to examine how these mechanisms bore theological identity in reciprocal ways across levels of a denomination was

---

12. Jackson Carroll and Wade Clark Roof, eds., *Beyond Establishment: Protestant Identity in a Post-Protestant Age* (Louisville: Westminster John Knox, 1993).

lacking. In a different sense, several of the faith practices identified by Dorothy Bass and her associates could also be understood as the local instances of possible mediating mechanisms.[13] With this treatment of such thoroughly theological matters as hospitality, testimony, discernment, or healing (to name a few) as a base, it would be intriguing to develop further how these individual and congregational practices might also become places of engagement with theological identity work initiated at the national level of a denomination.

The mediating mechanisms mentioned in the theological essays in the present collection can be grouped into three categories, by no means intended as an exhaustive typology. The first involves the *scripts* that establish some sort of coordinated basis for theological practices. Once again, hymns and liturgies are familiar examples of this (see the Episcopal and AG essays), but other examples include resolutions, procedural guides, and overt claims (see the LC-MS and RCA essays). Although often found as texts, scripts are not necessarily written. Appropriate worship behavior is a script preserved in familiar and repeated actions, while statements used in meetings may require nothing less than written form. Whether as plotted performances or inscribed declarations, scripts provide a concrete pattern for common work. Scripts are mechanisms that specifically mediate because they are also profoundly shaped by inputs from the national level, such as the approval or critique of specific practices or the language and limits that official documents give to local statements. At the same time, of course, congregations can affect these mechanisms in the opposite direction, as when worship resources are enriched by local recommendations or when resolutions are brought from the grass roots.

Another kind of mediating mechanism involves the *contacts* that enable serious interaction with other people. Sometimes this happens through the informal channels of relationship building, fellowship, or organizations whose main purpose is to create interpersonal connections. The NBC and Vineyard essays show the importance of such contacts for members to be able to see themselves as part of the denomination. At other times, contacts occur through more formal occasions, such as national gatherings, meetings with national or judicatory leaders, and informational events. These kinds of interactions are apparent in the UMC and LC-MS essays. Whether formally or informally structured, contacts like these are crucial for creating ordinary, accessible relationships for all participants. Contacts are mechanisms that specifically mediate because they require involvement by national level personnel not only so they might be known locally but also so they might in turn know people within congregations. Once

---

13. Dorothy C. Bass, ed., *Practicing Our Faith: A Way of Life for a Searching People* (San Francisco: Jossey-Bass, 1997).

again, the mechanism operates in a mutual fashion that humanizes the denomination and thus can prevent a sense of distance and disinterest.

One last kind of mediating mechanism involves the *visions* that evoke a shared direction and future for adherents. Although these may also involve scripts and contacts, their main focus is to create a horizon for action that leads to subsequent participation in a theological ethos. Such visions might be embodied as labor resources through service projects, social commitments, and movements, instances of which can be found in the UMC and AG essays. They are also embodied as ideational resources through orienting histories, originating purposes, and biographies of key figures, as the UCC and Vineyard essays demonstrate. Visions are mechanisms that specifically mediate because they give the national level a way to pass on the strongest commitments of the denomination in ways that ultimately must matter beyond that level. The challenge for such visions is that while they are easy to enunciate, they are difficult to put into specific practice. Without such enactment, however, the vision itself remains abstract and aloof, losing its ability to motivate and orient the entire denomination.

Other types of mediating mechanisms might be imagined, but for now a few summary comments merit emphasis. First, it is significant that these mechanisms have a *reciprocal* role, allowing different denominational levels mutually to affect each other. This study has focused on how the national level might deploy mediating mechanisms as a catalyst for building theological identity across the denomination. However, this should not prevent us from seeing how they can also become vehicles for congregations to influence, enrich, or even critique national practices. The entire network of relationships by which mediating mechanisms foster interaction between different levels in a denomination has yet to be examined, nor even have the specific features of these mechanisms and the categories into which they cluster been adequately described.[14] Such research would permit us to notice them more easily and thus give guidance at the national level for their use in strengthening theological identity. Related to this, we should next highlight that these mechanisms work in an *indirect* fashion. This is partly because, as already noted, they can only contribute to identity formation rather than deliver it fully formed. More than this, they mediate between levels of a denomination, not being under the complete control of any one of them. Because their use requires partnership between levels, they not only bear theological identity but also signify the type and strength of the relationship between levels. In this respect, mediating mechanisms are like Erving

---

14. Network theory could assist such research; see Martin Kilduff and Wenpin Tsai, *Social Networks and Organizations* (Thousand Oaks, Calif.: Sage, 2003).

Goffman's "tie-signs," evidence about significant and complex anchored relations between participants.[15] Looking at such mechanisms for what they say about the state of relationships with the national level might be a valuable indicator of denominational vitality. Finally, it is important to realize that such mechanisms are never singular but are *compound*. We already know that theological identity in denominations cannot be reduced to just one feature or expression. Likewise, mediating mechanisms that bear such identity are also multiple, offering several avenues to orient and shape members. Sometimes they are mutually reinforcing, while at other times they are not so easily reconciled. Provided that they avoid basic inconsistency and can tolerate moderate tension, however, they offer flexible and durable strategies for the national level to convey theological identity.

Mediating mechanisms are not really ends in themselves but truly matter insofar as they contribute to "identity narratives" in denominations. This poses the prior question of why identity formation, theological or otherwise, should be seen as having a narrative quality. In short, narratives are cultural constructions with the distinct ability to shape language toward a compact, shared, but paradoxical story reality. On the one hand, narratives create a sense of home, using words that build a world of the familiar and predictable, with all the richness and alternatives we might expect there. On the other hand, they create a sense of possibility, using words that allow us not only to anticipate problems (subjunctive potential) but also to imagine new ones (subversive potential).[16] Put another way, good narratives have both a mythic and parabolic character. While the mythic side of narrative mediates and reconciles, resolving tensions and evoking stability, the parabolic side challenges and disrupts, shattering any complacency with unforeseen and even disturbing possibilities.[17] Narrative requires these two aspects since both are intertwined in all of life. Without both of them, narratives quickly sound dubious. Stories with only a mythic sense of home are rejected as tiresome morality tales or propaganda, while those with only a parabolic sense of possibility are avoided as intolerably confusing or chaotic. We simply prefer to open ourselves only to a sufficiently plausible reality.

Identity formation has a narrative quality, then, because it concerns just this sort of open discovery within a plausible reality that exhibits both stability and newness. The stuff of our lives is given a backdrop that provides two things

15. Erving Goffman, "Tie-Signs," in *Relations in Public: Microstudies of the Public Order* (New York: Basic Books, 1971), pp. 188-237.

16. Jerome Bruner, *Making Stories: Law, Literature, Life* (New York: Farrar, Straus, and Giroux, 2002), pp. 3-13.

17. John Dominic Crossan, *The Dark Interval: Towards a Theology of Story* (Niles, Ill.: Argus Communications, 1975), pp. 51-57.

otherwise unavailable to us. One is the company of others, the belonging and mutual commitment that lend order and value to our lives. The other is coherent action strategies, an enriched inventory of tested ways to engage what we have not yet faced on our own. Identity is formed by narratives because these grant a broader terrain in which to find ourselves as ones who belong (sense of home) and act (sense of possibility). This is only amplified with theological identity formation, whether of individuals or groups, in which narratives must attend especially to ultimate realities about who we are and what we do as ones claiming a relationship with God. Such formation deploys narratives that tell the many tales of how a particular people of God, past and present, here and elsewhere, have voiced and enacted their theological commitments. Such narratives are therefore something like the repertoire of a dramatic troupe, a necessarily limited but nonetheless well-honed set of possible performances for different situations.[18]

This brings us back to how mediating mechanisms contribute to identity narratives in denominations. We saw that narratives supply the paradoxical basis for identity formation (sense of home and sense of possibility), but this is actually the result of quite specific raw materials.

> First, a narrative relies on some form of selective appropriation of past events and characters. Second, within a narrative the events must be temporally ordered. This quality of narrative requires that the selected events be presented with a beginning, a middle, and an end. Third, the events and characters must be related to one another and to some overarching structure, often in the context of an opposition or struggle. This feature of narrativity has been variously referred to as the "relationality of parts" or, simply, "emplotment."[19]

This simple trio of chosen elements (character, setting), ordered events (plot, direction), and structured relations (motive, energy) represents really the only materials needed by narrative to evoke its mythic and parabolic aspects. In large measure these are also the materials that mediating mechanisms provide for identity narratives in denominations. That is, such mechanisms are not only

18. Nancy T. Ammerman, "Religious Identities and Religious Institutions," in *Handbook of the Sociology of Religion,* ed. Michele Dillon (New York: Cambridge University Press, 2003), pp. 207-24. Narrative identity in denominations is also discussed in Nancy T. Ammerman, *Pillars of Faith: American Congregations and Their Partners* (Berkeley and Los Angeles: University of California Press, 2005), chap. 7.

19. Patricia Ewick and Susan S. Silbey, "Subversive Stories and Hegemonic Tales: Toward a Sociology of Narrative," *Law and Society Review* 29, no. 2 (1995): 200.

the *means* for conveying theological identity across levels and the *markers* of the quality of relationship between these partners, but they are also the *materials* that constitute identity narratives.

As a broad example of this, let us recall the typology of mediating mechanisms as scripts, contacts, and visions. The contacts mentioned in some of the essays in this collection surely gave participants a way to expand their theological ideas and practices (mechanism as means). At times contacts disclosed the depth and vitality of relationships in a denomination (mechanism as marker). Beyond this, though, they also provided the people and places essential for later telling or enhancing an identity narrative (mechanism as material). Just as contact mechanisms are like chosen elements (character, setting) in narratives, so also script mechanisms seem similar to ordered events (plot, direction), while vision mechanisms resemble structured relations (motive, energy). What makes these mechanisms important for denominations is, once again, that they attend to ultimate concerns and emerge from and for theological practices. For this reason, mediating mechanisms play a fundamental role in shaping effective theological identity narratives particular to denominations. Due to their mediating quality, this naturally remains a process of mutual negotiation between levels in denominations. As an active partner in that process, however, and due to its expansive horizon of history, connections, resources, and diversity, the national level is well positioned to take the initiative with such mechanisms in forming and reinforcing theological identity. Failing to do so would both abrogate its distinctive role and diminish the identity narratives that result.

In a more specific way, let us consider one case of how a denomination used mediating mechanisms from the national level to shape theological identity at the grass roots. The case involves the promotion of a twenty-eight-minute videotape by the Evangelical Lutheran Church in America (ELCA), primarily through its women's organization.[20] In brief, the videotape traces the journey of a quilt originating from a women's group in a rural Minnesota congregation to its destination in a refugee camp in Angola. Not only was this resource promoted through national structures for eventual use in congregations, its very development resulted from the denomination's financial support of an independent international aid agency, Lutheran World Relief. The denomination therefore utilized its organization, resources, and connections to deploy a mechanism that no other level could provide. Moreover, the global scope of the videotape's message was yet another way the national level made a distinctive contribution to what this mechanism conveyed. At the same time, its

20. *Angola's Piecemakers: The Quilt*, prod. WDAY-TV, Fargo, N.D., 28 min. (New York: Lutheran World Relief, 1996), videocassette.

true aim was to be viewed and discussed in congregations, ideally by the very women's groups that sewed the quilts portrayed. Without this local level of engagement and ownership, the videotape would have lost its mediating role.

To understand how this videotape operates theologically, it is important to know more about how the narrative it tells intersects with the identity narratives of its intended viewers. At the outset, such viewers meet persons much like themselves who are dedicated to the theological practice of helping those less fortunate. Any retreat into typical, paternalistic charity is quickly blocked, however, when several commonsense questions are asked and answered. Why are these quilts needed? Because their Angolan recipients live in refugee camps. Why are they refugees? Because a lengthy civil war has stripped them of their livelihood. How did this war happen? Because the viewers' own nation played a part in supporting it and still refuses to face the problem of land mines that threatens Angolans today. The videotape's narrative is more extensive, of course, showing the many ways that local funds (again, given by intended viewers) support relief and advocacy efforts. The basic strategy, however, is to cause a vision of charity to collide with a vision of violence so that one's theological identity narrative is reexamined. Viewers then begin to question their own complicity in events that cause a need for their quilts in the first place. Beneath this moral insight, however, rests a deeper aim about the theological meaning of gift. Any true gift, both ours to others and God's to us, creates a bond between the parties that calls forth further responsibilities. Beginning with an ordinary practice of grassroots Lutherans, this videotape creates a broader horizon that invites viewers beyond "Golden Rule Christianity"[21] into a particularly Lutheran theological identity, one that narrates giving, human or divine, as a theological practice of selflessness and resistance. This case of challenging and rethinking identity narratives using a mediating mechanism was instigated by a denomination's national level. It thereby suggests the significant way that any denomination at this level might orient its work and assess its best efforts.

Denominations and Resiliency

Beyond an initial review of insights from the theological essays, my argument thus far has been that all denominational work should be assessed in light of how it supports theological identity, and that the national level of a denomina-

21. Nancy T. Ammerman, "Golden Rule Christianity: Lived Religion in the American Mainstream," in *Lived Religion in America: Toward a History of Practice,* ed. David D. Hall (Princeton: Princeton University Press, 1997), pp. 196-216.

tion is best situated to catalyze this through mediating mechanisms that contribute to identity narratives. In this closing section, I wish to develop the implications of that claim for our understanding of the resiliency of denominations and what their larger theological value might be. We began this chapter by asking whether denominations are really *theological,* and found ample evidence across this entire study of the significant theological work they can do. We now close by shifting that initial question just a bit, pausing to wonder what exactly denominations *are,* theologically speaking.

When denominations are subjected to criticism, fair or otherwise, it is not their strengths that are scrutinized, of course, but their weaknesses. Interestingly, the understanding of identity narratives presented herein not only accounts for the former but also anticipates and explains the latter. The most profound failures of denominations, which are actually theological rather than merely organizational, can be best understood in narrative terms. Narrative theorists have long recognized that every effort to emplot characters, scenes, and other story elements in a motivated and compelling tale is a matter of selection. Focusing on some materials at the expense of others naturally limits the frame of reference and creates unavoidable blind spots. It is in just this way that the vested interests and approved ideology of the one making these decisions are written into the story.[22] Theological identity in denominations is subject to the very same forces. By not examining selectivity and the interests that drive it, however, the resulting limited perspectives can produce more serious organizational weaknesses. For example, a denomination historically rooted in one narrative (whether ethnicity, piety, or whatever) offers few ways for newcomers to hear their own theological identity someplace in the larger discourse of that group. Should the theological story become yet more isolated, the denomination may be left with a monaural, triumphant, self-congratulatory identity narrative that eventually becomes implausible even from within. In summary, narrow narratives leave denominations exceptionally vulnerable.

We learned through this study not only that effective, adaptive denominations promote strong theological identity narratives, but also that they do so by facing the blind spots inherent in those same narratives. This seems to happen in at least three ways. First, they simply recall mistakes and failures as part of the full story of the denomination. An anticipatory honesty prevails in such groups, using earlier tales of woe to keep later hardships from being entirely unexpected. Failure in the past teaches the theological practices for addressing it in the future. The NBC could speak with unflinching candor about the Lyons

22. Mieke Bal, *Narratology: Introduction to the Theory of Narrative,* trans. Christine van Boheemen (Toronto: University of Toronto Press, 1985), p. 104.

scandal, for example, because its identity narratives included a robust realism about human sin and the need for community solidarity. For the same reason, that scandal will doubtless be retold as a narrative theological resource in troubled times to come.

Related to this, a second way denominations deal with narrative blind spots is to retain or restore multiple narrative strands, especially those that have been marginalized or forgotten. By intentionally deploying different mediating mechanisms in diverse parts of the denomination, the national level can surface and conserve a wide range of stories about what it means theologically to be part of that group. Although some of these might not seem terribly important or equally relevant, they still represent a variety of theological strategies that may yet become useful in unexpected ways. When the UMC recovered a deeper appreciation of its specifically Wesleyan heritage, this underutilized narrative strand became a fresh theological resource for addressing contemporary social issues. If not by plumbing its historical roots, a denomination can also discover a range of identity narratives by attending to regional differences. Another option is to highlight a focal element whose rich symbolism allows for narrative variations among diverse adherents, as with the Episcopalian ritual aesthetic and concern for reconciliation. In any case, unsettled times seem to call for the development of multistranded identity narratives that together can bring durability to a denomination that might otherwise become quite brittle.

A third way denominations address their blind spots is by locating themselves within a larger ecumenical ecology of theological identity narratives. That is, such groups reject the pretense of theological self-sufficiency and, acknowledging their limited perspectives, seek connections with other denominations whose narrative resources supplement their own. Alliances are nurtured with groups whose complementary strengths offset internal weaknesses and thus enrich both denominations' practices and identities. The Vineyard showed a capacity for this through a network structure open to adaptive relations with others and an eagerness to absorb theological insights from outside groups into its own faith statements. The UCC also showed this capacity in its founding theological vision that guides its ecumenical commitments yet today. Whether capacities will translate into actual participation in a larger ecology remains uncertain. In principle, though, another strategy for greater resiliency is to rely on a diverse chorus of theological identity narratives to which each denomination adds its voice.

If resilient denominations promote their identity and minimize the debilitating effects of their weaknesses through the various narrative strategies mentioned in this chapter, this argues for retaining the distinctions and differences between denominations rather than viewing these as scandalous. The latter claim was, of course, quite forcefully enunciated seventy-five years ago by H. Richard Niebuhr.[23] His familiar critique of denominationalism is worth recalling since its theoretical assertions still persist, resting upon two theological claims that the present study calls into question. On the one hand, he viewed denominations as a surrender and accommodation to the sinful social structures of class, ethnicity, and so forth. Every effort to rationalize the existence of denominations, including theological ones, masked a distorted enmeshment with these secular origins. On the other hand, he viewed denominations as nothing less than a sign of division, scandalizing the body of Christ and defeating the church's ability to carry out its mission. The existence of denominations was therefore responsible for the ethical failure of the church to confront the world's evils with a united voice.

To be sure, there are egregious examples that support Niebuhr's position yet today. Arguing from the weakest cases hardly seems fitting, however, when so much is at stake. It would be more appropriate to ask what the diverse and strong cases in this study indicate in relation to Niebuhr's central theological claims, and what this in turn suggests about any legitimate theological purpose for denominations. Should the social structures reflected in denominations be treated as an evil that corrupts the church's identity? Should the differences reflected by denominations be equated with a division that impedes the church's mission? The answer to these questions, expressing essentially the twin threats of stain by the world and schism in the church, can benefit from the foregoing discussion of identity narratives.

Concerning the threat of stain, we can concede the interrelation between denominations and social structures without demanding its blanket condemnation. The influence of social structures upon the church is indisputable, unsurprising, and certainly not limited to the relatively recent emergence of denominationalism in America. The more pertinent question on the basis of this study is how social structures contribute to theological identity narratives in denominations. In those cases where secular forces indeed affected denominational forms, the theological concern is less about this supposedly scandalous influence than about how it is used in the identity narrative of the group. The RCA today remembers its Dutch ethnic and immigrant roots mainly in order to admit its own limitations as it seeks to reclaim a more effective mission. The NBC today recalls the forces of slavery and racism because this heritage is still essential for its theological strategies of resistance and support. That a denomination originates from or persists because of the impact of social structures

---

23. H. Richard Niebuhr, *The Social Sources of Denominationalism* (New York: Henry Holt and Co., 1929), pp. 3-25, 264-84.

surely merits critique only insofar as this legitimates an insular, self-serving identity narrative. To the extent that such a story engenders an honest engagement with the world, however, this more likely means that the denomination bears a distinctive theological identity narrative essential to the broader witness of the church.

Concerning the threat of schism, we can admit the distinctiveness of each denomination without this inevitably producing a rupture that undermines the church's witness. Clear differentiation between persons in a congregation is no predictor of disunion or disorientation, and may in fact give the strength to avoid just such pitfalls. The same is true for denominations. An important implication from this study is that denominations at their best construct distinct theological identity narratives when in relationship with other groups. In some respects this is simply the lesson of the New Testament canon, where multiple narratives create a powerful witness to Christ that resists homogenization into a single version. Indeed, it could be said that resilient denominations boldly witness to their trust in the sufficiency of God's ways when they honor precisely that which differs from their own theological identity narratives, even when this aspect of another group is disconcerting.[24] By contrast, a denominational narrative of self-reliant theological isolation is at first arrogant, then unsustainable, and ultimately powerless to witness to anything but internal preservation. At the same time, this should challenge denominations to remember that even their most cherished narrative strategies remain provisional. At a certain time, in a particular place, or for a special reason, distinct identity narratives may be required, while at another point they are no longer warranted. Denominations must always discern when, for the sake of mission, their theological identity narratives require separate organizational forms, and when they call instead for structural rearrangement, merger, or dissolution.

In the end, the theological value of denominations should be assessed on the basis of what they actually do (theological practices, especially those enabled by mediating mechanisms that contribute to identity narratives) rather than what they allegedly are (a priori suppositions of their stained and schismatic essence). Niebuhr built a surprising amount of his argument on the latter foundation, rejecting the theological legitimacy not just of denominations but of any social divisions. Interestingly, his assertions often deployed narrative strategies to support this, such as the compact claim "that East and West and South and North, Slav and Latin and Teuton, have parted the garment of Christianity among them, unable to clothe a single body of Christ with the seamless

---

24. Irmgard Kindt-Siegwalt, "Believing in Unity and Accepting Difference," *Ecumenical Review* 51, no. 2 (April 1999): 193-201.

vesture of his spirit."[25] The underlying story is, of course, the scene in Saint John's passion narrative when soldiers divide Jesus' outer garments and cast lots for his seamless inner tunic (John 19:23-24). Like Cyprian and Augustine and others before him, Niebuhr used this incident to create a tale of warning: dividing the church for whatever reason exceeds even the harm done by those who executed Jesus.[26] My intent in noting Niebuhr's brief account here (many others could have been selected) is to show that a different theological conclusion about church unity could be constructed on the basis of the same narrative materials. Not incidentally, this is exactly what this study has shown that denominations are able to do: promote distinctive identity narratives that enrich the witness of the church. Recasting Niebuhr's tale is therefore a useful demonstration of the theological purpose denominations can legitimately serve.

At its heart, Niebuhr used the incident of the seamless tunic to refer allegorically to the undivided church.[27] With the terms translated in this monovalent fashion, there is little choice but to say that church unity equals structural oneness, a claim that illumines one reason Niebuhr saw division as scandal. Is this, however, the only theological narrative that the seamless tunic can sponsor? Saint John already provided one alternative in verse 24, treating the incident as a fulfillment of Psalm 22:18. In that case the seamless tunic suggests the cry for deliverance embodied in that entire psalm, a psalm that in turn orients the theology of all the Gospel passion stories. Another narrative develops from noting that seamless weaving avoided mixing two kinds of cloth (Deut. 22:11), which meant that such garments were especially suited to the ritual strictness of the high priesthood.[28] In that case the seamless tunic suggests the role of Jesus as the pure mediator between heaven and earth in the very act of his execution. Both alternative narratives are rich with polyvalent meaning, turning away from a simple allegory about a tunic and toward a complex midrash about the significance of its wearer.

To be sure, Niebuhr used the incident of the seamless tunic to emplot not just any tale, but one that promoted an identity narrative about church unity. Intriguingly, the same possibility exists for the other narrative versions of this incident I just mentioned, although the implications are rather different. By di-

---

25. Niebuhr, *Social Sources of Denominationalism*, pp. 9-10.

26. Cyprian, *On the Unity of the Catholic Church* 7; Augustine, *Tractates on John* 118.4.

27. By way of further demonstrating narrative diversity, it is intriguing that Cyprian was more interested in how the tunic was woven (top to bottom, an allegory for how unity flows from heaven to earth) while Augustine focused on who received the outer garments (four Roman guards, an allegory for the church being entrusted to Gentiles and divided in all four directions).

28. Josephus, *Jewish Antiquities* 3.7.4; cf. Exod. 39:27.

recting us toward the central person in that incident and not a mere prop, these alternatives tell of church unity found in a source, not a structure. In such a reading the unity of the church is unharmed by different forms, for it rests upon the one whose dying cry incorporates the whole cosmic cry for deliverance. In such a reading, unity is unsullied by contact with sinful society, for it rests upon the one whose solidarity with the dying is a pure offering that brings abundant life. Structural differentiation, denominational or otherwise, is insignificant in light of this gift of unity — or perhaps more accurately, it becomes invaluable whenever it results in diversity of witness to the source of that gift. Such organizational work can rightly find a place for many theological identity narratives, including Niebuhr's salutary tale of warning. It is just this kind of work that denominations are especially equipped to do.

Contributors

Emily Barman is Assistant Professor of Sociology, Boston University.

Eugene W. Bunkowske is the Fiechtner Professor of Christian Outreach at the Oswald Hoffman School of Christian Outreach, Concordia University, St. Paul, Minnesota, and Director of the Master of Christian Outreach Program, Concordia University.

David L. Carlson is Associate Professor of Sociology and Chair of the Division of Social Science, Campbellsville University, Kentucky.

Mark Chaves is Professor of Sociology, University of Arizona.

John Coakley is L. Russell Feakes Memorial Professor of Church History, New Brunswick Theological Seminary, New Jersey.

Pamela D. Couture is Vice President and Academic Dean, Professor of Practical Theology, Saint Paul School of Theology, Kansas City, Missouri.

Quinton Hosford Dixie is Assistant Professor of Religious Studies, Indiana University–Purdue University, Fort Wayne, Indiana.

Ian T. Douglas is Professor of Mission and World Christianity, Episcopal Divinity School, Cambridge, Massachusetts.

David Emmanuel Goatley is Executive Secretary-Treasurer of the Lott Carey Baptist Foreign Mission Convention, and Executive Director of Lott Carey International.

Bill Jackson is the pastor of Black Mountain Vineyard, San Diego, California; Regional Coordinator for Vineyard Leadership Institute; and President of Radical Middle Ministries.

Shayne Lee is Assistant Professor of Sociology, University of Houston.

Donald A. Luidens is Professor of Sociology, Hope College, Holland, Michigan.

Paul Marschke is Emeritus Professor of History, Concordia University, Ann Arbor, Michigan.

Stephen Mathonnet-VanderWell is co-pastor of Second Reformed Church in Pella, Iowa, and Adjunct Professor of Religion, Central College, Pella, Iowa.

Gary B. McGee is Professor of Church History and Pentecostal Studies, Assemblies of God Theological Seminary, Springfield, Missouri.

William W. Menzies is President Emeritus and Chancellor, Asia Pacific Theological Seminary, Baguio City, Philippines.

Donald E. Miller is Professor of Religion and Sociology and Executive Director of the Center for Religion and Civic Culture, University of Southern California, Los Angeles.

Aldon D. Morris is Professor of Sociology and Associate Dean for Faculty, Northwestern University, Evanston, Illinois.

James R. Nieman is Professor of Practical Theology, Hartford Institute for Religion Research, Hartford Seminary, Hartford, Connecticut.

Jennifer M. Phillips is Vicar of St. Augustine's Episcopal Church, Kingston, Rhode Island.

Margaret M. Poloma is Professor Emeritus of Sociology, University of Akron, Ohio.

Russell E. Richey is Dean and Professor of Church History, Candler School of Theology, Atlanta, Georgia.

David A. Roozen is Director, Hartford Institute for Religion Research and Professor of Religion and Society, Hartford Seminary, Hartford, Connecticut.

Contributors

Roger L. Shinn is Reinhold Niebuhr Professor Emeritus of Social Ethics, Union Theological Seminary, New York.

William H. Swatos Jr. is a priest of the Episcopal Diocese of Quincy, living in Galva, Illinois; Executive Officer of the Religious Research Association and the Association for the Sociology of Religion; and Senior Fellow of the Center for Religious Inquiry Across the Disciplines, Baylor University.

Don Williams was serving as pastor of the Coast Vineyard Church, La Jolla, California, when he wrote his essay.

James Rutland Wood is Professor Emeritus of Sociology, Indiana University (Bloomington).

Barbara Brown Zikmund is former president of Hartford Seminary and a research fellow at Catholic University of America, Washington, D.C.